THE FALL OF THE ROMAN REPUBLIC
AND RELATED ESSAYS

THE FALL
OF THE
ROMAN REPUBLIC
and Related Essays

P. A. BRUNT

CLARENDON PRESS · OXFORD
1988

Oxford University Press, Walton Street, Oxford OX2 6DP
Oxford New York Toronto
Delhi Bombay Calcutta Madras Karachi
Petaling Jaya Singapore Hong Kong Tokyo
Nairobi Dar es Salaam Cape Town
Melbourne Auckland
and associated companies in
Berlin Ibadan

Oxford is a trademark of Oxford University Press

Published in the United States
by Oxford University Press, New York

British Library Cataloguing in Publication Data
Brunt, P. A.
The fall of the Roman Republic: and related
essays.
1. Rome — History — Republic, 265–
30 B.C.
I. Title
937′.05   DG254
ISBN 0-19-814849-6

Set by H Charlesworth & Co Ltd
Printed in Great Britain
at the University Printing House, Oxford
by David Stanford
Printer to the University

PREFACE

The title essay in the volume complements and occasionally revises the interpretation of the fall of the Republic offered in my *Social Conflicts in the Roman Republic*, 1971. Some of the more controversial views expressed there rested on my *Italian Manpower*, 1971, and on various articles, including those on the Equites which appeared in *Proceedings of the Second International Conference of Economic History*, 1962, published in 1965, and on *The Roman Mob* (*Past and Present*, 1966, reprinted with some changes in M. I. Finley, *Studies in Roman Society*, 1974); both were further revised for the German translations in *Zur Sozial- und Wirtschaftsgeschichte der späten römischen Republik*, ed. H. Schneider, 1976. Of these the former now furnishes a basis for entirely rewritten discussions in Chapters 3 and 4, while the latter is omitted from this collection, since most of the material it contained is found elsewhere in the present volume, and it has been my aim to confine repetition to a minimum compatible with clarity. The other articles on which I relied in 1971 reappear here, but with extensive revisions; I am indebted to the Society for the Promotion of Roman Studies for permission to reprint, in respect of Chapters 2 (*JRS* 1965) and 5 (*JRS* 1962), of which the latter supersedes the revised German version in Schneider's collection, and to the Cambridge Philological Society in respect of Chapter 7, which is derived from its *Proceedings* for 1965. Chapters 6, 8, and 9 are altogether new, except in so far as some material has been removed from the original version of Chapter 7 to Chapter 9. They too may serve to sustain some of the more debatable contentions in the first Chapter.

Annotation is generally restricted to citation of evidence, or where this could not conveniently be given, of modern works (preferably in English) which present and discuss it fully. In my judgement evidence and arguments count for more than arrays of modern 'authorities', which can seldom be complete, and which may often be more tedious and less useful, the more imposing their erudition appears. It has, however, been my aim to cite works representative of views opposed to my own, so that the student may be better able 'audire alteram partem'. Unfortunately my practice means that there is no systematic acknowledgement of my debts to other scholars (among them some with whom I differ most). Naturally these debts are countless, and many, incurred in nearly fifty years of study, now beyond recall.

P.A.B.

Brasenose College, Oxford
April 1987

CONTENTS

ABBREVIATIONS

Familiar abbreviations are used for standard works of reference, including epigraphic collections. For classical texts the practice of Liddell and Scott or the *Oxford Latin Dictionary* is normally adopted, but it should be explained that 'App(ian)' without adjunct refers to his *Civil Wars*, and that the sections in chapters of Plutarch's *Lives* are those used in the Loeb edition. A list follows of those modern works cited by the name of the author alone (with date of publication where necessary) or by other abbreviations.

ANRW	*Aufstieg und Niedergang in der römischen Welt*, ed. H. Temporini
Astin, 1967	A. E. Astin, *Scipio Aemilianus*
Badian, 1958 or *FC*	E. Badian, *Foreign Clientelae*
—— 1964	*Studies in Greek and Roman History*
—— 1967	*Roman Imperialism in the Late Republic*
—— 1972	*Publicans and Sinners*
Beloch, 1886	J. Beloch, *Die Bevölkerung der griechisch-römischen Welt*
Bleicken, 1955	J. Bleicken, *Das Volkstribunat der klassischen Republik*
—— 1972	*Staatliche Ordnung und Freiheit in der römischen Republik*
—— 1975	*Lex Publica*
Botermann, 1968	H. Botermann, *Die Soldaten und die römische Politik in der Zeit von Caesars Tod bis zur Begründung des zweiten Triumvirats*
Bruhns, 1978	H. Bruhns, *Caesar und die römische Oberschicht in den Jahren 49–44 v. Chr.*
Brunt, *IM*	P. A. Brunt, *Italian Manpower*, 1971
—— *Laus Imperii*	*ap.* P. Garnsey and C. R. Whittaker, *Imperialism in the Ancient World*, 1978
—— *Social Conflicts*	*Social Conflicts in the Roman Republic*, 1971
Buckland, 1908	W. W. Buckland, *Roman Law of Slavery*
Cherubini, 1983	G. Cherubini *et al.* (edd.), *Storia della società italiana*, 2, *La tarda repubblica e il principato*
Clementi, 1974	G. Clementi, *I romani nella Gallia meridionale*
Conway, 1897	R. S. Conway, *The Italic Dialects*
D'Arms, 1981	J. H. D'Arms, *Commerce and Social Standing in Ancient Rome*
De Laet, 1949	S. J. De Laet, *Portorium*
de Neeve, 1984	P. W. de Neeve, *Colonus* (Eng. ed.)
de Ste Croix, 1981	G. E. M. de Ste Croix, *The Class Struggle in the Ancient Greek World*

Earl, 1961	D. C. Earl, *The Political Thought of Sallust*
EJ	V. Ehrenberg and A. H. M. Jones, *Documents illustrating in the Reigns of Augustus and Tiberius*[3] (2nd ed. enlarged), 1975
ESAR	T. Frank *et al.*, *Economic Survey of Ancient Rome*, 1933–40
FC	See Badian
Finley, 1974	M. I. Finley (ed.), *Studies in Ancient Society*
—— 1980	*Ancient Slavery and Modern Ideology*
—— 1981	*Economy and Society in Ancient Greece*
—— 1983	*Politics in the Ancient World*
—— 1985	*The Ancient Economy*[2]
FIRA	*Fontees Iuris Romani Anteiustiniani*, ed. S. Riccobono *et al.*
Frier, 1980	B. W. Frier, *Landlords and Tenants in Imperial Rome*
Gabba, 1973	E. Gabba, *Esercito e società nella tarda repubblica romana*
—— 1976	*Republican Rome: the Army and the Allies* (tr. P. J. Cuff)
Galsterer, 1976	H. Galsterer, *Herrschaft und Verwaltung im republikanischen Italien*
Garnsey, 1970	P. Garnsey, *Social Status and Legal Privilege in the Roman Empire*
GC	A. H. J. Greenidge and A. M. Clay, *Sources for Roman History 133–70 BC*[2], revised by E. W. Gray, 1960
Gelzer, *Caesar*	M. Gelzer, *Caesar, Politician and Statesman* (tr. by P. Needham), 1968
—— 1969	*The Roman Nobility* (tr. by R. Seager)
Gruen, 1968	E. Gruen, *Roman Politics and the Criminal Courts, 149–78 BC*
—— 1974	*The Last Generation of the Roman Republic*
Harmand, 1957	L. Harmand, *Le Patronat sur les collectivités publiques*
—— 1967	*L'Armée et le soldat à Rome de 107 à 50 avant notre ère*
Harris, 1971	W. V. Harris, *Rome in Etruria and Umbria*
—— 1979	*War and Imperialism in Republican Rome*
Hatzfeld, 1919	J. Hatzfeld, *Les Trafiquants italiens dans l'orient hellénique*
Haug, 1947	I. Haug, *Das römische Bundesgenossenkrieg*, in *Würzburger Jahrbücher für die Altertumswissenschaft*
Hellegouarc'h, 1963	J. Hellegouarc'h, *Le Vocabulaire latin des relations et des partis politiques sous la République*
Herrmann, 1968	P. Herrmann, *Der römische Eid*
Hopkins, 1978	K. Hopkins, *Conquerors and Slaves*
—— 1983	*Death and Renewal*

Humbert, 1978   M. Humbert, *Municipium et Civitas sine Suffragio*
Ilari, 1974   V. Ilari, *Gli italici nelle strutture militare romane*
IM   See Brunt
Jolowicz–Nicholas, 1972   H. F. Jolowicz and B. Nicholas, *Historical Introduction to the Study of Roman Law*[3]
Jones, 1940   A. H. M. Jones, *The Greek City from Alexander to Justinian*
Kelly, 1966   J. M. Kelly, *Roman Litigation*
Keppie, 1983   Keppie, *Colonisation and Veteran Settlement in Italy, 47–14* BC
Kloesel, 1935   H. Kloesel, *Libertas* (diss., Breslau)
Kunkel, 1962   W. Kunkel, *Untersuchungen zur Entwicklung des römischen Kriminalverfahrens in vorsullanischer Zeit*
Latte, 1960   K. Latte, *Römische Religionsgeschichte*
Liebeschutz, 1979   W. Liebeschutz, *Continuity and Change in Roman Religion*
Lintott, 1968   A. Lintott, *Violence in Republican Rome*
Magie, 1950   D. Magie, *Roman Rule in Asia Minor*
Meier, 1966   C. Meier, *Res Publica Amissa*
Michel, 1962   J. Michel, *Gratuité en droit romain*
Mommsen, *StR*   T. Mommsen, *Römisches Staatsrecht*[3]
MRR   T. S. R. Broughton, *The Magistrates of the Roman Republic*, 1951
Münzer, 1920   F. Münzer, *Römische Adelsparteien und Adelsfamilien*
Nicolet, 1966, 1974   C. Nicolet, *L'Ordre équestre à l'époque républicaine*
OLD   *Oxford Latin Dictionary*
Oppermann, 1967   H. Oppermann (ed.), *Römische Wertbegriffe*
ORF   H. Malcovati, *Oratorum Romanorum Fragmenta*
Pohlenz, 1966   M. Pohlenz, *Freedom in Greek Life and Thought*
Premerstein, 1900   A. von Premerstein, *RE* iv. 23 ff., *s.v. Clientes*
—— 1937   *Vom Werden und Wesen des Prinzipats*
Raaflaub, 1974   K. Raaflaub, *Dignitatis Contentio*
RC   See Sherwin-White
Rice Holmes, 1923   T. Rice Holmes, *The Roman Republic*
Richard, 1978   J. C. Richard, *Les Origines de la plèbe romaine*
Rickman, 1980   G. Rickman, *The Corn Supply of Ancient Rome*
Rostovtzeff, *SEHRE*   M. Rostovtzeff, *Social and Economic History of the Roman Empire*[2],
—— *SEHHW*   *Social and Economic History of the Hellenistic World*
Rouland, 1979   N. Rouland, *Pouvoir politique et dépendance personelle dans l'antiquité romaine*
RR   See Syme
RRC   M. H. Crawford, *Roman Republican Coinage*, 1974
Salmon, 1967   E. T. Salmon, *Samnium and the Samnites*

Schneider, 1974	H. Schneider, *Wirtschaft und Politik: Untersuchungen zur Geschichte der späten römischen Republik*
—— 1976	(ed.) *Zur Sozial- und Wirtschaftsgeschichte der späten römischen Republik*
Schulz, 1936	F. Schulz, *Principles of Roman Law*
—— 1951	*Classical Roman Law*
—— 1953	*History of Roman Legal Science*
Scullard, 1973	H. H. Scullard, *Roman Politics 220–150 BC*[2]
Seager, 1969	R. Seager (ed.), *Crisis of the Roman Republic*
—— *Pompey*	*Pompey: A Political Biography*, 1979
Shatzman, 1975	I. Shatzman, *Senatorial Wealth and Roman Politics*
Sherk, 1969	R. K. Sherk, *Roman Documents from the Greek East*
Sherwin-White, 1973 or *RC*	A. N. Sherwin-White, *The Roman Citizenship*[2]
—— 1984	*Roman Foreign Policy in the East*
Simshäuser, 1973	W. Simshäuser, *Iuridici und Munizipalgerichtsbarkeit in Italien*
Smith, 1958	R. E. Smith, *Service in the Post-Marian Roman Army*
Staveley, 1972	E. S. Staveley, *Greek and Roman Voting and Elections*
Stockton, 1979	D. L. Stockton, *The Gracchi*
StR	See Mommsen
Suolahti, 1955	J. Suolahti, *the Junior Officers of the Roman Army in the Republican Period*
Sydenham, 1952	E. A. Sydenham, *The Roman Republican Coinage* (revised by G. C. Haines)
Syme, *RR*	R. Syme, *The Roman Revolution*, 1939
Taylor, 1949	L. R. Taylor, *Party Politics in the Age of Caesar*
—— 1960	*Voting Districts of the Roman Republic*
—— 1966	*Roman Voting Assemblies*
Treggiari, 1969	S. M. Treggiari, *Roman Freedmen during the late Republic*
Vetter, 1953	E. Vetter, *Handbuch der italischen Dialekte*
Ward, 1977	A. M. Ward, *Marcus Crassus and the late Roman Republic*
Weinstock, 1971	S. Weinstock, *Divus Caesar*
Whatmough, 1937	J. Whatmough, *The Foundations of Roman Italy*
Wilson, 1966	A. J. N. Wilson, *Emigration from Italy in the Republican Age of Rome*
Wirszubski, 1950	C. Wirszubski, *Libertas as a Political Idea at Rome during the late Republic and early Principate*
Wiseman, 1971	T. P. Wiseman, *New Men in the Roman Senate, 139 BC–AD 14*
Wissowa, 1912	G. Wissowa, *Religion und Kultus der Römer*

1

THE FALL OF THE ROMAN REPUBLIC[1]

I. The *res publica*; establishment of a monarchy by Augustus, for which the support of senate and Equites was indispensable; the change entailed no modification of the Republican class structure, but though merely political, can properly be called a revolution, and had momentous consequences. **II.** The 'mixed' constitution of the Republic not purely oligarchical; the monarchic nature of *imperium*; the powers of the people. **III.** The people not represented democratically in the assemblies. Limits on their competence. The great influence of the nobility, not entirely explained by clientship. **IV.** The conflicts of *populares* and optimates from which the Principate issued. They were not parties in the modern sense. No such parties could be formed at Rome; so too there were no large, durable factions within the nobility, based on the ties of kinship and friendship (ties morally less binding than the claims of the *patria* and in practice often subordinated to individual self-interest) and supported by faithful clients. **V.** The importance of public opinion and therefore of speeches and pamphlets appealing to public or sectional interests. **VI.** The nature of these interests and corresponding ideals. *Libertas. Otium cum dignitate.* **VII.** Cicero's 'fundamenta otiosae dignitatis' express generally accepted objectives; by realizing them Augustus assured the stability of his new regime. **VIII.** The failure of the senate to solve problems arising from imperial expansion in such a way as to ensure enough continuing and active support for its supremacy. The discontents of the Italian allies and the Equites, which generated the great crisis of 91–82, memories of which were potent on the minds of the next decades. The discontents of peasants, urban plebs, and soldiers, and the solutions devised by Augustus. Reliance of the senate on repression; the growth of violence; the overwhelming desire for *otium*. **IX.** The effects on the course of events at Rome of individual personalities and of developments outside the empire; the element of contingency; the impossibility of furnishing complete historical explanations, especially for a period of history for which adequate evidence is lacking.

---

[1] For verification of many statements in this essay the reader is referred to standard accounts of Roman history and the Roman constitution, and for dated events to *MRR*.

I

IN 104 BC Rome made or renewed a treaty with the little Greek city of
Astypalaea. The extant document designates the High Contracting
Parties as the people of Rome and the people of Astypalaea.
Treaties, like laws, were only of binding effect on Rome if approved by
an assembly of the citizens (n. 34). However, in accordance with normal
usage the treaty had also been sanctioned by a decree of the senate
(*senatus consultum*), and appropriate executive action, which neither
people nor senate could take, was committed to magistrates. Magistrates were expected to act 'e re publica fideque sua', in accordance with
the interest of the people and the trust reposed in them.[2]

'Res publica', as Cicero observed, was literally the same as 'res
populi', and denoted primarily 'the property or concern of the people';
by an extension of meaning it referred to the whole community, and is
then best rendered as 'commonwealth'; in some contexts it may seem
convenient to translate it as 'state', but it was only with some
embarrassment that Cicero could write of a monarchical *res publica*: with
a single ruler, there could hardly be the participation of the citizens in
affairs of common concern which the term naturally suggested.[3]

Already in the 50s and 40s the dominance of Pompey and Caesar made
Cicero complain that the *res publica* was lost: citizens and above all
senators had been deprived of effective political rights. Officially the *res
publica* continued to exist as late as Justinian, who declared that he was
upholding it (*Deo Auctore* 1), no doubt because his imperial authority was
still deemed to derive from a grant by the people (*Dig.* i. 3. 4. 1). But under
the Principate men often thought of the *res publica* as the system that
Augustus had finally overthrown: it had come to mean the Republic in
contrast with the imperial autocracy. Whatever his success in veiling this
autocracy from his contemporaries and making out that he was simply
Rome's leading man (*princeps*), later generations had no illusions. He had
founded a monarchy. As Tacitus put it, 'the political order had been
overturned (*verso civitatis statu*); nothing remained of the sound practice of
old times; abandoning equality, everyone awaited the orders of the
Princeps' (*Ann.* i. 4). It was characteristic that among Augustus' legal
prerogatives was that of concluding treaties on behalf of Rome.

Of course, no single man could govern an empire unaided. Senators,
who in the Republic had normally directed policy in their collective
capacity, and executed it as individual magistrates and promagistrates,
were now among the principal agents and advisers of the emperor, though

---

[2] Sherk no. 16; *FIRA* i². 31. 1, 32.

[3] *de rep.* i. 39, 43, 48. Latin lacked a word to denote constitution or form of government (*Att.* vii. 8. 4
used the Greek *politeia*); hence Cicero makes do with *res publica* or *rei p. status*, which uneasily embrace
monarchy. On the meaning of *res publica* Stark, 1967, is best; cf. Brunt, *Biblioteca di Labeo*, 1982, 238.

the senate's continuing role as the great council of state was of dwindling importance. Increasingly the emperors also made more use of Equites in administration and command and in their own councils; in the Republic this order, second in wealth and dignity to the senatorial, had already some, though a much smaller, share in the work of government, holding junior commissions in the army, judging cases, often political, at Rome, and undertaking public contracts, especially for the collection of taxes.

There was no sharp social or economic division between senators and Equites either in the Republic or in the Principate. Senators were indeed excluded by law from participating in the public contracts, and this form of investment had attracted the most affluent and best organized of the Equites and had involved them in some disputes with the senate. It is, however, a fallacy to think that the entire equestrian order constituted a 'business' class opposed to the 'landed interest' represented by the senators. The latter could also be involved in commerce, banking, and industry, but as land was the chief source of wealth in what we may regard as the 'under-developed' economy of the ancient world, it can be assumed that most members of both orders were primarily landowners. Most Equites were probably municipal gentry, the *domi nobiles*, who ruled the peoples of Italy, and whose number was swollen by the enfranchisement of the former Italian allies in the 80s and of the inhabitants beyond the Po in 49. They shared the same education, culture, and aristocratic outlook as the old Roman nobility; they mixed socially and intermarried with senators; they had the same interest in resisting any attack on property rights and in maintaining law and order. The conflicts that had arisen between the orders over judicial rights had been settled by compromise in 70. At all times, as senatorial families died out, or disappeared, probably from impoverishment, they were replaced by men of equestrian origin, but at any given point, in the Principate as in the Republic, men of this type were in a minority, and were soon assimilated. In the Principate, it is true, humble citizens could rise through the army to equestrian posts, but they too acquired wealth in their rise, and their advancement did not materially alter the character of the equestrian order. The cruelty and greed of some emperors were to alienate the senate, but it can be shown that in such cases equestrian officials were no more reliable than senators as instruments of tyranny. Even the gradual introduction of provincials into both orders after Augustus' time did not transform the attitudes prevalent in either, since they were recruited from the upper class overseas, whose ideas and economic interests did not diverge from those of their Italian counterparts and who readily absorbed the traditions which these had passed down.[4]

[4] Cf. ch. 3 and on the Equites in the Principate Brunt, *JRS* 1983, 41 ff.

We can thus fairly say that a ruling class still existed, continuous with that which had operated in the Republic, though distinctly enlarged.

According to Syme, 'whatever the form and name of government, an oligarchy lurks behind the façade, and Roman history, Republican or Imperial, is the history of the governing class'.[5] The truth of the first of these statements is somewhat banal. It depends on defining oligarchy quite literally as the rule of the few. In any system relatively few men direct the affairs of state; in our own, for instance, the leading members of the ruling party and the principal permanent officials, civil and military. None the less we call our system democratic, because these men are ultimately responsible to the representatives of the people and through them to the electorate. Oligarchy naturally denotes government by a set of men, privileged by birth or wealth, who are responsible to themselves alone. In this sense the senatorial order of the Republic is often thought to constitute an oligarchy; but this is to ignore or depreciate the powers of the people, which elected the magistrates, could occasionally bring them to account, and which at times was able to overrule the majority of the senate on issues of policy. Syme's second statement is gravely exaggerated for the Republic.

In the Principate substantial property was still requisite for both senators and Equites, and a high proportion of senators still consisted of men of hereditary status. However, they now depended not at all on the people, but wholly on the emperor. The senate as a body did little more than acquiesce in his decisions; individuals owed rank and promotion to his favour, and it was in his council that they might influence policy. There was no public decision, however trivial, that he was not free to make as he chose, and none of importance could be taken without disloyalty by anyone else, unless it had his sanction or was supposedly in accord with his wishes. In form each emperor was chosen by senate and people; in fact each could in one way or another determine the succession or, if he failed, a military coup was decisive. Some proclaimed their obedience to the laws, but they were not bound by existing laws and could themselves enact new ones. Prudence or principle might dictate respect for public opinion, or at any rate for that of the ruling class, and most emperors, those whose formative years had been passed in a private station within that class,[6] understood and commonly shared opinions prevalent among men who had once been their peers. However, so long as the emperor retained his lifelong power, he could not either in law or practice be brought to

---

[5] *RR* 7. My interpretation of 'the Roman Revolution' differs altogether from Syme's, whose book none the less furnishes an unsurpassed narrative of events during Augustus' career.

[6] All between 68 and 211 except Domitian, Marcus Aurelius, and Commodus.

account; at most he might be condemned and his acts reversed after death, if his successor consented. The property and lives of every individual subject, especially the most eminent, were exposed to the rapacity and suspicion of any ruler who was at once ready to exploit autocracy to the full and feared the effects of the hatred that he inspired. Only revolt or assassination could then give relief from oppression.

Although Syme himself acknowledges that Augustus founded a monarchy[7], he seems to see what he calls the Roman revolution as a transformation of the ruling class through the selection of Augustus' partisans at the expense of the old nobility. This may be questioned.

The term 'noble' is reserved by Syme and most scholars to men whose ancestors in the direct male line had held the consulship (or magistracies of an early period equal or higher in dignity); in my view it can also be applied to the descendants of praetors and curule aediles. Between 200 and 49 four out of five consuls belonged to the former category and most of the rest were probably or certainly noble in the wider sense; men such as Marius and Cicero, who could boast of no senatorial forebears, could very seldom reach the highest office. It was ex-consuls, or rather those of most talent and industry, who as *principes* normally guided the deliberations of the senate. At all times the nobility, however it be defined, was, like the senate itself, gradually recruited from below, as old families were extinguished or fell into oblivion. The disappearance of these families was quickened by the wars and proscriptions of the first century. It was therefore inevitable that from 49 the senate was composed to a greater degree than before of men of non-consular lineage and indeed of mere parvenus. Moreover, the greater part of the nobility espoused the losing side with Pompey or with Brutus and Cassius. They were naturally most attached to a system in which the senate had normally directed affairs, seeing that they dominated the senate. Men of equestrian and municipal origin were no doubt in general less devoted to a regime in which they had enjoyed much less power. It was in their number that Caesar, the triumvirs, and Augustus (initially at least) had to find most of their assistants, whom they were bound to reward. New men therefore had a much better chance of rising to the consulship and to the command of great armies after 49. However, once the generation of nobles who had fought to the last for the Republic had died out, Augustus allowed the names of ancient families to emblazon the roll of consuls almost as in the past; if he continued to use them less than new men in positions of high trust, it was perhaps because he was anxious to

7 *RR*, ch. XXXIII.

award these positions to talent rather than birth. In the senate at large, scions of families already consular by 49 BC actually appear to be proportionately as numerous as in 55 BC; however, the data are defective. Even if Augustus had to rely chiefly on new men in his ascent to dominance, he seems eventually to have been confident that his regime was accepted by virtually the whole senatorial order.[8]

We must not suppose that even men of equestrian and municipal origin were not affected by the force of tradition, and by veneration for what Cicero could quite casually designate as 'the ancestral institutions which the long duration of our empire validates' (*Mur.* 75). Both Equites and numerous senators of undistinguished houses are found among the Pompeians, the assassins of Caesar, and those who subsequently joined their cause (ch. 9 n. 117). In 44–43 the senate, full as it was of Caesar's nominees, stood for the Republic against Antony, albeit hesitantly. Cicero has doubtless exaggerated, but not entirely invented, the ardour that the cause of 'liberty' evoked in the towns of Italy, even in remote Cisalpina, where many owed their citizenship to Caesar.[9] Whole communities and hundreds of individuals were penalized by the triumvirs. Few of the proscribed whose names are recorded were of noble families (ch. 9 n. 118). Of course the triumvirs needed lands and cash for their troops, but it is a reasonable assumption that they selected as the victims of sequestration and proscription those prominent in the resistance to Antony.

After Philippi, for his own ends, L. Antonius proclaimed his intent to restore the Republic (App. v. 30, 39, 43, 54). The triumvirs themselves had assumed the commission 'rei publicae constituendae'; in fact they ruled autocratically without performing their task, but both Octavian (v. 132) and Antony (Dio xlix. 41. 6, 50. 7. 1, 22. 4) hoped to conciliate public opinion and gain an advantage in their contest for personal supremacy by promising to lay down their extraordinary powers. Octavian could also present himself as the champion of the old Roman

---

[8] *Nobilitas*: n. 54. Augustan consuls: Brunt, *JRS* 1961, 71 ff. My remarks on the composition of the senate are based on an analysis of the list of senators in 55 (not up to date) given by G. Willems, *Le Sénat de la république rom.*,[2] 1885, vol. ii, and that of Augustan senators in S. J. De Laet, *De samenstelling van den Rom. Senaat*, 1941. But the latter list has only 435 names, presumably under half of the true total, and the names of men of high birth were probably most apt to survive. *RR* is a mine of information on the new men. In AD 14 the consular legates of Nearer Spain, Dalmatia, and Syria were nobles; those of Pannonia and Moesia and the two commanders on the Rhine under Germanicus were new men. In Syria, if we adopt Syme's list in *Roman Papers*, iii. 869 ff., and include C. Caesar's consular advisers, there were 3 nobles out of 8 between 13 BC and AD 14 (or 4 on my definition of *nobilis*, which would apply to C. Sentius Saturninus). The provincial *Fasti* for the reign are in general very incomplete, and it may well be that earlier the proportion of *nobiles* was smaller. But it was perhaps a symptom of their reconciliation (Tac. *Ann.* i. 2) that M. Valerius Messala, who had fought with Brutus at Philippi, was Augustus' colleague as consul in the year of Actium and moved the conferment on him in 2 BC of the title of *pater patriae*.

[9] See endnote 1.

way of life against an orientalizing renegade, and 'mos maiorum' included the Republican institutions. Moreover, even new men who had advanced by his patronage, once they had risen high in the ranks of the senate, might hope to see its authority revived rather than diminished. Hence Augustus thought fit belatedly to fulfil his earlier undertaking, and in January 27 surrendered the commonwealth 'to the free disposal of senate and people' (*RG* 34). Thereafter he was careful to observe as much of the forms of the old system as was compatible with his retention of ultimate control. The forms might seem more important than they really were not only to the new men but to a new generation of the nobility: none knew from their own experience what it had been to sit in the senate when the senate truly directed affairs. The parvenu Velleius could actually eulogize Augustus for restoring 'that renowned ancient form of the commonwealth', noticing only one change—the creation of two new praetorships (ii. 89. 4)!

There seems to be no reason to suppose that Caesar and his successors could put themselves at the head of any party opposed to the Republic. Caesar's adherents in 49 included many who so bitterly detested his autocracy that they were to plot against his life or back the conspirators later. Some of the new men advanced by him or by the triumvirs and Augustus came from peoples which had rebelled in 90 or at any rate only been enfranchised as a result of the rebellion. Syme supposes that the former rebels continued to nurture resentment against Rome, or that this resentment was transmuted into animosity against the senate, which could have been held responsible for oppressing the Italians and frustrating their aspirations.[10] This might not be surprising, but there is no hint of it in our sources. On the contrary newly enfranchised communities, and their individual magnates, were among those who suffered in the Republican cause (n. 9). Nor do we find that Caesar, the triumvirs, or Augustus ever proclaimed a policy of promoting men of the type whose political

[10] *RR* 86–94, 286 ff., 339, etc. Syme implies an interpretation of Italian aims in 90 incompatible with that given in ch. 2 below. Bruhns ch. vi demonstrates that there is no reason to believe that Italians initially favoured Caesar in 49. On their attitude in 43 see endnote 1. If the municipalities marked out for veteran colonies by the triumvirs had been among those prominent in opposition to Antony, we may note that of the 18 first named the 7 identified by Appian were, except for Capua, all cities enfranchised in or after 90; similarly most of the places in which the triumvirs are recorded to have settled soldiers and therefore resorted to confiscations belong to the same class. It is not significant that numerous individuals from formerly allied communities rose to eminence under Augustus, since we naturally do not know the names of those who were ruined by having taken the losing side, apart from a few persons like Staius Murcus already prominent enough to be mentioned among Republicans in the conflicts that followed Caesar's death; cf. ch. 9 nn. 118 f. The most famous of those presumably connected with an insurgent leader of 90, who rose in the service of Caesar and the triumvirs, Asinius Pollio, seems to have had no ideological commitment to the anti-senatorial cause.

ambitions had been thwarted earlier by the arrogant exclusiveness of the nobility. If this was what they did, it was surely because it was in their ranks rather than in those of the nobility that they could discover the capacities and pliability that they required. We may think that these men gave their services not as members of a party, acting together for the deliberate transformation of Roman institutions, but as individuals who found themselves in a situation in which they could neither realize their own ambitions for some limited share in power nor render the state some service except by conforming to the will of a monarch.

By adopting this course they did more than satisfy their own selfish desires for office, rank, influence, and riches; they responded to the common interests of the propertied class, and indeed of the entire free population of Italy. The Republican liberty which had enabled each section of the community to contend for its own advantage had issued in 'twenty years of strife with no regard for custom and law' (Tac. *Ann.* iii. 28). Tacitus thought that Augustus won over everyone with 'the sweetness of tranquillity' (i. 2). But this might not have been enough to ensure the stability of the new order, as memories of the miseries of internal conflicts faded: sentimental attachment to the Republic might have revived. It was stability that Augustus sought to achieve. He expressed his wish in a proclamation that 'he might be permitted to establish the commonwealth firmly and securely in its settled state and to reap thereby the fruit he desired, of being called the author of the best system, and of bearing with him in death the hope that the foundations of the commonwealth he had laid would remain unshaken' (Suet. *Aug.* 28). For this purpose he had to contrive that his personal powers should be peacefully transmitted to a successor, but also to reconcile all those elements in the state whose disloyalty might shake it. He had to keep the urban plebs and the soldiery content, but above all to satisfy the interests and sentiments of the class whose collaboration was essential to the work of government: the armies themselves would remain loyal, if their generals and officers would, as in the mutinies of AD 14, preserve their fidelity. It was on this account that he observed Republican forms, so far as they were consonant with his ultimate control, making out that he had modified rather than overturned the old order. But every aspect of his policy is relevant to his general objective. As we shall see (section VII), he proved himself better able than the senate not only to secure internal peace and order but to fulfil all the ideals and aspirations which in the Republic had commanded the general assent of those who gave any thought to public affairs. The new regime was to be based not on the mere support of a faction of partisans whom he favoured, but on the more or less universal consent of all whose discontent might have jeopardized the settlement.

Thus the establishment of the Principate entailed no radical change in the composition of the ruling élite, nor indeed any in the class structure, in a Marxist sense of class, for instance (to take one recent definition) 'a group of persons in a community identified by their position in the whole system of social production, defined above all according to their relationship (primarily in terms of the degree of ownership or control) to the conditions of production (that is to say, the means and labour of production) and to other classes'.[11] Roman private law was developed in the Principate on the basis of Republican institutions in the interest of the propertied class.[12] Senators, Equites, and municipal oligarchs formed a single class, preponderantly land-owners, and in any case dependent largely, though not exclusively, on slave labour. In the century before Augustus many families of this class were exterminated or at least expropriated, but others took their place. Some large estates were broken up to make way for smallholders including veterans, but land was also found for the new settlers at the expense of other peasants; at other times the accumulation of acres by the rich had continued, as it was to do in the Principate. It is improbable that there was any net increase in the number of small farmers.[13] The great slave revolt in Italy of the 70s did not for long reduce the extent to which slaves were employed. Under the new regime, though a few individual magnates were unjustly victimized by tyrannical emperors, property rights were on the whole safer than in the civil wars of the Republic. If the use of slave labour declined, this was a later and gradual process, commonly explained on the assumption that slaves became dearer as imperial expansion almost ceased and the supply of those enslaved in Rome's foreign wars dwindled; whether or not this hypothesis is well founded, juristic texts suggest that the economy still rested on slave labour as late as the early third century.

To understand what the Roman revolution was not is important. But was there any revolution at all? This question has been recently debated in a waste of learned words best left in oblivion. In a Marxist sense there was none. But Marxists are no more entitled to dictate the usages of our language than the forms of our government. The word

[11] De Ste Croix, 1981, 43.

[12] What Schulz, 1951, 544 f., writes on the law of hire is generally applicable. Cf. ch. 1 endnote 5 on execution for debt.

[13] *IM*, ch. xix. The huge estates of the late empire (*massae*) were surely the product of the continuing concentration of landed property in a few hands, hidden from us in a period when political protest was impossible. My view of developments in the Principate and of the persistent importance of slavery is sketched in Cherubini *et al.*, 1983, ii. 95 ff.

'revolution' is customarily employed in English, as are its equivalents in other modern languages, to denote any momentous change, even one accomplished gradually like the Industrial Revolution, and particularly any violent constitutional change. Thus we speak of the French Revolution of 1830 and of our own 'Glorious Revolution of 1688'. Neither involved any modification in the social and economic structure. The latter, however, in setting bounds to the royal prerogative, secured a parliamentary government which, though for long aristocratic, peacefully evolved into democracy and the welfare state. Freedom broadened from precedent to precedent. The revolution consummated by Augustus was no less pregnant in consequences, as distant and as little imagined by anyone at the time as were those of the revolution of 1688, but precisely opposite in their tendency.

Mommsen, who attributed it to Caesar and who wrote as a nineteenth-century liberal, declared that an absolutist constitution which did not 'give play to the free self-determination of a majority of citizens was incapable of development' and 'therefore dead', only to contradict himself by continuing that 'the Roman absolute military monarchy . . . under the impulse of the creator's genius and in the absence of all material extraneous complications *developed itself* more purely and freely than any similar state'. For proof he referred to Gibbon; perhaps he had chiefly in mind the epilogue to the third chapter, where Gibbon reflects that the happiness of Rome's subjects, secured (as he held) by the beneficence of her rulers from AD 96 to 180, was unstable, since it 'depended on the character of a single man'; there was no guarantee against the recurrence of an oppressive tyranny, and in fact (as the sequel showed) it did often recur. In Gibbon's view the misery resulting was exacerbated in two ways. Unlike the subjects of an oriental despot, the victims were still imbued with ideals of liberty and felt its loss 'with exquisite sensibility'. Moreover, 'the empire of the Romans filled the world', and its ruler experienced no restraint, unlike autocrats in Gibbon's time, 'from the example of his equals, the dread of present censure, the advice of his allies, and the apprehension of his enemies', and there was no escape in foreign realms. It was no doubt in this sense that the Roman monarchy was for Mommsen not fettered by 'extraneous complications'.[14]

To Romans of high station like Tacitus liberty had long proved incompatible with the Principate; if Nerva and Trajan had reconciled them, the liberty they allowed was in reality precarious, as he surely perceived. Of course the liberty whose loss he deplored was chiefly or exclusively the right of men of high station to speak and write freely

---

[14] *Hist. of Rome* v, ch. xi (Everyman edn. iv. 439 f.).

and to take an independent part in public affairs. But it was not only this kind of liberty that was eroded as the system developed. Liberty in Roman conceptions could also include the citizen's right to personal protection under the law and indeed to equal treatment in the courts. To say nothing of arbitrary punishments inflicted by emperors, mostly indeed on the eminent, these rights were extinguished when citizens were subjected to penalties varying with their social status, or finally reduced to serfdom. In principle there were no limits to the exercise of absolute power, even though in practice the inefficiency of administration might frustrate enforcement of the emperor's decrees. It was not only in the centre that self-government was to vanish. The Republic left the cities of Italy and the provinces to manage their own affairs with little interference, and though from the first the cities were largely controlled by local oligarchies of birth and wealth, the common people often retained some political rights; gradually these disappeared, and ultimately the local oligarchies themselves were, in the general interests of the state as perceived by its master, reduced to being mere instruments of imperial will.[15]

How much restrictions on individual initiative and responsibility contributed to the marked absence of active patriotism in and after the third century, when it was once again needed to repel foreign attacks, must be a matter of speculation. The remedy that despotism devised to meet that crisis was ever more compulsion and regimentation, binding men and their children after them to any occupation which appeared vital for the survival of the empire. It is obviously still more hazardous to trace a connection between the disappearance of political freedom and the dearth of novelty and inventiveness in literature, science, and technology; this was an age in which the knowledge of past achievements was ever more widely diffused, yet little augmented. Even in law[16] and public administration there was little originality after the time of Augustus, and he and his contemporaries had themselves been formed in the Republic. Men were taught that the welfare of the state was safe in the hands of an all-wise monarch, and discovered that none the less his peace did not fulfil their search for spiritual peace (Epictetus iii. 13. 9 ff.). They might seek consolation in philosophic creeds which depreciated all material blessings or in the hopes infused by irrational religions of perpetual sabbaths in another world; this turn of mind was surely prejudicial to secular progress.

[15] See e.g. Jones, 1940, chs. VIII and XI. There is no comparable account of cities in the west (and relatively less evidence), but the juristic texts cited by Jones are of universal application. There had never been much local democracy in the west.

[16] Cf. Schulz, 1953, 99, on jurisprudence under the Principate: 'the heroic age of creative genius and daring pioneers had passed away with the Republic. Now their ideas were to be developed to the full and elaborated down to the last detail.' (cf. 125).

The ultimate beneficiary was Christianity. Its final success was also a by-product of the despotic system. By capturing Constantine and his successors, the faith of a minority conquered the western world, and this despite prolonged opposition in aristocratic circles. Guided by an intolerant Church, the emperors would now use their absolute powers to deny freedom of worship and to dictate the creed of their subjects. 'Cuius regio eius religio' was a principle that went back from the Treaty of Westphalia to the fourth century. At the same time the Church itself adopted internally the principle of monarchy; as Hobbes remarked,[17] 'the Papacy is not other than the Ghost of the deceased Roman Empire, sitting crowned upon the grave thereof'. Only in the continual conflicts of secular and ecclesiastical authority going back to Athanasius and Ambrose could freedom of a kind here and there emerge once more.

But if the Principate progressively eroded freedom, it ended and assuaged the fearful wounds of civil war, which at one time or another gravely affected most of the provinces as much as or more than Italy itself, and which was to recur in only two brief periods (68–9, 193–7) in the next two and a half centuries. Contemporaries of Augustus could visualize the collapse of state and empire, if internal concord were not to be re-established. In the event Roman dominion was also secure during the same stretch of time from serious foreign attack (except under Marcus Aurelius), and when such attacks came at last, accompanied by civil wars, it had the strength to hold out for many more generations. The 'immensa pacis Romanae maiestas' sheltered the continuance and diffusion of Graeco-Roman culture throughout its confines: in some parts of the west it was implanted so deeply that it could not be wholly uprooted even when the empire disintegrated. It may well be that this achievement was conditional on the readiness of local élites not so much to submit to Roman rule as to identify themselves with the rulers: they no longer had cause to consider themselves, as under the Republic, the subjects of an alien and oppressive power. As in other historical processes, gains offset losses. However we may strike the balance, the Roman revolution, though merely political, not touching the social and economic structure of the empire, had momentous consequences both for good and ill.

II

If the Principate was a monarchy which upheld the existing social and economic structure in the interest of the class from which the ruler

---

[17] *Leviathan*, ch. 47.

drew his advisers and assistants in the government, what was the regime it supplanted?

The Republic had no written constitution. Only the civil and criminal law had been codified in the fifth century BC; the extant fragments of the code show that it took existing political institutions for granted. One provision declared that whatever the people last commanded was binding; this meant that there were no 'entrenched' constitutional rules which the people could not change by statute.[18] But few of the rights possessed by people, senate, or magistrates had been established or modified by statute: most rested on custom or tradition.[19] Our term 'constitution' is indeed best rendered by Cicero's periphrasis: 'the political order most wisely instituted by our ancestors' (*Sest.* 137).

The Romans venerated tradition, but it was always evolving; it could actually be contended that change was characteristic of it. When Pompey's opponents in 66 argued that the conferment of a great command on him would be an innovation contrary to ancestral practices, Cicero could reply that it was traditional to adopt new expedients to meet new emergencies.[20] Hence what was constitutional could be a matter of controversy. The most recent practice could be challenged by resurrecting ancient precedents, and vice versa. This kind of uncertainty no doubt made it easier for Augustus to represent his own innovations as a modification rather than the subversion of the old order.

The system was, moreover, finely balanced: the rights of people, magistrates, and senate, if pressed to the uttermost, would lead to breakdown; and the balance depended on some degree of social harmony, which was dissipated in the late Republic.

In the hundred and fifty years before 133 the direction of affairs ordinarily belonged to the senate. Cicero could claim that constitutionally the senate had been placed in charge of the state with the magistrates as its virtual ministers; the senate ought indeed to respect

[18] XII Tables (*FIRA* i². pp. 23 ff.), XII. 5 (= Livy vii. 17. 12), cf. n. 52; ch. 6 nn. 9; 166. The only other surviving references to political institutions are IX. 1 and 4.

[19] Even the civil law of the XII Tables was brought up to date not so much by new statutes as by the actions taken by the praetors in virtue of their *imperium*; by creating new remedies they in fact made new law, supplementing and even setting aside that of the code (see Jolowicz-Nicholas, 1972, 97 ff.). No doubt they acted by the advice of a *consilium* (Schulz, 1946, 52) of notables, and they could have been restrained by consuls or tribunes if their innovations had not accorded with the public interest (as seen by their own class). Normally innovations were incorporated in the praetor's largely tralatician edict. Many provisions in the XII Tables had without being repealed fallen by custom into abeyance in later times (e.g. III. 5 f., VIII. 1, 18, 21, 23 f.); other *leges* could also fall into desuetude (e.g. ch. 6 n. 60).

[20] Livy iv. 4; Cic. *de imp. Cn. Pomp.* 60. Cf. *de rep.* ii. 2 (citing Cato), 30, 37; Polyb. vi. 10. 13 on the long constitutional evolution at Rome.

the freedom and interests of the commons, but he allots them no more than a passive role. Nominally this body of ex-magistrates sitting for life and incorporating political experience was a council summoned by magistrates to tender advice, and its decrees took the form of recommendations; in reality the magistrates could be expected to comply with their will. It is not necessary to enumerate the specific powers which it had acquired by custom, some of which will appear later: there was no matter of state on which it could not claim to be consulted, and as the people could act only on the initiative of magistrates, it could through them exert its influence on popular decisions. As we have seen, it was itself dominated by the nobility. Sallust viewed the regime as oligarchical: a few men, whom he more or less identified with the senate as well as with the nobility, monopolized power for their own advantage; the commons were too little organized to resist.[21] Modern writers usually accept his conception of the system as oligarchical, whether or not they are so ready to condemn the policies pursued.

Polybius, however, who lived at Rome in the heyday of senatorial ascendancy, did not agree. He was well aware of the great power the senate enjoyed. He emphasizes its supervision of public finance and of affairs in Italy, and its responsibility for Rome's diplomatic relations (vi. 13), which his narrative continually brings out. He points to certain ways in which the senate could bring magistrates and people into conformity with its will (vi. 15, 17). He admits that Greeks in general regarded it as supreme (vi. 13. 9). But he contends in effect that this conception was one-sided and that his own familiarity with Roman institutions enables him to correct it. He adopted the view long ago propounded by Greek theorists that the best attainable constitution, however it fell short of the ideal, was one in which monarchic, aristocratic, and democratic elements were mixed or balanced. Such systems were characterized by complexity and durability, both features manifest in the Roman. Polybius concluded that the Roman constitution was mixed.[22] The senate formed the aristocratic element, aristocratic and not oligarchic, since for Polybius oligarchs were men of birth and wealth who abused power for their own advantage (vi. 4. 3, 6. 8), whereas the senators owed their position to having been elected to magistracies for their services to the state (14, 9). The monarchic element was supplied by the consuls, the democratic by the assemblies (11, 12).

Cicero was to adopt a somewhat similar view. Without analysing

---

[21] Cic. *Sest.* 137; Sall. *BJ* 42 f., etc.

[22] Complexity: vi. 3. 3, 11. 11–13. Long evolution: n. 20. On the theories of Polybius and Cicero see most recently W. Nippel, *Mischverfassungstheorie u. Verfassungsrealität in Antike u. früher Neuzeit*, 1980, 142 ff., and J.-L. Ferrary, *JRS* 1984, 87 ff., with bibliographies. Nippel holds that the Roman system rested simply on the unity of the nobility and broke down when it was dissolved. This seems to me true only to the extent that popular discontents could find no effective expression without the leadership of individual aristocrats.

the functions of the different organs of government, as Polybius did, in order to show how one operated as a check on another, he detected a balance between the *potestas* of the magistrates, the *auctoritas* of the senate or leading men, and the *libertas* of the people, by which he certainly meant not only the protection of their persons but some degree of participation in political decisions (*de rep.* ii. 57); still, the duty of the magistrates was to conform to the will of the senate, and the system could work only if the people's share in power was largely specious (pp. 324 ff.). In fact Polybius too recognized that the aristocratic element predominated (vi. 51, xxiii. 14. 1). Was not the mixed constitution then essentially a sham? So Tacitus presumably conceived, in writing that 'All nations or cities are governed either by the people or the chief men or a monarch; a political system based on a selection and combination of these elements can more readily be commended than come into existence, or then long endure.' (*Ann.* iv. 33.)

By contrast Polybius and Cicero evidently held that the balance they discerned in the system contributed to that harmony, ensuring stability, which in Polybius' view had assisted Rome to come through the crisis of the Hannibalic war, and which Cicero's ideal statesman would contrive to restore and maintain (*de rep.* ii. 69). In the late Republic the consensus was indeed dissolved; none the less, an examination of the institutions in which Polybius and Cicero had seen monarchic and democratic factors at work may help us to understand the constitutional preconditions for revolutionary change.

It must seem paradoxical that Polybius viewed the consulship as a monarchic element. True, the Romans themselves supposed that the *imperium* which the consuls (and some other magistrates and promagistrates) possessed, essentially a discretionary power to do whatever the public welfare required, had been transmitted to them without restriction from the kings.[23]

Polybius noted (vi. 12. 2) that they were supreme over all other magistrates with the important exception of the tribunes. This was a half-truth. In practice the multiplicity of public business at Rome precluded them from regular interference in the functions of inferior magistrates, and in particular with the jurisdiction of the praetors, and if they had a theoretical right to give directions to promagistrates governing provinces and commanding armies, which some deny, it fell into desuetude. Moreover, as the office was collegiate, each consul was subject to the veto of the other, as well as to that of any of the ten tribunes. They were bound by oath to obey the laws, which included

---

[23] Cic. *de rep.* ii. 56; Livy ii. 1. 7 f. (accepted by Mommsen, dogmatically rejected by Ogilvie ad loc.).

restrictions on their power to condemn citizens to death and other heavy penalties.[24] Though they could not be arraigned for illegality while they held *imperium*, their tenure was for one year only, unless they were prorogued in military command or civil government outside the city by the people, or from the time of the Hannibalic war by the senate alone; and once they had demitted *imperium*, they could be brought to account before the people or a court constituted by the people (p. 20). For the rest of their lives they would mostly hold no further office. But they continued to sit in the senate. Their most permanent interest was therefore to exalt the authority of that body, in which they could hope to exercise long-lasting influence. This consideration would surely have enhanced the deference which a consul might generally be expected to feel for the opinion of his peers, but if he were recalcitrant, the senate could often restrain him through the agency of his colleague or of the tribunes.

However, the senate had no executive power; it could exert its will only through the magistrates, especially the consuls when they were in Rome. Thus in times of turbulence from 121 the senate would call on the magistrates to see to it that the commonwealth came to no harm. Though this decree cannot have had any force in strict law, it gave the magistrates the strongest moral support, if in coercing and punishing 'seditious' citizens they paid no regard to the right of trial by due process of law or to tribunician vetoes. Impeached for such action, Opimius, the consul of 121, was acquitted by the centuriate assembly in which the well-to-do, attached to the maintenance of order, preponderated. This was a precedent of moment. Thereafter no one denied in principle that the magistrates had extraordinary powers in a state of emergency declared by the senate, though it could still be argued that particular circumstances did not justify such a declaration.[25] But it was useless to declare it, if the consuls were present in Rome but not in accord with it; or rather it was impossible, as the senate could not even frame a decree without their consent.[26] Thus 'sedition' could not be repressed in 59, when the consul Caesar was its

---

[24] An oath to obey the laws was a precondition of assuming office (Livy xxxi. 50. 6 f.); at the end of their term magistrates swore that they had done so (Cic. *Fam.* v. 2. 7), a ritual still observed by Trajan (Pliny, *Paneg.* 65). For laws of late Republic that required an oath of compliance from senators as well as magistrates see ch. 2 App. IV; cf. Cic. *Att.* ii. 18. 2.

[25] Caes. *BC* i. 7; Sall. *Cat.* 29; Opimius, *GC* 120. Cicero argued that a citizen in arms against the state had forfeited citizen rights (*Cat.* iv. 10). *Populares* could hold that persons in custody were entitled to trial. This was the basis of the charge against Rabirius in 63 and of Clodius' persecution of Cicero: neither the *SC ult.* nor the decree procured by Cicero from the senate for the execution of the Catilinarian conspirators (the senate not being a court of law) was a defence of his procedure. All the evidence is discussed by Baron Ungern-Sternberg von Pürkel, *Unters. zur spätrepublikanischen Notstandsrecht,* 1970.

[26] See endnote 2.

author, or in 58, when the consuls had made a pact with the tribune Clodius. In any event the assumption of unrestricted power by the consuls in emergencies does not mean that the consular prerogative was normally monarchical.

Polybius' view was no doubt based on the position of the consul or proconsul as army commander or provincial governor. He then had life-and-death authority over soldiers and most subjects. There was no colleague or tribune to interfere. He was hardly accountable to public opinion at Rome, or to be restrained except by his own conscience.[27] He might on his return be impeached for violations of law, but the chances that charges would be both preferred and successful were probably not high, unless his misdeeds were peculiarly heinous. Polybius notes that he was still subject to control by the senate, in that it could grant or withhold money and supplies, and approve or refuse prolongation of his tenure and the coveted honour of a triumph (vi. 15). But space and time foiled close supervision.

Only the people in theory could make war and treaties. In practice the senate usually decided issues of foreign policy which were referred to Rome. Yet the commander in the field had a wide discretion. He might destroy a hostile community or receive its surrender on terms of his choosing.[28] He could admit a neutral people to the friendship of Rome,[29] and Rome, or her generals, when it seemed expedient, would then construe an attack on her friend's interests as an attack on her own. He could also negotiate a peace treaty: it required ratification at Rome, and if it were humiliating, it might be repudiated; but the authority of a victorious general was usually potent enough to secure acceptance of the provisions he had agreed to.[30] The senate would appoint ten legates to assist and guide him in the settlement of an area which Rome had taken under her administration or protectorate, but the victorious general commonly had his

---

[27] Cic. *Qu. fr.* i. 1. 22: in Asia 'tanta multitudo civium, tanta sociorum, tot urbes, tot civitates unius hominis nutum intuentur, ubi nullum auxilium [sc. of tribunes] est, nulla conquestio, nullus senatus, nulla contio'; *Qu. fr.* i. 2. illustrates the arbitrary conduct of Q. Cicero, which did indeed generate protests at Rome from those who had access to persons of influence there. Verres, whose conduct was incomparably more outrageous, disregarded all such representations, yet was twice prorogued. Of course governors could be charged on return with *repetundae*, maiestas, or *peculatus*, but the courts were often biased or venal; and the chance of conviction might depend on extraneous political circumstances.

[28] When the senate rejected the treaty that M. Marcellus (*cos.* 151) had negotiated with Celtiberians (the people, as usual, was not consulted), he accepted their *deditio* on terms similar to the treaty, and his successor, though avid for war, could not undo his action. (App. *Iber.* 48–50; Polyb. xx. 9. 10 f.).

[29] E. Badian, *JRS* 1952, 76 ff., for the Achaeans in 198.

[30] e.g. treaties with Carthage in 202 and 201, with Philip V in 197, and with Antiochus in 189. The case in n. 28 is exceptional; pacts with Numantia in 137 and with Jugurtha in 112 and 111 were disavowed as shameful.

way in the end, if there were dissension between him and any of the legates.[31]

Most wars were undeclared, resulting from what were taken to be acts of aggression by a foreign ruler or people against Rome or her allies or friends. Many were initiated on such pretexts by commanders in the field. The governor was not to make war or lead his forces beyond his province without the prior sanction of senate and people, but these restrictions, reaffirmed by a law moved by Caesar in 59, were often violated and hardly practical. Roman frontiers were not always clearly marked, and beyond them there were often predatory barbarian tribes. A governor might well be justified in conducting 'hot pursuit' of such tribes after an incursion, nor was it easy for those at Rome to see whether he had invented pretexts for a war, and really provoked it out of desire for booty and a triumph. In Spain, north Italy, and Macedon, new wars and extensions of Roman territory often came about in this way. Caesar's conquest of Gaul is only the most salient instance.[32] It was in the process that the army which enabled him to make himself master of the state had been hardened, and its allegiance secured by his liberality and charismatic prestige.

Of course Caesar was less inhibited in violating his own law because he and his political associates were dominant at Rome. Moreover, like Pompey in 67 and 66 he had received an extraordinary long-term command from the people. The holders of such commands were independent of the senate. It was in this capacity too that they could build up a military power of their own with which to put pressure on the senate or to defeat it in armed conflict. The extraordinary commands of the Republic furnished the precedents for the grant to Augustus of the provinces in which most of the legions were stationed. His consular *imperium* was the legal basis for his continuing military might (though it was also by military might that he had first obtained it), and as he kept it for life and had no colleague, *imperium* once again came to be truly monarchical, irresponsible, and unchecked.

Thus Polybius was percipient and prophetic in detecting a monarchic element inherent in the consulship, or rather, in the consular *imperium*. This is no less true of his valuation of the powers of the people, which in his own day was generally acquiescent in senatorial rule.[33]

[31] See Polyb. xviii. 45, 47; Livy xxxviii. 44–50 for disputes of Flamininus and Manlius Vulso with his legates. Flamininus' policy was adopted in the end, and Vulso's retroactively endorsed by his triumph.

[32] Aggressions by generals: Livy xlii. 7–9, 21 f.; App. *Iber.* 48–55, 59 f., *GC* 63 f., 86. Restraining laws: *JRS* 1974, 202; Cic. *Pis.* 50. Caesar: Brunt, *Laus Imperii*, 178 ff.

[33] For what follows on the powers of the people cf. Finley, 1983, chs. 4 and 5; F. Millar, *JRS* 1984, 1 ff.; both question if the Roman system was narrowly oligarchical. Millar, with whom I agree in general, is rather too much impressed by forms, and fails to bring out how little the people affected foreign policy and imperial administration in Polybius' time.

His analysis is no doubt very defective. He concentrates on formal rights exercised, as all his readers would assume, by assemblies meeting at Rome in which all citizens could vote. They alone could elect magistrates, decide on peace and war, try political offenders, and enact new laws (vi. 14).

What did these rights really amount to?

At elections, though it could be claimed that the people was free to choose whom it would (ch. 6 n. 114), candidates had to be men of wealth. Most of those returned to the highest offices were nobles; the reasons for this will be examined later. Nearly all were ready to defer to the senate's collective will. Still, in times of popular discontent the electors would return men prepared to defy the senate. The allocation of provinces to those elected was ordinarily a matter in part for the senate, in part for agreement among the magistrates. But the people would at times insist by clamour or through legislation that a particular magistrate of its own designation should be appointed to a particular command. It was in this way that Scipio Aemilianus secured commands against Carthage and Numantia, and Marius in the Jugurthine and Cimbric wars. Even in such matters the people retained sovereignty in the last resort.

Questions of war and peace were often referred to the people, and even debated before them, but there is no case in which the people in Polybius' time effectively overruled the will of the senate; indeed once a war had begun, a proposal for peace, so far as we know, was never submitted to the assembly without the senate's prior sanction. A treaty not approved by the people was not binding on it; none the less the so-called treaty with Gades, made by an officer in the field and later confirmed by the senate but not by the people, was not the only instance of its kind.[34] It was the senate too that most commonly granted privileges such as 'freedom' to provincial cities, and Polybius attests that it handled relations with the Italian allies. Not indeed that the senate itself was in full control of all affairs overseas; as we have seen, generals could on their own initiative launch wars, end hostilities, and accept obligations to new 'friends' of Rome, which might thereafter be treated as commitments of the state. None the less, the formal sovereignty of the people in foreign relations was frequently observed, and from the time of the Gracchi onwards the people could therefore be invited to exercise it against the will of the senate. Whereas it was in the senate that the policy of destroying Carthage's last remnant of power was discussed and decided, it was popular initiatives that forced on war à outrance against Jugurtha. The Gracchan agrarian law also

---

[34] Cic. *Balb.* 37; cf. Brunt, *CQ* 1982, 137 ff.

disturbed relations with the Italian allies and thereby led on to the moves of Fulvius Flaccus and Gaius Gracchus to extend the Roman citizenship by popular legislation.

The people had important powers of jurisdiction. In Polybius' time it was the law that every citizen (unless on military service) could appeal to the centuriate assembly against capital sentences imposed by a magistrate. Within the city the tribunes could enforce this right by interposing against a magistrate who sought to disregard it. Moreover, the tribunes had acquired the competence to bring capital charges themselves before the centuries, and charges on which the penalty was a fine before the tribes. Once they were out of office, former magistrates who had violated the citizen's right of appeal or to whom any other offence could be imputed were thus liable to impeachment before the people. It seems to me virtually certain that in practice, before Gaius Gracchus reinforced the right of appeal, it was not available to persons prosecuted for common crimes, who were given a fair trial by a magistrate with his *consilium*: on the other hand it was normally unsafe for magistrates even to attempt to try and sentence men accused of political offences which carried a capital penalty. These were brought not on appeal but in the first instance, before the people (cf. ch. 4, section VI and ch. 6, section XI). When Polybius asserts that the people determines all cases involving a heavy fine, especially those brought against men who had held high office, and can alone impose the death sentence (vi. 14), it is political trials that he must have in mind, as is only natural, given that his theme is the political balance of the constitution. But the people's power of jurisdiction meant that magistrates were accountable to the people. Even if prosecutions were brought or procured by aristocratic enemies of the defendants, it was the people that sat in judgment. This was not simply a guarantee of the private rights of citizens, who were in consequence less likely to suffer from wrongdoing by magistrates than Italian allies or other subjects: it was a weapon by which the people might make the magistrates attentive to its will. The constitution by the people of *ad hoc* courts to try men accused of bringing dishonour or disaster on the state, as under the Mamilian law of 108, served the same purpose, when they were composed of Equites and not of senators, who tended to be partial to their peers. From the late second century it became the practice to set up standing courts for the trial of certain statutory offences, and once these existed trials before the people went out of vogue. But except in the decade after Sulla's dictatorship these courts, to which the people delegated its capital jurisdiction, also consisted entirely or mainly of non-senatorial jurors; senators were not to be accountable to members of their own order alone.

Legislation was relatively infrequent. In the century before the Gracchi most of it was probably promoted at the desire of the senate, where debate, if it were controversial, would have taken place. Still, Flaminius' agrarian law of 232, which Polybius, no doubt reflecting aristocratic recollections in his own time, regarded as ominous of future demagogic corruption of the people (ii. 21. 8), and the Claudian law of 218 (p. 173), restricting the commercial activity of senators, passed against the will of the senate. These may not be the only cases. Livy's narrative of internal events between 218 and 167 is very defective; he records some laws which must have been more controversial than he reveals, and ignores altogether others like the Cincian law of 204 (ch. 8 n. 109) and the Porcian laws on appeal to the people (pp. 331 f.), almost certainly of this period, which served the interests of common folk and cannot have been pleasing to the rich and noble. He says nothing too of the law restricting holdings of public domain land (App. i. 8), which Tiberius Gracchus was to implement by distributing it among the poor; most scholars assume that it had been enacted after the Hannibalic war, and certainly Livy's failure to record it is no proof that it can be identified only with the attested but perhaps unhistoric Licinio-Sextian law of 367.[35] The Gracchi had their immediate precursors in tribunician agitators against conscription and in the authors of ballot laws, two of which preceded Tiberius' tribunate.[36] If the people had been for the most part quiescent in the previous century, it was perhaps partly because they were absorbed in foreign wars,[37] partly because the discontents expressed by the Gracchi were the result of a gradual process, and partly, as Sallust says (*BJ* 41), because their strength was unorganized until determined leaders emerged from the ruling class.

In any event the legislative prerogative of the people was undiminished. Most laws were proposed by tribunes. The tribunate had been instituted in the early Republic to protect the commons against the senate, then dominated by the patricians, of whom the nobility, including great plebeian families, were the successors in power. It was to perform this function that the tribunes had acquired both legislative initiative and a veto on the official acts of magistrates within Rome, and even on decrees of the senate (which magistrates might otherwise

[35] For non-controversial legislation see n. 38: it included the measures for land settlement from 200 to 173, which Livy sometimes refers to a *lex*, sometimes to a *SC*, sometimes to both; like other ancient historians he cared little for formalities: both were surely required (Millar, *JRS* 1984, 7 f., needs modification). Finley, 1983, 98, lists some possibly controversial measures mentioned by Livy.

[36] L. R. Taylor, *JRS* 1962, 19 ff.; cf. ch. 6 n. 103.

[37] Sall. *Hist.* i. 12; it was a commonplace in annalistic accounts of the conflicts between patricians and plebeians that they flared up in times of relative peace.

have been expected to carry out). The tribunate thus became traditionally a bastion of popular liberty, that is to say not only the freedom
of ordinary citizens from arbitrary oppression, but their right to share
in the control of the state. In Polybius' time indeed the tribunes, often
themselves nobles, commonly acted as convenient instruments of the
senate in promoting legislation it desired or impeding magistrates who
did not render it customary obedience.[38] But their original role was
not forgotten.

Polybius said that in exercising their veto they were 'to aim at doing
what the people wished' (vi. 16. 5). On such occasions, when they
could not consult the people, they were to judge for themselves what
the people's wish was. Their negative voice was decisive just because
they were deemed to personify the people. It would then be a
constitutional solecism if they were to use the veto actually to deny the
people an opportunity to express its will in legislation when the
opportunity was offered. Hence in 195 under strong popular pressure,
two tribunes abandoned the intention of vetoing the abrogation of the
Oppian law (Livy xxxiv. 5. 1), and in 188 other tribunes were induced
to withdraw a veto on the bill to enfranchise the citizens of Arpinum,
Fundi, and Formiae, on the ground that it was for the people, not the
senate (which presumably disapproved), to grant voting rights as it
pleased (Livy xxxviii. 36). In 137 a veto on a ballot law was similarly
withdrawn (Cic. *Brut.* 97). In 133 Tiberius Gracchus had probably
departed from constitutional practice in proposing the distribution of
public land without consulting the senate, but Octavius was guilty of a
graver impropriety in seeking to hinder the tribes from voting on the
proposal. Gracchus is said to have implored him 'not to frustrate the
earnest wishes of the people, to which as a tribune he should properly
yield'. Gracchus' deposition of Octavius could be assailed as a violation
of tribunician sacrosanctity, but he could reply that a tribune who
maimed the assembly by robbing it of its freedom to vote was no true
tribune.

Few attempts were made later to veto bills which manifestly had
overwhelming popular support. In 103 (?) the tribune Norbanus
overrode a veto by mob violence (a course that others would follow):
years later he was prosecuted for *maiestas*, and M. Antonius as his
counsel asserted that all magistrates 'ought to be in the power of the
Roman people' and that Norbanus was justified in adopting any
means to enforce the will of the whole citizen body. In 67 Gabinius
threatened a colleague who sought to veto the bill investing Pompey
with command against the pirates with the fate of Octavius; Cicero,

---

[38] Bleicken, 1955, is exhaustive on tribunician legislation and other activity 287–133.

who like Antonius could for forensic purposes flout his own principles, upheld his action on the ground that the voice and will of a single man should not prevail against that of the entire people (ch. 6 n. 157). Like Antonius he too could recall the early secessions of the plebs to show that force was warranted in the cause of popular freedom or sovereignty. It was a consummation of popular ideology when Clodius by a law of 58 removed virtually all the legal limitations on that sovereignty (ch. 6 n. 158).[39]

The legislative proposals made by the Gracchi as tribunes set the revolutionary process in train. From their time to Sulla's, tribunes continued intermittently to challenge senatorial control of the state in the name of the people. Having become master of Rome by force, Sulla thought it a sufficient check on the people's power to deprive the tribunes of their right to introduce bills, at least without the prior sanction of the senate, to curtail their right of veto, and perhaps to debar them from bringing impeachments before the assembly (ch. 6 n. 134). But he did not strike at the legislative initiative of consuls, and in 70 Pompey and Crassus in that capacity could carry a law that restored the full tribunician power. Once again tribunes became the instruments for asserting the people's sovereignty. A chain of events connects the law of the tribune Gabinius in 67 with the civil wars in which the Republic finally collapsed. Of course the Gabinian law was among those which in reality built up the power of dynasts like Pompey. None the less it was not enacted just to satisfy Pompey's inordinate ambition. It was demanded by the people, and was necessary in the public interest.

III

It is then a mistake to depreciate the constitutional rights of the people. It is far more debatable whether, as Polybius held, there was a truly democratic element in the Roman polity. What is meant by 'the people'? Even in Polybius' day there were some 400,000 adult male citizens, who could not possibly have been brought together in a single voting place nor accommodated in the city.[40] Many of them already lived at a considerable distance. In order that they should have an opportunity of attending assemblies, three weeks' notice of meetings and their agenda had, very properly, to be given; this meant in itself

[39] Cic. *de orat.* ii. 167, 199; Ascon. 72, 76 C., texts which make it plausible that Plut. *Ti. Gr.* 15 and App. i. 12 preserve authentic reports of Gracchus' case. Livy v. 29. 6 f. probably reflects the controversy (*contra* Ogilvie ad hoc.).

[40] *IM* ch. v; L. R. Taylor, 1966, ch. III, estimates that there was room for at most 70,000 in the Campus Martius.

that the people could never take emergency decisions.[41] Meetings were rare, and the people was never able to exercise that superintendence of everyday affairs which was vested in the assembly of democratic Athens. Nor could poor men afford to travel many days' journey to Rome, leaving their farms or shops. The enfranchisement of Italy made it only marginally more ludicrous to regard a primary assembly at Rome in which theoretically all citizens were entitled to vote as the true voice of the people.

The Roman practice of dividing the citizens into groups with the effect that a majority was composed not of heads but of these groups might conceivably have provided a remedy. In fact it did not.[42] For the tribal assembly which elected the tribunes and enacted nearly all laws, the citizens were registered in thirty-five local constituencies called tribes, four within the city of Rome, and thirty-one without. Probably in early times the urban voters were under-represented, while the 'rural' tribes, of which there were originally only seventeen, with areas closely surrounding the city, were more or less equal. But as Roman territory extended, even to very remote parts of Italy, some but not all of these tribes received exclaves, and fourteen additional tribes were progressively created, the last two in 241, with areas much larger and a far greater population than those still purely suburban. After 90 the new Italian citizens were more or less arbitrarily distributed among the existing tribes, with no attempt to introduce a greater equality between them. Hence a majority of tribes was by no means identical with a majority of citizens.

Elections to the higher magistracies, questions of war and peace, and capital trials were for the centuriate assembly. Here the people were divided into voting units, centuries, on the basis of property and age as well as tribal registrations. There were 193 centuries. Of these 18 belonged to those Equites to whom the censors had given a public horse, 70 to the first property class, one for *iuniores* (aged 18 to 44), and one for *seniores* (aged 45 and over) for each tribe. The second class contained 20 or 25 centuries. If among these centuries 97 concurred, they constituted an absolute majority, and no other classes would be called to vote. This was true even in elections: a candidate was returned once he had an absolute majority. The very poor, who probably composed almost half the citizen body as early as the Hannibalic war, still more later,[43] voted last and therefore in practice not at all, unless the issue were to be decided by a single century.

[41] A. W. Lintott, *CQ* 1965, 281 ff.
[42] I ignore the curiate asembly with its purely formal functions and the distinction between the tribal *concilium plebis*, from which the few patricians were excluded, and the *comitia tributa*, in which they could vote. For the tribes see ch. 6 n. 169; on the centuriate assembly ibid. nn. 162–4 with text.
[43] *IM* 64–8. Note Dionysius iv. 18. 2, vii. 59. 6.

There is some reason to believe that the well-to-do would attend meetings of this assembly from all parts of Italy, at any rate for the annual elections:[44] hence, if we ignore the distortions produced by the inequality of tribes and the disproportionate voting power of older citizens, commonly no doubt the most conservative of their own class, it was not wholly unrepresentative of men of property. Equally it was not in the least democratic. It is no doubt the people in this sense of which Polybius was thinking when he suggests that the senate could keep it under control by its right to vary the terms of public contracts in which 'nearly everyone' had an interest and because senators had a monopoly of deciding the most important civil suits in the courts (vi. 17). Poor men have no money to invest and no resources for litigation. The timocratic character of the centuriate assembly makes it easier to understand why it was ready to acquit Opimius (p. 16) and why the proposal to restore Cicero from exile was submitted to it (*post red. Quir.* 17) and not to the tribal assembly which normally enacted laws and which had approved his banishment; Opimius could claim that he had been the champion of order, and Cicero stood for property interests. None the less the centuries were capable of electing to the highest office men inimical to the nobility such as Marius in 108, Cinna in 88, and Caesar in 60. They were not always docile tools of the great houses.

However, the chief danger came from the tribal assembly. Some meetings were thinly attended, no doubt when legislation was a formality.[45] A few voters might then represent a rural tribe. At one time they would perhaps be its richer members, men who had an urban residence or the means to absent themselves from their country property and travel to Rome. However, there was always some immigration to Rome. When citizens changed their domicile, it was the duty of the censors to register them in a different tribe, but in the intervals between censuses they retained their existing registration. Moreover, we cannot be sure that all censors were diligent in their work. Between 70 and 28 no censors formally completed their tasks, and it is sometimes held (though it seems to me unlikely)[46] that the census rolls came to be wholly out of date. At any rate, it seems that in the late Republic the tribal assembly was dominated by urban dwellers, who must have commonly controlled the votes of nominally rural tribes. Hence, for instance, the importance of corn doles for winning popular support, and the clamour in 67 on Rome's food supply. In 133 Tiberius Gracchus' agrarian bill brought in a concourse

---

[44] ch. 2. nn. 108–10, n. 116, ch. 8, v.

[45] Taylor, 1949, 60, is, I think, mistaken in treating *Sest.* 105 as applicable to controversial bills.

[46] *IM* 105, 700–2.

of country voters, and this recurred in 100 and perhaps whenever the distribution of lands to peasants or veterans was broached. But these were exceptional occasions. Tiberius Gracchus himself, when seeking a second term as tribune, found that his rural supporters were busy with harvesting operations (probably the vintage), and he began to woo the urban proletariate. This could have been of little advantage if they had all been confined within four of the thirty-five tribes.[47]

In any event the assemblies, even though never truly representative of the whole citizen body, could express the will of sections of that body, which had interests distinct from those of the senatorial oligarchy and which were not always compliant to its will. It is true that their independence was limited in various ways, but the checks that the senate could employ were not effective when sections of the people were thoroughly aroused, had resolute leadership, and could command a majority in one of the assemblies.

The assemblies could do nothing except on the initiative of presiding magistrates.[48] They alone could admit men to stand for office, propose laws (which the people could accept or reject but not amend), and impeach political offenders. (It may incidentally be observed that the senate too could meet only on the summons of a magistrate and pass decrees only with his assent, and that in our own Parliament bills normally emanate from ministers of the Crown and are never carried against their will.) However, legally qualified candidates were never or hardly ever barred from standing (ch. 9 n. 14), and for legislation or impeachments there were ten tribunes, to say nothing of other magistrates, who could each take the initiative.

It is also alleged that there was little debate on questions laid before the people. This rests on a misunderstanding. There was no discussion in the formal meetings (*comitia*) at which the votes were taken, but on any controversial issue they were preceded by meetings (*contiones*), which could indeed be summoned only by a magistrate and addressed only by him or by persons he invited to speak; but as any magistrate could summon a *contio*, and not only he who would preside over the *comitia*, rival views on controversial questions would be fully presented.[49] No doubt the speakers were almost invariably senators, but they could include those who had defected from the senate's cause.

---

[47] App. i. 10, 14, 29 f., 32. Cic. *de leg. agr.* ii. 71 presupposes that there were urban dwellers in rural tribes. Cf. *ILS* 168 (AD 23): 'plebs urbana quinque et triginta tribuum' and Taylor, 1949, 200 n. 12, on *ILS* 6046: Mommsen, whom she cites, held that the figures related to new entrants on the register of dole-recipients; they would then suggest that in the Principate the great majority of urban dwellers were still in the urban tribes.

[48] Polybius did not note this; he could expect his readers to assume it from current Greek practice (Jones, 1940, 166 ff.).

[49] Taylor, 1966, ch. II.

Even in democratic Athens, where every citizen had a right to be heard, the 'orators' formed a class of more or less professional politicians, men who had the leisure to acquaint themselves with public affairs[50] and to cultivate the arts of persuasion; there too they must generally have been persons of some property and social standing.

Attempts could be made to obstruct the popular will in various ways. No more need be said of the tribunician veto, which proved ineffective as a barrier to proposals that had overwhelming popular support. Religious impediments might be discovered by magistrates or by the colleges of priests, composed mainly of aristocrats with the greatest political influence (Cic. *de dom.* 1). Cicero alleged that they had often been used to defeat seditious movements. But instances are hard to find. Bibulus' attempt in 59 to invalidate by one of these devices the legislation of Caesar and Vatinius had no success, though in 58 Clodius thought it well to bar similar action for the future.[51] A law of 98 BC empowered the senate to annul statutes passed in violation of specified conditions for their validity. It actually quashed the laws of Titius (tribune in 99) and Drusus (tribune in 91) by this authority, but it never ventured on this course against laws that retained widespread popular support.[52] Statutes might, indeed, be inoperative (like decrees of the senate) from the unwillingness of the magistrates to carry them out. In this way, for instance, the legal restriction on the amount of public land an individual might occupy had in 133 fallen into abeyance. The Plotian law of *c.* 70, providing for the allotment of lands to veterans, seems never to have been put into effect (ch. 5 n. 3). It was prudent for the authors of agrarian laws, like Tiberius Gracchus in 133 and Caesar in 59, to secure the appointment of commissioners with the power and will to execute them. In any event, the last century of the Republic is replete with examples of laws proposed or carried in conformity with popular demands against the will of the senate.

No doubt the magnates sought to apply pressure to voters by the exercise of political and economic power or by the claims of patronage. In modern accounts of Roman society the place of patronage has assumed enormous proportions.[53] It is often supposed that the great

[50] In this connection Arist. *Rhet.* i. 4 is too little pondered.

[51] Cic. *de leg.* iii. 27 (cf. ii. 30 f.) and his attacks on Vatinius' disregard of *obnuntiatio* and on Clodius' law restricting its use, e.g. *post red. sen.* 11, *Sest.* 33 f., *Vat.* 14, 18. In *de div.* ii. 28, 43, 75 he suggests, agreeing with his fellow-augur C. Marcellus (*cos.* 50), that some practices of divination had been invented for political expediency. Taylor, 1949, ch. IV, reveals without stating how little these devices served to obstruct popular legislation.

[52] Lintott, 1968, ch. x. The law was perhaps declaratory of traditional rules.

[53] My discussion of *clientela* here is based on ch. 8 (section v for elections). Ballot laws: ch. 6 n. 103; cf. p. 423. On elections Taylor, 1949, ch. III, probably has the best account (to be read critically), with too much stress on *clientela*, though less than Staveley, 1972.

families had hordes of clients who would vote at their behest. Yet assemblies in and after the time of the Gracchi, and occasionally before then, passed laws, and more rarely elected magistrates, contrary to the wishes of almost all the nobility. It follows that their clients were in a minority, or were not dependable. Patrons could most easily exert pressure when voting was open, but the ballot was introduced against the opposition of the nobility for elections in 139, most popular trials in 137, legislation in 131, and treason trials in 107. The first three of these laws, like the measures of Tiberius Gracchus, were actually carried by open voting. Cicero remarks that after the second of these laws defendants had to rely more on the effectiveness of their advocates (*Brut.* 106): there was less room for pressure, more for persuasion.

The importance of patronage is most plausibly used to explain the success of the nobility in elections to the higher magistracies (p. 5).[54] But it need not be the sole, nor even the chief, explanation.

We must not neglect the éclat of a splendid lineage. The names of aristocratic families were inseparably linked with the glories of Rome's past in which Romans of all sorts could take pride. Cicero himself could say, when addressing a mainly equestrian jury, that at elections 'all we good men always favour the nobility' (*Sest.* 21). This way of thinking persisted in the Principate. Tacitus (*Ann.* iv. 6) and the younger Pliny (*Paneg.* 69) approved when emperors advanced men for birth as well as for ability, and Seneca held that it was not unreasonable that even the most worthless aristocrats should be preferred to new men, however energetic: 'the recollection of great virtues is sacred, and there are more who delight in being virtuous, if the credit they gain does not expire with their own lives' (*de benef.* iv. 30); glory, like property, could be inherited. Yet Cicero, Tacitus, Pliny, and Seneca were all parvenus themselves. In the speech that Sallust puts into Marius' mouth (*BJ* 85. 4) we read that nobles would boast of their lineage and 'of the brave deeds of their ancestors'. Servius Sulpicius and Manius Iuventius thought it a plausible contention to argue that Murena and Plancius, candidates of less distinguished descent, could not have been preferred to themselves by the electors, unless they had resorted to corruption (p. 429). It might be hoped that like the emperor Tiberius (*Ann.* iv. 38), or such heroes of the past as Fabius Cunctator and Scipio Africanus, according to the tradition that Sallust reports (*BJ* 4. 5), nobles would strive to 'be worthy of their ancestors'; Marius and others could denounce them, precisely for degenerating from this standard (85. 37).

Great wealth was also an advantage in a political career.[55] Office as

[54] Brunt, *JRS* 1982, 1 ff.; Hopkins and G. Burton *ap.* Hopkins, 1983, ch. II.
[55] See generally Shatzman, 1975.

such and membership of the senate were unpaid. Ostentatious consumption, the gratification of the electorate with costly shows and feasts, and even outright bribery, enhanced the chances of competitors. Candidates were required by law to possess the equestrian census of 100,000 *denarii* (ch. 3 n. 3), but in fact most of them needed and possessed far greater resources. L. Aemilius Paullus (*cos.* 182, 168), who was not reckoned particularly rich for a senator, was said to be worth 370,000, with an income of perhaps 16,500 at a time when the legionary had to subsist on a wage of probably 120. Far larger fortunes are known from Cicero's day; he suggested that a man of high station needed 25,000 a year.[56] Aristotle observed that 'high birth is simply ancient riches and excellence' (*Pol.* 1294[a]13), and successful members of the Roman nobility must generally have inherited large properties. Though some houses probably decayed from extravagance, others were able to recoup the costs of political advancement from the profits, legitimate or illicit, of war and government. Sallust suggests that the oligarchs used their political dominance to line their own pockets.[57] The new men who competed with them necessarily belonged to the same economic stratum; they aspired to be accepted by the nobility and to found new noble houses; they might be associates of individual aristocrats. They did not then as such represent any interests or ideas opposed to those of the nobility, and there was no reason why the electorate should not prefer scions of famous families. It was rare for any candidates to come forward with a political programme or to be known in advance to favour one. But when it did happen that a candidate identified himself as an advocate of popular measures, which the senate was likely to oppose, he was more often a dissentient noble like Gaius Gracchus or Caesar than a new man.

The emperor Tiberius was to suggest that men might stand for office in reliance on *gratia* or *merita* (Tac. *Ann.* i. 81). That surely corresponds to Republican practice.[58] *Gratia* originated partly at least from the private services a candidate had rendered to all sorts of people, and not least to his munificence. Those who were under an obligation to him could be expected to give him their votes and to solicit the votes of others on his behalf. It is plain that in Cicero's time, as probably in earlier periods, it was necessary to woo uncommitted electors. For this purpose the candidate's public services and ability had to be magnified. In a parody of Roman elections Plautus says (*Amph.* 78) that a

[56] Cic. *Parad.* 49. Paulus; *ESAR* i. 209; for later fortunes cf. 387 ff.; Brunt, *Latomus* 1975, 619 ff. Army pay: Polyb. vi. 39. 12, on which see now M. H. Crawford, *Coinage and Money under the Roman Rep.*, 1985, 146 ff.

[57] *Cat.* 20. 7 f., *BJ* 31. 9, 19 f., 25; cf. ch. 1 endnote 7.

[58] See Cic. *Mur.* 20–42, *de offic.* ii. 48–51, 65 f. (on the relative value of military, oratorical, and legal distinction), ii. 52–64 (on munificence).

man should seek votes by his *virtus*, not by his partisans (*favitores*); in fact it was one task of the *favitores* to commend his *virtus*. Distinction in war counted for most. Marius boasted of his military prowess surpassing that displayed by nobles. But probably few parvenus could have outmatched aristocrats in this way. Gnaeus Plancius, for instance, had done nothing of much note (Cic. *Planc.* 60–2). We may guess that aristocratic generals tended to entrust commissions in which men could make their mark to officers of their own social standing.[59] Eloquence in the courts and juristic expertise were also of advantage. But at least until Cicero's time most eminent orators and lawyers were of high birth. No doubt numerous nobles succeeded, as Marius is made to allege, on the basis of the great deeds of their ancestors, the resources of their kin, and the number of their clients (*BJ* 85. 4), and not for any personal merits; but probably few parvenus had had much opportunity to prove their greater capacity for office.

This reference to patronage shows, of course, that it was one factor in the ascendancy of the nobility. Clients, who could include not only individuals, sometimes of standing, but entire communities, were under a hereditary moral obligation of *fides* to aid their patrons in various ways, and notably in voting for them at elections. Patronage did not belong exclusively to noble houses, but given the economic and political power they had enjoyed for generations, theirs must have been the most extensive. Thus a noble had a head start against a new man in competing for office, though not against all of his peers. But no less obviously none could thus command a majority of the electors. It is supposed, however, that families entered into alliances and that all the allies mobilized their own clients in a common cause. It does not matter for the present purpose whether these alliances were long-lasting, a question I shall discuss later; temporary combinations, at least between prominent individuals if not between whole families, there certainly were. We are not indeed told either that clients had a duty to vote not merely for a patron but at his behest, but it may well be that if they felt a genuine loyalty and respect for him, they would have voted on his recommendation. However, clients might have more than one patron and be faced with conflicting obligations; they were morally entitled to set what they saw as the public good above any duty to patrons (pp. 40 f.); they might find that patrons did little for them, and consequently follow their own interest. There is in fact no

[59] Thus 29 military tribunes killed at Cannae were said to be of consular, praetorian, and aedilician rank (Livy xxii. 49. 16). In Cicero's time senators were seldom military tribunes (but note I *Verr.* 30): they were more commonly legates or prefects. Young nobles might secure commissions as legates or prefects with little or no experience. Of 25 attested in 67, mostly under Pompey, probably 17 were of consular family; of 21 in 90 probably 12 (*MRR* ii. 147 ff.; cf. 28 ff.).

testimony that clients were mobilized in the way suggested, and the only detailed evidence we have for elections, which comes from Cicero's time and chiefly from his writings, hardly does more than hint at the value of patronage, whereas it clearly shows that candidates had to solicit the support of countless independent voters, and that birth, personal distinction, gratitude for services previously rendered, largesse, and outright bribery could all contribute to success. It is to be noted that admittedly in exceptional circumstances the electorate preferred both Marius against the united opposition of the nobility, and other new men about the same time, and that very few aristocratic families produced consuls in every generation (n. 54). Some sank into prolonged obscurity, and but for the success of some later scions, we might have supposed that they had died out; we can then assume that some of which we hear no more had not necessarily been extinguished but had passed into permanent oblivion, perhaps by impoverishment. They were not sustained by the loyalty of their dependants.

The importance of patronage has been exaggerated in many other ways. Some have thought that armed gangs and entire armies could be recruited from clients. But we hardly hear of their participation in the gang warfare of the 60s and 50s in the city: it reflected popular unrest. On very few occasions patrons are known to have enlisted their clients as soldiers; but in general it was material rewards rather than hereditary or personal fealty that bound some armies to their commanders, in civil wars; they behaved rather like the mercenaries of *condottieri*.[60] No man, said Crassus, could be accounted rich enough to be *princeps* in the commonwealth who could not support an army with his own money (Cic. *de offic.* i. 25). It has even been suggested that the relationship under which patrons and clients were expected to afford each other mutual aid divided Roman society vertically rather than horizontally and thus averted or mitigated the conflict of classes or sections. This is patently false. Patronage, often veiled under the appellations of friendship or guest-friendship (*hospitium*), extended to men of some social rank such as Equites and to foreign communities, among which we must count those in Italy before the Social war. But it is clear that it did not prevent the conflicts between senate and Equites or allay the Italian discontents, which ultimately broke out in insurrection. Patrons did not protect numerous peasants from expropriation nor sufficiently relieve social distress at Rome. Either they did not fulfil

---

[60] Sall. *BJ* 86. 3 (but note *IM* 406 ff.): 'homini potentiam quaerenti egentissimus quisque opportunissimus, cui neque sua cara, quippe quae nulla sunt, et omnia cum pretio honesta videntur'; App. v. 17, a brilliant analysis of the behaviour of troops in 41 (Pollio's?), applicable in some measure to earlier civil wars. Nepos, *Eumenes* 8, writes of Roman veterans commonly giving orders, not obedience, to their generals, Cf. ch. 5, III–IV.

their obligations to their dependants or there were masses of citizens with no attachment to them. There are some indications that the ties that bound patrons and clients had been stronger in earlier times, though even then they had not prevented grave social conflicts persisting down to 287, and that they were weakening in the late third and second centuries, partly because the claims of patrons were resented. The independence of the assemblies, especially in the last century of the Republic, is decisive proof either that clients of the nobility were a minority, perhaps small, of the citizen body, or that the loyalty of clients could not be counted on.

IV

The modern tendency to overestimate the political importance of clientship is also a basis for the conception that politics at Rome can be interpreted chiefly in terms of struggles for power within the ruling élite. It makes it possible to suppose that by entering into suitable combinations its members could simply manipulate enough voters to gain their ends, without appealing to distinct sectional interests and sentiments. We may then concentrate our attention on contests between aristocratic factions and neglect the attitudes of other classes or sections. This is a preconception not justified by the sources, and it bars comprehension of the real divisions in the citizen body, which in part decided the course of the revolution.

In Sallust's judgement the unbounded passion of the nobility for their *dignitas* and of the people for their *libertas* (both terms connoting political power) tore the commonwealth into two parts.[61] To use the terminology of the time, the politicians on one side, who upheld the authority of the senate, were the *boni* or *optimates*, the good or best citizens; their opponents *populares*. The latter term is also applied to measures, notably those proposed to alleviate social distress, which were carried against the will of the senate. The *populares* were indeed not simply social reformers, real or professed; more fundamentally, they asserted the sovereign right of the people to take decisions without prior sanction of the senate, but in the public interest, as they saw it. Cicero chose to define *populares* as those who merely said and did what would please the masses (*Sest.* 96), but politicians like Caesar who accepted the denomination could not have admitted that, and doubtless claimed that they were acting for the good of the people.[62] And

---

[61] *BJ* 41 f.; *Cat.* 37 f., *Hist.* i. 12; see endnote 3.

[62] *Sest.* 96–105, 136 f., idealizing the optimates (contrast *de rep.* i. 51, iii. 23), and numerous pejorative allusions in intimate letters both to the self-styled *boni* and denigrating the *populares* as demagogues careless of the state's good; as some politicians avowed the name (Cic. *de leg. agr.* ii.

though not democrats intent on making the assemblies responsible for systematically directing all the day-to-day business of the state, they had no scruple in 'proceeding through the people', whenever they saw, or professed to see, a need for the people to intervene. Thus, on learning that King Attalus had bequeathed the kingdom of Pergamum to Rome, Tiberius Gracchus is said at once to have invited the people to apply the royal treasure to equipping the settlers under his agrarian bill, and to have announced that he would make proposals concerning the cities of the kingdom, taking the matter out of the hands of the senate (Plut. *Ti. Gr.* 14); if this account is correct, he precluded the senate from deciding whether or not to accept the legacy, with its implications of closer involvement in Anatolian affairs, and thereby entrenched on the senate's traditional responsibility for finance, foreign policy, and defence. His brother promoted bills not only for the distribution of land allotments and cheap grain but on public works and taxes, the terms of military service, the mode of allotting consular provinces, judicial organization, and the enfranchisement of Italian allies. Hence he was 'unus maxime popularis' (Cic. *de dom.* 24).

The Gracchi set precedents for almost all later 'popular' activity. There was one notable post-Gracchan development. The people not only elected Marius as consul for 107 against the opposition of the nobility but gave him the command against Jugurtha (Sall. *BJ* 73), setting aside the tradition that the senate assigned consular provinces.[63] In 88 a law (undone by Sulla's coup) transferred to Marius as a private individual the command against Mithridates. The commands granted to Pompey in 67 against the pirates and in 66 against Mithridates, to Caesar in 59, and to Pompey and Crassus in 55, were carried through the assembly. These grants were also made for more than one year, the traditional period which it was for the senate to extend, and some of them gave the beneficiaries extraordinary powers.

---

10 etc., *Rab. perd.* 11 ff., *Cat.* iv. 9), they cannot have accepted this description. Popular measures include agrarian, frumentary, and ballot laws (cf. *Sest.* 103, *de leg. agr.* ii. 10, 27, 63, *de leg.* iii. 34–7 etc.), and in general defence of the people's rights or liberty, comprising both personal protection (e.g. *Rab. perd.* 13 ff., *Cat.* iv. 10, *de dom.* 80) and political powers (*de leg. agr.* ii. 17 f., 20, 27, *de leg.* iii. 27); the complete control of senate over the treasury, the subjects, the laws and courts, and foreign policy infringes *libertas* ('Memmius' *ap.* *BJ* 31), and the tribunician power is a 'telum libertatis' (Sall. *Or. Macri* 12), because it enables the plebs to exercise sovereignty. In Livy iii. 39. 9 it is *populare* 'per populum [not "per senatum"] agere', e.g. to confer extraordinary commands by plebiscite (*Phil.* xi. 17); this is not sufficiently stressed in Seager's excellent essay on *populares* (*CQ* 1972). See also *RE* xviii. 773 ff. (Strasburger on optimates); Suppl. x. 550 ff. (Meier on *populares*); Wirzsubski, 1950, ch. 2.

63 C. Gracchus' law *de provinciis consularibus*, which charged the senate with deciding which provinces should be consular in the following year but before the elections, so that the people might elect the men for the posts, is significant. The senate alone could best judge of military or administrative needs, but the people as sovereign was the fount of honour. Note, however, the very detailed provisions for executive action in the 'piracy' law of 101 (*JRS* 1974, 193 ff.).

Each of these laws was of course defended by appeals to the interest of the state: but for the people's intervention the right man would not have been appointed or given the necessary resources; thus in 67 it could be argued that the senate had done nothing to meet a pressing crisis. Repugnant to the senate, they ranked as 'popular' because they were emanations of popular sovereignty.

This antinomy between the authority of the senate and the rights of the people would issue in civil wars. Of course the causes of these wars were complex, and the reasons that led individuals to take one side or the other various. Still, the opposed principles were proclaimed in propaganda and surely had some effect on men's minds.

The matter is clearest in 49. Caesar defied the senate's expressed will in clinging to his command in Gaul; ultimately he marched on Rome rather than obey its decrees. The Pompeians stood for the authority of the senate: Caesar claimed that the senate was illegitimately overriding the vetoes of tribunes, the representatives of popular rights, and setting aside the people's enactment, which entitled him to stand in absence for a second consulship, and on his interpretation to retain his command until he could avail himself of that privilege. (He also alleged that the senate itself had been terrorized, but it is plain that even if the majority of the senate had no wish to precipitate armed conflict, it had at least freely pronounced that Caesar should give up his command.)[64]

Let us turn back to the 80s, where our evidence is scanty. In 88 Sulla marched on Rome when the people had passed a law depriving him of the Asian command allotted to him by senatorial decree. It was one of several laws carried by violence, and no doubt Sulla urged that they did not even represent the genuine will of the people; he professed that he was rescuing Rome from tyranny.[65] However, after occupying the city, he not only had these laws annulled on the ground that they had been illegally passed, but had it enacted that future legislation must receive the prior sanction of the senate. It would seem that this safeguard affected only legislation initiated by tribunes, for Cinna as consul in 87 was not precluded from proposing measures, perhaps to the centuriate assembly, which the senate did not approve. Cinna was expelled from the city by force and deprived of his magistracy by

---

[64] Caes. *BC* i. 1–9, 22, 32. The view of his opponents had already been stated by Pompey in September 51: 'dixit hoc nihil interesse utrum C. Caesar senatui dicto audiens futurus non esset an pararet qui senatum decernere non pateretur' (Cic. *Fam.* viii. 8. 9). For the senate's attitude see App. ii. 30. Caesar was of course demanding that he should retain his provinces after the expiry of the term granted by the *lex Pompeia Licinia* of 55, even if that be as late as March 49 and not, as I believe, in 50. I have stated my view rather more fully in *JRS* 1986. Cf. pp. 489 ff. below.

[65] App. i. 57. This was the inevitable plea to justify appeals to military force; cf. Caes. *BC* i. 22. 5; Augustus in *RG* 1.

senatorial authority. This gave him the ground for claiming that the senate had infringed the sovereignty of the people, which had elected him consul.[66] He and Marius fought their way back to power. Thereafter the senate itself was not a free agent. Sulla would certainly have been justified in asserting that he was bent on restoring its authority, although it was unable to give him its formal endorsement. And that was just what he did when victory had made him absolute master of the state.

The same kind of constitutional conflict did not persist in the years after Philippi. It needs no proof that Brutus and Cassius, and Cicero in 43, had sought to preserve or restore what they saw as a free commonwealth under the direction of the senate. They surely saw themselves as optimates. It is less clear that their adversaries appeared as *populares*, though in his initial struggle with the senate, then backed for personal motives by Octavian, Antony could claim to be exercising powers under legislation passed by the people; not that there is reason to think that it expressed any solid popular support. But once he had combined with Octavian and Lepidus and they had eliminated the Republicans, each was patently seeking personal supremacy, and all depended on force supplied by troops whose fidelity they had to purchase. In this rivalry both Antony and Octavian would vaguely profess to be champions of liberty and promise to reconstitute the commonwealth. In the end Octavian (or Augustus) would pretend that he had fulfilled his promise.[67] In appearance his regime was to allow more to the authority of the senate than to the rights of the people; in fact everything was subordinated to his will. The old conflict of optimates and *populares* had changed first into one between Republicanism and autocracy and then into a contest between rivals for a position in the state which was not responsible by any non-violent process to either senate or people.

Everyone now recognizes that neither *populares* nor optimates constituted parties of the modern type with a continuous existence and organization. The *populares* were individual politicians, or groups of politicians, who came forward only at intervals with particular proposals which they were ready to force through, if necessary, in defiance of the senate; on such occasions most senators united as optimates to resist the assault on the senate's authority. There could indeed be no parties of any kind as we know them in Rome. The *raison d'être* was lacking. Today they exist to win elections, which determine the composition of the government for perhaps years to come; men join or support a party because on the whole they have more confidence in

[66] App. i. 59 with Gabba ad loc., 65.
[67] App. v. 132; Dio xlix. 41, 1. 7; *RG* 34; cf. Vell. ii. 89.

the ability and policy of its leaders than in those of their rivals, though the necessary price may be compromising or surrendering some of their own interests or convictions. Elections at Rome did not serve a similar purpose. They decided only who should perform duties of administration and jurisdiction, command armies, and carry out policies properly prescribed by people or senate. Candidates seldom propounded a programme of legislation, and in any case by returning them the electors were not committed to voting for bills they might subsequently bring forward. They could and did choose as colleagues in the consulship men, like Caesar and Bibulus, deeply divided by personal and public differences. The tribunes too might be adverse to the consuls and not agreed among themselves. The magistrates collectively did not form a government in the modern sense. In normal times the senate approximates more closely to that conception, though it could be overruled by the people and could make its will effective only through the magistrates. But the composition of the senate, even though it consisted of ex-magistrates, was not affected by the elections of any one year. The senators sat for life; on every particular issue they could follow their own individual judgements, and even if many of them would tend to vote together and perhaps commonly accept the advice of some leading figure, they were not amenable to party discipline, or obliged to concur in a measure of which they disapproved as the price of retaining power. As for the assemblies, whose composition must have varied with the special circumstances that might induce citizens to attend, there was obviously no reason why men should vote for a party line rather than for what reason or passion prompted on the particular matter that was laid before them.

Thus optimates and *populares* did not and could not constitute parties as we know them. It is, however, curious that modern scholars who insist on this often proceed to construct groups or factions within the nobility hardly less cohesive and durable in their imagination than such parties.[68] In pre-Gracchan or pre-Sullan times, it is supposed, the aristocracy was divided between rival groups or factions, perhaps no more than two or three, consisting of whole families, allied by kinship and friendship sometimes for generations, which not only contended with each other for office, backed by their obedient clients, but were in

---

[68] The views on factions and friendship expressed here summarize those in chs. 7 and 9. Gelzer, who never subscribed to the theories of Münzer, Scullard, etc., provided powerful support for them by the importance he gave to clientship in his early monograph on the Roman nobility. It is only on the assumption that members of the rival factions could mobilize all their clients at elections and perhaps at some other meetings of the assemblies that they could have enjoyed the dominance, fluctuating between them, that is alleged. In his detailed accounts of events in the late Republic, the best of those written in this century, the mature Gelzer made nothing of this: he had too scrupulous a regard for evidence.

perpetual opposition on issues of policy, and which would seek to ruin their antagonists by criminal prosecutions.

The existence of these factions is not attested in the sources but is inferred by a process of induction based on a number of assumptions. (1) It is premised that the solidarity between not only agnates but also kinsmen by marriage was such that all normally took the same line in politics. (2) Friendship is taken to mean political co-operation, and any reference to friendship or instance of co-operation is regarded as evidence of enduring alliance. (3) Some suppose that the magistrates conducting elections had great influence on the results, and that therefore men who were colleagues in office or succeeded each other tended to belong to the same group. Exceptions to this rule are so numerous, however, even on the reconstructions offered by advocates of the theory, that other believers in 'family factions' discard this method of ascertaining their composition. (4) Prosecutions unquestionably presupposed enmity or produced it; on the theory under consideration the former explanation is generally preferred; they imply not so much that the accused was thought to deserve condemnation for his crimes, but that it was desired to eliminate or discredit a political adversary. Naturally this cannot be proved.

It is no doubt in the first two premises that the strength of this interpretation of Roman politics resides. Yet neither seems to be valid for the period for which we first have fairly copious testimony on the conduct of individual aristocrats, the time of Cicero. Kinsmen by blood and marriage were then often divided, and friendship was still more frequently transient and little more than nominal; moreover, men had so many intricate connections both of kinship and friendship with persons who came into conflict with each other that they were unable to oblige them all alike. Similar instances are on record from earlier times, but they are taken to be mere exceptions that do not invalidate the rule, without any systematic attempt to prove the rule, by showing how many more cases are actually known of long-enduring co-operation between either kinsmen or friends. Indeed men are assigned to a particular faction without any evidence at all of co-operation; if A is known to have worked with B, C, and D, then E as the kinsman of A by marriage must belong to the same faction, and so must F, who is identified as a friend of E, together with the entire families of E and F. If the same conjectural reasoning is applied to the reconstruction of political affiliations in the age of Cicero, when it can at last be tested, it yields conclusions that are ludicrously false. The evidence for that age shows that there were then no long-lasting, large coalitions of families as postulated for the second century. In default of comparable evidence for that time, we should indeed have to concede that there were such coalitions if their existence were recorded. But it is not, and we are simply asked to assume that the behaviour of politicians was quite different then from what we know it to have been later. This too is obviously conceivable, and if the prolonged collaboration of allied families were clearly attested, we could doubtless think up reasons why politicians later acted in a different way. However, the evidence cannot supply this proof. As already observed, coalitions of the kind envisaged could not have been kept in being by party discipline, but only by community of sentiments and interests and a sense of mutual obligation. They must therefore always have been exposed to continual disintegration as a result of the divergencies of individual advantage, of personal discords between kinsmen and erstwhile friends, and of considerations of the public good, which had a moral claim transcending all private obligations (see below).

Even advocates of the theory are forced to acknowledge that in Cicero's time factions are no longer composed of alliances of whole families. On one view they are now formed of the adherents of powerful individuals, to whom once again men are supposedly bound by ties of blood or marriage, or of friendship derived from benefits received. It is certainly true that in civil wars, when the state was split in two, the antagonists are labelled by ancient writers as Marians, Cinnans, Sullans, Pompeians, and Caesarians. But these appellations are used almost only of men who were fighting or had fought under the command of Marius etc. They were not members of factions which had previously supported their leader in peace or were bound to support him after victory. Pompey, for instance, had had very few consistent adherents. Many of his principal allies in 49 had long been in opposition to him and joined him only to resist the greater danger to the commonwealth which in their view Caesar presented. They included most of a coterie round Cato which had generally acted in collaboration. Similar coteries had probably existed at all times. Scipio Aemilianus and Lucius Crassus (*cos.* 95) seem to have had small groups of like-minded individual friends. More generally in Cicero's age politicians enter into shifting combinations, to promote their preferred personal or public ends at a given moment. I see no reason why this should not always have been true. It may also be noted that when issues arose, affecting the authority of the senate, men divided by private enmity or jealousy could unite in the common cause, as some did against the Gracchi. For the understanding of the political trends that led to the fall of the Republic, the differences between factions, even when this term is taken to refer to small and transient groupings, and not to the large, cohesive, and long-lasting alliances of modern invention, are of far less significance than conflicts of principle and interests which divided optimates and *populares*.

I do not deny that in Cicero's day close kinsmen and friends co-operated with each other in temporary competitions for office and on all sorts of minor questions which Christian Meier categorizes as 'routine politics'. In this collaboration mutual affection may sometimes have had its effect; more important is the fact that social morality inculcated a sense of moral obligation towards those with whom special connections subsisted.

Cicero recognizes that men have a duty to render each other services in proportion to their propinquity by blood or marriage, and to others in requital for services already received from them. (Patrons and clients might come in the last category, though he does not specifically mention them.) He gives a high place to obligations to friends. He was following the teaching of the Stoic Panaetius, but though very few Romans are likely to have been guided by Greek ethical theories as such, in this and in many other instances Panaetius' doctrine only reinforced customary morality.[69] Thus the stress Cicero lays on reciprocity is very Roman: the conception is embedded in the diverse connotations of the word *gratia* (p. 389). It is remarkable that in their wills Romans would give concrete expression to their sense of obligation to requite benefits. Advocates like Cicero charged no fees, but he averred in 44 that he had been bequeathed over twenty million sesterces by grateful clients (*Phil.* ii. 40). The tie between friends, like that between patrons and clients, was one of *fides*. Cicero could suggest that *fides* reposed on respect for the ancestral religion (*de nat. deor.* i. 14); a cult of Fides goes back at least to the third century. Its importance in Roman life is reflected in various legal institutions which rested on it.

None the less, the modern reconstructions of political factions exaggerate the extent or solidarity of connections derived from kinship and *fides*. It was only to the closest kin, to the degree of second cousins, that social morality and various prescriptions of the law recognized any special obligations (ch. 9 endnote 1). The web of intermarriages of the Roman aristocracy was probably so intricate that relationships among the nobles may have been all but universally embracing. Friendship was sometimes no more than a term for the observance of outward courtesies; and it could connect a man with others who were mutually opposed to each other. The most conscientious Roman might have to strike a balance between conflicting private obligations. Friendships in the sense of political alliances were easily dissolved. The closest kinsmen too may be found on different sides when large political

---

[69] *de offic.* i. 53–9 (similar grades of obligation appear in a treatise of the Stoic Hierocles *ap.* Stob., ed. Hense, iv. 671 ff.). Reciprocity: ibid. 47–9; cf. ii. 63, 69 f. Cf. pp. 415 f., 449 ff.

issues were at stake. In civil wars some families were divided. Co-
operation in 'routine politics' does not imply common membership of a
faction that would continue to act together, once a divergence of
personal interests or in views on the public good had appeared.

It need hardly be said that men do not always obey the dictates of
conscience or honour. No one will doubt that in Cicero's time many of
the most eminent figures in Roman public life acted unscrupulously for
their own personal advantage. It would be an assumption without
warrant that this had not always been true. However, in so far as men
were influenced by a sense of duty, it must never be forgotten that in
the Roman way of thinking duty to the fatherland was higher than
duty to family and friends. This is clearly acknowledged by Cicero in
the very context in which he sets out the order of private obligations
(n. 69). In his treatise *de amicitia* he is particularly concerned to lay
down that it is right to subordinate the claims of friendship to those of
the state. This is no doubt in part a polemic against Caesarians, who
had defended their conduct by their private obligations to Caesar. One
of them was Matius, who admitted that he had adhered to Caesar in
49, while disapproving of his cause (*Fam.* xi. 28. 2); he could very
probably have added that it had not been plain to him that the
Pompeians were acting any more than Caesar in that of the commonwealth. He maintains that his conduct after Caesar's death is in
keeping with the whole tenor of his life (ibid. 4), that of a true patriot;
the accusation that he is putting friendship before the fatherland rests
on the premises, which he cannot accept, that the killing of Caesar had
served the public interest (ibid. 2), and the services he has rendered to
Caesar's heir fulfilled his private duty without any implication that he
is neglecting those of a citizen (ibid. 6).

In fact the primacy of the fatherland's claims was a traditional
conception, voiced by Lucilius,[70] and enshrined in the legends of the
patriotic devotion of Horatius on the bridge, Gaius Mucius, Cloelia,
Marcus Curtius, the Decii, and Regulus. More strikingly still, an
earlier Horatius had struck down his own sister 'for forgetting her
fatherland'; L. Iunius Brutus had expelled the Tarquins, though his
wife was of the royal house, and had executed his own sons as traitors
to the Republic; a Postumius and a Manlius had also put to death a
son for breach of military discipline; Spurius Cassius had by one

---

[70] 1196–1208 Loeb (1326 ff. Marx): it is the mark of a good man 'commoda praeterea patriai
prima putare, deinde parentum, tertia iam postremaque nostra'. For the rest, he will be hostile to
bad men and helpful to good: no allusion to kin, friends, patrons, or clients. No doubt the verses
are affected by Greek ethics. But the dictum of Staveley, 1972, 194, that 'the bond established by
the conferment of a *beneficium* transcended all others in the Roman code' is patently false; many
other scholars tacitly presuppose some such premiss in explaining the conduct of Roman
aristocrats. See also pp. 355, 377–81, 416 with notes.

account been condemned by his own father for seeking to make himself tyrant; and the Manlii had shown their abhorrence of M. Manlius' similar design by ruling that none of their clan should again bear his *praenomen*.[71]

We need not consider whether any of these stories has a basis in fact, and we cannot even determine the antiquity of the legends, since there are so few surviving fragments of early annalistic or oratory: they were of course cited over and over again in Cicero's time, told in different forms with various embellishments, and thus mirror the moral views then accepted. Some of them at least are known to have been current in the second century. Accius wrote tragedies on the legends of Brutus and of the Decii. Polybius took patriotic devotion to be specially characteristic of the Romans, and illustrated his thesis by vague references to men who had fought in single combat for their country, or had proved that they set their country's good above natural ties by putting their sons to death; he cited in particular the tale of Horatius on the bridge, and held that the funeral orations of his own time served to strengthen the tradition of public service (vi. 54 f.). Sallust too had read that Fabius Cunctator and Scipio Africanus had been accustomed to say that ancestral busts incited new generations to valour (*BJ* 4); in the good old days men had pursued glory by serving the state (*Cat.* 6). The Horatii, Cloelii, and Curtii were families which never attained eminence at Rome or disappeared early from the *Fasti*; it seems unlikely that it was at a late date that they could obtain a general acceptance of legends that made members of their houses national heroes; and I think it improbable that the plebeian Iunii, who reached the consulship in the fourth century, could have induced everyone to believe that an invented patrician ancestor was the father of the Republic. But however ancient the tales were, they were deeply implanted in the consciousness of Romans in historic times; it is significant that it was thought to be a useful device in arousing Marcus Brutus against Caesar to remind him of the liberation of Rome by his forefather (Plut. *Brut.* 9).

In the historic period it is notable that after Cannae the senate declined to ransom Hannibal's prisoners (and so fill his coffers): Roman soldiers must learn to conquer or die; and yet the prisoners included many from the first families at Rome with numerous kin in the senate (Polyb. vi. 58). Similarly in 63 the Catilinarian conspirators were condemned to death by the senate, and none of their friends and kinsmen pleaded for mercy (cf. Cic. *Cat.* iv. 13). One man is said to have been executed by his own father. T. Manlius Torquatus (*cos.* 165)

---

[71] On the antiquity or historicity of the stories see *RE sub nominibus*. Cicero expected his hearers or readers to find it plausible that public men like himself were motivated chiefly by the hope of glory derived from service to the state (*Arch.* 26–30).

and M. Scaurus (*cos.* 115) banished sons from their sight, for provincial misrule and cowardice respectively; both committed suicide.[72]

Conceptions of the public good are inevitably subjective. It was no doubt easy for Romans to convince themselves, or to assume without reflection, that a course that suited their private interests or enabled them to satisfy their private obligations also conformed with patriotic duty. But this was not always so, even when the issue was merely who should be chosen to hold office. I see no reason to doubt that Fabius Cunctator sincerely dissuaded the centuries from returning as consul T. Otacilius, who was his niece's husband, on the ground that he was unfit to command against Hannibal (Livy xxiv. 8). It seems to me arbitrary to suppose that both Cicero and other advocates of the Manilian law were not influenced by the strong arguments which he used to persuade the people that Pompey's appointment was necessary to finish the war with Mithridates. In any case his speech exhibits the patent truth that in contests for any kind of public preferment it was necessary to show (if this could not be assumed) that the task to be performed was required for the public good and that the man proposed to perform it had the capacity to do so; no one could have come forward to say merely 'He is my sister's son'!

Equally, as spokesman for the triumvirs, Cicero would urge in 56 that on public grounds Caesar must be left to complete the conquest of Gaul. It must have been supposed that some senators would be impressed by this plea. No doubt there were some questions not of wide concern and not coming up for debate on which factions, however small or transitory, could gain their ends by covert intrigue, for instance in grants of *privilegia* voted in small houses (Ascon. 57 C.); but when a controversial matter evoked discussion in senate or assembly, politicians had to find means of persuading those who were not committed to their support, just as they needed the votes of more than their own friends and clients to secure the election of candidates they preferred. It was surely inevitable that they should then appeal to the public interest; they had to make out that their candidate was the man best fitted for a post, or that the senatorial decree or law they were advocating or resisting was conducive or prejudicial to the interests of the state. Of course they might represent in this light what best suited their own advantage, or that of the section of the community for which they spoke, and it would also have been natural enough if, as judges in their own cause, they had often too easily convinced themselves that what they told others was the truth.

In negotiations with Caesar, Pompey averred in 49 that he had acted

---

[72] Val. Max. v. 8. 3–5; there are other versions of these anecdotes.

only for the public good, and had always set the interests of the commonwealth before private ties. He implied that Caesar was not conforming to this standard; the charge was repudiated; Caesar replied that he was ready to submit to anything for the sake of the commonwealth (*BC* i. 7 f.). This exchange was surely typical at least of the language that all Roman politicians would employ. Nor need we assume with Sallust that the entire political class was corrupted by ambition, luxury, and greed and had no scruple in pursuing their personal ends.

Aristocratic ambition was in fact itself an obstacle to the formation of a party consisting of the adherents of some outstanding individual. Lucretius bewailed the infatuation of the ceaseless efforts of the nobility 'ad summas emergere opes rerumque potiri' ('to rise to the height of power and be masters of affairs', ii. 9 ff.). But such dominance was beyond the mark of any but the most exceptional figures favoured by the conjuncture of events, like Sulla and Pompey. In normal circumstances the most that a noble could hope to attain was that respect and deference to his judgement which the Romans called *auctoritas* and which derived from the offices he had held, his achievements, and his distinction in the arts of war and peace; such men ranked as *principes*, and their opinions tended to sway the senate and people.[73] But each was apt to incur the emulation and envy of those who would not concede his superiority; Scipio Aemilianus, for example, had his opponents and detractors (pp. 466 ff.); nor would ordinary senators readily tolerate any degree of eminence that jeopardized their own independence and dignity (pp. 327 ff.), much less dominance by any single man. Most of them could do no more than rise from office to office, augmenting their resources from the perquisites of war and government, and share in the general authority of the senate. The ladder of advancement narrowed at every stage. Under half the quaestors could reach the praetorship. No more than two of every six or eight praetors could become consuls. Not many consuls had the opportunity to gain glory and exceptional riches in a great military command, with the prospect of a triumph, and at most one in ten might later hold the censorship. The ambition of every individual demanded that the success of others should be restricted. This was perhaps one reason for the numerous, though ineffective, laws that limited both ostentatious consumption and largesse,[74] and electoral corruption, which might give an unfair advantage to wealthier rivals.

---

[73] See endnote 4.

[74] We should also take seriously the professed purpose of preserving or reviving *mores antiquos*, cf. J. Sauerwein, *Die Leges Sumptuariae als röm. Massnahmen gegen den Sittenverfall*; cf. ch. 6 n. 52. Caesar and Augustus must have had this in view in enacting such laws. Tiberius thought them futile (Tac. *Ann.* iii. 52–4).

More obviously it prompted the rules prescribed in 180, and a little modified by Sulla, that men must hold offices in strictly ascending order with minimum ages, and that they should be re-eligible for the consulship only after an interval of ten years, or (between 151 and 81) not at all. Though it was unavoidable to prorogue some consuls and praetors beyond their single year of office, since there were usually too many posts to be filled by eight or ten of these magistrates, the prorogation of consuls was rare in the second century.[75] Commanders were usually replaced after a year in the field with small regard to the exigencies of warfare. Hence frequent incompetence which damaged the interests of Rome and diminished the authority of the senate. Thus the bungling or corruption of senatorial generals and ambassadors in the Jugurthine war, and the disasters that generals brought on themselves in provoking or repelling the Cimbri and Teutones, led to the extraordinary advancement of Marius by the people's will.

After Sulla's dictatorship there was something of a change. He had perhaps intended each consul and praetor to hold a command for only one year after the expiry of his annual term at Rome. But a third at least of all consuls between 78 and 52 never went out to a province; the bloodletting of the 80s had resulted in a dearth of military experience and talent (Cic. *Font.* 42 f.); apart from operations in Gaul and Macedon, there were in the decade after his dictatorship serious wars in Spain, Asia Minor, and Italy itself; and several consulars held great commands for three years, Metellus Pius for nine, and Lucius Lucullus for eight.

It was in these circumstances that the senate had to employ the young Pompey in repressing Lepidus and Sertorius. His success, cumulating his great contribution to Sulla's victory, made him already the first man in the state, when he became consul in 70. But that must in itself have provoked the jealousy of other senators, which made it unlikely that he would obtain further opportunities for adding to his distinctions from the senate. In 70 he perhaps deliberately prepared the way for securing new commands from the people by restoring to the tribunes their right to initiate legislation; it was the people that appointed him with wide powers to deal with the pirates and Mithridates. He now counted as a *popularis*; optimate distrust aggravated the envy that his earlier career had aroused. The conception of some modern scholars that he could ever form a powerful faction of adherents within the senate seems to be quite erroneous. The resentments of his peers drove him into the coalition with Caesar and

---

[75] In the Hannibalic war a few men held commands for many years continuously; from 200 to 167 only 7 kept commands 2 or more years after their consulships; the incomplete *Fasti* from 166 to 90 yield 19 examples, but in most the ex-consul was only in the field for 2 full years.

Crassus. None of them ever seems to have had a numerous band of devoted partisans in the senate. Their dominance rested on the backing of the plebs, in particular of Pompey's veterans, and finally on armed force. When at last Pompey broke with Caesar, his chief allies were men who had long been engaged in his obstruction, but who had come to fear Caesar still more and would take advantage of Pompey's own jealousy of his erstwhile partner. The developments between 70 and 49 cannot be understood in terms of factions within the political élite as distinct from the ambitions of these few individuals, who found adherents primarily outside that élite (pp. 472 ff.).

V

Whatever machinations self-seeking politicians conducted behind the scenes, they commonly needed support beyond their own coteries within or outside the senate; and, as we have already seen, they then had to contend that the courses that suited their own interests conduced to the good of the state, which in their presentation of genuine belief might be coterminous with that of some section of the community, but which could hardly be overtly identified with the mere advantage of an individual or small faction. This explains why oratory, which was indispensable in the courts, where it certainly furnished means by which the advocate could extend his personal influence, also assumed great importance in the deliberations of senate and assemblies, and why pamphleteering was employed with rhetorical art to touch a wider audience. Rhetoric, which elicited its precepts from experience, much of it Greek, of the devices which were found to be persuasive, became a large element in the higher education that every Roman of rank received. Cicero could assert that the ideal *princeps* who would guide public deliberations would be a master of eloquence in the senate, the people and the courts (*de orat.* iii. 83), and that eloquence ruled the state (ibid. 76). There was some exaggeration here; knowledge of affairs carried no less weight in the senate than gifts of speech (i. 60, ii. 337), and men of experience and reputed judgement could sway that body without the graces of eloquence (i. 33, 38, 214 f.); but even a critic of the largest claims made for oratory could be represented as admitting that it was a valuable asset to a politician (i. 44).

In his *Brutus* Cicero unrolls a long catalogue of past notables distinguished for their eloquence; scrutiny indicates that they had displayed their talent mainly in forensic practice (which enhanced their *gratia*), but also in addressing the people on judicial and legislative business. It was perhaps a popular audience which the orator could most readily stir with the passions that suited his purpose (*de orat.* ii. 334, 337 f.); he had less scope in the senate, where tact compelled brevity, with so many others impatient to be heard themselves (ii. 333); still at least four of the orations that old Cato published (*ORF*[2] XLII, XLVIII–L) had been delivered to the senate, and L. Crassus excelled himself on his last appearance there (*de orat.* iii. 3). The Roman tradition of oratory, nurtured in part by the practice of funeral panegyrics, antedated the penetration of Greek rhetoric, and there is evidence independent of Cicero, who might be suspected of magnifying his own art, for the esteem in which it was held. Lucius Metellus (*cos.* 251) had been eulogized by his son for having attained his ambition to be the best orator as well as to be supremely successful in war, and P. Crassus Mucianus (*cos.* 131) had boasted of his eloquence as well as of his legal expertise (n. 73). Ennius praised M. Cornelius Cethegus (*cos.* 204) for his 'lips flowing with sweet words' (*Brut.* 58). Cicero himself conceded that prowess in war earned more prestige than fine oratory; none the less, his list of great orators included such men as the elder Cato and Scipio Aemilianus, who had triumphed for their victories. Caesar was an orator before he ever commanded an army, and owed to oratory his advancement to the point at which he could be vested with such a command.[76]

Eloquence in the courts explains the rise of the parvenu Cicero, but in 63 he applied his gift with great effect to 'saving the state' from sedition. We tend to be so conscious of the danger of seeing Roman politics in his time through his eyes, or to be so repelled by his conceit, that we can easily underestimate the influence that he attained by oratory. Dominant as they were in the 50s when in alliance, Pompey and Caesar did their best to attract his support or neutrality in 59; when they failed, they thought it prudent to connive in his banishment; and after his return from exile, they coerced him into acting as their spokesman.

The importance of the arts of persuasion can readily be illustrated in the prolonged discussions (*c.* 150 BC) on Roman policy towards Carthage,[77] in the effects of the eloquence of the Gracchi (Gaius' speeches were still admired nearly three centuries later),[78] in the clever demagogy with which C. Fannius (*cos.* 122) discredited Gaius' proposal to enfranchise the Latins (GC 41), paralleled in 63 by Cicero's skilful sophistries in defeating Rullus' agrarian bill, and not least in the great debate of 5 December 63, in which the senate was swayed first

---

[76] *Mur.* 20–5, 30, *de offic.* ii. 44–51, 65 (ranking jurisprudence below oratory). Caesar: *ORF*[2] 383 ff.

[77] Astin, 1967, ch. v and App. III with bibliography.

[78] Tac. *Dial.* 18. 2, 26. 1; Fronto 56 N. etc; Gell. x. 3. 1.

one way and then another by the arguments of Caesar and Cato, to both of whom Cicero allowed great eloquence (*Brut.* 118 f., 252 ff.). In 56 it would hardly have been possible to frustrate the will of Pompey and Caesar, nor therefore to refuse Caesar an extension of his command in Gaul, yet the dynasts were not content simply to rely on force: they put up Cicero to convince the senate in his *de provinciis consularibus* that this extension was required by the interest of Rome. They surely supposed that there were many senators open to persuasion. In my judgement this was frequently the case; neither senators nor citizens were necessarily or perhaps often committed to a decision in advance of discussion, as are most members of legislative assemblies and most voters today.

Speeches could affect only the relatively small audiences. However, as early as the second century some politicians, among them Cato, Scipio Aemilianus, and the Gracchi, published versions of some of their speeches. So of course did Cicero. As in his case, the orator might wish to pass down to posterity a memorial of his art and to immortalize his name.[79] But written versions of speeches could also influence opinion beyond the original audience, though they could reach directly only the reading public, persons of education and therefore of some affluence. This was surely the purpose for which Cicero circulated his *de provinciis consularibus*. He published only a small proportion of all the speeches he actually delivered, and we have to ask ourselves why he selected some and not others. This particular speech represented a political volte-face of which he was privately ashamed;[80] no doubt in publishing as in delivering the speech, he acted under pressure from Caesar, whose achievements it glorified. Similarly, Caesar's own *Commentaries* were clearly designed in part to demonstrate to public opinion the greatness of his services to Rome in Gaul and to justify his conduct in the civil war. Publicity could affect opinion far from the city. The excitement that political struggles could arouse among the citizenry in Rome itself was manifested at times by acclamations at the games, which Cicero could treat, when it suited him, as indications of their true feelings (*Sest.* 106).[81] It is more difficult to gauge the impact that they had outside the city, at least among the local gentry; presumably the peasantry knew and cared little about them. Early in 59 Cicero seems to imply that people round Antium did not bother their heads about the legislation of Caesar and Vatinius (*Att.* ii. 6. 2),

[79] Apparently the reason why Cicero wished to perpetuate his consular speeches (*Att.* ii. 1. 3); his earlier publication of some forensic speeches was no doubt intended partly to enhance his practice at the bar.

[80] This must be true, whether or not it is the palinode of *Att.* iv. 5. 1.

[81] A. Cameron, *Circus Factions*, 1976, 158 ff., collects the evidence.

but a few weeks later there was a ferment of indignation among the respectable people with whom he consorted at Formiae (ii. 13. 2; cf. 14. 2). He himself was dependent for news on private correspondence, and information may have been relatively sparse for others. At the beginning of 59 Caesar thought it advantageous to disseminate more widely proceedings in the senate and ordered their publication (Suet. *Caes.* 20. 1); he was thus appealing to opinion 'out of doors'; perhaps he hoped to make senators wary of advocating unpopular courses. In the ensuing years the proceedings would have contained records of the victories reported in his despatches and of the thanksgivings decreed on their account (*BG* ii. 35, iv. 38, vii. 50). We can only guess how much the prestige he gained in this way contributed to the feebleness of the resistance offered by the Italian towns, when he marched on Rome in 49.

Cicero's letters of that time are full of allusions to the reactions of the better sort to the progress of the campaign. Of course, given the possibilities of cancellation of debts and redistribution of property, of which there was much talk, they were deeply affected by the war. And it must never be forgotten that their attitudes might be of great importance, since the co-operation of local magistrates was vital in the levy of troops (ch. 5, App. I). A letter such as that which Caesar wrote to Oppius (*Att.* ix. 7c) advertising his aim 'omnium voluntates reciperare' and to avoid the harshness of Sulla was probably intended to be shown around, and exemplifies the widespread propaganda in speeches and open letters by which he commended his cause. Caesar's enemies countered with publications to defame him.[82] Even when he had made himself master of the state by blood and iron, appeals to public opinion still went on; freedom of speech had not been extinguished. Eulogies of the dead Cato were matched by attacks on his memory, in which Caesar joined himself.[83] The best-known political pamphlet is of course Cicero's second *Philippic*, an invective against Antony, written to be read in the form of a speech that was never delivered. But all the *Philippics*, though the others correspond to actual speeches, should be seen in this light. This collection of written versions of a series of speeches on the same political issue, which must have been disseminated at the time, is unique in Cicero's corpus. Copies were perhaps circulated to leading men in the Italian towns to strengthen their adherence to the Republican cause, partly by suggesting that it

---

[82] Cic. *Brut.* 218; Suet. *Caes.* 9, 49, 52. Despite his use of Oppius' life of Caesar (52 f.), Suetonius retails much of the (unreliable) propaganda of his enemies (e.g. 8, 12, 24. 3, 49–52, 54); treating him as the first emperor, he plainly regards him as beneficent in that role, but disapproves of his having usurped it (76).

[83] Gelzer, *Caesar*, 301 ff.

was already more strongly and enthusiastically supported, and there-fore safer to join, than it really was (cf. ch. 1 endnote 1). A war of words also preceded the decisive struggle between Octavian and Antony, whose conduct was convincingly maligned as a betrayal of Rome; his cause was lost before Actium, because in Syme's phrase 'created belief turned the scale of history'.

VI

Orators and pamphleteers obviously had to play on the sentiments and perceived needs of the public to which they appealed, even if it was their purpose to practise deception for their own ends. The very distortions and sophistries which Cicero for instance employs in resisting Rullus' agrarian bill or defending Rabirius in 63 are thus indicative of the attitudes of his audiences, since he was a master of the arts of persuasion, rather than of his own opinions; though in these cases he was perfectly sincere in desiring rejection of the bill and Rabirius' acquittal, the arguments to which he resorted were merely designed to sway the public. It was always necessary to profess attachment to the interest of the *res publica*. It cannot be doubted that jealousy and mistrust of Pompey inspired the opposition of the optimates to the grant of extraordinary commands to him in 67 and 66, but it appears that Catulus and Hortensius in resisting the proposals spoke of him in terms of the highest honour, and argued that it was inexpedient for military reasons to create the unitary commands proposed, and contrary to constitutional practice that so much power should be vested in a single man, in derogation of the rights that properly belonged to the annual magistrates entrusted with them by the people (Cic. *de imp. Cn. Pomp.* 51–63; Dio xxxvi. 31–5). There was a stock of ideals which commanded almost universal assent, though they could be interpreted in widely divergent ways and brought forward to justify the most diverse policies, by advocates who hoped to persuade their hearers (and had sometimes persuaded themselves) that they were embodied in the course of action recommended.

In this way measures of manifest and direct benefit to substantial sections of the people of Italy, land allotments for peasants including veterans, food distributions at Rome, citizenship for the allies, judicial rights for the Equites, and so forth could be both promoted and opposed by appeals to the welfare of the state and to recognized ideals, such as liberty, equity, tradition, and law. Thus the distribution of public lands to peasants was an ancient practice, and Tiberius Gracchus urged that it was necessary to resume it, in order to ensure an adequate supply of soldiers for the future, that the rich were holding larger tracts of the public domain than the law allowed, and that it was just to assist citizens impoverished in Rome's wars. Indeed any public assistance to citizens could be justified, on the basis that public property and funds could be said to belong to the people; the state was not regarded as an abstraction distinguishable from the citizens (p. 299). In reply it could be urged that it was inequitable to eject possessors of public land to which they had acquired a kind of title by the passage of time, or that it was unwise to deplete the treasury; it must be remembered that prudence required Rome, like other ancient states, to pile up reserves to meet heavy expenditure imperative in an emergency, since the modern practice of public borrowing in such contingencies was hardly thought of. Liberality with the citizenship again was part of the old Roman tradition, and the enfranchisement of the allies could be treated as just recompense for their loyalty and contribution to Rome's military strength (Vell. ii. 15). Of the case against it we know only that in 122 Fannius suggested that Latins would displace the old citizens from their places in public meetings and festivals at Rome (GC 41). The extension of judicial functions to the Equites in 123 could be represented not only as justified by the corruption of senatorial courts (App. i. 22), the argument endlessly repeated in 70, but as a mode of 'making liberty more equal' by enlarging the number of those who shared in political power; senators could object that by 'enslaving' them to the Equites it detracted from their proper responsibility to the people at large. It is easy to write off ideals like liberty as mere 'catchwords'; in fact they often corresponded to real interests, and also had a resonance of their own, vaguely associating some particular cause with others for which Romans had striven in the past.[84]

Liberty was often on the lips of politicians. It meant different things to different people (Chapter 6). For the ordinary citizen it comprised not only his safeguards for personal protection under the law but also his capacity as a voter, which the ballot enabled him to use with more independence; for the senator his right to speak freely on matters of state, and to have an effective voice in decisions; to both alike it was thus equivalent to a share in political power. The citizen could use his vote to secure material advantages, and the power of senators brought them lucrative perquisites. It is, however, unlikely that men consciously prized liberty as no more than an instrument for these purposes.

---

[84] Plut. *Ti. Gr.* 9, 15; App. i. 9, 11; Cic. *Sest.* 103; Florus ii. 1 encapsulate Gracchan controversies; cf. also n. 39; GC 78 for L. Crassus' speech. Cic. *de leg. agr.* ii is the fullest specimen of the kind of arguments that could be put before the assembly; probably he published it to exhibit to his upper-class readers the skill with which he could appeal to 'popular' slogans and arguments to defeat a 'popular' bill.

The liberty of the senator was inseparable from his share in the collective authority of the senate and from his individual dignity, his social rank, and esteem. Caesar was not alone in holding dignity dearer than life (*BC* i. 9. 4); his assassins were of just the same mind. In a hierarchic society everyone might value a place in the social scale that set him above others and desire to improve his status. Thus the Equites strove for control of the courts partly because it conferred 'splendour' on their order, freed them from subordination to the senators, and actually compelled senators to court their goodwill (Chapter 3). It is characteristic of this way of thinking that persons of respectable station resented the appellation of clients, with its connotation of inferiority and dependence (ch. 8 n. 31). The suffrage surely had something of the same consequence to a citizen. It set him above subjects and slaves. Every year at the elections grandees had to supplicate for his favour. He could feel himself to be one of the masters of a world empire, 'Romanos rerum dominos gentemque togatam'.

All this combined with the force of tradition to sanctify in men's minds 'the ancestral institutions which the long duration of our rule validates' (p. 6), which Polybius had seen as the source of imperial greatness (vi. 1), and which guaranteed to all their particular rights. Certainly this sentiment was strong among the senators, who had long in effect directed the state. On the reasonable view that the people was incompetent to take over this function, monarchy was the only practicable alternative, and any abridgement of the senate's authority was a step in that direction. Roman tradition, and the experience of the Greek and oriental world, taught them that monarchy was incompatible with freedom of any kind and with the rule of law; a king is 'one free to do as he pleases with impunity' (Sall. *BJ* 31. 26). We need not doubt that it was deeply abhorrent to them. It would be only natural that the masses should have simply accepted this aristocratic ideology; if they had been capable of political or historical reflection, they might have concluded that though the expulsion of Tarquin had in the first place only substituted the arbitrary government of the few for that of a single man, this change had proved to establish a basis on which their own rights could later be founded. In the no doubt largely invented stories of Spurius Cassius, Spurius Maelius, and Marcus Manlius, it was made out that these professed champions of the people had really aimed at tyranny, and had been discredited with the people on that account. These fictions at least presuppose that popular feeling could be aroused against anyone suspected of monarchic aspirations. So Tiberius Gracchus' opponents professed to see his encroachments on the senate's prerogatives as proof that he aimed at making himself 'king'. It was clearly hoped in this way to undermine his support.

According to Sallust (ibid. 31. 8), it was contended that 'the restoration of rights to the people prepared the way for kingship'; he puts the words into the mouth of a popular tribune, who treats the claim as partisan claptrap. Gracchus was hardly fool enough to entertain such an ambition, dependent as he was on the volatile favour of the masses and destitute of military force. But the autocracy of Caesar, who had previously adopted the same popular stance, had retrospectively justified such fears by the time when Sallust wrote. Not long before his death Antony publicly offered him the title of king. On the best evidence this provoked a popular outcry.[85] If that be true, even the masses were against the outward form and style of monarchy. They would perhaps be less conscious than senators that Caesar was already absolute as dictator. Once he was dead, it was enacted that no one should ever again be vested with this office. Augustus was to be careful to avoid this or any other formal appellation of supreme power. Still, the riots at Rome in 44, which made it unsafe for Caesar's assassins to remain there, and the popular clamour, which forced the senate itself in 22 to offer Augustus the dictatorship, show that the urban plebs at least no longer had any deep attachment to the Republic.[86] Gratitude to the monarch prevailed, though there is nothing to suggest that they or any other section of the people had deliberately worked for monarchy, or welcomed it before it had been in all but name established and brought them solid benefits.[87]

Sallust alleges that under the guise of the public good all politicians were striving only for their own power. He himself admitted some exceptions to his cynical generalizations;[88] in any event he was no better able than we are to read men's minds. As a spokesman of the optimates Cicero naturally implies that they acted in the interest of the whole commonwealth, whereas the *populares* were unprincipled demagogues (*Sest.* 96). In theoretical vein he could admit that men of wealth and high birth might arrogate to themselves the pretension of being the best, without possessing virtue or the art of government, and could

[85] Gelzer, *Caesar*, 321, cites the texts; only Nicolaus reported that the people approved of the offer.

[86] Antony (to please the senate, App. iii. 25) 'dictaturam quae iam vim regiae potestatis obsederat, funditus ex re publica sustulit' (Cic. *Phil.* i. 3). Cf. *RG* 5 with Gagé's notes. In fact the triumvirate was a dictatorship in commission.

[87] Caesar's desire for divine honours (J. A. North, *JRS* 1975, 171 ff.), the usual attribute of kings, is of course relevant; and such honours were freely to be given to Augustus in all parts of the empire and even in Italian towns. But he was careful not to seek official deification at Rome in his own lifetime, and even there the cult of his *numen* or *genius*, to which as a distinct entity sacrifices and prayers could be offered on his behalf (EJ 100 A), so far as it was not merely private, was entrusted to freedmen and slaves (L. R. Taylor, *Divinity of the Roman Emperor*, ch. VII); here again we can discern a difference of attitude between the masses and the political class, some of whom are said to have resented his aspirations to apotheosis (Tac. *Ann.* i. 10).

[88] *Cat.* 38; *Hist.* i. 12; cf. n. 61.

properly be called a faction (*de rep.* i. 51, iii. 23). High moral standards and devotion to the welfare of the governed were certainly not qualities commonly conspicuous among the Roman optimates. Many of them seem at times to have been motivated by purely egoistic aims of personal profit and advancement. None the less, it seems implausible to suppose that in general they did not believe that it was best for Rome to be directed by the senate, or were less sincere in this belief because the supremacy of the senate was identical with their own interest in retaining collective power. Class interest and constitutional convictions could coincide. The only optimate who attained personal dominance was Sulla, and he laid it down when he had re-established and fortified the authority of his order.

As for the *populares*, they would naturally have repudiated Cicero's imputation. It is not necessarily confirmed by the fact that they were themselves of senatorial rank and sometimes, like the Gracchi, of high lineage. In all times of social conflict members of the privileged élite have been found to take up the cause of the unprivileged on principle. Conceivably some *populares* genuinely thought measures they proposed to be necessary or beneficial to the state. It is rather less likely that they were truly attached to the popular sovereignty, which they had to defend in carrying those measures through the assembly. The Marians in the 80s, and Caesar, once in power both demonstrated contempt for it. But even if we take them to have been entirely unscrupulous, bent only on advancing their own careers or securing personal dominance, it is more significant that they found the means to their ends in giving effect to sectional grievances which the senate neglected.

The division between senate and people, or optimates and *populares*, is not to be explained in purely political terms. Men were accounted 'good', Sallust remarks, on the basis that they were defending the status quo 'in proportion to their wealth and capacity for inflicting wrongs' (*Hist.* i. 12). It was the use they made of this power that engendered the social discontents of the poor whom the Gracchi and later *populares* championed (*BJ* 42). In his revolutionary schemes Catiline could look to the support of the 'wretched' and 'needy' (Cic. *Mur.* 49–51): 'invariably men without substance of their own are envious of the good [!] and raise up the bad; in hatred of their own condition they strive to turn everything upside down; they are sustained without anxiety by confusion and riots, since destitution can hardly suffer any loss' (Sall. *Cat.* 37). Cicero was no less conscious of class conflict, and more openly prejudiced. In his eyes the urban plebs are 'wretched and half-starved, ready to suck the treasury dry', 'the dregs of the city'. Disloyal peasants too, 'who have never appreciated this commonwealth nor wished to see it stabilized', were for Cicero cattle rather than human beings. In the total breakdown of order after Clodius' murder rioters would kill anyone they met who wore fine clothes and gold rings (Appian ii. 22). Clodius' gangs were composed of slaves, criminals, at best hirelings, or so Cicero tells us; in reality many were probably craftsmen and shopkeepers. But that would not have commended them to Cicero; manual work, retailing, trade (unless carried on by rich men in a big way) were sordid occupations, and he could speak of 'artisans, shopkeepers, and all that scum'. No wonder if such people reciprocated with hatred the contempt of Cicero and his like. By contrast 'good men are made in the first place by nature, but fortune helps; the safety of the state is to the advantage of all good men but most clearly benefits those of fortune', which has been 'augmented and accumulated by divine favour'.[89]

For Cicero it was a primary function of the state to maintain property rights[90], and property owners were therefore its natural defenders, whom it was wrong to despoil; in gratifying the people at their expense, *populares* injured the welfare of the state (*Sest.* 103). Since the senators were in general exceedingly rich, they could be expected to protect the interests of the whole class to which they belonged; even if individual members were led astray by unscrupulous ambition or ruinous debts, the senate as a body would maintain the economic and social status quo. In Cicero's view it would deserve and obtain the consensus of all good men, a designation which like that of optimates he extended to all those citizens, even freedmen, whose personal affairs were sound and unembarrassed. By birth of equestrian status, and a scion of the municipal nobility of Arpinum, he saw his role as that of consolidating a *union sacrée* of men of property, 'our army of the rich' (*Att.* i. 19. 4). At first he aimed specifically at concord between senate and Equites, later at the consensus of all Italy, by which of course he meant that of the ruling class in the municipalities, to whom he often refers in letters as the 'boni'. It was the will, *interests*, and opinions of all such men that the true optimate leaders would serve (*Sest.* 97).[91]

[89] *Phil.* xiii. 16; *Cat.* iv. 19. Cicero on the urban plebs: *Att.* i. 16. 11, 19. 4, vii. 3, 5 (cf. *Flacc.* 18, *de offic.* i. 150 f.). Clodius' gangs: Brunt *ap.* Finley, 1974, 97 ff.; Lintott, ch. vi. Cicero's unpopularity: ch. 9 n. 80. In philosophic mood Cicero could recognize that the noble or rich were not necessarily the best, i.e. the most virtuous, and that their misrule could bring down aristocratic regimes (*de rep.* i. 51; cf. 48); self-styled optimates might be a mere faction (iii. 23); class conflict could ensue when politicians acted for sectional interests 'ut alii populares, alii studiosi optimi cuiusque videantur, pauci universorum' (*de offic.* i. 85 f.); and in private he often expressed disgust at the conduct of the so-called 'boni', whether aristocratic politicians or men of property in general, when they failed to seek the general good as he saw it.

[90] *de offic.* i. 15, 20 f. (with a curious disquisition on the origins of private property), ii. 73, *de rep.* iii. 24. In *Top.* 9 he remarks that *ius civile* had been established 'eis qui eiusdem civitatis sunt ad res suas obtinendas'. All Roman jurists would have concurred.

[91] *Sest.* 96 f. The boni (e.g. *Cat.* i. 32, iv. 14–17, *Fam.* i. 9. 13, v. 2. 8 and often) are the 'lauti et locupletes' of *Att.* viii. 1. 3, contrasted with 'multitudo et infimus quisque' (3. 4); they included in

What they demand is in his judgement 'otium cum dignitate',[92] of which the 'fundamenta' are 'religiones, auspicia, potestates magistratuum, senatus auctoritas, leges, mos maiorum, iudicia, iuris dictio, fides, provinciae, socii, imperi laus, res militaris, aerarium'. In 63, when he was professing to be 'vere popularis', that is to say one who genuinely cared for the people's good and not the kind of demagogue who commonly usurped the title, 'otium, pax, tranqillitas, fides, iudicia, aerarium' but also 'libertas' had appeared in a similar catalogue; in 57 he had claimed that with his recall from exile there also returned 'ubertas agrorum, frugum copia [!], spes otii, tranquillitas animorum, iudicia, leges, concordia populi, senatus auctoritas'.[93] *Otium* in this sort of context is clearly public order and internal tranquillity secured by the rule of law. But it is not enough if *dignitas* is wanting; indeed without *dignitas* it will vanish (*Sest.* 100). The 'dignitas rei publicae' certainly consists partly in Rome's imperial grandeur, inherent in some of the 'fundamenta' Cicero lists, but he surely has in mind also the conception that there can be no stability in a state except when every man is firmly fixed in his own social and political grade (*de rep.* i. 69); such gradations are required by equity (ibid. 43, 53) and characterize the traditional system at Rome (ii. 42).[94] At the apex stand magistrates and senate, or most specifically the senate, since the magistrates ought to be its servants, though the senate should ensure the 'splendour' of the orders next in rank (*Sest.* 137), above all the Equites (*de dom.* 74). The people should delight in its own tranquillity (*otium*), in the dignity of all the best men, and in the glory of the entire commonwealth (*Sest.* 104).

Neither liberty nor the 'rights of the people' figure in the catalogue of 'fundamenta'. The liberty Cicero prized was that of a senator, and it was implicit in 'senatus auctoritas'. In the *de republica* he would concede to the people only a sufficient appearance of liberty to keep them content, not a share in real power (pp. 324 ff.). Admittedly the true

general the Equites and municipal gentry. The concept of 'concordia ordinum', adumbrated in *Cluent.* 152 and realized in 63 (*Cat.* iv. 15, *Att.* i. 14. 4, 17. 10)—the phrase occurs in e.g. *Att.* i. 18. 3—in which agreement between senate and Equites was taken to be crucial, was enlarged later into 'consensus bonorum'. As already in I *Verr.* 54, Cicero could appeal to the common sentiments of all Italy, i.e. of the local ruling classes (e.g. *Cat.* i. 12, 27; ii. 25; iv. 2, 13) which had returned him as consul (*Pis.* 3), which would (he hoped) protect him against Clodius (*Qu.fr.* i. 2. 16), and which did in fact ensure his recall from exile (*Att.* iv. 1. 4 and often); cf. endnote 1 for its alleged Republican fervour in 43 BC. See H. Strasburger, *Concordia Ordinum*, 1931, reprinted in *St. zur alten Gesch.* i. 3 ff.

[92] *Sest.* 98. Wirszubski, *JRS* 1954, 1 ff., is best on this phrase, though he does not examine the 'fundamenta'.

[93] *de leg. agr.* ii. 8–10, *de dom.* 17; cf. *de har. resp.* 60: 'aerarium, vectigalia, auctoritas principum, consensus ordinum, iudicia', but voting rights also appear here.

[94] Under the Marian regime 'sine iure fuit et sine ulla dignitate respublica' (*Brut.* 227), perhaps in part because men of rank were mostly opposed to it (*Rosc. Amer.* 136).

statesman would aim at harmony between all orders for the sake of political stability (ii. 69), and in *pro Sestio* (137) he declares it to be the senate's duty to conserve and augment the liberty and interests of the people, but this is a task to be fulfilled at the senate's own discretion. The magistrates too are to be simply its executive agents (ibid.). If he elsewhere asserts their right to treat 'the safety of the state as the highest law', he surely has it in mind that they must still interpret this right in accordance with the will of the senate.[95] By contrast *populares* would leave to the senate the direction of affairs in normal conditions, without fettering the right of magistrates (including tribunes) to submit matters to the sovereign people when the senate had failed to take action which could be represented as required for the general good. Cicero's standpoint is here thoroughly optimate in the narrowest sense of that term.

VII

However, in the same context he has given optimates a much wider connotation, that embraces all the respectable elements of society. He hoped that senatorial government could be securely founded on their ·consent. This consent Augustus was to realize. He did so by fulfilling to a far greater extent than the senate had done the programme implicit in Cicero's catalogue of the 'fundamenta otiosae dignitatis'. Of course Augustus reserved ultimate control to himself, though careful to show an outward deference to the authority of the senate.[96] This deference would not have deceived or contented Cicero and his senatorial contemporaries, who knew what it was to share in real political power. Some indeed have suggested that in his *de republica* Cicero himself had acknowledged that the state needed a single wise statesman to guide its affairs, but this is a misconception (see Endnote 8); he never departed from his principle, stated in 46, that 'no one man should have more power than the whole commonwealth' (*Fam.* vii. 3. 5). But in all other respects Augustus' policies conformed with those which Cicero commended. That is not surprising. Analysis of the 'fundamenta' shows that they would have been at least in general terms acceptable even to *populares*, as to all who seriously concerned themselves with affairs of state. From this standpoint they merit further examination.

Of all the 'fundamenta' the most basic is 'mos maiorum'. This

---

[95] *de leg.* iii. 8; cf. *Phil.* xi. 28 defending Cassius' illegal seizure of Syria: he had acted 'Eo (iure) quod Iuppiter ipse sanxit, ut omnia quae rei publicae salutaria essent legitima et iusta haberentur.' D. Brutus was no less justified in similarly illegal action, as it accorded with the unexpressed will of the senate: 'voluntas senatus pro auctoritate haberi debet, cum auctoritas impeditur metu' (*Fam.* xi. 7. 2).   [96] Brunt, *CQ* 1984, 423 ff.

phrase and the like are ever on Cicero's lips; again he could count on unanimous respect for tradition.[97] He would quote with approval Ennius' line (*de rep.* v. 1).

Moribus antiquis res stat Romana virisque.

If only Romans were faithful to pristine standards, the state would last for ever (ibid. iii. 41). Admittedly following the model of Greek political treatises, he would prescribe a system of education in a part of his *de republica*, of which only fragments survive, designed to preserve or renew the national virtues. The frequency of sumptuary legislation (n. 74), and the censorial ban in 92 on Latin rhetoricians, as a novelty contrary to ancestral usage and custom and therefore to be disapproved (GC 124 f.), illustrate the same outlook. Cicero again would deny that anyone in private life was entitled to challenge on philosophical principles the accepted institutions and usages of his society (*de offic.* i. 148). In 46 he was to exhort Caesar to repress lusts, raise the birthrate, and correct with severe legislation the laxity and disintegration of moral values (*Marc.* 23). Caesar himself subscribed to these ideals by new sumptuary measures. Augustus could work up feeling against Antony by representing him as a renegade from the Roman way of life. Later, he would attempt to reinforce or revive the moral standards of 'the good old days'. Cicero was perhaps personally less concerned than Sallust professed to be with moral degeneration in private life, as distinguished from the loss of that public spirit and integrity which Roman heroes of the past had displayed (e.g. *de rep.* iii. 40 f.). Certainly 'mos maiorum' embraces more than private morality. The state religion is to be maintained, if for no other reason, because it is that which the ancestors devised (see below). By setting 'mos maiorum' between 'leges' and 'iudicia, iuris dictio' Cicero is perhaps suggesting, what was certainly true, that with its evolution by the praetors' edicts in mind (n. 19), the legal system rested on custom as much as on statutes. He makes it explicit that Rome's political institutions had the same basis (*Sest.* 137, *de rep.* iv. 3).

However, it was not only optimates who could compose variations on this theme. Popular rights were also part of the tradition. Ancient precedents could be cited for the resistance of the people to the senate. On Cicero's own view (n. 20), the constitutional evolution characteristic of Rome would justify innovations to suit changed needs; that could justify popular reforms. Moreover optimates as well as *populares* could be accused of violating established rules. Abuse of the *senatus consultum ultimum*, for example, involved disregard for law. We may

---

[97] H. Roloff, *Maiores bei Cicero*, 1938 (extracts in Oppermann, 1967).

also be sure that Clodius inveighed against the suppression by the senate of the rights of association which Numa was supposed to have established (ch. 6 n. 57).

The same respect for tradition was paraded and perhaps felt by Augustus. He was personally conservative in language (Quint. *Inst.* i. 7. 22) and dress (Suet. *Aug.* 40. 5). He restored temples (*RG* 20. 4; Livy iv. 20) and statues (Suet. 31), and revived ancient ceremonies (ibid.; cf. 43. 2). It was in accordance with ancestral practices, as he asserts, that he closed the temple of Janus (ibid. 13), refused unconstitutional powers (ibid. 6), and preferred to hand over Armenia to a vassal prince rather than annex the country (ibid. 27). Suetonius probably reflects his own presentation of various measures when he writes of his 'restoring the senate to its old proportions and splendour' by *lectiones*, which reduced its inflated number and removed men of low status (35), and of his reviving the censorship, a magistracy long discontinued (37), and the people's former electoral rights (40). He justified social and moral legislation by invoking past laws and senatorial decrees (Dio lvi. 6. 4), even citing the speeches of Republican worthies of an earlier century (Suet. 89). He himself says that 'by the new laws I promoted I brought back into use many exemplary practices of our ancestors which were disappearing in our time' (*RG* 8). If he then proceeds that he himself had transmitted many exemplary practices for posterity to follow, and thus admits to innovations, he conveys the impression, which was not false in regard to his legislation, that he was as it were continuing a path in the same direction as that laid out in the past; this sort of evolution was itself traditional at Rome.

In Cicero's list 'religiones, auspicia' have a conventional precedence. Religious observances traditionally accompanied every public act. It was a Roman conception attested from 193 BC (but doubtless much earlier in origin) to the time of Augustine that Rome owed her greatness to her peculiar piety and skill in winning the favour of the gods; Cicero himself voiced it with impressive eloquence.[98] Prayers, sacrifices, and divination presupposed the beliefs that the gods invoked existed, intervened in human affairs, could be placated by appropriate rituals, and gave signs of their will which, correctly interpreted, would avert evil from the state and the family. Among the highly educated élite theoretical scepticism, or at least indifference in practice, was perhaps not uncommon. Cicero himself was in my judgement devoid of personal piety, and as a philosopher he would adopt the agnosticism of Carneades. It was the élite who were responsible for maintaining the

---

[98] *de har. resp.* 19; *SIG*³ 601; Hor. *Odes* iii. 6. 1–8. Belief in divine favour may well have strengthened Roman morale, and consequent success have fortified the belief. Augustine was to polemize endlessly against it.

public cults, and their disbelief or doubts or mere indifference may
have been reflected in the neglect of some, certainly not of all, the
traditional practices. Caesar, for example, who was *pontifex maximus*,
was according to Suetonius (*Caes.* 59) never deflected from any plan by
religious scruples. In his *Commentaries* he acknowledges the importance
of unpredictable strokes of fortune (*BG* vi. 30), but allows no role to the
gods.[99] However, even philosophers who criticized the publicly accepted religion were always ready to conform outwardly, and their
theories would not and should not, in the view of men like Cicero,
penetrate the masses (ch. 6 nn. 49 f.). The frequency of Cicero's own
appeals to religion, when addressing the senate, upper-class jurors, and
the multitude alike, indicates that credulity was widespread even in the
higher orders.[100] Like many before him, Cicero held that religion was
the indispensable foundation of morality and of the sanctity of oaths
among the vulgar, and therefore of the social order.[101] Fortunately
too, its administration was confided to the leading men of state (*de dom.*
1). It could therefore be used by them as a political tool. Cicero avers
that it had often been of service in the repression of sedition (n. 51).
This kind of manipulation of religious scruples would betoken that
they powerfully affected the minds of many, if not of those who
resorted to it. In fact instances of its effectiveness are hard to come by.
Certainly Bibulus' employment of *obnuntiatio* in 59 was too blatant to
impose on people; it did not impede the enactment of measures
conforming to popular wishes and backed by force, nor could it secure
their subsequent nullification. Still, Clodius thought it well in 58 to
restrict by legislation any future abuse of the procedure (ch. 6 n. 158).

[99] Cf. Wissowa 70 ff.; Latte 164 ff. (on Cicero 285 f.); Schulz, 1946, on *ius sacrum*. Liebeschutz,
1979, ch. 1, is more reserved on the decadence of the state religion. Some of the 'proofs' are not
very cogent (e.g. the disappearance of some archaic practices which had lost their meaning), but
Cic. *de leg.* ii. 29, *de nat. deor.* i. 9, *de div.* i. 25, ii. 76; Livy viii. 11. 1, xliii. 13. 1; Varro *ap.* Aug. *Civ.
Dei* vi. 2; Horace (last note) can hardly be set aside; on private cults cf. *de leg.* ii. 52 f., *de div.* i. 27.
As for Caesar, such texts as *BG* i. 32. 4, ii. 31. 5, *BC* ii. 14. 3, 32. 6 show that like most Latin writers
he does not always hypostatize *fortuna* as a divine power; I doubt if he ever does, but see *contra*
Weinstock 112 ff., a work of immense learning but less judgement, which exhaustively examines
his religious measures as dictator; these at least show that he supposed the state religion to have
some impact on large numbers of men. On the Augustan 'restoration' see Wissowa 73 ff.; Latte
294 ff.; Liebeschutz, ch. 2.
[100] R. J. Goar, *Cicero and the State Religion*, 1978 (mistaken in my view in ascribing genuine
piety to Cicero).
[101] *de nat. deor.* i. 3 f., 14, 61, 63, 77, *de div.* ii. 70, 86; cf. Diod. xxxiv. 2. 47 (Posidonius; cf. *FGH*
87. F. 59); Polyb. vi. 56 (with Walbank's note), who thought that Romans feared punishment in
an after-life. The vehemence of Lucretius' attack on belief in immortality might suggest that such
fears were common, though not inculcated by state cults, but note *de nat. deor.* i. 85 f., *Tusc. Disp.* i.
36 f., 48, 111. The monuments only indicate an increased belief in the first century in the survival
of the individual soul (Jocelyn Toynbee, *Death and Burial in the Roman World*, 85). As to oaths,
soldiers at this time often violated the military *sacramentum*, and Caesar's assassins had sworn to
protect his life (Weinstock 223 ff.).

At his most sceptical Cicero still insisted that the public religion must be sedulously kept up. Apart from all other considerations, it was part of the *mos maiorum*, whose hold on men's minds might be weakened in general, if impaired at any point. But we have no warrant for supposing that *populares*, like Clodius, ever sought to impugn the authority of *religiones* and *auspicia*, as distinguished from what they surely argued was an improper resort to them. Of such overt impiety there is no evidence; and it is improbable that if the masses were superstitious, their avowed champions treated their beliefs with unveiled contempt. Clodius himself had consecrated Cicero's house to *Libertas*, and could contend before the pontiffs that on that ground its restitution to Cicero should be refused (*de dom.* 104–37). As dictator Caesar himself was active in the institution or renovation of cults (n. 99). How much this policy might have assisted in fortifying his hold over the masses can only be guessed. It is hard to see religion as a significant force in the course that events took down to Caesar's death, even though everyone probably paid it lip-service; thereafter it may well be that there arose some genuine feeling that the continuing strife, apparently endless, betokened divine anger, and Augustus' care in restoring temples, priesthoods, and cults very probably corresponded to such apprehensions.

Leges in Cicero's own theoretical writings must accord with the divine law of nature: statutes which do not fulfil this condition are not properly laws at all.[102] However, the Roman *ius civile* is superior to every other system (*de orat.* i. 196 f.); even the Twelve Tables, obsolete as they were, had instructed Romans in moral duty, and in particular taught them to distinguish *meum* and *tuum* (ibid. 181). But more recent statutes had been enacted which not only contravened moral criteria but had not been passed by due procedure; some had rightly been annulled by the senate on this ground; and the courts had refused to enforce a statute of Sulla's which infringed the principle that no Roman could be deprived of freedom or citizenship by mere enactment.[103] Laws of 59 and 58, which had been passed in disregard of the auspices and of previous statutes that prescribed the procedures for legislation, should equally have been regarded as void. Subject to these qualifications, *leges* form part of Roman *ius*, though much *ius* derived from immemorial or more recently developed practice (n. 19). The very term *ius* of course assimilated what was legally enforceable to what was morally right. *Ius* is sustained by the verdicts of the courts, and, as Cicero might have added, by magisterial 'iuris dictio'. The only

---

[102] *de rep.* iii. 33, *de leg.* i. *passim*, ii. 13. Cicero could not have sustained this position after he had reverted to Academic scepticism.

[103] *de leg.* ii. 14; cf. ch. 6 endnote 1.

alternative to legal process is the rule of force (*Sest.* 92). Stability is destroyed if court decisions are not upheld (*Sulla* 63). The courts guided by jurisconsults must respect the 'ius civile', which is the bond of life in society, the guarantee of property, and the source of impartial justice (*Caec.* 70). Law, duly administered by the courts, safeguards the liberty, rank, and possessions of the citizens (*Cluent.* 146, *de dom.* 33, 46).

Populares would hardly have dissented from any of this in principle. In asserting the people's unlimited right to legislate, they could have cited the Twelve Tables (ch. 6 n. 34). It was they who could claim to be upholding the rule of law in protesting against the arbitrary punishment of citizens, or in 133 against disregard of the legal limit on holdings of public land, and in 58 against the senate's abrogation of legal rights of association. It was also in the name of purity of justice that they could demand in 123 and 70 the termination of senatorial control of the courts, and that Cornelius in 67 required praetors to give juridical decisions in conformity with their own edicts; Cornelius also limited the senate's freedom to grant exemptions from the law, which had obviously been improperly exercised (Ascon. 57–9 C.). Despite the anarchic activities of a Clodius, it cannot be supposed that they would have contradicted Cicero's resounding assertions that men's life, freedom, and property rested on the rule of law.

Of Augustus it is enough to say that his re-establishment of order in itself reinforced the rule of law. In the course of that abdication of unconcealed autocracy which he dates to 28–27 (*RG* 34), he fixed the last day of 28 as the term after which 'the illegal and unjust regulations' of the triumvirate should cease to be valid (Dio liii. 2. 5). Thereafter he was so careful to observe property rights that he made his forum less spacious than he had planned rather than sequester land on which adjoining houses stood (Suet. *Aug.* 56). Tiberius was to avow that he had been entrusted with power that he might serve not only the state but private persons too (Suet. *Tib.* 29).

'Fides', which Cicero collocates in his list with 'iudicia' and 'iuris dictio', is in its most general meaning 'fidelity to promises and agreements', it can be seen as the basis of all just conduct (*de offic.* i. 23); and it has a wide range in Roman social life and legal institutions; but here perhaps it refers most specifically to 'credit'. Just as Cicero in 56 probably had in mind under *iuris dictio* the disruption of legal processes which had occurred in recent years,[104] so he was thinking principally when he spoke of *fides* here, of the insecurity of the money market at Rome that had resulted from the Mithridatic wars, and still more of the hopes that Catiline had held out to the 'wretched', as well as to the

---

[104] Especially in 58–57; cf. Brunt, *Liverpool Class. Monthly*, 1981, 227 ff.

ruined men of high degree among his accomplices, of remission of debts and redistribution of property.[105] In retrospect Cicero would write: 'What does relief of debts mean but this? You buy an estate with my money; you have it, and I lose the money ... Nothing holds the commonwealth together more strongly than *fides*, which cannot possibly subsist, unless men are obliged to pay what they owe. Never was there a stronger movement to prevent this than in my consulship ... Never was the burden of debt greater, yet never was it better or more speedily discharged; once hope of fraud had been dissipated, men had no choice but to pay up' (*de offic.* ii. 84). 'Would-be *populares* who bring up the agrarian question, with a view to driving possessors out of their seats, or think that moneys borrowed should be presented to the debtors, subvert the foundations of the commonwealth; and justice too is totally abolished if every man is not allowed to keep his own' (ibid. 78); by contrast, the true guardians of the commonwealth will exert themselves above all to ensure 'that every man keeps his own by the justice (*aequitas*) of law and court decisions in such a way that the weaker sort are not defrauded on account of their humble status and that envy does not hamper the wealthier sort in retaining or recovering what belongs to them' (ibid. 85).

In all this Cicero is unfair to the *populares*. In order to resettle the poor on the land, Tiberius Gracchus merely resumed public domains which the rich had occupied in contravention of an old law; admittedly they had been in possession so long and with such a sense of security that they had treated their holdings as private property, using it for dowries and family tombs, but strictly they were not being evicted from lands they owned (App. 7–10). Most subsequent agrarian schemes also involved redistribution of state lands or purchase from willing sellers. The only large expropriations before 41–40 were those of Sulla, reprobated by Cicero (*de offic.* i. 43, ii. 29);[106] Catiline who proposed to follow his example was one of his old partisans. The conception of equalizing wealth Cicero himself mentions as an absurdity that no one would entertain (*de rep.* i. 49). The Marian regime in 86 did enact that three-quarters of all debts should be remitted; this was a measure probably made necessary by the shortage of cash consequent on the Social war and the loss of Asia to Mithridates, and was perhaps partly designed for the benefit of an insolvent treasury (p. 159). In general *populares* hardly ever sought to relieve the poor of the burden of debt; Catiline is again the exception. Caesar's enemies expected in 49 that he would effect a remission of debts, but these fears were hardly justified.

[105] *de imp. Cn. Pomp.* 19, *de leg. agr.* i. 24, ii. 8. Catiline: *Mur.* 49–51, *Cat.* ii. 8, 17–22, *Fam.* v. 6. 2, *de offic.* ii. 84; Sall. *Cat.* 16. 4, 21. 2, 28. 4, 33.
[106] *IM*, ch. xix.

Initially he did no more than enable landed proprietors who were short of cash to satisfy their creditors by making over real estate to them at pre-war valuations (*BC* iii. 1); after prolonged agitation he was ultimately obliged to remit some arrears of rent due from urban dwellers in Rome and Italian towns, proof for Cicero of his inborn wickedness. The property of a debtor could be sold up by court order for the benefit of his creditors, with the result that he incurred through *infamia* the loss of many valuable civic rights; it may have been Caesar too who enabled him to escape this penalty by a voluntary cession of assets to meet his liability. But personal execution was open to the creditor where the debtor had insufficient assets for the purpose, or had concealed them; he could obtain a court order (*addictio*) enabling him to keep in bonds the debtor who had failed to pay the sum he was adjudged to owe or admitted owing; it seems that he might then be obliged to give the creditor forced labour. No *populares* even sought to mitigate this harsh procedure. The old laws restricting or banning interest on loans were allowed to fall into abeyance, though a praetor in 89 attempted enforcement, and was murdered (GC 150 f.).[107] Cicero could himself treat the maintenance of *fides* in the sense of credit as something the common people would approve (*de leg. agr.* ii. 8).

After *fides* Cicero finally names among the *fundamenta* 'provinciae, socii, imperii laus, res militaris, aerarium'.[108] He surely has in mind not only the preservation or extension of Rome's 'dominion over all peoples', ordained, as he was to tell the plebs, by the immortal gods (*Phil.* vi. 19), and resting both on military strength and on financial resources, but also the just administration and protection of Rome's subjects and vassals; perhaps *fides*, besides its more specific meaning as 'credit', by its collocation with what follows also suggests the idea that Rome was to regard her empire as a trust, and as in the good old days, exercise a 'patrocinium orbis terrae' rather than 'imperium' (*de offic.* ii. 27); the empire should be sustained by their goodwill (iii. 88). All this enhanced the *dignitas rei publicae*; for we must recall that *dignitas* had moral overtones and connotes 'worth' as well as 'rank'; imperial grandeur is both glorious and deserved. Again, there was nothing here that *populares* would have repudiated.

In principle everyone acknowledged that Rome had a duty to defend her allies and subjects and give them just government. Augustus' declaration that he wished all the provincials to know the care that the senate and he took that they should not incur wrongful exactions (EJ 311 v. 80) implied no new recognition of this duty; it was embodied in the *repetundae* laws designed for their protection

---

[107] See endnote 5.   [108] For what follows see Brunt. *Laus Imperii*.

(Cic. *Div. Caec.* 17), each allegedly of greater rigour than the last (*de offic.* ii. 75); *populares*, C. Gracchus, Glaucia, and Caesar, all introduced improvements, but Sulla too recodified the law. Gracchus, like the elder Cato, had denounced the oppression of the Italian allies before the people (Gell. x. 3), and Pompey in 70 that of the subjects overseas (I *Verr.* 45); Cicero in popular vein could expect to work up indignation on the same subject (II *Verr.* iii. 207, *de imp. Cn. Pomp.* 65). The mild and just principles on which he exhorted his brother to rule Asia (*Qu. fr.* i. 1) and on which he tried to act himself in Cilicia accorded with those of that most intransigent of optimates, the younger Cato (*Att.* vi. 1. 13, vi. 2. 8, *Fam.* xv. 5). It is another matter that the partiality and corruption of the courts made it hard for the subjects to obtain redress; still we must not conclude that most governors resembled Verres rather than Cicero. There was some improvement in the Principate, often exaggerated.

Even more obviously, all were agreed on maintaining Rome's imperial strength and prestige. In fact *populares* were most zealous for Rome's honour in the Jugurthine war, and brought to account commanders who culpably disgraced Roman arms in the north and imperilled the security of Italy during the next few years. None did so much to enhance Rome's power and glory as Pompey and Caesar, who owed their extraordinary commands to the people; 'imperii laus' is Cicero's chief theme in extolling the achievements of the former in 66 (addressing the people) and of the latter in 56 (speaking before the senate). Tiberius Gracchus justified his agrarian scheme at least in part by considerations of 'res militaris'; it would keep up the supply of citizens qualified for service in the legions.

Like later proposals for the distribution of land or grain, it was assailed as a 'largitio' that the treasury could ill afford. It is hard to see how these optimate criticisms could have been validated except perhaps in the period between 90 and the conquests of Pompey; imperial revenues were flowing in ample measure.[109] Although Cicero was perhaps not alone in arguing that Rome was entitled to tax the subjects in order to pay the armies needed for their protection (*Qu. fr.* i. 1. 34), Romans felt no compunction in treating the provinces as their possessions, producing income that they could apply to their own purposes. Probably no one saw any moral objection to Tiberius Gracchus' appropriation of the moneys available from Attalus III's bequest of the kingdom of Pergamum to fitting out the allotments under his agrarian bill. In a speech to the people, of which the context is mysterious, his brother claimed that his proposals were directed to

[109] See endnote 6, Ch. 3 n. 123.

'increasing your revenues, so that you may more easily serve your interests and the commonwealth' (Gell. xi. 10. 1). Cicero remarks that though responsible for huge largesses that squandered the treasury, he spoke as if he were its champion (*Tusc. Disp.* iii. 48). It may well be that additional income accruing from his reform of the Asian tax-system and new harbour dues covered his schemes of social relief. So too the cost of Clodius' free grain doles must have been found from the new revenues obtained through Pompey's eastern settlement, to which Clodius added a bonus, by providing for the annexation of Cyprus. Moreover, *populares* could retort to charges of extravagance with allegations that the ruling class lined their own pockets from the treasury. This was surely what many of them did, though the mechanisms by which they appropriated public funds without actually violating the law against peculation are somewhat obscure. Certainly it seems to have been within a general's discretion to decide what part, if any, of the spoils of war he would reserve for the treasury, or donate for public buildings and the like; and how much he would distribute to his officers and men; the former would get much larger shares, and he could retain for himself a proportionate sum.[110]

Once again it was Augustus whose reorganization of the armed forces, financial measures, and military and diplomatic triumphs did most to realize this part of Cicero's programme; the enhanced splendour of the city of Rome, which resulted from his munificence in building, symbolized her imperial greatness. These achievements were the more impressive because for contemporaries that greatness had seemed to be in jeopardy.

At a time when it seemed that civil wars might never cease, Horace was to lament that Rome was destroying herself by her own strength and express the fear that one day the clatter of barbarian horse would resound on the city's streets (*Epodes* vii and xvi), and Virgil would pray, with no firm confidence, that Octavian would prove a saviour not only from internal anarchy but from foreign dangers (*Georg.* i. 498 ff.):

Hinc movet Euphrates, illinc Germania bellum

Livy thought Rome strong enough to overcome all external foes only if the harmony that Augustus had then restored were perpetual (ix. 19. 17). No one of course could yet know that the capacity and impulse for conquest that had carried the Parthians from the Caspian to the Syrian border had now expired, or that there would not for centuries be a perilous revival of those German migratory movements which had

---

[110] See endnote 7.

threatened Rome in Marius' time: the fears of Maroboduus voiced by Tiberius are significant (Tac. *Ann.* ii. 63). But for Augustus' work continued anarchy might have exposed the empire to the same kind of irruptions which were gravely to damage the imperial structure in the third century AD.

In fact Augustus was to realize Cicero's ideal of enhancing the 'dignitas imperii'. Apart from completing the pacification of regions (especially in Spain) long nominally subject to Rome, and restoring Roman prestige in the east, tarnished by the defeats of Crassus and Antony, which might seem to portend greater disasters, by his annexations in the north he added more to Roman territory than anyone before him; and if in the end he was frustrated in his design to extend Rome's dominion at least to western Germany and Bohemia, and was far from fulfilling Virgil's prediction that he would accomplish her mission to conquer the world and thus establish universal peace (*Aen.* i. 235–7), he did bequeath to his successors an empire 'protected by the Ocean and remote rivers', relatively easy to defend (*Ann.* i. 9).[111] For both offensive and defensive purposes he required larger forces than the Republic had mobilized except in civil wars. There were now permanent squadrons to assure freedom of navigation on the seas; and the standing army numbered probably some 300,000 men, as against about 75,000 in 60 or 125,000 in 53; at the same time the burden of military service was lessening for Italians, since about half the soldiers were probably provincials, and the proportion of provincials was growing.[112] New financial resources were required for these military commitments (and indeed for increased domestic expenditure, which also tended to magnify the splendour of the city of Rome itself); the richer Italians had to make some contribution, and Augustus assisted from his vast personal wealth; the rents of his ever increasing estates supplemented the yield of taxes. But the revenue from the provinces must also have been buoyant: of the new acquisitions Egypt at least produced a huge surplus over occupation costs, and everywhere peace must have augmented prosperity, and more efficient methods of taxation must have enabled the state to take its due

---

[111] It is generally held that Augustus sought only to establish defensible frontiers, and failed to advance them in the north to the projected Elbe–Danube line; I argued in *JRS* 1963, 170 ff., that he hoped to realize the ideal of world-dominion in prudent stages, and that it was only after the Illyrian and German revolts of AD 6–9 that he (or Tiberius) adopted a purely defensive posture. However this may be, the great extent of his conquests and the stress he himself laid in *RG* on the military glory he had won are facts beyond dispute.

[112] Cf. *IM*, chs. xxv f., for legionary strengths. My estimate of the Augustan army includes a highly conjectural figure for the *auxilia*; and it ought to be borne in mind that provincial *auxilia* were used in the late Republic, though not on the same scale or so sytematically as in the Principate. Conscription in Italy was less oppressive under Augustus and was normally discontinued from Tiberius' time (*IM* 414 f.; cf. *Scripta Class. Israelica*, 1974, 90 ff.).

proportion of the rising gross product of its dominions.[113] Pursuing a peaceful and economical policy, Tiberius could lay up a great reserve (Suet. *Gaius* 37. 3).

We can hardly estimate the effects of these achievements in reconciling opinion to the new regime: it was known by its fruits. But most patently it was vital to Augustus' political success that he re-established and maintained 'otium'. After the miseries of civil wars, he captivated everyone 'dulcedine otii' (*Ann.* i. 2), prescribing laws 'under which we might live in peace with a prince' (iii. 28); 'it was in the interest of peace that all power should devolve on one man' (*Hist.* i. 1). Horace could say quite simply that under Augustus' sway he did not fear to die by violence (*Odes* iii. 14. 16). Of the most turbulent sections of the community in the late Republic, Augustus kept the urban plebs content by better provision for the food supply (not to speak of that of water, or of the public works that gave them employment[114]), and the soldiers with gifts, and above all by guaranteeing them the means of livelihood on discharge. Velleius' panegyric on his work (ii. 89) is reminiscent of Cicero's ideals: 'civil wars were extinguished, foreign wars buried, peace was recalled, armed frenzy everywhere laid to rest, force restored to the *laws*, authority to the *courts*, majesty to the *senate*; the power of magistrates was reduced to its ancient limits . . . The famous and *traditional* form of the commonwealth, as it had been *of old*, was brought back to life. Cultivation returned to the fields, respect to *religion*, security to men; everyone was safely in possession of his own.'[115]

Velleius chose to say nothing of the variety of devices by which Augustus had assured himself of ultimate control of the state. The fundamentally monarchic character of the new settlement probably dismayed parvenus of his type less than the nobility, and less than it would have dismayed Cicero, who had shared in the senatorial ascendancy and risen to an eminence now beyond the reach of any private man. Some have indeed supposed that Cicero himself had helped to prepare men's minds for the Principate by his account of an ideal 'moderator rei publicae' in his *de republica*. But Cicero's 'moderator' is no more than the model statesman; there is nothing to show that Cicero contemplated that he should be vested, except perhaps in a

[113] Caesar had probably substituted collection by local governments of the direct taxes not only in Asia but throughout the east for collection by publicans, who had probably been little used for this purpose in the west. Augustus' institution of periodic provincial censuses permitted the government to base tax demands on fairly realistic estimates of presumably increasing wealth. See A. H. M. Jones, *The Roman Economy*, 1974, ch. 8; Brunt, *JRS* 1981, 161 ff.

[114] Brunt, *JRS* 1980, 81 ff.

[115] Vell. ii. 126 adulates Tiberius in similar terms, as if Augustus' work had to be done over again.

short emergency, with any extraordinary legal powers such as Augustus possessed (see endnote 8). In any case for all the adulations of provincials or Roman poets, who could frankly recognize that Augustus was monarch and credit him with divinity or divine aid, there appears to have been no ideological enthusiasm for monarchy among the élite, whose collaboration Augustus most needed (Section I). For their attitude the best evidence is his own caution in posing as no more than the first man at Rome and parading his *civilitas*.[116] Tacitus makes his admirers acknowledge that the rule of one man was the only remedy for the discords of the state, but praise him for not assuming the style of king or dictator and affecting to remain merely *princeps*; like Velleius, they too enlarge on what his measures achieved (*Ann.* i. 9). The new regime was approved by the *boni et beati* because Augustus did what Cicero's optimates were to have done: he gave effect to their 'will, interests, and opinions' in the matters men of prosperity cared for most.

VIII

Why did the senate fail to achieve that consensus which Augustus obtained? Clearly at times it alienated the Italian allies, the Equites, the urban plebs, the peasants, and the soldiery. It did so because of its inability to solve problems that arose from Rome's expansion.[117]

It is a mere dogmatic assertion which explains nothing to say that an aristocracy as such cannot rule an empire. (The Venetian aristocracy did.) At least in its acquisition the Roman aristocracy had shown the most remarkable sagacity. In the early period of the Republic, when Rome was still struggling first for survival and then for hegemony among her neighbours, the patricians had made prudent concessions to popular grievances and absorbed the leading plebeian families in a new nobility, more open to talent, and thereby preserved the degree of internal harmony necessary for external success. The conquests that Rome made permitted large distributions of booty, allotments of land, the repayment and from 167 the discontinuance of direct taxes. Victories enriched the ruling élite, but there was enough to satisfy the common people as well. Very probably the former were the more

---

[116] On *civilitas*, which was cultivated by all of those successors of Augustus who sought like him to retain the goodwill of the élite, see A. Wallace-Hadrill, *JRS* 1982, 32 ff.; perhaps it might be added (*a*) that the emperor who eschewed monarchic trappings was likely to be more accessible to their views and (*b*) that the pretence that he was 'unus ex nobis', while not detracting from his real power, maintained their *dignitas*. In my view *civilitas* or its absence is of the first importance for understanding an emperor's relations with the higher orders, and not only with the senate: it is a prominent theme in the portrayal of emperors by the Eques Suetonius.

[117] Compare what follows in this section with the illuminating analysis in Hopkins, 1978, ch. 1.

ready to allow them a share in the profits because the measures that answered this purpose also contributed to Rome's military strength and thus to further expansion. Allotments of land enabled the peasants to increase and multiply and thus augmented the number of legionaries. They were also commonly granted in colonial foundations, Roman or Latin, placed at strategic points for the control of Italy. The reservoir of manpower, which even the huge losses inflicted by Hannibal could not exhaust, and which made Rome immeasurably superior to kingdoms in the east, was further increased by extensions of the citizenship. This liberal policy, without precedent in that of other city-states, also helped to win the loyalty of some Italians, those who were incorporated in the Roman state. The 'allies', though entangled in wars not of their choosing, were at least assured of Rome's protection, a matter of special moment so long as fear of Gallic inroads persisted (Polyb. ii. 23), and were accorded internal autonomy; the oligarchies, which usually controlled them, might have close relations of friendship with the Roman nobility. Numerous revolts occurred as late as the Hannibalic war, but even then most of the Italians stood by Rome, some perhaps from a justified belief in her eventual victory. They were rewarded by a century of internal peace, of which the forty years before Hannibal's invasion had given a foretaste.

Once acquired, the empire was indeed ill-governed. Mutual rivalries and jealousies made the senators ready to entrust mediocrities with the tasks of administration and defence; at the same time they were too partial to their peers, moving in the same social circles, to impose effective restraints on their treatment of the subjects. Hence the provincials were often oppressed and inadequately defended. Many or most detested Roman rule. However, it was not their discontents that brought the Republic down. The improvements made under the Principate in imperial government, and the reconciliation of the provincials, or of their élites, may furnish a retrospective justification for the revolution, but have no bearing on its origins. Italian voters and Italian swords destroyed senatorial supremacy. The same rapacity and arrogance that earned the hatred of Asians or Spaniards were visited by senators on their fellow-citizens and Italian allies. Moreover, grievances at home arose from the effects of imperial expansion on society, economy, and political institutions. Perhaps the very solidity of Roman might led the senate to neglect the preservation and repair of the internal consensus which had been a condition of Roman conquests. There seems to be some truth in the common Roman view that danger from without had promoted harmony within, and that harmony tended to dissolve once external danger had apparently been removed.

Early in the second century north Italy was pacified, apart from marauding raids, and whatever apprehensions the Hellenistic monarchies may at first have aroused were allayed by a succession of easy victories. Rome's military strength was so overwhelming that the old methods of sustaining it were allowed to fall into disuse. The process of colonization was halted after about 173.[118] Enfranchisement of Italians ceased. No pressing need was apparently felt to keep up the number of citizens qualified by property for military service. Legionaries were recruited mainly by conscription; it was hated, and if the proportion of allies in Roman armies was allowed to increase in the later second century, as was probably the case, this was perhaps one of the reasons. It was also a device that relieved the Roman treasury, which paid legionaries from imperial revenues, whereas the Italian communities had to pay their own contingents. (It is not really true that Rome exacted from her allies a tribute only of blood and not of cash as well.)[119]

For reasons that I have attempted to explain in Chapter 2 the allies came to desire parity of rights with the Romans. The revolt of Fregellae is proof that this desire was already latent among the Latins, when the issue was raised by M. Fulvius Flaccus; no doubt it had been stimulated by the Gracchan agrarian law, imperilling the possession of Roman domain land which was held by oligarchs in the Italian communities, though enfranchisement would hardly have occurred to anyone but for Rome's earlier tradition of extending her citizenship. It may well be that in the first instance the senate rejected the demand precisely because it emanated from *populares*, and concession might have strengthened their political influence. It was evidently easy enough to rouse the opposition of the plebs. In a hierarchic society any order may feel satisfaction in seeing others lower in the scale. Among the allies themselves the demand for enfranchisement cannot as yet have been either universal or deeply felt. No more is heard of it for almost thirty years. But once the idea had been implanted, it must have silently flourished. Senatorial leaders recognized its strength in 91, but half-heartedly and temporarily. When Drusus' proposal foundered, there was a widespread revolt. Nearly all the Latins (who were mostly of Roman descent) remained loyal, and some other communities; we can assume that each people followed the lead of its own *principes*, who could differ on the prudence of taking arms. But the course of events seems to show not only that the rebels sought

---

[118] Over 40,000 received allotments 200–173 (*ESAR* i. 122 ff.); there may have been a little unrecorded settlement after 167, when we no longer have Livy's narrative, the source of previous information.

[119] Conscription: *IM*, ch. xxii. Italian contingents: ibid. 677 ff., cf. Ilari, 1974.

incorporation in the Roman state, and independence only if that were denied, but that the loyalty of the rest could not be assured unless they were given precisely what had previously been refused. The senate deserves some credit for seeing this, and at last acting accordingly, but it then tried to nullify the benefit by restricting the voting power of the new citizens. Their consequential discontent was the precondition of civil wars and of the Marian seizure of power. Amid this turmoil it proved necessary to extend the citizenship to the former insurgents too, but the practical effect was still minimized by the failure to register most of the new citizens on the census rolls until 70.

The attitude of the senate to Italian aspirations is not explained in our sources and is hard to understand. It is most unlikely to have been due to a conception that any further increase in the number of citizens and in their geographical distribution would break the bounds of a city-state. This doctrinal thinking was alien to the practical Roman mentality; and in any case with over 400,000 adult male citizens, many already living hundreds of miles from the city, Rome was and had long been a city-state of a wholly anomalous kind. It may be that some nobles feared that with an enlarged electorate in the centuriate assembly, in which the Italian magnates at least could be expected to exercise their voting rights, their own order would lose control, and perhaps even be confronted with more new competitors. If such apprehensions were entertained, they were belied by experience in the post-Sullan generation. Fiscal considerations may have counted for something. Perhaps we must simply invoke a mental inertia generated by the conviction that Rome's imperial power was now so great that it was no longer necessary to take account of allied sentiments.

Imperial expansion also produced the conditions for the intermittent conflicts of senate and Equites (Chapter 3). There was a vast increase in public revenue and expenditure and therefore in the scope of state contracting, whether on public works, or supplies for the armies, or in the collection both of rents on public domains such as mines and of provincial taxes. It had already proved necessary that the contractors for these enterprises should be organized in companies, and investment in them was widely spread among the rich. Their interests could often conflict with those of the treasury and the taxpayers, of which the senate was the proper custodian, while their organization and voting strength in the centuriate assembly afforded them some means of political pressure. The wealth of such men and their consciousness of the importance of their public functions enhanced their sense of a dignity which was imperfectly recognized in the existing structure. They resented the monopoly of judicial rights possessed by senators in all important cases (Chapter 4). Though the senate itself was recruited from their ranks, as older families died out or were impoverished, those among them who sought a political career may have chafed at the arrogance with which the nobility looked down on newcomers. Gaius Gracchus was to enlarge their opportunities for profit in public contracting, and the *splendor* of their position in the state by conferring on them judicial rights; in particular they alone were to sit in judgement on senators accused of extortions from the subjects, a privilege extended by later popular legislation to other political offences. The tenacity with which they clung to these rights shows that he had detected ambitions which the senate had ignored and which it now long tried to frustrate.

In this case it is easy to comprehend the senate's attitude. Senators wished to be responsible to their peers alone, except in so far as they were bound by constitutional practices, which they could not dream of upsetting, to recognize the electoral, legislative, and judicial rights of the people: they could of course also assert with some reason that it was not for the good of either treasury or subjects that they should be amenable to the new pressure that publicans could exert on them through control of criminal courts.

The discord between the senate and the equestrian order, or rather its most affluent members organized in the publican companies, came to a head at the same time as the Italian insurrection. There was intense bitterness within the propertied class at Rome. This was one reason why the Social war issued in civil war.

It may, however, appear that these conflicts had little to do with the ultimate collapse of the senate's supremacy. That was restored by Sulla. At latest in 70, when the censors more or less completely registered the new citizens, and certainly those among them who wished to exercise political rights at Rome, and when the long contest for control of the courts was settled by a durable compromise, both Italians and Equites had secured their essential aims. In fact, despite occasional disputes arising from the public contracts and the existence among those Equites who aspired to office of some resentment at aristocratic exclusiveness, there is no evidence of any great cleft dividing the two higher orders; equally there is none of animosity among the Italian gentry against the senate (p. 7). But recollection of the fearful sufferings of the wars that lasted from 90 to 82, which did result from the senate's resistance to equestrian and Italian ambitions, had an enduring effect on the minds of all who stood to lose from their repetition, and conditioned them to accept any regime that was most likely to secure them in their lives and property (p. 67). The Equites and the gentry who controlled the Italian peoples and had no more sympathy than senators with the grievances of the poor, were not prepared, as Cicero hoped, to take a strong stand in defence of the senate's authority when it was threatened by 'dynasts', whose strength had its origin in the indifference of the senate to the needs of the masses.

The acquisition of empire sharpened the division between rich and poor. Booty from some of the foreign campaigns doubtless enriched the more fortunate of Rome's peasant soldiers,[120] but far more of them must have been ruined by service overseas, which could take them away for years together from their small farms. Not indeed that military service was probably the main cause of the decline in the number of peasant owners. At all times the subsistence farmer must have been unable to survive a series of bad harvests without falling into debt. Many of them must have had holdings too small for the maintenance of a family without benefit of usage of public domain land or of additional plots leased from the larger landowners or of seasonal employment by the latter. The profits of warfare, government, and public contracting now furnished the rich with large sums to invest, which they preferred to put into the aggrandizement of their holdings of land. They would thus have been more ruthless in foreclosing on the farms mortgaged to them as security for credit; we are told that some actually seized by force the properties of their weaker neighbours. At the same time they were occupying and enclosing more and more of the domain land for arable cultivation, besides grazing ever larger herds on the common pastures. They also imported large numbers of slaves, taking the view that slave labour was more economical than free labour on their estates. Hence the peasant who lost his own holding had less chance of leasing a farm, or of getting hired employment except for seasonal work, for which the permanent labour force of slaves was insufficient. The expropriated peasants might migrate to Rome or other towns, but though with the great increase of the 'national income' that we must postulate, there must also have been an increased demand for manufactured goods and services, this demand too could be largely met by slaves and freedmen, who were already possessed of the skills that the peasant lacked, or could be trained at the cost of their owners or patrons; there was little for the peasant but casual unskilled work. In Rome at least the swollen population lived in squalor and on the edge of starvation. It is unlikely that the rural poor, once deprived of their own farms, were less wretched than the under-employed agrarian proletariate of southern Italy a few generations ago.[121]

---

[120] Harris, 1979, 58 ff., 102 ff.

[121] See e.g. F. M. Snowden, *Violence and Great Estates in the South of Italy*, 1986, for vivid illustrations. On the Roman agrarian question cf. ch. 5, I and the further statement of my views

In some measure the concentration of landed property in fewer hands was a process that must always have been in operation. Until about 173 it was continually counteracted by the creation of new colonies or by viritane allotments of land in Italy which Rome had conquered. It is clear that after 173 there still remained a considerable stock of such land in public domain. Tiberius Gracchus proposed to resume the traditional policy of distributing it. If it had been intermitted, it was partly perhaps because the senate saw no strategic necessity for it (p. oo), partly because the senators themselves were among the chief beneficiaries of the conversion of domain land into what were in effect private estates. Gracchus was indeed to argue that there was still a military reason for reviving the tradition on the footing that Roman power rested on a sufficient supply of peasant soldiers. It does not seem to have occurred to him that in so far as military service in itself prejudiced the viability of small farming, it must impair the prospects of his new settlers, nor that other factors would still operate against small owners. We are told that in fact the Gracchan colonists ultimately failed to make good, just like the veterans to whom Sulla later gave allotments. Yet land distribution continued to be the panacea for assuaging rural discontent, although the quantity of domain land available must have been severely reduced by the Gracchan measure, so that it later became necessary to resort to purchase with state funds, whether compulsory or from willing sellers, or else to outright confiscations from those who had taken the losing side in civil wars. The opponents of such settlements rested their case on the sanctity of private property or the need to conserve the resources of the treasury. Allotments of land could temporarily increase the number of small owners (though they too were among the victims of Sullan and triumviral sequestrations).[122] No one seems to have discerned that in the long run these measures were doomed to futility.

That does not diminish the political importance of the demand for agrarian reform. It is hard to overestimate the significance of Tiberius Gracchus' initiative. In order to carry out his plan, he challenged senatorial authority comprehensively, and set the precedent for all future popular movements. Moreover, it was in the course of its

---

ap. Cherubini, 1983, 99 ff., with select bibliography. The alienation of small farms no doubt occurred usually by sale or *fiducia cum creditore* (n. 107). Ti. Gracchus (App. i. 10, 27), Sulla (Cic. *de leg. agr.* ii. 78), and Caesar (App. iii. 2, 7) all made allotments inalienable; they could then not legally be sold or given as security; the settler had only his chattels to pledge in return for a loan. But the threat of personal execution (ch. 6 n. 7) might force him to surrender usufruct to his creditor and, on the creditor's demise, to his successor; alternatively the law was ignored, because no one would challenge the creditor's title in the courts when he took possession. An inalienability clause in the Gracchan law was eventually rescinded, in regard to Sullan allotments not observed.

[122] Sall. *Or. Lepidi* 12. 24; Hist. i. 65, Dio xlviii. 9. 3; cf. *IM*, ch. xix (iii) and (vi).

implementation that the problems of Rome's relationship with the allies first became controversial and the initial stimulus was given to their claim for enfranchisement. It is possible that it was partly or mainly to win further support for the work of the land commission that Gaius Gracchus turned both to the urban plebs in instituting the corn dole, and to the Equites. A generation later, the younger Drusus, bent on granting the citizenship to the Italian allies and restoring control of the courts to the senate, felt it necessary to woo the plebs, which probably cared little for either proposal, with more distributions both of grain and land. We cannot tell how far in the result this demagogy actually estranged some of those who might have sympathized with his main objectives. At any rate all these issues were intertwined, and solutions for any of them may have become all the harder.

A great concourse of rural voters came in to Rome to pass Tiberius Gracchus' agrarian bill. We do not hear that this recurred later, except when the primary beneficiaries of land allotments were demobilized soldiers, themselves of rustic origin. The more recent migrants into the city were doubtless always interested in any opportunity to regain a livelihood on the land, but they do not seem to have constituted an effective pressure group. Widely scattered throughout Italy, most of them remote from Rome and unable to attend the assemblies, the dispossessed peasants other than the veterans found no determined champions after the Gracchi; the ease with which Rullus' agrarian bill of 63 was defeated is significant.

For the mass of the urban plebs the first consideration was the price of grain. The senate showed as little solicitude for them as for the rural poor.[123] The cost of the dole instituted by Gaius Gracchus was reduced either by raising the price or by limiting the number of recipients or by both devices. Sulla abolished it altogether. It is true that it was revived on a small scale by a consular law of 73 and greatly extended by a measure that Cato proposed as tribune in 62. These measures were plainly concessions extorted by popular unrest. Before 73 high prices had provoked serious rioting; and it is probable that the constant disorders in the city in the next twenty years were linked with scarcities. At the time of Cato's law Catiline was still in arms, and the senate was bound to be apprehensive that he would be aided by an outbreak of insurrection in the city. It was left to the *popularis* Clodius to abolish the charge always made hitherto for the grain distributed by the state and apparently to make them available to virtually anyone who claimed a share.

By organizing the clubs in which the humbler people at Rome had

---

[123] Rickman, 1980, chs. III and VII on measures to ensure the procurement of sufficient grain, as well as those for its cheap or free distribution.

been accustomed to associate and which the senate had sought to suppress, he also deprived the senate of the means of keeping order there. It is notable that the senate had no troops or police permanently at its disposal for the purpose. No doubt the very concept of a police force was unfamiliar in the ancient city-state, but then the huge agglomeration of inhabitants at Rome was itself almost a unique phenomenon; it must at least be said that the senate lacked the discernment to devise a new remedy for an unparalleled problem. It might well have feared to entrust to any one of its own members power that might have given him dominance. The remedy was found by Augustus, who had thousands of troops stationed in or near the city under officers of his own choice.[124]

Not that he relied chiefly on repression: he also made far better provision for the material welfare of the Roman poor. In particular he finally created permanent machinery for ensuring the procurement of grain. It was idle to promise the plebs free or cheap rations at the public expense if insufficient supplies reached the city; moreover, especially before Clodius' law, the dole did not meet all the require-ments of the population; and later too many still had to buy at market prices. Gaius Gracchus' construction of public granaries shows that he recognized the problem, but it was never solved in the Republic. The prevalence of piracy before 67 interrupted shipments and caused prices to soar; even when Pompey had rooted it out, scarcities could still arise, and in 57 he had to be given a new extraordinary commission to organize procurement. The crisis of 67 had, however, already crucially affected the course of the political revolution. A chain of events connected the Gabinian law with the subsequent grants of great commands to both Pompey and Caesar, from which the civil war of 49 issued and the ultimate overthrow of the senate's supremacy.

In 67 the votes, and the violence, of the urban plebs were decisive. By 59, when Caesar in turn received his command in the north, the strong arms of Pompey's veterans had enabled the 'triumvirs' to control the assemblies and to disregard the wishes of the senate. What they wanted above all was land, and it had been Caesar's first task as consul to fulfil their demand. The agrarian question had entered a new phase as early as Saturninus' efforts to settle the veterans of Marius (Chapter 5). Even before Marius enlisted men without any property for the legions, a precedent which seems to have been followed thereafter, many of the legionaries had possessed little of their own; and though conscription, which remained the normal mode of recruitment, especially in crises, must still have brought owners and tenants of small

---

[124] Cf. W. Nippel, *JRS* 1984, 20 ff.

farms under the standards, they were likely, as in the past, to lose them, if retained in service for years. The *proletarii* themselves, volunteers and conscripts alike, seem to have been drawn almost exclusively from the rural population (including small towns). These soldiers had 'no stake in the country'; they were ready to take any opportunity of enriching themselves. The prospect of booty induced them to join up with Marius in 107 and to obey Sulla's orders to march on Rome in 88; at all times they would seek plunder, donatives, rises in pay; but what they most desired was some assurance of a livelihood after discharge, and it was natural for them to look for this in the competency of a holding of land. Sulla no doubt promised allotments, to win recruits in 83, and he did allot lands to all who served him in the civil war, but he failed to provide for similar rewards to legionaries in the future, and the senate invariably obstructed grants or (as in 43) aroused suspicions that it would not honour promises made.[125] It was only through the dominance of successful generals regardless of its will that veterans obtained lands in 59, under Caesar's dictatorship and under the rule of the triumvirs.

It is indeed evident enough that the senate had nothing to fear from small armies regularly garrisoning provinces, and even from large armies under the command of men like Metellus Pius and L. Lucullus faithful to senatorial government. We may account for the disloyalty of soldiers to the regime on the basis that they came from a class which the senate had done nothing for, and consequently would not feel that they owed it anything. But equally we have no reason to suppose that they had any positive ideological repugnance to the regime, that they conceived themselves as representatives of the down-trodden peasantry. It was their own material welfare that they cared about, and probably they seldom objected if other peasants were expropriated to make way for them.[126] They threw up no leaders of consequence from their own ranks. They depended on their generals to provide for their interests. But the generals in turn depended on them to enforce their own will on the state. Sulla, Pompey, Caesar, the triumvirs, and Augustus himself all owed their power to their troops, and it was primarily by enriching them, and especially by promises and grants of land, that they secured their allegiance.

The most fatal error that the senate made was thus its failure to keep the soldiery content. Even the pay was low till Caesar doubled it, and

[125] On the senate's promises see p. 266, *IM* 325 f. The discontent in Octavian's army was apparently due in part to the exclusion of some from the benefits, in part to failure to make immediate payment in full of a promised donative (App. iii. 86–90; Dio xlvi. 41–3); but Appian also makes Octavian suggest that the senate could not be trusted to implement undertakings for land allotments (iii. 87).

[126] They could protest at the expropriation of their own kin (Dio xlviii. 9. 3).

no regular provision was made for veterans after demobilization. Augustus himself came to see the necessity for this only in 13 BC, though he had continually been settling veterans on the land in Italy or overseas, and doubtless his soldiers had come to expect such rewards. Of course it was impossible, without never-ending sequestrations of property, to satisfy their hopes of allotments in Italy; since the time of Caesar it had been necessary to place some of them in overseas colonies, at the expense of provincials, 'lesser breeds without the law', rather than of Italian proprietors.[127] In 13 it was only (substantial) bounties in cash that were guaranteed after so many years' service. The promises then made were not wholly kept, and it appeared in AD 6 not only that the term of service must be lengthened, but that the richer citizens must be made liable to new taxation, in order to meet the expense. Senators resented the burden, and it is easy to imagine that they would in the Republic have rejected any similar scheme, if they had seen that they would have to bear any part of the cost. It was the price in cash that they had to pay for the benefits of the *otium* established by the Principate; if they had had the foresight to accept its necessity earlier, they might have preserved their own *libertas* as well.[128]

The senate succumbed to force, which it had been the first to employ. Tiberius Gracchus was lynched, his followers later persecuted with a travesty of justice. His brother afforded a pretext for armed suppression; there was no clear justification for the subsequent massacre of his adherents. Sallust observed that these harsh measures 'increased the fears of the nobility more than their future power' (*BJ* 42. 4); he knew that the descendants of those who had taken the sword were to perish by it. The Gracchi were posthumously honoured as martyrs; their fate implanted a longing for retribution, which the Mamilian commission was to satisfy. Popular hatred of the nobility was expressed not only in the election of Marius and other new men as consuls in 107 and the next few years but also in the condemnation of aristocratic generals about the same time for the disasters they had incurred in the northern wars.[129] Saturninus learnt from the example of the optimates to rely on force; in the end it proved that they still had

---

[127] Legionaries of provincial origin, an ever increasing number, would not even want lands in Italy; that might also be true of Italians long stationed in a province which became a new home for them, but note Tac. *Ann.* i. 17. 3.

[128] *IM*, ch. XIX (vii). At the figure fixed in AD 5 the cash bounty for a legionary was more than equal to 13 years' annual pay. In *IM* 341 I doubted if it would purchase much land. But we do not know: calculations of the average price of land in Italy based on Colum. iii. 3. 8 (337 n. 3) are unreliable (cf. R. Duncan-Jones *ap.* M. I. Finley, *St. in Roman Property*, 1976, 11). On the new taxes see Dio lv. 25, lvi. 28.

[129] Plut. *C. Gr.* 18; GC 68 f. (cf. Sall. *BJ* 30. 3, 31. 2, 65. 5).

the preponderance, and they would slaughter him and his associates after they had surrendered and might have been brought to trial. Politics became more vindictive. The bitterness evoked by Drusus' proposals was seen in his own assassination and in the vendetta conducted against his friends arraigned on trumped-up charges of treason under the Varian law. In 88 Sulpicius copied Saturninus' violent methods. He too miscalculated. Sulla marched on Rome, occupied the city, had the laws of Sulpicius repealed or annulled, and outlawed him and his associates, notably Marius, the saviour of his country. The optimates thus inaugurated military coups and proscriptions. Marius and Cinna were soon able to retaliate; their victims too were not many, but included some of the leading men of the state. A few years later Sulla wrought vengeance on a far larger scale; hundreds of his opponents were proscribed, their sons barred from office, and great tracts of land throughout Italy confiscated and made over to his soldiers and favourites.

War, as Thucydides said, is a teacher of violence; civil war was most brutal in its discipline. Appian conceived the Social war as a civil war, and with some justice, so many were the ties linking the Romans and the loyal allies on the one side with the rebels on the other. Probably it induced a temper of mind which made it easier to treat fellow-citizens without compunction as enemies. Be that as it may, one conflict merged into another, and for nine years with only a short interval there was fearful loss of life, sacking of cities, devastation of the land, and disregard for the rights of property.[130] The impact of these miseries must have been the greater as Italy had for a century become accustomed to internal peace. No doubt Sulla claimed to have restored stability and tranquillity; his critics could call it 'otium cum servitute'. But his claim was false. He was hardly dead when Lepidus raised a new insurrection, relying chiefly on the 'innoxia plebs' whom he had dispossessed in many parts of Italy to make room for his veterans.[131] This was crushed in 77, but with no troops stationed in Italy to maintain order, Spartacus' slave revolt could gather enough strength to defeat consular armies in 72; devastations again ensued, and the wealthy must have sustained heavy losses, if only from the defection and eventual slaughter of thousands of slaves; it was not till 71 that the revolt was suppressed. With fighting still in progress in Spain, Macedon, and the east as many as 200,000 Italians, perhaps a sixth of all adult males, had been recruited for the legions by 72.[132] As always,

---

[130] *IM*, chs. XVIII, XIX (iii).

[131] Sallust's *Or. Lepidi* antedates his agitation but gives a fair impression of the causes of discontent (cf. GC 233–5).

[132] *IM*, ch. XXV.

conscription must have aggravated the economic difficulties of the peasantry, including the Sullan settlers. By 63 debt was rife in all regions of Italy, and Catiline could hope that rural discontent would furnish him with the means for a new coup; a former officer of Sulla, he looked to new proscriptions and confiscations to enrich himself and his partisans. It was a mad enterprise in the sense that even initial success would have attracted retribution from Pompey with his large and efficient army in the east, but it was the vigilance and energy of Cicero that prevented the insurrection from assuming large proportions. However, broken men from all these wars and revolts could hold out in the remote uplands. Kidnapping was common, and travel unsafe without an armed escort (Ascon. 31 C). Moreover, violence had become a habit. Rome was infested with armed gangs; in the countryside the proprietors of large estates would employ their slaves to eject weaker neighbours by force; the adoption of sharper legal remedies indicates the prevalence of the evil. It was left to Augustus to re-establish security.[132]

Though some of the Pompeians in 49 hoped like Catiline to replenish their fortunes by a victory of the Sullan type, far more of the propertied class must have dreaded the renewal of such a 'calamity for the commonwealth'. Sulla's victims had clearly included not only his committed adversaries but rich men who had incurred the private enmity or aroused the cupidity of members of his entourage, or who had been simply implicated in resistance to him through decisions taken in their home towns, perhaps under the coercion of his opponents, if they happened to have military control in the district. In 49 the *boni et beati* desired peace on almost any terms; once Caesar had overrun Italy with a rapidity that minimized the destruction of war and had convinced them that he was unlikely to effect a social revolution, they were on his side, especially as the Pompeians meant to blockade Italy, and perhaps reconquer it by arms, and threatened reprisals even against neutrals (pp. ooo ff.).

Italy suffered little from the civil wars in Caesar's lifetime. But it was otherwise after his death. Already in 44–43 cities were sacked and farms pillaged in the north. The fact that many of the municipalities had committed themselves against Antony gave the triumvirs a pretext for systematic severities; and they needed cash and lands to satisfy their soldiers. Hundreds were proscribed; the territory of sixteen of the most flourishing cities were set aside for distribution to veterans; their armies were quartered on the civil population; heavy contributions were levied from the rich, who had borne no direct taxation since 167.

[132] *IM*, App. 8.

Though it was again outside Italy that the triumvirs defeated their opponents, the assignation of lands to the veterans produced renewed civil war there in 41–40. Nor was there a cessation of sufferings when this fighting ceased. For years Sextus Pompey as master of the seas could cut off imports of food, and he offered a refuge in Sicily to thousands of slaves on the Italian estates. It was after eliminating him that Octavian could boast that he had restored peace by land and sea (App. v. 130).[134] But there was no prospect of its permanence so long as power was divided between him and Antony. The drain on Italian manpower continued till Octavian had established his sole supremacy; in 49 there were probably 80,000 men in the legions, and 420,000 more were enlisted between then and 32.[135] It was still necessary to impose taxes on the richer citizens (n. 134). As Octavian was actually in possession of Italy, it must have been evident, as it had been in 49, that more distress would be caused if victory ultimately went to the party centred in the east; in addition Octavian could represent himself as the champion of Italian traditions against his orientalizing rival.[136] Thus if one man were to be supreme in the state, it would be better that he should be Octavian; and after 'twenty years of conflict with no regard to custom and law' (Tac. *Ann.* iii. 28) the class of men whose conservative instincts would naturally have favoured the preservation of senatorial rule were now content to accept monarchy. It was their consent that did most to ensure the stability of the regime which the revolution had brought to birth,[137] but which they had never previously desired or envisaged.

IX

Thus in the changed conditions created by imperial expansion the senatorial aristocracy, blinded in part at least by short-term views of its own political and economic advantage, failed by timely concessions to satisfy the needs or aspirations of the Italian allies, the best-organized Equites, the urban plebs, the peasantry, and the soldiers. To maintain

---

[134] *IM*, chs. xviii, xix (vi), App. 8., App. v. 15, 18, 25, 34, 67, 74, 77 writes of famine in Rome and even in Italy. Rome must in fact have been fed chiefly from Italy, but the disruption of agricultural operations will have diminished the harvests there. Financial exactions in 43–42: App. iv. 5. 31 f.; Dio xlvii. 14, 16 f., in 42–40: App. v. 22, 24, 67 f.; Dio xlviii. 3 f., 9. 5, 10, 12. 4, 13. 6, 31; in 38: App. v. 92; Dio xlviii. 43. 1, 49. 1. There were some remissions in 36 (App. v. 130; Dio xlix. 15), but more exactions in 32 (Dio l. 10, 20), followed by remissions and personal liberalities of Augustus in 29 (Dio li. 17, 21). Details in Appian and Dio are not all perspicuous.

[135] *IM*, ch. xxvi.

[136] Syme, *RR*, ch. xx; it is another matter that Antony was to some extent misrepresented (ibid. ch. xix).

[137] It is highly significant that the grave mutinies of AD 14 could not ripen into revolt because the generals and officers were all loyal to Tiberius.

or reassert its ascendancy, which was not based on unchallengeable legal or customary rights, it turned to coercion and force; but despite the traditions of respect for the senate as such, and for the noble families which preponderated in its ranks, it ceased to possess that measure of consent, or rather of resolute commitment to its cause, which was required if it was to retain a superiority of force; in the end it could not assure peace and order, and forfeited the firm allegiance of the naturally conservative propertied class, who would otherwise have had no quarrel on political, social, or economic grounds with its supremacy. Almost everyone would then acquiesce in the establishment of a monarchy, which almost no one had ever regarded as intrinsically desirable.

However, this analysis or any other which is confined to general factors, to political, social, and economic institutions and their development, indispensable as it is to understanding the Roman revolution, cannot completely explain it. The senate's control was undermined by laws the assemblies passed, and destroyed by rebellious armies. However, the assemblies could act only on the initiative of magistrates, and the troops obeyed their disloyal commanders. If the history of the late Republic is too often written as if its course was determined merely by the rivalries of great political figures contending for power and drawing their strength from ties of personal fealty and friendship, while the discontent with the senatorial regime which gave them a following is ignored or minimized, we must not fall into the opposite error of neglecting the vital role performed by the leaders in promoting the revolution, though none of them before Caesar in his last years designed it.

From the time of Marius and Sulla military leaders struck the most damaging and ultimately fatal blows at the old order. They needed not only exceptional talents but also exceptional opportunities. The Numidian and German wars set Marius in an unprecedented eminence, which he failed to exploit and which did not quench his thirst for military glory. Mithridates' invasion of Asia appeared to offer him one more chance to satisfy this craving; Sulla's determination not to be deprived of the fame and riches attendant on victory in the east led on to the civil wars of the 80s, and it was Sulla's successes in Asia that ensured him the loyalty of the veteran army without which he could not have reduced Italy to submission. It was in these wars, and their aftermath in the rising of Lepidus and the suppression of Sertorius in Spain, that Pompey rose to the foremost position in the state, which he was to consolidate by extirpating piracy and finishing off Mithridates, and which evoked the insuperable jealousy and suspicion of the optimates. He was driven into alliance with Caesar, of which the price was Caesar's Gallic command; as Cicero remarked, 'he nurtured, aggrandized, and armed Caesar against the commonwealth' (*Att.* viii. 3. 3). Caesar too could never have made himself master of the Roman state if he had not first subdued Gaul, acquiring not only immense riches but the devotion of an 'incomparable army' (*Fam.* viii. 14. 3). And probably Pompey and the optimates would never have ventured to provoke him into marching on Rome, if the Parthians had not eliminated the great army of Syria under Crassus, a rival for whose goodwill Caesar had better reason than Pompey to hope.

No doubt it was in part Roman activity or inactivity that made Jugurtha, the Cimbri and Teutones, Mithridates, and the pirates formidable or at least troublesome to the Roman state, and Roman policy may in each case be fundamentally explicable in terms of the political, social, and economic structure of Roman Italy. But all these enemies of Rome had their own aims and their own strength which must be attributable in part to the conditions that obtained in and around their homelands. So too, while Crassus' attack on the Parthians was surely inspired by his personal ambition, dictated by the political developments at Rome, to emulate the military achievements of Pompey and Caesar, the capacity of the Parthians almost to annihilate his forces was the result of developments in Iran entirely extraneous to the factors that operated in Italy or the Roman empire. The *Völkerwanderung* of the Cimbri and Teutones from the Baltic coast of Germany far beyond Roman horizons must have been stimulated by causes (of which we know little or nothing) unconnected with affairs in the Mediterranean, even though the ineptitude of Roman generals in making probably unnecessary attacks on them and incurring disastrous defeats first made them a danger to Italy. Caesar clearly embarked on the conquest of Gaul, most of which was altogether outside the sphere of previous Roman influence, with the purpose of making himself the first man at Rome, but his ambition and skill as a general, and the valour of his troops, are not enough to account for his success; to say nothing of the fertility of the land and the facility of communications within it, which made it far easier to subjugate than western Germany was to prove in Augustus' time, the Gallic peoples were riven by domestic discords and internecine rivalries, and Caesar's own account goes far to justify the claim 'vere reputantibus Galliam suismet viribus concidisse' (Tac. *Hist.* iv. 17). Even though we may think that Caesar himself did not destroy the Republic beyond repair, that this was the work of the triumvirs, and that it was Augustus who first created a monarchic system, it is no less evident that they could do what they did only in a situation which he had brought about, and that Caesar's autocracy, temporary and vulnerable as it was, is inconceivable but for the conquest of Gaul and the conditions within Gaul that made the conquest possible. Hence it is an abstraction from the complex historical reality to explain the Roman revolution solely by factors internal to Rome and her empire.

On a metaphysical view all historical events are fully determined. The historian as such, who examines the evidence empirically, cannot confirm or refute this thesis; though he assumes, as we all do in daily life, that there are causes for men's actions as well as for the purely physical phenomena that affect their lives, his evidence does not allow him to demonstrate this, still less to deny the individual agent all freedom of action. In any event historians since Thucydides have all had to allow for the element of chance, or contingency, at least in the sense that there can be intersections of different chains of caused events, which could not be predicted in advance and cannot be explained in retrospect. Thus it may have been inevitable that Jugurtha and the Cimbri and Teutones should come into conflict with Rome, but it must appear to be sheer coincidence that Roman generals in the north should have incurred by unusual folly a fearful disaster at Arausio, leaving Italy open to invasion, just at the moment when Marius was free after his prestigious completion of the Numidian war to step forward as Rome's saviour from the German peril. It would be easy and needless to multiply parallels.

The very existence of particular individuals of such and such character exemplifies the element of apparent contingency in history. We may grant that the mental and corporeal qualities of every man are fully determined, but if this is true it is evident that the factors that make him what he is are not just those of his environment and his own past actions (which may at any given moment limit his freedom of choice in the future): they must be in part genetic, and these factors elude investigation by the historian, no matter what the period be that he is studying. To say nothing of a man's talents, desires, and passions, his very capacity to survive presumably depends in part on his physiological make-up, and in part too on the risks of death to which he is exposed. The incidence of disease is relevant, and the history of diseases can hardly be written for antiquity, nor can the susceptibility of any individual of any era be fully explained. Given that the Roman's expectation of life at birth was not more, and probably much less, than thirty,[138] it was statistically improbable that any of the figures who made a great mark in public affairs should even have survived to the time when they did their most notable work. Augustus himself was over thirty at the time of Actium. It may also be noted that he had

---

[138] Hopkins, 1983, 100 f.

already been wounded in Illyricum: if the wound was not mortal, that must have been because the assailant's blow happened to lack the right strength or direction. An illness in 23 BC almost proved fatal; at that time the Principate was not yet stabilized, if only because there was no one who could easily have taken over his powers. In the event his unpredictable longevity helped to habituate men to the new regime.

Some would depreciate the effects on the course of history of the unique personality of individuals. We all recognize from contemporary experience that the great majority of men behave in much the same way as others of the same social and economic background. It is on this basis that we can venture on generalizations about the attitudes of Roman senators, Equites, etc. The conduct of any particular representative of a given category may often seem of small consequence. In the 60s Pompey gave great offence to certain prominent nobles, for example to Q. Metellus Creticus and L. Lucullus, but he was almost bound to have estranged many such persons of rank and influence in rising to pre-eminence; perhaps it is of little moment which of them had come to view him with the greatest aversion and distrust. The great figures who apparently contributed decisively to the process of political change, like the Gracchi, Pompey, and Caesar, were themselves Roman aristocrats, and we can assume and sometimes show that they were imbued with ideas and desires common to their class. However, it is equally clear that it was chiefly in virtue of talents, beliefs, and ambitions which set them apart from their peers that they affected the actual course of history. Nor can we be sure that the peculiar characteristics of quite insignificant persons may not in a particular conjuncture determine how events proceed. A riot, or rout, may begin when one man throws a stone, or panics in battle; we cannot aver that but for his impulse it would have occurred at all. In 49 most senators, though hostile to Caesar, desired to avoid war (p. 489); they were precipitated into decisions that brought it on by the bellicose resolve, among others, of two men otherwise of little consequence, C. Marcellus (*cos.* 50) and L. Lentulus (*cos.* 49). It is not obvious that the senate would even have been invited, still less pressed, to pass the fatal decrees of January 49, if the electors had returned as consul Caesar's partisan, Ser. Galba, in place of Lentulus. A Pompeian victory at Pharsalus would have changed the course of history, at least for the time. Caesar avows his debt for his success to the outstanding courage of the *evocatus* Crastinus (*BC* iii. 91, 99). Conceivably the example he set decided the day.

In this connection we must not forget that whatever general institutional causes may be found for the fall of the Republic, it was the outcome of hard fighting, in which the issue, not predictable to contemporaries, derived from the skill and valour of the combatants. In the end the battles at Philippi proved fatal to Republican liberty. Brutus and Cassius had command of the sea, and though their army was inferior, they had occupied almost impregnable lines; if the triumvirs could not break through, shortage of supplies would eventually compel them to withdraw. The effect of such a retreat on the morale of their troops might well have been disastrous; on both sides the soldiers were fighting primarily in the hope of rewards, and these hopes would falter, if the prospect of victory receded. Antony's attempt to breach the enemy's position failed, but after an initial success, which Cassius in premature despair thought complete, he killed himself. Left in sole command, the less-experienced Brutus lost patience; he launched an attack, and all was lost. It is plausible that better generalship would have reversed the issue of the campaign.[139]

Brutus too, we are told, had persuaded his fellow-conspirators to kill Caesar alone, and to spare Antony. In hindsight Cicero pronounced this to have been a fatal error.[140] He was surely right. After Caesar's death the executive power in Italy for some time lay with Antony and Dolabella as consuls; the senate was virtually impotent, and it was in the tangle of events brought about by Antony's ambitions that the young Octavian found the means and pretexts to lay the basis of his own personal power. It is very hard to suppose that the Republic would not have lasted longer, if Antony had been put out of the way. Counter-factual propositions of this kind, concerning the role of individuals, appear just as legitimate modes of expressing historical causation as statements in the same logical form which relate to more persistent factors in the historical process, e.g. that senatorial power would have been more enduring, if the senate had not alienated the affections of urban plebs or peasantry; and in some cases, like that just given, their credibility is more directly perspicuous from the evidence at our disposal. They do not of course imply that the unfulfilled condition was capable of fulfilment. There may have been necessary reasons why the senate, perhaps for the sake of the greater profits to be obtained from the employment of slaves rather than free men, should have been careless of the welfare of the poorer citizens, and equally why Brutus, being the man he was, should have insisted on shedding no blood but the tyrant's. In the latter case, however, the explanation lies in secrets of his personality, which we are bound to presume but cannot fathom. If in fact his decision was fully determined, what we commonly think of as his freedom of choice means only that another man in the same situation, being differently constituted, might have

---

[139] See e.g. T. Rice Holmes, *Architect of the Roman Empire*, 1928, 84 ff.
[140] Plut. *Brut.* 18; Cic. *Att.* xiv. 21. 3, *Fam.* x. 28. 1.

chosen, and been bound to choose, differently. This is a problem for philosophers.

On this occasion Brutus, perhaps a man of modest abilities (though, we are told, of strong resolve), failed to turn what *we* know to have been the course of history. But others, more highly gifted, appear from the evidence to have given an impetus to events which they in some measure designed, as mediocrities could not have done. The outstanding eloquence and passionate determination of the Gracchi, and the comprehensive grasp shown by Gaius at least of the problems of the state, or alternatively of the variety of means for embarrassing the senate, set the revolutionary process in motion. It was consummated and ended by Augustus. Not only did he found a stable monarchy; in various degrees he reorganized or remodelled the armed forces, the finances, the administration of the city, and the empire. Unlike all his successors, at any rate before Diocletian, who (as Fergus Millar has perceived) did little more than react to events and make minor adjustments in the system, he was an innovator on a large scale, and his innovations endured. It is of course perfectly true that the conditions favoured his work. The blood-letting since 49 had removed potential opponents. Everyone yearned for peace and order. When he became master of the Roman world, he still had a long life before him, and could proceed step by step. He was able to win general consent for his work. But nothing suggests that anyone without his peculiar gifts could have achieved what he did. Caesar and Antony alienated their own followers. The mature and experienced Tiberius, a man of proven ability, who set out to imitate Augustus,[141] failed to retain the goodwill of the élite whose co-operation was essential to the new system. It was surely only because Augustus had built so solid a structure that it could survive the odium which many of his successors, especially in the next hundred years, would provoke. No doubt the empire needed a monarch. But only a Pangloss will affirm that the hour brings forth the man. If that were true, states would never decline nor empires disintegrate. Contemporaries feared with reason that Roman power would collapse in perpetual anarchy. It was partly due to the genius of Augustus that it did not. That genius eludes explanation no less than the genius of Virgil. He too was the product of his age, as all great poets and artists are, but he was able to transcend the conditions by which his coevals were limited; the same can be said of Augustus.

Even if a providential dispensation, or mechanistic laws, which metaphysicians or sociologists can discern, inexorably determine that all things happen as they do, even if the chain of events, linking causes and effects, is unbreakable and the individual agent is not free to

---

[141] Brunt, *CQ* 1984, 484 f.

behave in any other way than that in which he does behave, his actions remain among the links in the chain, and they can no more be removed than any other links; if none the less we imagine the possibility of their removal, we may not then go on to suppose that the later links would be all unchanged. Obviously the removal of a particular human agent would not alter the effect of non-human forces, such as the conditions of soil and climate or the incidence of disease (unless he were one who actually like Pasteur discovered remedies for it), but we cannot be confident that it would also not affect 'institutional' factors. We may give them abstract designations like 'the social system' or 'the market', but such terms are themselves convenient shorthand for an infinity of individual human actions, produced by the complex reactions of each man to the behaviour of others, and there is no a priori reason for rejecting the overwhelming impression that we receive both from our daily experience and from historical evidence, that a decisive influence can be exercised on general behaviour by the actions of a particular man; especially one set apart from the rest by a combination of external circumstances giving him power over others and of personal qualities, which furnish him with exceptional ability to effect his aims, and which may also make those aims different in material respects from those that might have been predicted of one with his particular place in society.

The success of natural scientists in 'explaining' the infinite variety of the phenomena they study, by showing how their correlation can be expressed in relatively few and highly generalized hypotheses or 'laws', has encouraged the hope that political or social 'scientists' will be able to account for phenomena in a similar fashion. So far this hope does not seem to have been realized. Scientific laws command assent only in so far as they cover all the known phenomena; once it is seen that they fail to do so, they must be discarded or amended. No hypotheses have been formulated with a like combination of simplicity, exactitude, and exhaustiveness to make all the phenomena of human behaviour in society intelligible. For example, suppose that Marxism fully elucidates the transitions from one 'mode of production' to another: it still appears to leave unexplained the great variety of 'superstructures', political, social, and cultural, supposedly erected on the economic basis of society, which can coexist and change with an identical 'mode of production'. In the Marxist view the 'slave mode of production' governed the economy both of democratic Athens and of the Roman world; how then do we account for the innumerable differences between them? The great political change at Rome from Republican to monarchic institutions is equally inexplicable by Marxist theory.

Such general theories, like the economic or social models, which some historians have learned to employ, presuppose a degree of uniformity in human behaviour and in the effects and development of institutions (themselves partly dependent on the physical features of the environment in which particular societies are moulded) which, though founded on empirical observations, they tend to exaggerate. Like the mere use of analogies between conditions in societies which resemble each other at certain points, analogies which models systematize, they may enable the historian to devise lines of inquiry which the simple inspection of the evidence at his disposal for the period he studies, and of the interpretations placed on it by writers within that period, might not have suggested; and closer scrutiny may uncover indications that factors were at work similar to those more amply documented for other ages or lands. Still, conclusions that arise from this procedure must be tested by the whole body of relevant facts that his evidence discloses; they must at least be shown to be congruent with those facts, and they are susceptible, if congruence is lacking or incomplete, of refutation or modification; in the nature of things they can never be entirely verified, any more than scientific 'laws', which are no more than provisional hypotheses that account for the phenomena so far observed. I am of course aware that the very concept of historical facts can be treated with scepticism, but then this scepticism must apply with equal force to all the general theories or models, since they too rest on the premises that there are facts that can be discovered about human behaviour which can also be systematically correlated.[142]

In practice no systematic theory can explain without remainder the complex interweaving of human activities, especially if the course of events can be altered by the apparently contingent influence of individuals. And on this premiss the historian can never provide any complete explanation of the past. The origins of the personality of every individual are necessarily hidden from him. Moreover, he can seldom comprehend it as it was. His only direct evidence would be a man's own intimate revelations of his ideas and feelings, and even then doubts would arise whether any man truly understands himself. Such revelations are rarely available, and in the late Republic for none but Cicero, or rather for Cicero only in the last twenty years of his life. In default of direct evidence, what can the historian make do with?

In our dealings with those around us, we may start by supposing that they act for much the same reasons as we think from introspection that we ourselves do; when it becomes manifest that their conduct cannot be so explained in all cases, we take account of what they and

---

[142] See endnote 9.

others say of the motives that inspire them, or of current views, derived
from experience, about the general springs of action. As we must allow
that men in other ages and lands did not necessarily behave in exactly
the same way as those in our own society, we must similarly consider
how they interpreted their own conduct or that of their contemporaries
and what kinds of desire they supposed to have decisive effects.
Thucydides (i. 76 f.) makes Athenian spokesmen plead that the policy
of their city was dictated by the three most powerful impulses, honour,
fear, and material gain. In this analysis there is nothing 'desperately
alien' from our own perceptions, though we might be less ready to
accord so large a place in human motivation to 'honour'; certainly to
Greeks, and also to Romans, the pursuit of power, status, prestige,
fame among living men and in the recollections of posterity, seemed to
be as dominant as the passion for economic gain, and just as rational;
we must beware of thinking that Greeks or Romans conformed to
models of human behaviour constructed by political economists; the
value that Romans set both on *dignitas* and on *libertas* is significant in
this regard. Thucydides ignored here any influence of moral impera-
tives, which he probably thought irrelevant to inter-state relations, but
which he could elsewhere recognize as capable of influencing men's
treatment of their fellow-citizens; and we must always allow for the
possibility that men felt themselves bound to fulfil traditional obligations both to the state and to those with whom they had private ties;
this too, if they reflected on it, might be part of their honour. However,
any such general identification of possible types of motive hardly
enables us to determine which motive, or what mixture of motives,
operated on a particular individual in a particular conjuncture,
though it may be more helpful for an understanding of the objectives of
states, or of whole classes or orders within states. If we try to discover
why Pompey, for instance, acted as he did, then in default of direct
evidence, we have to resort to conjectures based on an estimate of his
personality, which we construct, partly from what was said of him by
contemporaries who knew more of him than we do, or by later writers
who had read contemporary accounts now lost, partly by an interpretation of all his recorded overt actions; coherence is the test of
plausibility. But contemporaries might be biased or insensitive; and
they too had to resort to the same kind of interpretation. Cicero knew
Pompey and Caesar well, but he often found Pompey inscrutable, and
certainly misjudged Caesar in 49. Moreover, we may have too little
information about a man's life to be able to use the criterion of
coherence to explain his behaviour on the few occasions on which he
stands before us. To take an extreme case, Italian leaders like
Poppaedius Silo, who brought about the revolt of 91–90, are mere

names to us. On the available evidence even the Gracchi can be variously supposed to have been inspired by injured pride, rancour, ambition, solicitude for the poor, or zeal for the true interests of the state; though it was enemies who put the worst construction on their actions, enemies are not inevitably mistaken.

The difficulty in discerning the true personality of an individual and ascertaining the reasons for his actions at any given moment besets all historians. It is compounded for the historian of Rome by his frequent ignorance about the most important events. Their relative order, not to say their absolute dating, is sometimes uncertain; when the sequence of events is unknown, it is more than usually hazardous to trace causes and effects. Little may be recorded of the content of laws which we can none the less see to have been pregnant with grave consequences: how can we say what the legislator intended when we cannot be sure what he did? An intelligible account of the great wars from 90 to 82 can hardly be written. Continually we have to draw on meagre excerpts and summaries of detailed histories now lost, whose identity and reliability cannot be established, made by late writers whose ignorance and carelessness distorted what they transmit; comparison with the contemporary evidence supplied by Cicero, especially in his letters, shows how prone to error they were, and they cannot be more trustworthy in those parts of their works which we cannot check in the same way.[143] To a surprising extent, because of the gaps in Cicero's correspondence and its allusive character, these late 'authorities' still remain indispensable for Cicero's time, when we must also get what information we can from the *ex parte* statements in his speeches. Eyewitness accounts are rare, documents few and fragmentary. The personality of a leading figure may not be the most dubious element in any modern reconstruction. For Aristotle history is concerned with what Alcibiades did; poetry, with which we may associate fiction, with what a man like Alcibiades necessarily or probably would do. But we must sometimes conjecture what Alcibiades did in accord with our picture of what he was likely to have done. The line separating the historian from the novelist becomes faint: it is principally in their intentions that they differ. The novelist aims at a lifelike and coherent plausibility to illustrate universal aspects of human nature; for the historian plausibility is a tool by which he seeks to find what actually happened.

The ideal history in my judgement would combine analysis of

---

[143] On the defects of epitomators cf. Brunt, *CQ* 1980, 477 ff. It is part of my purpose in including ch. 4 in this collection to exhibit the kind of problems that the inadequacy of our evidence presents, and to illustrate the methods by which we may reach solutions that can hardly be regarded as more than probably correct.

enduring physical and institutional factors with a narrative exhibiting the contingent effect of individual actions. For the historian of Rome the former task, to which this volume is largely devoted, is no less difficult than the latter. With the dearth of archival material and the lack of statistics accessible to modern and to a lesser degree to medieval historians, he has to draw his analyses of political, social, and economic conditions in large part from the same inadequate sources from which a narrative is constructed, supplemented by allusions and anecdotes; he can but seldom turn to contemporary descriptions, such as the Roman writers on agriculture supply; and these are far from being comprehensive and are notably deficient in the numerical data required for economic history. It is easier to establish that the evidence does not justify some modern analyses than to see just where the truth lies. It may well be that I have asserted my own conclusions at times with undue confidence. It is irksome to present what it seems reasonable on the evidence to believe with reiterated provisos that some degree of probability is the most that can be justly claimed. The historian of Rome can be likened to a man standing at the entrance of a cavern of vast and unmeasured dimensions, much of it impenetrably dark, but here and there illuminated by a few flickering candles.

2

ITALIAN AIMS AT THE TIME OF THE
SOCIAL WAR*

I. THE DEMAND OF THE ITALIANS FOR CITIZENSHIP must have existed in the Gracchan period, but grew in intensity in the next thirty years until it became almost universal among the Italian *principes*, including the Etruscans, Umbrians, and Samnites; it was satisfied by the *lex Iulia* enfranchising the loyal Italians and by the later grants of citizenship to *dediticii*, the ex-rebels. **II.** THE CONCEPT OF ITALIAN UNITY: ROMANIZATION. Significance of the organization of the rebels in the new state Italia. The concept of Italia. Spread of the Latin language and of Roman institutions. **III.** THE VALUE OF CITIZENSHIP TO THE ITALIANS. The allies had already lost true independence and were subject to heavy military and financial burdens; on the analogy of Roman municipalities already existing in 90, they could expect to preserve, after enfranchisement, substantial local self-government. Events in 88–87 show that what they wanted was political rights at Rome which would enhance their *dignitas* and indirectly favour the material interests of the Italians, especially of the *principes*; without them the *ius provocationis* itself was unlikely to afford much protection. Probably their ambitions and sense of Rome's dependence on them had been stimulated by Marius' career and the Cimbric crisis.

THE Social war broke out when Rome refused to grant the allies' demand for citizenship. Any explanation of this refusal is conjectural (p. 71). I am here concerned rather with the attitude of the Italians. I shall argue, like Gabba, that they sought a share in political power, though not only, if at all, for the reasons he

* This essay had its origin in a paper read to the Fourth International Congress of Classical Studies in Philadelphia in August 1964, which was enlarged for publication in *JRS* 1965, 90 ff.; there I acknowledged my debt for suggestions made by M. W. Frederiksen and E. T. Salmon, to whose survey of the pre-90 Romanization of Italy in *The Beginnings of the Latin World* (Report of the Canadian Historical Association, 1960) I paid tribute. The present version is extensively revised in the light of some more recent treatments, notably of the second thoughts of A. N. Sherwin-White in *RC*[2] and of H. Galsterer, 1976 (with whom I am in little accord); the work of M. Humbert, 1978, is of great value wherever relevant. The most stimulating discussion already available in 1964–5 was that of E. Gabba, *Le origini nella guerra sociale e la vita politica* (*Athen.* 1954), which I now cite as republished in Italian in 1973 and in English in 1976; it deals with some matters not considered in detail here and impinges on the subject of ch. 3, but except for a few bibliographical additions Gabba did not seek to bring his treatment up to date, apart from a

suggested; and that their desire to become Romans reflects the success of Rome in unifying them in sentiment and was stimulated by the Cimbric war and by the career of Marius and other *novi homines* of his time.

I. THE DEMAND OF THE ITALIANS FOR CITIZENSHIP

In explaining the origins of the Social war Appian went back to the proposal made in 125 BC by the consul M. Fulvius Flaccus to enfranchise 'all the Italians'; thwarted at that time, he was jointly responsible with C. Gracchus for similar proposals, which also failed, in 122 (i. 21. 86–7, 34. 152). In fact, as Appian knew (n. 6), Gracchus' bill provided for the enfranchisement of the Latins and the conferment of Latin privileges, which included the right to vote at Rome in one tribe chosen by lot (*StR*^{3} iii. 643), on the other Italians. Flaccus himself had offered the *ius provocationis* as an alternative for Italians who did not wish for the Roman citizenship. Valerius Maximus, who alone mentions this (ix. 5. 1), writes as if choice lay with individuals, and if this is correct, Flaccus was not proposing the incorporation of whole peoples as in the past and in the manner of the enfranchisements of the 80s but the enrolment as citizens of such members of the Italian peoples as applied. Unless he simultaneously proposed to abrogate the rule under which Roman citizenship was incompatible with that of any other city (n. 5), this would have wrecked the political and military organization of Italy; some communities would have been deprived of their ruling élites and of manpower required to meet Rome's demands for military contingents. It seems to me more likely that Valerius Maximus has expressed himself with the carelessness typical of most of our sources, and that it was communities that were to have the option between incorporation and the *ius provocationis* for their own citizens.

Appian reports that Flaccus' sole or primary aim was to reconcile the Italians to the resumption of Roman public land in their possession, so that the Gracchan triumvirs might make more land allotments to the poor. Political gain was to outbalance economic loss. For this purpose he 'incited' the Italians to demand enfranchisement. And it proved (he says) that they actually preferred citizenship to possession of the land. Moreover, they were inflamed by the failure of Flaccus and Gracchus: they could not bear to be subjects rather than

brief reply to his critics in the initial note to the new version; cf. also *ANRW* i. 772 ff. I remain unconvinced that commercial motives had much influence either on the policy of Rome or on the aspirations of the Italian allies (cf. n. 113), but I fully concur with him that it was a share in political power that the *principes*, who guided the allied peoples, aimed at; this was true both of those who rebelled and those who remained loyal.

partners in empire. It seems to be clear on the one hand that Flaccus cannot have conjured up their desire for citizenship, and that he must have had reason to believe that many would regard it as recompense for loss of land, and that on the other hand the desire cannot yet have been so strong and widespread as Appian makes out. The alternative offer of *ius provocationis* indicates that Flaccus himself was conscious that not all might wish to merge their separate civic identities in the Roman, and it is manifest that Italy cannot have been seething with discontent for the whole period from 122 to 91. Appian has retrojected to the Gracchan era sentiments which took time to become so pervasive and powerful that they resulted in a great crisis in the relations between Rome and the allies, but he is probably right in ascribing significance to the abortive proposals of the 120s. By recognizing aspirations to equality of rights among the allies and treating their satisfaction as a practical issue, Flaccus and Gracchus surely promoted their extension; beneath the surface of apparent tranquillity more and more Italians were fastening their hopes on enfranchisement until the moment came when they were ready to accept no denial to their claim.

Individual Italians had long manifested a wish to change both their domicile and citizenship for Roman. The Latins and perhaps some other Italians enjoyed reciprocal rights of *commercium* and *conubium* with the Romans; the former right entitled them to acquire real property in Roman territory; and they might also obtain Roman citizenship by migrating to Roman territory. In 195 Hernicans, who had the same rights as Latins, had sought to have their names accepted for new Roman colonies and to be recognized as Roman citizens on that basis; the senate had rejected their claim (Livy xxiv. 41). In 187, 177, and 172 measures were taken against Latins who had exercised or abused the *ius migrationis*, which was not abolished but more restrictively defined (xxix. 3, xli. 8 f., xlii. 10. 3); although Livy thought that they, or most of the thousands concerned, had moved to the city of Rome, this may not have been true of all; the rule was that unless they had complied with the conditions prescribed they were not to be registered at Rome, sc. as Roman citizens; the *ius* was certainly not confined to those who legitimately domiciled themselves in the city itself. It may be that the migrants were primarily seeking a more economically attractive domicile, especially in Rome itself, but we cannot be sure that they were not at least as much attracted by the higher dignity of Roman citizens; at any rate they were ready to exchange their old citizenship for it. On these occasions the Roman government acted at the prompting of the allied communities themselves, who represented that the emigration would make it hard for them to supply the military contingents required by Rome (xliii. 8. 7); the implication is that Rome did not regularly adjust military demands to the number of men available for service, as in 193 (xxxiv. 56. 6). It may be noted that there is no evidence for Galsterer's view that henceforth no individual Italian could exercise the *ius migrationis*, even under the conditions laid down, without the formal consent of his home government.[1] We do not know if further expulsions occurred after 168, when Livy's record is lacking.

In 126 the tribune M. Iunius Pennus passed a law, which C. Gracchus opposed, expelling foreigners from Rome. The exact terms of the law and its motive are not attested. It is generally and plausibly assumed that it was intended to prevent a swarm of Italians coming to the city and exerting pressure in favour of Flaccus' law. In 122 the senate adopted a similar precaution before Gracchus' enfranchisement bill was to be put to the vote.[2] Flaccus, it is true, was not yet in office in 126, but he might already have advertised his proposals. If this interpretation of the measure is correct, it is confirmation that the proposal was thought likely to evoke enthusiasm among the allies. Galsterer supposes that it was actually promoted by the Italian governments, like the senatorial measures of 187, 177, and 172. Cicero cannot have been aware of this, for he pronounced it to be 'inhumanum'.[3] In 122, according to Plutarch (*C. Gr.* 12. 2), men thronged from all parts of Italy to support Gracchus' enfranchisement bill, and the senate caused an edict to be issued, presumably by the consul Fannius, requiring them to leave the city (n. 6). Here again we have evidence that there was wide desire in Italy for political rights at Rome, even though it had not yet reached the strength which would lead to a general insurrection.

The failure of Flaccus' proposal, which seems never to have come to a vote, did indeed lead to an isolated revolt, that of the Latin colony of Fregellae. It was razed to the ground by the praetor, L. Opimius, who as consul was later to repress C. Gracchus and his supporters. Cicero says that on both occasions he freed the state from the gravest perils (*Pis.* 95, *Planc.* 70). But the Roman state was not threatened by the rebellion of a single Latin city. Opimius was evidently supposed to have nipped in the bud what might have been a more general insurrection. There are other indications that discontent was not confined to Fregellae. Gracchus was accused of trying to bring about the revolt of allies as well as of complicity in the actual defection of Fregellae (Plut. *C. Gr.* 3). That city had of course no chance of

---

[1] Galsterer 162; *contra* Brunt, *CQ* 1982, 144–6. See endnote 1.
[2] Cic. *de offic.* iii. 47; Festus 388 L.; date: Cic. *Brut.* 109. Cf. *FC* 177.
[3] Galsterer 178, completely distorting Cicero's meaning: he *contrasts* Pennus' action with the *lex Licinia Mucia* (which elsewhere he could regard as ill-judged, but not barbarous).

withstanding Roman power by itself, and must surely have counted on support elsewhere, though wrongly. Although the origins of the revolt are not explicitly recorded, it is natural to assume that it was sparked by Flaccus' failure. One of the local notables, Q. Numitorius (*RE* xvii. 1405), betrayed the town and was evidently rewarded; his daughter was to marry M. Antonius, *pr.* 74, but as he was put on trial (Cic. *de inv.* ii. 105), he must have been formally party to the revolt, which had naturally been decided by the local senate. Galsterer, who seems to deny that the insurrection indicates desire for enfranchisement, has no alternative explanation, and minimizes the severity of the punishment inflicted, which was surely designed as a deterrent; he even thinks that the inhabitants all received the citizenship in the new town of Fabrateria Nova, founded in 124 (Vell. i. 15) in the former Fregellan territory: of this there is no evidence; it is far more likely that most Fregellans lost their lands as well as their city.[4]

About this time Rome probably did make a conciliatory gesture in granting the Latins the right to obtain the citizenship *per magistratum*, a concession designed to secure the loyalty of the aristocracies in the Latin cities and thereby that of the cities themselves, which could hardly rebel like Fregellae except with leadership from above. For this purpose it was obviously necessary that the local magnates who acquired the Roman citizenship *per magistratum*, together with their descendants, should remain qualified to direct the affairs of their own communities, and that they should therefore retain their local political rights. It is then likely, though there is no direct evidence, that the rule by which a Roman citizen could not possess the citizenship of any other city was relaxed in their case.[5]

Gracchus, as we have seen, proposed to grant citizenship only to the Latins, and the Latin right to the other allies.[6] Perhaps as yet the desire

---

[4] See also *Per.* Livy lx; Vell. ii. 6; Obsequens. 90; Val. Max. ii. 8. 4; Ascon. 17 C. says that by taking Fregellae Opimius 'ceteros quoque nominis Latini socios male animatos repressisse'; *de vir. ill.* 65. 2 alleges the revolt of (non-Latin) Asculum; this might betoken that there was an abortive insurrectionary movement there. We do not know the occasion of the speech in the senate by L. Papirius of Fregellae 'pro Fregellanis colonisque Latinis' (*Brut.* 170); he was a contemporary of Ti. Gracchus, and his speech may belong to a time of agitation before the revolt. The total destruction, even of the temple of Aesculapius, at Fregellae (M. H. Crawford and L. J. Keppie, *PBSR* 1984, 32. ff.) suggests the ferocity born of fear that the revolt inspired, *contra* Galsterer 179 ff. He says that the political effects were 'according to our sources astonishingly small'. Who can say, especially as our sources for the period are so meagre, that Roman action did not restrain revolts for thirty years and warn the Italians in 91 not to rebel except in organized concert?

[5] G. Tibiletti, *Rend. Istit. Lomb.* 1953, 43 ff. See endnote 2.

[6] Badian, *FC* 299 f. on App. i. 23; Plut. *C. Gr.* 12. Badian 190 infers from Appian's version of the edict banning from the city those with no voting rights that it did not affect Latins, but this may overestimate the accuracy of Appian's language. As the Latins were to be the chief beneficiaries from Gracchus' bill, it was their support (more from intimidation than from their limited voting power) that his opponents had most to fear. .

for Roman citizenship was keenest among the Latins, who were mainly of Roman descent,[7] except in the old Latin towns, Tibur, Praeneste, and Cora, and in the Hernican communities which enjoyed the Latin right (Appendix IV), but these too were at least culturally not distinguished from the Romans, and so near to Rome that it was particularly easy for them to take an active part in Roman politics. The ethnic and cultural connections of all Latins to Rome made it easier to advocate their enfranchisement. However, the consul Fannius was able to play demagogically on the reluctance of the urban plebs to share the advantages of citizenship with Latins (*ORF*[2], p. 144), and it was safe for the tribune Drusus to veto the bill (App. i. 23. 100).

Appian thought that the allies were already passionate for equality with the Romans in political rights. But were they yet ready to surrender their own autonomy? Did they regard the Roman citizenship itself as valuable, chiefly because of the protection it might provide against arbitrary punishments by Roman magistrates?[8] Such treatment was certainly a substantial grievance. C. Gracchus adduced instances of Roman cruelty and oppression to them in pleading their cause. Gellius, who preserves these extracts from his speech, quotes in the same context passages in which Cicero indicts Verres' barbarity to Roman citizens.[9] This was by no means the only count against Verres, and it would be illegitimate to infer from the fragments of Gracchus' oratory that he had nothing to say of other allied sentiments. However, Flaccus had envisaged that some of the allied peoples might prefer the *ius provocationis* to absorption in the Roman states, and in 122 the tribune Drusus countered Gracchus' bill by a bill offering *provocatio* to Latins; it was never enacted.[10] Under the Gracchan and a later law successful prosecutors for *repetundae* were offered the right as an alternative reward to citizenship.[11] Presumably it would have been valid not only against Roman magistrates but also against those of

---

[7] See endnote 3.

[8] In my judgement the *ius provocationis* was effective in ensuring that political charges were heard in the first instance by the people and that defendants on other charges were at least given a fair trial, and after C. Gracchus by courts constituted by the people's authority, only in so far as the magistrates were *either* conscientiously respectful of the law, *or* afraid to violate it because of penalties that the people might later visit on them; cf. ch. 4, VI; ch. 6, XI. There was much less danger to them if they infringed the rights of those who had no political rights at Rome.

[9] Gell. x. 3. 2 ff. Cato had earlier castigated the unjust treatment of Bruttians (ibid. 17 ff.). Gracchus cites cases from Latin cities (Cales, Ferentinum, Venusia) and from Teanum Sidicinum.

[10] Plut. *C. Gr.* 9 says it applied to Latins even on military service. Diod. xxxvii. 12. 3 and Cic. *Att.* v. 11. 2 prove that it never passed; Marcellus flogged a Comensian to show that on his view Caesar's grant of citizenship to the Latins of Comum was invalid. Sall. *BJ* 69. 4 is irrelevant, see n. 118 with text.

[11] See n. 5. In my view the imposition of an oath in the Tarentum law suggests that it is part of Glaucia's *repetundae* law, like the *lex Servilia* cited in Cic. *Balb.* 53 ff. (cf. Brunt, *CQ* 1982, n. 33).

their own communities. It may be observed that in that case its grant was an infraction of local autonomy. This is not an objection: successful prosecutors also obtained exemption from military service, which must have provoked at least as much discontent among the allies as it did among Roman citizens,[12] and from other public duties. By an exercise of sovereign power Rome gave them privileges as against their fellow-citizens. The autonomy of the allies, which of course did not secure them from contributing men and money to Rome's wars, was very imperfect.

It is easy to see that an *individual* might prefer to obtain personal protection and privileges, rather than to accept for himself alone the Roman citizenship and thereby cut himself off from the political life of his native community, if under Roman law he could not retain his old citizenship along with the Roman (n. 5). In 216 some Praenestine cavalrymen had declined the Roman citizenship, not wishing to forfeit their own (Livy xxii. 20 2). However, some other Italians, as we have seen, had been prone to emigrate to Roman territory, in order to change their citizenship, long before Gracchus' time. This kind of infiltration was to give Rome serious concern in 95 (see below). Even some Italian notables acquired the franchise, legally or illegally, before 90.[13] But the proposals of Flaccus and Drusus, which offered the *ius provocationis* for whole communities, indicate that in the 120s it was believed at Rome that there was no universal wish among the allies for absorption in the Roman state. And certainly Appian has exaggerated the strength of the Italian demand at this time for full citizenship. Despite his explicit statement, the Italians remained tranquil for a generation after Gracchus' failure.

Any explanation of the origin of the Social war must account for the very different reception in Italy of the defeat of Gracchus' bill and of that of the younger Drusus. During this interval the desire of the allies for the citizenship evidently became more widespread and more intense. It was recognized by Marius, for instance in his enfranchisement of a group of horse from Camerinum, and perhaps by Saturninus, if his agrarian and colonial schemes provided for the participation of Italians on a large scale (see Appendix I). Unfortunately the details of his proposals cannot be recovered, and though it is possible that his ultimate failure aggravated Italian discontent, no authority tells us that this was so. What we do know is that in 95 it was supposed that many Italians had crept on to the census rolls illegally. This process the *lex Licinia Mucia* was designed to check, by

---

[12] L. R. Taylor, *JRS* 1962, 19 ff.

[13] Wiseman 16–19. Most of his examples are conjectural. Val. Max. iii. 4. 5 says that M. Perperna was found not to be a citizen after being consul in 130. Cf. Harris, 1971, 192 ff., 319 ff.

establishing a judicial procedure to deprive of the citizenship those who had usurped it. Diodorus may suggest that the status of tens of thousands was still in question in 91 (n. 20). On this occasion the Romans were not acting (as Galsterer holds against the evidence), as in 187, 177, and 172, at the allies' request or with their consent. Cicero could call it inexpedient and pernicious to the state, and the learned Asconius, commenting on his words (67 C.), observes that the Italians were mastered by a passionate desire for the citizenship, that a great number were posing as citizens, and that the law so provoked the Italian *principes* that it was the chief cause of the war that broke out over three years later.[14]

Here the mention of *principes* is especially significant. It recurs in the *Perioche* of Livy's seventy-first book, where the epitomator tells that Livy recorded the conspiracies and speeches of the Italians late in 91 'in consiliis principum'. The Italian communities were of course ruled oligarchically—by the *domi nobiles* of whom we hear something in the time of Cicero.[15] It was they alone who could make known their views officially in deputations to the senate or informally in dealings with their patrons and *hospites* among the Roman aristocrats.[16] It was they who determined, in unison or by the will of a dominant faction, the course their communities were to take. Their ambitions and interests were decisive, and it is their motives in seeking the citizenship that we must try to discover, not those of Italian peasants who would for the most part be ready to follow the lead they gave.[17]

Asconius' statement may seem puzzling on two counts. It is not very easy to suppose that many Italians of rank and mark had acquired the citizenship surreptitiously, despite the story of Marcus Perperna (n. 13). If the *lex Licinia Mucia* offended the *principes*, it was perhaps chiefly because the intransigence it displayed dashed their hopes of a general and legal extension of the franchise. Secondly, it may seem strange that if the law was so provocative the crisis was delayed for more than three years. To this difficulty there are two answers. The

---

[14] The legalistic defence of the law in *de offic.* iii. 47 does not cancel his earlier condemnation of the law *ap*. Ascon. 67 C. in political terms. The *quaestiones* under the law (*Balb*. 48 ff.; *Brut*. 63) show that it was directed against alleged usurpations of citizenship: there is no reason to suppose that it removed any existing legal right by which foreigners could properly acquire it, e.g. *per migrationem*; even if 'ius' is read in *Balb*. 54 (*contra* Brunt, *CQ* 1982 n. 33), there is no implication that any right was abrogated.

[15] Sall. *Cat*. 17. 4; many examples in Syme, *RR* 82 ff.; Wiseman, 89 ff. For Etruria see Harris, 1971, chs. IV and VI.

[16] e.g. relations of Poppaedius Silo with Drusus (Plut. *Cato Minor* 2) and Marius (Diod. xxxvii. 15. 3) and of Vettius Scato with Pompeius Strabo (Cic. *Phil*. xii. 27). Cf. *Rosc. Amer*. 15, *Cluent*. 165, 176 f., 198, ch. 8 n. 28.

[17] Not that the *principes* need always have represented the views or interests of the local peasants; in 129, for instance, they need not have done so (*contra* Badian, *FC* 175). Cf. Harris (n. 15); n. 33 below.

fate of Fregellae had demonstrated that armed revolt required careful preparation,[18] and I doubt if preparation for so widespread and concerted a rebellion as occurred in the winter of 91/90 can have been deferred until Drusus' inability to keep his promises had become plain in the autumn of 91, the time to which Livy's account of Italian *coniurationes* and Appian's of negotiations and exchange of hostages relate; of course final meetings to implement earlier and provisional plans must have occurred then.[19] In any case revolt was their final recourse. Diodorus has a story that the Marsian leader, Q. Poppaedius Silo, was marching on Rome with ten thousand armed men drawn from those fearing the results of judicial investigations, presumably under the *lex Licinia Mucia*, to demand citizenship at the point of the sword, when he was persuaded by some Domitius to submit his plea to the senate peaceably, since the senate was already well disposed to grant it (xxxvii. 13). The story, preserved in an excerpt, has no context and is hard to fit into the sequence of events: it may be fiction,[20] or rather a hostile rumour based on the known fact that large numbers of Italians under Poppaedius' leadership mustered at Rome to put pressure on senate and people; it is indeed attested that there was a plot, revealed by Drusus, to kill the consul L. Marcius Philippus, the chief opponent of enfranchisement, at the Latin festival (*de vir. ill.* 66. 12). But, whatever truth there may be in Diodorus' tale, it illustrates the fact that the allies preferred to rely at first on pressure and persuasion. In this policy they all but succeeded: Drusus had the backing of the majority of the senate until the death of L. Crassus in September 91, and it was only when he had failed that a large number of the allies acted on an alternative plan of revolt.

Sherwin-White (*RC²* 137) has recently toyed with the notion that the author of the work *de viris illustribus* was right in stating that Drusus,

---

[18] *Ad Her.* iv. 13 (cf. 16) gives an extract from a speech (real or fictitious) which clearly purports to relate to charges of treason under the *lex Varia* and to be at an early stage of the revolt, which it attributes to treasonable incitements by Romans (cf. Ascon. 22, 73 C.); it suggests that the allies are mostly loyal (doubtless the revolt spread, or was reported, gradually), that the rebels lack sufficient men, money and good generals, and should have learned from the example of Fregellae.

[19] i. 38. 169 f. Appian, as often, is indifferent to chronology and misplaces the outbreak after the *lex Varia* and the resultant trials. It is clearly dated to (late) 91 by Obsequens 54 and Oros. v. 18. 1, i.e. by Livy, who recorded scattered operations in winter 91–90 in lxxii; cf. also Diod. xxxvii. 2. 2; Ascon. 67 C. Ascon. 22, 73 C. shows that the *lex Varia* was the sequel, as implied by Val. Max. viii. 6. 4: the law 'iubebat quaeri quorum dolo malo socii ad arma ire coacti essent'; he then adds that it brought the war about! Trials doubtless began early in 90; C. Cotta, rejected in his candidature for the tribunate a few days after L. Crassus' death in Sept. 91, was banished some months later (*de orat.* iii. 11).

[20] Diod. xxxvii. 13 tells of Poppaedius Silo marching on Rome and saying that if he could not persuade the senate to grant citizenship, he would ruin Rome with fire and sword. Haug thinks this fiction. It is hard to see where it could be fitted in. Who could have been his 10,000 followers fearful of *euthynai*? Were trials under the *lex Licinia Mucia* still pending?

like Gracchus, proposed to enfranchise only the Latins; it was they in his account who plotted Philippus' murder (ch. 66). Similarly, Orosius says that Drusus won over all the Latins with the hope of freedom, and after failing to carry his proposal, raised them to arms (v. 18. 2)! Both writers no doubt depend on Livy. This account of Drusus' proposal cannot be accepted. It is contradicted not only by Appian (i. 35) and Diodorus (xxxxvii. 21), but by the epitomator of Livy (lxxi) and by Velleius (ii. 14), who is also likely to have drawn on Livy. The *de viris illustribus* itself has a famous anecdote in which Poppaedius, the advocate of 'the cause of the allies', was staying with Drusus as his guest-friend (ch. 80; cf. Plut. *Cato Minor* 2). In Valerius Maximus' version (iii. 1. 2) Poppaedius is made out to be a leading man among the Latins, preferring their claims. But it is absolutely certain that he was a Marsian.[21]

Similarly, Florus writes of the revolt of 'all Latium' (ii. 6. 7), whereas in fact the Latins were almost solidly loyal. It would be unintelligible if Drusus' failure to carry a scheme of primary benefit to the Latins provoked a revolt not among the Latins but among those peoples who had nothing to gain from it, or at most Latin status. However, the errors of these late epitomators, who doubtless hardly understood the distinction between Latins and other allies, are most easily explained on the assumption that they read in Livy that the Latins too were agitating for citizenship.

If they remained loyal, Venusia excepted (n. 42), when the insurrection broke out, we may account for this by the ties of blood and language that bound them to Rome, perhaps too by the privileges that they, and especially their *principes* (n. 5), already enjoyed, and even by the smouldering of ancient animosities between them and neighbouring Italian peoples in whose confiscated lands Latin colonists had been originally settled. In any case the revolt was not universal among the allies; elsewhere too there would be leaders who were pro-Roman or simply expected a Roman victory. But the Romans evidently felt that they could not count on the continuing aid or quiescence of the Latins or any other Italians, and realized that the Latins were not (as sometimes supposed) perfectly content with the rights of acquiring Roman citizenship by change of domicile, or by holding local magistracies (from which few could benefit). Hence after one year of fighting Rome conceded to the loyal Latins and allies the very demand for citizenship, the refusal of which had caused the rest to revolt.

Diodorus has preserved the terms of an oath in which men swore allegiance to Drusus on condition that he secured the citizenship for

---

[21] Diod. (n. 20); *Per.* Livy lxxvi etc.; cf. *RR* 91.

them (xxxvii. 11). Its authenticity is a subject of debate,[22] and unfortunately the excerpt does not tell us who swore it. It is, however, a natural view that (if genuine) it was to be taken by Italians at large. All our authorities are indeed agreed in Justin's words that 'all Italy was now demanding not freedom but a share in government and citizenship' (xxxvii. 4. 13).[23] The term 'freedom' is ambiguous: in this context it is 'independence of Rome', whereas when Orosius (v. 18. 2) says that the Italians hoped for freedom, he means exactly what Justin contrasts with it; at Rome freedom is often synonymous with political rights. In his account of the outbreak of the war with the Latins in 340, which probably owes something to experience of events in 91–90, Livy makes the Latins demand liberty in the sense of equality of power within the Roman state (viii. 4. 3–6, 4. 11, 5. 4). According to Appian, once the insurgents had organized, they made a last appeal to the senate to grant citizenship (i. 39. 176). During the hostilities further colloquies seem to have turned on the same question. In 90 Marius and Poppaedius discussed 'peace and the desire for citizenship' (Diod. xxxvii. 15). In recording a meeting between Pompeius Strabo and the Marsian Vettius Scato, Cicero indicates that the citizenship was still demanded (*Phil.* xii. 27; see p. 109). If Sulla was unable to negotiate peace, presumably in 89, it was surely because he was not empowered to grant the rebels' terms (Frontinus, *Strat.* i. 5. 17). Sherwin-White, in an effort to minimize this evidence (RC^2 146), writes that in 87 the Samnites 'refused an offer of citizenship, because it did not entirely restore their *status quo ante*'. The texts (n. 55) say nothing of the *status quo ante*, which would have been that position of dependent alliance which the rebels sought to escape from: according to Licinianus, the Samnites would not make peace unless citizenship were granted to them and to all deserters from Roman armies, and unless their own property were restored (20 F.); Dio (fr. 102. 7) agrees as to the citizenship, but adds that they would not give up their booty and demanded the return of all deserters and captives from their own ranks. By this time the senate was desperate for help against Marius and Cinna, and the Samnites could raise their demands because they could expect Marius and Cinna to accede to them all. Citizenship was still what the rebels wanted. The undoubted fact that they had seceded, which Sherwin-White stresses (RC^2 144 ff.), by no means implies that their true desire was independence of Rome, as he supposes.

There was no question of the allies being satisfied with *civitas sine*

[22] Herrmann, 1968, 55 ff.
[23] Diod. xxxvii. 2. 1, 13, 15; Cic. *Phil.* xii. 27; Strabo v. 4. 2; Vell. ii. 15; Florus iii. 17. 6, 18. 3; Pluto. *Cato Minor.* 2; App. i. 35. 155, 38. 169, 39. 176, 49. 212 f., 53. 231.

suffragio. I think it probable that the class of persons who had once had this status no longer existed. The *ius suffragii* had been granted to some or all[24] of the Sabines in 268, and to the three Volscian towns of Arpinum, Formiae, and Fundi in 188. Velleius (i. 14) alone records the first grant, and Livy (xxxviii. 37) the second; it may be that he mentions it only because it gave rise to a constitutional wrangle (the senate had not given its prior consent to the law). We cannot assume that Livy would have registered every similar act of enfranchisement; his narrative of domestic events in the second century is patently incomplete (p. 21). Still less can we expect the wretched epitomator to mention such grants where the text of Livy is lost: the grants made in 268 and 188 are both absent in the *Periochae*. In 188 the senate so far relented towards the Capuans as to permit them once more to be enrolled as citizens (Livy, loc. cit.); this did not mean indeed that they were given the vote, and we might conjecture that in view of their earlier disloyalty they would have been among the last *cives sine suffragio* to be promoted. Latinization might well have been a criterion for grant of the franchise. Cumae began to use Latin officially instead of Oscan in 180;[25] at Capua the first datable Latin inscription erected by the local *magistri* is of 112 or 111.[26] Caere no doubt clung longest to its native language, Etruscan; and it seems to me probable that the lists of *cives sine suffragio* were known as *tabulae Caeritum*, precisely at a time when Caere was the last community of citizens who still lacked the vote[27] (whether or not the Capuans, who no longer had communal status, also lacked it). At any rate, we cannot argue that only those few enfranchisements had occurred of which we happen to be told; on the other hand, it appears to me unlikely *(a)* that if the class of citizens *sine suffragio* had still existed (apart perhaps from the Capuans) in the period of agitation among the allies for enfranchisement, there would have been no suggestion that as a compromise the allies might be given 'half-citizenship' (to use Mommsen's term), which would have included the *ius provocationis*, rather than the Latin right, which did not include it, or *(b)* that there would have been no trace, particularly during the Social war, of discontent among the half-citizens at the inferiority of their status. It may also be remarked that even in 90 there

---

[24] In my view all (*Latomus*, 1969, 121 ff.).

[25] Livy xl. 42. 13: 'Cumanis petentibus permissum, ut publice Latine loquerentur et praeconibus Latine vendendi ius esset'. The inference sometimes drawn that Rome had hitherto forbidden Cumae the official use of Latin seems absurd. Presumably the Cumaeans, to ingratiate themselves, intimated their wishes and Rome gave a sanction that was not required legally.

[26] *ILLRP* 705 ff.; these inscriptions are collected and discussed by M. W. Frederiksen, *PBSR* 1959, 80. ff.

[27] *IM*, App. 1. *Alii alia*: I see no reason to alter my views in the light of Harris, 1971, 45 ff.; Sherwin-White, *RC*² 200 ff.

is no testimony to their being upgraded, and that the argument *e silentio* against their earlier promotion applies equally against their promotion at this time too, though it is clear that there were no half-citizens left in Cicero's time. But if promotions occurred in the second century, they must have raised hopes of enfranchisement elsewhere, which were frustrated only because Rome departed from that liberality with the citizenship which had earlier been a mark of her policy.[28] (See Appendix III.)

To say that the Italians desired citizenship is to generalize. There could have been exceptions,[29] though the Samnites were not among them. Sherwin-White supposes that many would still have preferred the *ius provocationis*, for which there is no evidence so late as 90; he assumes that they were reluctant to surrender that degree of independence which they enjoyed, and which the rebels actually chose to restrict further in creating the new state of Italia when Rome rejected their initial demands (see below). Certainly, the Romans themselves reckoned with the *possibility* of this particularism when, at the end of 90, they passed the *lex Iulia* and left the loyal allies free to accept or refuse the Roman citizenship (Appendix II). But none refused it.

At Heraclea and Naples indeed a large number preferred 'foederis sui libertatem' to Roman citizenship. But even here the objectors must have been in the minority and were overcome. Cicero singles out these cities for their temporary hesitation in accepting the Roman offer; it is a reasonable inference that there were hardly any other instances. Both were Greek cities, and Greeks were more attached (we may think) to preserving their separate identity than the properly Italian peoples. The attitude of a minority of their citizens, however substantial, is therefore far from supporting Sherwin-White's conception: the isolation of these cases argues the very reverse.[30]

In Appian's account the *lex Iulia* was designed to appease unrest in Etruria and Umbria, where in the winter of 90/89 the people were being incited to join the revolt. News of the law was hastily sent to Etruria (and presumably to Umbria), where the citizenship was gladly accepted (App. i. 49. 211 f.). The Etrurians and Umbrians had thus been on the point of revolt, and now changed their minds (216 f.). There had in fact been some fighting in Etruria and Umbria which Appian neglects. He may be corrected from the Livian tradition. Orosius actually says that the Etruscans and Umbrians were reduced 'plurimo sanguine impenso et difficillimo labore' (v. 18. 7). But it is

---

[28] Cic. *Balb.* 31, ignoring the long temporal gap.

[29] In App. i. 49. 212 no exceptions are allowed; μόνον should not be changed to μόνον οὐ; cf. Gabba ad loc.

[30] Cic. *Balb.* 21; cf. *Arch.* 5 ff., *Fam.* xiii. 30.

always part of his purpose to dilate on the magnitude of Rome's past sufferings (*praefatio* 9 ff.), and he is surely exaggerating. It is clear from the *Perioche* of Livy lxxiv that this fighting took place at the very end of 90[31] and that it was soon over; L. Porcius Cato defeated the Etruscans while still praetor, and next year, as consul, he was fighting the Marsians (*Per.* lxxv). The insurrection was probably half-hearted and localized (e.g. at Faesulae, which was sacked, according to Florus ii. 18. 11); for that reason Appian ignored it.[32]

The alacrity with which the Etruscans and Umbrians accepted the citizenship in 90 is relevant to their attitude to Drusus in 91. Appian says that the very Italians on whose behalf Drusus was acting objected to the agrarian schemes by which he hoped to win over the Roman plebs; they feared to be deprived of Roman *ager publicus*, the use of which they enjoyed illegally (i. 36. 162).[33] These fears operated particularly on the Etruscans and Umbrians, whom Appian curiously distinguishes from the 'Italiotai' here (163) but not elsewhere (212 f.).[34] Probably the Etruscans at least were ruled by a particularly narrow oligarchic class; it is likely enough that their *principes*, more than any others, had extensive holdings of *ager publicus*. Appian says that they came to Rome really to murder Drusus but nominally to oppose the law, and that at the time when he was killed they were awaiting the day of the *dokimasia* of a law. It is commonly thought that the law is the enfranchisement bill, and that the Etruscans and Umbrians were therefore opposed to it. Carcopino explains this by supposing that their magnates feared that the grant of the citizenship would introduce a dangerous equality within their communities. There is no certain evidence for this hypothesis or for holding that the abortive revolt of the Etruscans and Umbrians in 90 can be accounted for by any kind of internal revolution.[35] In fact this interpretation of Appian is mistaken. The context shows clearly that the law of which he is writing is Drusus' agrarian or colonial law. Now that law had undoubtedly been passed, and long before the autumn of 91, when

---

[31] Haug 201 ff. showed that Livy followed a fairly strict chronological order.

[32] Harris, 1971, 216 f.; Sherwin-White, *RC*[2] 149 n. 1.

[33] Compare the complaints made in 129 by the Italians against the Gracchan land commissioners (App. i. 19; Cic. *de rep.* i. 31, iii. 41); those aggrieved were surely local magnates who were *possessores* of Roman *ager publicus* within their territories, though they could purport to speak for their cities. For such *ager publicus* in Etruria cf. Harris, 1971, 105 f., 203 ff. On relevant evidence of the *Liber Coloniarum* see now Keppie, 8 ff; Cf. n. 68.

[34] Probably his source for the first passage distinguished the Etruscans and Umbrians from the other Italians. We are always entitled to assume that Appian was slipshod like other epitomators (Brunt, *CQ* 1980, 477 ff.) in summarizing his sources, and that he could be inaccurate and inconsistent in use of terms.

[35] *Contra* L. Piotrowicz, *Klio* 1930, 334 ff.; J. Carcopino, *Hist. Rom.* ii. 368; J. Heurgon, *JRS* 1959, 43; see now Harris 1971, 218 ff.; cf. 31 ff. against the view that Vegoia's prophecy can be used for events of 91.

Drusus was killed. Badian therefore concluded that the *dokimasia* to which he alludes must be not the vote in the assembly for the enactment of the law but that in the senate, which resulted in its nullification. Appian's narrative is in any case radically defective in that he does not mention that Drusus' laws were annulled, and before his death. It has been objected that *dokimasia* normally refers to an affirmative vote in the *comitia* (cf. i. 10. 42, 29. 132, iv. 7. 27); if this objection is decisive we ought not to infer that Appian, contrary to his plain meaning, has the enfranchisement bill in mind, but rather that by associating the *dokimasia* with Drusus' death he has made one of those grossly confusing chronological connections which disfigure his narrative of the 50s (e.g. ii. 14), and that it was much earlier when the Etruscans appeared in the city to agitate against the agrarian law. In view of their readiness to accept the citizenship in 90/89, it is incredible that in 91 the Etruscans and Umbrians had opposed their own enfranchisement in principle. At most we can say that they objected to the price that Drusus thought it necessary for them to pay, if the Roman plebs was to be won over, a price not demanded under the *lex Iulia*. Taking Badian's view of the meaning of *dokimasia*, I previously argued that by the time they appeared in Rome to support the annulment of the agrarian law, they had nothing to lose, since there was no longer any prospect of his carrying the enfranchisement bill. Harris has replied that the consuls must have organized resistence to the agrarian distributions at a time before Drusus' cause was manifestly lost. I am not convinced that the timetable is such as to make this contention compelling. But dogmatism on such a point is not in place where the evidence is so defective.[36]

The *lex Iulia* was the only law that offered the citizenship to Italian communities in general. Many scholars have, however, supposed that in 89 the *lex Plautia Papiria* offered the franchise to individuals in the rebel communities who might come over to Rome. But (as Badian observed) nothing is known of the terms of the *lex Plautia Papiria* except that it granted citizenship to a probably small class of *ascripti* of federate cities, foreigners who had received the citizenship of cities like Heraclea, which were enfranchised under the *lex Iulia*, and were domiciled in Italy and registered at Rome within sixty days (*Arch.* 7). Badian has also shown that the law was passed, if not as late as December 89, at any rate in the last part of that year. Thus even if the law did grant citizenship to individual insurgents, it came too late in the year 89 to change their determination to fight on. And the later it is put in 89, the less likely does it become that the Romans then made any

---

[36] *Historia* 1962, 225 ff.; cf. Harris 212 ff.

concession of the kind supposed. By the autumn of 89 most of the rebels had already been reduced by hard fighting to unconditional surrender, and there was no reason to stimulate desertion in the rebel ranks.[37]

Velleius (ii. 16. 4) says that the Romans gradually recovered their strength by 'recipiendo in civitatem qui arma aut non ceperant aut *deposuerant maturius*'. The words italicized are taken by Sherwin-White[38] to mean that the citizenship was offered by the *lex Iulia* to rebels who should have laid down their arms by a given date. But if Velleius be interpreted thus, he finds no support in Appian's account of the *lex Iulia* (or in any other testimony). According to Appian (i. 49. 212–3), it was only the loyal allies who were offered the citizenship; he adds indeed that the grant made the rebels hope for like concessions and weakened their resistance, a statement which finds no confirmation from the bloody fighting that went on through 89, but which strictly implies that no concession had yet been made to them. And Velleius surely means that the citizenship was offered to cities that had taken up arms but had already submitted; this is the natural force of the pluperfect 'deposuerant'. Moreover, his statement covers both 90 and 89, and he might have had in mind extensions in 89 of the benefits of the *lex Iulia* to ex-rebel communities, as distinct from those reduced by force, to whose enfranchisement he refers when rehearsing events of 88 or later (ii. 17).

In some cases an anti-Roman movement may have been quelled from within. Though Sherwin-White was right to deny that there is evidence from the Social war of divisions on class lines within the Italian peoples, he was not right in claiming that there is no sign of *any* internal divisions, that 'a state was either for [Rome] or against her'.[39] It would have been extraordinary if this had been so in communities in which hostile factions are certainly documented, as at Rome itself.[40] In fact we find that Minatius Magius of Aeclanum (Vell. ii. 16) and perhaps Publius Sittius of Nuceria[41] took the Roman side against their own compatriots, that several cities were brought over to the insurgents by force or treachery,[42] that Pinna stood sieges both from the

---

[37] Badian, 1964, 75 ff. (esp. n. 34); cf. *Historia* 1962, 228; in *JRS* 1973, 125 ff., he clinches the case. But Sherwin-White is misleading in saying on the basis of Cic. *Balb.* 21 that the *lex Iulia* was the only general law of enfranchisement: it was the only law that offered citizenship to loyal allies, who became *fundi* of it; the rebels as *dediticii* received citizenship later by Rome's unilateral grant.
[38] *RC²* 148.   [39] Ibid. 135.
[40] For local Italian *inimicitiae* cf. the Oscan Table of Bantia (App. *IV*), cap. 1; Cic. *Rosc. Amer.* 17, *Cluent.* 21 ff.; for *stasis* in the war Sisenna iv. 78: 'denique cum variis voluntatibus incerta civitas trepidaret'.
[41] Cic. *Sull.* 58. Nuceria may not have revolted, but cities federated with her did; cf. Gabba on App. i. 42. 186.
[42] Venafrum, though Roman (Festus 262 L.), was betrayed, presumably by local Italian residents (App. i. 41. 183); likewise Nola (ibid. 42. 185), which was to hold out till 88 (Vell. ii. 17). The rebels reduced some Apulian cities by force; here Latin Venusia came over of its own accord, but surely not without internal opposition (ibid. 42. 190). Dio, fr. 98. 3 attests division in the Picentes.

Italians and the Romans,[43] and that Vidacilius killed his enemies at Asculum in 89, presumably on charges of treason.[44] Magius, of whom we know something only because he was Velleius' grandfather, could not carry the people of Aeclanum with him, but elsewhere pro-Romans may have crushed an abortive revolt. Our information is far too sparse to reject this *e silentio*. It is a hypothesis that is particularly plausible for the Etruscans and Umbrians, where the revolt was so brief. Conceivably in such circumstances the *lex Iulia* still reserved to the Romans the right to investigate the facts and determine whether on the whole such a community deserved the reward of loyalty. This may explain why a special law was necessary to confer the citizenship on Umbrian Tuder.[45] Finally, it is not at all likely that the Romans held out any hopes of pardon to the rebel leaders. In the Hannibalic war, while sparing the masses, they had been ruthless to the authors of revolt,[46] and in the age of Marius and Sulla they had not become more merciful. It is significant that when the Marsians had to submit, Poppaedius Silo evidently fled to the Samnites; and later the Samnite general Papius Mutilus had no expectation of amnesty.[47] It was very natural for the rebel peoples mostly to remain loyal to their leaders; if the latter were not offered pardon, they had no choice but to go on fighting. 'Quidquid delirant reges plectuntur Achivi.'

Among the central Italian peoples there are signs that even during the war relics of friendly feeling towards the Romans survived. Diodorus (xxxviii. 15) preserves a story of fraternizing between the troops of Marius and Poppaedius in 90, which ended in fruitless negotiations between the generals. Cicero was an eyewitness of a meeting in 89 between Pompeius Strabo and another Marsian general, Vettius Scato, who described himself as 'voluntate hospitem, necessitate hostem'. He adds: 'erat in illo colloquio aequitas; nullus timor, nulla suberat suspicio, mediocre etiam odium. Non enim ut eriperent nobis socii civitatem, sed ut in eam reciperent, petebant' (*Phil.* xiii. 27). Of course this is rather idealized; there had been, and was to be, bitter fighting; and massacres occurred, as in later civil wars; war is a βίαιος διδάσκαλος. But I do not see

---

[43] Diod. xxxvii. 19 f. (cf. *ad Her.* ii. 45) with Val. Max. v. 4. 7.

[44] App. i. 48. 207 ff. (chronologically misplaced, see Gabba ad loc.).

[45] Sisenna iv. 119: 'tamen Tudertibus senati consulto et populi iusso dat civitatem'. Harris 230 suggests that a *SC* was necessary to give effect to the *lex Iulia* in the case of a people still in arms when that law was passed.

[46] Livy xxiv. 47. 10, xxvi. 15, xxix. 8. 1 f., 36. 10–2.

[47] Poppaedius, Diod. xxxvii. 2. 9; *Per.* Livy lxxvi; Papius, Licin. 32 F.; *Per.* Livy lxxxix. Few of the recorded Italian generals can be connected with any Italians later eminent at Rome; Asinius Pollio (*cos.* 40), Papius Mutilus (*cos.* AD 9), and an officer named Poppaedius Silo (*RR* 91) were presumably collaterals, if not descendants. But App. iv. 25 says that the rich Samnite senator Statius, proscribed when eighty in 43 BC, had rendered the Samnites great services in the war; no doubt he was one of the Samnites who went over to Sulla (Diod. xxxvii. 2. 14; cf. E. T. Salmon, *Athen.* 1964, 67 f.).

why we should question the essential truth of Cicero's picture; the Marsians were still anxious to become Romans: it was Rome that still obstructed an accommodation. The Romans persisted until they had reduced the peoples of central Italy to surrender, and it was only when they needed reinforcement against the Marians in 87 that the senate was prepared to enfranchise them (Appendix II). As *dediticii* they were probably not given the option of declining incorporation under the *lex Iulia* (n. 37), but it was well known that this was what they desired.

It is more plausible to hold that the Samnites at least preserved some of their ancient animosity to Rome, which had made most of them, unlike the peoples of central Italy, go over to Hannibal. Some Italian coins show an Italian soldier with his foot placed on a Roman standard or the Italian bull trampling on the Roman wolf.[48] When the coins bearing these symbols are inscribed, the legends are in Oscan; some of them have the name of the Samnite general Papius Mutilus. 'Safinium', perhaps equivalent to Samnitium, is written on another of his issues.[49] The Samnites, with the Lucanians, held out longest of the rebels; they had not been suppressed when the civil war of 87 broke out. It was they who entered into negotiations with Mithridates in 88.[50] Indeed some or all of the coins mentioned may belong to the last desperate stage of resistance in the south.[51] In 82 most of the Samnites and Lucanians again took up arms against Sulla,[52] and everyone knows the story that their general Pontius Telesinus, 'vir penitus Romano nomini infestissimus', declared that Rome must be totally destroyed, for Italy would never be free until the wolves had been rooted out of their lair (Vell. ii. 27). But who reported these words (uttered, if at all, to his own Samnite troops) to a Roman, and how were they transmitted? Very probably they originated in an invention circulated by the memoirs of Sulla,[53] who had good reason to

---

[48] Sydenham, 1952, nos. 627 f., 630, 641.

[49] Ibid. 639.

[50] Posid. (Jacoby no. 87) F. 41; Diod. xxxvii. 2. 11. Date: Gabba, 1973, 248 = 1976, 88. Some Italians eventually fled to Mithridates (Front. *Strat.* ii. 3. 17). Gabba, 1973, 323 = 1976, 113, connects with all this the negotiations between Sertorius and Mithridates (Plut. *Sert.* 23; App. *Bell. Mithr.* 68). Two of the rebel coin issues (Sydenham 632, 643) can be associated with their overtures to him.

[51] So A. Voirol, *Schweizer Münzblätter*, 1953/4, 64 ff.

[52] Salmon, 1967, 377 ff., demonstrated that the Samnites were not continuously in arms from 87 to 83 and that they did not obstruct Sulla's march in 83 from Brundisium to Campania. But it seems to me unwarranted and incredible that Sulla, who needed any support he could get, would not seek it from the Samnites, and actually proclaimed a crusade against them, before they mostly rallied to the Marian side; like many other Italians, they doubtless did so because they could not trust his promises, esp. in view of their role in 87. Cf. n. 47.

[53] Haug argued that Velleius drew indirectly on these memoirs. They certainly lie behind Plutarch's description of the Samnites and Lucanians as peoples most hostile to Rome (*Sulla* 29. 4). Sisenna, if regarded as an alternative source, no doubt adopted Sulla's bias. For Sulla's treatment of the Samnites see App. i. 87. 400, 93. 432; Strabo v. 4. 11; Salmon, 1967, 386 ff.

denigrate the Samnites at Rome, in order to justify his massacres and devastations; Appian tells how he killed all his Samnite prisoners and remarked that the Samnites had always been dangerous to Rome, and Strabo that he declared that Rome would never have peace so long as they had not been broken up. In fact Pontius Telesinus and his men were now Roman citizens, and were fighting not against Rome but against one Roman faction. The other evidence does not amount to much. Rome had shown from the first, as had to be expected, that she would not recognize the new Italian state; the Italians were therefore committed to a life-and-death struggle, and it is not surprising that they announced symbolically in their coins that the victory would be theirs, or that Samnites sought to revive memories of their own heroic past.[54] As for Mithridates, even Romans in civil wars did not scruple to seek foreign aid.

But there is more solid evidence for Samnite sentiments. In 87 the senate tried to come to terms with the Samnites and Lucanians. The negotiations broke down because they demanded citizenship not only for themselves but for those who had deserted to them, together with the restoration of their property and other conditions. Cinna and Marius accepted all their demands.[55] Thus, as Appian (i. 53. 231) observes, they too got what they wanted—the citizenship. In 66 Cicero thought that it would assist the cause of his client, Cluentius, that 'Boviano totoque ex Samnio cum laudationes honestissimae missae sunt tum homines amplissimi nobilissimique venerunt' (*Cluent.* 197) This hardly suggests that there was much sense in Rome of Samnite hostility to her power.

II. THE CONCEPT OF ITALIAN UNITY: ROMANIZATION

Of course when in 91 the rebels were frustrated in their claims to the citizenship they were obliged to seek a different solution for their problems. This was the creation of a new state, Italia, at Corfinium, 'a common city for all the Italians in place of Rome'[56] a sort of anti-Rome (in the same sense as we speak of anti-Popes). It is far from clear, perhaps it was not clear to the Italians, just what consequences this entailed. As Rome would not acknowledge the new state, Rome had to be defeated. Diodorus says that the Italians were now fighting for their own hegemony (xxxvii./xxxviii. 22). The possibility that Italy might

[54] Gabba, 1973, 279 = 1976, 101, concedes too much in holding that an appeal was made to the desire for independence among the masses, of whose sentiments we naturally know nothing at all.

[55] Licin. 20 F.; Dio, fr. 104 7; App. i. 68. 309 f.

[56] Strabo v. 4. 2; more details in Diod. xxxvii. 2. 3 ff.; cf. *CIL* i². 848: 'Itali, T. Laf[renius] pr[aetor]'. For name Italia or Vitelliu see the coins.

be divided between two states, with momentous effects on the empire overseas, was not one to which they needed to give any consideration, because the Romans were not prepared to contemplate such a compromise. If they could not force the Romans after all to concede their original demands—and the readiness of Poppaedius Silo in 90 and of Vettius Scato in 89 to enter into *pourparlers* suggests that they still had this in mind—they had to make the Romans surrender. Whether they would have decided to incorporate a defeated Rome into the new Italia we shall never know.

The rebel state has been variously represented as unitary[57] or federal. Our information is meagre, but Diodorus stresses the imitation of Rome. Even the coins were mostly copied from Roman issues.[58] There was to be a senate of five hundred members, two consuls, twelve praetors, and since a spacious forum as well as a council house were planned (they can hardly have been built), a primary assembly to meet in the forum was surely envisaged. All this favours the first alternative. It is denied by Sherwin-White, only because he is convinced, without good reason, that the rebel peoples were passionate for local autonomy. Since the state was new, the senate could not consist, as the Roman senate did, of ex-magistrates, but must have comprised magnates of the rebel peoples, chosen, naturally enough, on some proportionate basis; similarly, of the first two consuls one was a Marsian and one a Samnite, and doubtless most of the other insurgents were allowed a praetor apiece. No system of representation need have been written into a constitution. There was no machinery to draft a constitution; for immediate needs the senate received 'autocratic power', and enacted a law for the election of the two consuls and twelve praetors. A passage in Strabo (v. 4. 2) might be read as meaning that they were elected by the rebel host mustered at Corfinium, but that necessarily unrepresentative body can have done no more than acclaim the names propounded by the senate, from whose ranks, we are told, the persons were to be chosen who were to rule and conduct the war: these persons were probably none other than the magistrates. The differences between the initial arrangements for the government of

---

[57] H. D. Meyer, *Historia* 1958, 74 ff. Salmon, 1967, 348 ff.; cf. *TAPA* 1958, 89 ff., holds that App. i. 39. 175 gives an official Italian list of 12 rebel peoples each entitled to one praetor; in that case the number of praetors was not fixed until the relatively late adherence of Pompeii, Venusia, and some Apulian cities; and further adhesions would presumably have created a claim for more praetors. It is also an objection that the peoples named were of very unequal strength. Salmon's assignation of different generals to specific peoples is often highly conjectural; and we cannot always distinguish (e.g. i. 40. 181) between local and 'federal' commanders. The hypothesis is unsound.

[58] This invalidates Carcopino's hypothesis (*Hist. Rom.* ii. 378) founded on the coins of a league between central and southern rebels: see Sydenham's notes on the coins and Voirol (n. 51).

Italia and the Roman system can largely be explained by the necessity of improvisation in the winter of 91/90.

The rebels had hoped for political unity and equality within the structure of the Roman state. When this was denied, they sought to achieve the same aims without Rome and against her, but they still could not escape Roman influences. There is no trace here of the passion for freedom and autonomy which had informed the separatist revolts of Athens' subjects. That is not surprising. We need not rely for an explanation merely on an unfathomable difference between the national characteristics of Greeks and Italians. The long internal peace within Italy, which had lasted for a century since Hannibal's departure, had no precedent in Greek experience and had demonstrated the advantages of political unity to peoples of whom many had once struggled hard against Roman domination. It had bound them together in culture and sentiment. And it had made possible the acquisition of a dominion overseas which Italians as well as Romans had been able to exploit.[59] We should expect Justin to be right when he says that they desired 'consortium imperii'.

Even the concept and name of Italia or Vitelia are significant.[60] To Metternich Italy was no more than a geographical expression, and the political unity which the rebels wished to maintain was not to be regained, once Rome had fallen, until the nineteenth century. The name Italia had once stood only for Calabria. It was the Romans who gave it a larger extension and a political connotation by distinguishing from their allies or subjects overseas the Italians whose duty and privilege consisted in finding soldiers for Rome's armies, not money for her treasury, the 'socii nominisve Latini quibus ex formula togatorum milites in terra Italia imperare solent'.[61] Here with a common dress as

[59] In distributions of booty to soldiers Italians are recorded to have received the same as Romans on three occasions (Livy xl. 43. 5, xli. 7. 1 ff., xlv. 43. 4); half as much on another, but this was evidently thought novel and unfair (xli. 13. 6. ff.), and is unlikely to have been a precedent; however, the proceeds of booty not distributed went, like indemnities and taxes, to the Roman treasury. In 173 Latins received smaller viritane allotments than Romans, p. 513, Ilari 141 n. 74. On Italian business activity in regions under Roman rule or hegemony cf. p. 168.

[60] F. Klingner, *Rom. Geisteswelt*[2] 13 ff.; Ilari 3 ff., though Galsterer 37 ff. has shown that 'Italia' *can* also denote merely the *ager Romanus* in Italy. On the Romanization of Italy see esp. G. Devoto, *Scr. Min.* i. 287 ff. (who rightly remarks that the view of the Social war as a final protest against Roman rule contradicts the story of Romanization, Samnium perhaps excepted), and some parts of his *Gli antichi italici* and *St. della lingua rom.*; J. Whatmough, 1937 discusses it regionally; cf. now Salmon, 1967, ch. 9, and Harris, 1971, ch. v, on Samnium, Etruria, and Umbria. I am not familiar with further researches on this subject.

[61] *Lex agraria* (*FIRA* i[2]. no. 8) 21, 50; on the formula see *IM*, App. 6; Ilari, ch. III (largely confirming my views). Cf. *FIRA* i[2]. no. 30 (186 BC): 'neve nominus Latini neve socium quisquam'; the Gracchan *repetundae* law (ibid. 7) 1: '[Quoi socium no] minisve Latini exterarumve nationum'. There is a threefold classification: (1) *socii* (in Italy); (2) *nomen Latinum*; (3) other foreign peoples. In the 'piracy law' (*JRS* 174, A cols. II 6 and III 31), the Greek text in my view mistranslates the Latin original 'socii nominisve Latini' by οἱ σύμμαχοι ὀνομάτος Λατίνου or τοὺς

symbol of a common status[62] was the germ of the later conception of 'Romanos rerum dominos gentemque togatam'. Officially Italy ended still at the Aesis, but both Cato (n. 83) and Polybius (i. 6, 13, ii. 14) carried it to the Alps, and the *lex Pompeia* of 89, by granting Latin status to the Transpadani, implies a half-recognition of the larger limit. Only the Alps provided a natural boundary, and the unity discerned in the earlier official terminology was clearly not so much geographical as cultural, sentimental, or national. If any such sense of unity already existed, it was the work of Rome. To have created it, though without deliberate purpose, was a remarkable achievement.

In Italy the mountain ranges are only less divisive than in Greece, and in the pre-Roman era the Italians were not bound together by those ties of common blood, language, religion, and manners of which the Greeks were conscious (Hdt. viii. 144): they were peoples of diverse origin and tongues. Even the affiliation of Oscan and Latin is more perceptible to the comparative philogist today than it can have been to Italians living in 90; and some of the Italians spoke languages that were not Italic; that of the Etruscans was not Indo-European. Since language influences thought, the extension of Latin was not only an outward sign of developing unity but one of the chief factors in its promotion.

Pliny (*NH* iii. 39) was to say that it was Italy's achievement 'tot populorum discordes ferasque linguas sermonis commercio contrahere'. Latinization within Italy prepared Italy to fulfil this task, and followed the same process as can later be observed in the empire at large. Once Rome had become the ruling power, the very diversity of the Italian linguistic pattern gave Latin the advantage as a lingua franca. Roman magistrates (it was alleged[63]) in old days refused to speak Greek, or doubtless any alien tongue; and the Italian *principes* needed Latin to communicate with the senate, or with patrons and *hospites* at Rome. In the army Latin was the language of the high command, and perhaps too the only intelligible medium of intercourse in or between allied cohorts. (Mommsen plausibly conjectured that the contingents of small cities must have been often amalgamated in a

συμμάχους Λατίνους. 'Socii nominis Latini', where it occurs in our texts of Livy (e.g. xxxviii. 44. 4), is also probably an error of Livy or a copyist.

[62] Ilari 4 n. 11. Sallust uses *togati* and *Italici* as equivalents (*BJ* 21. 2, 26). Cisalpina is already *togata* in 43 (Cic. *Phil.* viii. 27). Strabo (vi. 1. 2) says that the distinctive languages, armour, and dress of the Lucanians, Samnites and Bruttians had all disappeared, but though often dependent on earlier sources, he is here no doubt reporting what he was told and saw on his own travels (v. 3. 6), when Samnium had not recovered from Sullan *Schrecklichkeit* (v. 4. 11), and when the Lucanians (as of course the rest) were Romans (vi. 1. 3). I doubt his testimony as to the language at least of the masses; cf. n. 76.

[63] Val. Max. ii. 2. 2; Harris, 1971, 170 f.

single unit.[64] According to Velleius (ii. 110. 5), Pannonians who rose against Rome in AD 6 had learnt from service in Roman armies to speak and actually to read Latin;[65] and if they acquired this facility in one generation, how much more must Italians have done so in two or more centuries. A great block of Roman territory (including that of Latin cities) extended from north Campania to south Etruria and north-eastwards from Rome, with the Via Flaminia as its artery, to Picenum and Ariminum.[66] Within this area Latin displaced the native speech of Faliscans, Volscians, Aequians, and Sabines[67] and influenced the contiguous Italians. Outside this solidly Latin region there were pockets everywhere of Latin-speakers, the strategically situated Latin colonies, lands confiscated after the Hannibalic war in the south, where some Gracchan settlers could find homes,[68] as earlier Scipio's veterans had been assigned allotments in Samnium and Apulia (Livy xxxi. 4. 2), or simply groups of Roman citizens or Latins living in allied cities, like those who were massacred at Asculum or captured at Nola and in some Apulian towns in 90 (App. i. 38, 174, 42. 185 and 190). And Roman roads penetrated allied lands; presumably they were kept up by the *viasiei vicani*, who were probably Roman (*FIRA* i². no. 8. 10 f.). We should not underrate the actual mixing of populations. Not only were Romans or Latins domiciled in allied towns; Samnites and Paelignians migrated to Latin Fregellae (Livy xli. 8), other Italians to Narnia (xxxii. 2, 6); non-Latin forms in early inscriptions or coins from Luceria (*ILLR* 504), Spoletium (ibid. 505), Pisaurum (ibid. 23), and Beneventum (Conway, *Italian Dialects* no. 159) suggest that the colonists were not all of Roman or Latin stock; to Rome itself of course Italians were much attracted, despite occasional expulsions.[69] Diodorus thought that the combatants in the Social war were linked by marriages, owing to the custom (νομός) of *conubium* (xxxvii. 15. 2), and though this is clearly attested only between Romans and Latins, it may have become more extensive; at least we know that Pacuvius from Latin Brundisium was sister's son to Ennius from Messapian Rudiae (Pliny, *NH* xxxv. 19).[70]

---

[64] *StR* iii³. 674. The *extraordinarii* (Ilari 143 ff.) were presumably mixed. Livy xliv. 40. 5 f. records how Marrucinian and Paelignian cohorts were marshalled with Samnite *turmae*, and a Vestinian cohort with Latin cohorts and *turmae*.

[65] But Mócsy (*RE* Suppl. ix 767) is probably right to refer this to the officers alone.

[66] It is right to speak of Romans and Latins together, cf. Ennius (Vahlen) 466: 'qui rem Romanam Latiumque augescere vultis'. In Latin colonies *coloni* or *incolae* of alien extraction would tend to be assimilated: cf. Harris, 1971, 158 f.

[67] R. S. Conway, *Ital. Dialects* i or Vetter under each people named.

[68] See G. Tibiletti, *Rel. del* x *congresso di scienze stor.*, 1955, ii. 262 ff., for enclaves of Roman land in allied territories; hence Gracchan *cippi* at Volcei, Lucanian Atina, and Aeclanum (*ILLRP* 469–71, 473) and at Ligures Corneliani (?) (A. Russi and M. Valvo, *Quinta Miscellanea*, 1977, 205 ff.). See K. J. Beloch, *Rom. Gesch.* 1926, 494 ff., on Grumentum and Telesia; cf. n. 33.

[69] Cf. nn. 42 (Venafrum), 66.   [70] Beloch, *Ital. Bund* 153.

The effects of all this are not easy to gauge or date, given the sparsity of early inscriptions. It is clear that Latinization had made much progress among the Abruzzi peoples who were nearest to the great central block of Roman territory. The Latin alphabet was used from the first by the Volsci, Marsi, Paeligni, Vestini, and Marrucini; it also appears on Frentanian coins; before the Social war it had been adopted in the Umbrian towns of Iguvium, Fulginiae, Asisium, and Tuder, and in Apulian Bantia and Teate. Asisium used Latin officially a little before 90.[71] In Marsian territory we find Latin inscriptions of the Gracchan period, and one of the third or even the fourth century.[72] Marsians and Asculans could each produce a Latin orator in the second century (Cic. *Brut.* 169). The fact that the insurgents of central Italy inscribed their coins with Latin legends suggest that they had by now adopted Latin officially. In Etruria, Umbria, and the south the native languages were still in public use locally. In the mid-second century the comic poet Titinius could refer to men who spoke Oscan or Volscian and had no Latin.[73] Yet Latin must have been understood over a wide area. That would best explain the erection of Latin inscriptions, whether on local initiative or at Roman behest, at Bantia, Clusium, and elsewhere,[74] indeed in districts so remote as the lands of Genua and the Veneti.[75]

The gentry at least (and it was they who counted) must have become bilingual. Hence, once they had obtained the citizenship, they were ready at once to adopt Latin. Nearly all the notables of Apulian Larinum born before 90, whom Cicero mentions in his defence of Cluentius, have Latin *praenomina*. Even in Etruria, as Harris has shown, Latin had ousted Etruscan on tombstones by the time of Augustus. Most tombstones were set up by the relatively affluent. We know from other parts of the empire that the epigraphic monopoly enjoyed by Latin (or Greek) is no proof of the extinction of the native tongues. The actual disappearance of the non-Roman languages in Italy may have been the result of a process far more prolonged than our evidence

---

[71] See Conway (n. 67) or Vetter under each people or city named, and cautious remarks on Umbria in Harris 184 ff. Devoto, *Ant. Ital.* 60, observes that adaptation of the Latin alphabet in Paelignian and Volscian inscriptions shows that it was not imposed.

[72] *ILLRP* 7 (late 4th c.; Devoto, *Storia* 195, puts it in the third); cf. 285; *CIL* ix. 3827. The Volscians seem to have adopted Latin in the late third century, Conway 266 ff. See also Conway on the earliest Latin inscriptions of other peoples. Devoto, *Storia* 201, notes Latin influence on the Oscan *cippus Abellanus* (Conway no. 95, mid-second century).

[73] *CRF* (Ribbeck) 104.

[74] *FIRA* i². no. 6; cf. App. IV, *CIL* i². 595–7. I do not cite here the *SC de Bacchanalibus* (*FIRA* i². no. 30), since the *ager Teuranus* where it was set up was probably Roman (Gelzer, *Kl. Schr.* iii. 259 n. 15). The *repetundae* law found at Tarentum (n. 5) provides for publication in all allied cities.

[75] *FIRA* iii. no. 163; *ILLRP* 476 f. G. E. F. Chilver, *Cisalpine Gaul*, 1941, 72, illustrated early Romanization in nomenclature.

reveals. Modern parallels indeed suggest that the language of epitaphs need not be that actually spoken by the deceased and his kin.[76] No doubt the old forms of speech lingered longest in the fields and the market-place,[77] and in some views they have left an impress on the evolution of modern Italian.[78] But when all reservations have been made, their rapid abandonment after 90 and sometimes earlier by men of rank indicates how easily they would assimilate themselves culturally to the master-people, especially when they had been admitted to membership of it.

Contemporary experience shows that the adoption by the subjects of the language of rulers is not enough to create common sympathies. In 225 the Italians had gladly co-operated with Rome against the Gauls, not out of loyalty to Rome or Italy, but because they saw that their individual interests were menaced by the invaders (Polyb. ii. 23. 12, 31. 7).[79] By 90 they had transcended this particularism. We can see this process at work in the inscriptions abroad, where they designate themselves as Italici, perhaps as early as 193 in Sicily, and not as members of their particular communities.[80] A Roman magistrate adopted the same conception in the second century when he claimed that as praetor in Sicily he had rounded up 'fugiteivos Italicorum'.[81] It was indeed the Romans who contrasted the Italians with external peoples (n. 61). Cato, in particular, in his *Origines* made it his task to trace the origins of every Italian people; and, according to Dionysius, he was not alone in this: C. Sempronius Tuditanus and many others did likewise.[82] Cato seems also to have had little to say of Rome's early wars against the Italians; perhaps he preferred to celebrate the enterprises in which Rome and the Italians fought side by side.[83] Military camaraderie probably played a large part in promoting a national sentiment. The poet Ennius served Rome as a soldier; and

[76] Harris, 1971, 169 ff. Cf. my remarks in D. M. Pippidi (ed). *Assimilation et résistance à la culture Gréco-romaine*, 1976, 170 ff., on the survival of vernacular languages in provinces where only Latin or Greek was used officially or commonly attested by inscriptions.

[77] Thus among the Paeligni (Conway, p. 234) and at Pompeii not long before its destruction (ibid. nos. 60–7). A Vestinian inscription in Latin of 58 BC seems to preserve Oscan words (*ILLRP* 508). Rudorff noted the survival in Roman times of Oscan and Umbrian measurements (*Grom. Veteres* 281).

[78] Whatmough (n. 60) 302 f, cf. 279 f. He also dates some Messapian inscriptions to the late Republic (232).

[79] *FC* 145 on Polyb. iii. 90 *fin.*

[80] *Italici: ILLRP* 320, cf. 343 and many post-90 inscriptions; cf. Hatzfeld 238 ff.

[81] *ILS* 23 = *ILLRP* 454.

[82] Dionys. Hal. i. 11. 1 (*pace* Harris, 1971, 20 n. 3); Nepos, *Cato* 3; Serv. on *Aen.* ix. 600: 'Italiae disciplina et vita [a Vergilio] laudatur, quam et Cato in originibus et Varro in gente populi Romani commemorat'. See Peter, *HRF*; Cato, frs. 42, 45, 47–51, 53, 56, 58 f., 61 f., 69 f.

[83] Three books were devoted to the origins of Rome and other Italian peoples, and the fourth began with the first Punic war.

then this Messapian, the man with three hearts who spoke Greek, Oscan, and Latin, chose to sing the glories of Rome in his *Annals*.[84] He was one of the many Italians who helped to make Rome the cultural as well as the political centre of Italy. Plautus and Accius came from Umbria, Naevius and Lucilius from Campania, Pacuvius from Brundisium, Caecilius from Cisalpina. The Oscan farces of Atella were naturalized at Rome.[85]

Admiration for Rome led some of the Italians to invest their magistrates with Roman titles or to adopt Roman constitutional and legal forms.[86] Ignoring Latin cities and the older Roman *municipia*,[87] we find Latin titles adopted at Falerii (senate, praetors, aediles, quaestors), Pompeii (quaestors and aediles), Abella (senate, quaestors, *legati*), Potentia in Lucania and Vicus Supinus in Marsian country (quaestors), Alfedena in Samnium (aediles); tribunes are also attested from Teanum Sidicinum and either Nuceria or Pompeii, and a quaestor, who may be merely the official of a sacred guild, at Umbrian Iguvium.[88] An Oscan law from Bantia in Lucania shows that that small and remote place had gone far in imitating Roman institutions. The old Oscan *meddiss*[89] has ceased to denote the chief magistrate and means simply 'magistrate' in the generic sense. The specific offices except for the censor have Latin names; there are even tribunes, perhaps borrowed immediately from the neighbouring Latin colony of Venusia. As in some other Italian cities the use of the Latin term 'senate' is clearly derived from Rome at a time when it had lost its original significance as a council of elders. Various rules reflect Roman constitutional practice. It has recently been contended that the law is

---

[84] Cf. *Ann.* 545 (Vahlen): 'nos sumus Romani qui fuimus ante Rudini'.

[85] Strabo v. 3. 6 says that they were performed in Oscan (in his time or that of his source?). See Whatmough (n. 60) 390. Harris, 1971, 184 n. 2 is dubious on Plautus' origin.

[86] G. Camporeale, *Terminologia magistratuale nelle lingue osco-umbre*, 1956; I do not accept all his views.

[87] Latin colonies naturally were modelled on Rome; so there is nothing 'extraordinary' in the archaeological discovery of group voting at Cosa (*contra* M. H. Crawford, *JRS* 1981, 155); and one would expect the institutions of the older Latin cities to be very similar to Roman. The titles of some chief magistrates in *municipia*, three aediles in the Volscian cities of Arpinum, Fundi, and Formiae (*ILLRP* 546 f., 595 f., 601–4), praetors at Cumae (576), a dictator and aedile *iuri dicundo* at Caere (*ILS* 5918a), and the Sabine *octoviri* (see endnote 4) in my view indicate Latinization of indigenous titles; cf. Humbert 289 ff.

[88] Falerii, Vetter 264, 317, 320 (= *ILLRP* 238); Bantia, App. IV; Pompeii, Vetter 8 f., 11 f., 16–18, 20; Abella, ibid. 1; Potentia, ibid. 180, 181a; Vicus Supinus, ibid. 228d (= *ILLRP* 286); Alfedena, ibid. 143; Teanum, *ILS* 6298; Nuceria (?), ibid. 6445a (= *ILLRP* 1143); Iguvium, *Tab. Iguv.* va 23 b 2. U. Laffi in *Les Bourgeoisies munic. ital. aux IIe et I^e siècles av. J.-C.*, 1983, 59 ff., at 67 cites some further instances. There seems to be no warrant for holding that the *kvestur* was the chief magistrate at Iguvium replacing the *uhtur* (from the same root as *auctor*), cf. III. 7 f.; the *uhtur* may be a religious official (Vetter ad loc); see also Harris, 1971, 189 ff.

[89] F. Sartori, *Problemi di st. cost. italiota*, ch. 1 gives a lucid summary of evidence and theories on the *meddiss*.

of Sullan date and reveals the earliest institutions of Bantia when it had already become a Roman *municipium* and that the rules in question betray the influence of Sulla's constitutional measures. However, as argued in Appendix IV, they do not correspond at all closely to Sulla's innovations, but rather to the normal practice of the Roman system in the second century; everything suggests that the Bantians were not Roman citizens, and there is no good reason to date the law later than about 90, or perhaps late in the second century; moreover, whenever it was engraved, the abbreviations of the titles of magistrates suggest long familiarity with the Latin terms.

The document also refers to a *legis actio*, to *manus iniectio* on the *pro iudicato*, and (actually using the Latin term) to *dolus malus*. Thus Bantian civil law had also been in some respects assimilated to Roman. This process is likely to have gone furthest in less out-of-the-way Italian communities and must have made the full reception of Roman law in the new municipalities created after the Social war all the easier. Latin colonies had probably assisted in its promotion, affording models nearer at hand than Rome herself. It so happens that an inscription from Latin Luceria also refers to 'manus iniectio'.[90] But even without any such testimony we should have to assume that the civil law of the colonies was identical with that of Rome at the moment of their several foundations. No doubt in course of time, as Roman law developed, differences would arise. But the fact that in 90 the Latins, or rather some Latin cities,[91] still allowed an action for damages for breach of promise to the disappointed bridegroom which was not available at Rome merely shows that they had preserved an archaic Roman institution.[92] At some points the Latins kept their law in agreement with the Romans by freely adopting Roman statutes such as the *lex Furia de testamentis* and the *lex Voconia de mulierum hereditatibus* (Cic. *Balb.* 21). It would be rash to infer from Cicero's words that no other Italians did so.[93]

Evidence on these subjects is very meagre. The literary authorities are silent or generally non-technical on the forms of government or law in the allied cities, and inscriptions are seldom informative. The Oscan

---

[90] *ILRRP* 504. In the Iguvine Tables the words *aŕputrati* (va ii) and *stiplo* (vi a 2; cf. *steplatu* i b 13) are held to be of Latin origin by e.g. Vetter, but cf. Devoto, *Ant. Italici*[2] 1951, 273, on the first. The second borrowing does not imply adoption of Roman law; there is no analogy between the use of the last two words and Roman *stipulatio* (U. Coli, *Il diritto pubblico degli umbri*, 1958, 25 f.). See L. Mitteis, *Röm. Privatrecht*, 1908, 3 ff.

[91] *Ius Latii* meant that the citizens of Latin cities enjoyed on a reciprocal basis certain rights in Rome and in other Latin cities, not that each Latin city had the same public or private law.

[92] Gell. iv. 4; cf. Varro, *LL* vi. 71; M. Kaser, *Röm. Privatrecht*[2], 1971, 75 f.

[93] Livy ix. 20. 10: 'nec arma modo sed iura etiam Romana late pollebant' has typical value; on the circumstances cf. *RC*[2] 80 ff. On the extension of Roman legislation in private law to 'Italia' (e.g. Gaius iii. 121 ff.) see Galsterer 37 ff.

law of Bantia is the only document of its kind. But it is plausible to suppose that at least in cities more accessible to Roman influence the extent of borrowing would not be less than at Bantia. This is strongly suggested by what is known of the constitution of Italia itself with its senate, consuls, and praetors. Even the Samnite Papius Mutilus calls himself *embratur* or *imperator* in the manner of a victorious Roman general.[94]

III. THE VALUE OF CITIZENSHIP TO THE ITALIANS

The demand of the Italian peoples for the Roman citizenship and their readiness when that was denied to merge in the new state of Italia imply that they were not concerned to preserve their individual statehood. Hence it is unlikely that the infractions, real or supposed, of their internal self-government by the senate constituted an important source of their discontent.[95] As municipalities either of Rome or Italia the cities would have less and not more autonomy at home. The surrender of local rights was no doubt acceptable, as a necessary price to be paid for the preservation of peace in Italy and empire abroad, and for a share in the control of that empire. There was no independence to be surrendered: that belonged to the dim past; outside Etruria[96] it had probably left no coherent native record.

For two centuries Rome had decided questions of foreign policy and fixed the military contributions they had to make. These contributions must have involved them in a financial burden.[97] Cicero recalls that the allies and Latins used to meet the costs of pay and food for their soldiers (II *Verr.* v. 60), and though Polybius says that no deduction was made from the pay of allied soldiers, as it was from that of legionaries, to cover the cost of grain (vi. 39. 15), this may mean not that it was borne by the Roman treasury but that the allies were paid proportionately less; he also mentions that the allied cities had to appoint a paymaster for their troops (vi. 21. 5). Certainly the Latins provided *stipendium* in the Hannibalic war and some complained of it as a heavy burden (Livy xxvi. 9, xxix. 15. 9), no doubt because the allies, like the Romans themselves (xxiii. 31; xxiv. 11), were paying a direct tax on property at much more than the usual rates. Indemnities, booty, and provincial revenues enabled Rome in 186 to repay the

[94] Sydenham 640 f.

[95] Polyb. vi. 13. 4 f. with Walbank ad loc.; cf. Badian, *FC* ch. vi; Salmon, 311 ff.; J. Goehler, *Rom u. Italien*, 1939, 53 ff. Rome's interventions were no doubt almost all designed to preserve general tranquillity, but though Rome was prepared to suppress any local movements subversive of the authority of the local *principes* (Harris 1971, 129 ff.), there was no continuous interference in local administration.

[96] Harris, 1971, ch. i.   [97] C. Nicolet, *PBSR* 1978, 1 ff.

surtaxes on citizens levied in the past twenty-five years (xxxix. 7. 5), and from 167 to remit *tributum* altogether (Plut. *Aem. Paull.* 38); the allies had no such resources enabling them to act in the same way. The grant of citizenship would have been a substantial financial relief to the Italian cities; if they lost the right of taxing themselves, they were also freed of the need to do so. It is true that we hear nothing of any financial grievance: but we hear so little of the Italians' case that this argument from silence is not decisive.

How much autonomy could the Latins and Italian allies hope to retain on incorporation in the Roman state, and how much did they actually preserve? It was obvious that the Roman state, with its limited apparatus of magistrates, was unable to administer local affairs throughout Italy in any highly centralized fashion. The existing *municipia* and colonies had certainly enjoyed for the most part a considerable degree of local self-government. It is true that Capua, after her revolt to Hannibal, had lost her own magistrates and that her former territory was administered by Roman officials, though even here some sort of parochial local government seems to have sprung up (n. 26). Anagnia too was deprived of self-government on incorporation, but these measures were surely exceptional, and at Anagnia temporary. There is nothing to show that the *praefecti iuri dicundo* sent out to the parts of Italy where citizens were already extensively scattered, to make justice more easily accessible to them, had any general administrative functions within Roman colonies or *municipia*, which, unlike Capua, kept their own magistrates. The survival into the Principate of dictators, aediles, and *octoviri* as the chief magistrates in places which were *municipia* before 90 is in my view best explained by the hypothesis that Rome had let them keep the magistracies that they had had in the period of independence. This indicates that Rome had interfered little in their internal organization when they were incorporated in the Roman state. The Roman colonies too had come to enjoy a considerable degree of local self-government.[98] Given the extent to which the senate already intervened in the affairs of allied cities (n. 95), their *principes* could reasonably feel that if their cities became *municipia* their local powers would not be sensibly diminished. They could have seen that an existing *municipium* like Arpinum, where in this very period proposals for a local ballot law engendered a keen controversy,[99] did not lack its own lively political activity.

If they made calculations of this kind, they were not wholly disappointed. It is true that in most of the newly enfranchised communes the magistrates henceforth have a uniform titulature, which

---

[98] See endnote 4.   [99] Cic. *de leg.* iii. 36.

was presumably imposed by Rome, and that Roman legislation prescribed qualifications for membership of local councils and tenure of local offices, and defined their rights and duties in some detail; in the assemblies the Roman system of group voting probably became universal. In effect power was reserved to men of property; there was nothing new in this, and naturally it suited the *principes*.[100] It was not until the second century AD that the central government attempted any close supervision of municipal administration; in the Republic the necessary bureaucracy did not exist. Pompeii was surely not the only place in which local elections were vigorously contested.[101] Rome was so far from requiring rigid uniformity that the public use of Greek was still tolerated at Naples.[102]

The chief magistrates had powers of jurisdiction. In Transpadane Gaul after its enfranchisement in 49 certain types of civil case were reserved to the courts at Rome; and we may assume that there were similar regulations affecting those communes which received the citizenship after the Social war (n. 100); we may recall, however, that in classical Roman law any recognized court, whatever the limits on its competence, could decide civil suits beyond those limits, by agreement between the parties (*Dig.* v. 1. 1). Justice did not then become more remote and inaccessible because the Italians had obtained the Roman right. Moreover, the *praefecti iuri dicundo*, once sent out to various parts of Italy, disappeared; the local courts were then in the charge of magistrates who had been chosen locally.[103] The extent of municipal criminal jurisdiction is disputed: I cannot believe that it embraced capital indictments (ch. 4 endnote 1).

How far were the new citizens bound by the rules of Roman law? Criminal law was mainly defined by Sullan and post-Sullan statutes which were clearly applicable to them. It is often held that the *municipia* were entitled to retain their own customs and laws, at any rate in the private sphere. Gellius (xvi. 13), apparently summarizing or elaborating a speech of the emperor Hadrian (ibid. 4), which he perhaps misunderstood, thought that at one time *municipes* were not bound by any Roman *lex* unless their own people had adopted it ('fundus factus est'), but he adds that in his own day the rights of *municipia* had fallen into oblivion and were no longer in use (ibid. 6, 9). Though we may doubt if the antiquarian writers on whom Hadrian .and Gellius presumably relied had any accurate information on the position of the

---

[100] See endnote 5.   [101] *ILS* 6398 ff.; cf. ch. 8 n. 127.
[102] Sartori (n. 89) 31 ff., see e.g. *IGRR* i. 429 ff.
[103] The annually elected *praefecti Capuam Cumas* probably had no duties long before the office was abolished in 13 BC (Dio liv. 26). No doubt the praetors ceased to appoint the other prefects, first in one place, then in another, as they were no longer required. The continued designation of some places as *praefecturae* meant only that they had once been the seats of prefects; see endnote 4.

earliest *municipia*, generally composed of *cives sine suffragio*, it may well be thought that at first Rome had no motive and no means for imposing on them her own *ius civile*, especially in days when they were hardly familiar with Latin, a language they might officially adopt at a much later stage (n. 25), given that legal procedure in the archaic Roman law often required the nicest linguistic precision. However, as we have already seen, there are hints (and we could expect no more) of the reception of Roman law even among the Italian allies before 90; this development was the more natural since Roman law itself was being adapted, as local systems probably were not, to suit the conditions of a more complex society, and was becoming a more convenient instrument for Italians in general. Both Latin and allied communes had become 'fundi' of various Roman statutes in the second century: Cicero, who tells us this, does not mention that *municipia* took the same course (*Balb.* 20 ff.). It may be that their right to follow their own laws and customs was already defunct. It is at any rate certain that the law to be administered in Transpadane courts is Roman, whether cases are to be decided at Rome or locally, and that the juristic writers never allude to any divergence between Roman and municipal law. Moreover, Gellius himself notes that the peculiar Latin law on *sponsalia* ceased to be valid after the Latins became Roman under the *lex Iulia* (n. 92). It is everywhere assumed in the law-books that all citizens must conform to the *ius civile*. One exception was admitted under the Principate; in making a will a citizen was bound to institute an heir who would succeed to both the debts and assets of his estate (and to use various prescribed formulae both for this purpose and for leaving bequests): the will was invalid in default of an heir. But serving soldiers, and no other citizens, were exempt from these strict requirements. Moreover, if a foreigner received the citizenship individually, his kinship relations in the absence of any special provision were automatically dissolved; hence they lost any right of intestate succession, and if still foreigners, they could not receive under a will. Nor can any citizen contract a marriage with a foreigner unless *conubium* exists; the grant of citizenship *may* be accompanied by that of *conubium* with foreign women. Under the Flavian charters that governed the Spanish cities which had newly received the status of Latin *municipia* not only are the public institutions modelled on those of Rome, but private relationships are entirely regulated by the Roman civil law, which the local courts are within prescribed limits empowered to administer; for example, Latins as well as Romans can possess *patria potestas*, which Gaius (i. 55) thought peculiar to Roman law. This makes it still harder to believe that in Hadrian's day there were any *municipia* with the Roman right that still retained their earlier legal

institutions. It seems to me overwhelmingly probable that in principle
the reception of Roman law in Italy itself went back to the enfranchisement of Latin or allied communes, and in Cisalpine Gaul to the
conferment of Latinity by the *lex Pompeia*.[104] It was surely typical that
disputes arising over possession of land *in agro Tarquiniensi*, formerly
allied territory, in which the Volaterran Caecina was involved, were
settled under Roman law—in this case indeed by a court at Rome;
both parties obtained the advice of Roman jurists.[105]

A *municipium* was part of the Roman *civitas*, a term which in this sense
means the collectivity of (Roman) *cives*; no question of the duality of
citizenship arose. In Cicero's time it was the general rule (which some
men forgot) that a Roman could not be a citizen of any other *civitas*,
and therefore not even of one which was in fact subject to Roman
control (n. 5). From the time of the triumvirate this rule was so far
abrogated that a foreigner who obtained the Roman franchise could
still be required to fulfil his old civic obligations to the city of his origin.
In my view this did not mean that he was not in all other respects as
subject to Roman law as an old Roman. In any event the legal status of
such persons has no bearing on the question of whether whole
communities could retain the private law they had previously enjoyed
after incorporation.[106]

It was not necessarily a hardship if they could not. We cannot be
sure that Roman law was very strange and unfamiliar in the Italy of
the Social war. In so far as it was administered by local courts, it may
at first have been applied with little rigour, not least because the courts
understood it imperfectly. It was of clear economic and social advantage
that the same system should operate throughout the peninsula, and all
the more because it had been developed, and was continually being
adjusted, to meet the needs of changing economic and social conditions
as perceived by the propertied class, to which the Italian *principes*
belonged.

[104] Military wills; *Dig.* xxix. 1. 1. Kinship relations; Pliny, *Paneg.* 37 f. (concerned with
consequential tax liability); cf. Gaius i. 93–5. In Latin cities the *patria potestas* and patronal rights
of those who secured Roman citizenship *per honores* were therefore specifically conserved, *FIRA* i².
23 (on which cf. *RC*² 378), xxii f. Ibid. xxix concerns *tutoris datio*. It is obvious that in Latin cities
there must have been both *commercium* and *conubium* between those who had already got Roman
citizenship and their fellow-*municipes*. Flavian charters: See ch. 4 endnote 2. The most common
examples of *conubium cum peregrinis mulieribus* granted along with citizenship are in the *diplomata* for
auxiliary soldiers.

[105] The case is fully discussed by B. W. Frier, *The Rise of the Roman Jurists*, 1985, esp. ch. 1.

[106] On the questions of dual citizenship and the applicability of *ius civile* to new citizens see for a
summary treatment Jolowicz-Nicholas 71 ff, 469 ff.; cf. *RC*² 295 ff. I concur in the traditional view
that it did apply, even though in practice and eventually by official recognition the *ius civile* was itself
modified by the partial adoption of institutions prevalent in the east. At all times of course Romans
could make contracts with foreigners enforceable in forms other than those admitted in Roman law.
Romans resident in a privileged city might be required to obey local laws (*SIG*³ 785).

They could then reckon that enfranchisement would not substantially reduce their local control, and they could also think that any loss of autonomy was well purchased by a share in political power at the centre. It seems clear to me that the demand for citizenship was essentially a demand for the vote and even for the chance to hold office at Rome. The importance of the vote is shown by the events of 88 and 87. The attempt of the senate to circumscribe the voting strength of the new citizens (at this time those who had remained faithful to Rome in 90) by confining them to eight or ten tribes (App. i. 49) and thus, as Velleius says (ii. 20), preserving the superior rank (*dignitas*) of the old citizens led to the agitations first of Sulpicius and then of Cinna. Appian reiterates that each enjoyed the support of the new citizens, whom they proposed to enrol in all the thirty-five tribes. Sulpicius carried his measure by force, and Sulla then marched on Rome. No doubt he acted because of the transfer to Marius of his command in the east: he could justify his coup only on the ground that all the Sulpician laws had been carried by violence (Cic. *Phil.* viii. 7). All were annulled (App. i. 59). The grievance of the new citizens was unremedied. In 87 Cinna took up their cause: according to Velleius (ii. 20), 'ingentem totius Italiae frequentiam in urbem acciverat'; the forum was choked with bodies and ran with blood (Cic. *Cat.* iii. 24) because of the dispute on the voting rights of the new citizens (*Phil.* viii. 7). All this was not just 'a scuffle over the tribal distribution of the new voters' (RC^2 135). Cinna, expelled from the city, reinstated himself in a great civil war for which he won support at first from the new citizens in Latium and then more widely (App. i. 65 f.; Vell. ii. 20); Marius found recruits among the Etruscans, who were no less anxious for full voting rights (App. i. 67. 306). In 83 Sulla and Lucius Scipio negotiated 'de auctoritate senatus, de suffragiis populi, de iure civitatis' (*Phil.* xi. 27); later, according to Appian (i. 86. 388), Sulla attempted to treat with Scipio's colleague Norbanus, perhaps, so Appian conjectures, from fear that the greater part of Italy would rally to his adversaries. I do not see how Sherwin-White is entitled to assert (RC^2 144 n. 13) that they were only discussing 'the powers of the popular assemblies at Rome', especially as Appian attests that the Marians relied on the new citizens (i. 76. 348) and had initially most support in Italy (86. 388, 393). The new citizens could fear that Cinna's legislation would be annulled by Sulla, just like that of Sulpicius, and he was only able to recruit on a greater equality when he had promised to respect their rights.[107] All this shows that the

---

[107] Sulla's promises: App. i. 77. 352 (perhaps put too early; cf. *Per.* Livy lxxxvi). Supporters are attested at: Brundisium, 79. 364; Suessa, 85. 385; among the Marsi (Plut. *Cr.* 6); more generally in App. i. 86. 393. We do not know whether Pompey's recruits in Picenum, a region of early Roman settlement, were old or new citizens.

Italians were content with nothing short of full political equality or 'liberty' (pp. 337 ff.).

It may be objected that they could have had little interest in the vote because most of them were too distant from Rome to exercise it often, if at all. But even if we ignore the allied communities which were nearer to Rome than many previously existing Roman townships, some indeed like Tibur very close, this is no more than a half-truth. The peasant in allied Samnium or Lucania could no more make frequent visits to Rome than the peasant in Roman Picenum, but the *boni et locupletes* could and did. 'Routine' politics revolved round the elections to the higher magistracies, and in these elections, conducted in a timocratic assembly, the votes of such men—'homines honesti atque in suis vicinitatibus et municipiis gratiosi'—counted heavily. There was nothing very exceptional in the great concourse from all Italy that gathered for the elections and games as well as for the census in 70 (I *Verr.* 54). We have numerous references to the importance of municipal votes in the Ciceronian age, even to the votes of towns in remote Cisalpina.[108] Cicero refers to the value of the support he enjoyed from Etruscan Volaterrae and Campanian Atella (*Fam.* xiii. 4. 1, 7. 4). On extraordinary occasions at least even soldiers exercised influence,[109] and the local plebs might turn up to vote.[110]

Our sources insist on the allies' demand for justice and equality. 'Petebant eam civitatem cuius imperium armis tuebantur' says Velleius (ii. 15); latterly they had contributed perhaps twice as many soldiers to Rome's armies as the citizens (n. 109); it was by their efforts that Rome had won her empire, and yet the empire permitted the Romans 'homines eiusdem et gentis et sanguinis fastidire'. This sounds like a relic of allied propaganda;[111] it illustrates at once the sense of kinship with the Romans that made the allies wish to be Romans themselves and the craving for rank and dignity that was always so strong in Roman society. The resentment of Italians at being unjustly treated as inferiors may be thought a merely emotional motive for their conduct, but men are often guided by passion, and this explanation of Italian discontent deserves the strongest emphasis. But this should not disguise the fact that political rights could bring solid benefits. To hold

---

[108] Cic. *Mur.* 47; even the votes of the ex-magistrates of the Latin communes in Cisalpina were important for electoral success; cf. *Att.* i. 1. 2; Hirtius, *BG* viii. 50. 1, 51. 2 (of course most of the communes south of Po and a few to the north were already Roman). Cf. pp. 428 ff.; Taylor, 1949, 57 ff.; 1960, 292.

[109] Cic. *Mur.* 37 f.; cf. p. 429. Probably more than half the legionaries were drawn from the former Latins and allies; it is unlikely that enfranchisement altered their proportion in Roman armies (*IM*, App. 26, Ilari 148 ff.).

[110] Cic. *Planc.* 21 (communes fairly near Rome).

[111] Cf. Diod. xxxvii. 22; App. i. 39. 176; *ad Her.* iv. 13. Livy viii. 4 f. perhaps retrojects the ideas of 90 to the time of the Latin war in 340.

that the Italians desired full citizenship is not therefore, as Sherwin-White suggests (RC^2 143), to make their motive 'narrowly political'.

The vote itself was a marketable commodity in times of electoral corruption, and apart from outright bribes, the richer citizens, whose suffrages counted for most in the centuriate assembly, could doubtless barter their support in return for all sorts of favours. We must always bear in mind that the Italian communities were governed oligarchically, and that the interests of the local *principes*, who could expect their peoples to follow their lead, were of primary importance. Many of them could expect equestrian status along with the franchise, and to share in the rights of jurisdiction and social dignity which belonged to the order. At trials the testimony of such men would now carry increased weight.[112] Above all everyone liable to taxes, needed to pay for the cost of allied contingents in the Roman army, would obtain relief, once Italians were entitled to serve in the legions at the expense of the Roman treasury.

Gabba argued that *negotiatores* from the allied communities, who were numerous among the Italian businessmen overseas, desired the citizenship as the instrument by which they could press Rome into a more expansionist foreign policy required by their commercial interests. The underlying premiss that political rights were indispensable for influence on Rome's policy seems to me correct. But its particular application is doubtful. In my judgement Gabba overrates the importance of trade in the predominantly agrarian economy of ancient Italy. Certainly he has not established the necessary correlation between the rebel leaders and the business interests concerned. Moreover, in the past Rome had been ready enough to afford personal protection to Italian no less than Roman businessmen in foreign parts, while neither before nor after the enfranchisement of Italy does it appear that commercial interests in any other sense promoted Roman aggrandisement, nor even that businessmen sought to urge expansion on a reluctant senate.[113] It is perhaps more plausible to suppose that Italians hoped as citizens to have a share in lucrative public contracts, though in fact there are only two instances of first-century publicans originating from among the new citizens.[114]

---

[112] Cic. *Cluent.* 197 f., where the *principes* of formerly rebel peoples are mentioned with as much respect as those of communes that were Roman before 90 in *Planc.* 21 f.

[113] Gabba, 1973, ch. IV = 1976, ch. III. See the reviews of his earlier version by J. P. V. D. Balsdon, *Gnomon* 1954, 343 f., and A. N. Sherwin-White, *JRS* 1955, 168 f. (cf. RC^2 142), and ch. 3, III–IV.

[114] Nicolet, 1966, 344 ff., lists known publicans, among whom note P. Ventidius Bassus, but omits P. Caesius (ib. 420). None of the *negotiatores* he lists (376 ff.) are known to come from the enfranchised peoples. In both lists there are some non-Latin *nomina*, but as such *nomina* can be borne by pre-90 *cives* they do not determine origins.

Carcopino supposed that the rebels were inspired by alarm for their holdings of public land.[115] If this were true, it would be odd that Drusus should have hoped to win Italian support by the franchise at the same time as he redistributed the public land, or that the insurrection should have broken out just when his laws had been annulled and the danger to their holdings had receded. Still, it is beyond question that the interests of Italian landholders were better protected when Roman politicians had to take account of their votes. Hence the concern Cicero displayed for the lands of the Volaterrans and Arretines (*Att.* i. 19. 4, *Fam* xiii. 14).

It is likely that the military levy caused as much hardship and discontent among the Italians as we know that it did among the Romans (n. 12)—more, perhaps, if the Italians had to bear an unfair incidence of the military burden (n. 109). Landowners were hardly less affected than small farmers if conscription took their tenants or labourers from the plough. Observe then the practice of Murena in 64: 'habuit proficiscens dilectum in Umbria; dedit ei facultatem res publica liberalitatis, qua usus multas sibi tribus quae municipiis Umbriae conficiuntur adiunxit' (*Mur.* 42). Many tribes: the Umbrians must have controlled Clustumina and been important in at least two others.[116]

Some lay the greatest stress on the arbitrary and oppressive behaviour of Roman magistrates as an allied grievance, and the value of the *ius provocationis* as a protection from it. I have already pointed out that in the 90s there is no suggestion that the grant of this right alone was any longer proposed as a compromise settlement of allied claims. This is not to say the Italian *principes* made no appeal to this grievance. The harsh threats of Servilius at Asculum actually sparked off the revolt, and a Latin there saved himself from death by pleading that he too was subject to the rods.[117] But what was the value of the *ius provocationis*? A magistrate could always override it, if he was not impeded by another magistrate with equal or greater power, or deterred by the fear that he would be prosecuted and condemned after demitting office. It was far more probable that these checks would operate effectively to protect a man whose kin and fellow-townsmen had votes which a Roman politician might need (n. 8). In the Jugurthine war Turpilius, a citizen of Latin stock, was summarily put to death in a manner unusual for officers precisely, we may suspect, because he did not count politically,

[115] *Hist. Rom.* ii. 372 ff.

[116] Taylor, 1960, 271 ff. (Lemonia and Pupinia); cf. Harris, 1971, 240 ff. Most of the first 17 rural tribes had probably had few citizens on their rolls before 90, and thereafter newly enfranchised communes fairly near Rome may have a very strong influence in some of them, e.g. Tibur in Camilia, Sora in Romilia, and a few ex-Latin communes in Papiria. But cf. n. 120.

[117] Diod. xxxvii. 13. 2 (cf. App. *BC* i. 38. 173).

his fellow-townsmen being unenfranchised.[118] In the last resort, as Romans found under the imperial autocracy, the guarantee of personal and private rights is a share in political power.

All these considerations of course had been valid in the time of Gaius Gracchus when the Italians seem to have been neither so united nor so fervent in the demand for enfranchisement. We must ask what had changed their attitude. We may suppose that the question of enfranchisement, once raised, had to be answered in the end; that, as years passed, the Italians became more conscious of their unity in sentiment, more attracted by the benefits of the citizenship, more convinced that they had little to lose by surrendering part of the attenuated autonomy still left to them. Perhaps we should not expect less than a generation to be required before old prejudices were surmounted. But this process of rethinking was probably accelerated by the Cimbric war. In 91 the allies emphasized how much Rome was indebted for her empire to Italian arms. But it could best be seen just how indispensable the Italians were, when, for the first time since Hannibal Rome was threatened by a crisis that seemed to imperil her very survival, when it became necessary to forbid all able-bodied men to leave Italy.[119] Marius' readiness to reward some Italians for their valour in the war must have looked like recognition of what was due to all (Appendix I).

In this crisis Marius was the saviour of the state and six times consul. No Roman had ever achieved such a distinction in so short a space of years; and Marius was not only a new man, but he came from Arpinum, a town that had received the full citizenship in 188. And in his generation he was not the only new man to rise to or aim at the highest honours at Rome. Cn. Mallius Maximus (*cos.* 105), C. Flavius Fimbria (*cos.* 104), C. Coelius Caldus, (*cos.* 94). and C. Billienus, who narrowly missed the consulship, were of the same class, and very probably *municipales.* Earlier still there had been the Etruscan, M. Perperna (*cos.* 130). If the Italian *principes* could hardly expect to vie with Marius in virtue and fortune, they might more reasonably hope that they or their descendants could emulate such lesser men, if only their communities had equal privileges with Arpinum. Their communities: for it was an advantage to them not only to have the citizenship for themselves as individuals but to be able to call on the support of their townsmen. Even the plebs of a municipality would come to vote for a 'favourite son'. When the young Plancius stood for the aedileship the whole people of Atina was in Rome to support him in the tribal assembly, not to speak of the *equites* and *tribuni aerarii* with which that prosperous prefecture abounded. 'Non modo enim tribum Teretinam,

---

[118] Sall. *BJ* 69. 4; App. *Num.* fr. 3.
[119] Licin. 14 F. Yet Rome seems to have deployed only 6 legions against the Cimbri (*IM* 431).

sed dignitatem, sed oculorum coniectum, sed solidam et robustam et adsiduam frequentiam praebuerunt' (*Planc.* 21). The neighbouring communities too were there in force, Allifae, Casinum, and Venafrum, likewise registered in Teretina, Arpinum the largest community near Rome enrolled in Cornelia, Sora, which dominated Romilia.[120] It so happens that most of these communities, though not Sora, already had the citizenship in 91; but can anyone doubt that the newer *municipia* manifested the same kind of enthusiasm when one of their own *principes* sought office at Rome? The Paelignians proudly recorded that Q. Varius Geminus was the first among them to hold senatorial offices (*ILS* 932).

He lived under Augustus. A long interval had passed since the Social war, though no longer than that between the full enfranchisement of Arpinum and the rise of Marius. Many Italian peoples saw their 'favourite sons' advance earlier than the Paelignians. Gabba did good service in assembling the evidence for their presence in the post-Sullan senate.[121] From Caesar onwards they flooded the *curia*. It may seem risky to argue from the effects of enfranchisement to the motives for which it was sought; but only a little imagination is needed to see that these effects could already be hoped for in the age of Marius, and that what the Italian *principes* desired was not only the *ius suffragii* but the opportunity to hold office in Rome.

---

[120] Taylor, 1960, assigned only one other commune to this tribe, Ateste, not enfranchised till 49. But very many communes cannot be assigned to any tribe, or only by hazardous conjectures; cf. Badian, *JRS* 1962, 208.

[121] See endnote 6.

APPENDIXES

I. Roman Politics and the Italian Question

Marius is often held to have been well-disposed to the Italians. This view rests on flimsy evidence. His illegal grant of citizenship to a troop of horse from Camerinum (Val. Max. v. 2. 8; Cic. *Balb.* 46. etc.) may have been a merely impetuous act. Appian (i. 29. 132) alleges that the *Italiotai* were the chief beneficiaries under Saturninus' agrarian or colonial legislation, but this text is isolated, and Gelzer's view (*Kl. Schr.* ii. 75, 91 ff, iii. 288 f.) that he often misunderstood references in his sources to Roman *agrestes* is particularly plausible in this instance (*contra* Gabba ad loc.), since elsewhere (29. 132, 30. 134 and 139) he speaks only of *agrestes* backing Saturninus (cf. Galsterer, cited in n. 60). There would be some confirmation for Appian's view, if in *Balb.* 48 we amend 'ternos' to 'trecenos' and suppose that Saturninus authorized Marius to enfranchise 300 Italians in each of the colonies to be founded; otherwise the number is trivial and the authority given perhaps not unprecedented (cf. Cic. *Brut.* 79). But there is no compelling reason for the emendation. The colonies were never founded, but at least one Latin, Matrinius, was enfranchised by Marius under Saturninus' law. Naturally Marius defended him when his title to the franchise was impugned under the *lex Licinia Mucia* of 95. This was no doubt a test case for all Italians who purported to have received the citizenship under Saturninus' law, but L. Crassus too appeared for the defence (*Balb.* 48); we must infer that he, as joint author of the law of 95, had been concerned to annul mere usurpations of the franchise and not the grants Marius had made. Badian conjectures (1958, 211 f.) that infiltration had been favoured by the censors of 97, but the parallel of the expulsions in 187, 177, and 172 suggests that it was a gradual process, and Badian's further supposition that the censors of 97 were Marius' men rests in part on debatable prosopographic inferences and still more on a general conception of Roman politics which I give reasons for rejecting in Chapter 9 (see especially pp. 459 ff.).

But though it follows that we have no grounds for asserting that Marius was favourable to Italian claims, equally we do not know that he was adverse to them. His political attitude in the year of Drusus' tribunate is not on record. Though he may well have delighted in the condemnation of Rutilius, which prompted Drusus to propose his judiciary reform, he had been on good terms with some of Drusus' backers, notably L. Crassus and P. Sulpicius Rufus (p. 460). His Fabian strategy in 90 (Plut. *Mar.* 33) and negotiations with Poppaedius (p. 103) may suggest that at that time he favoured concessions to the rebels. In 88–87 he was leagued with Sulpicius and then with Cinna, both of whom pressed for the grant of equal voting rights to the new citizens. Of course it may be that in 88 it was only the eastern command that he cared for, and in 87 he naturally joined Cinna to effect his own restoration in the state. His attitude to the allies may always have been decided by the expediency of the moment.

No one doubts that Drusus, advised by L. Crassus and M. Scaurus, acted in 91 in the interests of the senate. Diodorus (xxxvii. 2. 2 with some support from *Per*. Livy lxxi) makes the promises to the allies come from the senate. Sherwin-White's suggestion (*RC²* 148) that Diodorus (or rather Posidonius?) was simply drawing an inference from Drusus' role as *patronus senatus* can hardly be refuted. But it seems to me implausible that Crassus at least was not fully committed to his programme (as scholars cited by Harris, 1971, 228, have held), and Crassus dominated the senate till his death in September (*de orat.* iii. 1–8). Hostile to allied claims in 122 and 95, the optimates had surely changed their policy. They perhaps needed the help of the Italians to carry the judiciary bill by force (if necessary) even before they had the vote, or hoped that, once enfranchised, they would vote against its repeal. But the success of Fannius' demagogy in 122 and the attitude of the old citizens to the voting rights of the new in 88–87 show that the allied cause was not popular, and the Equites could exploit this unpopularity to the detriment of the judiciary bill; I therefore believe that the majority of the senate must have had other reasons for favouring enfranchisement, that they must have held that allied discontent could only be allayed by concessions, if the disasters allegedly foreseen by L. Crassus and others (*de orat.* i. 26) were to be averted. 'Mors Drusi *iam pridem* tumescens bellum excitavit Italicum' (Vell. ii. 15).

With the death of Crassus Drusus' influence crumbled. His laws were repealed; officers were sent to keep order in Italy; the allied ultimatum was rejected; later (n. 19), to establish a 'consensus bonorum' in the crisis, the *quaestio Variana* (by which the Equites vented their animosity on supporters of the judiciary bill under the pretence that they had stirred up the war) was authorized by the senate to sit when all other courts had been suspended (Ascon. 73 C.; Cic. *Brut.* 304). The change in the senate's attitude demands explanation. We may perhaps find it in the increasing violence, or threats or rumours of violence, among the allies as the year proceeded; we do not know what truth there was behind the stories of the oath taken to Drusus, of Poppaedius Silo's march on Rome (Diod. xxxvii. 11, 13), or of the plot to kill the consuls at the Latin festival (*de vir. ill.* 66). That festival was normally held in early summer (*Inscr. Ital.* xiii. i. 143 ff.), but may have been iterated later in a year full of evil omens (Obsequens 54). It was an old Roman tradition not to yield to coercion, and probably the more pressure the allies applied, the more they alienated the sympathy of men who had once been ready to follow Drusus and Crassus.

II. The Enfranchisement of the Allies

The *lex Iulia* offered citizenship to all the Latins (Gell. iv. 4. 3), presumably excepting Venusia which was in revolt, or rather to Latins and allies (Cic. *Balb.* 21), sc. to those who were loyal (App. i. 49. 212 ff.), including those who had laid down their arms (p. 108). It also authorized commanders to enfranchise soldiers 'virtutis causa' (*ILS* 8888); otherwise it made grants only to communities.

Appian, without naming the measure, clearly describes it and dates it between the major operations of 90 and 89, that is to say in the winter (cf. i. 50. 217). This is plausible in itself; the consul L. Iulius Caesar (whom Appian wrongly calls Sextus) had been unable to return for the consular elections (which in 105 were held after the news of Arausio, fought on 6 October, had reached Rome; cf. Sall. *BJ* 114 with Licin. 11 F.) at the normal time (App. i. 44. 196). Presumably, then, he was not free to move his law until the very end of the year. Moreover, Appian couples the law with the conscription of freedmen, which is mentioned in *Per.* Livy lxxiv. The next sentence in the *Perioche* refers to fighting against the Umbrians and Etruscans, and Appian too at least recognizes a disloyal movement in Umbria and Etruria at the time the law was passed. Livy followed a fairly strict chronological order (n. 31), and the events of 89 seem to begin in the same *Perioche* immediately afterwards with a reference to Asian affairs. G. Niccolini (*Rend. Acc. Linc.* 1946, 110 ff.) put the *lex Iulia* early in 90, but he confused Lucius with Sextus Caesar (misled by App. 48. 210) and assumed that the consul was not in Rome after June 90; who then conducted the elections?

Sisenna iv. fr. 120 reads: 'milites, ut lex Calpurnia concesserat, virtutis ergo civitatis donari'. Since Pompeius Strabo granted citizenship to Spanish troopers 'virtutis causa' under the lex Iulia (*ILS* 8888) in November of a year which must surely be 89 rather than 90 (he is styled *imperator* and this implies that he had an independent command, and was not legate as in 90; cf. further C. Cichorius, *Rom. St.* 181 ff.), it seems to follow that the *lex Iulia* had superseded the *lex Calpurnia*, which must belong to 90 (on the assumption that it is not before the war). Presumably it was under the latter law that Caesar himself, as consul commanding in the field, was empowered to enfranchise a Cretan (Diod. xxxvii. 18). An objection arises. Sisenna seems to have alluded to an event of 89 as early as his third book, in fr. 44: 'Lucium Memmium, socerum Gai Scriboni, tribunum plebis, quem M. Livi consiliarium fuisse callebant, et tunc Curionis oratorem . . .'; for the date cf. MRR ii. 38 n. 4. However, fr. 120 (cf. the pluperfect 'concesserat') may well relate to an earlier incident inserted parenthetically. Moreover, there is another possible reference to the author of the *lex Calpurnia* in the third book (fr. 17): 'Lucius Calpurnius Piso ex senati consulto duas novas tribus . . .'. It was in 90 that this Calpurnius moved, though he need not have passed, some measure to enrol new citizens in two new tribes. (Whether these two tribes along with the eight mentioned by Velleius ii. 20 make up the ten tribes in which the new citizens were to be enrolled after the *lex Iulia*, according to Appian 49. 214, must be left uncertain.) It would seem that some measure of enfranchisement preceded the *lex Iulia*. We may think that Italian individuals who took the Roman side in defiance of their own communities, like Minatius Magius and his followers (Vell. ii. 16), may have been offered the citizenship even earlier than the loyal communities.

Probably the *lex Iulia* itself restricted the new citizens to eight or ten tribes. L. R. Taylor denies that this restriction applied to the Latin colonies (1960, 107 ff.). She supposes that tribes had been assigned to each Latin colony, as probably later to the Latin communities in Transpadana, in which ex-magistrates who had obtained the citizenship in virtue of holding office were to be enrolled, and that when the Latins in general were enfranchised in 90, the people of each colony were to be registered respectively in the tribes in which such ex-magistrates were registered already. The Latin colonies were certainly distributed in the end among 16 tribes. This, however, tells us nothing about the way in which they may have been distributed in 90. Supposing Taylor to be mistaken, they would originally have been assigned to newly created tribes, which were abolished in the 80s; and no trace of this original registration could survive. Her view is based (a) on the assumption that Rome could not have treated the Latin colonies so unfairly; (b) on the denial that the Latins are named among the new citizens who were discontented with their registration. The first contention can carry little weight. On any view the *lex Iulia* provided primarily for the enfranchisement of loyal allies: so it was they who were unfairly treated at *this* time. It is another matter if the *later* distribution of all the new citizens, including ex-rebels, among all the tribes was so made as to discriminate in favour of Latins and other loyalists against ex-rebels (cf. Harris, 1971, 236 ff.). Moreover, if in 90 the Latins were already distributed in all the tribes, it would be odd if the not very numerous other loyalists were assigned to as many as eight or ten new tribes. That would actually have favoured them. The second contention compels her to draw a distinction between the Latin colonies and such older Latin towns as Tibur and Praeneste, which certainly adhered to Cinna (App. i. 65. 294). Such a distinction, she thinks, already existed in that the grant of citizenship to ex-magistrates had not applied to them. For this view she deploys (107 n. 19) two arguments: (a) Asconius 3 C. says that before 90 the right had belonged to the Latin colonies. But the colonies were so much the larger element in the *nomen Latinum* that Asconius might well have ignored Tibur etc. (b) 'Two citizens of Tibur, who from Cicero's description (*Balb.* 53 f.) should have been in the office-holding class not long before the Social War, were not citizens, for they acquired citizenship through successful prosecutions.' But prosecutors were often young men, and these Tiburtines need not have been ex-magistrates themselves, nor sons of men who had held a magistracy after the *ius civitatis per magistratum adipiscendae* had been devised. The text she cites refers to 'Latinis, id est foederatis'; this does not of course mean that *all* Latin communities had *a foedus* with Rome (the colonies owed their status to their foundation charters), but shows that some had: viz Tibur and the other members of the old Latin league, which had not been incorporated in the Roman state on its dissolution in 338, and which were now bound to Rome by individual treaties; though *foederati*, they were also Latins. Hernican towns like Ferentinum, which were not absorbed by Rome when the Hernican league too was dissolved, also counted as Latin by assimilation (cf. Livy xxxiv. 42; Mommsen, *StR*. iii. 622): so *a fortiori* did Tibur etc. Had this not been the case, the *nomen Latinum* would have been first obliterated in 338 and then artificially revived with the foundations of Latin colonies. (See also Brunt, *IM* 47 f., 528, *CQ* 1982, 144; Galsterer 1976, 87 f.)

On the *lex Plautia Papiria*, probably late in 89, see pp. 107 f.

After recording the campaigns of 89, Appian i. 53. 231 says that the war raged until all the Italians got the citizenship except for the Samnites and Lucanians, who apparently obtained it later. This might suggest that the enfranchisement of the rebels had in the main already been completed by the end of 89. Similarly Velleius ii. 17 records the beginning of the year 88 in the corrupt words 'finito ex maxima parte . . . Italico bello, quo quidem Romani victis adflictisque ipsi exarmati quam integris universis civitatem dare maluerunt', and however this may be amended, it seems to point to the same conclusion. But the vague language of Appian and Velleius is inaccurate. It was only in the course of the fighting between the Marians and the senate in 87 that 'dediticiis omnibus civitas data qui polliciti multa milia militum vix XVI cohortes miserunt', sc. to the senate (Licin. 21 F.). Licinianus makes this follow the abortive negotiations between the senate and the Samnites and Lucanians and the acceptance by the Marians of all the terms of these rebels, who were still in arms, including the citizenship (20 F.; cf. App. 68. 309 f., Dio fr. 102. 7). The *Perioche* of Livy lxxix is confused ('Italicis populis a senatu civitas data est. Samnites, qui soli arma recipiebant, Cinnae et Mario se coniunxerunt') but is in rough agreement. The *dediticii* are clearly the peoples who in 89 had had to surrender unconditionally; cf. *Per.* Livy lxxv: 'Cn. Pompeius Vestinos in deditionem accepit . . . Compluraque oppida in deditionem acceperunt . . . L. Sulla aliquot populos recepit [sc. in deditionem]'; lxxvi: 'Cn. Pompeius procos. Vestinos et Paelignos in deditionem accepit'. It can be assumed that all peoples who were forced to submit were *dediticii*. This means that the new citizens who backed Sulpicius and Cinna must have been those enfranchised by the *lex Iulia*, and if all Latins were not included among them, we cannot explain how they were so numerous. Slow to reward the loyal allies, the Roman government would naturally have had no inclination to enfranchise rebels but for the emergency of civil war in 87.

As the *dediticii* did not respond to any great extent to the senate's appeal for help, it may reasonably be held that Marius and Cinna had no party motive for not putting the senate's grant to them into effect. Nor would they have wished to dishonour their promise to the Samnites and Lucanians, who in fact mostly took the Marian side in 83–82. It is therefore strange to find in *Per.* Livy lxxxiv 'novis civibus S.C. suffragium datum est'. This suggests that not until 84 did the Marians fulfil their promises. Another entry in the same *Perioche* runs: 'Libertini in quinque et xxx tribus distributi erant'. Again this seems to imply that a proposal made by Cinna in 87 (*Schol. Gronov.* 286 St.) was only now put into force.

The explanation seems to lie in the conduct of the censors of 86–85. According to Eusebius (*ap.* Jerome, 233 Froth.), they registered only 463,000 citizens. Figures are easily liable to corruption, and Beloch (1886, 352) amended to 963,000. This is palaeographically easy, and the figure now stands in an intelligible relation with the 910,000 enrolled in 70–69, considering the enormous losses sustained in 83–82, which could not yet have been fully made good. None the less, I believe the transmitted figure is sound: if the censors had failed to register most of the new citizens, and they remained voteless, we can understand the entry in *Pero* lxxxiv. Similarly, the censors doubtless refused to distribute the freedmen among the tribes. When we consider the censors were L. Philippus, Drusus' old enemy, who was to fight for Sulla in 83–82, and M. Perperna, who survived the Sullan proscriptions and probably made his peace early with the conqueror, we need not be surprised that they should deliberately have sought to sabotage Cinna's policy. Of the independence of the senate and senators under the so-called *dominatio Cinnae* this is not the only specimen. It may be asked why Cinna let Philippus and Perperna be chosen as censors; the answer is probably that he had few partisans and that he had to regard all as for him who had not been strongly against him, see p. 461. The *Perioche* is elliptic; probably the senate in 84 at the insistence of the Marians promised that a new census should be held in which new citizens and freedmen would be fairly registered; without the appointment of new censors there was still no machinery to implement the promises. Naturally no new censors were appointed, as the civil war was now impending, and the effective registration of the Italians as citizens with voting rights must have been deferred until 70–69. Cf. *IM*, ch. VII.

III. The End of *Civitas Sine Suffragio*

Sherwin-White found 'two direct indications that some *municipia* survived *sine suffragio* down to the decades before the Social War' (*RC²* 213 f.). He admits that his second text is ambiguous: Appian (i. 10. 41) refers to opposition to Gracchus' agrarian bill coming from men from the colonies and cities with equal civic rights. As Humbert has shown (23–32, 205–7, etc.), this *isopoliteia* denotes the Latin status, not *c.s.s*, and Appian should have had in mind (*a*) Latin colonies and (*b*) other communities like Tibur with Latin status (App. II). Sherwin-White lays more weight on the reference in the *lex agraria* of 111 (*FIRA* i². no. 8. 31 f.) to Roman and Latin colonies, *municipia*, pro-colonies, and *pro-municipia*. He assumes that 'the term *municipium* should refer technically to a self-governing commune of *cives s.s*, while the *pro municipiis* should be either fully enfranchised *municipia* and *oppida c. R.*, or else the category of small communes just discussed as duoviral prefectures, formed out of mere fragments of former *populi* and *gentes*.' In dismissing what I said on this in the original version of this essay, he takes no notice of my later suggestion in *IM* 527 f., that the term *municipium* was never reserved for communes of *c. s.s.*, but also embraced once independent communes like Tusculum, which had been incorporated in the Roman state *optimo iure*, while retaining some measure of local self-government. This view has since been confirmed by Humbert (cf. esp. 192–5, 271 ff.). We must, however, beware of thinking that all the terms implicit in the law had any precise technical significance. The intention of the legislator was surely to use language so vague and all-embracing that it would cover the enjoyment of Roman public land by any Roman or Latin communities. The Latin were mostly Latin colonies founded by Rome, but those non-colonial cities which had survived the dissolution of the old Latin and Hernican leagues without being incorporated as *municipia* in the Roman state possessed the same rights, and were for the legislator's purpose equivalent to Latin or Roman colonies or Roman *municipia*: in the Republic Latin *municipia* did not exist. In 173 both Latins and Romans had been given viritane allotments in Cisalpina, and in this and other areas of scattered settlement urban centres would develop at places where markets were held or *praefecti* administered justice; and these places would gradually acquire local administrative functions with common funds and no doubt communal landholdings, without at once acquiring the status of colonies or *municipia*. Some of the latter also had such large territories that they were divided into *pagi* or *vici*, which may well have had parochial functions and possessions of the same kind. Later lists of Roman communities enumerate *praefecturae, fora, conciliabula*, and sometimes *pagi, vici, castella (FIRA* i.² no. 13. 83; cf. no. 12, no. 19. XXI etc; in 13. 89 and 142 we have only *praefecturae*, as in no. 20; later legal draftsmen too did not achieve uniform completeness and accuracy). On such communities see e.g *RC*² 161; Galsterer 24 ff.; Humbert (see his Index s. v.). I suggest that all are loosely covered in the formulation of the *lex agraria*; it protects the enjoyment of public land by any Roman or Latin communities, however designated, just as in v. 30 the relevant powers of any Roman magistrate or 'promagistrate' are defined without specification of the various titles (consul, proconsul, praetor, propraetor, etc.). There is nothing in the terms of the law to prove or disprove that there were still *c. s.s.* in 111.

It is also odd for Sherwin-White to argue from another phrase in the law (23: 'id oppidum coloniamve ex lege . . . constituit deduxit conlocavitve') that in 111 '*municipia* in the later sense did not yet exist', meaning (I suppose) that no *civitas* which had been absorbed in the Roman state with full rights was yet called a *municipium*. The clause refers to the creation of a new town or colony, and could not refer to places like Tusculum or Arpinum, which already existed as self-governing communes when they were incorporated with full rights or raised from half to full citizenship, and which, according to our evidence, represent the original *municipia*; it was no doubt a later development when an *oppidum*, a *forum*, or *conciliabulum* received the same appellation. In my view *oppidum* is a generic term for a town, including a *municipium*, with no precise juristic definition (*IM* 583).

In *Collection Latomus*, 1969, 121 ff., I argued for the old view that all the Sabine *c.s.s.* were enfranchised fully in 268, and not only the people of Cures. This is again contested by Humbert 234 ff. His argument from Polyb. ii. 24. 5 (n. 110) is in my view met by the hypothesis (*IM* 49) that Polybius distinguishes the Sabines from the Romans because there had been a tumultuary levy in the *ager Sabinus*, whether or not I was right in thinking that *c.s.s.* served in the legions. He also notes that the Sabines are classed as *socii* in Livy xxvii. 45. 14 f. as late as 205. Strictly the term does not suit any *cives*, with or without the franchise. But Livy can improperly use it of Roman colonists (xxii. 14. 3, xlii 3. 3, cited by Galsterer 54). The reliability of xxviii. 45 is anyhow questionable (*IM* 548 n. 3, 656 n. 1). Humbert rejects my view that most of the Sabines enfranchised in 268 could have been transferred in 241 to the new tribe Quirina as 'unjustified' (n. 110), but the old citizens who had received allotments from Manius Curius in what came to be the area of Quirina must then have been transferred to that tribe (Taylor, 1960, 63 ff.);

why not enfranchised Sabines too? His own interpretation of Livy xl. 51. 9 (below), if I understand it, implies that such transfers could take place.

Humbert dates to the mid-third century the full enfranchisement of Volscian Velitrae (184 ff.); the commune had survived with *meddices* when Romans were settled there *viritim* (338) and the tribe Scaptia constituted in its territory (332), but the Octavii of Velitrae obtained Roman offices in the late third century (Suet. *Aug.* 1). Sherwin-White (p. 212) objects that the *nomen* shows that they were of Roman stock, but as Humbert remarks, the cadet branch of the family continued to hold offices in Velitrae itself, and fusion had presumably taken place. Similarly, Volscian Privernum lay at the centre of tribus *Oufentina*, created for Roman settlers in 318; commenting on the verse of Lucilius 'Priverno Oufentina venit fluvioque Oufente', Festus 212 L. remarks that others from different cities were later enrolled by censors in this tribe, which certainly implies that the people of Privernum were at some date so enrolled. One would indeed expect the Volscians of Velitrae and Privernum to have received the full franchise earlier than the more distant Volscians of Arpinum etc. in 188. A similar consideration applies to Volscian Frusino, and still more strongly to Anagnia, in view of the old Hernican connection with Rome. Sherwin-White himself seems to concede it as probable that Atina, just beyond Arpinum, had the full franchise at least from the mid-second century; it was in the Teretine tribe, as were Casinum, Venafrum, and Allifae to the south; it seems reasonable to suppose that all were promoted together. Here the non-Roman population was probably Samnite, and if men of this stock were given the vote before 90, we may wonder to whom it would have been denied. As for the Sabines, even if Cures alone benefited from the grant of 268, Cicero surely implies that all were fully enfranchised earlier than 90 (*Balb.* 32, *de offic.* i. 35, which also mentions the Aequi), and Livy (xl. 46. 12) might seem to put this earlier than 179 (a very insecure inference).

Following Taylor (1960, 17 f.), Humbert argues from Festus (quoted above) that the censors could enrol *c.s.s* in the tribes and thereby give them the vote (347 ff.). He has to meet the objection that a special *lex* was required for Arpinum etc. He remarks that these three communes had never lost any of their territory by confiscation and that in consequence no settlement of Roman citizens *optimo iure* had taken place there. On his view the censors were entitled to act wherever as a result of such settlement fusion had occurred between citizens of the two categories. However, he also suggests that the censors of 189/8 were specifically instructed by the *lex Terentia* (Plut. *Flam.* 18. 1) to act in this way; that the enfranchisement of Arpinum etc. and the registration of Capuans at Rome, both in 188, were to round off their work; that in 179 'some reorganization of the map of the tribes' was found necessary; and that this explains why the censors then 'mutarunt suffragia, regionatim-que generibus hominum causisque et quaestibus tribus descripserunt' (Livy xl. 51. 9). All this is highly conjectural (as he admits); the content of the *lex Terentia*, which Livy ignores, and the meaning of Livy's statement cannot be safely determined (but see L. Grieve, *CQ* 1985, 417 ff.). It seems to me that a *lex* would have been necessary, wherever the *c.s.s.* had still been organized in a self-governing commune, whether or not that commune had ever had to surrender lands to Roman viritane settlers; and that if Humbert's hypothesis is basically correct, the *lex Terentia* might merely have required the censors to enrol in a tribe all *c.s.s.* resident within its area, i.e., in Sherwin-White's formulation, where there were 'small communes, formed out of mere fragments of former *populi* or *gentes*'. Humbert's survey in ch. v of the probable extent of earlier grants of *c.s.s.* involves conjectural combinations of evidence for confiscations, formation of prefectures, and anomalies in the later municipal organization, and it is not always easy to determine whether a community had retained such local self-government as Arpinum etc. had. Cumae and Caere at least surely belonged to this category, and Humbert (p. 352) does not profess to know when they were promoted (nor when the Capuans received the vote); we cannot, I think, dispense with the hypothesis that there were other laws besides that of 188, of which no record survives. The loss of Livy's narrative from 168, and its deficiencies for domestic events in the period it covers (p. 21), make this easy to accept. In any case the known instances of full enfranchisement seem to presuppose others that are not documented, and Humbert is to my mind right in holding that the category of *c.s.s.* to which no additions had been made, so far as we are informed or can conjecture, since perhaps 268 (pp. 244 ff.), was regarded as anomalous and provisional, and is likely to have been progressively eliminated.

IV. The Tabula Bantina

The famous bronze tablet of Bantia is inscribed on one side in Latin, on the other in the local Oscan (*FIRA* i. 26, 16; cf. Vetter 13 ff. for Oscan text). It was generally supposed that the Oscan was the earlier text, until a new fragment published by Torelli showed that the tablet was first nailed to the wall when the Latin text was engraved. It was then turned and re-used for the Oscan text, presumably when the Latin text ceased to be of concern to the Bantians. That text contains the final clauses of a Roman *lex*, which has been variously and uncertainly identified. Galsterer (*Chiron* 1971, 191 ff., with full bibliography; cf. A. W. Lintott, *Hermes* 1978, 125 ff., on the Latin law), who adopted the view that it was part of the *lex Appuleia de maiestate*, held that this was superseded by Sulla's law, and that it was only then, as it ceased to be operative, that the Bantians could re-use the bronze for the set of rules in Oscan relating to local administration and processes of law. (In fact the *lex Varia* of 91/0 may have already incorporated the terms of the *lex Appuleia*, though it dealt specifically with charges of treasonable conspiracy with the Italians (GC 136 f.). Varius himself was later to be condemned under his own law, (ibid. 151), surely not on any such charge, but perhaps for disregarding the vetoes of his colleagues (App. i. 37; Val. Max. vii. 6. 4); cf. Ascon. 59C. on the charge brought against Cornelius, *tr. pl.* 67; presumably too that brought against Norbanus under the *lex Appuleia*, Cic. ii. *de orat.* 197). Galsterer deduces that the rules of the Oscan law were in force when Bantia had become a *municipium* after the Social war. This conclusion is surely insupportable.

The Oscan text reveals a community with an assembly, senate, and magistrates bearing the titles of censor, praetor, quaestor, and tribune of the plebs. The Latin terms are borrowed for all cases but 'people' or 'comitia' and censor. In later Roman municipalities we occasionally find a senate, as distinct from the *ordo* of *decuriones*, and *comitia* (*ILS* Index 674 ff.), and magistrates sometimes bear names of Roman origin, like those at Bantia, which are best explained as having been retained from the era when they had had allied or Latin status. Normally Italian municipalities have as chief magistrates not praetors but *quattuorviri* or *duoviri iuri dicundo*, who are dignified with the appellation of *quinquennales* when at five year intervals they discharge local censorial functions. Bantia itself had *duoviri* (*CIL* ix. 418 in Torelli's reading). The regime of the Oscan text was therefore not that which later existed in municipal Bantia. Moreover, there is nothing in the document to suggest that Bantia was already a municipality. The censors are to register the citizens of Bantia in the Bantian people. They are not required as in the Table of Heraclea to follow the formulae published by the magistrates responsible for taking the census at Rome, a requirement which in my judgement goes back to the 80s (*IM* 38, 519 ff.). The Bantian censors are to sell the persons and property of the citizen who fails to register without due cause. This corresponds to the Roman rule (ibid. 33. n. 3), but once the Bantians had secured the Roman franchise, the power would hardly have remained with a local magistrate; what if the Bantian had removed to some other place in Roman territory, as being a Roman citizen he was entitled to do? Other clauses concern the procedure for trials by the Bantian *comitia*; it is modelled on the Roman, except that five and not four hearings are prescribed and the citizens give judgement under oath. On the most favoured but not uncontested interpretation of the Oscan terms, the *comitia* can impose capital sentences. It seems to me unlikely that after the Social war the municipalities still possessed any capital jurisdiction (ch. 4 endnote 1).

Galsterer held that some provisions of the Oscan law reflect Sullan constitutional innovations. The first extant clause enacts that in circumstances which were set out in the lost part of the text some magistrate, perhaps a tribune, is entitled to impose a veto on comitial proceedings only after taking an oath that he is acting for the public good and in conformity with the views of the majority of the senate. Perhaps the restrictions that Sulla imposed on the tribunician right of veto, which he did not entirely abolish (GC 212), were of this kind. But in pre-Gracchan days tribunes had commonly been the instruments of senatorial policy, useful in restraining other recalcitrant magistrates, and Bantia could have borrowed this rule from what was taken to be the proper constitutional practice in second-century Rome. The Oscan law also provides that no one may be censor without having been praetor, nor praetor without having been quaestor. Whether or not, as Galsterer but not all other scholars thinks (cf. A. E. Astin, *Collection Latomus* 1958, for full discussion), such a rigid rule was first imposed at Rome by Sulla; once again it certainly corresponds to normal Roman practice before his time. The Oscan law also forbids anyone to hold the tribunate after other offices. This is very different from the Sullan bar on ex-tribunes holding any higher magistracy. It is surely incredible that the tribunate, which was so rooted in Roman tradition that even Sulla ventured only to remove its claws and not to destroy it, was actually introduced at Bantia in the time of his ascendancy. It may perhaps be said that it had been imported when Cinna was dominant and that no steps were taken under Sulla to abolish it. But the fact that the alien Latin terms for praetors, quaestors, and tribunes were not only borrowed from Rome but abbreviated as 'pr.' 'q.' and 'tr. pl.' suggests that the Bantians had long been familiar with them. It is then best to suppose that they went back to the period of independence and had been adopted from the neighbouring Latin colony of Venusia, which had tribunes (*CIL* ix. 438), though admittedly the titulature of its other magistrates is not documented for the colonial era.

Venusia itself joined in the allied revolt; and we must assume that Bantia, like the other Lucanians, took their part. It would have been only natural if it had then turned any Roman law set up there to the wall, as no longer operative. Thus even if the Latin text belongs to Saturninus' *maiestas* law, we do not need to assume that the bronze tablet was re-used only when and because it had been superseded by any other Roman law. Moreover, granted that the Oscan text was engraved as late as 90, it by no means follows that all or any of the provisions preserved were then novel. The use of the abbreviations mentioned above is against this. We should have only a *terminus ante quem* for the borrowings from Roman practice and for the use of Latin terms. These borrowings extend to civil law; we read of a 'legis actio', and the Latin legal phrases 'manum adserere' and in the new fragment 'dolus malus' are taken into Oscan.

The date and nature of the Latin law is probably an insoluble puzzle. It was surely a controversial, probably a popular, measure, since it makes magistrates and senators who wilfully violate or neglect it liable to fines (para. 2), and requires an oath of obedience from present and future magistrates and from senators (paras. 3, 4). Both these provisions find close parallels in the piracy law of 101 (*JRS* 1974, 195 ff.; cf. 215 for comparison with our law; the relevant provisions are in reverse order, and it looks to me as if the Greek text is in part only an inexact paraphrase of the technicalities of Roman legal drafting), and of course in Saturninus' agrarian law. The literary sources mention the oath to that law only because Metellus Numidicus preferred exile to taking it (*GC* 105 ff.). Probably he did not dispute the propriety of an oath but only the validity of a statute which had been passed by violence: the imposition of an oath to a particular law was not an innovation; the *lex agraria* of 111 shows that there were precedents (*FIRA* i^2. 8. 40–2). The analogy of the piracy law also shows that a law to which successive magistrates were obliged to swear was not necessarily one which would be of permanent duration (cf. the obscure relics of col. v of the Cnidus text of the piracy law). It appears from vv. 7 f. and 14 of our law that it constituted a *iudicium publicum* and that it concerned an offence which was not capital but which may have been subject to a pecuniary penalty; in any event conviction entailed elements of *infamia* (para. 1). However, this too is no proof that it was concerned with a permanent *quaestio*; we might recall the courts set up by the Peducaean and Mamilian laws. It is thus possible that the law was of quite temporary effect, and in that case the tablet might have been re-used for the Oscan text well before 90.

Traditionally the law was dated between 133 and 118 on the ground that the magistrates who are to take the oath in future years include agrarian triumvirs; and no such triumvirs are attested except for those appointed under Gracchus' law. If this highly persuasive argument were unanswerable, attribution to Saturninus would be excluded. But it has been pointed out that the list also includes the dictator and *magister equitum*, who were not appointed annually and who had in fact not been appointed since 202. The legislator might then have named agrarian triumvirs in case the office was revived. (The mention of the triumvirs in the list of the current magistrates is merely a dubious restoration.) The law could not, however, be after 100, since Saturninus seems then to have constituted a decemvirate of land commissioners (*MRR* i. 577).

It is hardly credible that Roman laws were normally placed on view, still less inscribed, in allied towns. Any identification of our law should therefore explain why this was done at Bantia, whether by Roman command or by the wish of the Bantian authorities. It ought to be of some concern to Bantians. Various possibilities can be envisaged. It might have afforded protection or offered rewards to Bantians (like *repetundae* laws; cf. n. 74), or affected their interests in land, as agrarian laws could (cf. n. 68). It might have rendered Bantians liable to penalties, or have provided for trials in which they could be required to bear witness. The extant clauses unfortunately fail to indicate its relevance to an allied community.

The first extant paragraph merits a little further consideration for its possible connection with my thesis in Chapter 4. The culprits for some unknown offence are subjected to specified disabilities (all of which appertain to Roman citizens, not Bantians) by dint of imposing on Roman magistrates the duty not to allow them certain rights; the magistrates themselves are penalized for contravention in the next paragraph. In the lines that can be read the appropriate magistrate is forbidden (*a*) to ask for the *sententia* of the culprit either in the senate or in a *publicum iudicium*; (*b*) to let him give evidence; (*c*) to appoint him as *iudex*, *arbiter* or *recuperator* (the restoration here is certain); (*d*) to let him wear in public the senatorial *praetexta* and *soleae* (*StR* iii[3]. 886 ff.); (*e*) to let him vote in the assemblies; (*f*) to enrol him or let him remain in the senate (a probable restoration). Some of the rights withheld are exclusively senatorial, and all are those which senators could exercise, at least if they were not already as such debarred from judication. Let us assume, though this is obviously uncertain, that the culprits under the law can only be senators or aspirants to senatorial status. Would it then follow that men of this category were, when the law was passed, still eligible for judicial functions? It may be noted that two types of judication are mentioned. Giving a *sententia* in a *iudicium publicum* is distinguished from acting as a *iudex*, *arbiter*, or *recuperator*. Lintott (*ANRW* I. 2. 246 f.) supposes that the former term here refers to a trial in the assembly, without denying that it can also mean a criminal court of *iudices*, as in the Gracchan law (v. 11), where in my view 'quaestione iudiciove publico', sometimes amended without reason to 'quaestione iudicioque publico', is more or less tautologous, like 'lex plebiscitumve' (in this point I differ from Kunkel, 1962, 51 ff., at n. 211). But in a *iudicium populi* each citizen did not deliver a *sententia* but merely cast a vote; and the culprits are disqualified from voting in the assembly by the separate prohibition in (*e*) laid on every magistrate who may preside over the assembly from taking their votes. The prohibition in (*a*) is directed to the magistrate who presides either over the senate or over a court. The president of a court need not be the same magistrate who enrols men in the *album iudicum* or appoints a *iudex* in a particular case; and there is thus no overlap between the provisions in (*a*) and (*c*), just as there is no overlap between the direction to the magistrate presiding over the senate not to invite the *sententia* of the culprit and that to the censor not to place him on the roll of senators; the former is not exonerated from his obligation by the failure of the censor to act as directed. It seems to follow then that the culprits belong to a class eligible for both criminal and civil judication, and that this class may be senatorial. Yet I do not take this as confirmation, however slender, of my thesis that senators retained rights of judication after 123, even on the basis that our law is later than Gracchus' judiciary legislation. The author of our law may have wished to provide that senatorial culprits should be excluded from judiciary rights, even if under any subsequent legislation senators should be qualified to exercise them.

As already observed, it is implicit in the first paragraph that the culprits have not been condemned to a capital penalty. Prima facie it follows that the law cannot be one which imposed such a penalty, as the *lex Appuleia maiestatis* surely did. The same objection arises with Lintott's suggestion that it is a *lex de sicariis*. If our law were one which set up or remodelled a court for a capital crime, we should have to suppose that the first paragraph related only to persons guilty of some ancillary and less heinous offence. I doubt if Lintott has provided a solution of this kind. He himself has exposed the difficulties in various other theories, and though I could add to their number, speculations are idle, which it is possible sometimes to refute but never to prove. In general Republican statutes which modified both criminal and civil law are passed over in narrative sources, and known, if at all, from chance allusions which tell us little of their contents (pp. 218 f.). In this case we must be content with ignorance. We may then think that the most natural inference from the mention of the agrarian triumvirs is correct, and that the law enacted between 133 and 118 may have ceased to operate long before 90; hence the Oscan text may be a generation earlier than the Social war.

3

THE EQUITES IN THE LATE REPUBLIC*

I. The term Equites may designate either *Equites equo publico* or all with the same birth and property qualifications. Interrelations of Equites and senators: they formed a single class with largely identical interests. **II.** Discord between the two orders arose from *(a)* conflicts between the senate and equestrian publicans; *(b)* competition for rights of judication; *(c)* perhaps to some extent equestrian resentment at the political exclusiveness of the nobility. The evidence of Polybius. The work of Gaius Gracchus. The bitter conflicts in and after Drusus' tribunate, which are not to be explained by any contradiction in the economic objectives of the two orders. Even then the equestrian order not united. The judiciary compromise of 70 terminated the division between the orders. **III.** Further consideration of the thesis that the orders embodied conflicting economic interests. Equites chiefly landowners. The special importance of the publicans; their occasional conflicts with the senate. *Negotiatores* abroad; among them traders had relatively little influence. Senators also engaged in overseas 'business'. *Laissez-faire* the norm in public policy. **IV.** Roman imperialism prompted in part by economic motives, but not by the aim of increasing 'business profits'; nor can it be proved that Equites exercised pressure on the senate for that purpose. **V.** Summary and epilogue on the Augustan settlement so far as it concerned the Equites.

I

DISCORD between senate and Equites has a large place in the struggles that marked the tribunate of Drusus in 91 and the succeeding years, struggles which culminated in civil wars. The most manifest cause was clearly rivalry for control of the criminal courts. The judicial rights obtained for the Equites by Gaius Gracchus

* This essay is based on the lecture given at the Second International Conference of Economic History, 1962, and published first in its *Proceedings* in 1965, and then in Seager, 1969, and in a revised German translation in Schneider, 1976. I have found it most convenient to rewrite it, although the thesis remains the same. In great measure my conclusions were confirmed by the independent and exhaustive work by Nicolet, i. 1966 (cf. his prosopographic supplement in ii. 1974), and accord with those of Meier, 1966 (see Index s.v. Ritter), and Badian, 1967 and 1972. The once orthodox interpretation of the role of the Equites is represented most fully by H. Hill, *The Roman Middle Class in the Republican Period*, 1952.

conferred *splendor* on the equestrian order, and derogated from the prestige and independence of senators. Considerations of *dignitas* were doubtless no more alien to the mentality of the former than of the latter. Moreover, some Equites aspired to a senatorial career, at least for their sons, and may well have resented the arrogant exclusiveness of the nobility, dominant in the senate, which tended to limit the advancement of new men. In addition, economic causes of conflict have been discerned. The equestrian *iudices* were chiefly selected from the class of rich Romans who invested in the state contracts, for the supply of armies, for the construction and maintenance of public buildings, and above all for the collection of certain taxes. Senators were debarred by law from participation in these contracts,[1] and it was the duty of senate and magistrates to control the publicans in the cause both of treasury and taxpayers. This was certainly the origin of occasional disputes. The judicial power of Equites gave them the means of exerting pressure on senators to maximize their profits, and thus afforded material advantages as well as enhancing their honour. In a more general way it is often supposed that the Equites can be identified with the 'businessmen' of Rome, bankers, money-lenders, merchants, and shipowners, as well as publicans, whereas the senate was composed of landowners, who tended to neglect business interests, from which their own might diverge. However, businessmen in general, as distinct from the publicans, were not organized and did not render such manifestly essential services to the state as the publicans; they appear to have enjoyed relatively little influence. Moreover, as will be seen (pp. 163 f.), most Equites were also in fact landowners, no less than the senators; and the latter too could engage in peripheral business activity. Nor is there proof of any contradiction between the landed and commercial interests that would have divided the orders.

In a narrow sense the Equites consisted of 1,800 or perhaps 2,400 of the richest citizens enrolled by the censors in the eighteen centuries of those who were given a public horse, with which they were required to serve in the army. But as early as 400, according to annalistic tradition (Livy v. 7), others with property which enabled them to keep their own horses had been admitted to the cavalry. In 225 the Roman cavalry numbered 23,000 (Polyb. ii. 24), though at least 4,000 (the

---

[1] Ascon. 93 C; Dio iv. 10. 5, lxix. 16; Paul *Sent.* fr. Leyd. 2 (ed. G. G. Archi *et al.*): 'senatores parentesve eorum, in quorum potestate sunt, vectigalia publica conducere, navem in quaestum habere . . . prohibentur; idque factum repetundarum lege vindicatur'. Cf. comparable municipal regulations in *lex Irnitana* J and texts cited by the editor, *JRS* 1986, 161, 212 f. See Badian, 1972, 16, for evasions of the rule in Cicero's time; cf. pp. 100 ff.; it seems to me unlikely that they were common; no sign of them at least in what we read of the dispute in 67 (n. 53). Cf. also Wiseman 197 f.

Campanians) were not full citizens (Livy xxiii. 5. 15). By the late Republic military service had ceased in practice to be obligatory for the wealthy; Equites, however, filled most commissions as tribunes and prefects in the army (n. 58). Enrolment in the eighteen centuries had thus come to be a social distinction, which was also of political advantage: it conferred exceptional voting power in the centuriate assembly. In the first century, and on the general view since a law of 129 BC, the purpose of which is obscure, men had to surrender the public horse and ceased to be enrolled in the eighteen centuries on elevation to the senate; thus the equestrian order, though comprising men of senatorial families, excluded the senators themselves. The indispensable property qualification under the *lex Roscia* of 69, which gave privileged seating in the theatre to holders of the public horse, was 400,000 sesterces; it may have gone back to the Hannibalic war. Under the *lex Visellia* of AD 24 they also had to be men whose paternal grandfathers were of free birth; this qualification is not attested in the Republic but may well have been in force. In Cicero's time, if not earlier, all who were possessed of the same qualifications could be described as Equites in a wider sense. The *lex Aurelia* of 70 created three panels of *iudices*, senators, Equites, and *tribuni aerarii*; the second class undoubtedly consisted only of holders of the public horse (Cic. *Phil.* i. 20), but Cicero himself could describe the third too as Equites (e.g. *Flacc.* 96), and this is only explicable on the basis that by property and birth they too were of equestrian standing. The term retained this broader range in Augustan and later usage.[2]

Almost certainly senators in the Republic had the same census qualification as Equites, though probably on average they were richer, and Augustus would more realistically raise the senatorial census to a million sesterces.[3] The equestrian minimum, measured by Roman plutocratic standards, could be slighted by Cicero (*Fam.* ix. 13. 4), and was doubtless far exceeded by the richer and more influential members of the order, even if none is credited with the immense fortune of a Crassus or a Pompey. Equites were not, however, tempted so readily as senators to a life of ostentatious consumption; Atticus could restrict current expenditure in his town house at Rome to 36,000 a year.[4] Many surely lived on their estates or in country towns, where they constituted the local nobility. After the enfranchisement of Italy the order must have been augmented with many more *domi nobiles* from all parts of the peninsula, whose ideas and economic background cannot

---

[2] See endnote 1.   [3] Nicolet, *JRS* 1976, 20 ff.

[4] Nepos, *Att.* 13. 6. Cicero claims to have saved from an income of 100,000 from his estates (*Parad.* 49, misunderstood by Frank, who collects data on great fortunes in *ESAR* i. 208 ff., 295 ff., 387 ff.). At 5 per cent the minimum equestrian capital yielded 20,000.

have differed essentially from those of the old Roman aristocracy, with whom they might previously have enjoyed relations of guest-friendship (*hospitium*). Such men might visit Rome perhaps only once a year for the elections and games.[5] The more affluent, like Atticus, would also have had their residences in Rome. It must have been a practical necessity for active publicans to live in or near the city, and the Gracchan *repetundae* law confined the choice of equestrian jurors to persons domiciled there or nearby.[6]

Equites were often linked with senators in social intercourse and might be styled their friends, an appellation sometimes veiling clientship (p. 393 f.). They shared the same kind of education and culture. They might follow the same pursuits as jurists and advocates. Intermarriage occurred, and the brothers of some senators remained mere Equites, probably many more than we happen to know of. The equestrian order was at all times the 'seminarium senatus' (Livy xlii. 61. 5); Equites filled the gaps left by the extinction or impoverishment of old senatorial families; the process was quickened when Sulla doubled the size of the senate (p. 155). Admittedly they could seldom rise in a single generation to the highest offices. But the Equites of highest standing (and some had possessed their status for generations) belonged to the same social milieu as senators. It is significant that Cicero could assume that the father of C. Trebonius (*cos. suff.* 45), a 'splendidus eques Romanus', had been known personally to senators in general (*Phil.* xiii. 23).[7]

Men of this stamp had no class sympathy with proposals for the allotment of lands to peasants or veterans, or for doles of cheap or free grain to the urban poor, or for the relief of debtors. They were thus not natural allies of popular politicians embroiled with the senate. It is not surprising that they opposed Tiberius Gracchus.[8] His brother sought their support by giving them judicial rights and enlarging their scope for profiting from public contracts; none the less they turned against

[5] Cf. Cic. I *Verr.* 54 (on which see *IM* 36): it must have been Equites of this sort who demonstrated against the 'triumvirs' in July 59 (*Att.* ii. 19. 3; cf. p. 161).

[6] On Mommsen's restoration of *FIRA* i². vv. 13, and 17 within a mile, but he admitted that this was uncertain (*Ges. Schr.* i. 51); 20 miles for senatorial *iudices* under the *SC Calvisianum* (*FIRA* i². no. 68 v. 109, on which see F. de Visscher, *Les Édits d'Auguste découverts à Cyrène*, 1940, 144 n. 2).

[7] Nicolet 214–84, and on equestrian culture 101 n. 73, 441 ff. (cf. L. R. Taylor, *TAPA* 1968, 469 ff.); Wiseman, 1971, esp. 53 ff.; Gelzer (n. 2). Note, for instance, equestrian friends of M. Antonius, *cos.* 99, and L. Crassus, *cos.* 95 (Cic. *Brut.* 168, *de orat.* ii. 2 f.; Val. Max. ix. 1. 1): Cicero's family had noble friends or patrons; the connections of an Atticus or Balbus need no documentation. Jurists: W. Kunkel, *Herkunft u. soz. Stellung der röm. Juristen*, 1952, 50 ff.; cf. F. Schulz, 1953, 46–8. Advocates: Cic. *de orat.* ii. 2, 262, *Brut.* 131, 167 f., 205, 241 f., 246, 271, 280 ff., *Fam.* xiii. 12. 2, 22. 1. Marriages: e.g. Cic. *Sulla* 25, *Planc.* 27 (cf. R. Syme, *Roman Papers*, 605 ff.), *Pis.* fr. 9–11.

[8] *Per.* Livy lviii; Vell. ii. 3. 2; cf. Cic. *Sest.* 103 (the audience of his speech was mainly equestrian); Badian, 1972, 55.

him.[9] The sources furnish no explanation. It may be that they disliked his policy of extending the franchise to Italians, perhaps in the apprehension that there would be increased competition for public contracts; later they were to oppose Drusus, though of course his attack on their judicial rights is enough in itself to account for this (pp. 206 ff.). Perhaps they were alienated from Gracchus by his eventual readiness to resort to violence. The preservation of order and the sanctity of property must have been their first consideration. Hence they would rally to the senate against Saturninus in 100,[10] and against Catiline,[11] who (it was feared) designed to remit debts and redistribute property. Thus in 63 Cicero could realize his ideal of 'concordia ordinum', which he later broadened into 'consensus Italiae', the union of his 'army of the rich' extending throughout the ruling class of the Italian towns; the programme of 'otium cum dignitate' which he outlined in 56 was indeed calculated to meet the desires and interests of all men of property. The programme included direction of affairs by the senate.[12] But there is no sign that Equites rejected this in principle. If order were maintained, and if the senate acquiesced in their claim to at least a predominant share in judication, as it did under the *lex Aurelia* of 70, and was complaisant to the publicans, they were likely to be content.

II

On this analysis there was more to unite the two orders than to divide them. How then should we account for the conflicts which did undoubtedly occur? Their origins can be detected in Polybius' explanation of the dependence of the people on the senate; by the people he means primarily the Equites.[13] This dependence he ascribed to two causes.

(1) Almost everyone (he says), i.e. in the upper-class milieu, of which he had personal acquaintance, was engaged in innumerable public contracts, and those contracts, when found disadvantageous, could be cancelled or modified only by the senate. Among these contracts he specifies those let by the censors for public buildings in Italy, and

---

[9] Sall. *BJ* 42; we may surmise that the senate made it clear that it would not attempt to repeal the judiciary legislation (ch. 4), and would thus allow the Equites a significant share in government ('spes societatis'). The acquittal of Opimius by the timocratic *comitia centuriata* tends to confirm Sallust's testimony; cf. also Plut. *C. Gr.* 14. 4, and E. Skard in Oppermann, 1967, 185, on Opimius' dedication of a temple to Concordia.

[10] Cic. *Rab. perd.* 20–27; Plut. *Mar.* 30. 3; Val. Max. iii. 2. 18; Oros. v. 17. 9.

[11] e.g. Cic. *Cat.* iv. 15.   [12] See pp. 55 f.

[13] Pol. vi. 17; cf. Walbank ad loc.; Nicolet 382 f. Cicero too virtually equates people with Equites in I *Verr.* 38, *Cluent.* 151, *Phil.* iv. 15, viii. 8.

collection of revenue from rivers, harbours, gardens, mines, land, and everything under Roman power.[14] He does not mention taxes, and there is indeed no evidence that the collection of provincial tribute, as distinct from rents or *scriptura* on public domains, was farmed to Romans before the annexation of Asia in 133. Now there was no legal requirement that public contracts should be leased only to Equites, and we happen to know of a freedman contractor for road repair, probably of the Sullan period (*ILS* 5799). Nor was it essential that in all cases the contractors should be organized in companies like those which later collected the Asian tithe. On the other hand, it was only rich men acting together who could undertake contracts for which considerable capital and organization were required.[15]

Army supplies and transport, and in the third century the construction of ships for Rome's great fleets, must have come in this category, though Polybius fails to mention them. We hear of a company, evidently resembling those later attested for tax-farming, that contracted for army supplies in 215, and in 212 the senate was nervous of punishing the fraud of one such contractor lest it might offend the 'ordo publicanorum', which was influential clearly because its operations were indispensable to the state. Contracting for army supplies is again attested in 195 and 167, and must always have been in use, except in so far as troops could be supported by requisitioning from the subjects or by plunder from the enemy.[16]

Large sums were also spent on public works, for instance 6 million *denarii* on the Roman sewage system in 184; the revenue of one year was appropriated to buildings for the quinquennium beginning in 179, and half a year's revenue to censorial works in 169; the cost of the Marcian aqueduct started in 144 was 45 million *denarii*. It is not surprising that in 184 those interested in such huge expenditure could attempt, with initial success, to sabotage the efforts of the censors to curb profiteering, or that in 168 they secured the impeachment and

[14] Walbank supplies some illustrations; add Cato frs. 103 M². ('salinatores aerarii', farmers of salt tax), 106 (contract for supply of wine for an unknown public purpose). Though military roads were normally built by consuls or praetors, much of the work was surely done by contract even if military labour was to some extent employed; the censors contracted at least for roads in and near Rome (Radke, *RE* Suppl. xiii. 1431 ff.).

[15] Evidence for public buildings and costs from 200 to 80 is assembled by Frank, *ESAR* i. 144, 183 ff., 226 f., 258 ff. In App. ɔ to the original version of this essay I refuted his attempt to minimize the importance of these contracts and those for army supplies (n. 16); Badian, 1972, chs. I–II, now makes a fuller and better case against it.

[16] Livy xxiii. 48, xxv. 3, xxxiv. 9, xliv. 16. 3 f. Admittedly Harmand, 1967, ch. v, produces no testimony for public contracting at Rome for the army in the first century, but cf. *JRS* 1974, 201, Col. II 28 ff.; supplies were perhaps largely obtained then in the provinces or in enemy territory, though generals may still have relied on private entrepreneurs for procurement. Hucksters who followed the camp, trafficking with the soldiers (e.g. App. *Lib.* 115 ff.; Sall. *BJ* 44. 5; Caes. *BG* i. 39, *B. Afr.* 75. 3), are in another category.

almost obtained the conviction in the centuriate assembly of another censor who had followed a similar course.[17]

Polybius explicitly refers to mines, and the evidence, which must come from a lost part of his work, that in 168 the senate would not lease the Macedonian mines to Roman publicans for fear of their oppressing the subjects, indicates that it already had experience of the power that could be wielded by lessees of state mines; this in turn implies that these lessees must have been well organized (n. 71). This experience must have been obtained in Spain, where the large-scale employment of slave labour in the mines, of which Diodorus gives a lurid account (v. 35 f.), presumably derived from Posidonius, shows that the entrepreneurs, 'a multitude of Italians attracted by the high returns', must have disposed of great capital. By Strabo's testimony (iii. 2. 10), expressly drawn from Polybius, the state's share in the proceeds from the silver mines near New Carthage was 25,000 *drachmae* (*denarii*) a day; that of the contractors can only be surmised. It is true that in the Principate small men could obtain concessions in a mining area in Spain, but this mode of exploiting public property was hardly feasible without close supervision by the imperial bureaucracy of procurators assisted by the emperor's freedmen and slaves, which had no Republican antecedents. Thus, though it is true that in theory the state could have exploited the Spanish mines without leasing the actual extraction of the ore to publican companies, as distinct, for example, from entrusting publicans with collection of rents from the extractors, and though there is no direct evidence that it did in the Republic adopt the former system, we can plausibly infer from the indications cited that it was that system which it chose.[18]

(2) Senators were judges in the most important criminal and civil cases. As to the former, we may recall the trial by the consuls of 138 with a senatorial *consilium* of publicans who had obtained the contract for manufacturing pitch on Sila and their servants for an alleged massacre (Cic. *Brut.* 85 ff.). I shall, however, argue in Chapter 4 that it was more commonly civil jurisdiction that would have produced resentment.

Thus Equites were subject to control by a body dominated by the nobility, in which men originating in their order could seldom attain high rank,[19] and whose members, whatever their origin, were not

---

[17] Livy xxxix. 44 (cf. Plut. *Cato Maior* 19, *Flam.* 19), xliii. 16.

[18] *Contra* J. S. Richardson, *JRS* 1976, 139 ff. (whose general views on the Spanish mines I also reject) at 143 f. Richardson did not dispute my rejection (in App. 1 to the earlier version of this article) of Frank's view that until 179 the state directly exploited the Spanish mines, which it had no means of doing; see now Badian, 1972, 31 ff., who also attributes to Cato in 195 the introduction of publicans (the best interpretation of Livy xxxiv. 21. 7).

[19] Among new men in the senate P. Rupilius (*cos.* 132) and T. Aufidius (*pr.* 67?) had previously been engaged in tax collection (Val. Max. vi. 9. 7). Diod. xxxiv–xxxv 38. 1 makes it

entitled to share in the public contracts and would hardly represent the peculiar interests of the publicans. This control must have been a source sometimes of economic loss, and often of irritation. In the pre-Gracchan period more than one dispute had occurred between the publicans and the senate or magistrates (nn. 16 f.). Gaius Gracchus did not create a cleavage between the orders, as hostile sources suggest;[20] rather, friction already existed, and he sought equestrian support by enhancing the power, dignity, and profits of members of the order. His new regulation of the taxes of Asia, which became the model for that of eastern provinces acquired later, and also his introduction of 'nova portoria', and his public works, gave the publicans new opportunities for profit and added to their influence; the state relied heavily on the taxes they collected.[21] He did not touch the senate's control over contracts,[22] but he made it more likely that it would be responsive to the claims of the Equites through their monopoly of seats in the *repetundae* court, where they could sit in judgement on senators themselves. [See also Addendum, pp. 526 ff.]

According to Diodorus (xxxiv–xxxv. 2. 31), who surely drew on Posidonius, the governors of Sicily in the 130s had not dared to repress the banditry of slaves for fear of alienating their masters, landowners who were mostly Roman Equites and who thus belonged to the order which controlled the courts at Rome. This explanation of the governors' pusillanimity is of course anachronistic for that decade, but reflects the subservience of many governors to equestrian interests which Gracchus' measures probably produced later, and which is implicit in Posidonius' assertion that Gracchus sacrificed the subjects to the rapacity of the publicans (ibid. 25). Cicero himself, despite his close connections with the publicans, and his readiness in 70 to eulogize the

likely that this was also true of Marius; *pace* T. F. Carney, *Biography of C. Marius* (*Proc. Afr. Class. Ass.* Suppl. 1), 23, there is no proof that he illegitimately retained an interest in public contracting after entry to the senate; nor do we know that the Spanish Mons Marianus and the mines there took their names from him. New men as consuls: Brunt, *JRS* 1982, 1 ff.

[20] e.g. Cic. *de leg.* iii. 20; Varro *ap.* Non. Marc. 728 L.; Diod. xxxiv–xxxv 25. 1 (from Posidonius and ultimately Rutilius Rufus); *Per.* Livy lx.

[21] Cic. *de imp. Cn. Pomp.* 17: 'publicani . . . suas rationes et copias in illam provinciam [Asiam] contulerunt, quorum ipsorum per se res et fortunae curae esse debent. Etenim si vectigalia nervos esse rei publicae semper duximus, eum certe ordinem qui exercet illa firmamentum ceterorum ordinum recte esse dicemus.' *Planc.* 23: 'flos enim equitum Romanorum, ornamentum civitatis, firmamentum rei publicae publicanorum ordine continetur'. These statements were largely true, until Rome could adopt a different method of tax collection. Cf. *de prov. Cons.* 11, and see R. Rowlands, *TAPA* 1965, 369; Badian, 1972, 42 ff. Cf. n. 56. *Portoria*: Vell. ii. 6. 3 (cf. S. J. De Laet, 1949, 45–58). Gracchus professed a concern for public revenues (Gell. xi. 10; Cic. *Tusc. Disp.* iii. 48), which he needed to increase, to pay for his schemes that involved greater public expenditure. Public works: Plut. *C. Gr.* 6; App. i. 23; Festus 392 L.

[22] In 61 the Asian publicans petitioned the senate for a modification of their liabilities 'lege Sempronia' (Schol. Bobb. 157 St.); cf. n. 53. For the senate adjudicating in disputes between publicans and provincials see Nicolet 347 ff.

incorruptibility of equestrian *iudices* (I *Verr*. 38), could admit that 'wicked and rapacious magistrates' in the provinces curried favour with the publicans (II *Verr*. iii. 94): Verres still found collusion with them expedient,[23] though at a time when Equites had been deprived of their judicial functions, and we may think that this kind of behaviour was still more common when a governor was amenable to conviction by an equestrian court. Even a man of high principle might then think it prudent to conciliate the publicans at the expense of the taxpayers; this is the course that Cicero in effect recommends his brother Quintus to pursue as proconsul of Asia in 59; and when governing Cilicia, he was careful to try to satisfy their claims, though with the least possible injury to the provincials. At the same time he could press other governors, perhaps less scrupulous than himself, to concede the demands of publicans or of Equites with other interests in their provinces.[24]

It is true that there is little evidence in our meagre records that equestrian *iudices* actually used their judicial powers for the unjust conviction of senators who sought to restrain their malpractices. Indeed very few senators are known to have been condemned by the equestrian *repetundae* court. Of course our records are incomplete; still of 18 certain or probable prosecutions listed by Gruen between 123 and 91 only 4 issued in convictions.[25] Perhaps most governors were too apprehensive of the power of the Equites to stand up to the publicans, and some may have chosen to share in their illicit gains. It may perhaps be taken as illustrative of their enhanced influence that Marius worked through Equites active in Africa to impugn Metellus Numidicus' conduct of the Jugurthine war.[26] As proconsul of Asia, Q. Mucius Scaevola curtailed their extortions, and is said to have suffered from equestrian malice, but we do not know how; perhaps they kept him out of the censorship. Of course they did procure the unjust conviction of his legate P. Rutilius in 92, and it was this notorious miscarriage of justice that provoked Drusus to assail the order's judicial rights.[27] In a later period L. Lucullus incurred the hostility of the Equites for protecting the provincials from them (Plut. *Luc*. 20), but there were certainly other reasons, arising from the public interest and perhaps

[23] II *Verr*. ii. 169–91 concerning the contractors for the *portoria*; his relations with the farmers of the grain tithe are irrelevant here, as they were only by accident Romans or Equites.

[24] *Qu. fr.* i. 1. 32–5 (as he expressly says, he and his brother were under peculiar obligations to the order, sc. for political support; hence his attitude in 61 to the publicans' claims (n. 53), which he thought shameless (*Att.* ii. 1. 8)). Cilicia: *Att.* v. 14. 1, v. 21. 10, vi. 1. 4, and 15 f., 2. 5. The Asian tithe-farmers looked to Cicero for support (v. 13. 1), and he put pressure on other governors to favour publicans and other *negotiatores*, one of them a senator (*Fam.* xiii. 9, 53–9, 61–3, 65).

[25] Gruen, 1968, 304 ff.

[26] Vell. ii. 11. 2 speaks of publicans and other *negotiatores*: Sall. *BJ* 65. 4 (cf. 66. 4) specifies 'equites Romanos, milites [sc. officers] et negotiatores', a term which can include publicans.

[27] Scaevola: Cic. *Fam.* i. 9. 26; cf. *Planc*. 33. Rutilius: GC 125 ff.

from the jealousy of his peers, for the gradual limitation and eventual termination of his unusually long command in the east.[28] Gabinius too set himself against the publicans in Syria, and was finally convicted of *repetundae*, but only after he had been narrowly acquitted of *maiestas* (Cic. *Qu. fr.* iii. 4. 1), of which he was manifestly guilty; we must also recall that in the 50s senators formed one third of the courts, and that Gabinius' past activity as a popular tribune and continuing connection with Pompey must have made him many enemies among senatorial *iudices*.[29]

However, it is not only the decisions of the *repetundae* court we have to take into account. Gracchus' reformation of that court became a model for the constitution of the *ad hoc* court set up by the Mamilian law of 109, and for the permanent court created by Saturninus to try charges of *maiestas*, which presumably took cognizance of those brought under the Varian law of 90. There was a heavy toll of distinguished senatorial victims under the Mamilian and Varian laws. It was under the impact of trials on the former occasion that L. Crassus in 106 could plead that senators should be rescued 'from the jaws of those whose cruelty can be satiated only by our blood' and that senators should have no masters but the Roman people.[30] As this second remark implies, though senators could not deny their traditional responsibility to the people on impeachment before the centuriate assembly, they desired otherwise to be judged only by their peers; it was demeaning that they should be made accountable to men of a lower order.

In my view Gaius Gracchus did more than give the Equites control of the *repetundae* court; he also gave them a share in judication in other criminal cases that came before permanent courts, and in determining those civil suits which had hitherto been reserved to senators; thereby he relieved them of that dependence on senators the importance of which Polybius had stressed. This is argued in Chapter 4.

The value of the Asian tax contract cannot be estimated with any precision. According to Plutarch, Pompey's conquests added a revenue of 85 million *denarii* to the existing revenues of 50 million; the figures probably refer only to the provincial revenues received in cash.[31] Asia must have previously been the chief source.[32] In 47 Caesar substituted collection there by the city authorities for tax-farming and reduced by

---

[28] See endnote 2.

[29] Cic. *de prov. cons.* 9–11, *Pis.* 41, *Qu. fr.* ii. 12. (11) 2, iii. 2. 2; cf. Sherwin-White, 1984, 271 ff. Dio xxxix. 59. 2 says that he failed to protect the tax-farmers against brigandage.

[30] GC 68 f., 78 (Cic. *de orat.* i. 225), 141 (Cic. *Brut.* 304 f.).

[31] Plut. *Pomp.* 45, on which see Badian, 1967, 70 f.

[32] Broughton, *ESAR* iv. 562 ff. (perhaps 15 million coming in to the treasury: I cannot believe, as he infers from Philostr. *v. Soph.* ii. 1. 548, a poor source, that in Hadrian's time it had sunk to 7 million).

a third the total sum payable by the subjects. Since he was short of money at the time and was filling his coffers by various impositions, it is unlikely that he intended to reduce government receipts; rather he was cutting out the takings of the companies.[33] We may therefore infer that the publicans kept perhaps up to half of what the provincials paid, partly as a legitimate profit arising from the difference between the sum they guaranteed to the treasury and that which was legally due from the taxpayers, and partly by illicit exactions.[34]

Thus Gracchus' measures favoured the material interests of the Equites; they also assured them of a place of independence and even of splendour and dignity in the republic.[35] We should not underrate the importance they attached to this new political standing, nor their craving for *gratia, auctoritas*, and even *honores*.[36] From two well-known passages in Cicero's speeches (*Cluent.* 150 ff., *Rab. Post.* 13 ff.) it might be concluded that the prominent Equites of the pre-Sullan epoch were men who had abjured the advantages and risks of political life and preferred the quiet and security of private enrichment. But this was only true of some among them. Cicero himself describes them as men 'qui summum locum civitatis *aut non potuerunt* ascendere aut non petiverunt' (*Cluent.* 151). As early as 111, if we may believe Sallust (*BJ* 31), Memmius was declaiming against the nobility's monopoly of office, and in the next decade Marius was not the only new man who rose to high office.[37] Sallust also says that at this time the plebs preferred new men (ibid. 65), but in elections to the consulship and praetorship the votes of the rich counted for most, and in any case the electors could not have shown this preference, unless there had been candidates of equestrian families who sought high office.

It was not a meaningless gesture when Drusus proposed, in depriving Equites of their control of the courts, to enrol many of them in an enlarged senate. We are told that some were aggrieved at not being placed on his list.[38] Sulla carried out his plan. Not only his new recruits

---

[33] Plut. *Caes.* 48; Dio xlii. 6; App. v. 4. If the province paid 22.5 million, of which 7.5 went to the publicans, reduction of their liability by one third would leave the treasury no worse off; it would gain if the publicans' share was larger.

[34] Broughton, op. cit. 580.

[35] Cic. *Rab. perd.* 20 ('magnam partem rei publicae atque omnem dignitatem iudiciorum'); the optimates could not endure this 'equestrem splendorem' (*Rosc. Amer.* 140); cf. *Cluent.* 152; Florus ii. 1. 4; Nicolet 520.

[36] *Splendor, Sest.* 137; *dignitas, Att.* i. 17. 9, *de prov. cons.* 10, *Pis.* 41, *Cael.* 3 ('quaecumque in equite Romano dignitas esse possit, quae certe potest esse maxima'); Nepos, *Att.* i. 1, 6. 2 (cf. last note); Brunt, *JRS* 1961, 76, on social privileges which illustrated equestrian rank; Nicolet 212 ff. *Gratia* and *auctoritas*, see e.g. *Planc.* 32, *Att.* i. 2. 2; Nepos, *Att.* 6. 2. Equestrian *clientelae*: p. 397. Equites claimed, and optimates objected to, unfettered freedom of speech, *Planc.* 33 ff.

[37] Cn. Aufidius, C. Billienus, C. Flavius Fimbria, and Cn. Mallius Maximus happen to be known.

[38] App. i. 35, *de vir. ill.* 66; cf. p. 207.

but later entrants into a senate now doubled in numbers must have been chiefly of equestrian family. According to Cicero, all but one of the candidates for the curule aedileship of 54 were of this category (*Planc.* 17), among them Cn. Plancius, son of the leading publican of his day, who had the backing of the whole order of publicans, 'because they reckoned that his distinction was one for their order, and that they were acting in the interests of their own sons' (ibid. 24). No doubt a high proportion of these upstarts, like those later adlected by Caesar, also belonged to the municipal aristocracies. Cicero says that the post-Sullan senate was chosen from all Italy (*Sulla* 24), and that in 43 almost all senators came from the Italian towns (*Phil.* iii. 15); the elder Plancius himself was a notable from Atina, and one of Caesar's more distinguished recruits, L. Aelius Lamia, came of an old family at Formiae. Still, Plancius was prominent as a publican, as was Lamia, 'princeps equestris ordinis', who had many other business interests.[39]

Evidently many Equites did not share the attachment of Atticus to 'honestum otium'; in fact Atticus, who could certainly have followed a political career, carried his aversion to public life so far as to abstain from any part in judication and public contracting; he is surely untypical.[40] To some extent the arrogant exclusiveness of the Roman nobility must have irritated Equites, like Plancius and Lamia, who could harbour political ambitions for themselves or their sons, and this resentment may well have contributed to breaches between the orders.[41]

Still, in comparison with the struggle for control of the courts this was at most a secondary source of friction.[42] Caepio's law of 106 creating mixed courts for *repetundae* (p. 204), though not long in force, enraged the Equites against him, and Glaucia won their gratitude by its repeal. The condemnation of Rutilius and Drusus' consequential attempt to restore senatorial monopoly produced the fiercest acrimony. Drusus' proposed enlargement of the senate was no compensation; the men associated with the ruin of Rutilius would hardly be the beneficiaries, and Equites elevated to the senate would cease *eo ipso* to represent the equestrian order and in particular the publicans, in whose contracts they would be debarred from sharing. Drusus further inflamed their anger by seeking to make the former equestrian *iudices* criminally liable for bribes they had taken. If they feared competition in bids for the public contracts from the richer of the Italians whom he

---

[39] Plancius and Lamia: Nicolet 981 ff., 762 ff.

[40] Nepos, *Att.* 6; cf. Cic. *Att.* i. 17. 5; Suet, *Aug.* 2; Nicolet 699–722.

[41] The attacks made by Cicero on the *pauci*, not the senate (II *Verr.* v. 180 ff., *Cluent.* 152, etc.), and by Sallust mirror feelings presumably common among senators of equestrian origin.

[42] For discussion of all laws and proposals relating to judication see ch. 4. Most of the evidence is readily found in GC.

designed to enfranchise, they may also have been averse to his enfranchisement bill. After the failure of all his proposals and his own assassination, they carried by violence the Varian law of 90, under which they pursued a vendetta against his friends on the pretence that they had treasonably instigated the Italian revolts. There was a reaction against this persecution in 89, when they were deprived by the Plotian law of the monopoly of judication at least in the *maiestas* court. Sulla was later to exact vengeance on the 'old *iudices*' who had come into conflict with Drusus (Cic. *Cluent.* 151-3). On their side they were perhaps so incensed against the senatorial majority that they were ready to take any action which caused it offence.

This may explain the alliance made in 88 by the tribune Sulpicius Rufus with the Equites, although he was a former associate of Drusus and was seeking to undo the restrictions the senate had imposed on the voting rights of the newly enfranchised Italians, and thereby to implement Drusus' more liberal policy. He surrounded his person with an escort of 600 Equites and called them his 'anti-senate'. Our information on the political manoeuvres in the 80s is so scanty that the actions and reactions of individuals and sections of the citizen body are hardly intelligible, and Sulpicius in particular is shrouded in mystery.[43] But it may be that a common antagonism to the senatorial majority connected him with the politically active Equites. He also proposed that the command against Mithridates should be transferred to Marius from Sulla, to whom as consul it had been allotted. Obviously he hoped that Marius' influence would assist him in his main design. In the past Marius had himself enjoyed equestrian backing, and Sulpicius' alliance with Marius may well have contributed to his *rapprochement* with the Equites. Some have supposed that at this time Marius was in league with Equites who favoured imperialist expansion in Anatolia for the promotion of their 'business' activities. It will be convenient to anticipate at this point a more general discussion of the impact that issues of foreign policy may have had on the relations of the orders, and to examine whether this hypothesis is necessary or plausible, if we are to account for the political conjunctures in 88.

Early in the 90s Marius had visited Asia Minor and met Mithridates, and Plutarch (*Mar.* 31) purveys a hostile story that he secretly hoped to secure a new command and win additional glory and wealth by stirring up war with him. Yet at that time Marius had no prospect of such an appointment even if a war had broken out, and there is no evidence in any case that Equites were then pressing for an imperialist

---

[43] See especially C. Meier, 1966, ch. vi; A. W. Lintott, *CQ* 1971, 442 ff. Cf. also pp. 459 ff.

initiative. The senate itself subsequently took action to check the expansion of Mithridates' power. Ultimately Mithridates was provoked into war by the conduct of Roman representatives in the east in 89. We are told that they acted without authority from senate and people (App. *Bell. Mith.* 15, 17, 19). Some have taken them to be associates of Marius, but there is no good reason to think that even Manius Aquillius, who had been on good terms with him, was merely his tool, or that the other leading figures had any connection with him. In any case their aim, so far as we can tell, was not to extend Roman territory but to build up other vassal kings in Anatolia against Mithridates; nor do they seem to have been preparing the way for an extraordinary command to be vested in Marius, which they could have had no reason to expect: they hoped to win the war themselves and augment their own riches and distinction. As they had at best a very small force of Roman troops at their disposal, and Rome's military resources were still fully employed in subjugating the revolted Italians, their initiative was so reckless that we must not only believe that it had not been sanctioned by the senate, but also doubt if it could have had the prior approval either of Marius, whose military experience could scarcely have commended such rashness, or of the head offices of the publican companies with so much to lose, if Rome's possession of the province of Asia were put in jeopardy. Admittedly local Roman *negotiatores*, who had lent large sums to king Nicomedes of Bithynia, also urged him to attack Mithridates on the footing that they could expect repayment only from the plunder he would obtain (ibid. 11); even if they were local agents of principals at home, including publican companies, they need not have acted under instructions from them, any more than Aquillius and his associates proceeded on the senate's authority. Naturally, once Mithridates had overrun Asia, the home government had no choice but to dislodge him as soon as possible; this must also have been the principal care of the publicans and anyone else with business in the province. It is perfectly conceivable that they backed Marius' candidature for the job, not because they knew that he would be more responsive than Sulla to their interests, but out of animosity to the senate, coupled with faith in his capacity as the general who would most rapidly defeat Mithridates.[44]

Another explanation has been propounded for equestrian discord with the senate in and after 88. There was a credit crisis. Debtors who had suffered loss from the wars were unable to meet their obligations for principal and interest. The praetor Asellio in 89 countenanced attempts they made to revive an old and obsolete law that barred the

---

[44] For the unsatisfactory evidence and some discussion of modern reconstructions of Rome's relations with Mithridates, see now A. N. Sherwin-White, 1984, ch. v.

taking of interest. He was murdered in public; the assassins could not be found; allegedly the money-lenders covered everything up. In the following year the consuls Sulla and Q. Pompeius passed a law which may either have scaled down debts by a tenth or imposed a maximum of 12 per cent a year on the interest recoverable, a limit that was later to be normal and may already have corresponded to the usage thought reasonable.[45] It is very probable that in 89 the embarrassed debtors were primarily to be found among not only small farmers but larger landowners who had been unable to harvest their crops or get in rents in regions which had been theatres of war, though by 88 the loss of investments in Asia consequent on Mithridates' invasion must have more widely affected liquidity (n. 98). The consular measure of 88 was required by conditions similar to those which led Caesar in 49 to rescue landowners from the temporary difficulties caused by the outbreak of war.[46] We can assume approval by the senate. Asellio's more extreme attitude need not have had much support. In any event senators as well as Equites could make loans (p. 173), and equestrian landowners were just as liable as senatorial to have sustained losses in the war. We cannot then safely infer a clash between the economic interests of the two orders as such.

It is true that Sulpicius, though allegedly in debt himself, proposed the exclusion from the senate of anyone owing more than the inconsiderable sum of 2,000 *denarii* (Plut. *Sulla* 8). The purpose of this measure is not recorded, but it need not have been intended to reduce the supposedly great influence of debtors as a class in the senate rather than to remove some particular adversaries of Sulpicius or his equestrian allies; it has also been conjectured that he was seeking to force senatorial landowners to repay loans by selling up land, perhaps at prices advantageous to equestrian purchasers.[47]

It has also been held that Equites had suffered from a depreciation of the silver coinage which, according to Pliny (*NH* xxxiii. 46), had been effected by Drusus, but the extant coins prove that Pliny was in error; some depreciation did occur, but not till 88–87, and it was then doubtless necessitated by a shortage of bullion due to the massive new

---

[45] Asellio: App. i. 54; *Per.* Livy lxxiv; Val. Max. ix. 7. 4. The 'old law' is variously identified with the *lex Genucia* of 342 and the *lex Marcia*, which *may* also be of the fourth century. In that period the plebs had constantly agitated for relief of debts and limitation of usury. In 193 the provisions of 'multae faenebres leges' had been extended to loans made by allies as secret agents of Roman creditors (Livy xxxv. 7). About this time aediles collected fines for their violation (e.g. xxxv. 41). It is uncertain if these measures did not relate merely to interest exceeding a reasonable rate. See *RE* vi. 2187 ff. (Klingmüller) for full discussion. Law of 88, Festus 516 L.: 'unciaria lex appellari coepta est, quam L. Sulla et Q. Pom(peius Rufus) tulerunt, qua sanctum est ut debitores decimam partem . . .'. A senatorial decree of 51/50 (n. 111) again imposed the 12 per cent maximum. All such enactments tended to be ineffective.

[46] M. W. Frederiksen, *JRS* 1966, 126 ff.   [47] Meier, 1966, 83 n. 115.

issues needed to pay the troops.[48] A *lex Papiria* dated by Crawford to 91 had introduced the semuncial *as* and apparently resulted in confusion about the value of the bronze coins used in petty market transactions, which was ended by a measure of the praetors of 85; M. Marius Gratidianus annexed the credit for the reform and endeared himself to the populace. The problem was hardly a matter of grave concern to great financiers, but if it had been, and had determined the policy of the Marians, they would hardly have deferred remedial action for a year after they had secured possession of Rome.

The credit crisis must indeed have been exacerbated since 89, not only by the continuance of fighting in Italy but by the loss of Rome's dominion in the east, with the consequential diminution in public revenues and in the income that publicans and other *negotiatores* had been receiving. It was the Marians who took the most drastic action for relief of debtors by the *lex Valeria* of 86, which reduced all liabilities by three fourths.[49] The beneficiaries must have included not only the owners of great estates unable to repay their loans but countless small men as well; the treasury too was presumably enabled to scale down any arrears due to public contractors. The losers were just those moneyed men who had not themselves been affected by the disappearance of their eastern investments. The measures can only have been justified by what was taken to be the general good, or by sheer necessity; it affords no support to those who see the Marian party as in league with 'big business'.

In fact not all Equites were Marians. Many must have sided with Sulla in the civil war or stayed neutral, and it was among them that he must have recruited most of the new senators needed to double the total number; he chose them, we are told, 'ex equestic ordine', or 'from the best of the Equites'. Cicero, who took no part in the fighting and was too young for enrolment, was probably typical of the recruits; of hereditary equestrian status and from a ruling family at Arpinum which had enjoyed the patronage of Roman nobles.[50] It does indeed seem probable that Sulla deprived the Equites of their valued privilege of reserved seats at the games, since the Roscian law of 67 is said to have *restored* it; we do not know when it had been first conferred, except that the date must be later than the grant of a similar privilege to senators in 194 (ch. 6 n. 155), and Cicero speaks of his hatred for the

---

[48] *RRC* 569–72, 616 (cf. 78 f., 362). Crawford allows that Drusus may have proposed depreciation to pay for his projected largesses (cf. Florus ii. 5).

[49] *RRC* 77 f., 610 f.; Cic. *de offic.* iii. 80; Pliny, *NH* xxxiii. 132, xxxiv. 27. Lex Valeria: Vell. ii. 23; cf. Sall. *Cat.* 33.

[50] Stockton, *Cicero*, ch. 1. Sulla's senators: *Per.* Livy lxxxix; App. *BC* i. 100; they included a few of less repute (Sall. *Cat.* 37; *Or. Lepidi* 21; Dionys. v. 77); see Gabba, 1973 ch. IX = 1976, ch. V.

order, but in the very same breath he refers to the bitter retribution he visited on the old 'iudices', that is to say on the politically prominent section of the order that had been embroiled with the senate in the last few decades (*Cluent.* 151). As often (nn. 56 f.), Cicero has the publicans primarily in mind. It is true that according to Appian (*BC* i. 95) some 1,600 Equites as well as 40 senators appeared on his first proscription list; Florus (ii. 9. 25) says that in all there were 2,000 senators and Equites, most of whom obviously belonged to the second category, among his victims. The number surely exceeded those of the leading publicans whose rancour against Drusus and his friends had been so marked in 91–89. But naturally the chief men in communities which had espoused the Marian side, often of equestrian census, will also have figured in the proscription lists.

For all Sulla's detestation of the publicans he could not dispense with the tax-farming system. The notion that he abolished it in Asia is not warranted by the evidence. In 84 he had had no choice but to demand lump sums from the Asian cities, since the head offices at Rome were under the control of his enemies, and the local organization must have been disrupted by Mithridates. But it is not attested that he essayed any permanent change in the system, and we soon find it in full work once more.[51] Between the time of Polybius and Strabo (iii. 2. 10) the Spanish silver mines passed into private ownership; whenever the state sold them (and there is nothing to show that it was Sulla who did so), it was presumably intended not to disoblige the publicans but to produce a windfall of ready cash for the treasury; former publicans are likely to have been among the purchasers.

To the economic interests of Equites Sulla was probably indifferent. He was, however, resolved, in accordance with his general policy of fortifying the senate's supremacy, to give senators complete control of the criminal courts and to satisfy those 'qui equestrem splendorem pati non potuerunt' (Cic. *Rosc. Amer.* 140). The Equites, irrespective of their past attitude to Sulla, cannot have been content with this forfeiture of their dignity and influence, and doubtless fomented the general indignation aroused by the corruption of senatorial *iudices*. In 70 the senate could not resist the clamour, but a durable compromise was at last achieved; senators were still to constitute one third of the *album iudicum*, Equites in a broad sense two thirds (n. 2).

Once this issue had been resolved, there was no persistent quarrel between the orders. It is significant that in some subsequent trials in which the voting of the different panels of *iudices* is recorded, senators, Equites, and *tribuni aerarii* were all divided: they did not vote as

---

[51] Brunt. *Latomus* 1956, 17 ff.; cf. Badian, 1972, 95.

blocks.[52] Sallust, as Nicolet observed (p. 638), never alludes to the conflict of the orders; it had ceased well before he entered public life. Cicero hoped that they would act together in the unison exemplified in their common opposition to Catiline. He lamented indeed that this concord was disrupted in 61 by the refusal of the senate to meet the claim that the Asian publicans made for a reduction in their contractual liabilities to the treasury, and by a proposal to make equestrian *iudices* subject to penalties for corruption. In 59 Caesar satisfied the demands of the publicans.[53] However, the importance of the controversy was exaggerated by Cicero. It was not primarily to gratify the publicans that Pompey, Crassus, and Caesar formed their coalition, and it was not by their aid that they dominated Rome; they came together for their own ends, and relied on sheer force (pp. 473 ff.). Nor had they the support of the whole equestrian order, since in July 59 Equites, presumably municipal gentry, demonstrated against them (n. 5). We may also note that the move to penalize the corruption of equestrian *iudices* having lapsed, there were suggestions made in the senate in 55 that equestrian officials should be liable for *repetundae*, but they were rejected in a full house (Cic. *Rab. Post.* 13). The senate entertained no strong antipathy to the Equites.

In 50 Caelius assumed that the *iudices* as well as the senate would side with Pompey, now allied with the optimates, against Caesar in a civil war (*Fam.* viii. 14. 3). and Cicero in March 49 could say that they had been Pompey's special admirers (*Att.* viii. 16. 2); admittedly he had also opined in December that the publicans were most friendly to Caesar and that rich people outside the senate would settle for peace at almost any price (vii. 7. 5). Soon they were increasingly alienated from Pompey, when they came to think that their lives and property would be safer if Caesar won; they were in general not prepared to make sacrifices in the senatorial cause.[54] Still, many individual Equites fought for Pompey in 49, and later were hostile to the triumvirs; 2,000 are said to have been victims of triumviral proscriptions.[55] Individuals

---

[52] See esp. Cic. *Qu. fr.* ii. 4. 6; Ascon. 55 C. (cf. 28, 53, 56, 61; Cic. *Att.* i. 16. 5, iv. 15. 4, *Qu. fr.* iii. 4. 1). We must allow for corruption, pressure, and some respect for evidence and law as well as sectional bias.

[53] Cic. *Att.* i. 17. 8–10, 18. 3, 7 and 19. 6, ii. 1. 8, 16. 2, *Planc.* 35, *Rab. Post.* 13, *de offic.* iii. 88; Suet. *Caes.* 20. 3; App. ii. 13; Dio xxxvii. 7. 4; cf. n. 22.

[54] e.g. *Att.* viii. 13, 16, ix. 12. 4, 13. 4; cf. *Fam.* viii. 17. 2 (Caelius). Meier, 1966, 92 (esp. n. 176), argues that their real sympathies lay with Pompey, partly because many who remained neutral and flattered Caesar thought that Cicero should take Pompey's side, but on this see Brunt, *JRS* 1986, 12 ff; his rank and past conduct were deemed to place him under a special obligation.

[55] Dio xli. 18. 6 says that most senators and Equites ultimately joined Pompey, a statement not true even of senators (cf. 43. 2); Appian that 40 leading Equites fell in battle for him (ii. 82). Equites or senators of probably equestrian origin are attested among Pompeian officers (*MRR* ii. 266–71, 279–84, 292, 303, 312 f.). Proscriptions: App. iv. 5.

decided for themselves; in the last crises of the Republic we cannot detect any conflict between the higher orders as such, for both were divided, but can at most say that Equites, naturally enough, cared more for their own security than for the preservation or restoration of the senate's supremacy, which those who shared in its privileges were most apt to equate with liberty.

III

So far then it seems that the intermittent conflicts of Equites with the senate, though perhaps aggravated by the arrogance displayed by nobles to those Equites who themselves aspired to high office, were primarily due to disputes arising from the public contracts, which (as Polybius may indicate) were more frequent than the few actually recorded, and still more to competition for judiciary rights; by securing these rights Equites could attain a position of dignity in the state and free themselves from dependence on the senators, but as a result the authority of the higher order was impaired, and senators themselves became dependent on persons of lower degree. Of course the publicans could also exploit control of the criminal courts to deter magistrates and governors from curtailing the profits of their operations; the contest also affected their material interests. It was the publicans, who could be described as 'the flower of the order',[56] who were most active in performing judicial functions, and who as early as 168 dominated the eighteen centuries (Livy xliii. 16); their organization gave them alone among the Equites the means as well as the incentive to intervene continually in politics and they were therefore equated with the order,[57] although it certainly comprised other elements. To a large extent the quarrels considered above arose between the senate and the publicans.

But was there not a deeper and broader conflict between the orders? The Equites have often been conceived as a 'business' class, in contrast with the great landowners who composed the senatorial aristocracy. Is this conception true? And if so, was the landed class indifferent or actually hostile to the 'business' class? Was the senate under pressure from this class to be more attentive to its interests, and in particular to pursue a policy of imperial expansion from which it hoped to derive profit but which the senate was reluctant to undertake? In that case

[56] See n. 21; cf. Cic. II *Verr.* ii. 175 ('principes equestris ordinis'); *Rab. Post.* 3: 'C. Curtius, princeps equestris ordinis, fortissimus et maximus publicanus'; cf. n. 39 on Plancius and Aelius Lamia.

[57] II *Verr.* ii. 174, iii. 94, 168 ('si publicani, hoc est si equites Romani iudicarent'); cf. n. 27 on Rutilius' condemnation. Florus ii. 5 identifies Drusus' equestrian opponents ('robora populi Romani', Cic. *Cluent.* 153) with the publicans. In Cicero's view the senate's resistance to their demands in 61 dissolved the *concordia ordinum* (n. 53); he could refer indifferently to the terrorization by Clodius in 58 of the Equites (*de dom.* 55, 96) and of the publicans (*Qu. fr.* i. 4. 4).

how successful was the pressure? And in so far as the senate did in fact oppose or neglect business interests, must this be explained by the divergence of the interests of landowners, or can quite different reasons be supplied? Something has already been said, especially in regard to the conflicts of the 80s, which bears on these questions, but they need further discussion.

In the first place, the suggested dichotomy of equestrian and senatorial interests is too sharply cut. Equites as well as senators were landowners, and senators could have their hands in 'business'. I shall begin by considering the different sources of equestrian wealth.

There are of course no statistics by which we can determine their relative importance. Among individuals who were certainly or probably holders of the public horse Nicolet finds 16 publicans, 46 *negotiatores* (a vague and ambiguous term), and at least 50 landowners; but some of them appear in more than one of these categories, and the relative tally of *negotiatores* is swollen by the disproportionate number of allusions in Cicero's speeches and letters of recommendation to persons with *negotia* in the provinces as distinguished from municipal gentry; moreover, *negotia* could include the ownership of land overseas. These data do not then prove (nor does Nicolet suppose) that a majority of Equites were 'businessmen', not landowners.[58] General considerations warrant the view that land was the main source of wealth for most Equites, as for senators; in fact, there are few instances to illustrate the thesis, which no one disputes, that the latter drew their income chiefly from Italian estates, apart from their gains in war and government.[59]

Real estate was the safest and, perhaps chiefly on this account, the most respectable investment.[60] No doubt urban property for renting was often a valuable source of income,[61] but in a largely agricultural society farms, sometimes leased to tenants, must have formed the greater proportion of the assets of the rich. The publicans themselves had to find security in Italian *praedia* for the huge sums they might owe the treasury on their contracts.[62] The leading publican in Cicero's day,

---

[58] Nicolet, 1966, 247–468; see the Tables at 312, 344, 376 (but cf. pp. 297, 341–3), and 416 for Equites (or senators of equestrian birth) of attested municipal origin or active in local government; many of the municipal notables listed on 420 ff. were also surely Equites. At 272 ff. he lists attested Equites who were military tribunes or prefects; in my view (cf. *JRS* 1983, 43), J. Suolahti, *Junior Officers of Roman Army in Rep. Period*, 1955, was justified in assuming the equestrian status of all such officers; this was not an Augustan innovation.

[59] Shatzman, 1973, has collected and analysed what evidence there is; cf. Wiseman, App. III.

[60] Cato, de agric. pr.; Cic. de offic. i. 151 on agricultural property; cf. n. 64.

[61] Frier, 1980, esp. ch. II (which cites the sparse Republican evidence).

[62] Polyb. vi. 17 (οὐσίας); Livy xxii. 60. 4; Cato, fr. 106 M. *FIRA* iii. no. 153 i. 7, iii. 13 (*lex Puteolana*); Cic. II *Verr.* i. 142 f.; *FIRA* i. no. 24, LXXIII f. (*lex Malacitana*, based on Roman practice); Ps.-Ascon. 252 St. *Praedia* (which can include urban property) had to be in Italy; Cic. *Flacc.* 79 f.; Schol. Bobb. 106 St.

Gnaeus Plancius, was a man of hereditary distinction in the flourishing rural district of Atina.[63] The successful merchant did well to invest his gains in land, a course that even freedmen like the fictional Trimalchio followed.[64] Most men of equestrian census, especially after the enfranchisement of Italy, must have been found among the municipal gentry, the *domi nobiles*, like those who came up from Picenum to help in suppressing Saturninus in 100 (*Rab. perd.* 22), from Larinum and neighbouring towns to intercede for Cluentius in 66 (*Cluent.* 197 f.), or from Atina and its vicinity to support the younger Plancius at his trial (*Planc.* 21 f.). Nicolet lists 49 attested Equites of municipal origin and another 23 persons who held municipal offices, possibly or probably Equites; naturally his lists are no more than illustrative (n. 58). Though some men in this class also had 'business' activities, who can doubt that most were men like Sextus Roscius of Ameria, worth 16 million sesterces with 13 estates in the Tiber valley (*Rosc. Amer.* 20), or Cicero's father, who bequeathed lands in Arpinum to his sons?[65] The security of landed property was thus a common economic interest for both senators and Equites.

Still, landowners who invested large sums in the public contracts may well have obtained therefrom a much higher proportion of their income than from their estates. Certainly they had distinct economic interests. Moreover, whereas municipal gentry played only a limited role in Roman public life, chiefly as voters in the centuriate assembly (unless, like the Cicero brothers, they actually embarked on a senatorial career), the publicans were active as a pressure group, with influence which it is easy to comprehend.[66]

They performed functions vital to the state in the absence of a bureaucracy (n. 21). The capital required and profits expected[67] were so great that the co-operation of many was indispensable and forthcoming. Cicero could claim that a company farming Bithynian taxes was 'pars maxima civitatis' and was actually composed of other such companies; so in this instance at least there was interlocking membership (*Fam.* xiii. 9. 2). For large undertakings the publicans formed joint

---

[63] Cic. *Planc.* 32; cf. 21 f. For his equestrian friends in the neighbourhood see n. 39.

[64] Cic. *de off.* i. 151; Petronius 76 f. D'Arms, 1981, ch. 5, is right that Trimalchio should be treated as typical only with great caution. The great landed wealth of the freedman C. Caecilius Isidorus, reported by Pliny, *NH* xxxiii. 135 from his will of 8 BC, perhaps came principally by inheritance from a Metellus (Brunt, *Latomus* 1975, 624 ff.); he claimed liquid capital, available in part for commercial investment, amounting to 60 million HSS, and implied that he had hundreds of thousands of acres under cultivation or pasturage.

[65] Cic. *de leg.* ii. 3, *de leg. agr.* iii. 8; other evidence in O. E. Schmidt, *Ciceros Villen*, 1899, 9 ff.

[66] See endnote 3 for what follows.

[67] The losses of a publican mentioned in Cic. *Fam.* xiii. 10 were no doubt incidental to the civil war; the Pompeians seized on the funds publicans held locally in Asia and Cyprus (Caes. *BC* iii. 31, 103).

stock companies, in which numerous investors could take shares
(Polyb. vi. 17). They differed from all other partnerships (*societates*)
recognized in Roman law, which were automatically dissolved by the
death or withdrawal of any of the partners, subject to discharge of the
mutual obligations incurred while the partnership still subsisted, and
in which each partner had a personal liability to third parties arising
from his actions pursuant to the purposes of the contract, even though
he might be able to recover a proportionate share of his liability from
his partners. The state could not have tolerated the similar dissolution
of companies engaged in performing essential functions as a result of
contingencies that could not be foreseen or controlled when it let out
the contract. The publican companies must therefore have remained in
being until they had completed their contractual obligations, for
example for the construction of a building or for the collection of taxes
for the prescribed period, commonly five years. Indeed, on the expiry
of that period much the same group of *socii* may usually have obtained
a renewal of their rights, as it would have been hard for rivals to have
carried on work for which the former contractors had assembled a
large and experienced staff of freedmen and slaves.[68] Tacitus seems to
suggest that some companies that farmed *portoria* had had a continuous
existence in Nero's reign since the Republic (*Ann.* xiii. 50. 3). The head
offices of such companies were at Rome, where the *socii* could meet in
conclave under *magistri* and pass *decreta*,[69] sometimes on political
questions not directly related to their business. It was the easier to take
their views as expressing those of the whole equestrian order (n. 57), in
which they tended to be the most notable figures, as the companies
alone, not the order, had corporate organization; though a statue was
dedicated to L. Antonius as patron of the eighteen centuries, it was
perhaps individuals who paid and affected to be their representatives;
and there was no precedent (Cic. *Phil.* vi. 13).

Now on occasion the senate or magistrates withstood the publican
companies, indispensable as they were, in their current operations or
circumscribed the future extension of their operations. But it is hard to
detect any economic interests of their own order that can have
prompted such actions. They must have been proceeding in what they
saw as fulfilment of their responsibility as custodians of the treasury or
of the welfare of the subjects (nn. 13, 17, 53). Doubtless they more
commonly failed to protect the subjects, partly because they were

[68] 'Familiae maximae' in Asia: Cic. *de imp. Cn. Pomp.* 16; cf. *Brut.* 85; Caes. *BC* iii. 103. 1; *Dig.*
xxxix. 4. 1. However, competition is attested in Livy xliii. 16; Cic. II *Verr.* i. 143 (small
undertakings), and presumably implicit in the overbidding which would lead the Asian publicans
to seek a reduction in payments to the treasury in 61 (n. 53).

[69] Cic. *de dom.* 74, 142, *Sest.* 32, *Vat.* 8 (on Cicero's banishment and recall), II *Verr.* ii. 172
(honouring governors), *Flacc.* 37 (letters to all senators).

apprehensive of the political power the publicans possessed or were illicitly sharing in their profits, partly because the public revenues depended on the work the publicans did. It must have been for fiscal reasons that some senators actually objected to the abolition of Italian *portoria* in 60, which also involved an obvious loss to those who could profit from the contract. No doubt others thought the measure fiscally defensible after the great accretion of revenues from Pompey's settlement of the east (n. 31), and there was general relief for Italians, consumers as well as traders, which probably gratified most Equites among others.[70] There was no clash here of the economic interests of the two orders.

In certain cases not so far fully considered the senate denied or restricted opportunities for gain from public contracting. There is no actual record of protests from the potential investors, though this may be due to deficiencies in our sources. In 167 it refused to lease the Macedonian gold and silver mines to Roman companies and closed them altogether, on the ground that it was unsafe to let them to the natives and that publicans would prove oppressive.[71] There was to be no Roman army of occupation in Macedon, and it was probably realized that publicans could not safely operate there except under its protection. In 158 the mines were reopened, but not necessarily leased to Roman publicans; they may have been worked for the benefit of the local governments, which issued much silver in the next few years.[72] Pliny tells us of a *lex censoria* that forbade publicans to employ more than 5,000 men in the gold mines near Vercellae (until 42 within the province of Cisalpine Gaul), and of an old decree of the senate that forbade all mining in Italy, a prohibition that certainly did not affect the iron mines of Elba. The date and reasons for these regulations are unknown. Frank conjectured that the companies which mined in Spain desired to restrict competition and that the senate perhaps wished to conserve domestic ores.[73] There is at any rate no ground for supposing that conflict between the orders arose from these enactments. So far as concerns the

[70] Dio xxxvii. 31; Cic. *Att.* ii. 16. 1; cf. *Qu. fr.* i. 1. 33. Badian, 1972, 105, remarks that publicans were compensated by the new contracts for taxes resulting from Pompey's conquests.

[71] The agreement between Diod. xxxi. 8. 6 and Livy xlv. 18. 5 shows that Livy's specific reference to the publicans is not his own interpretation anachronistically imported from the later influence of the publicans, which already in 169 had all but ruined a censor (Livy xliii. 16); both surely drew on a fuller statement in Polybius.

[72] Cassiod. *Chron. Min.* (ed. Mommsen) ii. 130. Gaebler (*Z. f. Num.* 1902, 143 f.) pointed out that the Macedonian communities minted much silver in the succeeding years. The senate may have become less apprehensive of a local rising. If so, Andriscus' revolt was a shock. Annexation followed, with the installation of a Roman garrison (*IM* 428 f.). We know that in 63 the old royal domain in Macedon was leased by censors to Roman publicans (n. 75), not whether this was also true of the mines.

[73] *NH* xxxiii. 78, iii. 138, xxxvii. 202. Elba: Strabo v. 2. 6; cf. Frank, *ESAR* i. 180.

farming of taxes and of rents on public domains, Roman companies farmed the *portoria*[74] and dues on public lands[75] in all cases for which we have any records, but so far as we know it was not until the Gracchan era that they were employed, in the east, to collect tribute. In Spain, for example, and probably in all western provinces except Sicily, the government was content to demand lump-sum payments from the local communities.[76] No doubt in the wilder areas publicans could not have operated safely. But the case of Sicily is striking. The tithes on grain were farmed city by city not to Roman companies but to individual contractors, who might be Romans but commonly were not, and it was not till 75 that a Roman company was authorized to collect the quotas on fruits. Again we do not hear of any equestrian pressure, which the senate had to resist,[77] to change the Sicilian system. Conceivably the capital available for Roman companies was absorbed in other public contracts, notably tax-farming in the east.

The publicans were of course not the only Equites whose capital was employed in 'business'. We also hear much of *negotiatores*, among whom they are only included at times. It is their activity beyond Italy with which I shall primarily be concerned, since it is often thought that it affected imperial policy. Both before and after the Social war Italian *negotiatores* are amply attested in the east, not only within Roman provinces but in many other places where Rome exercised a hege- mony; much of our evidence comes from inscriptions. In the west there is no comparable epigraphic testimony, but literary allusions suggest, what we should in any case expect, that they were no less numerous, for instance, in Sicily, Spain, and Africa.[78] Even Transalpine Gaul,

[74] Italy n. 70; Sicily, Cic. II *Verr.* ii. 171 etc.; Asia, *Att.* xi. 10. 1 (cf. n. 97); Cilicia, *Att.* v. 15. 4; Syria, *de prov. cons.* 10 (note 'vectigalis'). The farming of *portoria* attested under the Principate also in Gaul, Africa, and Spain (De Laet, 1949, 376 ff.) obviously went back to the Republic.

[75] e.g. in Bithynia, Chersonese, Macedon, and presumably other public domains listed by Cic. *de leg. agr.* ii. 50 f. Note also allusions to *scriptura*, levied on cattle pastured on public domains in Asia (Lucilius 671 M; *Att.* v. 15. 4), Sicily (II *Verr.* ii. 169 etc.), Africa (*FIRA* i². 8. 82 etc.), Cilicia (*Att.* v. 15. 4). *FIRA* l.c. shows that publicans also collected rents or tithes from cultivable land in Africa, which must have been chiefly public land, since 'plerique Poenorum', like the Spanish communities, paid lump sums as tribute to Rome without intervention by publicans (II *Verr.* iii. 12). If Sherk 12 antedates C. Gracchus' regulation of Asian tribute, the publicans already active then and in dispute with the Pergamenes may have been collecting tithes only from the old royal domain. Cf. n. 77 on Sicily.

[76] See last note for Spain and Africa. Probably the same practice was adopted in Transalpine Gaul; Caesar demanded a fixed sum from the peoples he subdued (Suet. *Caes.* 25).

[77] II *Verr.* iii. 18. See in general V. Scramuzza, *ESAR* iii. 237 ff., 253 ff., 340 f. *Ager publicus*, e.g. at Leontini, was subject both to tithes leased locally and to a rent leased at Rome, 258 ff.

[78] See esp. J. Hatzfeld, 1919; cf. *BCH* 1912, 5–218 (Delos), whence most material in *ESAR* iv for Greece and Asia. See *ESAR* iii. 334 ff. for Sicily; iii. 135–7, 143 f. for Spain (cf. Gabba, 1973, 289 ff. = 1976, 105 ff.); iv. 26 ff. for Africa (cf. S. Gsell, *Hist. anc. de l'Afrique du Nord* vii. 58 ff.); G. Clementi, *I romani nella Gallia meridionale*, 1974, for Gaul; Frank, *ESAR* i. 387–92 selects examples. The evidence for all areas is also reviewed by Wilson, 1966, and in *IM*, ch. xiv.

only fifty years after its occupation, was so packed, Cicero alleges, with Roman *negotiatores* that no payment was made which did not go through their accounts,[79] and archaeological evidence reveals a vigorous Italian wine trade even beyond the confines of the province.[80] In 57 Caesar dispatched a force to overawe Alpine tribes and open up the route, apparently over the Great St Bernard, which merchants had been accustomed to cross with great peril and on payment of heavy tolls (*BG* iii. 1). Caesar's story shows how traders would follow the Roman standards, among other things assisting in the procurement of supplies; a massacre of such people at Cenabum heralded the revolt of Vercingetorix (vii. 3).

Who were these *negotiatores*? In the east many, even though Greeks might call them Romans, were in the pre-Sullan period not Roman citizens, much less Equites, as they came from communities (some of them Latin) not yet enfranchised.[81] Thus in the very period in which conflict between the orders was most acute, people of this status can have had no part in shaping it. It is another matter if their discontents contributed to the revolt of the Italian allies, but this too is a hypothesis which seems to me unfounded (p. 127).

The Roman *negotiatores* overseas were themselves not all wealthy. In Cyrenaica, Augustus was informed that in 7/6 BC only 215 had assets worth 10,000 sesterces on census valuations.[82] Some were freedmen and other persons of low degree; of course the humbler *negotiatores* may often have been agents for big men. Still, some of those domiciled abroad, as well as the principals of such agents, had substantial means and included Equites.

They were certainly not all traders. The term *negotiatores* and its equivalents ('qui negotia habent' or 'qui negotiantur') are ambiguous.[83] Cicero could speak of 'all the publicans, farmers, stock-breeders and the rest of the *negotiatores*' operating in Transalpine Gaul:[84] 'The rest' must embrace bankers or money-lenders, merchants, and ship-owners. Men in 'business' are here conceived as all those active in the

---

[79] *Font.* 11–13, 46.   [80] Clementi (n. 78) reviews the evidence.

[81] Wilson, 1966, ch. VIII; Latin nomenclature is of course no proof of Roman citizenship, nor Oscan of allied status; cf. p. 515; Hatzfeld, (n. 78) 238 ff. The designation 'Italici' in Sall. *BJ* 28, 47; Diod. xxxiv/xxxv. 31 for expatriates in Africa, and *ILS* 864; Diod. xxxiv/xxxv. 2. 27–34 (where the reference to Roman Equites in 31 is, given the context, unreliable) for those in Sicily, suggests that they were not all Roman.

[82] *FIRA* i². 68, 1; 1 ff. In some provinces, hardly here, there were peasant immigrants from Italy, e.g. veterans, but in my view (*IM*, ch. XIV) they were not numerous before the 40s, nor would they have been classed as *negotiatores*.

[83] Cf. Wilson, 1966, 4–6; Nicolet 358 ff.; from both I differ at least in nuance.

[84] *Font.* 46; cf. *Fam.* xiii. 53. 2 for *negotia* inland. For substantial Roman estates abroad see Wilson, 1966, 49 ff. (Africa), 56 (Sicily, where we find senators among them, Cic. II *Verr.* iii. 93, 97, 152; the list in Scramuzza, *ESAR* 337 f., is unreliable on the occupations of Roman residents), 159 ff. (the east); cf. *IM* 213.

management of property of every kind. But elsewhere Cicero differentiates *negotiatores* from publicans, landowners, and merchants alike. Evidently he is then appropriating the terms to bankers and moneylenders.[85] Individuals whom he mentions as 'in business' often fall in this category. On the other hand, the *negotiatores* who clashed with the Asian publicans in 59 (n. 97) were patently shippers. We know also of 'mercatores qui Alexandri[ai] Asiai Syriai negotiantur' (*ILS* 7273). In 46 the expatriate community at Utica included 300 affluent Romans; it is inconceivable that they were mostly occupied in providing credit facilities rather than shipping grain.[86] The same is surely true of the 'Italici' or 'cives Romani' who were 'in business' at Agrigentum and Panhormus (*ILLRP* 380, 387), ports where their presence is naturally connected with Sicilian grain exports. Many Italians at Delos were probably engaged in the slave-trade, of which Delos was the most notable centre; this particular form of trading, indispensable to the ancient economy, was probably despised (as it was by American slave-owners), and is therefore seldom avowed.[87] Bankers and moneylenders were often, perhaps invariably, very rich, as appears from their ability to finance princes, cities, and Roman magnates. Such men cannot have been numerous. Their wealth doubtless brought them social esteem, so that a Cicero could count them among his 'friends'.

The various business activities of Italians overseas could be interlocking. Land was perhaps often acquired by money-lenders to whom it had been offered as security for loans never repaid.[88] Contractors for army supplies and the extraction of ore (and within Italy for construction work) necessarily had to buy, sell, and move commodities (including slaves). The tax-farmers would have huge sums in cash at the disposal of their local representatives, pending remittances to the state or to the investors,[89] which could be employed on any enterprise that promised a lucrative return; they certainly used it on making loans, banking, and trading.[90] In sum, the groups of Italians said to

[85] e.g. II *Verr.* ii. 153, 168, 188, *Font.* 12, *Cluent.* 198, *Planc.* 64.

[86] *B. Afr.* 88, 90. Plut. *Cato Minor* 59 describes the 300 as bankers and merchants. There were also important *conventus* at e.g. Hadrumetum, Thapsus, and Zama (*B. Afr.* 97).

[87] W. V. Harris, *Mem. Amer. Acad. Rome* 1980, 117 ff. (129 ff. on slave-traders). Delos: Strabo xiv. 5. 2.

[88] Cic. *Flacc.* 51 affords one example.

[89] Caes. *BC* iii. 31, 103; this explains 'vectigalium residuis' in Suet. *Aug.* 101.

[90] Loans: Cic. II *Verr.* ii. 186 f. It would seem that Nicomedes III of Bithynia met his debts on loans from publicans by making over to them his subjects to be sold as slaves (Diod. xxxvi. 3). The indemnity of 120 million *denarii* imposed by Sulla in 84 on the Asian cities is said to have swollen to a total liability of 720 million, of which half had actually been met by 70, when Lucullus scaled it down; the province was oppressed by 'publicans and money-lenders' (App. *BM* 63; Plut. *Luc.* 7, 20). It can be presumed that publicans were among the creditors. Probably Sulla extracted from the cities the last penny they could pay, and they were so exhausted thereafter that they could meet arrears of the indemnity, annual Roman taxes, and their own expenditure only by

'be in business' in overseas centres comprised bankers, landowners, publicans, and their agents, as well as traders. Probably the last class outnumbered the rest, but were of less account.

Moreover, merchants as such were not only persons of relatively low standing; they were destitute of the organization which the publicans possessed. As already observed, they could not form joint stock-companies in which the concentration and accumulation of capital would give them economic power, and the corporate capacity to exert political pressure at Rome. In local centres indeed where Romans overseas congregated, they were in Cicero's time often associated in 'conventus civium Romanorum', whose members (not, of course, all of them merchants), by reason of their riches or status as citizens of the imperial state, might dominate the indigenous communities.[91] Very probably governors were often responsive to their wishes, if only from prejudice in favour of their co-nationals. Otherwise Roman 'busi-nessmen' could only seek as individuals the intervention of powerful patrons on their behalf. The thirteenth book of Cicero's letters *ad Familiares* contains a corpus of letters mostly recommending to men in official positions his friends or clients and their 'affairs' in provinces. Those for whom he solicits assistance include senators, Equites, provincials, and others of unknown status. The 'affairs' are sometimes unspecified; others are explicitly related to landholding or loans, only one mentions trade (xiii. 75). In Cicero's eyes the trader was disrepu-table, unless he were engaged in large-scale importation and distribu-tion (*de offic.* i. 151); it was surely their wealth that gave merchants of this kind respectability. It is significant that few Romans called themselves merchants.[92] They preferred the term *negotiator* or equiva-lent phrases, which veiled their true occupation and assimilated them to those whose 'affairs', consisting in public contracts, landowning, and providing credit facilities, were better regarded. Cicero allows that some of those at Puteoli, the port where most of Rome's grain imports arrived, were 'honesti'; they were 'homines locupletes'. But overseas traders, who seldom visited Rome, 'homines tenues, obscuro loco nati',

borrowing, especially from Italians, at rates of interest determined by the paucity of liquid funds and the poor security offered, only after Sulla's pacification of Italy; cf. Sherwin-White, 1984, 247–52. Cic. *Att.* vi. 1. 16, 2. 5 shows that publicans in Cilicia debited the cities with arrears, if possible at usurious rates of interest; this was a paper transaction in which no money passed from the publicans, who in fact found it hard to collect on these loans. Banking: Cic. *Fam.* v. 20. 9, *Att.* xi. 2. 3. Trade: under the *lex Antonia de Termessibus* (68 BC) publicans are exempt from the local tolls on commodities conveyed by land or sea through their territory. Termessus is not on the seaboard; Magie 1176 f. rightly inferred that this was a standard provision, applying to other 'free' cities.

[91] *IM* 220 ff.

[92] Nicolet 367 notes that only 3 *mercatores* appear in the Index to *ILLRP*, and that no Eques is so described. Cf. J. Rougé, *Recherches sur l'organisation du commerce maritime en Méditerranée sous l'empire rom.*, 1966, 274 ff.

the sort whom Verres thought it safe to flog, cast into the quarries, and execute, Roman citizens though they were, were probably more typical, and obviously possessed neither equestrian status nor political influence.[93] Though Cicero's client Rabirius Postumus certainly engaged in trade on a large scale, it is his more respectable activities as publican and money-lender that Cicero chooses to stress. Specific allusions, literary or epigraphic, to merchants are rare, and no prominent Eques known to us was primarily a merchant. Atticus, for instance, drew his income from urban property, estates in Epirus, and banking and money-lending.[94]

The *Commentariolum Petitionis* illustrates the electoral importance of the publicans (3, 50) and of the eighteen centuries (33); there is no mention of traders.[95] In 49, when Cicero enumerates the various categories of 'boni' in Italy, i.e. of 'locupletes', he mentions only publicans, money-lenders, and landowners, and in lamenting the hardships that Pompey's projected blockade must inflict on Italy, he has not a word of the losses that traders will incur.[96] Cicero adjured his brother as proconsul of Asia to conciliate the publicans and others there whose business had enriched them and who thought that they owed the security of their fortunes to his consulship. Since he prided himself in restoring credit in 63 (*de offic.* ii. 84), the 'others' he had in mind were probably money-lenders. It was also Quintus' duty to care for the provincials; Cicero admits that it was a hard task to mediate between them and the resident Romans; it is plain that he was thinking primarily of the excessive claims of the publicans, though he was somewhat perturbed by the arbitrary dealings of Quintus with some other individual Romans, including one Catienus, 'homo levis ac sordidus [perhaps then a trader] sed tamen equestri censu'. When the farmers of the Asian *portoria* were involved in a dispute both with the provincials and the local Roman shippers, Cicero thought that the latter were in the right, but he hoped for a compromise and in the last resort was prepared for political reasons to back the publicans.[97]

[93] II *Verr.* v. 154 (Puteoli), contrast iii. 96, v. 140–68, esp. 167. *Negotiatores* of higher rank in Sicily (e.g. ii. 69, iii. 148, iv. 42 f.) need not be merchants.

[94] Rabirius: Nicolet 1000 ff. (cf. 762 ff. on Aelius Lamia); Atticus: *RE* Suppl. viii. 516 ff. (Fager); Nepos, *Att.* 14. 3 is incorrect in deriving his wealth almost entirely from his Epirote land, see e.g. Cic. *Att.* i. 13. 1, 19. 9, 20. 4, iv. 15. 7, 16. 7, v. 13. 2, vi. 1. 25, ix. 9. 4.

[95] Note also 29 on 'multi homines urbani industrii, multi libertini in foro gratiosi'. The votes even of freedmen, presumably engaged in trade and industry at Rome itself, were worth canvassing, doubtless because they controlled the centuries of the first class in the four urban tribes. The *Tabula Hebana* (EJ 94a. 23, 33) implies that few, if any, senators or Equites were registered in two of these tribes (Succusana and Esquilina) in the early Principate.

[96] *Att.* vii. 7. 5, ix. 9. 2, 10. 3.

[97] *Qu. fr.* i. 1. 6 f., 33, i. 2. 6, *Att.* ii. 16. 4 (with Shackleton Bailey ad loc.; text and interpretation in detail are difficult).

Cicero's speech in favour of the Manilian law is of some significance in this connection, not least because it is necessarily his cue to dwell on those considerations which he expected to have most effect on a popular audience. In arguing that Pompey was the right man to finish off the war with Mithridates, he naturally expatiated on his success against the pirates. Their depredations had obviously been injurious to all sea-borne trade, and Cicero refers to this, but he makes more of the losses of revenue, the difficulty of transporting troops, the sufferings of Roman *socii*, the damage to Rome's prestige; above all he insists on the danger to the vital corn-supply. As for Mithridates, Rome's honour requires his elimination; it is in this connection that Cicero recalls, but in a rather colourless way, his massacre of Italians in 88, i.e. of *negotiatores* as well as publicans. Economic interests also have a large place in the argument. Cicero reminds his audience that many Romans besides the publicans have property in Asia, and that if this property is put at risk there may be a recurrence of the credit crisis at Rome itself which had followed Mithridates' invasion of Asia in 88. It would seem that he was thinking chiefly of Italian bankers and money-lenders in the east, though he also implies that the interests of merchants were at stake, when claiming that in the past Rome had fought many wars in defence of her merchants. Rome's duty to protect her subjects is far more often his theme; and he insists principally on the necessity of securing the state's revenues and of protecting the publicans on whom the treasury relied for collection.[98] The relatively low importance that he lays on purely commercial interests reflects not merely or chiefly his own attitude, but that which he assumed to be prevalent.

If all this be true, *negotiatores*, traders, and even bankers or money-lenders had no such means at their disposal as publicans for operating as political pressure groups or determining the attitude of the Equites as an order. There is, however, nothing to show that senators evinced any antagonism to their interests. Senators too could take part in all sorts of 'business' enterprises. Some owned lands overseas (n. 84). Others defied or evaded the ban on their sharing in public contracts (n. 1). Others again engaged in trade and money-lending. All this was compatible with social prejudices against trading or money-lending, partly because the involvement of senators in business could be effected through intermediaries, partly because their wealth and status did not

[98] Pirates, *de imp. Cn. Pomp.* 31 ff.; effects on trade, 31 f.; on *socii* 32; on revenues, 32; on armies, 32; on grain imports, 33 f.; cf. 44. It is implicit that Pompey restored the state's honour, as emphasized in the *lex Gabinia Calpurnia* (best text in Nicolet *et al.*, *Insula Sacra*, 1980); that is again involved in the Mithridatic war (6 ff.). Mithridates: massacre, 7 (cf. *Flacc.* 60); *socii*, 4, 6, 12, 14, 19, 21, 45; *negotiatores*, 6, 17 ff.; credit crisis of 88, 19; wars fought for merchants, 11; *vectigalia*, 4 f., 6 f., 14 ff., 21, 45; publicans, 15–17.

depend on these activities. In any case there could be no objection to the trading that was integral to the management of their own estates.

It is true that in 218 a law proposed by the tribune Q. Claudius enacted that no senator or his son might possess a ship with a capacity of over 300 *amphorae*, enough, it was held, for the conveyance of the fruits of his own estates. We do not know why it was passed, but Livy's explanation that 'all commercial gain appeared unbefitting to senators', though it accords with the prejudices expressed by Cicero, cannot have represented aristocratic sentiments at the time, since it is said to have been solidly opposed by the nobility; that suggests incidentally that it is unlikely to have been enforced. Cicero in prosecuting Verres, who had as governor of Sicily built and operated a ship, concedes Hortensius' plea in defence that the old laws Verres had violated were dead. That in turn suggests that Verres' conduct, though probably unusual, was not without preced-ent.[99] Senators were necessarily interested in commerce, to the extent that even the Claudian law recognized as legitimate, in so far as they had to market surpluses of their estates. They might also manufacture wine and oil from their grapes and olives, rather than contract the work out or sell the fruits.[100] The produce of their lands might include material for making bricks, tiles, pottery, and fuller's earth, and they might have their own kilns and workshops for these purposes. Their wine and oil might be shipped in their own *amphorae*. Some *amphorae* bear the marks of a great noble, Appius Claudius Pulcher, perhaps the consul of 38; and the Sestii of Cosa, who probably first attained senatorial status in the first century, operated in this way on a fairly large scale.[101]

Senators also did not refrain from money-lending. Though Cato the censor approved the old legal rule that a usurer was to be mulcted fourfold, it was already obsolete in his own day. He himself partici-pated in bottomry loans, which could be distinguished from other loans at interest, since they were in part a form of insurance on ships and cargoes, and almost indispensable to sea-borne commerce. And even the moral disapprobation of usury still voiced by Cicero did not deter eminent aristocrats of his time, Pompey and Marcus Brutus, from

---

[99] Livy xxi. 63. 2 (modern interpretations are various and all conjectural); Cic. II *Verr.* v. 45. Paul (cf. n. 1) says that the ban was reimposed by Caesar's law *de repetundis* of 59; cf. *Dig.* xlix. 14. 46. 2; l. 5. 3.

[100] Contrast Cato, *de agric.* 10–13 with 144–7.

[101] D'Arms, 1981 (admirably indexed), chs. 2–4, and for the early Principate ch. 7, though some of his examples are too speculative or partly vitiated by his misconception about Roman 'company law' (n. 66). Cf. Wiseman 198 f.

lending to princes or cities at rates of interest exceeding those allowed by law. They acted through men of straw who, as it happened, were almost certainly Equites.[102]

The rich, including senators, would naturally have large liquid sums at their disposal, not all of which they would wish to see lying idle in their coffers or on deposit with bankers. These moneys were surely used not only to make loans of the kind made by Pompey and Brutus or to supply credit, as Marcus Crassus did, to other Romans of standing, but also to finance the business undertakings of their own slaves and freedmen. Slaves could carry on many transactions with their *peculium*, money or other assets which belonged in law to their masters, but which for certain purposes was treated as their own.[103] Obviously the masters took a share in the proceeds. Such slaves would tend to obtain manumission, and continue in the same business, often still supported by patrons. To judge from inscriptions, in Rome and to a lesser extent in other Italian towns men of servile status or extraction had a large, sometimes a preponderant, share in many trading and industrial enterprises (cf. n. 95). They might amass great wealth, some part of which their patrons might often have the right to inherit on their decease. But it is unlikely that they could have started without capital provided by their owners or patrons, who may often have had a continuing interest in their ventures.[104] C. Caecilius Isidorus (n. 64) may well have laid the basis of his fortune with money that a Metellus placed at his disposal. Some freedmen in business in the east bear the gentile names of proud aristocratic families.[105] By these means senators could, without soiling their own hands, draw profits from sources that they did not need to acknowledge and that Cicero disparaged. 'Multis *occulto* crescit res faenore' (Hor. *ep.* i. 1. 80).

Very possibly some Republican senators had no stake in 'business';

[102] *De agric. pr.* 1; Cic. *de offic.* ii. 89; cf. i. 150; Plut. *Cato Maior* 21. Brutus and Pompey: Cic. *Att.* v. 21. 10–12, vi. 1. 3–7, 2. 7–9, 3. 5, *Fam.* xiii. 56. As Brutus' agents held prefectures under Ap. Claudius or Cicero, I regard them as Equites (cf. n. 58). Cic. *Parad.* 16 indicts Crassus for 'dimissionem libertorum ad defaenerandas diripiendasque provincias'; by contrast to eminent Romans he lent free of interest (Plut. *Cr.* 3. 1), putting political obligations on many senators (Sall. *Cat.* 48. 5). The provincial *negotia* of other senators (*Fam.* xiii. 41 f., 55, 57) were no doubt loans. Q. Considius who was owed 15 million HSS in 63 by other Romans was perhaps a senator (Nicolet 848 f.). For Cicero himself see J. Carcopino, *Cicero, The Secrets of his Correspondence*, 1981, 55 ff. Cf. also Wiseman 199 ff.

[103] Buckland, 1908, chs. viii f.: the little Republican evidence (A. Watson, *Law of Persons in the Later Roman Rep.*, 1967, 178 ff.) is sufficient to show that essentially the relevant classical law goes back to the Republic.

[104] Treggiari 91–106. Most Capuan manufacturers in M. W. Frederiksen, *PBSR* 1959, 107 ff., are freedmen. The data analysed by Gummerus, *RE* ix. 1496 ff., are chiefly imperial, but what Republican evidence there is fits his picture; probably the 'statistics' somewhat underrate the part played by the freeborn in trade and industry (*IM* 387).

[105] Wilson, 1966, 110.

those who had could probably have said, like the younger Pliny in a later time: 'I am almost entirely in real estate, but have some money out at interest' (*Ep.* iii. 20. 8). Their own interests in business would have then been marginal. But many besides Cicero would have had 'friends' or clients in the business world, and senators who had to resort to borrowing had reason perhaps to ingratiate themselves with their creditors in their political conduct.

Yet just as the senate, or individual governors of the most various political complexions, Lucullus and Gabinius, Caesar and Cicero, could at times withstand the pressure of publicans for the benefit of treasury or taxpayers, so they could also set themselves against the excesses of usury.[106] The primitive laws that forbade or limited the taking of interest were indeed obsolete.[107] In the relatively complex economy of the late Republic the provision of credit facilities was indispensable, and it was recognized that it could not be obtained unless there were a reasonable return on loans. When good security was available, the normal rate of interest was not high. At Rome it had been no more than $\frac{1}{3}$ per cent per month in 54, when it doubled because so much liquid cash was taken up in electoral corruption (Cic. *Att.* iv. 15. 7). In such conditions the maintenance of credit was considered a necessity. In 63 under Cicero's leadership the senate would grant no relief to debtors and forced them to fulfil their obligations in full.[108] Credit (*fides*) was among the 'fundamenta otiosae dignitatis' on which Cicero expected all good men to agree (pp. 61 f.). Mithridates had to be eliminated among other reasons because insecurity in Asia could lead to a crisis in the money-market (n. 98). It was only in exceptional conditions due to civil wars in the 80s and 40s that special relief was given to debtors (pp. 158 f.).

However, the ancient prejudice against usury persisted to the extent that attempts could be made to limit rates of interest to those which were considered fair; but these attempts reflected traditional moral views rather than the self-interest of a landed class in Italy which was supposedly in constant financial embarrassment. Lucullus banned usury in Asia for the sake of the provincials, not of Italian landowners;

---

[106] Lucullus in Asia limited the rate of interest to 1 per cent (compound?) monthly, deducted interest already paid (at a higher rate?) from principal due for repayment, and provided that no creditor should receive more than a quarter of a debtor's income: it is said that all loans were then paid off in four years (Plut. *Luc* 20). Caesar would allow creditors in Spain to take no more than two thirds of debtors' incomes (*Caes.* 12; we may note that usurious exactions were not confined to eastern provinces; cf. Cic. *Mur.* 42; Sall. *Cat.* 40 for indebtedness in Transalpine Gaul, which doubtless led to the Allobrogic revolt of 62, Dio xxxvii. 42 etc.). Gabinius: n. 29. Cicero: *Att.* v. 21. 11–13 (maximum interest fixed at 1 per cent compound a month), vi. 1. 16, 2. 5; he would appoint no *negotiator* in his province as prefect (v. 21. 10).

[107] For what follows see generally *RE* vi. 2187 ff. (Klingmüller); ch. 6 n. 60.

[108] Cic. *de offic.* ii. 84; cf. Dio xxxvii. 25. 4; Cic. *Cat.* ii. 18–21; Sall. *Cat.* 21. 33.

Cicero says that the 'aequitas' of his regulations was such that they were observed for the next twenty years.[109] He himself took similar measures in Cilicia and announced them in an edict he terms tralatician (*Att.* vi. 1. 15 f.). They probably accorded with those commonly adopted in principle since Q. Scaevola's government of Asia (*c.* 95), even if Lucullus' predecessors in Asia left them in abeyance there. It was probably for the benefit of provincials that the senate itself passed a decree of unknown content in 60, which had the effect of preventing Atticus from collecting what he thought his due from the free city of Sicyon. Cicero imputes it partly to malice (i.e. against *negotiatores*), partly to the conception that it was fair. The second explanation is more plausible than the first. The decree not only had the support of Cato, who proclaimed his devotion to the welfare of the subjects, but of the *pedarii*, the very section of the senate in which men of equestrian origins and connections can be presumed to have predominated.[110]

In 51–50 the senate decreed that at Rome interest should be limited to 1 per cent per month.[111] We do not know why this measure was passed; the maximum fixed much exceeded that to which the rate had risen in 54; perhaps fear of civil war had already reduced liquidity. A critic alleged that this was subversive of credit, but the rule then established seems to have remained nominally in force throughout the Principate, though it did not apply to bottomry loans with the greater risks that they involved. We should not ascribe it to sectional interest or hostility to 'businessmen', many of whom, no less than landowners, would have benefited from relatively easy terms of credit. It is of course unwarranted to assume that the senate was never actuated by considerations of justice and the general welfare, even though it might be too ready to grant exemptions to persons of influence without scrutiny; in the same way individuals like Atticus (*Att.* vi. 1. 5) or Cicero himself (n. 24) could apply pressure on governors to accede to the claims of their friends without regard to merits of those claims, which they might choose not to inspect too closely.

Limitation of interest rates was a deviation from the normal *laissez-faire* attitude of ancient states, Rome included, an attitude not inspired by economic theory, of which there was none,[112] but conditioned by the lack of government machinery to make interference effective. There was hardly any regulation of trade or industry. They might

---

[109] *Acad. Pr.* ii. 3.   [110] *Att.* i. 20. 4, ii. 1. 10; cf. i. 13. 1, 19. 9.

[111] Cic. *Att.* v. 21. 13 (the allusion to C. Iulius is obscure). On the Gabinian law forbidding loans at Rome to foreign embassies, see M. Bonnefond in C. Nicolet (ed.), *Des ordres à Rome*, 1984, 61 ff.; it was not designed to restrain money-lending to provincials.

[112] M. I. Finley, 1985, ch. vi.

indeed be subject to taxation. Ancient states were loath to tax citizens directly; they preferred to rely on rents from public domains, including mines, on transit and customs dues, monopolies, taxes on sales or on particular occupations, and so forth. All these revenues could be, and commonly were, collected by publicans in default of a civil service. For the same reason there could be no effective control of private commercial and industrial enterprises, and laws like those on usury were apt to fall into desuetude; the enforcement of laws too commonly rested on the private efforts of delators incited by rewards. Customs duties were normally levied with no regard to the ownership or provenance of the goods or the ships carrying them. This was, for instance, the Roman practice both in Italy and the provinces. The aim was to raise revenue; no one thought of giving preference to native producers or merchants; in fact duties were generally low.[113] There is indeed one important qualification to be made in regard to this *laissez-faire* habit. Governments were always concerned to ensure the importation of essential supplies, especially food. They would therefore intervene when private enterprise could not be expected to meet the need. At various times the Republican government took steps to procure imports of grain when a dearth threatened shipments to Rome. The construction by magistrates in the second century of harbour works, *emporia*, and the like also facilitated the city's imports; there is no need to invoke the influence of traders, even though it was of advantage to them.[114]

Trade was undoubtedly important in the Italian economy. The city of Rome had become dependent on imports of grain, especially from Sicily, Sardinia, and Africa. Even grain collected as tithes had to be transported by private enterprise, and much more must have been bought and shipped by merchants on their own account. Storage too was probably provided chiefly or entirely in private granaries.[115] Naturally Italian business communities were especially conspicuous in Sicily and Africa. There were also substantial imports of luxury goods and of slaves. It is often thought that most slaves imported were captives made by Roman generals, but even these would normally be sold in the camp, and placed on the Italian market by slave-dealers; and in fact many or most of those who reached Italy came from regions where Rome had fought no wars, and must have been purchased by traders, partly among the victims of piracy or of fighting between

[113] De Laet, 1949, Part I. Low *ad valorem* rates are attested in Republican Sicily (Cic. II *Verr.* ii. 185: 5 per cent) and in the Principate, except for tolls at imperial frontiers; in Gaul duties on wine varied from place to place (De Laet 79 ff.).

[114] Rickman, 1980, chs. I–II.

[115] Rickman, 1980, chs. V and VI. Some *horrea* were owned by senators.

peoples beyond the frontiers. The importance of Delos as an *emporium*, and the prominence of Italians there, probably depended in part on the slave-trade (n. 87). The cost of imports was met not only from the profits of empire but by exports, for instance of wine. Italians presumably had some advantage in supplying the needs or shipping the products of their own country; moreover, the influx of wealth into Italy may well have meant that Italians tended to have more capital than others for all kinds of commercial undertakings, notably of course for banking and money-lending. But in general the Roman government in the Republic had no incentive to promote Roman or Italian trading activity. This was not the result of hostility to or contempt for the 'business' community, nor to deliberate indifference to its interests; it was the product of a habitual and unconscious attitude which kept the state aloof from commercial activity, except in so far as it was a source of public revenue or indispensable to the procurement of vital supplies.

It is true that in the first century it seems to have been Rome's policy to require exemption from the tolls imposed by cities within Rome's dominion for goods transported by publicans (n. 90). This was a privilege procured by their exceptional power and the importance of their public functions, and it would not have been needed, if citizens as such already enjoyed the same immunity. Probably then the insistence of the government in 187 that Ambracia should free all Italian traders from her tolls is an instance as isolated as it is inexplicable of a policy favouring them.

In 168 Rome made Delos a free port. The effect, and probably the intention, was to divert much traffic from Rhodes, to diminish her revenue from customs duties, and in consequence to weaken her naval power. Delos became the principal *emporium* of the Aegean, especially after the destruction of Corinth in 146, which was, so far as we can tell, a purely vindictive punishment for disloyalty. Certainly Italian *negotiatores* flocked to Delos, but so did others of various nationalities: the Italians had no special privileges.[116]

To an increasing extent sea-borne commerce in the Mediterranean suffered from the depredations of the pirates. These naturally affected the necessary imports of peoples under Roman rule or protection, and eventually of Rome herself. In 102 the senate made its first attempt to suppress the evil by dispatching M. Antonius to Cilicia. A more systematic assault was planned in 101 or 100. There is reason to think that it was promoted by *populares*. The extant fragments of the law that they carried declares that it is designed to enable Romans, Latins, and

[116] Livy xxxviii. 44. 4 (Ambracia); Polyb. xxxi. 10 (Delos). Harris, 1979, 94 (among others), takes a somewhat different view; cf. n. 120.

all peoples in the friendship of the Roman people to sail the seas in safety and obtain what is right.[117] On this footing it was not inspired by merely Roman commercial interests.

The measures taken at this time had at best only temporary success. By 67 the pirates had all but closed the seas. Rome's prestige was damaged, and the population of Rome was in danger of famine. It is clear that these were the chief considerations that made the demand for the appointment of Pompey to clear the seas irresistible. If the senate opposed it, it was for political reasons: the senators were jealous and apprehensive of Pompey. It has been conjectured that they had been less ready to initiate effective action because the pirates contributed to the abundance and cheapness of the slaves whose labour they needed on their estates. There is no proof of this, and it seems more likely that their inertia is an example of their general incapacity at this time for the efficient conduct of affairs; probably too no one but Pompey had the insight to discern that the evil could be suppressed only by an organization extending over all the seas under a unified command.[118] It was also only under popular pressure that in 57 Pompey was granted the *cura annonae* for five years, with the *imperium* needed to requisition crops and stocks in the hands of merchants and to divert corn ships from other destinations to Rome. These powers were not obviously agreeable to merchants, but they were necessary for the provisioning of the city.[119] Both in 67 and 57 this quite traditional concern lay behind extraordinary measures. As was often the case, the senate failed to discharge its accepted responsibilities, but its hand was forced not by sinister commercial interests but by popular clamour.

IV

The mentality implicit in the normal *laissez-faire* policy, not sustained by any doctrinal justification but followed unthinkingly, makes it unlikely not only that the senate would have deliberately furthered commercial enterprises by systematic state intervention but even that Roman businessmen would have conceived the possibility of seeking this support; nor, as we have seen, were they organized to press for it. It was another matter that considerations of honour and prestige imposed on the government an obligation to protect the lives and property of its citizens, and for that matter of other allied and friendly peoples who

---

[117] *MRR*. i. 568. M. Hassall and others combine and comment on the Delphi and Cnidos fragments of the 'pirate law' from which I quote II 6 ff. in *JRS* 1974, 195 ff.

[118] See e.g. Magie, 1950, ch. XII; cf. n. 98. Strabo xiv. 5. 2 stresses the pirates' part in making slaves.

[119] Cic. *Att.* iv. 1. 7, *Qu. fr.* ii. 5, *de dom.* 14–31, etc.

happened to be active in affairs outside Roman territory. The
publicans, it is true, who were actually exploiting public lands and
revenues, might easily have entertained the hope of extending the field
of their activity; yet in fact, as already remarked, their scope continued
at all times to be somewhat restricted, and so far as we know, without
protest on their part. None the less, it has been held that publicans or
negotiatores or both favoured imperial aggrandizement for their own
profit, and either resented the senate's reluctance to respond to their
wishes or forced the senate to comply.

The notion that their interests had any effect on the senate's foreign
policy, at least in pre-Gracchan times, has been denied in particular by
those modern historians who discount any economic motives for the
expansion of Rome's power, and who are partial to Roman claims
that, apart from some unauthorized campaigns initiated by generals
greedy for plunder and military glory, Rome fought only to repel
attacks on her own territory or on her friends and allies, or at worst to
anticipate and prevent future aggressions which were sincerely, if
sometimes unreasonably, feared.[120] Many wars which resulted in the
extension of Rome's dominion can certainly be explained in this way.
But various reservations must be made. Certainly the supposed
reluctance of the senate to annex new provinces is not proof that its
policy was essentially defensive.

(a) We must not neglect the Roman craving for 'glory' or what we
might prefer to call honour or prestige, which was to be obtained by
victory in war and the subjection of other states to Rome's will;
individuals too in all ranks craved for military distinction. Annexation
was not necessary to satisfy this impulse. The Roman empire was
conceived as extending to all peoples that could be expected to submit
to Rome's instructions and not merely to those under direct administration. By Cicero's time Romans could already think that they were
destined by the gods to rule the world (*Phil.* vi. 19). Any resistance to
them could then be treated as unjustifiable.

(b) Rome showed no reluctance to make overseas annexations in the

---

[120] See e.g. T. Frank, *Am. Hist. Rev.* 1912/3; cf. *Roman Imperialism passim, contra* e.g. G. de
Sanctis, *St. d. Rom.* iv. 26 n. 58, 554 n. 161; E. Gabba, 1973, 219 ff. = 1976, 78 ff., who invoked the
authority of Rostovtzeff; but the latter came to agree with Frank on the treatment of Macedon,
Rhodes, Corinth, and Carthage (*SEHHW* 737 f., 787 f.); it is no longer necessary to discuss these
matters fully. In what follows I am in general agreement with Harris, 1979, though he allows
some commercial influence on Roman policy (93 ff.); cf. *Papers and Monographs of the American
Academy in Rome* 1984, 13 ff.; the volume contains other interesting essays on Roman imperialism
with bibliographies, notably Gruen's able but unconvincing depreciation of economic motives.
Cf. also Brunt, *Laus Imperii*; it need not be denied that the Romans waged many wars in
accordance with their own peculiar and biased conception of what a defensive war was. Harris,
1979, ch. IV, rightly traverses the doctrine, accepted by e.g. Badian, 1967, of the senate's
deliberate aversion to annexations.

third century, when the provinces of Sicily, Sardinia, and Hither and Further Spain were constituted. Admittedly two generations passed before additional and still limited annexations were made. Certainly the senate pursued no plan of systematic aggrandizement. This is not least clear in the case of Spain. The limits of the provinces there were pushed forward only intermittently and on the initiative of individual governors; it was left to Augustus to pacify the whole peninsula, which he did in a decade by deploying exceptionally large forces. (Incidentally, it was only thereafter that the rich mineral resources of Asturia could be exploited.) The senate seems to have been incapable, as we might expect from a body already in pre-Sullan times composed of 300 members, of the insight, resolution, and consistency to devise and execute this kind of expansionist strategy. It reacted to contingencies as they arose, as indeed did most of Augustus' successors. If we suppose that it was guided by considerations of gain as well as of mere defence, we may then note that the treasury was for decades as amply fed by indemnities paid annually as it might have been by the imposition of tribute on provincials. Moreover, the burden of military service bore heavily on the citizens; the senate was bound to have some regard to public opinion before prolonging a war à outrance when submission and indemnities could be more easily obtained, and perhaps (as in Spain and Macedon) incurring the subsequent necessity of installing permanent garrisons, to keep the subjects down and ward off external attacks; even on a financial reckoning the costs might then exceed the return. In some cases the ease of annexation has been overestimated. And no doubt the senate might be jealous of the pre-eminence that an able general might attain from outstanding military success, and fearful of disaster, if armies were led incompetently.

(c) It is not plausible that Romans were ever unconscious of or indifferent to the profits of conquest. Rome's expansion in Italy before 264, and later still in the north, involved great accretions in territory where the wealthy could aggrandize their landholdings and peasant colonists could increase and multiply. The booty that many acquired in the Italian campaigns prompted the hope in 264 that intervention in Sicily would prove no less lucrative, a hope that contributed to the outbreak of the first Punic war[121] and the extension of Roman power overseas. At all times generals and soldiers could be incited to offensive operations by the same prospect, though campaigning which brought few rewards was unattractive. In the second century imperial revenues filled the treasury, and made it possible to suspend indefinitely direct taxation on Roman citizens. Members of the ruling order, not to speak

---

[121] Polyb. i. 11. There were other powerful reasons both for and against intervention (cf. 10).

of the publicans, were enriched by the profits of war and government. At a later stage the populace received manifest benefits from annexations.[122] We cannot be sure that but for popular demand the senate would have accepted Attalus III's bequest of his kingdom; in any case Tiberius Gracchus appropriated receipts to fitting out his settlers on Roman public land, and Gaius Gracchus presumably found the money for his corn dole and public works by a more efficient exploitation of the new province. The conquests of Pompey financed greatly increased expenditure for the benefit of the urban plebs and settlers on the land. Clodius also promoted the annexation of Cyprus, perhaps to assist in meeting the cost of the corn dole.[123] But even if we allow that the profits of empire were both perceived and desired, the profits envisaged derived from plunder and the augmentation of public revenues, and they advantaged many sections of the citizen body.

For Thucydides (i. 76 f.) profit, fear, and glory were the three motives that decided men's actions. Roman policy illustrates this diagnosis. Which, if any, was dominant at any given moment, it would often be hard to say. But in so far as we give weight to profit, it is not necessary to contend that either publicans or other *negotiatores* played a significant part in disposing men to imperialist policies: there were much more evident economic benefits for Romans of all sorts. The special interests of publicans and *negotiatores* it may be added, were not precisely the same. *Negotiatores* could and did flourish beyond the frontiers of provinces, wherever they could expect local governments to be too apprehensive of Rome to threaten their security or even curb their activity: publicans could farm taxes and rents on public domains or extract ore from state-owned mines[124] only after annexation. There were also profits to be made from the supply of armies, though wars must have interfered with much other commerce.

Cicero asserted in 66 that Rome had often fought to redress wrongs to her merchants and shipowners (n. 98). A few possible instances can be cited. In the 230s Rome forced Carthage to liberate Italian traders

---

[122] Badian, 1967, stressed this.

[123] Sherwin-White, 1984, 268 ff., who rightly notes that Clodius and his friends could not gain personally from the annexation, suggests that he was motivated by rancour against the king. Be this as it may, he must have justified his measure publicly in other ways. Sherwin-White seeks to show that the treasury did not need additional resources. His calculations are speculative, but in any case Cicero could in the years 59–56 assert or believe that the extravagance of the *populares* was exhausting the treasury; see *Att.* ii. 16. 1, 17. 1, *post red. sen.* 18, *de dom.* 28, *Vat.* 5–29, *Pis.* 28. 57; we may perhaps give some credence to *Qu. fr.* ii. 5. 1, *de har. resp.* 60, *de prov. cons.* 11; and Clodius could build on such allegations, whether true or not, when advocating the acquisition of Cyprus. Cf. ch. 1 endnote 6.

[124] Polyb. xxxiv. 10. 10–12 (cf. Walbank ad loc.), however, attests that Italians for some time joined in working the gold mines in Noricum beyond the frontier, but were expelled by the natives, who wished to monopolize the profits.

arrested for supplying her rebel mercenaries in Africa; their ill-treatment afforded a justification for seizing Sardinia under threat of war. In 229 an expedition was launched against the Illyrians on the plea that they had robbed and killed Italian merchants. But in both cases we can adduce other possible or probable reasons for action. Sardinia was to be a source of revenue, and the Romans may have desired to extend their power across the Adriatic.[125] In any case injuries to any citizens or persons under Rome's protection were affronts to Rome's honour, and in so far as they were true causes of war, it still does not follow that the aim was to promote business interests.

This consideration is relevant to the claim that the Jugurthine war was inspired by economic motives. It is clear enough that there were numerous Italian *negotiatores* not only in the province of Africa but in the Numidian kingdom. At Cirta they defended king Adherbal against Jugurtha's attacks, and as a consequence Jugurtha massacred them (Sall. *BJ* 22, 26). There was a popular outcry at Rome, and the senate was finally forced, against the inclinations of those who had the most influence in its deliberations, to undertake a war for the destruction of Jugurtha. The senators held to be responsible for its earlier failure to protect Adherbal and for the failure of the first campaign were suspected of corruption, a charge that Sallust took to be proven and that was presumably accepted by the court established by the Mamilian law. The 'Gracchani *iudices*' who composed the court and condemned the defendants were evidently Equites, a fact that Sallust does not notice.[126]

The speech of the tribune Memmius which, whether or not it is drawn at least in part from some authentic account of what he said, represents Sallust's own interpretation of anti-senatorial agitation at the time, accuses the senate of sacrificing not the economic interests of any section of the people but the *maiestas* or *imperium* of the state.[127] It is also replete with bitterness at the arrogant exclusiveness of the nobility which monopolized power. If this motif is authentic, it no doubt reflects the attitude of some men of equestrian origin like Sallust himself, who aspired to a share in government (n. 41).

Sallust also stressed the hatred felt by the plebs for the nobility, exacerbated by the cruel suppression of the Gracchi. It is the plebs that is determined on Jugurtha's destruction (30, 33. 3), yet so far from suggesting that it was actuated by genuine care for Roman honour, he

---

[125] *De imp. Cn. Pomp.* 11; Harris, 1979, 65, 195–7.

[126] Corruption: *BJ* 13, 15 f., 25. 29, 32–5, 40. 1, 80. 5. Mamilian court: GC 68 f.

[127] *BJ* 31 (sections 9 and 25 for *maiestas* and *imperium*). Cic. *Brut.* 136 does not indicate that any of his speeches were extant.

asserts that it was moved chiefly by factious spite (31. 2, 40. 3). But not the Equites. By his account the state was split between the senate or nobility and the plebs (41 f.), and the senate had had equestrian assistance in crushing the Gracchi (n. 9); he does not then regard the Equites as necessarily opposed to the senate. He does indeed inform us that Marius prevailed on Equites in Africa, both *negotiatores* and officers in the army, to intrigue for his election to the consulship and appointment to replace Metellus (n. 26). But they were simply induced to believe that Metellus was protracting the war and that Marius could finish it off more rapidly; they were impelled by 'hope of peace'. He actually conveys the impression that as candidate for the consulship Marius depended chiefly on the backing of the common people (73. 6), though, as he and his readers would have known, he could not have been returned without the votes of men of property.

But if Sallust has not sufficiently brought out the part played by Equites in these transactions, both as members of the Mamilian court and as electors in the centuriate assembly, we should not conclude that he neglects the true reasons why they too shared in the revulsion against the senate's conduct of affairs. The massacre at Cirta was an extreme provocation to Rome's honour; Cicero in 66 was to adduce Mithridates' slaughter of Italians only to show the necessity of its vindication (*de imp. Cn. Pomp.* 11 f.). The allegations of corruption surely found general credit and may have been true. An irresistible and almost universal demand for vengeance on Jugurtha was perfectly natural. Once Rome had embarked on the war, it was of course not only considerations of honour that required its victorious and swift termination. The early restoration of peace and order was also conducive to the prosperity of trade. Metellus' successes were indecisive. It was easy enough for men including army officers to believe that Marius could complete the job more efficiently.

Certainly there is not the least hint that Marius held out the prospect that he in contrast to Metellus would annex any part of the Numidian kingdom. In the event he did not do so. Annexation would presumably have alienated Bocchus, who helped decisively to end Jugurtha's resistance, and have entailed much more prolonged military effort at the very time when Italy itself was thought to be menaced by the German hordes.[128] No one is known to have had it in view. In so far as Marius promoted the settlement of veterans on public lands within the province of Africa, it can only have diminished the revenues derived from them and collected by publicans.

Commercial influence has also been detected in the conquest of that

---

[128] Harris, 1979, 151.

part of Transalpine Gaul which was later called Gallia Narbonensis.[129] However, the pretexts at least for war were afforded by pleas for succour from Massilia and the Aedui, with whom Rome had contracted obligations of alliance or friendship. Rome had previously aided Massilia against her Ligurian neighbours in 154 (Polyb. xxxiii. 8–11). It might well now have appeared that only a permanent military presence in the region could guarantee the security of Rome's allies. Moreover, control of the region safeguarded the land route to Spain. It is significant that the construction of the Via Domitia immediately followed the conquest, and that the province had a permanent garrison. It may also have been envisaged that it would prove a valuable source of supply for armies operating in north Spain, as it did in the 70s (Cic. *Font.* 8, 13, 16, 26); it was no doubt for this purpose that Fonteius was then improving the road (ibid. 17). There was a vigorous and increasing export trade in Italian wine to south Gaul, but that does not warrant the view that conquest was undertaken to promote its growth. The customs dues Fonteius imposed on wine in the 70s may actually have damaged Italian exporters by raising prices. Noricum too attracted Roman traders from the second century, but there was no move to annex it till Augustus' time;[130] the Roman government had not intervened even when the natives expelled Italian mining operators in Polybius' day (n. 124). And it was left to Caesar to extend Roman territory in Gaul beyond the narrow limits of Narbonensis.

In the fictitious dialogue of his *de republica* (iii. 16) Cicero makes L. Furius Philus assail the injustice of a ban Rome had imposed on the planting of vines and olives by 'Transalpine peoples'. The dramatic date is 129 (i. 14); the ban should then have been earlier. The only such peoples in any sense then subject to Rome were the Ligurian tribes defeated in 154. The text is not evidence that it was later extended to those conquered in and after 125. The accumulating archaeological evidence for the Italian wine trade in the region cannot in its very nature show that there was no indigenous production, still

---

[129] GC 28, 47–9, 53 f., assembles most of the scattered texts; I need not discuss chronological problems, nor cite the various and idle speculations on Cic. *de rep.* iii. 16. On Narbo see also Strabo iv. 1. 6, 12, 14, iv. 2. 1. By AD 12–13 Equites must have been so numerous there (cf. Gades and Patavium, Strabo iii. 5. 3, v. 1. 7) that some belonged to the local plebs and not to the local council (*ILS* 112a); no doubt trade accounts for this. The Via Domitia followed an old route known to Polybius (iii. 39. 8, xxxiv. 6). Garrison: *IM* 463 ff. My table on 432 f. should probably allow for legions there in each year before 91. See generally Clementi, 1974; C. Jullian, *Hist. de la Gaule* iii. ch. 1.

[130] G. Alföldy, *Noricum*, 1974, 44 ff.; cf. n. 124. It appears from Strabo iv. 6. 7 that the Romans did in the Republic deprive the Alpine Salassi of their gold workings, but failed until Augustus to prevent them from selling to the publicans the water required at extortionate rates (cf. also Dio, fr. 74, liii. 25).

less that it was prevented or restricted by Roman action, or that Cicero
has dated the ban too early. We cannot indeed know that it was ever
effective anywhere; how was it enforced? Furius is made to say that it
was designed to increase the value of Italian vine and olive plantations;
in that case the intention was at least as much to benefit landowners as
merchants. But we have to recall that Furius had assumed the role of
advocatus diaboli; there was to be a reply from Laelius, of which only
fragments survive. Laelius may have answered that the ban had been
imposed at the request of Massilia for the profit of her wine producers;
it was in her defence that Rome had fought in 154. The text casts no
light on Roman motives for subsequent aggrandizement.

At an early date after the conquest a Roman colony was founded at
Narbo. This too has been adduced as evidence for the commercial
inspiration of Roman aggrandizement. The place was already and
long remained an important trading centre. It had a port and
relatively easy communications up the valley of the Aude with that of
the Garonne, and it also lay athwart the ancient route from east to west
on which the Via Domitia was built. It was a point of strategic
importance for the same reasons that made it a thriving mart. That
was surely why it was selected as the site of a colony and as the
provincial capital. The colony bore the cognomen Martius; for Cicero
it was a 'specula populi Romani ac propugnaculum' (*Font.* 13). That is
a description which fits the traditional role of a Roman colony. No
doubt the cognomen also recalls those which C. Gracchus bestowed on
his colonies, for example Carthage-Junonia. But despite the historic
role of Punic Carthage in Mediterranean commerce, the settlers whom
Gracchus took out, though 'respectable' and therefore not mere
peasants, received allotments of land.[131] However Junonia might have
developed, if it had been permitted to survive, the basis of its economy
was initially to be agrarian. That may be no less true of Narbo.
Romans believed that the best soldiers were to be found in the rural
population, and in any case those who were, if need be, to defend a
strategic stronghold were best given a permanent attachment to the
soil; lands were no doubt confiscated from the natives. On this view the
foundation, which was a 'popular' measure, could have found favour
with the rural plebs; the objection of the senate to transmarine
settlement was probably based on a hidebound prejudice against
dispersing Italian military manpower, or if merely factious, ostensibly
justified in these terms.[132] It makes little sense to suppose that the

---

[131] App. *Pun.* 136, *BC* i. 24; Plut. *C. Gr.* 11. Plut. 9. 2 refers to respectable citizens to be settled
in other colonies: *FIRA* i². 8. 59 indicates that those despatched in Junonia received up to 200
iugera.
[132] *IM* 39, 700.

senate simply wished to deny the desire of Equites to develop the place commercially, especially so soon after it had secured equestrian support against the Gracchi, and at a time when it abstained from any move to deprive Equites of their new judiciary rights.

It has already been argued that Roman aggression against Mithridates in 89 was the responsibility of Manius Aquillius and other senators in post in Asia, abetted by some money-lenders in the area, and that there is no evidence that they were acting at the instance of powerful equestrian interests at home, nor that they themselves meditated actual annexations.[133] The reprisals taken by the king for their aggression had to be avenged, like Crassus' defeat at Carrhae; no matter that the Romans acknowledged in both cases that their generals had flouted their own conception of a just war. In both cases too extraneous circumstances retarded the restoration of Roman honour. For obvious reasons Sulla in 84 had to be content with the recovery of the lands Mithridates had overrun; later he disapproved Murena's premature resumption of hostilities with inadequate resources. But the peace he patched up was never ratified at Rome, and in the next few years Roman armies were engaged in securing territory to the south of the Pontic kingdom, whence a new offensive could be launched. In 74 the senate did not hesitate to accept the bequest of the kingdom of Bithynia; it can hardly have been a surprise that Mithridates, who could not be unaware of Roman ill will, treated this as a *casus belli*. Publicans had at once gone to work collecting revenues in the new province,[134] and we cannot doubt that they heartily approved of the annexation; but just at this time, when Equites were still excluded from judication, their influence on the senate was surely minimal; it may be significant that it was before the Aurelian law had been enacted that Lucullus felt able to adopt strong measures in Asia against equestrian extortions. Already committed to the costly deployment of large forces in Anatolia from fear of Mithridates and hope of vengeance, the senate itself must have welcomed the accession of new revenue from Bithynia, and probably saw no other means but annexation to make it safe from his attacks.

Equally, once Mithridates had been dislodged from his own kingdom, there was little alternative to bringing Pontus itself under direct rule. Very probably this was Lucullus' intention, though he failed to carry it out as a result of his entanglement in an Armenian war, which permitted Mithridates to make a come-back. It was therefore left to Pompey to constitute the new conjoint province of Bithynia and

---

[133] Cf. p. 157. For what follows see esp. Sherwin-White, 1984, chs. VII–IX, where the meagre evidence is fully given.

[134] Plut. *Luc.* 8; App. *BM* 71; Memnon (*FGH* no. 434) 27. 5 f.

Pontus. He also brought Cilicia Campestris and north Syria under direct Roman rule. In theory they had hitherto formed part of the Seleucid kingdom, but Antiochus XIII, though recognized by the senate as king about 73 and again by Lucullus in 69/8, had probably never enjoyed any authority in Cilicia,[135] and had been expelled from Syria. Pompey dethroned him. It is plausible to conjecture that he took into account the potential threat from the Parthians, who for generations had been expanding their power, and who could not therefore be counted on to accept the Euphrates as its limit. Pompey preferred to maintain or establish vassal princes in central and eastern Anatolia and south Syria, but this sort of barrier to Parthian aggrandizement was likely to be most firm, if it were supported by a Roman military presence in the fertile plains of Cilicia and north Syria, where Rome could find the usual co-operation from the local administrations of Hellenized cities,[136] and could extract revenue through tax-farmers that would meet or more than meet the expense.

There is then no reason to think that Pompey was the instrument of equestrian business interests. Of course the Equites active in Asia had no love of Lucullus and must have approved of his removal from the command, but by 66 this was in any case inevitable, whatever their attitude (n. 28). It would also have been natural for them to have backed the Manilian law, simply because like everyone else they must have thought Pompey the best general to conclude the war rapidly and restore that peace and security in the east which conduced to all their operations there. That they knew in advance that he alone would pursue a policy of annexation and thus enlarge the scope of the tax-farmers for profit is a mere conjecture with no foundation in the sources (cf. n. 135). The decisions he eventually took were probably prompted by the knowledge of conditions he obtained on the spot. It is not attested that he had any close connection with the publicans either then or later. The notion that he had helped in 70 to restore the system of tax-farming in Asia abolished by Sulla is groundless. Even if there were evidence for abolition by Sulla, it had been revived before 70 (n. 51), i.e. during Pompey's absence in Spain. Unlike Crassus, he is not known to have seconded the claim made in 61 by the farmers of the Asian tribute for a reduction in their liability to the state; admittedly it was Caesar, his ally, who satisfied them in 59.

Sherwin-White also argues that the constitution of vassal states in

[135] Magie, 1950, 1178 n. 37. Pompey settled ex-pirates in Cilicia (ibid. 1180 n. 43); it has been suggested that this made his intention of annexation clear before the Manilian law was enacted, but his action may not have been taken, or at any rate not known at Rome, so early. Whether or not Marius granted lands to Romans in Numidia (ch. 5, App. II), annexation did not follow.

[136] In Pontus he founded new cities to provide this infrastructure for Roman government (Sherwin-White, 1984, 229).

preference to annexation indicates his indifference to the profits of publicans, whose scope was thereby more restricted than it might otherwise have been. This is not so clear. Judaea was certainly not the only vassal state that was now made subject to tribute, as the Macedonian and Illyrian republics had been in 168. Caesar as dictator was to exclude Roman publicans from rights of collection in Judaea, and it is imprudent to assume that he was confirming what Pompey decreed.[137] In the wild regions in which these vassal states were found it would doubtless have been hardly safe for publicans to collect direct from the taxpayers; but in the provinces settled by Pompey they did not do so: they made bargains (*pactiones*) for lump sums with the city governments.[138] Similar bargains were certainly made with dynasts in Syria (Cic. *de prov. cons.* 9). We should perhaps suspend judgement. Roman money-lenders at least could make usurious loans to vassal princes. In 51 the Cappadocian king was heavily in debt to Pompey himself, and we need not share Cicero's good opinion of the modesty of his demands (*Att.* vi. 1. 3). But all in all Pompey's arrangements can be adequately explained by his conceptions of the interests of the Roman state.

The failure of Equites to induce (or perhaps to invite) the senate to annex lands in which publicans might have operated is remarkably illustrated by Rome's dealings with Cyrenaica and Egypt.[139] Ptolemy Apion bequeathed the former kingdom to Rome in 96; the Roman

[137] Badian, 1967, ch. v. Cic. *Att.* ii. 16. 2 refers to tribute from Antilibanon, i.e. from the Ituraean prince, Ptolemy (*RE* xxiii. 1766 no. 60). Judaea: Jos. *AJ* xiv. 201 (cf. 74); Sherwin-White, 1984, 232 n. 115, doubts the natural inferences from Cic. *Flacc.* 69; *de prov. cons.* 10 on the use of publicans there before Caesar.

[138] Sherwin-White, 1984, 232 n. 116. The evidence comes only from Bithynia, Cilicia, and Syria, except that *Fam.* xiii. 65. 1, which raises special problems, seems to relate to *scriptura* in Asia. Sherwin-White supposes that in the past the Asian publicans (like those in Sicily) had made *pactiones* with the individual taxpayers, not the cities. This may be true, though Cicero's reference to their large staff employed 'in agris' (*de imp. Cn. Pomp.* 16) may refer only to collection of rents from former royal lands outside city territories. I believe but cannot prove that *pactiones* with cities came in after Sulla directly assessed the Asian cities for an indemnity in 84; that the publicans were thereafter insurers, not collectors, of the direct tax imposed on cities; that this system was simply adopted for the new provinces; and that it made it simple for Caesar to eliminate the publicans in Asia too(n. 33). (In my view Sherwin-White wrongly interprets *Flacc.* 91, which relates to local tax of Asian Tralles, farmed out not by the governor Globulus, but simply when he was governor; cf. Broughton, *AJP* 1936, 175 ff.; the cities could fulfil the *pactiones* from the proceeds of local taxes.)

[139] See generally Sherwin-White, 1984, ch. xi, better than Harris 154 ff. Speculations on senatorial policy concerning Cyrene are idle; we must be content with ignorance. It is particularly implausible that in this case there was jealousy of the éclat to be won by any organizer of the province. In 75 a quaestor was given the task. So too the quaestor sent out regularly to Lilybaeum may have been Rome's first magistrate in Sicily: men of quaestorian rank could be commissioned to govern Hither Spain in 65 and to annex Cyprus in 58; we have further particulars which show that there were special reasons for these appointments; otherwise they too would be incomprehensible.

government apparently laid hands on his treasure, but took no steps to organize a province till 75; it was then presumably that the former royal lands were first leased to publicans;[140] if any revenue came in from Cyrenaica before, it must have been through the agency of the free cities. In 88 king Ptolemy Alexander I likewise left Egypt to Rome, or so it was claimed, by a will the authenticity of which was disputed. The senate did not hesitate to authorize seizure of moneys he had deposited at Tyre. But it did not attempt annexation. Ptolemy Lathyrus, who had disputed the crown with Alexander, was able to take over; on his death in 80 Sulla dispatched a son of Alexander to assume the diadem; but he was soon murdered, and Ptolemy Auletes, an illegitimate son of Lathyrus, installed himself as king, unrecognized but undisturbed by Rome. Given Rome's preoccupations in the 80s and 70s, it was natural that no effort was made at occupation. That would have required a considerable armed force. In 65, when other difficulties were at an end, Crassus supported a bill that the inheritance of Egypt should be taken up. It was defeated by optimate opposition. Cicero spoke against it before the people; it was one of only three appearances of this kind that he made before his consulship. We may think that he wished to ingratiate himself with the optimates, but he would hardly have chosen this occasion to take their part, if he had feared that it would alienate the good will of the publicans with whom he had close associations; silence would have been more prudent.[141] Auletes was to be recognized in 59 on the proposal of Caesar, in which his fellow 'triumvirs' presumably concurred. Auletes paid such large sums to this end that his measures to recover the expense from his subjects provoked his expulsion; again he resorted to bribery to obtain his restoration by Roman arms, which Gabinius ultimately effected. Rabirius Postumus was probably not the only equestrian financier who hoped to recoup himself from the subsequent exploitation of Egypt. But the publicans never appear to have pressed for annexation, despite the wealth of the Nile valley. Sherwin-White supposes that the bureaucratic system of administration in Ptolemaic Egypt must have been well known in Rome and that its 'peculiarity' was one decisive consideration against annexation. In fact, however, the Ptolemies did

---

[140] Cic. *de leg. agr.* 50 f. implies that in 63 they had been leased by censors; in Pliny's day publicans collected *scriptura* (*NH* xix. 39).

[141] The fragments of his speech with comments by the Bobbian Scholiast (91–3 Stangl) are our best evidence. Crassus backed the claims of the Asian publicans in 61 (n. 53), but this can be explained not by any financial connections with them, on which our sources, e.g. Plut. *Cr.* 2 f., 6 f., are significantly silent, but by his wish to disrupt their good relations with the optimates; the enmity, generally covert, between him and Cicero, their consistent advocate, is notable. And nothing suggests that his Parthian war was prompted by anything but his own pursuit of glory and wealth.

farm out some taxes and monopolies, though with all sorts of checks.[142] One may doubt if publicans understood the Ptolemaic system well enough to see that it would afford them very limited prospects of profit, or if they did, would have assumed that the Roman government would and could make no changes to enlarge their scope for gain. It may well be that all their available capital was absorbed in existing undertakings and those which they could expect to result from Pompey's conquests. The controversies that concerned Egypt in the 60s and 50s seem to have divided the senatorial order, not to have separated it from the Equites; rival politicians advocated different courses from personal greed or ambition or mutual suspicion and distrust.

It remained for Augustus to annex Egypt, and then not to open it up to Roman businessmen but to exploit it for the state and to augment Rome's corn-supply. With Egypt as a base he was also to attempt the conquest of Arabia, the most flagrant exception to the defensive policy which modern writers generally (and in my view erroneously) impute to him, because he was impressed by what he had heard of the riches of the country; we hear nothing of any plan to secure for Rome's subjects a greater share in the spice trade on which the sheikhs levied lucrative tolls.[143] This was a typical specimen of economic imperialism of the ancient kind; the aim was to divert these tolls into Rome's treasury.

V

We may then conclude that there is no proof either that the foreign policy of the senate was inspired by any economic aims other than that of adding to the reserves and revenues of the state, or that it was subjected to pressure by business interests. The publicans too gained by the accession of new revenues, so far as they were entrusted with the collection, but they appear in general to have been satisfied with the opportunities they already had at any given time, and are not known to have urged further annexations on a reluctant senate. Traders and money-lenders could prosper beyond the limits of Roman administration, wherever the extension of Roman power afforded them protection; if injuries to them aroused indignation and led to retribution, this was no more than Rome's honour required.

The intermittent conflicts of the orders do not call for an explanation

---

[142] I prefer the account in Wilcken, *Gr. Ostraka*, i. 515 ff., to that of e.g. C. Préaux, *L'économie royale des Lagides*, 1939, 450 ff.

[143] Strabo xvi. 4. 22. Tolls: Pliny, *NH* vi. 101, xii. 63–5, 84. Rome also imposed high duties on the frontiers (De Laet, 1949, 306 ff., 333 ff.).

in terms of their divergent economic interests. Some Equites presumably resented that aristocratic exclusiveness which limited their own ambition to rise or see their sons rise in a political career. At times the senate provoked the publicans by fulfilling its proper responsibilities to the treasury and the taxpayers. But the root of discord lay in the competition for judicial rights. When vested in the Equites, they conferred something of that *dignitas* which was dear to Roman hearts, and also allowed the publicans, the leading and only organized section of the order, to exert undue pressure on senators in maximizing their profits from state contracts; to senators this dependence on Equites was a hateful diminution of their own prestige and freedom. This quarrel certainly did much to exacerbate the discords at Rome in and after Drusus' tribunate, and thereby contributed to bringing on the civil wars of the 80s. The memory of the fearful experience of this time and the failure of Sulla to heal the wounds inflicted were in turn to colour or determine men's attitudes in the age of Caesar. In this way the discord of the orders had a share in the ultimate fall of the Republic, though in the meantime it had been allayed by the compromise of the Aurelian law. The Equites in general were doubtless less ready to make sacrifices for that political supremacy of the senate which optimates identified as the cause of Republican liberty, and more prone than senators to yearn for peace and order at almost any price; yet many were found among the adversaries of Caesar and his heirs; the order as such took no side in the political struggles after 70 and the civil wars they generated.

We may briefly look forward to the Augustan settlement so far as it concerned the Equites.[144] Nothing suggests that Augustus restored to the publicans the function of collecting direct taxes in the east of which Caesar had deprived them (nn. 33 and 137), though they continued to farm indirect taxes and rents on public lands and were even given the collection of the new death duties on Roman citizens. Other businessmen received no more favours from the state than they had ever done. If Augustus needed to secure the loyalty of the order, he did not conceive that for the purpose he had to assist them in business activities. Equites retained their judicial rights, but in Augustus' reign the process began whereby senators were to be tried for alleged crimes only by their own peers (unless by the emperor himself); they were no longer to feel a galling dependence on an inferior order. In this, as in other ways, Augustus and his successors were ready to uphold the dignity of senators without imperilling their own control of the state. Equally, they would promote the social esteem of senators. The Equites

---

[144] See Brunt, *JRS* 1983, 42 ff.

too were to be set apart from and above the people at large.[145] It is characteristic that Augustus records that in 2 BC he was hailed father of his country by the senate and equestrian order as well as by the entire Roman people (*RG* 35). New men of equestrian origin, chiefly the *domi nobiles* from Italian towns, now had a better chance of rising to the summit of a senatorial career. Those who did not choose or could not attain this eminence now had increased opportunities of distinction in public service. In an enlarged standing army there were more military commissions for them to fill. Some of these officers could advance to higher posts in the fiscal administration and as governors of provinces and holders of great prefectures at Rome. A few might be numbered among the emperor's most intimate counsellors. It has even been held that emperors were more confident of the loyalty of Equites than of senators and aggrandized the former to protect themselves against the latter. This theory perhaps draws some of its persuasive power from the belief that there had already been in the Republic a fundamental cleavage between the orders, recollections of which might make a ruler congenial to Equites if he had lost senatorial goodwill. But no such cleavage had existed. An emperor whom the senate had cause to hate would also forfeit the loyalty of most Equites, even though the senate might be the focus of discontent. This was only natural. In the Principate, as in the Republic, the two orders formed a single class with common economic interests as large property owners, and their members were often bound together by birth, marriage, education, and social intercourse. It was only evanescent conditions that had ever intermittently sundered them.

[145] Brunt, *JRS* 1961, 76 ff The Larinum *SC* provides a new illustration (B. Levick, *JRS* 1983, 97 ff.).

4

JUDICIARY RIGHTS IN THE REPUBLIC[1]

I. The Problem. **II.** The conflicts and ambiguities of evidence on C. Gracchus' legislation: his probable aims considered in the light of Polyb. vi. 17. **III.** The thesis that C. Gracchus gave Equites a monopoly of judication only for the *repetundae* court and created a mixed *album* of *iudices* for other criminal and civil cases not inconsistent with other relevant legislation between 123 and Sulla's time, in particular with Drusus' proposals. **IV.** The inaccuracy of most ancient evidence on the *lex Aurelia*, and the general inadequacy of sources on criminal legislation. Why the testimony of Plutarch, and probably Livy, on Gracchus' judiciary legislation should be preferred. **V.** This testimony cannot be rejected on the premiss that in 123 there was no standing criminal court except for *repetundae*; most of the standing courts of the post-Sullan period certainly antedated Sulla, and some are almost certainly pre-Gracchan. **VI.** In any case Gracchus' restriction on the inappellate criminal jurisdiction previously exercised by magistrates almost necessitated the creation of some standing criminal courts, if they did not already exist. **VII.** The importance of the *album iudicum* for civil cases. **VIII.** Summary of conclusions.

I

IN 149 BC the *lex Calpurnia* provided for the establishment of a large standing court before which Rome's subjects and allies could seek reparation from magistrates who had illegally enriched themselves at their expense. The jurors were all to be senators. It seems quite certain from the narratives of Appian and Diodorus and from the extant fragments of the *repetundae* law engraved on the *tabula Bembina*

---

[1] I here restate with minor modifications the thesis adumbrated by M. Gelzer (*Kl. Schr.* i. 222) and developed in App. II to the original version of ch. 3; my aim is partly to meet criticisms made by M. Griffin, *CQ* 1973; Gruen, 1968 (ch. III); and Stockton, 1979; and partly to show how my reconstruction of Gracchus' judiciary reform coheres with later measures affecting judication. The bibliography is large, but I shall refer only to those works of which it is necessary to take account for presenting my thesis; J. P. V. D. Balsdon, *PBSR* 1938, 1 ff., remains fundamental, and W. Kunkel, 1962, revolutionized our understanding of Roman criminal procedure in the Republic to an extent which has not been grasped by all later writers on these problems. This essay has been improved by critcisms from Mr. Stockton.

that Gaius Gracchus substituted Equites for senators in this court. However, according to all explicit testimony Gracchus' legislation also concerned judication in general, that is to say the right and duty of acting as *iudex* in all criminal and civil processes. All but one of our sources which purport to record such legislation make out that he transferred judication in general to the Equites: Plutarch alone says that *iudices* were to be drawn from a mixed *album* of senators and Equites, a plan he also ascribes to Tiberius Gracchus (n. 21), without noticing that Equites were to have a monopoly in the *repetundae* court. It is clear that of all Gracchus' measures his reform of judication was considered the most momentous. It must therefore have been fully described by Livy. In my judgement Livy would have given a correct account of its main features. Unfortunately what he reported is lost, or rather it is garbled by the *Perioche* of his sixtieth book, where we read that Gracchus passed a law for the enrolment of 600 Equites in the senate itself, thereby trebling its size. I shall argue that what lies behind this nonsense was an account basically agreeing with Plutarch's, and that in fact Gracchus created a mixed *album* of senators and Equites for all cases but *repetundae*. Plutarch forgot the exception: other writers were so much concerned with the exception, because of its political consequences, that they overlooked the rule. It is important always to bear in mind that we depend throughout on mere epitomators of the full accounts that once existed, written when the facts were well known, and that it was the prevailing vice of ancient epitomators to distort the accounts they followed, by loose and inaccurate formulations and by arbitrary selection of material.[2]

My reconstruction of the Gracchan legislation on judiciary rights inevitably requires me to adopt particular views of later judiciary legislation. This essay will therefore survey the whole field, though without attention to some details, such as the organization of judicial decuries in Cicero's time, or the special provisions of the *lex Licinia de sodaliciis* of 55 or the *lex Pompeia* of 52, or more than incidental

---

[2] Brunt. *CQ* 1980, 477 ff. Besides statements quoted in the text see Vell. ii. 6. 3, 32; Tac. *Ann.* xii. 60. Anyone who reads Velleius' narrative of the period consecutively will see that it is rhetorical, vague, and untrustworthy. Let Tacitus speak for himself: 'cum Semproniis rogationibus equester ordo in possessione iudiciorum locaretur et rursum Serviliae leges senatui iudicia redderent, Mariusque et Sulla olim de eo vel praecipue [!] bellarent'. 'Semproniae rogationes' can be rhetorical plural for a single law. The Servilian law of Caepio in some measure restored senatorial judication; that of Glaucia deprived the senators of whatever rights Caepio had given them. I have a high respect for Tacitus' testimony on the Principate, but he had not had occasion to study Republican history, and in the whole chapter is perhaps summarizing a typically muddled speech by Claudius (cf. R. Syme, *Tacitus* 705); see, however, n. 21. Pliny, *NH* xxxiii. 34 (cf. ch. 3 n. 2): 'Iudicum appellatione eum [equestrem] ordinem primi omnium instituere Gracchi [!], discordi popularitate in contumeliam senatus' is also inaccurate rhetoric, and anyhow does not attest an equestrian monopoly of judication.

comment on the substantive criminal or civil law.[3] The argument is complicated and conclusions are summarized in the final section.

II

I may begin by remarking that, although Appian and Diodorus show by incidental remarks that they were particularly concerned with the *repetundae* court, they and all other writers who expressly refer to Gracchus' judiciary legislation do not limit it to the *repetundae* court, and that some actually imply that Gracchus defended it on grounds that were hardly applicable to that court at all. According to Appian, having bought the support of the urban plebs by corn distributions, Gracchus then sought that of the Equites by transferring the courts to them: he boasted that he had thus overthrown the senate (i. 22. 91, 93). Plutarch represents him as seeking to curtail the power of the senate by abolishing their monopoly of judication (*C. Gr.* 5). In the view of Varro (*ap.* Nonius 728 L.), 'he transferred the *iudicia* to the equestrian order and thus made the state two-headed': that phrase recurs in Florus (ii. 5), who might well have drawn on Livy; perhaps Gracchus used it himself. Florus also seems to be echoing Gracchan propaganda[4] when he asks what could be more productive of 'equal liberty' (cf. p. 338) than an arrangement by which, with the senate governing the provinces, the authority of the equestrian order had a basis in dominion of the courts (ii. 1). Diodorus tells of harangues in which Gracchus spoke of destroying aristocracy and setting up democracy: in Latin parlance he attacked the *pauci* and championed *libertas* and the *iura populi* (xxxiv-xxv. 25). According to the same writer (xxxvii. 9), 'when the senate threatened war on Gracchus on account of the transfer of the courts, he made the bold reply that if he were to die, he would still leave the sword implanted in the flank of the senators'. Like other somewhat similar reports of his belligerent sayings,[5] this may be an invention of his enemies. Whatever his tirades against the senators and whatever his real motives, he must have overtly defended his judiciary legislation by arguments, however specious, that the cause of justice would be served by extending judicial rights to the Equites.[6] Diodorus and Florus might suggest that he contended that this would make a better balance in the constitution

---

[3] On the Gracchan law itself see from this standpoint A. N. Sherwin-White, *JRS* 1982, 18 ff.; and on Republican developments in the law of *repetundae* A. W. Lintott, *SZ* 1981, 162 ff.; cf. Brunt, *Historia* 1961, 189-97.

[4] Stockton, 1979, 225.   [5] Cic. *de leg.* iii. 20; Diod. xxxiv/xxxv. 27.

[6] Sherwin-White (n. 3) shows that the Gracchan law cannot be interpreted as a merely partisan measure; the details illustrate a concern for the rights of all under Roman rule or protection. [Roman citizens too could benefit, pp. 526 ff.]

and promote the cause of liberty. An appeal to liberty, that is to say to popular rights, hardly seems apposite, if Gracchus was simply concerned with *repetundae* suits, which were primarily, if not exclusively, designed to secure compensation for Rome's allies and subjects. Plutarch of course thought that he was abridging the judication of senators over citizens, and he notes that it was in advocating this measure that Gracchus symbolically departed from the traditional practice by which orators had turned their faces when speaking towards the senate and for the first time began to face the people. What he was proposing was allegedly at least in their common interest.

Now Polybius had held that the 'people' were dependent on the senate, not only because the senate controlled all public contracts, but 'most of all' because senators were 'judges in the majority of both public and private transactions [συναλλάγματα], where the complaints [ἐγκλήματα] were grave' (vi. 17. 2). The terms he uses show that he has civil cases partly or chiefly in mind. 'Public transactions' could indeed refer both to criminal trials and to the disputes that might arise from public contracts, which magistrates would decide with a *consilium* under administrative law.[7] They might also include *repetundae* cases, given that citizens as well as foreigners could bring charges under the *lex Calpurnia* and later laws, and that Polybius wrote or revised his sixth book after 149, when the *lex Calpurnia* was passed. But he was surely thinking chiefly of cases in which the defendants might be 'from the people', and in the Republic charges of *repetundae* lay only against senators or persons who were at least of the senatorial order (n. 10 with text). In any event Polybius' allusion to 'private transactions' must refer to ordinary civil suits, and those who, like Fraccaro (n. 99), deny that senators could have had any monopoly of judication in any class of such cases in effect tax him with error, without warrant as I hope to show later.

Dionysius also supposed that senators were given a monopoly of civil judication in the regal period (ii. 14, iv. 25, 36); I presume that nothing was known of the legal institutions of that remote age, but also that the annalistic invention which Dionysius adopted was probably, like many such fictions, a retrojection of later practice. So too Plutarch held that before Gracchus 'senators alone decided court cases', and that 'in consequence they were formidable to the people and to the Equites'. Polybius of course does not go so far: he restricts the senatorial monopoly to important cases. It need not have been based on statute rather than on usage maintained by the discretion of the praetors, but to alter the usage a statute would have been required: senatorial

---

[7] Liddell and Scott s.v. On administrative law see Mommsen, *StR* i[3]. 169–85, 314; for the right of citizens to prosecute for *repetundae* [see pp. 526 ff.].

magistrates were unlikely to have exercised their discretion to reduce the influence of their own order. We can easily guess that the Equites resented dependence on senators. To ingratiate himself with them, and to make them fully capable of balancing senatorial power, Gracchus needed to remove the monopoly.

According to Appian, the senatorial courts had been discredited by corrupt acquittals in the recent past of Aurelius Cotta, (Livius) Salinator, and Manius Aquillius. The senate was therefore ashamed to resist transfer of the courts to the Equites. Cotta was certainly charged with *repetundae*, and so presumably were Salinator and Aquillius.[8] Hence Appian was at least primarily concerned with legislation that affected the *repetundae* court. He goes on to tell that in course of time the equestrian *iudices* made unjust and corrupt use of their power over senators, suborning accusers 'of the rich' and abolishing prosecutions for the bribery of judges. The former allegation also appeared in L. Crassus' invective on equestrian judication in 106 (n. 16). Appian's source evidently had the same kind of bias. Diodorus too, presumably following Posidonius, when he condemns Gracchus for 'designating the Equites as *iudices* and thus making the inferior element in the state supreme over their betters', is thinking only of the *repetundae* court and perhaps of others modelled on it which were to try the offences of senators.[9]

However, Appian also thought that after Gracchus' enactment Equites sat in judgement on *all* Romans and Italians, and in *all* matters affecting property and civic rights. Does this not imply that the Gracchan legislation was not restricted to cases of *repetundae*? It may be said that the Gracchan *repetundae* law itself extended beyond senators. It covered offences by all magistrates down to quaestors, *tresviri capitales*, and the tribunes of the first four legions, together with their sons if the fathers were themselves senators (on the best interpretation of the surviving words in v. 2).[10] It did not, like a formula in the Sullan law *de sicariis*, probably derived from another of Gracchus' laws,

---

[8] See Gruen, 1968, 297. I suspect that the major count against senatorial *iudices* was not corruption but partiality towards defendants of their own order, amply attested in the Principate (Brunt, *Historia* 1961, 217 ff.). Appian probably mistook references to the shame felt by some individual senators for a general acquiescence by the senate in Gracchus' law, see *contra* Diod. xxxvii. 9. The judiciary or *repetundae* law may well be that which passed by a majority of only one tribe (ibid. xxxiv/xxxv. 27).

[9] Posidonius, whom Diodorus presumably followed, was no doubt particularly concerned by the oppression of the provinces, which in his view was exacerbated by collusion between senatorial governors and equestrian *iudices*, among whom the interest of the publicans was decisive (cf. xxxvii. 5).

[10] Sherwin-White (n. 3) 19, commenting on v. 2 of the Gracchan law, restored by analogy with vv. 16 and 22, where holders of minor magistracies are again assimilated to senators; but cf. J.-L. Ferrary, *Labeo* 1983, 71 f. Persons indictable under the law who were not senators would almost certainly be *equites equo publico*. Cf. n. 19.

embrace all who had given opinions in the senate (*Cluent.* 148; cf. 151), a category which would probably have included *quaestorii* even before their enrolment (Livy xxiii. 32; Festus 454 L.; Gell. iii. 18. 7). It would be prudent to assume that, as in the Principate the office of *triumvir capitalis* was normally held before the quaestorship, which gave access to the senate, most Republican holders of that office were not yet senators in any sense; and though as late as 70 senators could be military tribunes (I *Verr.* 30), there were 24 each year and the majority cannot have been members or had any hope of entering it. However, the distinction drawn between the tribunes of the first four legions, who were elected by the people (*StR* ii[3]. 575), and the other tribunes, who, like *praefecti*, had just as good opportunities for extortions, is significant; the former counted as magistrates, and election was an honour, which was probably most sought by men of senatorial lineage. The extension of the coverage of the law to sons of the magistrates listed, provided that they had senatorial fathers, may suggest that a high proportion of the minor magistrates in question would at least be of senatorial family, and in itself indicates an intention to strike at men of senatorial rank in a loose sense.

It may also be noted that the penalty under Gracchus' law was only pecuniary (cf. n. 15): condemnation did not entail the loss of civic rights or banishment of which Appian speaks. Appian is not then thinking merely of the Gracchan *repetundae* law, even so far as 'men of senatorial rank' are concerned; and of course he suggests that all Romans and Italians were affected. Stockton, however, has rightly observed that he does not strictly imply that it was Gracchus himself who transferred judication in cases other than *repetundae* to Equites: he is indeed looking forward to a time after Gracchus when (as he alleges) 'the Equites used to combine with the tribunes and make themselves formidable to the senate'.[11] He might have had in mind what he had read in his source of the establishment of courts such as those set up by the Mamilian law and by Saturninus' and Varius' laws on *maiestas*, in which judication was vested in the Equites on the Gracchan model.[12] But this will still not account for his view that all Romans were affected. If we take this seriously, we must posit a general law breaking that partial monopoly of judication both in civil and criminal cases which Polybius attests. If such a general law was enacted after Gracchus, we might even in our meagre sources have expected some hint of it. (It needs no proof that praetors would not of their own volition have used their *imperium* to modify the monopoly.) Stockton

---

[11] Stockton, 1979, 147.

[12] I now take the general view that 'Gracchani iudices' in Cic. *Brut.* 128 means that the Mamilian courts (*BJ* 40) were equestrian. For Saturninus' law see Cic. *de orat.* ii. 199–201.

himself attributes to Gracchus such a general law giving Equites in turn a monopoly of all judication. But we know of senators who still acted as *iudices* in civil cases, between the tribunates of Gracchus and the dictatorship of Sulla.[13] This evidence could be explained on the assumption that with the praetor's consent litigants could still have been free to choose any *iudex* by agreement among themselves, though one party could hardly have insisted on the choice of a person who was not on the list of recognized *iudices*. Still, it is obviously compatible with Plutarch's testimony that Gracchus' law itself constituted such a list of both senators and Equites, testimony which Stockton simply rejects.

There are two obvious objections to Plutarch's account. (*a*) Why should Gracchus have given Equites a monopoly of judicial functions only for *repetundae*, and how could he have justified a distinction between that process and other processes? (*b*) How can we explain the statements in most of our sources that the *iudicia* were simply transferred to the Equites?

(*a*) Gracchus could well have argued that senators were too biased to do equal justice in cases of a kind in which members of their own order were always defendants and that experience had proved this. There was no like reason why they should fail in their duty when deciding either civil suits or charges of crimes such as murder, or even *ambitus*, in which senators themselves would be the aggrieved as well as the allegedly culpable parties. Granted that non-senators resented the exclusive right of senators to determine the most important civil suits, it did not follow that there was a demand to deny them any part in civil judication. Legal expertise was still chiefly found among the senators. Many were doubtless of known integrity. It is true that even if they were excluded from the *album* litigants could still choose such men to act as *unus iudex*, but as will appear later, that would not suffice to ensure that senators were available for all civil judication, for example, as *centumviri*, even when their suitability was not open to question. These were considerations by which Gracchus could have justified a distinction between *repetundae* cases and all other cases, both in public and in his own mind.

(*b*) By creating a mixed *album* of senators and Equites from which *iudices* were to be chosen in cases hitherto decided by senators alone, and an *album* in which Equites perhaps outnumbered senators by two to one (see below) Gracchus did in a vague sense 'transfer *iudicia*' to the

---

[13] *Dig.* xxiv. 3. 66 *pr.* (P. Mucius (*cos.* 133): dowry of Gracchus' widow); Cic. *de offic.* iii. 66 (M. Cato, died before 91: sale of house), ibid. 77 (C. Fimbria, *cos.* 94: *sponsio*); *ad Her.* ii. 19 (C. Coelius Caldus, *cos.* 94: *iniuria*); Val. Max. viii. 2. 3 (Marius: dowry). Cic. *Rosc. Com.* 42 gives apparently the only attested instance of an equestrian *iudex* under the Republic: it was the conduct of eminent men in this role that was remembered.

Equites. Similar language could be employed by Cicero himself (II *Verr.* iii. 223),[14] Plutarch (*Pomp.* 22), the *Perioche* of Livy xcvii, and Ps.-Asconius (206 St.) to describe the effect of the *lex Aurelia*, which did in fact constitute a mixed *album*. The inaccuracy was the more pardonable in regard to the Gracchan system, since the Gracchan *lex de repetundis*, and later laws setting up similar courts for *maiestas*, gave Equites a judicial monopoly and made senators responsible to them in precisely those *iudicia* which most attracted the attention of political historians and of orators concerned with politics. Judgements on civil suits or on criminal prosecutions of lower-class offenders would arouse no political controversy. By contrast conviction for *repetundae*, if it involved financial ruin and *infamia*, could make the defendant prefer exile, as Verres did.[15] Even in a civil suit, when it threatened bankruptcy and *infamia*, it could be said that a man's fame and fortune (*Quinct.* 8), and indeed his *caput* (ibid. 29, 33) and life-blood (ibid. 39, 46), were at stake. Hence in 106 L. Crassus could plead with the people to rescue senators from the cruelty of equestrian *iudices*, which 'can only be satiated with our blood', another figurative expression; he may also have hoped that if the equestrian monopoly of the *repetundae* court was destroyed, it would be less likely that the Equites would be given exclusive judication in extraordinary courts like that set up by the Mamillian court, which could impose 'capital' penalties resulting in banishment. At any rate the composition of the *repetundae* court was the source of political controversy in the last decade of the second century; and still more bitter conflicts followed the notoriously iniquitous condemnation of P. Rutilius in *c.*92 and the proceedings under the *lex Varia*.[16]

Now it is indeed certain that Gracchus made Equites alone *iudices* in *repetundae* cases. It should never have been questioned that the fragmentary *lex repetundarum* preserved on one face of the *tabula Bembina* (*FIRA* i². no. 7) is a Gracchan law.[17] It requires the peregrine praetor

---

[14] Stockton, *Historia* 1973, 216 ff., canvassed again the possibility that Cotta's first proposal was more extreme, but see Gelzer, *Kl. Schr.* ii. 168 ff.: Cicero's rhetoric should not be taken literally.

[15] C. Cato (*cos.* 114), though condemned for *repetundae*, but only to pay 8000 HS (Cic. II *Verr.* iii. 184, iv. 22; Vell. ii. 8), retained his consular status till conviction under the Mamilian law in 110 (Cic. *Brut.* 128). *Infamia*, which involved loss of status and disabilities in private law, was not prescribed by the Gracchan law as incidental to condemnation, but probably first by Glaucia (*ad Her.* i. 20; cf. Lintott (n. 3) n. 133). Compare the disabilities imposed by the Latin law of Bantia (ch. 2, App. iv). When condemnation involved both social and financial ruin, men might prefer voluntary exile; they could then take their liquid assets with them beyond Roman jurisdiction; and their wealth and continuing connections at Rome might earn them influence in their new home (cf. Cic. *Att.* v. 11. 6 on C. Memmius at Athens, and Strabo x. 2. 13 on C. Antonius in Cephallenia).

[16] GC 63 f. (Mamilian court), 78 (L. Crassus), 125–7 (Rutilius), 136 f. (*lex Varia*).

[17] Stockton, 1979, 230 ff.; cf. Sherwin-White, *JRS* 1972, 83–99.

to empanel 450 persons from whom juries are to be chosen for trials in the current year; in subsequent years the praetor appointed to preside over the court is to do the same. All present and former members of the senate, together with holders of offices which gave a claim to future membership of the senate, and the fathers, brothers, and sons of such persons, are ineligible; the positive qualification is lost in lacunae of the text, but there is no doubt that it was in some sense equestrian, whether the *iudices* were to be past and present holders of the public horse, or to be merely of free birth and equestrian census. They also had to be resident in Rome;[18] so they were not likely to be mere country gentlemen, but the richest members of the order, notably publicans who needed a Roman domicile for their business. Persons indictable under the law are among those ineligible; they would have included some Equites.[19]

There is a seeming difficulty for my case in that the *repetundae* law provided for 450 equestrian *iudices*, while the judiciary law posited provided probably for 600 or 300. But this can easily be met. We have only to postulate that the judiciary law was passed later (hence it was impossible to define the positive qualifications of *iudices* in the *repetundae* law by reference to it), and, if we accept the figure of 600, that a larger panel was now seen to be required for the more multifarious duties with which the more general law was concerned.

Appian and Diodorus, as we have seen, inform us, without explicitly stating, that before Gracchus senators had judged charges of *repetundae*, and that he substituted equestrian juries for that offence. It may be said that as on my own view Appian and other authorities are misleading in suggesting that senators were excluded from judicial functions, they might also be wrong about the *repetundae* court. The epigraphic law abrogates two preceding statutes on *repetundae*, the Calpurnian, which had first set up a permanent court (n. 69), and the Junian, which is otherwise unknown. Cicero alone refers to an Acilian law which clearly provided for equestrian jurors and which was proposed by the father of M'. Acilius Glabrio, praetor 70 (I *Verr.* 51).[20] Could not the Junian law have been Gracchan, instituting mixed juries, and the Acilian a more extreme measure of later date? That is

---

[18] Tradition and sound practical reasons dictated this rule (Sherwin-White (n. 3) 22), though I doubt if it excluded '*many* Roman financiers' (my italics); he also in my view underrates the importance publicans already enjoyed before 123; cf. pp. 148 ff.

[19] See n. 10; many or most of the minor magistrates and sons of senators would be Equites. But under the Julian law Equites (unless minor magistrates) were still immune (*Rab. Post.* 13.); the scope of the *repetundae* process was only extended to other equestrian officials under the Principate (Brunt, *Historia* 1961, 198). Cic. *Cluent.* 104, 114, *Rab. Post.* 16 show only that in Republican *repetundae* law Equites could not be prosecuted for taking bribes as jurors.

[20] He would have been an *aequalis* of Gracchus (Badian, *AJP* 1954, 374 ff.).

hard to credit. The total extrusion of senators from the court by a post-Gracchan law would have been a controversial measure that could not have failed to leave some other mark even in our meagre tradition. If the Acilian law was post-Gracchan it must have done no more than modify Gracchus' measure in technical details; alternatively, it can be identified with Gracchus' statute on the basis that Acilius, like Rubrius, was a colleague who acted as his agent. The Junian law, on the other hand, is best regarded as a measure which introduced some minor modification into the arrangements made by the Calpurnian. We can safely conclude that Gracchus did entirely replace senatorial with equestrian *iudices* in the *repetundae* court.

Let us now turn to Plutarch. He states that Gracchus 'provided for the enrolment of 300 Equites in addition to the 300 senators and confided judication to the 600 together'. In itself this is ambiguous, and it might mean that Gracchus enrolled 300 Equites in the senate. Such an enlargement of the senate was to be proposed by Drusus in 91 and effected by Sulla for the very purpose of enabling the senate alone to provide all the *iudices* required—at a time when more were undoubtedly required than in Gracchus' day. However, elsewhere Plutarch resolves the ambiguity: he means that there was to be a mixed *album* of 300 senators and 300 Equites.[21] Like our other authorities, he does not explicitly refer to *repetundae*, but unlike them he makes it clear that he is thinking of all kinds of judication, of cases in which defendants were not necessarily *senatorii*.

The *Perioche* of Livy lx, which does not mention any judiciary measure at all, alleges that Gracchus passed a law that 600 Equites should be enrolled in the senate, which then consisted of 300 members, with the result that the equestrian order was twice as strong in the senate as the former members. The author is wretchedly inaccurate. It may well be that he did not draw on Livy directly but on an epitome (n. 43). He probably lived at a time when the *album iudicum*, which in Livy's day included both senators and Equites (p. 231), had ceased to exist. We can readily assume that Livy, like Plutarch, wrote of the constitution of such an *album*, and that an abbreviated statement of his account was misunderstood by a writer to whom the concept of an *album* was unfamiliar and unintelligible: unlike the fuller description of Gracchus' proposal, which Livy himself must have given, it may have been as ambiguous as the first formulation in Plutarch which I quoted. This is the view taken not only by those who accept the

---

[21] *C. Gr.* 5 with *Comp.* 2. Plutarch ascribes the same proposal to Ti. Gracchus when standing for re-election (*Ti. Gr.* 16), whereas Dio, fr. 83 makes him propose transference of the courts to the Equites. See Stockton, 1979, 73. Conceivably Tacitus (n. 2) had in mind Ti. Gracchus' proposals as well as his brother's laws.

evidence of Plutarch but by some scholars who suppose that Plutarch and Livy both refer to a proposal made by Gracchus and later abandoned by him in favour of purely equestrian courts. I shall consider this hypothesis later. It would make it easy to explain the discrepancy between Plutarch and the *Perioche* as to the number of equestrian *iudices*. If both were concerned with an abortive plan, we could conjecture that Gracchus toyed with alternative numbers. But it is also conceivable that if both are reporting a judiciary law actually carried, Plutarch misconstrued a statement that the number of equestrian *iudices* was double that of the senators as meaning that the number of persons on the *album* was double that of the senate. The emphasis that the *Perioche* lays on the total number may deserve credit, and the number of *iudices* was probably that established by the *lex Aurelia* of 70, viz. 900. Gruen (p. 88) and others contend that both Plutarch and the *Perioche* are discredited by their disagreements. The truth is that they, and all our other sources, are continually inaccurate, and that their inaccuracies produce conflicting statements, each of which may none the less have some basis in facts more complex than any one of them reveals.

III

Now all our sources which refer to any judiciary legislation of Gracchus purport to record a general *lex iudiciaria*, some alluding in particular to the *repetundae* court. Miriam Griffin remarks that in this respect all may give inaccurate reports of a measure with more limited scope; she adduces what she takes to be parallels.[22] Certainly no precision on such a matter can be expected of them. However, as she admits, they are not always wrong. The *lex Aurelia* was indisputably (as they state) a judiciary law. In my view Drusus in 91 also proposed such a measure (see below). On the other hand, Miriam Griffin is right about the *lex Servilia Caepionis* of 106, although it is styled 'iudiciaria' by Cicero (*de inv.* i. 92); he could equally use the phrase 'omnes iudiciariae leges Caesaris' to denote Julian laws concerned with particular offences (*Phil.* i. 19; cf. 21).

The Servilian law may be considered here, because its terms might seem to be inconsistent with the hypothesis that Gracchus had set up a mixed *album*. Cicero tells us that it was hateful to the Equites 'cupidos iudicandi' (*de inv.*), and that they were hotile to Caepio 'propter iudicia' (*de orat.* ii. 199). Tacitus confusedly writes of 'Servilian laws' that restored the 'iudicia' to the senate (n. 2). Late authorities, dependent on Livy, state that it provided for mixed senatorial and

---

[22] *CQ* 1973, 108 ff. Much of what follows replies to this article; cf. also Lintott (n. 3) 186 ff., 197.

equestrian courts.[23] Balsdon gave strong reasons for preferring their account, and I accept it.[24] However, on my view jurisdiction was in general already shared between the two orders. If so, it follows that Caepio's law concerned only the court *de repetundis*; it was no doubt likely to affect any extraordinary courts to be set up for political charges. Cicero can be taken to mean that the Equites resented loss of their control of political courts. It is evident that Saturninus' law on *maiestas* gave them such control of the new court it established (n. 12), and that Caepio's law was soon repealed by the *lex de repetundis* of Servilius Glaucia, under which a vindictive equestrian jury was enabled to convict Rutilius.[25]

Miriam Griffin also regards Plutarch's account of Gracchus' legislation as inconsistent with certain statements by Cicero and with Drusus' judiciary proposal in 91.

(*a*) In 70 Cicero declared that there had been not the least suspicion of judicial bribery in the fifty years in which Equites had continuously enjoyed judication ('cum equester ordo iudicaret'), in contrast to the notorious corruption rife after the transfer of *iudicia* to the senators (I *Verr*. 38). If this were true, there was an astonishing moral degeneration in the order after 70. Cicero could perhaps venture on his claim, however false, simply because no equestrian *iudex* had been actually convicted of taking a bribe. However, it contradicts the no less partisan testimony of Appian's sources on their misconduct, and cannot be reconciled with the attempt made by Drusus, which the Equites strenuously resisted, to impose retroactive penalties on them for corruption (see below). But memories are short, and the suspicions which had certainly existed despite Cicero's assertion could have faded in comparison with what was believed to be the proven guilt of senatorial *iudices* in the more recent past. Cicero's assertion thus had enough plausibility for his rhetorical purpose, that of impressing on the court the necessity of restoring the reputation of senatorial *iudices*, if the senatorial monopoly of judication were not to be swept away. We are not to look for any truth or precision in Cicero's statement. Moreover, in fact he does not strictly imply that Equites had possessed *sole* judication for fifty years; he had not necessarily overlooked Caepio's law, and there is no need to think that he meant that in cases other than *repetundae*, on which he was focusing attention,[26] senators had

---

[23] Obsequens 41; Cassiod. *Chron. MGH* xi. 132 (on which see Mommsen, *Ges. Schr.* vii. 668 ff.).

[24] *PBSR* 1938, 98 ff.

[25] Cic. *Scaur. ap.* Ascon. 21 C., *Brut.* 224. Cf. n. 16 with text. 'Propter iudicia' could mean 'because of trials', sc. of one kind of case, rather than 'because of courts' established for various kinds of case.

[26] I *Verr.* 38. Admittedly he goes on to mention cases in which senatorial *iudices* in other post-Sullan courts had taken bribes.

always been excluded from the courts, as Equites had been excluded by Sulla.

Again, in his speech for Cornelius he said: 'Memoria teneo, cum primum senatores cum equitibus Romanis lege Plotia iudicarent, hominem dis ac nobilitati perinvisum Pomponium causam lege Varia de maiestate dixisse.'[27] Under the *lex Varia* many senators had been condemned for treason by the malice of the Equites, who then controlled the court *de maiestate*; the *lex Plautia* of 89 provided for the election of *iudices* on a tribal basis, not excluding senators nor even 'plebeians', but probably only *iudices* to hear charges under the *lex Varia* (n. 122). In the context Cicero's words do not imply that senators and *iudices* had never shared judicial functions in any other court before, or that neither Caepio nor Gracchus can have set up mixed courts.

We may notice here another text which on its most natural interpretation refers to mixed courts in the pre-Sullan period. The author of the treatise *ad Herennium* gives a model passage from a speech, actual or fictitious, in which a prosecutor for parricide appeals successively to *iudices* 'who love the name of the senate', to those 'who wish the station of an Eques to be most splendid in the state', and to those who have parents or children (iv. 47). This would make little sense unless the court *de sicariis* or *de venenis*, which also took cognizance of charges of parricide (n. 71), included both senators and Equites. The *lex Plautia* can of course be invoked to explain it by those who believe that law to have had a wider extension than I think plausible.

(*b*) As for Drusus, we are told in the *Perioche* of Livy lxxi that he proposed that the *iudicia* should be equally shared between the senate and the equestrian order. If this has any basis in Livy's text, we might suppose that the proposal was really limited to the courts *de repetundis* and *de maiestate*, of which the Equites admittedly had sole control: it would therefore not show that a mixed *album* did not already exist for other purposes. However, this would mean that Drusus did not seek to effect what, according to the *Perioche* of book lxx, the senate actually desired, viz. the outright transference of the *iudicia* to itself. And yet in conformity with Cicero's delineation of Drusus' policy,[28] the *Perioche* acknowledges that he was the champion of the senate's cause. Moreover, Appian (i. 35) states that he proposed to re-establish a senatorial monopoly, and so far Velleius (ii. 13) agrees; Appian adds that for this purpose the senate was to be enlarged by the adlection of 300 Equites.

---

[27] Ascon. 79 C. I also agree with Balsdon (n. 24) that 'cum primum' can mean 'as soon as' and not necessarily 'when for the first time', but even if it is construed in the latter sense, it has to be considered in the context. I follow Badian (*Historia* 1969, 475) in amending 'Cn. Pompeium' to 'Pomponium'; we do not need to think that Cicero was an 'adherent' of Pompey to see that he could not have vilified Pompey's father in 65.

[28] *de orat.* i. 24, *Mil.* 16; cf. Diod. xxxvii. 10; Vell. ii. 13; Ascon. 68 C.

It is evident that whereas no such enlargement had been necessary in 106, when all that was done was to give senators a share in membership of the one court from which they were then excluded, a senate of 300 members was too small to provide all the *iudices* required for other duties, both civil and criminal. Hence it would not be surprising that Drusus should have intended to anticipate the course taken by Sulla. The author of the work *de viris illustribus* (66) also says of Drusus that 'equitibus curiam, senatui iudicia permisit', and, as Appian tells more fully, that the proposal evoked jealousy on the part of the Equites who were not to gain admission to the senate and objections from senators who did not wish to see the aristocratic composition of the senate diluted. Perhaps on this account the senate was in the end the readier to quash Drusus' laws.[29]

There is no difficulty in supposing that the epitomator of Livy once again mixed up the senate with the *album iudicum*, especially as his summary of Drusus' law is incongruent with his own account of the senatorial objective that Drusus championed, and that Velleius has simply omitted mention of the proposed adlection of new senators (which of course never took place).

It is true that Appian's account is not free from error and confusion. He cannot have been right in thinking that the senate had been reduced by seditions below its normal number, as was to be the case in 81; even when recording how Sulla increased its size (i. 100), he did not understand that this was necessary if senators were to man the courts, and supposed that he was merely filling gaps in the roll of senators created by the civil wars. He was surely providing his own ignorant gloss on Drusus' proposal. He also says that the Equites 'suspected' that the admission of some of their order to the senate would only be a prelude to their exclusion from the courts, although by his account it must have been apparent that this was precisely what Drusus intended. But of course *individual* Equites, once Drusus' plan had been published, would have suspected that they might personally lose their judicial rights by not being enrolled in the senate, a promotion some might not even have desired; Appian could easily have garbled a statement to this effect in his source. The detailed account that both he and the writer *de viris illustribus* give of the attitudes of both senators and Equites to Drusus' bill presupposes that their version of it, which is also that of Velleius, is correct; and it seems to me incredible that it could have been sheer fiction. Of course there can have been no uncertainty about its content, all the more as it was passed into law, though annulled before implementation. Livy would not have been in error,

<hr>

[29] Cic. *de dom.* 41, 50, *de leg.* ii. 14, 31; Diod. xxxvii. 10.

and Velleius may well reflect what he wrote;[30] a confusion by the contemptible epitomator is easy to credit.

Drusus also enacted penalties against *iudices* who took bribes. Miriam Griffin contends that as in the post-Sullan era charges of this offence normally came before the *repetundae* court,[31] Drusus' law must have been a *lex de repetundis* and not a *lex iudiciaria*. That would carry the unacceptable implication that he did not attempt to change the equestrian composition of the *maiestas* court. Moreover, we do not know (i) that Drusus, whose laws never came into operation, intended the same procedure for trying charges of judicial corruption as that established by Sulla, or (ii) that he did not propose a separate law on judicial corruption penalizing equestrian *iudices*. The provision of such penalties is often taken to be incompatible with the exclusion of Equites from the courts. But that is not the case, if the penalty applied to past corruption. Of the two texts in which Cicero refers to its applicability to Equites, one permits and the other requires us to believe that it was retroactive. The second text has been unwarrantably emended, with no linguistic justification, to remove this implication, on the premise that retroactive legislation was contrary to the spirit of Roman law.[32] That is indeed a principle stated by Cicero, but with a significant exception: 'nisi eius rei quae sua sponte tam scelerata et nefaria est ut, etiamsi lex non esset, magnopere vitanda fuerit' (II *Verr.* i. 108). Judicial corruption was the more suitable to be treated as such an exception since it had actually been a capital offence under the Twelve Tables.[33] Evidently this law had fallen into desuetude. However, in 142 the praetor L. Hostilius Tubulus had been flagrantly guilty of taking money when presiding over a murder court, in 141 a plebiscite authorized his trial by a *quaestio* under the presidency of one of the consuls, and he went into exile;[34] if we may believe Asconius (23 C.),

[30] *RE* viii. A 644 (Dihle); cf. Haug, 1947, 100 ff.

[31] Op. cit. (n. 22) 116; see Cic. *Cluent.* 104, 114; this was not the only possible procedure (ibid. 115 f.; cf. Ewins, *JRS* 1960, 99). *Rab. Post.* 16, cited by Griffin, is here irrelevant, and her inference from the Gracchan *repetundae* law v. 28 seems to me unsound; it cannot have been Gracchus' deliberate intent to exempt Equites from penalties for taking bribes, *contra* Nicolet, 1966, 511 ff.; even though Gracchus' law neglected to penalize them, that could not mean that in taking bribes they were 'taking money *in accordance with* this law' (surely a patent absurdity); Sherwin-White (n. 3) must be right that the clause relates to persons indictable under the law, who would include some holders of the public horse (n. 10), when they had taken money less than the minimum (v. 2) required for indictment.

[32] *Rab. Post.* 16: 'si quis ob rem iudicatam [sometimes unwarrantably amended to 'iudicandam'] pecuniam accepisset'; *Cluent.* 153: 'ei qui rem iudicassent' (which could but need not represent a future perfect in the terms of the statute; in any event Cicero need not be *quoting* the terms, *contra* Lintott, op. cit. in n. 3, n. 125). Appian and Diod. xxxvii. 10. 3 also strictly imply that he provided for retrospective charges, though their accuracy could be impugned.

[33] Gell. xx. 1. 7; cf. n. 34.

[34] Cic. *de fin.* ii. 54: 'cum praetor quaestionem inter sicarios exercuisset, ita aperte cepit pecunias ob rem iudicandam, ut anno proximo P. Scaevola tr. pl. ferret ad plebem, vellentne de

his extradition was ordered, and he took poison. Evidently at that time there was no *lex* defining the offence and setting up a permanent *quaestio* to try it, even when it had been committed by a senator, yet it was considered so monstrous ('magnopere vitanda') that a retroactive capital penalty could be imposed. It is true that the condemnation of Rutilius, which clearly set Drusus off on his anti-equestrian pro-gramme, is not ascribed in the numerous sources to judicial corruption, but simply to the conspiracy of the publicans against a man who had curbed their extortions;[35] but there is nothing to exclude the possibility that some of the *iudices* were believed to have been bribed by his enemies, or that other cases of corruption were alleged; Cicero's bland denial of this has virtually no weight (see above).

Miriam Griffin makes much of the statement made by Drusus' chief opponent, the consul Philippus, that he needed a 'consilium' other than 'illo senatu'. This of course presupposes that the senate was at the time (September 91) still on Drusus' side. 'That senate' is simply pejorative: from Philippus' standpoint it had ceased to act in the public interest.[36] There is a parallel to, or reminiscence of, this complaint in that which Livy (ii. 57. 4) attributes to Ap. Claudius, *cos.* 495: 'non consulem senatui sed senatum consuli deesse'. Griffin's notion that Philippus is implying that he intended to constitute an equestrian anti-senate, and that an abortive plan of Drusus' adversary has been made the basis for a false account of Drusus' law, seems to me sheer fantasy.

Thus Drusus sought to do what Sulla actually did, restore the senatorial monopoly of the courts. And even if Drusus proposed mixed courts, there could be no question of Plutarch mixing up Gracchus' proposals with his, or for that matter with Caepio's; he never had any occasion to write of the activity of Caepio and Drusus,[37] and even if the presumably rather detailed source or sources which he used for Gracchus made any comparison between his judiciary proposals and those which were made later, that would have made plain to him what Gracchus actually did. There is of course a clear analogy between the enlargement of the senate which the *Perioche* of Livy ascribes to Gracchus and that which Drusus proposed and Sulla effected; but nothing in the habits of its writer suggests that he would have read on

ea re quaeri. Quo plebiscito decreta est consuli quaestio Cn. Caepioni; profectus in exsilium Tubulus statim nec respondere ausus; erat enim res aperta.' Tubulus was long remembered as a prime scoundrel (*MRR* i. 475). The incident shows that whatever procedure the XII Tables had prescribed had fallen into desuetude; cf. ch. 1 n. 19.

[35] GC 125–7.

[36] Cic. *de orat.* iii. 2. Philippus said in a *contio*: 'videndum sibi esse aliud consilium [a council that behaved differently', so too in Val. Max. vi. 2. 2; 'alio senatu']; illo senatu se rem publicam gerere non posse'. For the usage of 'ille' see *OLD* s.v. 4 c. Cf. also Quint. *Inst. Or.* xi. 1. 37.

[37] He names Drusus only in *Cato Minor* 2.

to books lxxi and lxxxix and misconstrued Gracchus' plans in the light of what he found there. Livy himself cannot have been in error (see below). We cannot explain away the testimony of Plutarch and the *Perioche* by confusion with subsequent legislation, which, if mentioned at all in their sources, would have been mentioned only by way of contrast with the Gracchan scheme.

IV

The conflicts of evidence on the judiciary measures of Gracchus, Caepio, and Drusus make it worth while to turn to the evidence on the *lex Aurelia*, as similar discrepancies occur, though the truth is known beyond question. Scholiasts on Cicero testify that the *iudicia* were equally shared by senators, Equites, and *tribuni aerarii*;[38] two allusions in Cicero's letters confirm this.[39] However, Cicero treats the *tribuni aerarii* as Equites and even as 'principes equestris ordinis',[40] and can therefore say that the courts were now shared between senators and Equites.[41] This is only comprehensible if the panel of Equites proper consisted of past and present holders of the public horse, while the *tribuni aerarii* were also Equites in the looser sense of possessing the equestrian property qualification. We can only conjecture why the panels were constituted in this way. Cicero had remarked in 70 that the corruption imputed to the senatorial *iudices* had created a demand for the appointment of censors who would be able to purify the courts by removing the unworthy from the senate and thereby from the *album iudicum* (*Div. Caec.* 8). It was reasonable for Cotta in proposing his reform to have provided that the new equestrian jurors should likewise be subject to censorial scrutiny. The enrolment of *equites equo publico* was a matter for the censors, and we may readily assume that they were also responsible for designating the *tribuni aerarii*; it had once been their

---

[38] Ascon. 17 C. etc.; cf. Schol. Bobb. 94 St.: 300 from each category (cf. Cic. *Fam.* viii. 8. 5; Pliny, *NH* xxxiii. 31).

[39] *Att.* i. 16. 3, *Qu. fr.* ii. 4. 6.

[40] *Font.* 41, *Rab. Post.* 14; cf. *Cluent.* 121, 130, *Flacc.* 4, 96, *Planc.* 41. Pompey's regulation of 55 that *iudices* of all three orders should be selected 'amplissimo censu' (Ascon. 17 C.) merely means they were to be among the richest of those possessed of the formal qualifications (which for all comprised a minimum of 400,000 HS). Schol. Bobb. 91 St., perhaps derived from Cicero, says that a *iudex* might disqualify himself by losing 300,000 or 400,000 HS; naturally this does not imply that he is contemplating the loss of a man's entire fortune, and therefore that 300,000 was the minimum required for *tr. aer.* Caesar eliminated them (Suet. *Caes.* 41; Dio xliii. 25), but apparently retained the minimum census qualification of 400,000 (Cic. *Phil.* i. 20). Augustus' creation of a fourth decury of men with only 200,000, entitled to judge only 'de levioribus summis' (n. 110), is of course not evidence that the *tr. aer.* had once formed an intermediate grade, esp. as their competence was not restricted. Cicero's testimony is in any event decisive against conjectural combinations of this kind.

[41] *Cluent.* 130. So too he ignores 'plebeian' *iudices* under the *lex Plautia* (n. 27).

function to pay the legionaries, and that might well have meant that they were not only drawn from those whose property furnished security in case of their embezzlement of public funds in their care, but that they could be cut off from the list by censors for misconduct.[42] Their office had become a sinecure, just as the *equites equo publico* were no longer required to serve in the cavalry, but in the one case as in the other the censors could have retained the right to award or withhold a title of social distinction which raised them above others with the same property qualification. Thus two thirds of the new *album* were in some sense Equites. Velleius says that judicial rights were shared between senators and Equites 'aequaliter' (ii. 30), which we may perhaps render as 'fairly', though in the absence of other evidence 'equally' would be more natural. The preponderance of Equites in the broad sense explains why Plutarch (*Pomp.* 22) and the *Perioche* of Livy xcii write of transference of the courts to them. We can similarly account for a misconception of Gracchus' judiciary law. True, Velleius expressly contrasts the compromise of 70 with the Gracchan system of purely equestrian courts and the Sullan of purely senatorial (loc. cit., cf. ii. 6. 3), presumably because he is thinking of the exclusive control of *political* courts by Equites in the Gracchan system. It is clear that but for the survival of commentaries by the diligent Asconius and of the letters of Cicero the content of the *lex Aurelia* would be as disputable as Gracchus' judiciary legislation, for which we have no evidence better in kind than Velleius and the *Periochae* of Livy.

None should doubt that Livy, writing when there was a mixed *album*, was perfectly well aware of the terms of the *lex Aurelia*, and that the error in the *Perioche* is one of many that must be attributed to his miserable epitomator.[43] It seems to me no less certain that if we had Livy's account of events from the Gracchi to Sulla, though it might fail to bring to light those 'clandestine, private maneuvers' which, according to Gruen[44], are the 'genuine stuff of politics', and though it might reflect the bias of his sources in analysis of the motives and intentions of rival politicians, we should not lack accurate information on overt facts known to all contemporary observers of the political scene. The period was perfectly familiar to historically minded Romans in the first

---

[42] C. Nicolet, *Tributum*, 1976, 46 ff., also for the possibility that they collected the *tributum* (not levied since 167) and had to advance the sums due to the treasury. Of course senators too were liable to be removed by the censors. (The distinction drawn in a Sullan law between members of the senate and those with a right 'in senatu sententiam dicere' (*Cluent.* 148) seems to imply that Sulla had assumed that there would be regular censorial *lectiones* through which ex-quaestors embraced in the latter category would normally become full senators.)

[43] Many scholars have held that the *Periochae* derived from an earlier and fuller epitome of Livy: Kroll disagreed (*RE* xiii. 824 ff., with bibliography).

[44] Gruen, 1968, ch. 1.

century BC. Hence Cicero can casually refer, for example, to such incidents as Pennus' law of 126, the *lex Thoria*, and the prosecutions under the *lex Mamilia*, without giving any explicit account of them:[45] he could take it for granted that his audience or readers knew the circumstances. What he says in the last instance would be as problematic to us as the other two allusions but that Sallust's *Bellum Iugurthinum* was preserved as a masterpiece of Latin prose writing. That work in itself shows the wealth of material deriving from contemporary narratives and speeches that was available to a writer three generations later.

Exactly what sources were used by Livy or Sallust, or by other derivative writers such as Claudius Quadrigarius, Valerius Antias, or Aelius Tubero, whom Livy might have followed, it is impossible to tell. We can name some writers of contemporary history in the period, such as Cn. Gellius, L. Coelius Antipater, Sempronius Asellio, C. Fannius, and P. Rutilius Rufus, but so little is known of the scope of *their* works, and that from a few chance allusions or citations, that we cannot even be sure that there were no other sources lost in total oblivion. The memoirs of Scaurus (*cos.* 115) were available to Cicero and are probably cited later; Plutarch, or his sources, could cite the memoirs of Catulus (*cos.* 102).[46] Numerous speeches from the second century were extant, including some published by Tiberius and Gaius Gracchus, of which the latter evoked Cicero's strong admiration.[47] They have probably left some traces even in our meagre tradition.[48] Livy certainly used speeches, Cato's in particular, and it is extremely unlikely, given his rhetorical training, that he was not as familiar with those of Gaius Gracchus, whom Cicero had rated so highly, as with those of Cato; in fact, we may infer from *Perioche* lix that he drew on Gaius' speech for the *rogatio Papiria* (131 BC), which was long extant in antiquity.[49] It is true that, whereas he needed a book for 1.8 years in his third decade, and for just over 2 years for his narrative of events from 200 to 168, and no less than 18 books for the period from 91 to 79 (which is also poorly documented in our extant sources), 13 sufficed for the years from 133 to 92. It was not a time of great wars, on which he

---

[45] *De offic.* iii. 47, *Brut.* 136, 127 f.

[46] Cf. Peter, *HRR* i. *sub nominibus.*   [47] *Brut.* 103, 125 f.

[48] Malcovati, *ORF²*, no. 48, 16–20. She reasonably assumed that Gracchan speeches are reflected in some passages of Plutarch (*Ti. Gr.* 9, 15, *C. Gr.* 1, 3, 8) and Appian (i, 11, 22).

[49] xxxviii. 54. 11, xxxix. 42 f., *Per.* xli, xlix (Cato's speeches, which may also have been used where this is not stated, e.g. in xxxvii. 57; there is a puzzle about the reference in *Per.* xli to Cato's speech on the *lex Voconia*, which belongs to 169 and is not mentioned by Livy in xliii, where it belongs; perhaps there was a forward allusion to it in one of the gaps in xli. 18–21, conjecturally in connection with the undated *lex Furia*, which it strengthened.) Cf. *Per.* xlix (Galba) lix (Q. Metellus), lxx, where Livy evidently relied on a statement of Cicero for the trial of Manius Aquillius in default of other evidence (GC 116).

loved to expatiate. But within this period he could still write at length on major internal commotions. Tiberius Gracchus' tribunate occupied virtually the whole of book lviii (apart from some material on the Sicilian slave war), and the activities of Gaius must have consumed most of books lx and lxi, which ran from 126 to 120 BC. It is our misfortune that both Appian and Plutarch have not chosen to tell us as much of the transactions of 123–122 as of 133; both must once have been amply recorded. Our information on the turbulent year of Saturninus' second tribunate, to which Livy devoted a whole book (lxix), is just as scanty.

The period from the Gracchi to Sulla is therefore not one in which we should expect to find different 'traditions' about public events, one of which can be regarded as authentic, while others can be rejected as fictions devoid of all foundation; the discrepancies in our evidence must rather be explained by the rhetoric, bias, and inexactitude of many of Cicero's allusions, and by the carelessness characteristic of epitomizers, which we often find in the secondary accounts of events in the 50s. Here their errors can generally be exposed by collation with the testimony of Cicero: it is this alone, for instance, that proves that those late narratives are right which credit Caesar in 59 with two agrarian laws, and not with only one; if it were lost, Ockham's razor would doubtless have been confidently applied.[50] It is never sufficient simply to dismiss one version of events and to prefer another, without showing how the error of the former can be explained.

No source of error is so common as the undue brevity and looseness of hasty epitomizers. The *lex Aurelia* gave the Equites preponderance in the courts: it was then easy to say that it transferred jurisdiction to them. The *tribuni aerarii* were Equites in a wide sense (n. 40): it was natural not to differentiate them from those who were formally entitled to the appellation. Even if Asconius were a generally unreliable authority, and even if his testimony were not confirmed by Cicero, it would have been right to believe that they formed one third of the *album iudicum*, simply because it would have been impossible to see how their inclusion could have been invented, and perfectly comprehensible that it should have been ignored. The more detailed our testimony is, the more it is likely to preserve (perhaps in a confused and inaccurate form) some elements from the earlier and fuller evidence, which rival versions have omitted, or obscured in imprecisely general phrasing. So too in regard to Gaius Gracchus' legislation on the courts, if he did not exclude senators but gave Equites a share or preponderance, together with an actual monopoly in the court that was of most

---

[50] Cf. Brunt, *CQ* 1980 471 ff., esp. 492.

political importance, epitomes and casual allusions could easily credit
him with transferring the courts to the Equites; on the other hand, the
contradictory statement made by Plutarch, which must be right if it
has the backing of Livy, is less easy to explain except on the basis that it
is true.

In fact only one other explanation merits serious consideration. It is
the theory adopted by many scholars, including Stockton, that
Plutarch and (probably) Livy recorded an initial proposal of Gracchus
which he eventually abandoned. Some discovered an analogy by
imputing to him a change of plan for the extension of the franchise:
Stockton himself has refuted this, and I shall waste no words on it.[51]
Others sought support for the theory in what we are told of his
enactment (perhaps part of some more general measure) 'ne quis
iudicio circumveniretur', which prescribed penalties for senators
alone.[52] They supposed that this expressly related to the acceptance of
bribes by *iudices*, and found it inexplicable that only senatorial *iudices*
were liable, not only if senators were excluded from the courts, but also
if Equites were even eligible. Hence they dated it to a time when
Gracchus did not intend to touch the senatorial monopoly, and
conjectured that the *Perioche* of Livy, rather than Plutarch, has
preserved the truth, and that at one stage he designed simply to
enlarge the senate and leave senators in possession of the courts. But it
has been shown that, though the terms of the enactment were so wide
and vague that they could cover a corrupt vote for condemnation, that
was not its true purpose: it was devised to limit the undue exercise of
power by senators, making it a criminal offence for them to procure a
man's unjust condemnation by any wrongful means, of which bribery
was only one.[53]

Most advocates of the two-stage theory dated the law or laws to 122
and the abortive plan to 123. In my judgement it is far more likely that
in order to consolidate his power Gracchus sought to win equestrian
support in his first tribunate, both by his judiciary legislation and by
his regulation of the Asian tax system. Moreover, whether or not the
bill that passed by only one tribal vote be identified with a judiciary
law (n. 8), the conferment of judication on the Equites can have had so
little appeal to the masses that it would have been safe in 122 for

---

[51] Stockton 143–9, 237–9.   [52] Cic. *Cluent.* 115 f.; cf. U. Ewins, *JRS* 1960, 94 ff., at 99.
[53] *Cluent.* 148, 157; Ewins, art. cit.; cf. Stockton, 1979, 122–6. Sulla incorporated this
Gracchan law in his *lex de sicariis* (*Cluent.* 151). It may be that it had been part not of the Gracchan
law 'ne de capite . . .' (n. 88 with text) but of an otherwise unattested Gracchan law *de sicariis*; as
shown in section VI, the law 'ne de capite . . .' necessitated the creation of a *quaestio de sicariis* if it
did not already exist; and if it did, Gracchus may have wished to amend its terms of reference.
The absence of any express testimony to such a Gracchan law is certainly no proof that there was
none (cf. pp. 216 ff.).

Drusus to have exercised his veto.[54] Indeed the influence of Gracchus waned in 122, and in the early part of that year, when it was perhaps still strong, he had to spend seventy days organizing the settlement of Iunonia (Plut. 11. 1). All this is not decisive against a date very early in the second tribunate, and the *repetundae* law at least must be placed early in either 123 or 122, since it envisages that a panel must be enrolled for the current year, in which charges under the new procedure may still be brought;[55] Stockton, who favours 123, can hardly be right in dating it to the autumn. Holding with more entire confidence than the evidence permits that the judiciary legislation belongs to early 123 (which I still think most probable), I previously argued that there was no time for a change of plan. However, there is no force in this contention. Plutarch and Livy could have recorded a scheme that he contemplated but abandoned after a week or two. Nor can we make anything of the mere fact that both refer to a law (*lex*, νόμος), not a *rogatio*. In the very same context Plutarch writes of the 'law' for enfranchising Latins, which never passed, and the author of the *Periochae* (book iii) can use the term *leges* of agrarian bills which were not enacted. However, Plutarch makes clear his belief that the law as he described it was actually passed. He adds that Gracchus himself selected the new equestrian *iudices*. This is incompatible with the mode by which *iudices* are to be empanelled in the *tabula Bembina* and under later legislation.[56] Probably Gracchus' enemies made out that they were his creatures, and Plutarch has here mistaken hostile propaganda for truth.

Whether Gracchus' supposed change of plan evinces greater moderation or less, we might expect that some explicit hint of it would be

[54] It may be objected that, according to Cicero *ap*. Ascon. 78 C., the populace demanded the Aurelian law and the Roscian; but his claim in regard to the Roscian is highly dubious (ch. 6 n. 155); in any case the notorious corruption of senatorial *iudices* in the 70s, which could affect defendants of all degrees charged with murder, peculation, or forgery, might account for a universal demand for reform (cf. I *Verr*. 44). Stockton, 1979, 226 ff., reviews other chronological arguments on the chronology of Gracchan laws, all in my view indecisive. Perhaps the order of the notices in *Per*. Livy lx has some weight, but we cannot be sure that it follows Livy's. In my view Appian narrates events to explain the rise and fall of Gracchus without exact attention to chronology; he even fails to note that he was killed in the year after his second tribunate; cf. ch. 9 n. 61.

[55] It is not very material that the praetorian provinces for the year had already been allocated (vv. 12, 16), since that might have been done at the end of the preceding year, but significant that the law envisages prosecutions in the very year of its enactment. It seems to me that the repeated mention of 1 Sept. (vv. 7, 9) implies that a charge under the law would not be heard in the year in which it was brought unless preferred before that terminus, even though the lacuna in vv. 6 f., makes it impossible to determine what happened if it were preferred later (cf. W. W. Buckland, *JRS* 1937, 42).

[56] Cic. *Cluent*. 121: 'praetores urbani ... iurati debent optimum quemque in selectos iudices referre'. In 52 Pompey was apparently empowered to nominate for a special *album* (Ascon. 38 C.), but this was more appropriate for a consul than for a tribune.

found in some of our sources, and more particularly in Plutarch, who brings out how Tiberius Gracchus was inflamed by opposition to his first agrarian bill and made it more severe, and how Gaius abandoned his persecution of Octavius.[57] Stockton replies that it is no less remarkable that Plutarch fails to mention that he altogether excluded senators from the *repetundae* court. That is not so. Plutarch was not an historian but a biographer. His primary concern was not with the actions of any of his heroes for their intrinsic importance but with the way in which they illustrated the man's personality, his virtues, and faults (e.g. *Alex.* 1). Gracchus' legislative programme interests him because it shows Gracchus 'gratifying the people and overthrowing the senate' (5. 1) and thereby obtaining almost monarchic power (6. 1). If he was right that Gracchus subverted senatorial dominance by abolishing their monopoly of jurisdiction, his special regulation of the *repetundae* court was a detail that did not essentially affect Plutarch's picture.[58] But it would have been very different if Gracchus had changed his mind, because he was either exacerbated by resistance or ready to defer to objections. It is then unlikely that Plutarch found in his source any evidence that Gracchus ever propounded a judiciary reform other than that which he brought into operation.

V

It will be seen that the two-stage theory is not capable of decisive refutation. But I do not think that scholars in general would have been disposed to accept it, had they not been unduly influenced not only by the apparent testimony of some sources that Gracchus simply transferred the *iudicia* to the Equites, but also by the belief that there were no other judicial functions besides service in the *repetundae* court, from which senators were admittedly excluded, to which his legislation *could* have applied. To this contention I now turn.

So far as crimes are concerned, it is said that no other permanent *quaestiones* yet existed. It might be added that it would have been futile for Gracchus to have prescribed the composition of any future court constituted *ad hoc*, since its composition could always be determined by the very measure by which it was constituted.

In the post-Sullan system permanent criminal courts existed at least:[59]

---

[57] *Ti. Gr.* 10, *C. Gr.* 4.

[58] The law on *repetundae* has little interest for most narrative sources in its own right, as distinguished from the composition of the court (cf. n. 64 and text).

[59] GC 219 ff., assemble the chief texts. I ignore the novel *lex Cornelia de iniuriis*, as the process was certainly civil (*Inst.* iv. 4. 1; Gruen, 1968, 263, is apparently unaware that *poena* and *iudicium* are terms of civil as well as of criminal process), and we do not know that there was a *quaestio* (Kunkel, *RE* xxiv. 742). *Vis*: see Lintott, 1968, ch. VIII.

1. *de sicariis et veneficis*
2. *de falsis, testamentaria, nummaria*
3. *de repetundis*
4. *de maiestate*
5. *de ambitu*
6. *de peculatu*
7. *de vi*

The last was certainly created after Sulla under Lutatian and Plautian laws; the others are known to have operated under Cornelian laws, except for *peculatus*, of which this is presumed. The Cornelian statutes *de sicariis* . . . and *de falsis* . . . remained the basis of the relevant criminal law throughout the Principate; the other statutes were superseded by Julian laws *de repetundis* (59 BC), *de maiestate*, *de ambitu*, *de peculatu*, and *de vi*, which likewise remained in force thereafter; for our purpose it does not matter which of them were the work of Caesar or of Augustus.[60]

The imperial jurist Pomponius, having recorded the institution of the urban and peregrine praetorships (*Dig.* i. 2. 2. 27 f.), observes that 'after the conquest of Sardinia, then of Sicily, also of Spain and next of Narbonensis', an enumeration of the creation of new provinces which is chronologically disordered and omits the pre-Sullan annexation of Achaea, Macedonia, Africa, and Asia, additional praetors were appointed to govern them, and that then Sulla 'quaestiones publicas constituit, veluti de falso, de parricidio, de sicariis, et praetores quattuor adiecit'; Caesar was to add two more, and there was thus a total of twelve (ibid. 32). Pomponius' count of praetors is inaccurate: after 179 there were always six, and in Cicero's time only eight;[61] of course in the Sullan system praetors stayed at Rome in their year of office to administer justice, and went out thereafter to provinces as promagistrates. Nor was there any permanent court *de parricidio*; trials on this charge seem to have come before the court *de sicariis* (see below), though the offence was regulated not by the Cornelian law but by a Pompeian law of unknown authorship and date (*Dig.* xlviii. 9). Pomponius' testimony is thus so inaccurate that we could not properly infer from it that Sulla created (even if that were what 'constituit' unambiguously means) the three *quaestiones* he specifically mentions, or any others.

The fact that a Sullan statute defined the law to be applied by a permanent court to a particular crime or group of crimes is plainly no proof that any such court was first set up by Sulla. We *know* this to be untrue of the courts *de repetundis* and *de maiestate*.[62] We also have

---

[60] *Dig.* xlviii. 4. 6–8, 9–11, 13.

[61] Cic. Sest. 87, *post red. sen.* 22 f. for 57 BC.

[62] The trial of Norbanus in *c.* 95 under the *lex Appuleia maiestatis* proves that that law created a permanent court (*de orat.* ii. 107, 197 f.; cf. GC 91 ff.).

allusions to pre-Sullan trials by *quaestiones* for murder, *ambitus*, and *peculatus* (see below). Some or all of these have been construed to refer to *ad hoc* courts set up on special occasions. A passage in Cicero seems to draw a distinction between *ad hoc* and permanent courts: 'cognosce alias quaestiones, [i] auri Tolosani [104], coniurationis Iugurthinae [sc. under the *lex Mamilia* of 110]; repete superiora: Tubuli de pecunia capta ob rem iudicandam [142]; posteriora; de incestu rogatione Peducaea [113]; [ii] tum haec cotidiana: sicae venena peculatus, testamentorum *etiam nova lege* quaestiones'; elsewhere too he shows that Sulla established a new permanent court for forgery.[63] The 'cotidiana' are clearly crimes repressed by permanent courts, but among them Cicero differentiates between forgery, which was a novelty, and those which by implication were the subject of earlier legislation. So there was nothing fundamentally new in Sulla's law 'de sicariis et veneficis' or in the post-Sullan repression of *peculatus* (a Sullan law is not actually attested); and there is no evidence that he first created any criminal court, except for forgery. In fact no historical narrative for the period mentions his constitution of any courts at all. Velleius (ii. 32) merely says that he transferred judiciary functions to 'the senate', an inaccurate term to represent 'the senators'. Appian does no more than mention that he adlected new senators, without making it clear that he doubled the size of the senate with the aim, as Tacitus alone remarks (*Ann.* xi. 22), of enabling it to provide sufficient *iudices*. There is of course equally no ancient authority for the myth widespread in modern works that he performed an outstanding service by remodelling the criminal law in substance; in fact, his laws, except on forgery, may have been tralatician apart from points of detail.

This silence on the part of *narrative sources* is typical. They were not interested in the establishment of new courts, or in the designation of certain acts as criminal, or in subsequent modifications of criminal law. Just as they are silent on almost every statute that reformed the civil law in substance or procedure, so too they do not mention the *lex Calpurnia de repetundis*, nor any later legislation on the offence including the *lex Iulia*,[64] except in so far as it changed the composition of the courts, nor the *lex Appuleia de maiestate* (n. 62), nor the *lex Pompeia de parricidiis*, nor the statute under which men were prosecuted for *ambitus* in the pre-Sullan period, nor any statute on *peculatus*, nor the Lutatian

---

[63] *de nat. deor.* iii. 74; cf. II *Verr.* i. 108: 'Cornelia testamentaria, nummaria, ceterae complures (leges) in quibus non ius aliquod novum populo constituitur, sed sancitur ut, quod semper malum facinus fuerit, eius quaestio ad populum pertineat ex certo tempore', from which we may deduce that in respect of at least some of the offences listed in Sulla's forgery law an injured party could previously have brought a private action; cf. Kunkel, 1962, 64.

[64] Yet the narratives of domestic events in 59 are fuller than for any year between 132 and 79. Dio liv. 16 also neglects the enactment of Augustus' adultery law.

and Plautian laws on *vis*, nor Caesar's laws on *vis* and *maiestas* (*Phil.* i. 21). We can learn much of those laws which were in force in Cicero's own day, chiefly from speeches in which he was pleading under their terms, and much of those still operative in the Principate from the comments of jurists on their interpretation and later extension; statutes which had become obsolete in Cicero's lifetime are known, if at all, from a few chance literary allusions,[65] or from the equally fortuitous survival of epigraphic fragments. It is therefore illegitimate to argue *e silentio* that at any particular date no law was in force by which a permanent *quaestio* had been constituted, because we do not happen to know of it, or to assume that Sulla was the first to establish such courts, if they are not clearly attested before his dictatorship.

Cicero recalled that Servilius Glaucia used to warn the people to be wary of any bill that set up a new *quaestio* before which any citizen, and not simply ex-magistrates, might be indicted for offences committed after its enactment; it is evident that at least proposals of this kind had become familiar before the end of the second century.[66] With no police or public prosecutor, the state had to rely on delators to bring crimes to light and to encourage them with rewards. A class of professional accusers seems to have come into existence before 80, who were active *inter alia* in preferring charges of murder; some time earlier it had become necessary to penalize false accusations by a *lex Remmia*,[67] which was perhaps the work of a Remmius attested as tribune in 91,[68] but which is unlikely to have been enacted until the abuses of the practice of delation had become apparent over a period of some years.

It is only sheer prejudice that obliges some scholars to put a wholly unnatural construction on a passage in which Cicero indicates that several permanent *quaestiones* predated Gracchus. He says that C. Carbo (*cos.* 120, and born therefore *c.* 165) was distinguished as an advocate at a time when 'plura fieri iudicia coeperunt; nam et quaestiones perpetuae hoc adulescente constitutae sunt, quae ante nullae fuerunt; L. enim Piso tr. pl. legem primum de pecuniis repetundis tulit' (in 149). Gruen holds that this 'in context surely means that the institution of *quaestiones perpetuae* dated to 149, not that several *quaestiones* were constituted about that time'.[69] But the Calpurnian law created only one such *quaestio*, and it seems to me the plain sense of the text that for Cicero it was the precedent for others set up in

[65] Fullest for Glaucia's *repetundae* law (GC 100 f.), whose provisions, continued in later legislation, Cicero cites in three forensic speeches.

[66] *Rab. Post.* 14.

[67] Cic. *Rosc. Amer.* 55–7; cf. also 8, 90; *Dig.* xlviii. 16. 1. 2; Kunkel, 1962, n. 343. Dio, fr. 100 names a delator notorious in 88.

[68] *De vir. ill.* 66. 2 (not in *MRR*).

[69] *Brutus* 106; Gruen, 1968, 87 n. 44, is followed by Griffin.

the next two decades. If he had been thinking only of trials ('iudicia' could be so translated) in the *repetundae* court, he would simply have omitted the words 'nam et . . . fuerunt'. What other courts could have been established?

It is most natural to think of *quaestiones de sicariis* and *de venenis*, which took cognizance not only or primarily of murder but of carrying weapons and procuring poisons with evil intent, though it will be convenient to refer to them as murder courts.[70] Murder of close kin was parricide and under the *lex Pompeia* known to us by name only from imperial jurists, it carried a peculiarly barbarous penalty; Cicero tells that a few years before his defence of Sextus Roscius in 80 a charge of parricide brought by a delator had been tried by a jury, probably in a court *de sicariis* or *de veneficiis*.[71] His pre-Sullan treatise *de inventione* provides an example of delation for both poisoning and parricide, and alludes to a case in which there was an attempt to bar a civil action for *iniuria* on the footing that a decision would be prejudicial to a future trial 'inter sicarios'. The roughly contemporary work addressed *ad Herennium* offers specimens of oratorical pleas for men accused before *iudices* of parricide or murder. All these cases were pre-Sullan. When Roscius was charged with parricide, but before the court 'inter sicarios', Cicero says that that court was meeting in 80 after a 'long interval'; however, the president M. Fannius, who was then praetor, had actually presided in some previous year, presumably as *aedilicius* (nn. 74–6); the interval need be no longer than that of the civil war (83–82) plus a subsequent period in which Sulla might have dealt summarily with criminals as dictator. Cicero refers to the countless professional informers who were accustomed to bring charges 'inter sicarios et de veneficiis' evidently before this 'interval'.[72] Sulla's statute (which Cicero never mentions in his defence of Roscius) need have done no more than consolidate and elaborate the previous law; though it embraced both types of offences under the heading 'de sicariis et veneficis', Sulla did not necessarily envisage that one court would suffice; in 66 two courts *inter sicarios* and one *de veneficis* were sitting simultaneously.[73]

---

[70] Kunkel, 1962, 64 ff.; cf. J. D. Cloud, *SZ*, 1969, 260 ff.

[71] *Lex Pompeia*; *Dig.* xlviii. 9. I do not see why it may not be pre-Sullan. The court which heard charges before Sulla (*ad Her.* iv. 47, *de inv.* ii. 58 f., *Rosc. Amer.* 64 f.) was probably, as after Sulla (*Rosc. Amer.* 11 with 28), the *quaestio inter sicarios* or *de venenis*. This may have been prescribed either by the *lex Pompeia* itself or by pre-Sullan and Sullan legislation on the other 'murder' charges, which might have enacted that the penalty should be that laid down by the *lex Pompeia* in the cases to which that law applied. Similarly the *lex Iulia de repetundis* may have incorporated heavier than pecuniary penalties when the offences proved would also have been indictable under e.g. the Sullan law *de maiestate* (cf. Cic. *Pis.* 50; A. N. Sherwin-White, *PBSR* 1949, 12 ff.).

[72] Cic. *de inv.* ii. 58–60, *Rosc. Amer.* 11, 28, 64 f., 90 (cf. n. 67), *ad Her.* iv. 47, 53; cf. nn. 67, 75.

[73] Cic. *Cluent.* 147 f.

In the 90s C. Claudius Pulcher (*cos.* 92) had, as *aedilicius*, served as 'iudex q[uaestionis] veneficis'. So too in the post-Sullan period there were often too few praetors to preside over all the *quaestiones*, and their place was supplied by a *iudex quaestionis* or *quaesitor*.[74] The writer *ad Herennium* refers to such *quaesitores* in murder cases, among them L. Cassius (*cos.* 127), who was long remembered for asking in that capacity 'cui bono fuisset perire eum de cuius morte quaeritur'.[75] It is most probable that he exercised the function as praetor or after his aedileship, i.e. before 123; in the late Republic the presidents of standing courts, if not praetors, were *aedilicii*, like C. Claudius.[76] Finally, the praetor Hostilius Tubulus 'quaestionem inter sicarios exercuit' in 142 (n. 34). Gruen considers it likely that he was in charge of an extraordinary *quaestio*, since such a *quaestio* was set up in 138 to try publicans and their agents for murder, and he supposes that to have been unnecessary, if a standing court were already in being. (He also thinks, contrary to the evidence, that the permanent court is not known to have existed before Sulla.)[77] His argument has no force. In 52, although permanent courts for *vis* and *ambitus* already existed, Pompey promoted new legislation for the trial of offenders, which aggravated the penalties, speeded the procedure, and provided for a special *album* of *iudices* and for the election of a consular to preside over the court to hear the charges arising from Clodius' murder.[78] In 138 the publicans of Sila were alleged to have procured the death of 'men of note', and given the probable influence of the defendants and 'the magnitude and atrocity' of the crime imputed to them, the consuls themselves were commissioned to take cognizance of the matter. The establishment of a special court for this affair is therefore no ground for denying that there was a regular court to try what Cicero calls the 'daily' crimes of low-class *sicarii*.

Peculation was another offence of the 'daily' type (n. 61) which could be committed by men of relatively low rank,[79] and for which

[74] *ILS* 45. The *lex Cornelia de sicariis* envisaged that the president of the court might be 'iudex quaestionis' (*Coll.* i. 1. 3; *Dig.* xlviii. 8. 1. 1). The term 'quaesitor' (I *Verr.* 29, *Font.* 21, *Cluent.* 55, 74, 89) is in my view used to denote the president, whether a praetor or such a *iudex*. *Aliter* Mommsen, *StR²* ii. 582 ff., whose theory need not be examined here.

[75] *Ad Her.* iv. 47 with Ascon. 45 C.

[76] M. Fannius (n. 72), *aed.* probably in 86 (*RRC* i. no. 351), C. Iunius in 74 (cf. Cic. *Cluent.* 79), C. Flaminius in 66, Caesar in 64, C. Octavius in 63(?), Crassus Dives in 59 were all *aedilicii*, like C. Visellius Varro (*Brut.* 264), *ann. inc.*; this can be true of all other such *iudices* recorded in *MRR* ii. under 86, 70, 66, 62. Consulars and praetorians are attested only for extraordinary courts set up by the laws of Peducaeus (113), Mamilius (110), and Pompey (52).

[77] Gruen, 1968, 261, on Cic. *Brut.* 85–8. It is another matter that there was a special *quaestio* to try Tubulus (n. 34).

[78] Ascon. 38 f. C.; App. ii. 23. Plut. *Cato Minor* 48; Tac. *Dial.* 38. 2; cf. Cic. *Mil.* 15, *Att.* xiii. 49. 1.

[79] e.g. Cic. *Mur.* 42; Plut. *Cato Minor* 16. 3; Livy xxx. 39. 7.

there was a pre-Sullan permanent court. Naturally we seldom hear of prosecutions except when a man of high station was accused, as L. Lucullus was probably accused in 102 and Pompey in 86. Gruen concedes that a permanent court probably existed by 102, but argues that it must have been constituted after 104, when there was an extraordinary investigation into the embezzlement of the Tolosan gold (n. 63). But the eminence of the principal defendant on that occasion, Q. Servilius Caepio (*cos.* 106), and the complexity of the affair, in which a great number of persons were probably implicated, might well have made it seem appropriate to set up a special tribunal with its own procedure and an exclusively equestrian jury, unlike that of a permanent court already in existence.[80]

The existence of some permanent criminal courts which would have been senatorial as early as 133 would be certified, if we were to accept Plutarch's story that when seeking re-election Tiberius Gracchus propounded a new legislative programme (n. 21), including a bill creating a right of appeal to the people from their verdicts, unless we suppose that the putative bill merely reinforced the right of such appeal when a citizen was condemned by the magistrate acting by advice of his *consilium*, perhaps under the authority of a senatorial decree (cf. section VI). Tiberius might also have proposed to make even the sentences of courts set up by the people appellate, as Antony proposed in 44 to provide for appeals from sentences of the courts *de vi* and *de maiestate*.[81] Some scholars, however, take his alleged programme to be merely a fictitious retrojection of Gaius' measures: I incline to think this view implausible, on the ground that even if Tiberius was seeking re-election simply for his personal security, he still needed to furnish public reasons for his candidature, and to win additional popular support.

VI

Whether or not there is evidence for the existence before 123 of any permanent court except that *de repetundis*, the question of the establishment of such courts before Sulla needs to be reviewed in the light of Kunkel's reconstruction of pre-Sullan criminal processes.

On Mommsen's theory, which became canonical, citizens could be tried by a magistrate for crimes, but they could always appeal to the people against sentences of death, flogging, and fines over a certain limit; as a result proceedings in the magistrate's court were mere formalities, and the substantive trial took place on appeal, to the

---

[80] Plut. *Luc.* 1, *Pomp.* 4; cf. Gruen, 1968, 176 f., 244 ff. For the *aurum Tolosanum* see GC 80, 85.
[81] Cic. *Phil.* i. 21 f.

centuriate assembly on capital indictments, and to the tribal when the penalty was a heavy fine; no other procedure was known until permanent or *ad hoc* courts were set up for particular offences or types of offence.[82] Numerous trials before the people are in fact recorded, but critics of Mommsen were able to show that in all historic cases, except for the trials of C. Rabirius in 63, the people acted as a court of first instance, hearing indictments by a magistrate, normally a tribune.[83] Moreover, almost all the cases are those of political offences. Kunkel supposes that magistrates acting by the advice of a *consilium* could exercise inappellate jurisdiction, e.g. for murder, on prosecutions brought by kindred of the victim or by delators appearing in the public interest.[84]

His complex and plausible arguments cannot be rehearsed here, but at first sight his conclusion is barred by an insurmountable difficulty. That citizens had a right of appeal against capital convictions in the second century is beyond question. It cannot be believed that this right was rendered inoperative just because the magistrate tried a man with a *consilium* which he could choose at his own will and which could share his own bias. Defendants on political charges could then have been at the mercy of a hostile court. There seems to be no doubt that in practice magistrates did not venture to hear such charges, which came before the assembly in the first instance. This was ensured not only by the *ius provocationis* and by the tribunician *ius auxilii*, which was available only within the city of Rome, but precisely by the competence of tribunes to impeach before the people any magistrate who violated the former right. However, it is another matter to suppose that tribunes would give protection within the city to persons prosecuted for common crimes, or impeach, or threaten to impeach, magistrates who would not allow appeal on conviction, when there was no reason to think that he and his *consilium* would fail, or had failed, to give them a fair hearing. Hence in actual usage non-political crimes could have been dealt with as Kunkel suggests. Indeed it seems inconceivable that the cumbrous procedure of the centuriate assembly, with hearings on four days (n. 82), was the normal mode of bringing common criminals to justice.[85] Some cases have been adduced when it was used for such trials, but all have exceptional features which can explain the adoption of an unusual process.[86] Good sense suggests that the peasant who

[82] *StR* iii[3]. 751 ff. [83] Bleicken, *RE* xxiii. 2444 ff.; cf. endnotes 8 f.

[84] Kunkel, 1962 (cf. my review in *Tijdschr. voor Rechtsgeschiedenis* 1964, 440 ff., and lucid discussion by Nicholas in Jolowicz–Nicholas, ch. 18), *RE* xxiv. 721 ff.; he strengthened, perhaps without proving, his case that the magistrate was bound by the majority of his *consilium* in *Kl. Schr.* 1974, 111 ff.; no doubt this was the custom.

[85] In my view Polyb. vi. 14 relates only to political trials. Cf. ch. 6, xi.

[86] A. H. M. Jones, *Criminal Courts of the Roman Republic and Principate*, 1972, 5 f., tried to show that ordinary crimes were tried by the people, citing Oros. v. 16. 8; Val. Max. vi. 1. 8, but on the

killed an unfaithful wife, or the footpad of the city streets and rural highways were more summarily treated. No doubt many culprits whose guilt was flagrant or admitted ('manifesti' or 'confessi') could be punished out of hand, but many must have had some defence to offer, and they would hardly have renounced the right of appeal if that right had been respected. But in that event the assembly would have been kept in almost continuous session: cases under the Sullan murder law occupied three courts simultaneously in 66 (n. 73).

On occasion in the second century the senate instituted *quaestiones* that exercised inappellate capital jurisdiction.[87] This too was possible because, given the kinds of crime to be repressed, public opinion approved, and the tribunes would not interfere. But it may be thought that these senatorial decrees were unnecessary and unintelligible, if magistrates were regularly repressing such crimes in the ordinary course of jurisdiction. This difficulty can easily be met: it would have been reasonable for the senate to take special note of what was seen as a 'crime wave', and then either (as in 186 and 130) to direct the consuls to act, though they did not normally exercise jurisdiction at all, or (as in 184, 180, and 179) to free particular praetors from other responsibilities for the purpose.

However, the establishment of the permanent court *de repetundis* may well have suggested the desirability of creating similar courts *de sicariis* and *de venenis* by statutes, which would have provided *inter alia* like Sulla's law (n. 74), that in default of a praetor jurisdiction should be vested in a *iudex quaestionis*, like C. Claudius Pulcher, and ensured that there was a panel of suitably qualified *iudices* readily available to the president of the court. There is nothing against this hypothesis, and what we are told about the *quaestiones* of Hostilius Tubulus and L. Cassius (nn. 76 f.) makes in its favour.

In 132 the senate actually commissioned the consuls to try without appeal those who had allegedly engaged in a revolutionary conspiracy with Tiberius Gracchus. This was a violation of the rule hitherto observed that it was for the people to hear capital charges of a political character. No tribune had the will or courage to intervene, but in 123 C. Gracchus secured the banishment of at least one of the consuls concerned, P. Popilius, for his infraction of the rights of citizens. He

first incident see Kunkel, 1962, 47 n. 179; the second was also peculiar: 'non enim factum tunc, sed animus in quaestionem deductus est; plusque voluisse peccare nocuit quam non peccasse profuit'. The sovereign people could be induced to convict when a court could be expected to reject the charge. Both defendants were also of high degree.

[87] Livy xxxix. 14, 18 (cf. *SC de Bacchanalibus*, *FIRA* i². 30, 186 BC; Livy xl. 19. 9 f., 181), 41. 5 (184: poisoning), xl. 37. 4 (180: poisoning), 43. 2 (179: poisoning), *Per.* xlviii. (cf. Val. Max. VI. 3. 8, 152: poisoning); cf. n. 77. No doubt as under Domitian (Dio lxvii. 11. 6) undiagnosed epidemics were confused with mass poisoning.

also carried a new law 'ne de capite civis Romani iniussu populi iudicaretur'.[88] In some degree this law must have been merely declaratory. Gracchus was re-affirming the principle of the Valerian and Porcian laws (pp. 331 f.) which Popilius was properly held to have violated. But the provisions of a Gracchan law cited by Cicero under the rubric 'ne quis iudicio circumveniretur' (nn. 52 f.), which penalized all those in the senatorial order who combined to procure by illicit means, for instance bribery, the capital condemnation of a citizen in a *iudicium publicum*, may have been part of the same enactment. More important, that law provided that any senator, and not merely a magistrate, who voted for the capital condemnation of a citizen contrary to its terms, should himself be liable to a capital charge before the people. Henceforth any member of a consular *consilium* exercising capital jurisdiction without the people's sanction would be placing himself at risk. Gracchus' law did not of course preclude the constitution of such extraordinary tribunals by statute; courts set up in this way would exist 'iussu populi'. It is surely no accident that after 123 we hear nothing of courts created by the senate alone even to try common crimes.[89] To dispose of the seditious, the senate would now resort, for the first time in 121, to passing 'the last decree' (ch. 1 n. 25); the magistrates were thus encouraged on their own responsibility to execute agitators or 'conspirators' summarily as enemies of the state. But it seems reasonable to suppose that after 123 the senate thought it prudent that there should be a statutory basis for the inappellate trial of common criminals. The institution of the permanent *quaestiones* that pre-existed Sulla, in so far as they were not already in being in 123, may be seen as the necessary result of Gracchus' law.

A theory has recently been advanced that before and after Sulla, and until some unascertainable date in the Principate, municipal courts could impose capital penalties on citizens. If this be true, after 123 (if not before) they must have obtained this authority by statute. We know that the municipal jurisdiction of communities in Cisalpina enfranchised in 49 was regulated by statute, and presumably there had been similar legislation for the communities enfranchised as a result of the Social war, if not for those incorporated earlier. However, even in civil actions the competence of Cisalpine courts was restricted where the defendant would incur *infamia*, and it is *a fortiori* hard to credit that criminal courts in the Cisalpine communes could deprive a citizen of

---

[88] GC 13, 31. Note Cic. *Cat.* iv. 10, *Sest.* 61; Dio xxxvii. 14. 5.

[89] Diod. xxxvi. 15 tells how probably in 101 Saturninus was tried for his life by senators for outraging Mithridates' envoys. Despite *StR* ii³. 112 n. 3, I think this inaccurate; cf. Gruen, 1968, 168 f. He was acquitted after agitating with the plebs. I think we must assume that if condemned he could have appealed to the people under Gracchus' law.

his *caput*, nor is it likely that they were denied a power which other local courts had retained.[90] The arguments adduced for the contrary view are not probative.[91]

What has been said seems to prove that permanent courts *de sicariis* and *de veneficiis* must have existed before 123 or have then been established. Nor need we think that there were no others. Charges of *ambitus* before a *quaestio* are attested in 116, 97 and 92. Gruen himself concedes that it is reasonable to posit a standing court, though the law under which it was established is not recorded.[92] Since the evidence is so scanty, and preserved by chance, we can as well date it before 123 as afterwards. Nor should we infer that a *quaestio de peculatu* was post-Gracchan because the only known pre-Sullan trials are of 104 or later (n. 80). Not many cases are attested in Cicero's heyday, though he speaks of them as 'daily occurrences' (n. 63). The defendants might be, and perhaps generally were, clerks rather than ex-magistrates (n. 79). Both courts might none the less have furnished theatres for Carbo's forensic displays (p. 219).

In this period and later the penalty for *ambitus* was no longer, as it had once been, capital.[93] Conviction for *peculatus* resulted in pecuniary damages.[94] Persons condemned on either charge might therefore be among those who were excluded by the Gracchan *repetundae* law from acting as *patroni* or *iudices* because they had been condemned 'quaestione ioudiciove puplico'[95] and were on that account not to be enrolled in the senate. I do not, however, press this as confirmation that there was more than one *permanent* court in 123, since we might also think of *ad hoc* courts, nor can we be sure that at this date *iudicium publicum* might not refer to trial by the people. Manifestly the draftsman did not have in mind persons who had suffered a capital sentence, e.g. for murder!

To sum up, one text of Cicero, naturally interpreted, shows that the *repetundae* court was not the only permanent *quaestio* in existence before 123. There is no objection to supposing that similar courts had been set up for murder, peculation, and electoral corruption; and the general state of our evidence is such that absolute corroboration would have been wholly fortuitous and indeed unlikely. Moreover, if we accept Kunkel's theory, magistrates sitting with a *consilium* had been accustomed to exercise capital jurisdiction over common criminals, and except when this procedure had already been superseded by the

---

[90] *FIRA* i². 19 f., esp. 20. 1–9.   [91] See endnote 1.

[92] Gruen 260 f. (with evidence and two other speculative cases). The laws against *ambitus* of 181 and 159 (Livy xl. 19, *Per.* xlvii) cannot have set up a standing court; cf. n. 69.

[93] Polyb. vi. 56. 4 makes this out to be true in his day; more probably the penalty was ancient, but already obsolete. Cf. Mommsen, *Strafrecht* 865 ff. Capital penalties under XII Tables (VIII. 1, 8–10, 21, 23, IX. 3) also seem to have become obsolete.

[94] *Strafrecht* 760 ff.   [95] I take these terms to be probably tautologous (ch. 2, App. IV).

creation of statutory courts before 123, the enactment of Gracchus' law *ne de capite civis Romani iniussu populi iudicaretur* now made the creation of such courts imperative. Admittedly the composition of the jury could have been separately regulated in each law establishing a new permanent *quaestio*, but we are not entitled to say that there was no occasion in Gracchus' time for any general measure like the *lex Aurelia* to regulate judication in criminal cases, and that for that reason alone Plutarch's account of his judiciary legislation must be incorrect.

VII

The *lex Aurelia*, however, also concerned civil judication (n. 121), and this was a matter of more concern to the Equites than criminal judication, except when the charges, like *repetundae*, touched senators, whom the judicial authority of Equites might make obsequious to equestrian desires.[96] Their power and dignity were not much enhanced by the right to sit in judgement on men accused of common crimes, who would rarely be of their own order, whereas their individual interests might be deeply affected by the settlement of disputes arising from public contracts, by claims to inheritances and bequests, by contractual suits often involving large sums, or by civil actions on delicts, which could entail fines (*poenae*) and the loss of full civic status (*infamia*). It would have been at least galling if they were compelled to accept the adjudication of senators, and this could have been to their disadvantage, if it was with senators that they were in dispute. Let us again recall the testimony of Polybius, which critics of my hypothesis have passed over in silence, that it was chiefly by their monopoly of judication in important public *and civil* cases that the senate secured the dependence of 'the people'. Moreover, it is clear that in Cicero's time judication in civil as well as in criminal cases enhanced a man's dignity,[97] which was dear to every upper-class Roman. It would have been natural for the Equites to desire to break a senatorial monopoly, and for Gracchus to satisfy this ambition. We should not be the least surprised that a change in civil judication does not enter into our historical record, when we reflect that that record ignores the introduction of the formulary system and virtually every other change made by statute in the civil law. In the previous statement of my thesis I laid the greatest emphasis on the importance of this feature of Gracchus' judiciary measure; my critics generally ignored this part of the argument.[98]

---

[96] So Diodorus (n. 9).   [97] Cic. *Rosc. Com.* 15, 42.
[98] Not Stockton (1979, 146 ff.), whose view necessitates the two-stage theory of Gracchus' judiciary legislation (*contra* pp. 214–6).

Of course no such reform can be imputed to Gracchus if (as some think) Fraccaro proved that there was no senatorial monopoly of civil judication to be broken, and that Gracchus could not have created an *album iudicum*, however composed, whose members were alone qualified to determine some civil cases. Fraccaro, indeed, gave the classic exposition of the view I am contesting, because he did at least confront the implication of Polybius' testimony.[99] He supposed it to be largely mistaken, as he accepted a theory of Wlassak, which for long had the authority of a dogma. At Rome litigants would first appear *in iure* before a magistrate, generally a praetor, who could accept or deny the right of action, would define the issue that was to be decided, and would instruct one or more private persons, the *unus iudex* or occasionally *recuperatores* to decide it. Wlassak accounted for this division of legal process by the hypothesis that originally the parties had freely accepted arbitration by persons of their own choice; the state did no more than give its approval and regulate the forms. This hypothesis rested partly on explanations of other features in Roman civil procedure. Here it will suffice to say that so far from being unquestionably true, it has now been generally abandoned.[100] It cannot therefore have the conclusive force which Fraccaro gave it. However, one of Wlassak's arguments, endorsed by Fraccaro, is of particular relevance to our theme.

Cicero claims that the degradation (*nota*) of a man by the censors is not to be reckoned as a judgement on him, since 'neminem voluerunt maiores nostri non modo de existimatione cuiusquam sed ne pecuniaria quidem de re minima esse iudicem, nisi qui inter adversarios convenisset' (*Cluent.* 120). This claim was taken to demonstrate that the *unus iudex* was in and before Cicero's time always freely chosen by the parties, and therefore that there could have been no requirement that for certain types of case he had to be selected from the senate or from any *album iudicum*, however composed. But Cicero does not purport to be speaking only of cases that would be settled by an *unus iudex*. He is chiefly concerned with judgements that affected a man's *existimatio*. Now condemnation in a *iudicium publicum* could result in *infamia*, not to speak of heavier penalties, and it was obviously untrue that the *iudices* in criminal cases were chosen by free agreement between the prosecutor and defendant: they had only limited rights of

---

[99] *Opuscula* ii. 255 ff.; p. 259 states Wlassak's doctrine without citing him.

[100] Jolowicz–Nicholas 176–9; more fully, with bibliography, M. Kaser, *Röm. Zivilprozessrecht*, 1966, 6 f., 14–16, 20, 23, 31–6; 41–4; he accepts that Wlassak's theory is more plausible for *arbitri*, but O. Behrends, *Die röm. Geschworenenverfassung*, 1970, 97 ff., thinks that they were originally expert assistants of the magistrate. Kaser 36 n. 39 cites especially Fraccaro for the view that Gracchus' law concerned the *repetundae* court alone, which he thinks 'perhaps' right; but clearly he cannot have been impressed by Fraccaro's legal arguments.

rejecting a specified number of names. Nor were all civil cases decided by an *unus iudex*. Some administrative cases, and some actions for delict, in which condemnation might entail loss of *existimatio*, as well as pecuniary loss, went to *recuperatores*. The *lex agraria* of 111 provides that claims made by publicans against users of public land are to be decided by *recuperatores*: the magistrate propounds eleven names, and plaintiff and defendant are each entitled to reject not more than four. A mode of appointment which allowed the parties a limited right of rejection seems to be normal.[101] It falls far short of free agreement between the litigants. At least in the post-Gracchan era inheritance disputes came before the *centumviri* (see below); here again there was a numerous jury, and the litigants can at best have exercised a comparable right of rejection, which may be presumed, though it is not apparently documented. In Cicero's time it was for minor magistrates, the *decemviri litibus iudicandis*, to determine if a man was free or slave; to say nothing of the importance of the issue to the man whose liberty was at stake, the party who claimed him as a slave might stand to lose or gain an asset worth much money. The *decemviri*, if not already senators, were doubtless always of the senatorial class, and could easily have been embraced in Polybius' concept of senators.[102] Again we might conjecture that either party could reject particular *decemviri* as biased. But it is plain that in all these cases the free agreement of the parties must be reduced to at most a limited right of rejection, and that Cicero's rhetoric is misleading.

To allow his claim some specious plausibility, which we should beware of denying to any of his forensic assertions, however false, we may suppose that it had rather more applicability to the appointment of the *unus iudex*. We know in fact that the plaintiff or defendant could 'ferre iudicem', i.e. tender the name of a *iudex*, and that the other party

---

[101] In *FIRA* i[2]. no. 8. 36 f., the *recuperatores* need not be either senators or Equites. Of course any law after 123 could modify qualifications required by a Gracchan law. Here we can divine a reason for deviation. The appointment of *recuperatores* may be made by a promagistrate, i.e. outside Rome, and must be made within ten days of application. The dispute to be settled could arise far from the city, in an area where there were too few senators or Equites immediately available for the prompt adjudication that was desired. Cf. also n. 135. On *recuperatores* see generally Kaser (n. 100), pp. 143 f. (citing *FIRA* i[2]. no. 67. 67–9; II *Verr*. iii. 140 etc.); J. M. Kelly, *Studies in the Civil Judicature of the Rom. Rep.*, 1976, ch. II.

[102] Cic. *Caec.* 97, *de dom.* 78; cf. *RE* iv. 2260 ff. (Kübler). In the Principate, when the *decemviri* had been transferred to take some part in the organization of the centumviral courts (n. 135), they were young men who had not yet held the quaestorship, but *ILS* 915 f., 948, show that this was not always true under Augustus and Tiberius; in *ILS* 9 we cannot be sure if Cn. Scipio (*pr.* 139) gives all his offices in strict order. One might doubt if judication in *causae liberales* was normally left to men in their twenties, or whether the office might not be held, as military tribunates still were in 69 (I *Verr*. 30), by senators, i.e. men over thirty. Admittedly it is not listed among 'senatorial' offices in *FIRA* i[2]. 6. § 3 (Bantia), 7. 22 (*tab. Bemb.*), but any decemvir who was already a senator would have been covered *qua* senator (6. § 4, 7 loc. cit.). Plaut. *Rudens* 713 might suggest that a senator could be expected to determine a *causa liberalis*.

could accept (*sumere*) that name; Cicero provides us with two instances in which a *iudex* was chosen by this kind of agreement, one a senator, the other an Eques.[103] A *iudex* thus appointed could still be taken from the *album*; Seneca can write of 'accepting' a *iudex* 'ex turba selectorum' (n. 107), and though in the Principate choice was not so circumscribed,[104] it could not fall on anyone in categories wholly disqualified by law;[105] that must always have been true, and represents another limitation on agreement between the parties that Cicero could overlook. He more than once mentions the right of either party to reject on oath (*eiurare* or *eierare*) a person nominated as 'unfair' (*iniquus*). This corresponds to the right of a litigant in the Principate to 'refuse' or 'reject' a *iudex* appointed by lot from the *album*; we hear no more of an oath, which had perhaps become obsolete.[106] I can find no evidence that *eiuratio* was in order only when a *iudex* had been proposed by the adversary, and not also when he was taken from the list. In the Principate the alternative to free choice by the parties was sortition,[107] evidently from those members of the *album* who had been assigned to civil judication (n. 118); the younger Pliny suggests that sortition was the normal course (n. 106). We cannot say if it was employed in the Republic as distinct from nomination by the praetor. It may be that agreement between the parties was then more common, but it cannot always have been forthcoming. A litigant would in any case have found it hard to resist the nomination by his adversary of a person who was on the list of those officially qualified to act, unless he could allege that the nominee was 'unfair'; nor would the praetor have tolerated the endless rejection of one name after another, a course that could have prevented the suit from ever coming to trial. Social and magisterial pressure would thus probably have ensured that most *iudices* in important cases were taken from the list by a procedure that could always be represented as involving the agreement of the parties, given their right of *eiuratio*. None the less Cicero could contemplate that an advocate might have to plead before a hostile *iudex*, and his use of the singular shows that he had an *unus iudex* in mind (*de orat.* ii. 72). Thus even in relation to this kind of civil process the rhetoric in *pro*

---

[103] *De orat.* ii. 263; e.g. *Quinct.* 32, *Rosc. Com.* 42.

[104] *Dig.* v. 1. 80 (Pomp.), xlii. 1. 57 (Ulp.). Quint. *Inst.* v. 6. 6 warns against leaving to the adversary choice of *iudex.*

[105] *Dig.* v. 1. 2. 3 (Paul); cf. i. 9. 2 (Cassius).

[106] 'Eiurare [or 'eierare'] iudicem iniquum': Cic. II *Verr.* iii. 137, *de orat.* ii. 285, *de fin.* ii. 119, *Phil.* xii. 18. I cannot find this phrase documented after Cicero. Tac. *Dial.* 5. 1 uses 'iudicem recusare'; cf. Pliny, *Paneg.* 36. 4: 'Sors et urna fisco iudicem adsignat [i.e. a *iudex* is now appointed in the normal way for fiscal cases]; licet reicere, licet exclamare: "hunc nolo" . . . '.

[107] Agenn. Urb. (*Gromatici* 74. 22 L.); Pliny, *NH pr.* 6–8; Behrends (n. 100) implausibly presses this to show that there was an alternative only between sortition from the *album* and selection from outside the *album*. But cf. Sen. *de benef.*, iii. 7.

Cluentio 120 is very economical of the truth; there were limits and exceptions to the ideal practice of 'our ancestors' which he did not care to specify.

Agreement between the parties and magisterial nomination are also distinguished in Republican legal texts which speak of 'iudicis recuperatorum datio', of 'reciperatorum [or 'iudicis'] datio addictio', of 'iudicis arbitri recuperatorum datio addictio'.[108] There should be a distinction between 'datio' and 'addictio'. Now Servius Sulpicius referred to a *iudex* 'ex conventione litigatorum addictus' (*Dig.* v. 1. 80), and according to Festus (12 L.), 'addicere' means 'dicere et adprobare dicendo'. We may then infer that the magistrate was said 'iudicem addicere' when he approved the choice of the parties; the term 'iudicem dare' is wider, and in the Table of Heraclea the magistrate is required 'iudicem dare' in circumstances in which the consent of the defendant would hardly have been apposite; similarly there is nothing to suggest that it was ever obtained for the appointment of *recuperatores*.[109] Thus the terminology indicates that in the Republic the *iudex* could be 'given' without such consent.

Since there is hardly any Republican evidence for the assignment of *iudices* on the *album* to their various functions, we may first consider what is known of the system in the Principate; that too is not abundant.

At the outset of Augustus' reign there were three decuries of *iudices*, consisting of senators (n. 116) and Equites only (cf. n. 40); Augustus added a fourth, composed of men with a census of only 200,000 HS and qualified to decide only 'de levioribus summis', and Gaius a fifth, no doubt subject to the same limitation;[110] since some 'select *iudices*' boast on inscriptions of being 'inter quadringenarios', we may infer that equestrian census was required only of those whose judication was not restricted and so more honourable.[111] The emperor took over from the urban praetor (n. 56) the function of enrolling men on the *album*.[112] Nominally each decury now comprised 1,000 members, but they were not always at full strength;[113] though selection was an honour, as the inscriptions show, some were reluctant to perform the duties, and Augustus allowed a year's vacation to each decury in turn.[114] The *Tabula Hebana*, a law of AD 19, modelled on one of AD 4, refers to the Equites of all the decuries constituted for the public *iudicia*, and Gellius says that he was chosen by the praetor among the *iudices* to determine

---

[108] *FIRA* i². 8. 34–7 (*lex agr.*), 12 V (= *Gromatici* 263 f. L.), 20, 15; cf. 7 (*fr. Atest.*). See endnote 2.
[109] Ibid. 13. 44. I suspect the Gromatic text (n. 108) which refers to 'addictio' of *reciperatores* without collocation of 'iudicis'. Contrast *FIRA* i². 21. XLV (Urso).
[110] Suet. *Aug.* 32. 3, *Gaius* 16. 2; Pliny, *NH* xxxiii. 33.   [111] *ILS* 4093, 6523, 6772.
[112] Suet. *Aug.* 29. 3, 32. 3, *Tib.* 41, 51, *Cl.* 15. 1; Pliny, *NH* xxix. 18.
[113] Pliny, *NH* xxxiii. 30. A senatorial decury could never have been 1000 strong.
[114] Suet. *Aug.* 22. 3; Pliny, *NH* xxxiii. 30; Dig. l. 5. 13 (Ulp.).

the *iudicia* called private; the elder Pliny also distinguishes between those qualified to condemn a man to exile and those who could only decide pecuniary suits.[115] However, these texts do not imply that *iudices* entitled to determine criminal cases might not also exercise judication in important civil processes. There can be no such implication, since senators employed on other public business could be exempted in 11 BC from both public and private *iudicia*,[116] and the Eques Ovid served in the *centumviri* and as *unus iudex*, as well as in criminal courts.[117] No doubt the *iudices* competent only 'de levioribus summis' also had no part in criminal judication. It appears that at the beginning of each year the *iudices* were assigned by lot to different civil and criminal functions;[118] Dio refers to their allotment to the centumviral court under Augustus, and the spacious *forum Augusti* was partly intended to accommodate the 'sortitiones'.[119]

Obviously the system in the late Republic was not identical with that in the Principate: we know of some modifications made by Augustus and his successors, and there may have been more, introduced by Augustus' ill-documented judiciary laws.[120] However, it is at least clear from one remark made by Cicero that after the *lex Aurelia* the same *iudices* he addressed in a case of *repetundae* would also determine civil suits. Not, we may think, necessarily in the same year in which they were available for the *repetundae* court.[121] It appears that it was already the practice for *iudices* of the *album* to be assigned by lot to the various criminal courts and presumably to civil judicature by a sortition carried out by the quaestors after they came into office on 5 December;[122] as Gellius shows (n. 115) this function had passed to the urban praetor by the second century AD.

The number of *iudices* on the *album* was much greater from Augustus' time than it had been in the Republic. Under the *lex Aurelia* there were only 900 (n. 38); Sulla had reserved judication to some 600 senators; the Gracchan *album* which I have posited comprised 600 or, more probably, 900, but before 123 the senators numbered only 300. It must therefore be asked whether senators could have monopolized judication even in the most important cases before Gracchus, especially as a considerable number would be at any given time exempt by reason of

---

[115] EJ 94a. 9; Gell. xiv. 2. 1; Pliny, *NH* xxix. 18.

[116] Front. *de aquis* 101: for senators on the *album* cf. Sherwin-White on Pliny *ep.* v. 29. 2 (but Mommsen withdrew his suggestion that they had ceased to serve in *StR* iii. 897. 3).

[117] Ovid, *Tr.* ii. 92–4, *Ex Ponto* iii. 5. 23 f.; cf. *ILS* 6747.

[118] See Behrends (n. 100) 17–70.   [119] Suet. *Aug.* 29. 1; Dio liv. 26. 6.

[120] S. Riccobono, *Acta Divi Aug.*, 1945, 142 ff., collects the evidence; see esp. *Vat. fr.* 197 f.

[121] *Flacc.* 12, which does not prove that the same men alternated in the same year, *contra* Behrends (n. 101) 63, though this may have occurred, as *indices* allotted to some criminal courts would have had little or nothing to do in many years.

[122] Dio xxxix. 7. 3 with Cic. *Qu. fr.* ii. 1. 2 f., rightly interpreted by E. Meyer, *Caesars Monarchie*

age, infirmity, or other public duties, and indeed how even 600 or 900 persons could cope with the judicial business that occupied so many more in the Principate.

We may first notice that the amount of such business was continually growing.[123] Granted that two or three permanent *quaestiones* besides that for *repetundae* had been created before 123, or were at latest established in that year, others were certainly added subsequently to deal with *maiestas* (Saturninus), *falsa* etc. (Sulla), *vis* (soon after Sulla), and adultery (Augustus); the scope of the court or courts *de vi* was enlarged by the *lex Julia de vi privata*. Unless municipal courts could impose penalties affecting the *caput* of the citizen (n. 91), the enfranchisement of the communities of peninsular Italy in and after 90, and of those of north Italy in 49, must have greatly increased the work of those Roman courts which tried common crimes, including after Augustus' legislation adultery. Equally it must have enlarged the business of civil judicature. It is clear that the jurisdiction of local courts in Transpadana was restricted by pecuniary and other limits,[124] and similar limits no doubt applied to those in the other Italian communities.[125] That did not prevent litigants accepting local jurisdiction outside the limits,[126] but we can readily suppose that one of the parties would often insist on his right to sue or be sued at Rome;[127] very likely this involved delay and additional costs, which would commonly suit the wealthier litigant. The tendency to refer cases to Rome might well have grown, as the memories of former autonomy faded in Italy after 90 BC.

We have also to consider the size of the jury courts. Under the Gracchan law *de repetundis* the jury was to be 51 strong. But in 171 the senate had appointed only five *recuperatores* to hear Spanish complaints of *repetundae*. This was a standard number for *recuperatores*.[128] It could have been adopted by the Calpurnian law. The senatorial *repetundae* courts constituted by the *SC Calvisianum* of 4 BC were to have only nine

---

u. das Principat des Pompeius, 109 n. 3; cf. Brunt, *Liv. Cl. Monthly*, 1981, 2–4 ff., against Behrends (n. 100) 64 ff.

[123] Suet. *Aug.* 29. 1 refers to the increased 'hominum et iudiciorum multitudo' which necessitated the construction of the *forum Augusti*.

[124] I need not enter into the interpretations of *FIRA* i². nos. 19 f. (see e.g. Simshäuser, Ch. v).

[125] The *lex Irnitana*, esp. LXIX, LXXXIV, furnishes new evidence on municipal jurisdiction, see *JRS* 1986, 227–30, for commentary citing the principal texts known previously. See endnote 2. We cannot be certain how far rules attested for the Principate go back to the late Republic. [126] *Dig.* v. 1. 1 (Ulp.), l. 1. 26 (Paul).

[127] Cato, *de agric.* 149. 2 perhaps supplies an early instance. Note Paul, *Dig.* ii. 1. 20: 'extra territorium ius dicenti impune non paretur'. If a man from town A desired to sue one from town B, on a claim that could be tried *either* in town B (but not in town A) *or* at Rome, he might naturally find resort to Rome more convenient.

[128] Livy xliii. 2. 5; cf. Kaser (n. 100).

members.[129] Gracchus might well have opted for a much larger
repetundae court, to minimize the chances of corruption. Both permanent and extraordinary courts after 70 had juries of over 50 and even
over 70, the number perhaps varying with the kind of *quaestio*. But it
looks as if in the Sullan system, with only senators entitled to serve, the
juries were smaller. In the trial of Oppianicus for murder only 32 *iudices*
voted (*Cluent.* 74), and Cicero suggests that the eight *iudices*, who would
have ceased to sit in the trial of Verres had it been protracted into 69,
constituted 'a large part' of the court (I *Verr.* 30, II i. 30).[130]

Of all civil cases the most important on the whole were probably the
inheritance cases, which were heard as early as the time of L. Crassus
(*cos.* 95) by *centumviri*; it was these which engaged great orators like
Crassus and in the Principate the younger Pliny.[131] No other category
of civil cases is more likely to have been reserved to senators before
Gracchus. In Pliny's day the *centumviri* numbered at least 180 and
normally met in four different courts.[132] Festus, however, tells us that
they had once numbered 105, three persons being 'chosen' (by a
process that is not recorded) from each of the thirty-five tribes, and
that they were then called *centumviri* for convenience.

This precise arrangement cannot have gone back beyond 241, when
the last two tribes were created. Many scholars argued that the
centumviral court was therefore first constituted after 241, perhaps
much later; Wlassak was bound to regard it as a 'modern' invention,
since its character did not accord with his theory that civil judication
was originally arbitration by persons whose decisions the parties
consented to accept. A late date has now fallen out of favour chiefly
because of the archaic features of centumviral procedure (n. 132).
Conjectures have been advanced to explain why from the first a fairly
large jury rather than an *unus iudex* should have been responsible for
settling inheritance disputes. Kelly supposes that the tribal organization of the court was primitive; but since there is some evidence that

---

[129] On Mommsen's supplement of the *tabula Bembina* 7 f., *recuperatores* decided certain charges
of *repetundae*, but supplement and sense are very uncertain (W. W. Buckland, *JRS* 1937, 42 ff.).
Tacitus refers to the court, which could award simple damages for *repetundae* under the *SC
Calvisianum* (*Ann.* i. 74. 6; cf. *FIRA* i². 68, v) as *recuperatores*.

[130] Other evidence in Mommsen, *Strafrecht* 217 f. J. Lengle, *SZ* 1933, 275 ff., made it probable
that under the Sullan system the senate was divided into ten decuries, one of which was available
for each permanent *quaestio*; in that case no jury could consist of more than 60—x *iudices*, where x
represents senators necessarily excused from service on particular occasions.

[131] Cic. *de orat.* i. 173, 177, 180, etc.; Tac. *Dial.* 38. 2; Pliny, *Ep.* vi. 33. 2, ix. 23. 1 (with
Sherwin-White's notes). Cf. Kelly (n. 90) 34 ff., and ch. III on the statistical importance of
succession cases; it is clear (apart from his figures) that the jurists paid most attention to the law of
succession.

[132] Pliny, *Ep.* vi. 33. 3. See in general Wlassak, *RE* iii. 1935 ff., for evidence on the court. For
recent discussion of its antiquity see Kunkel, 1962, 118 ff., and Kelly (n. 101), ch. I (with
bibliography); he rejects views that it had jurisdiction beyond cases of succession.

juries of *quaestiones* were chosen on a tribal basis in the first century, it might rather be thought that Festus was describing the centumviral organization as it was in that era.[133] Certainly he was only explaining the name of the court, which had ceased to be apposite in the Principate, by reference to a time when it approximately corresponded to the number of *iudices*; he does not even profess to know, and could hardly have known, that it had been constituted in the way he describes from its very inception. For instance, if we suppose that the *iudices* concerned always numbered about 100 and were tribally selected, the number of *iudices* per tribe could have varied as more tribes were created (25×4, 33×3, etc.). Alternatively, the total number and the name might both have changed, just as the *decemviri sacris faciundis* became *quindecemviri*. Again, senators alone, or senators and Equites, might have been enrolled on a tribal basis; or that basis may itself have been a later innovation. The retention of archaic procedure in the Principate does not of course exclude the possibility of all kinds of other reforms at different dates: we actually know that in that period the total number of *iudices* enrolled had increased, and that the *decemviri litibus iudicandis* had been given by Augustus a novel, though problematic, part in the organization.

It therefore follows that we cannot be sure that the organization described by Festus had not been first created in or after 123 (the name of the court is not attested earlier), or, that the number he gives the panel did not reflect the influence of Gracchus. Before 123 the total number of *iudices* required for inheritance cases need not have been so large that they could not all be drawn from a senate of 300 members. Not indeed that we must assume that it was ever normal for all *centumviri* to sit together; in Pliny's day a jury in ordinary cases presumably numbered about 45, and in the late Republic the *centumviri* may already have been split into similar divisons. There must have been some unrecorded statute which prescribed the tribal representation and which could also have determined the number in each division. Perhaps of Gracchan origin, this statute will have instituted the system that Festus describes, operative in the time of L. Crassus.

[133] 47 L.: 'Cum essent Romae triginta et quinque tribus, quae et curiae sunt dictae [!], terni *ex* [not 'a'] singulis tribubus sunt electi ad iudicandum, qui centumviri appellati sunt: et licet quinque amplius quam centum fuerint, tamen, quo facilius nominarentur, centumviri sunt dicti' (cf. Varro, *RR* ii. 1. 26). Tribal composition is compatible with a requirement for senatorial or equestrian qualifications, cf. perhaps the *tabula Hebana* (EJ 94a). We do not need to see any close parallel with the *lex Plautia* of 89, under which 'tribus singulae ex suo numero quinos denos *suffragio* creabant qui eo anno iudicarent; ex eo factum est, ut senatores quoque in eo numero essent, et quidam etiam ex ipsa plebe' (Ascon. 79 C.); Festus does not imply *election*. In my view the *lex Plautia* need have applied only to the *maiestas* court, since in 90 it had been the only court active, according to Cic. *Brut.* 304. Tribal representation was also provided by the *lex Licinia de sodaliciis* of 55 (Cic. *Planc.* 36) and perhaps had some place in *quaestiones* generally after 70 (Kunkel, *RE* xxiv. 753 ff.).

The statements that Sulla transferred the *iudicia* to senators are made by authors who were concerned with the *quaestiones*.[134] It may well be that no attempt was made to withdraw from the Equites that share in civil jurisdiction which they had acquired. The enfranchisement of Italy must have increased the volume of litigation at Rome, and even with an enlarged senate it might not have been convenient to restore to senators their monopoly of deciding the most important civil cases.

The constitution of a mixed *album* from which *iudices* were to be selected for both criminal and civil cases decided at Rome naturally did not preclude the subsequent enactment of legislation which might widen or restrict the choice of *iudices*. One may recall the abortive attempt to establish a special jury for the trial of Clodius in 61, the *lex Vatinia de reiectione iudicum* of 58, and the *lex Pompeia* and the *lex Licinia de sodaliciis* of 55; similarly in the pre-Sullan era senators could be excluded from newly created special or permanent *quaestiones* under the Mamilian and Appuleian laws by which they were set up. The qualifications for judication outside Rome could also be quite different from those prescribed for Roman courts: thus *recuperatores* to be appointed under the *lex agraria* of 111 are simply to be drawn from citizens of the first class, and *iudices* or *recuperatores* appointed by municipal magistrates or by provincial governors would also not require equestrian census.[135]

VIII

Conclusions

1. According to Polybius, before 123 senators had a monopoly of judication in the most important administrative and civil cases. They also provided *iudices* for *repetundae* trials, and presumably composed the *consilia* of magistrates who exercised jurisdiction for common crimes, which were in practice not subject to appeal.

2. The Gracchan law 'ne de capite civis Romani iniussu populi iudicaretur' put an end to this inappellate jurisdiction.

3. Under a Gracchan law Equites obtained exclusive control of the

---

[134] Cic. I *Verr.* 37 etc.; Vell. ii. 32; Tac. *Ann.* xi. 22.

[135] For provincial lists of qualified *iudices* see Sherwin-White on Pliny, *Ep.* x. 58. 1. I do not agree that those in Bithynia would not act in civil cases, for which the governor would use his own *comites*; in Republican Sicily, though there was as yet no provincial *album*, it was proper for the governor to select local Roman residents or *negotiatores* by lot (Cic. II *Verr.* ii. 32–4 etc.). In Cyrenaica the census qualification for murder trials raised by Augustus from 2,500 *denarii* to 7,500 was low (*FIRA* i². 68. 1). In municipalities where *iudices* or *recuperatores* were appointed by the local magistrates *iuri dicundo* (e.g. *FIRA* i². 20 f.), no high property qualification can have been required in law or practice.

repetundae court, which was broken by Caepio's law of 106, but soon restored by Glaucia (*anno incerto*).

4. The *ad hoc* court set up by the Mamilian law and that permanently established for *maiestas* by Saturninus were also equestrian.

5. Drusus proposed in 91 to reinstate the senatorial monopoly for criminal judication (this has been questioned, but wrongly).

6. The *lex Plautia* of 89 provided for the election of *iudices* from the senate, Equites, and even *e plebe*, but this probably concerned only the *maiestas* court.

7. Sulla restored to senators the monopoly of at least criminal judication.

8. The *lex Aurelia* of 70 constituted an *album* of 300 senators, 300 Equites (*equo publico*), and 300 *tribuni aerarii* (who possessed equestrian census, a fact sometimes denied, but wrongly), from which *iudices* were to be taken for both criminal and civil cases (including centumviral cases) decided at Rome, though the parties to a civil dispute could also agree on a *unus iudex* outside the *album*.

9. According to all sources, Gracchus passed a general law on judication which *either* constituted a mixed *album* somewhat as the *lex Aurelia* did (Plutarch and probably Livy) *or* vested judication entirely in the *Equites* (other authorities): Appian as well as Plutarch indicate that after Gracchus Equites could judge cases in which non-senators were defendants, i.e. cases other than *repetundae*.

Some scholars deny that any such law was passed, holding that there was no purpose in any general regulation of judiciary rights, since (*a*) no permanent *quaestiones* existed in Gracchus' time besides that for *repetundae*, and (*b*) civil litigants were free to select *iudices* as they wished and could not be restricted to those whose names appeared on any *album*. These objections are unfounded.

As to (*a*):

10. On the natural interpretation of *Brutus* (106) Cicero implies that other *quaestiones* besides that for *repetundae* were set up before 123; in any event the establishment of some such statutory courts became imperative on the enactment of Gracchus' law *ne de capite*

. . . .

11. Sulla is known to have created only one such court; the *quaestio maiestatis* existed from 103, and permanent courts *de sicariis*, *de veneficis*, *de ambitu*, *de peculatu* may be pre-Gracchan (they are certainly pre-Sullan).

As to (*b*):

12. The theory that litigants were invariably free to choose an *unus*

iudex is not demonstrable nor plausible; they certainly could never choose *centumviri, decemviri, recuperatores*; hence there is no warrant for rejecting Polybius' testimony that in his time all *iudices* in *important* civil and administrative cases had to be taken from a senatorial *album*.

It therefore follows that:

13. The testimony of the sources should *certainly* be accepted that Gracchus passed a general judiciary law, in addition to a *repetundae* law.
14. If his aim was to reduce the power of the senate by enhancing that of the Equites, he should have ended that senatorial monopoly of judication which Polybius stresses by constituting an *album* for civil as well as criminal cases which was *either* wholly *or* partly equestrian.

How can we choose between these alternatives? If we had a full record of the period from 123 to 70, such as Livy provided, the uncertainties which so often exist for us about overt facts of importance, like judiciary laws, would surely vanish; they arise only because we have to depend on inaccurate historical summaries and loose allusions in which rhetoric may distort the truth. The contradictions in our miserable sources about the proposals of Gracchus, Caepio, and Drusus are matched by their conflicting statements on the *lex Aurelia* itself. It is only because this law was operative in Cicero's time that we happen to have evidence from his writings which proves that the most complex version of the purport of that law is correct: epitomizers tend to simplify. In all these cases discrepancies do not originate from rival traditions (or fictions), but from the failure of any of our authorities to give precise and complete statements of the truth. We must not then pin our faith to any one source, but try to elicit the truth by discovering how all may reveal it in part, and yet distort it by carelessness. Since Gracchus undoubtedly gave Equites a monopoly in the *repetundae* court, and since courts later set up to judge political offences were modelled on it, it would have been quite natural for writers who were chiefly or only concerned with judication, in so far as it remained a constant source of political controversy, to say baldly that he transferred the *iudicia* to the Equites, and to neglect the more general reform of the *album* recorded by Plutarch and, conjecturally, by Livy (whose testimony would be decisive, if we only knew what it was). The error was the easier if Equites preponderated in the *album*, as under the *lex Aurelia*, which some writers once again represent, falsely, as eliminating senators from judication. To account for Plutarch's version on the footing that it is incorrect seems to me less easy; there is nothing to be said for the supposition that he confounded Gracchus' proposal with that of any later reformer, and the theory that he mentioned only a plan from which Gracchus resiled and not that which he actually enacted, though it cannot be refuted, is incompatible with Plutarch's biographical interests. Plutarch of course is also one-sided in ignoring the *repetundae* law. This is just the kind of omission that is typical of epitomators.

15. We may then conclude that it is probable that except for *repetundae* Gracchus created a mixed *album*; Caepio (in my view) applied the same principle to *repetundae*, while Drusus (as the evidence independently proves) anticipated Sulla in proposing to restore a senatorial monopoly, at least in criminal judication, and to enlarge the senate for the purpose.

5

THE ARMY AND THE LAND IN THE
ROMAN REVOLUTION*

I. Continuing importance of the agrarian problem after the Gracchi. Most Italians countrymen; the influx into Rome, where, as in other towns, freedmen and slaves had a disproportionate share in all skilled work. Structure of rural population; well-to-do landowners, small peasant owners and tenants, day-labourers. The labour force on great estates not entirely servile. Desire of the free *rustici* for farms of their own. **II.** The army recruited from *rustici*, who were still often conscripted after Marius. Length of continuous service in the legions, even if the norm was six years, enough to ruin small farmers; they needed land on discharge. **III.** Indiscipline and disloyalty among the troops. Purely political appeals for their support. Few of them bound by personal allegiance. The ties of religion. Material inducements to loyalty: booty and illicit enrichment; donatives. **IV.** Above all they demanded land allotments. The senate adverse to their demands. Refutation of views that they saw allotments merely as assets to dispose of, and that they commonly regarded military service as a profession they had no wish to give up. Land the most natural provision for their retirement. Why they sometimes failed as farmers. **V.** Epilogue on Augustus' measures.

I

THE Roman revolution had its origin, as Sallust (*BJ* 41 f.) saw, partly in the misery of the poor, in a social crisis; it began with the Gracchi and with agrarian reform, and agrarian reform remained a leitmotiv in the turbulent century that followed. I need only mention the laws or bills of Lucius

* This version of an essay published in *JRS* 1962 is partly rewritten, especially in section I, with notes renumbered, and supersedes the German version of 1976. For documentation given in 1962 I have now often referred to fuller statements in *IM* or elsewhere. The argument is essentially unchanged: to my knowledge it has never been refuted. It built on the work of R. E. Smith, 1958, and on articles by E. Gabba in *Athenaeum* 1949 and 1951, since republished with some changes in Gabba 1973 (Eng. tr. 1976). But in crucial points I differ widely from Gabba: for example, I think it misleading to describe the army of the late Republic as 'professional'; I rate much lower the importance of clientship; and I think Gabba wholly mistaken in holding (e.g. 1973, 117 ff. = 1976, 120 ff.) that normally veterans had no wish to return to the land. In the revised versions of his essays Gabba takes no account of my contentions. I repeat here my original acknowledgement of helpful suggestions made by M. H. Crawford, P. J. Cuff, M. W. Frederiksen, A. H. McDonald, and R. E. Smith.

Philippus,[1] Saturninus, Sextus Titius,[2] and the younger Drusus, the settlement of the Sullan veterans, the proposals of Plotius,[3] Rullus, and Flavius, the agitation of Catiline, the legislation of 59 BC, and the later allotments of Caesar, the Triumvirs, and of Augustus himself. Modern accounts tend to obscure or even deny the unity of this theme throughout the period.[4] It is true that in the earlier phase reformers were more concerned to find remedies for social distress as such, and in the later to provide homes for veterans. But the Gracchan settlers and the veterans had two things in common: they were mostly countrymen, and they desired to obtain a secure livelihood by owning their own land. According to Appian, whose testimony we have no right to reject, the work done by the Gracchi was not lasting (cf. n. 1). Hence the distress they had tried to alleviate persisted or revived; the governing class remained indifferent. Unorganized and unarmed, the followers of the Gracchi could save neither their leaders nor their own interests; men of the same class, with arms in their hands, were the essential instruments for bringing down the Republic.

2   In the economic life of ancient Italy agriculture was of dominant importance. Land was the safest investment, and the chief basis of wealth. The total number of men, women, and children of citizen status in AD 14 was on my estimate not much above 4,000,000, of whom 5–600,000 were domiciled at Rome. Of the rest some lived in towns; their number cannot be estimated, but many towns must have been centres from which most of the inhabitants went out to till the adjacent fields. The great majority of citizens obtained their livelihood from the country. There were also two or even three millions of slaves, most of whom again must have been employed in agriculture and pasturage; the higher the figure we adopt, the larger their share would have been in rural employment, for it is a fair assumption that trade

---

[1] Cic. de offic. ii. 73: Philippus' assertion 'non esse in civitate duo millia hominum qui rem haberent' illustrates and exaggerates the failure of the Gracchi (App. i., 27).

[2] Obsequens 46; Val. Max. viii. 1, Damn. 3.

[3] Plut. Luc. 34. 4; Dio xxxviii. 5. 1–2 probably refer to the lex Plotia agraria (Cic. Att. i. 18. 6) of 70 (?) BC (MRR ii, 128); cf. E. Gabba, Par. del Pass. 1950, 66 ff.; R. E. Smith, CQ 1957, 82 ff.; contra Smith, Dio shows it was not implemented.

[4] Gabba 1973/1976, ch. II passim, like Velleius i. 15. 5, too sharply distinguishes veteran settlements in the first century from almost all previous allotments of lands. In fact the extensive allotments, colonial or viritane in the early second century, as in previous times, probably served both to augment the number of peasants, from whom the armies could be recruited (cf. App. i. 7), and to reward soldiers with part of the land they had conquered (cf. Livy xxxi. 4. 1–3, xxxv. 9. 7 f., 40. 5 f., xxxvii. 57. 7 f., xl. 34. 2–4); G. Tibiletti, Athen. 1950, 234 ff., and H. H. Scullard, JRS 1960, 62 ff., conjectured that the agrarian bills of Laelius and Ti. Gracchus respectively were in part designed for the benefit of veterans. The social motives of the Gracchan scheme (cf. Cic. Sest. 105) were adduced for later agrarian proposals (Cic. de leg. agr. i. 22, ii. 70, 97, Att. i. 19. 4; Dio xxxviii. 1. 3; Suet. Caes. 41. 1). See also K. Hopkins, 1978, chs. I–II, a valuable analysis of 'the impact of conquering an empire on the political economy of Italy', which is relevant to most of this essay.

and industry cannot have occupied more than 10–20 per cent of the total population.

Clearly the *total number* of those so occupied must have risen, as the population itself gradually increased, if only through the influx of slaves, and the *proportion* surely became greater, as Italy was enriched by the acquisition of imperial possessions overseas and by the internal peace which obtained, except in the north, for a century after the Hannibalic war.[5] The increase of population would have required an enlarged supply of food; this demand was met partly by imports, partly by clearance and drainage bringing new lands under the plough, partly perhaps by improved methods of cultivation; but a rise in total purchasing power, however unevenly distributed, must have meant that there was also an enlarged demand for manufactured goods and for the services of those engaged in trade, transportation, and construction. Naturally this was greatest at Rome itself, where the ruling class were domiciled and there was the greatest concentration of both private and public expenditure. The growth of the population there can be dimly traced in the need for additional water supplies, which required the construction of great new aqueducts in 144–127 and again under Augustus.[6] Some peasants drifted into the city, and doubtless into other towns.[7] But the population of Rome was chiefly augmented by slaves and freedmen.[8]

Many of these belonged to the households of the rich, securing their luxury and ostentatious dignity. But more important, thousands of inscriptions suggest that at Rome, and to a lesser extent in Italian towns, trade and industry were chiefly in the hands of slaves and freedmen. Most are imperial, but what we have from the late Republic or the Augustan period is congruent with the later data. For instance the fine ware made at Arretium in the first century BC

---

[5] *IM*, ch. x, giving the results of II–IX.

[6] *IM*, ch. XXI, which requires some modification in detail, not affecting the general conclusions. Livy xxxix. 3. 4–6, xli. 8. 6 ff. refer to migration of Italians to Rome in the early second century; the language may be anachronistic. Italians with 'ius migrationis' could gain the citizenship thereby, if they settled anywhere in the *ager Romanus*; cf. xxxiv. 42. 5 f. (with R. E. Smith, *JRS* 1954, 18 ff.). A. H. McDonald adhered to the view that there was a drift to Rome and other towns from the early second century; cf. *Camb. Hist. Journ.* 1939, 126 f., 132. Cf. n. 13 below. Note that Marian veterans did not migrate to Rome (App. i. 29).

[7] Some town-dwellers cultivated the adjoining fields, see e.g. Cic. *de leg. agr.* ii. 89 on Capua, which must be true *a fortiori* of towns less developed as manufacturing and trading centres; P. Garnsey, *Proc. Camb. Phil. Soc.* 1979, 1 ff., a valuable discussion of the extent to which peasants lived in villages and scattered homesteads (a pattern of settlement surely more common after Rome had established internal peace in the peninsula), misunderstands this text, which means that Capua, after losing civic self-government in 211, *remained* a 'receptaculum aratorum'.

[8] For what follows see (besides the chs. in *IM* and Hopkins cited in nn. 4–6) Brunt *ap.* Cherubini, 1983, and on free labour at Rome, *JRS* 1980, 81 ff., defending and amplifying views in *The Roman Mob* (Finley, 1974, ch. IV).

was manufactured by freedmen and slaves. Conceivably the epigraphic evidence somewhat exaggerates their predominance. It can be conjectured that for various reasons humble men of free birth were less able or willing to leave memorials of themselves and of their manual employment. Moreover, there are few inscriptions of those engaged in unskilled, often casual, labour, which must have given a livelihood to some displaced peasants; on the other hand, they possessed neither the skill nor the capital to compete in the crafts or even in trade. The wealthy could import slaves who were already trained, or could pay the cost of training them. It is evident that rightly or wrongly entrepreneurs supposed that slave labour under their absolute control brought in the greatest profits, at any rate if the slaves, who had to be maintained continuously, could also be kept continuously at work; this was a proviso well understood by Cato in regard to farming,[9] and it must have been seen to apply equally to urban employment. In order to obtain efficient service from skilled slaves, owners were indeed obliged to allow them a share in earnings, and often to reward them with freedom before they had come to the end of their working lives. But in manumitting them they could require continued service from them, even without payment if they were given maintenance. The freedmen engaged in industry and trade were doubtless mainly pursuing the same activities as in their days of servitude; and though they might become rich themselves, it is probable that initially at least they were financed by their former masters in return for a share in profits.[10] The impression derived from inscriptions of the preponderance of slaves and freedmen in the population of Rome is fortified by Cicero's allusions to the plebs, especially to Clodius' gangs, which in fact comprised numerous artisans and shopkeepers.[11] At a much earlier date Scipio Aemilianus had berated the Roman plebs as consisting of men 'to whom Italy was but a stepmother'.[12]

[9] Implicit in Cato de agric. 2. 2 f., 5. 2, 39. 2.

[10] Treggiari, 1969, 11–20, 68–81; P. Garnsey, Klio 1981, 359 ff., differentiates between freedmen who became independent of patrons and others. Statistics on craftsmen etc.: H. Gummerus, RE ix, 1496 ff.; A. M. Duff, Freedmen in the early Roman Empire 109 ff.; cf. Treggiari, 1969, 91–105 for the Republic

[11] The Roman Mob (n. 8) 95 ff.; Lintott, 1968, ch. vi, to be preferred to Gruen, 1974, 433 ff. Gruen 361 n. 9 notes that in de leg. agr. ii Cicero implies that the urban plebs was of native stock; but in this speech he aimed at flattery of the plebs urbana.

[12] Vell. ii. 4. 4; Val. Max. vi. 2. 3; de vir. ill. 58. 8. P. Fraccaro, Studi sull' età dei Gracchi (Stud. stor. per l'antich. class., 1912), 387 ff., connected this mot with Scipio's efforts to limit land allotments in the interest of the Italians. This would imply that the urban mob were interested in land allotments. I do not believe this. The sources make Scipio reply with this mot to the outcry when he had pronounced that Gracchus was 'iure caesus'. This is perfectly plausible; the killing of Gracchus was a violation of provocatio, to which the humblest citizens were profoundly attached, as Cicero found to his cost. See also A. E. Astin, CQ 1960, 135–9.

None the less some peasants did drift into Rome,[13] and doubtless into other towns. They could at any rate hope for casual employment, for which it was uneconomic to maintain slaves. They might go out into the fields to assist in seasonal operations (p. 249). As there was little navigation in the winter, the work of dock-labourers and of porters and carriers must have bunched in the summer months. Building activity of all kinds was to some extent seasonal; and the demand for labour on great public works was extremely intermittent. At Rome immigrants might also receive doles from the great houses, purchasing their loyalty, as well as bribes from candidates for office.[14] In the brawls at Rome before Sulla's time the nobility could call on the aid of urban clients (doubtless including their freedmen) against the rural supporters of 'popular' agitators.[15]

It was perhaps to undermine this attachment, and not or not merely from genuine compassion, that Gaius Gracchus instituted cheap distributions of grain at the public cost. This measure in any event testifies to the existence of an urban proletariate of free men at Rome, which had already been formed before state doles were available. The public expenditure on grain distributions was in some way reduced by a *lex Octavia*, probably towards the end of the second or early in the first century; and they were totally abolished by Sulla. Consequential resentment may explain why in Cicero's time the nobility had lost control of the urban plebs; if so, it had not been allayed by the revival of distributions for a limited number of beneficiaries in 73, nor by Cato's law of 62 extending them much more widely: the poor could perceive that these were concessions extorted by fear. Only in 58 did P. Clodius make distribution free, and the number of recipients was soon vastly swollen, probably because slave-owners took the opportunity to manumit their slaves on a large scale, retaining a legal right to their services and transferring much of the cost of maintenance to the state.[16] However, the urban poor could not live on bread alone: they needed other food, clothes, and shelter. At all times the possibilities of obtaining casual employment for wages must have been the primary cause of migration into Rome, and no doubt to some extent into other

[13] Sall. *Cat.* 37. 4–7; Varro, *RR* ii *pr.* 5; App. ii. 120; Suet. *Aug.* 42. 3; the last three texts refer to conditions after 58.

[14] Sall. l.c.; Cic. *Verr.* ii. 3. 215, *de offic.* ii. 55, 57–9; Plut. *Cic.* 8. 1; Pliny, *NH* xv. 2, xviii. 16. Trebatius, *Dig.* ix. 3. 5. 1 indicates that patrons might give clients free housing.

[15] e.g. in 100 (n. 43), 88, and 87 (App. i. 55. 243 f., 64. 288; the 'old citizens' are surely chiefly those resident at Rome); cf. pp. 432 f.

[16] *IM* 376–82, but for date of *lex Octavia* H. Schneider, *Wirtschaft v. Politik*, 1974, 36 f. I now think that males were eligible for the doles from puberty, amending 'undecimo' to 'quarto decimo' in Suet. *Aug.* 41; cf. J. R. Rea, *Oxy. Pap.* xl p. 13. It is only an assumption that the ration was always, as in 73 (Sall. *Or. Macri* 19), 5 *modii* a month, compared with 3 for legionaries (Polyb. vi. 39), and 3–4½, varying with the heaviness of their labour, for Cato's slaves (*de agric.* 56).

towns, where there were no regular public doles at all. Suggestions in our sources that the drift of peasants into Rome was principally due to the public grain distributions are thus exaggerations. Only Sallust makes this the reason for migration as early as 63. He speaks of peasants preferring life in the city to 'ingrato labori' in the fields (n. 13). In truth, they could not subsist anywhere in entire idleness; and if they moved into the towns, it must have been largely because it was even harder to procure a livelihood in the country. Not that they can have prospered in Rome. In the crowded and insanitary conditions there mortality must have been very high. Probably few could raise a family; the dole, given only to males above the age of puberty, though more than enough for a single man, was inadequate for a wife and children as well; and the continuing influx of free immigrants will not have resulted in a steady and substantial net increase in the total of free-born inhabitants.[17]

Thus in my view the majority of the population of Rome had no roots in the soil of Italy and little interest in agrarian reform.[18] Equally, as will appear later, they contributed few recruits to the legions. Their riots fill a large part in our records, and in 67 their discontent forced through the Gabinian law; this was certainly an essential link in the chain of events that led on to the fall of the Republic. But in the end it was the disloyalty of the soldiers to the established regime that was decisive; it is their behaviour which above all requires elucidation; and they were drawn from Italy rather than from Rome itself. Now the free inhabitants of Italy outside Rome, though there were obviously craftsmen[19] and traders in other towns, many of them freedmen, and sailors and fishermen on the coasts, must principally have obtained their livelihood from agriculture and pasturage.

Something may first be said of the substantial landed proprietors. In the late Republic there were over 300 towns in Italy excluding Cisalpine Gaul,[20] and the curial class, together perhaps with some rich freedmen, may well have numbered over 50,000.[21] Each city councillor, even where the census qualification was as low as 100,000 sesterces, might have owned a farm of the model size of 100–300 *iugera*, 25–75

---

[17] *IM* 385 ff.; cf. ch. xi.   [18] Cic. *de leg. agr.* ii. 71.

[19] Varro, *RR* i. 16. 4 shows how such craftsmen might serve surrounding farms.

[20] Beloch, *Bevölkerung* 391, counted 431 in the Principate; some were constituted in the late Republic, and before 49 BC some fifty in Transpadana lacked citizen rights.

[21] *Curiae* of 100 members, Cic. *de leg. agr.* ii. 96 (Capua); *ILS* 6121 (Canusium, AD 226); cf. *Diz. Ep.* s.v. *centumviri*, but smaller numbers are known, e.g. *CIL* xiv. 2458, 2466. The property qualification might be 100,000 HSS (Petron. 44; Pliny, *Ep.* i. 19. 21; cf. Dio lxxii. 16). In many towns, as in Patavium (Str. v. 1. 7) or Narbo (*ILS* 112) under Augustus, there must have been well-to-do men outside the *curiae*, notably freedmen corresponding to the later Augustales.

hectares, described by the agronomists. Of course the great Roman magnates were immensely richer; Lucius Aemilius Paulus was worth 370,000 *denarii* at his death in 160, and Crassus (*cos*. 70) was reputed to have invested 50 millions in real estate. Since average land-values are unknown, we cannot estimate the size of their holdings, but plainly they were vast. By purchase or violence, or by taking lands pledged to them as security for debts that could not be repaid, some of them chose to annex the farms of their poorer neighbours and to possess themselves of extensive continuous tracts of land; others, like Pompey, preferred to acquire discrete properties in different regions, so as to minimize the risk of adverse climatic conditions in a particular locality; in either case they may well have preferred to divide their property into the relatively small units which the agronomists envisage, that could either be efficiently managed by a *vilicus* with a score or so of slaves or be leased to small tenants. Thus in the early first century Roscius owned thirteen separate *fundi* in the territory of Ameria (Cic. *Rosc. Amer.* 20). Naturally ranching required far more extensive land for pasture, but flocks and herds could be grazed partly on the great expanse of public land in return for a fee (*scriptura*) paid to the publicans.[22]

The great mass of free men in rural Italy must, however, have been composed of owners or tenants of small farms and of agricultural labourers. According to tradition, the typical holding of the peasant citizen had once been only 7 *iugera*, and some allotments made to settlers in the early second century were at least below the size of 20–30 *iugera* which were needed, except on unusually fertile soil, to support a family. Such peasants had to supplement the produce of their own farms either by working on larger estates or by exploiting adjacent public land, but their enjoyment of public land was progressively reduced by the ability of the rich to occupy and enclose cultivable parts of this land for their exclusive use, or to pasture on it their flocks and herds. Hence the decline in the peasantry, which was observable by 133. Not of course that the class of smallholders was then (or ever) extinct. Probably they held out longest in the more mountainous, infertile, and inaccessible regions, which were least attractive to rich investors in land. The decline was perhaps checked by the Gracchan allotments, though we are told that they ultimately proved ineffective (n. 1), and by settlements of veterans in the first century, though to a

----

[22] K. D. White, *BICS* 1967, 63 ff., collected evidence on *latifundia* and on large landholdings generally. The *word* is first attested in Pliny, *NH* xvii. 135, where it evidently excludes such discrete holdings as Pompey's. Wealth of magnates: *ESAR* i. 208 ff., 295 ff., 387 ff., cf. Brunt, *Latomus* 1975, 620 ff., on the huge landholdings of L. Domitius Ahenobarbus (*cos*. 54 BC) and of a freedman of the Metelli (*ob*. 8 BC). Stockton, 1979, admirably summarizes the agrarian situation in 133 and explains the use of *ager publicus* (ch. 1 and App. 1).

considerable extent other peasants were displaced for their benefit.[23] The same factors, which cannot be discussed here, that militated against smallholders in the pre-Gracchan period continued to operate thereafter.[24] None the less, at no time in the late Republic were smallholders eliminated. Varro briefly notes that a very large number of poor men were still cultivating their own fields with their own labour and that of their families in the 30s; he was probably thinking not only of peasant proprietors but of tenants, such as Horace's Ofellus, 'cum pecore et gnatis fortem mercede colonum'.[25]

We know little of the rural poor.[26] They hardly ever left epigraphic records of their existence. In certain areas archaeology reveals the presence of small farms; but their dating is insecure, and material remains cannot show if the farmers were owners or tenants; it is also often unsafe to assume that what was true in one place and time applies to any other.[27] Extant literature, written by or at least for the élite, takes little interest in the rural poor, except when (as in 133) they contributed directly to political conflict. Even the agronomists, Cato, Varro, and, at a date beyond our period, Columella did not aim at describing the rural economy of Italy, but only at instructing substantial owners how best to exploit their estates. They tacitly assume that in optimum conditions slave labour brought in the highest profits. Slaves provide the permanent labour force on Cato's model farms. Varro takes it for granted that they will perform routine operations on farms and act as herdsmen for stock-breeders. Though we cannot be confident that landowners invariably followed the precepts of the agronomists, since in other ages the practices recommended by experts and pursued by the majority of farmers have differed widely, generalizations in our sources indicate the extensive employment of slaves. Their number cannot be determined, but there is hardly a hint that the mortality among slaves attendant on Spartacus' revolt, in which at least 150,000 may well have perished, seriously denuded the land of slave workers.[28] Still the agronomists themselves conceded that it was uneconomic to use slaves on lands that were unhealthy (probably malarial), where the depreciation rate would have been excessive, or so

[23] *IM*, ch. xix (ii) and (vi).

[24] See pp. 73 ff. Conscription still aggravated other factors (*IM*, ch. xxii).

[25] Varro, *RR* i. 17. 2; Hor. *Sat.* ii. 2. 115.

[26] The then known evidence was collected and analysed by W. E. Heitland, *Agricola*, 1921. Cf. K. D. White, *Roman Farming*, 1970, ch. xi, Brunt *ap.* Cherubini, 1983, 95 ff.

[27] *IM* 352 f. Much subsequent archaeological work is used in A. Giardina and A. Schiavone (eds.), *Società romana e produzione schiavistica*, 1981, but is overlaid by dogmas on the nature, extent, and development of the 'slave mode of production'; cf. the reviews by D. W. Rathbone, *JRS* 1983, 160 ff., and M. S. Spurr, *CR* 1985, 123 ff.; whether these are right or wrong, the archaeological evidence is too patchy and ambiguous to demonstrate.

[28] *IM* 122, 287–9.

distant that the owners could not exercise sufficiently close supervision; Columella also applied this advice to lands desolated by the severity of the climate or the barrenness of the soil (which might have been unsuited to vines or olives and have produced a scanty yield of cereals).[29]

In such conditions Varro recommends employment of free wage-earners, Columella leasing to tenants. Tenancy was also known in the Republic, for instance to Varro himself.[30] It so happens that there is no allusion to it earlier than a fragment of the agronomist Saserna (*ap.* Colum. i. 7), writing perhaps at the beginning of the first century. But the silence of previous literature, given its small bulk and its subject-matter, is no indication that tenancy was not in use, perhaps in common use. Even Cato was not aiming to describe the rural economy of his time. In my view it is an accident that we also hear little of it in any Republican or Augustan sources; most of our information comes from the younger Pliny and from imperial jurists. But Cicero too leased his farms in the territory of Arpinum; only he does not, like Pliny, tell us anything of the process and problems. Juristic texts are sparse before the second century of our era; it is all we can expect that the fragments of Republican and Augustan legal writers contain a dozen references to the law governing tenancy of farms.[31] It is also probable that the juristic texts of all periods chiefly concern substantial tenants who, unlike the poor, were capable of taking disputes with landlords to court.[32] Some possessed slaves of their own. It is significant that juristic and some other allusions to tenancy show that lands under vines and olives, in which considerable capital would often have been invested, might be leased; the rents would then be relatively high, and beyond

---

[29] Varro i. 17. 3; Colum. i. 7 (who thought that in *these* conditions slaves were specially unsuited for cereal production).

[30] i. 2. 17, ii. 3. 7; see also nn. 31, 32. P. W. de Neeve, *Colonus*, 1984, is exhaustive on tenancy in this period. His analysis of the evidence is acute, but I tacitly differ from him on several points.

[31] Ser. Sulpicius, *Dig.* xix. 1. 13. 30, 2. 15. 2, 2. 35. 1 (?); Alfenus Varus, xv. 3. 16 (slave 'quasi colonus', cf. also xl. 7. 14), xix. 2. 30. 4; Aelius Tubero, xix. 1. 13. 30; Labeo, vii. 8. 10. 4, xix. 2. 60. 1 and 5, xx. 6. 14, xxxiii. 2. 30 (?), 2. 42 (?), 7. 12. 3 (slave 'quasi colonus'), xxxiv. 3. 17 (?) (mentioning 'reliqua colonorum'), xxxix. 3. 5, xl. 7. 14. (Allusions to 'reliqua colonorum' do not necessarily prove that tenants were prone to default on rent, of which there is other evidence in Pliny; as rent was payable in arrears, the sums due were among the assets of an estate, which the owner might devise by his testament). De Neeve's view that the texts cited suggest that the relevant law (of *locatio–conductio* of farms) was still at an early stage of development (pp. 45 ff.) seems to me subjective; the introduction of new remedies against defaulters, probably in the first century, may however suggest that it was only now that there were some substantial tenants capable of litigation. Contracts for leases could of course have been made by stipulation, before the contract of *locatio–conductio* was devised. If *colonus* in the sense of tenant is not attested before 100, it is also then found only in Cato in the basic meaning of cultivator.

[32] Cf. J. M. Kelly, *Roman Litigation*, 1966, i–iii. Well-to-do tenants: de Neeve pp. 82–6, 100, 195, with erroneous interpretation of Pliny *Ep.* x. 8. 5, where 'colonus' is singular for plural, as the allusion to 'remissiones' proves.

the capacity of poor men to pay, or at any rate to find adequate sureties for payment. It may be observed that large owners might choose to lease their lands for reasons other than those which the agronomists mention. A woman or a minor, or a man likely to be long absent from his estates, might all adopt this course, if it was recognized that operation through a *vilicus* demanded the close personal supervision that they could not provide. Some owners might also prefer a fixed return to the supposedly higher profit of direct management with its attendant risks. It was perhaps partly for this reason, as well as to reward faithful service, that some owners actually set up their slaves as quasi-tenants, rather than appointing them as *vilici*.[33] If land was almost entirely under cereals, which do not require continuous cultivation throughout the year, the employment of slaves would not have been economic, as for vines or olives or (and this was probably most common) for mixed farming. But we can hardly doubt that most tenants were small men. Horace's modest Sabine estate comprised a home farm worked by eight slaves and five holdings leased to tenants. Such men would be economically dependent on their landlords and probably be their clients, though the notion that patrons assigned land to clients on a precarious basis without rent is in my view without foundation (p. 411). Hence Catiline in 63 and Domitius Ahenobarbus in 49 could raise troops from their tenancy.[34]

Even when farms were directly managed, the labour force was not necessarily servile, or at least not entirely servile. Cato alludes to arrangements in which free men performed some of the cultivation in return for a share of the produce.[35] Varro, as we have seen, envisages that all the work might be done by hired labourers. When slaves did constitute the permanent labour force, it did not pay the owner to maintain enough hands for seasonal work such as harvesting grain, picking and pressing olives, gathering and treading grapes. It is partly implied, partly stated by Cato that such work was put out at contract. For such seasonal work the contractor needed free labourers, not slaves whom he would have had to maintain for the rest of the year.[36] Varro (*RR* i. 17. 2) expressly says that for those 'opera rustica maiora' gangs of hired free labourers were employed. There are a few other extant allusions to 'messores' or 'vindemiatores', or to other hired labourers on

[33] P. Veyne, *R. Ph.* 1980, 233 ff., *Rév. hist.* 1981, 3 ff., does not convince me that this was common.

[34] Hor. *Ep.* i. 14. 1, *Sat.* ii. 7. 118; cf. n. 87.

[35] *De agric.* 136 f. as interpreted by de Neeve 201 ff.

[36] *De agric.* 144–6; cf. E. Brehaut, *Cato the Censor on Farming*, 1933, xxxiv ff., on the implications of his calendar of farm work. Free 'custodes' in 13, 66 f. Cato's 'operarii' are not free (Brunt, *JRS* 1958, 165), nor are the 'pastores' of 149 f., who can be pledged.

the land.[37] Caesar required graziers to employ free men up to one-third of their labour force (Suet. *Caes.* 42); the enactment may have been ineffective, but can hardly have been patently futile: it implies that free workers were available. The picture drawn in the parable of labourers waiting to be hired for work in the vineyards (Matt. 20: 1 ff.) may have been as familiar in ancient Italy as in Palestine. We cannot tell how these agricultural labourers found a livelihood when they were not engaged by the large proprietors. Some no doubt dwelt in Rome or in other towns, where they could get casual employment. Many probably had small plots of their own or under leases, which neither sufficed for the subsistence of a family nor (especially if under cereals) demanded their labour throughout the year. But underemployment and near starvation must have been chronic in ancient Italy, as in modern times, among the rural poor. Marius' backers for the consul-ship included 'opifices agrestesque omnes, quorum res fidesque in manibus sitae erant',[38] and these were clearly the people who gladly embraced the prospect of hard, dangerous, and ill-paid service in the legions, which did at least assure them of clothing and food.

It is only to be expected that the partisans of land allotments should be found not among the urban plebs, but among the rural poor, very small owners, the younger sons of yeomen whose farms brooked no subdivision, tenants who wished to own rather than rent their land, and day-labourers whose work in the fields hardly sufficed for subsis-tence, agriculturists born, who had not found that 'fundit humo facilem victum iustissima tellus'. On the whole this expectation is confirmed by the evidence. Diodorus[39] and Appian[40] make it plain that Tiberius Gracchus' supporters came from the country. Cicero and Plutarch say the same for Gaius. It was in country districts near Rome that in 123 he sought votes for the bill against Popilius Laenas.[41] Though he also wooed the urban plebs by his frumentary law, at the end it could be taken for granted that 'harvesters' would be his partisans.[42] Saturninus called up veterans from the country to pass a colonial bill: the 'optimates' mobilized the urban population.[43] In 63 Rullus' bill evidently gave preference to the rural tribesmen, and

[37] Plut. *C. Gr.* 13. 2, *Mar.* 41. 2; Cic. *de orat.* iii. 46; Hor. *Sat.* ii. 6. 11; Pliny, *NH* xiv. 10 (cf. W. Kunkel, *Eos* 1957, 207 ff.); Suet. *Vesp.* i. 14; Sen. *Ep.* 47. 10 (cf. E. Gabba, 1973, 93 n. 119.) Cic. *de offic.* i. 41, 50 need not refer to agricultural workers, and *Caec.* 58, 63 may allude to 'servi alieni'. The labourers who migrated to Rome (Sall. *Cat.* 37. 7) need not have been completely divorced from the land.

[38] Sall. *BJ* 73. 6; cf. Gabba, 1973, 38 = 1976, 16.

[39] xxxiv/xxxv. 6. 1 = Posid. (Jacoby, no. 87), F 110 (b).   [40] i. 13. 57, 14. 58 f.

[41] Cic. *Cat.* iv. 4; Plut. *C. Gr.* 3. 1; cf. the title of his speech 'de Popillio Laenate circum conciliabula' in Gell. i. 7. 7. Livy vii. 15. 13 ('novorum ... hominum ... qui nundinas et conciliabula obire soliti erant') may reflect the practice of *populares* in the late Republic.

[42] *Peregrini* were so disguised, Plut. *C. Gr.* 13. 2.   [43] App. i. 29. 132, 30. 134, 31. 139 f.

though it is clearly nonsense when Cicero suggests that they would be men of property (*de leg. agr.* ii. 79), it is likely enough that his intention was to allot lands first to country-dwellers. It is true that residents in the city were not excluded, and that Rullus, Cicero in 60, and probably Caesar in 59 all talked of draining off the urban proletariate and at the same time repeopling the deserted parts of Italy (n. 4). But probably only some of the most recent migrants into the capital would have been attracted back to the land. Cicero in 63 appealed with demagogic skill to the mob's love of the bribes, games, and festivals enjoyed chiefly by those domiciled at Rome. Livy's story of the early colonization of Antium is probably coloured by later experience; few, he says, would enrol: 'cetera multitudo poscere Romae agrum malle quam alibi accipere'. Similarly, later conditions are probably reflected in Dionysius of Halicarnassus' story that king Tullus Hostilius distributed royal and public domains to men who would otherwise have had to work for wages on the estates of the rich.[44] In other words, for the urban proletariate an agrarian agitation was not serious; or rather, it did not seriously desire to receive land so much as to blackmail the senate into other concessions. The agrarian agitation of 63 was followed by Cato's law of 62 greatly increasing the number of recipients of cheap corn.

In 63 the urban plebs at first supported but finally deserted Catiline; they were alienated by Cicero's skilful allegation that the conspirators intended to burn down the city.[45] It was among 'agrestis homines, tenuis atque egentes' (Cic. *Cat.* ii. 20) that Catiline found his most faithful followers. The threat which his movement presented to order, property, and the interests of Cicero's 'exercitus locupletium' (*Att.* i. 19. 4), 'the men whose fortunes had been augmented and accumulated by the favour of the gods' (*Cat.* iv. 19), is the clearest indication we have of the distress and discontent which is the social background of the political revolution in this period. At the consular elections in 63 Catiline had already forfeited the support of Crassus and Caesar;[46] he appeared in public, surrounded by impoverished Sullan colonists and the very peasants they had dispossessed;[47] it was reported that he had privately declared his resolve to place himself at the head of the 'miseri', and he openly boasted in the senate that he would not fail to give leadership to the class whose one weakness was that it had lacked a leader.

Defeated at the polls in a timocratic assembly, he proclaimed then, if

[44] Cic. *de leg. agr.* ii. 71; Livy iii. 1; Dionys. Hal. iii. 1. 5.

[45] Sall. *Cat.* 37. 48. 1 f; cf. Cic. *Cat.* iii. 22, iv. 17; Dio xxxvii. 1. 3.

[46] At least there is no evidence for it, and Crassus defended Murena. His, and Caesar's, complicity in the plot was a partisan invention.

[47] Cic. *Mur.* 49; cf. *Cat.* ii. 20; Sall. *Cat.* 16. 4, 28. 4. Cf. Harmand, 1967, 476.

not earlier, a programme of remission of debts and redistribution of lands.[48] Fighting and devastation in the 80s and again in 78–77, the persistence of violence in the countryside thereafter,[49] the great slave revolt of 73–71, and the indirect effects of pirate depredations and the Mithridatic war had naturally led to a social and economic crisis. The exceptionally large number of legions required between 78 and 71[50] had inevitably involved conscription of peasants, including no doubt many of the Sullan colonists, many of whom would have been ruined by absence from their farms. The burden of debt had never been greater than in 63, according to Cicero's own admission, and some bill had been promoted, but not passed, at the beginning of the year 'for the cancellation of debts'. Cicero said that in every corner of Italy all who were oppressed with debt rallied to Catiline.[51] These people certainly did not consist mainly of men with great possessions, like Catiline himself, who could perhaps have paid their debts off by selling part of their property, and it would be uncritical to suppose that debts were incurred only through extravagance, or that in Cicero's language all those who were 'egentes' or 'malis domesticis impediti' were 'improbi' or 'furiosi'.[52] A succession of bad harvests would inevitably force the yeoman to borrow and the tenant to default on his rent; the harsh law then left him at the mercy of his creditor, who could keep him in custody, and perhaps even make him work as a bondsman;[53] Manlius' letter, as reported by Sallust (*Cat.* 33), claims that many farmers had lost 'fama atque fortunis'—their property had been sold up and they had suffered loss of 'existimatio'—and that they were not even allowed 'amisso patrimonio liberum corpus habere'.

It is not surprising that the revolutionary movement spread to all parts of Italy;[54] 'tanta vis morbi ac veluti tabes *plerosque* civium animos invaserat' (ibid. 36). Etruria was the chief centre of disturbance, as in Lepidus' time, but outbreaks are also attested in Cisalpina, Picenum, Umbria, the Paelignian land, Campania, Apulia, and Bruttium.[55] It is almost a catalogue of the recruiting areas for the Roman legions. But Catiline lacked a show of legitimate authority and a trained and disciplined army. It was otherwise in 49, when 'numquam improbi cives habuerunt paratiorem ducem' (Cic. *Fam.* xvi. 11. 3); Caesar too

---

[48] Dio xxxvii. 30 puts this after the elections of 63, perhaps too late; Sall. *Cat.* 21. 2, in 64, much too early, when the plutocrat Crassus was still backing Catiline.

[49] *IM* ch. xviii and App. 8. Texts which purport to refer to early Rome may also retroject later conditions, e.g. Cassius Hemina, fr. 17 P.; Sall. *Hist.* i. 11. Note also Cic. *Phil.* ii. 41. On removal of boundary stones cf. Dionys. Hal. ii. 74. 5; Grom. Vet. 350 f. L. (fr. of Vegoia).

[50] *IM* 446 ff.   [51] Cic. *de offic.* ii. 84, *Cat.* ii. 8; Dio xxxvii. 25.

[52] e.g. *Cat.* ii. 17 ff., *Sest.* 97, *de off.* ii. 84.   [53] Ch. 6 n. 7 with text.

[54] Cic. *Cat.* ii. 8, iv. 6; Cato's speech, Sall. *Cat.* 52. 15.

[55] Cic. *Cat.* ii. 6, *Sull.* 53, *Sest.* 9; Sall. *Cat.* 27. 1, 28. 4, 36. 1, 42. 1; Plut. *Cic.* 10. 3, 14; App. ii. 2; Dio xxxvii. 30. 4, 31. 2; Oros. vi. 6. 5–7. Cf. n. 47.

was suspected of intending to remit debts (*Att*. vii. 11. 1), and his failure to fulfil this expectation led in 48 and 47 to riots and revolt.[56]

II

The rural population not only provided partisans for land distributions; it was they who supplied Rome with her soldiers. Velleius (ii. 15. 2) says that before 90 BC two-thirds of Roman armies were drawn from the Italian allies: this proportion may be too high,[57] but no one will question that they then provided over half the recruits; and surely they continued to contribute on much the same scale after their enfranchisement.

Before Marius' first consulship in 107 the Roman legionaries had normally been *assidui*, citizens possessed of some property, and therefore for the most part peasant proprietors. But whether or not the property qualification had been reduced in the Hannibalic war and again in the Gracchan era, a theory advanced by Gabba, modified by me, and widely adopted,[58] it was certainly so low by 107 that it can hardly have exceeded the value of a dwelling and a garden plot; the soldiers no longer supplied their equipment which the state provided, deducting the cost from pay. Marius enlisted *proletarii*, and our authorities imply that his example was followed thereafter. They censure him for opening the army to men without 'a stake in the country', and modern writers, including even Gabba, have generally held that he introduced a fundamental change in its composition.[59] But in social terms the difference between men who in civil life had lacked economic independence, and those totally destitute of property is minimal, and the significance of Marius' reform was very small. It will be seen that it did not create a professional army of volunteers, as Gabba still supposed. In any event it did not alter the rural provenance of most soldiers.

There were never many recruits from the urban proletariate. We

---

[56] See p. 505 at 5.   [57] *IM*, App. 26; cf. Ilari, 1974, 148 ff.

[58] In the original version of this essay, as in *IM* 74–83, 402–8, I supposed that a decline in the number of those qualified for legionary service (*a*) led to reductions in the qualification in the Hannibalic war and in the Gracchan era, and (*b*) alarmed Ti. Gracchus and his contemporaries; the fall in the total number of citizens registered in the army between 165/4 and 136/5 is not very considerable, but if it concealed a disproportionately greater fall in the number of *assidui*, they would have known it, as we do not. This is all conjectural; see J. W. Rich, *Historia*, 1983, 288 ff., for acute though perhaps not decisive objections. Rich also shows in effect that as a result of devaluations in the coinage from the time of the Hannibalic war the property qualification for legionary service must have progressively fallen in real terms unless it was actually raised in monetary terms.

[59] Sall. *BJ* 86. 2; Val. Max. ii. 3. 1; Gell. xvi. 10. 14; Florus i. 36. 13; Plut. *Mar.* 9. 1. Cf. Gabba, 1973, 1976, ch. 1.

hear of levies throughout Italy in 87, 84–82, 52, 49, 43, and 41 BC, and more particularly on various occasions in Cisalpina, Etruria, Picenum, Umbria, the Sabine country, near Arpinum, in Campania, Samnium, Lucania, Apulia, Bruttium, among the Marsi, Paeligni, and Marrucini. The levy was probably conducted through the *municipia* and *coloniae*, just as before 90 allied cohorts had been levied under the *formula togatorum* from the Italian towns.[60] Discharged soldiers under the Republic, as in Augustus' reign, return to their home towns. By contrast references to recruitment at Rome are rare. In Rome freedmen preponderated; they were normally ineligible for legionary service, and only in emergencies were they formed into special units, as in 216, (Livy xxiii. 57. 11, xxiv. 14. 3) 90,[61] and AD 6 and 9.[62] On these occasions city-dwellers of free birth were also conscripted for the legions; the result was not very encouraging; in 89 the army of Lucius Cato, chiefly drawn from the city, was undisciplined (Dio, fr. 100), and I need hardly do more than allude to the 'vernacula multitudo, lasciviae sueta, laborum intolerans' serving in AD 14, to such men as Percennius 'dux olim theatralium operarum, . . . procax lingua et miscere coetus histrionali studio doctus' (Tac. *Ann.* i. 31; cf. 16). In 83 the consuls Scipio and Norbanus, Appian tells us (i. 82. 373), levied the best army they could from the city and joined it to the army from Italy. Perhaps Appian has garbled a contrast between troops drawn from old and new citizens; however if this is not so, it is relevant to recall that Scipio's army had so little stomach for fighting that it soon deserted to Sulla (i. 85). Levies in or near the city are again recorded in 49 and 43, but these too were at moments of exceptional crisis.

There is indeed no doubt, though the contrary has been affirmed,[63] that the armies of the late Republic were overwhelmingly rural in origin, just as the legionaries and praetorians enlisted in Italy during the Principate hardly ever came from the city of Rome, but generally from the central and northern regions.[64] Marian veterans came in

[60] See App. 1. It is not clear that in 63 Cicero actually levied any of the urban plebs (Dio xxxvii. 35. 4). In my view (*contra* Harmand, 1967, 246, 254) Dio xxxix. 39 does not imply that the conscription of 55 either extended to them, or that conscription had become abnormal (cf. n. 70); protests against the levy were known earlier (n. 69; *IM*, App. 21), when it was certainly the usual way of raising an army. Livy viii. 20. 4 probably reflects later experience, whereas vii. 25. 8 is out of line with other evidence. Cf. also Sall. *Or. Macri* 26 f. with *IM* 643.

[61] App. i. 49. 212 (cf. Gabba ad loc.); *Per.* Livy lxxiv; Macrob. i. 11. 32.

[62] Pliny, *NH* vii. 149; Suet. *Aug.* 25. 2; Dio lvi. 23. 3; Macrob. i. 11. 32; EJ[3] 368 = *ZPE* 1974, 161 ff. Tac. *Ann.* i. 31. (cf. 16) and Dio lvii. 5. 4 refer to such *ingenui* in the legions; freedmen served in special cohorts.

[63] M. Cary, *Hist. of Rome*, 1947, 303; cf. *CAH* ix. 492. Most books are vague on the point, but create the wrong impression. The truth was seen but not fully argued by W. E. Heitland, *Agricola*, 1921, 175 f.; J. Carcopino, *Hist. Rom.*[2], 1940, 486; and Gabba, 1973, 56 ff. = 1976, 24 ff.

[64] G. Forni, *Reclutamento delle legioni*, 1953, ch. IV; cf. 157 ff.; A. Passerini, *Coorti pretorie*, 1939, 148 ff.; for exceptional enlistment of soldiers at Rome in AD 132–3; cf. J. F. Gilliam, *AJP* 1956, 359 ff.

from the fields to back Saturninus (n. 43). Sulla returned to Italy in 83 with five legions, but he allotted land to twenty-three; with the possible exception of men from Scipio's four legions (Plut. *Sulla* 28. 3), which had deserted to him, his reinforcements came from the country; he did not control the capital when recruiting in 83.[65] Cicero describes Caesarian veterans, when he is in complimentary vein, as 'homines rusticos, sed fortissimos viros civisque optimos', but when they took Antony's side as 'homines agrestes, si homines illi ac non pecudes potius'.[66] For Horace the typical soldier captured by the Parthians was a Marsian or Apulian (*Odes* iii. 5. 9); in fact we happen to know that a strong Lucanian contingent served under Crassus (Pliny, *NH* ii. 147). In the twenty years after Caesar crossed the Rubicon, some 200,000 Italians were often under arms; hence 'squalent abductis arva colonis'.[67]

It has generally been supposed that from Marius' time the army was composed mainly of volunteers. The supposition was natural, given the misery of the poor, which in modern countries too has always tended to make the voluntary principle effective (cf. Tac. *Ann.* iv. 4). Yet it is not correct. Conscription was frequently employed, as R. E. Smith showed in his excellent book,[68] in times of civil war, but not only then. Conscription must have affected the peasants who still owned or rented small farms. Pompey in 49 took it for granted that cohorts raised in Picenum 'quae fortunas suas reliquerunt' (*Att.* viii. 12B. 2) included men of property. We know that the levy had been resented bitterly in the second century,[69] and this was still true in the first.[70]

The period of service remained uncertain, and might be long. The legions which Lucius Valerius Flaccus took out to Asia in 86 were not discharged for twenty years;[71] on the other hand those raised by Lucius Piso in 58 were disbanded in 55.[72] I do not agree with Smith that any distinction can be drawn in theory or practice between standing armies in the provinces and legions raised for special pur-

[65] App. i. 79. 363, 81. 370, 85. 387, 86. 393, 100. 470 (with Gabba's notes) show how Sulla's army grew; for its numbers see *IM* 441 ff; cf. 305.

[66] *Fam.* xi. 7. 2. *Phil.* viii. 9; cf. x. 22. See also *Arch.* 24, Hor. *Ep.* ii. 2. 39.

[67] *Georg.* i. 507; cf. Lucan i. 28 f.; App. v. 18. 72, 74. 314; *IM* ch. xxvi.

[68] Smith, 1958, 44 ff.

[69] Livy xxxiv. 56. 9, xxxvi. 3. 5, xxxix. 38. 6 ff., xlii. 32. 6–35. 2, xliii. 11. 10, *Per.* xlviii, lv, and *Oxy. Epit.* of lv; App. *Iber.* 49, 78; Sall. *BJ* 41. 7; App. i. 7. 30; Plut. *Ti. Gr.* 8. 3. P. J. Cuff thinks that harsh discipline in the mid-second century (Pol. vi. 37; *Per.* Livy lv; Front. *Strat.* iv. 1. 20) was a particular grievance; later it was relaxed; cf. n. 100.

[70] *IM* 408 ff. with App. 20. Conscription in Italy, though not in the provinces, first fell into desuetude (with some later exceptions) under Tiberius; cf. Brunt. *Scripta Class. Israel* 1974, 90 ff.

[71] Cic. *de imp. Cn. Pomp.* 26; Plut. *Luc.* 34 f.; App. *Mith.* 90, which must refer only to the Valerians; Dio xxxvi. 14–6, 46. 1.

[72] Cic. *de prov. cons.* 5, *Pis.* 57 with 47, 91–2. There were no legions in Macedon in early 49; cf. Caes. *BC* iii. 4.

poses.[73] Some part of Metellus Pius' and Pompey's armies in Spain must have remained as garrisons there after the end of the Sertorian war.[74] Pompey took over troops in the east from Lucullus and various commanders, including the legions that had been sent to Cilicia in 78 under Servilius Vatia, and on his return to Rome he left legions in Syria and Cilicia, whose survivors were still there in 49. The nucleus of the army that conquered Gaul consisted of four legions which before 59 had constituted the garrison of Cisalpine and Transalpine Gaul.[75] But a tabulation of the number of legions in the field during the post-Marian period shows that many soldiers must have been discharged after a campaign or two, while it was no novelty that there were permanent garrisons in some provinces, though they were now more numerous. In the first century as before soldiers had a claim to be demobilized after serving six years (nn. 123, 124). If some served far longer, that had been true also of legionaries in the Hannibalic war. No recruit could foresee how long or where he would be called on to serve.

This means that it is misleading to speak of a professional army; no one who enlisted could count on making a career in the army which would occupy most of his active life. As will appear later, the evidence makes it doubtful if many would actually have entertained this ambition. They often pressed for demobilization, though they hoped then to obtain rewards that would secure their future livelihood. Those who had previously been small farmers would often have nothing to return to; even two or three years in the legions might have been enough to ruin them. As in the second century, when 'the people were oppressed by military service and lack of resources' (Sall. *BJ* 41. 7), the incidence of conscription continued to aggravate the perennial factors which imperilled the viability of small farms. The pathetic story Valerius Maximus (iv. 4. 6) tells of the consul Regulus will be remembered. During his absence for a year in Africa the steward of his farm of seven *iugera* had died; his hired man had run away with the farm stock, and his wife and children were in danger of starvation. Such must have been the fate, not of a consul and a noble in the third century, but of many a peasant in the second and first centuries. Thus, even when the legionary was a man of some property, army service would soon reduce him to the same economic level as his proletarian comrades.

---

[73] Smith, 1958, ch. III; *contra IM* 218–20, 227–32. For provincial garrisons see now my tabulations of legions in *IM* 432 f., 449.

[74] Smith 21. 2; cf. *IM* 452–63.

[75] *IM* 463 ff.

III

The political attitudes of the legionaries in the late Republic were varied and complex. Mommsen once wrote of the soldier in the post-Marian army that 'his only home was the camp, his only science war, his only hope the general'.[76] This opinion is rather exaggerated; at least the soldier was often not inexperienced in agricultural work. It remains true of course that he was commonly a man who had lost his property or never possessed any, and that while he might make or repair his fortune in an army, he had little prospect of continuous and remunerative employment in civil life after discharge. It is clear from the conduct of troops who served under Sulla, the Marian leaders, Caesar, and the dynasts who struggled for power after Caesar's death that he might feel more loyalty to his commander than to the government at Rome. In all these cases, however, conditions were abnormal; the legitimacy of the government at Rome could be denied. The frequency of indiscipline, mutinies, and even the desertion of generals by their armies in civil wars indicates that commanders could not count on the implicit loyalty of their troops. It is also too easy to assume that the soldiers were entirely indifferent to constitutional and political issues and guided wholly by personal attachments, still more by hopes of material rewards,[77] although the assumption was made in antiquity. Some, says Sallust (*BJ* 86. 2), explained Marius' enrolment of *capite censi* by his ambition: 'homini potentiam quaerenti egentissimus quisque opportunissimus, cui neque sua cara, quippe quae nulla sunt, et omnia cum pretio honesta videntur'; and other writers echo the same accusation (n. 59). Sallust wrote out of his experience in the triumviral period, and as Appian said in a notable analysis of the conduct of the soldiery in 41 BC, they were then serving their generals rather than the state, and did not scruple to desert them for rewards, since they knew that the generals needed them only for personal ends.[78] But we have reached a time of which Tacitus could write 'nulla iam publica arma' (*Ann* i. 2), and yet even now (as Appian says) generals and soldiers veiled their infidelity with the pretence that they were acting for the general good.

In earlier days it is still clearer that the armies were wooed with political propaganda; men may act from mixed motives, and we

---

[76] *Hist. of Rome* iv. 6 (Everyman edn. iii. 188).

[77] A. von Premerstein, 1937, 25, and Gabba, 1973/1976, ch. II, stressed personal attachment; *contra* Gruen, 1974, 365 ff. Indiscipline: Harmand, 1967, 272 ff., assembled the evidence down to 50. Note also the mutinies against Caesar in 49 and 48–47 (nn. 126–7); also in Spain (Dio xliii. 29). In 44–40 examples are too numerous to cite; there was also a serious mutiny against Octavian in 36 (n. 128).

[78] App. v. 17; cf. Plut. *Sulla* 12. 6–9; Nepos, *Eumenes* 8. 2.

cannot be sure that this propaganda was of no effect. When he marched on Rome in 88, Sulla could point to the violence at Rome by which legislation adverse to his interests and views had been carried, and argued that he was doing no more than meeting force by force; though all but one of his leading officers abandoned him, such pleas may have affected the common soldier. In 87 Cinna claimed that his deposition violated popular sovereignty.[79] Both of them certainly appealed to the cupidity of their troops as well, but how can we determine that this appeal alone was decisive? The regime that Cinna established rested on force, and flouted constitutional rules; its legitimacy could be doubted. In 83 Sulla sought support by guaranteeing the rights of the new citizens and advocating a compromise peace, which the troops of his enemies longed for.[80] Both Caesar and the Pompeians spoke, however insincerely, of their attachment to the Republic and the constitution (Dio xli. 57 1; cf. 17. 3), and addressed such propaganda to the armies. The Pompeians stressed the authority of the senate. We are told that the sincere and passionate eloquence of Cato's appeals to patriotic duty inspired their troops at Dyrrhachium.[81] Caesar, while inflaming the cupidity and personal loyalty of his men, also harangued them on his own services to the senate, the unconstitutional acts of his opponents, and the violation of tribunician sanctity; his soldiers on the Rubicon shouted that they were ready to defend his dignity and the rights of the tribunes.[82] In Spain he told the soldiers that he preferred a bloodless victory over fellow-citizens. On the eve of Pharsalus he reiterated the story of his vain efforts to secure 'quietem Italiae, pacem provinciarum, salutem imperii', and the veteran Crastinus plunged into battle with the cry: 'Caesar shall recover his dignity and we our freedom'.[83] H. Drexler has argued that the simple soldier who wrote the *Bellum Hispaniense* saw the campaign of 45 BC as one that was fought between armies that owed a merely personal allegiance; but even this author notes that, as in the past, Caesar was striving to save Spain from devastation and oppression.[84] Brutus and Cassius surely showed some skill when they combined with lavish gifts to their troops appeals to the ideal of liberty: Caesar, they said, had held the sanctity of tribunes and the electoral rights of the people in contempt, and the triumvirs were

---

[79] App. i. 65. 298 f.; for bribes, Vell. ii. 20. 4; *Schol. Cron.* 286 ff. On the conduct of armies in the 80s cf. Meier, 1966, 237 ff. On propaganda and its effects see also Harmand 303–12, 418 ff.

[80] App. i. 85 (with Gabba's notes); *Per.* Livy lxxxvi. Cf. n. 130.

[81] Plut. *Cato Minor* 54; App. ii. 50 ff.; Dio xliii. 5.

[82] Caes. *BC* i. 7 f. (cf. App. ii. 33; Dio xli. 4. 1), 22, 85.

[83] Caes. *BC* i. 9. 71 f., 80, 85, iii. 90; cf. 19, 57; App. ii. 47.

[84] *Hermes* 1935, 208 ff., stressing *B. Hisp.* 17, 19. 4; cf. *B. Afr.* 45; but cf. *B. Hisp.* 1, 42, *B. Afr.* 25. 5. Cf. also Gruen's just comments (1974, 375) on Drexler.

oppressing Italy. Their legions, many raised by Caesar, fought hard for their victory.[85] Other Caesarians, it is true, behaved differently; at one moment in 44, when Octavian professed to be an obedient servant of the Republic, ready to oppose Antony, he lost the favour of veterans who cared chiefly for vengeance on Caesar's assassins and the retention of their land allotments (App. *BC* iii. 41 f.). But at least in 40 Octavian's men were unwilling to fight Antony in a purely personal quarrel (ibid. v. 59), whereas in 31 they showed no like reluctance to take part in a struggle against one who had been branded as a traitor to Roman traditions and interests.

Appeals to the citizen's sense of duty to the commonwealth and to the public good may then have had some effect on the soldiers; how much we can hardly estimate. But the issues were seldom clear in times of civil war, and the soldiers, even if they were able to assess them, were surely more decisively influenced by personal considerations.

It is allegiance to commanders that is most commonly emphasized. The armies of the late Republic, it is often said, came to be almost private armies attached to their generals rather than to the state. This kind of assertion has plausibility only in relation to armies that took part in civil wars. No one will believe that, for instance, the garrison legions in Macedon or Spain were private armies of the successive proconsuls appointed to command them. And even in civil wars some armies deserted their generals. Cinna was actually killed by his own troops. The legions of the consuls of 83 went over *en masse* to Sulla. In 44 two of Antony's legions transferred their allegiance to Octavian. This can hardly be explained by their hereditary allegiance to Caesar's adopted son. They had been formed by Caesar in or after 49, and other legions of the same vintage were to fight for Brutus and Cassius against him.[86]

The personal loyalty imputed to the soldiers is commonly connected with clientship. It is supposed that generals often enlisted their own clients or that the troops under their command were converted into their clients. The recruitment of clients is attested, but rarely. In 134 Scipio Aemilianus had raised 4,000 volunteers for the Numantine war, but of these only 500 consisted of his friends and clients, and of course he also took over the two legions already in the field. In 83 Pompey mustered ultimately three legions, the kernel of which was evidently composed of his father's old soldiers or dependants in Picenum. One might wonder how he paid them; can Crassus have had his success in mind when he said that no one could be esteemed rich who could not

---

[85] App. iv. 89–99, 133.

[86] *IM* 474–88; *legiones* Martia and IV were not part of the Gallic army. For other desertions cf. Harmand (n. 77).

support an army from his own resources (Cic. *de offic.* i. 25)? Sulla's other officers could not vie with him, but the younger Marius was able to induce veterans who had probably served his father to re-enlist, and they may have acted from hereditary loyalty. In general Sulla collected troops by 'friendship, fear, money, and promises' (App. i. 86); presumably his opponents did likewise; both sides brought pressure on the Italian communities in the course of recruitment (Diod. xxxviii–xxxix. 13). 'Friendship' can be an euphemism for clientship, and we may conjecture that municipal as well as aristocratic adherents of the warring parties procured soldiers among their own clients, or, like L. Visidius in 43 (Cic. *Phil.* vii. 24), encouraged enlistment by exhortations and grants of money. The tenants who followed Catiline in 63 and L. Domitius Ahenobarbus in 49 *may* have been their clients (p. 249). But in 49 both the Pompeians and Caesar relied on conscription; men were reluctant to serve. In 44–43 Octavian could re-engage veterans of Caesar, who doubtless looked on him as their hereditary patron, though they had other motives for taking arms (see below); so could Antony and Lepidus, who had other claims on their support; some had received lands under a law moved by Antony, which he and his associates were charged to execute; and Lepidus had probably organized colonies for veterans in Gaul, and was their patron in his capacity as *deductor*; Antony perhaps had a similar relation to beneficiaries of his law.[87]

The nucleus of Caesar's faithful Gallic army was formed of four legions raised to protect Cisalpine and Transalpine Gaul years before he became their commander; so too Pompey in 66 took over ten or more legions already in the east.[88] Conscripts or volunteers, these troops were not initially their clients; no more were any armies in being the clients of those who succeeded to their command. No doubt time and habit might forge a personal allegiance. Labienus reckoned that in three years the Pompeians had made their forces in Africa 'loyal by custom' (*B. Afr.* 45). But success in war, especially if prolonged and gained over foreign enemies, contributed most (cf. Caes. *BC* i. 7); Caesar makes Curio say that 'successful actions win the goodwill of an army for commanders and reverses make them hated' (ii. 31. 3). Sulla, Pompey, and Caesar had pre-eminently enjoyed success. We are too

---

[87] Scipio: App. *Iber.* 84; Pompey: Vell. ii. 29, *B. Afr.* 22. 2, etc.; Diod. xxxviii–xxxix. 10 makes Sulla express surprise that his other leading partisans had not even obtained aid from their *oiketai*; (can this term indicate a misunderstanding of *familiares* or *clientes*?); Marius: Diod. ibid. 12; Catiline: Sall. *Cat.* 59. 3; Domitius: Caes. *BC* i. 34, 56; P. J. Cuff suggested to me that the Domitii were patrons of the Marsi, where he recruited troops (cf. Diod. xxxvii. 13); conscription in 49: *IM* 409; recruitment in 44–43 by Octavian, Antony, and Lepidus: *IM* 481–3; *lex Antonia*: 324 ff; Lepidus' colonies: 589; cf. Celsa in Spain (592). *Deductores* as patrons: Harmand, 1957, 23 ff.

[88] *IM* 457 f., 466 f.

apt to treat them as typical. Victories might also give the general the means of largess; Caesar delicately refers to his 'perpetui temporis officia' (iii., 90) to the Gallic legions, whom he had continually enriched (n. 97). No doubt all this was not enough; Lucullus' soldiers secured much booty (n. 95), but he could not convince them that he had a genuine concern in their welfare; moreoever, in the end he suffered reverses. He may also have lacked the personal magnetism that Sulla perhaps, and Caesar, possessed. Caesar claims that he was so loved that his men would refuse no danger for his safety (*BC* iii. 26. 1); one particularly striking example of devotion is on record (*B. Afr.* 44–6), and it was exhibited posthumously in their insistence on retribution for his assassins. Still, it was confined to those who had long served him in Gaul; the two legions he sent back to Italy in 50, which had been formed not long before, were to fight for Pompey (*BC* iii. 88. 2), and many of those raised in or after 49 followed Brutus and Cassius, admittedly in the hope of great rewards, which equally prompted their compeers to serve the triumvirs (see below).[89] The Gallic veterans were themselves capable of mutiny (nn. 126–7), and their loyalty to Caesar's memory was sharpened by apprehensions that his enemies would deprive them of their land allotments.[90] Nor is there comparable evidence for fidelity to Pompey among his former soldiers (pp. 437 f.).

Religion sanctified the soldier's loyalty. He had sworn to obey his general and not to desert the standards.[91] Obviously this traditional oath (*sacramentum*) had never been conceived to justify taking arms against the commonwealth. But in a civil war, when the legitimacy of the regime in power at Rome was itself in dispute, it may be that legionaries, to whom the rights and wrongs of the quarrel were obscure, saw their clearest duty in literal fidelity to their oath. In 49 and later, however, rival generals sometimes thought it expedient to order their men to swear a new oath of fealty, and those who had transferred their allegiance might be sworn in again to their new commander. It is difficult to assess the effect of such oaths; the sanction was fear of divine wrath, and we do not know how lively this was. Certainly oaths were often violated; perhaps the mere reiteration of solemn formulae weakened their force. In any case they have nothing to do with clientship; no one tells us that clients as such were sworn to obey patrons.[92] It is also hard to discern how much soldiers may have

---

[89] *IM* 485 f.

[90] See generally on Caesar's troops in Gaul Plut. *Caes.* 16 f.; Suet. *Caes.* 67–70. Their attitude after his death: Nic. Dam. *FGH* 90 F 130. 41, 46, 49, 56, 103; 118; App. ii. 133, iii. 12, 32, 40, 43, etc.; for full analysis see Botermann, 1968.

[91] Harmand, 1967, 299 f.

[92] Caes. *BC* i. 23, 76, ii. 28–32, iii. 87; App. ii. 47, 193, iv. 62. 268, 116. 487. Cf. also ch. 8, vii.

been ready to see the victories of their general as proof of divine favour, legitimizing his cause.[93]

Clientship itself was a moral tie, resting on *fides*. If there is no proof that soldiers in general became clients in the strict sense, bound by a hereditary attachment to their generals, it is also true that in Roman morality the conferment of benefits created an obligation to requite them when possible. None the less, duty to the commonwealth was a higher claim on every citizen's conscience. But the influence of any of these moral claims can easily be exaggerated. Gratitude for past favours might count less than expectation of those to come; and soldiers might be most faithful to generals with the best chance of victory and of fulfilling promises of future benefits. The chief need of the poor was subsistence, and the strongest motive for the soldier was the prospect of material gain.

The rate of pay is disputed, but certainly was low, till 'doubled' by Caesar to 225 *denarii* a year: and pay might fall into arrears. So far as the legionary depended on *stipendium*, he could expect only a mere subsistence, with nothing for his family or future. But there was also the hope of booty or donatives.[94] Marius attracted volunteers for the Jugurthine war by the chances of plunder (Sall. *BJ* 84. 4), and he fulfilled their hopes (ibid. 87. 1, 91. 6, 92. 2). Warfare in the east was particularly lucrative; even Lucullus, though he was accused of meanness to his troops and tried to restrain them from sacking Greek cities, allowed them to plunder Tigranocerta with its immense stores of wealth, and by his own account distributed 950 *denarii* to every one of his soldiers; we hear of their riches and luxury.[95] Pompey rewarded his legionaries in the eastern campaigns with 1,500 *denarii* apiece.[96] Caesar enriched his soldiers in Spain after a minor campaign in 61 (Plut. *Caes.* 12. 2), and his liberality in Gaul was evidently vast.[97] Then, as on other such occasions, officers did proportionately better. Of course booty and donatives accrued chiefly to men who served in large armies and in great wars. Much less was to be made in the guerilla fighting

---

[93] J. Rufus Fears, *Princeps a Dis Electus*, 1977, 90–111, with my reservations in *JRS* 1979, 170 f.

[94] Pay: H. C. Boren, *Historia* 1983, 427 ff., reviews all the hypotheses and produces a new one: it is only certain that the legionary received about 120 *denarii* in Polybius' time and 225 in AD 14; cf. ch. 1 n. 56. Donatives: Fiebiger, *RE* s.v. *donativum*; *IM* 392 ff. Booty: Harris, 1979, 102 f., and Rich (cited in n. 58) justly stress that the prospect of booty could be a motive for volunteering. Resistance to conscription (Taylor, *JRS* 1962, 19 ff.) was doubtless most apt to occur when the prospect was small, and hardship and danger more certain.

[95] Plut. *Luc.* 14, 17, 19, 29 with 26. 2 (cf. App. *Mith.* 86 with 78), 30, 37. Cf. App. *Mith.* 82. Further texts in Harmand 1967, 411 n. 18; cf. 420 f., especially Hor. *Ep.* ii. 2. 26–40.

[96] Pliny, *NH* xxxvii. 16; Plut. *Pomp.* 45. 3; App. *Mith.* 116. Booty and Tigranes' gifts (Str. xi. 14. 10; Plut. 33. 6; App. 104) are not included.

[97] Plut. *Caes.* 17; Suet. *Caes.* 67 f.; App. ii. 47; cf. Dio xli. 26; Caes. *BC* iii. 6, 90, *contra* Lucan v. 273; see, more generally, Nic. Dam. *FGH* 90 F 130. 41.

endemic in many provinces. In 48–47 Quintus Cornificius took some Illyrian forts and was able to distribute some booty, 'quae etsi erat tenuis, tamen in tanta desperatione provinciae erat grata' (*B. Alex.* 42. 3). Octavian in 36 tried to make his soldiers believe that they could be enriched by plunder in Illyricum (App. *BC* v. 28), but the country was poor (Dio xlix. 36) and the prospect probably illusory.

We have also to reckon with opportunities for illicit enrichment. Some commanders could not maintain discipline (n. 77), and were careless of the rights and interests of the civil population. The Cypriots paid governors of Cilicia 200 talents a year to be spared the winter quartering of troops (Cic. *Att.* v. 21. 7). Lucullus and Pompey made their armies winter under canvas;[98] but this was perhaps exceptional. According to Cicero, the entry of Roman soldiers into a provincial city differed little 'ab hostili expugnatione', and he justly surmises that the sufferings of the subjects must have been worse than those recently inflicted in Italy itself.[99]

Civil wars accentuated the sufferings of civilians and the opportunities of soldiers. In the Social war Sulla ingratiated himself with his troops by relaxing discipline and by allowing them to pillage Aeclanum.[100] Proscribed and dependent on the loyalty of his army in 84, he quartered them on the Asian cities and ordered their unwilling hosts to pay each man 12 *denarii* a day, about as much in ten days as their annual *stipendium* (Plut. *Sulla* 25. 2). In Italy he won golden opinions at first, important for his final success, by keeping his men to a pledge to abstain from plundering;[101] but as the war developed, he had to live off the country;[102] whole cities were sacked.[103] Caesar tried to spare Italy from plunder and punished soldiers who resorted to it;[104] even in the provinces he was generally scrupulous and preferred, as in Africa, to impose heavy fines out of which he could reward his soldiers.[105] But his own deputies were laxer in control (*B. Alex.* 48. 2, 49, 65). The Italians suffered severely from military depredations in the years 44–40, as in the 80s;[106] in the winter of 43–42, for instance, the triumvirs quartered their armies on the Italian towns, which had to provide the men with free board and to submit to their illegal rapine (Dio xlvii. 14. 3 f.). Servius Sulpicius and the Augustan jurist Labeo

---

[98] Plut. *Luc.* 33. 3; Cic. *de imp. Cn. Pomp.* 39.

[99] Cic. *de imp. Cn. Pomp.* 13, 37 f.; *Pis.* 86, 91.

[100] Plut. *Sulla* 6. 8 f. (cf. 12. 9; Sall. *Cat.* 11); App. i. 51. 223.

[101] Plut. *Sulla* 27. 3; Vell. ii. 25; Dio, fr. 108 f. [102] App. i. 86. 389.

[103] App. i. 94. 438 (Praeneste); 88. 401 (Sena Gallica); Cic. II *Verr.* i. 36 (Ariminum); Florus ii. 9. 28 (Sulmo). Cf. *IM*, ch. xviii.

[104] Dio xli. 26; cf. Caes. *BC* i. 21, *B. Afr.* 54. *BC* i. 28. 1 points a contrast with Pompey.

[105] Caes. *BC* ii. 22 (but cf. iii. 56, 80), *B. Afr.* 3, 7, 26. 5. But note Suet. *Caes.* 54. 3.

[106] Cic. *Phil.* iii. 31, vii. 15. 26; App. iv. 35.

had occasion to discuss the incidence of liability as between landlord and tenant in Italy 'si exercitus praeteriens per lasciviam aliquid abstulit'; or to take a concrete instance, when the tenant had fled in terror at the mere approach of the soldiery, and they had removed the window-frames and everything else from his farmhouse (*Dig.* xix. 2. 15. 2, 2. 13. 7). As in AD 69 and the later empire, the soldiers showed little sympathy or solidarity with the peasantry from whom they themselves were drawn.[107] They did, however, insist in 41 that their own relatives and the fathers and sons of their comrades who had fallen in battle should be spared the confiscation of their lands (Dio xlviii. 9. 3).

Desire for plunder made the soldiers readier to follow their generals in civil wars, irrespective of the cause they professed to represent; 'praemia miles dum maiora petit, damnat causamque ducemque' (Lucan v. 246 f.). Sulla, the first to turn his army against the government at Rome, probably appealed to their cupidity; his soldiers almost forced him to march on Rome in 88, as, according to Appian (i. 57. 252), they were afraid that if he were replaced in the eastern command, other legions would enjoy the spoils of Asia. In 83 he employed bribes and promises as well as appeals to friendship and coercion in raising reinforcements (ibid. 86. 393). When Caesar crossed the Rubicon, a gesture he made led his soldiers to believe that he was promising to make every man among them an *eques* (Suet. *Caes.* 33). Certainly neither he nor his opponents spared promises of great rewards.[108] At his triumph in 46 Caesar gave each veteran 5,000 or 6,000 *denarii*.[109] After his death rival commanders and the senate itself vied in undertakings to enrich the soldiers.[110] Ruthless exactions in the east enabled the high-minded Brutus and Cassius, after paying one donative, to promise their men 1,500 *denarii* apiece, and after the first battle of Philippi Brutus actually distributed 1,000. At the same time the triumvirs promised their soldiers 5,000 each. Not since Cannae had there been such a slaughter of Italians, and it was primarily for

---

[107] N. H. Baynes, *Byz. Studies* 307 ff. (= *JRS* 1929, 229). See for instance Tac. *Hist.* ii. 87. 2.

[108] For Caesar cf. Caes. *BC* i. 39. 3 f.; iii. 6, *B. Alex.* 77. 2; Suet. *Caes.* 38. 1; App. ii. 47, 92; Dio xli. 23. 1, xlii. 52. 1, 54. 2 (perhaps nothing had been paid by Sept. 47; cf. Cic. *Att.* xi. 22. 2 with App. ii. 92). For Pompeians, Caes. *BC* i. 17, 21, ii. 28, iii. 82. Curio: Caes. *BC* ii. 39. 3.

[109] 5,000: App. ii. 102; Dio xliii. 21; 6,000: Suet. *Caes.* 38, perhaps including 1,000 promised (App. ii. 92) or actually paid (Plut. *Caes.* 51; cf. Dio xlii. 54. 2) during the mutiny of 47 BC, or else an extra largess after Munda, when he feasted the plebs (Suet. 38; Pliny, *NH* xiv. 97) and perhaps gave the soldiers another donative. Or perhaps Gallic veterans received 1,000 more than the rest.

[110] Thus in 44 Octavian gave veterans 500 *denarii* (Cic. *Att.* xvi. 8. 1; App. iii. 40) and then 500 more, with a promise of 5,000 (App. iii. 48), ratified by the senate (ibid. 65, 86, cf. Cic. *Phil.* v. 53, vii. 10, etc.); the senate's attempt to delay payment in full was one factor that enabled Octavian to march on Rome in 43, when the senate vainly offered 5,000 to all his troops (App. iii. 86, 89 f.; ch. 1 n. 125); Antony's parsimony and attempt to impose strict discipline caused desertions (ibid. 43; cf. *Phil.* v. 22, etc.). For bribes offered to Spanish legions, cf. *Fam.* x. 32. 4.

mercenary motives that the armies fought.[111] The lavish monetary gifts made or at least promised to soldiers on whom their generals were dependent might much exceed the sum of 3,000 *denarii* which Augustus thought adequate as a bounty to legionaries who had served for twenty years or more (Dio lv. 23. 1). But in the late Republic the soldiers were not content with money: they wanted land.

IV

In and before the early second century allotments of land had sometimes been made to veterans (cf., n. 4). But there is no good evidence that the senate continued this practice after about 150 BC. It could take no credit for Saturninus' laws, providing for grants of land to Marius' veterans (Appendix II). The colonization of soldiers by Sulla was his personal policy, not that of the senate. R. E. Smith indeed argued that after Marius it became 'accepted practice' for grants of land to be made to veterans.[112] Thus he suggests that governors customarily gave men demobilized from the standing armies in the provinces 'a piece of land, probably in the vicinity of the garrison town, or a sum of money with which to buy a property for themselves'. He has shown that legionaries sometimes settled in provinces where they had served, and it is likely enough that they were farmers or at least landowners; there was no other investment that offered better security than land, and few of them had any civilian experience except in agriculture. But we can readily suppose that they acquired land by purchase out of their military profits, or even by sheer violence. Only in Spain have we records of a very few colonial foundations such as Italica (205 BC), where soldiers were or may have been settled, apart from the settlement of Marian veterans in Africa, Corsica, and perhaps Cisalpina (Appendix II).

As for troops discharged in Italy, it is plain that they had little or no chance of securing land allotments there from the voluntary action of the senate; they had to look to their generals (cf. Cic. *de leg. agr.* ii. 54), and few generals had the influence and the lack of constitutional scruples to force through agrarian bills. The senate is said to have approved land allotments to veterans of the Sertorian war, probably under a *lex Plotia* of 70 BC. But the situation was revolutionary; Pompey did not disband his army in 71 and used his power to undo part of Sulla's work; the senate was perhaps not a free agent.[113] Cicero

---

[111] App. iv. 89, 100, 120; Plut. *Ant.* 23. 1.   [112] Smith, 1958, 51 ff.

[113] See *contra* A. N. Sherwin-White, *JRS* 1956, 5–7. But the conduct of Metellus Pius in 71 (Sall. *Hist.* iv. 49) and Pompey in 62 (Vell. ii. 40. 3; Plut. *Pomp.* 43; Dio xxxvii. 30. 6), when he did not realise fears evoked by his conduct in 71, shows that it was irregular for him to retain his army even till his triumph on the last day of 71; cf. R. E. Smith, *Phoenix* 1960, 1 ff. Sherwin-White's

condemned the *lex Plotia* (*Att.* i. 18. 6), and in 59 BC it had still not been implemented. In 63 Rullus' bill was defeated; ostensibly, according to Cicero, it was designed to settle the poor on the land (p. 251); but if it had been passed, Crassus and Caesar would have been able to make a deal with Pompey; he required lands for his troops, and they would have had lands to dispose of.[114] The optimates resisted Flavius' proposals to settle the Pompeian veterans, and Caesar's bills in 59 could be carried only by violence against their continued opposition; the senate could not meet force with force, because the triumvirs had at their bidding the veterans themselves, and Caesar's army.[115] After Caesar's death in 44 his veterans feared, not without reason, that if the optimates recovered power, their allotments would be in jeopardy.[116] These fears combined with their affection for Caesar to make them irreconcilable with the 'Liberators'. At last in 43 the senate saw the necessity of satisfying the desire for land at least of those soldiers on whom it depended for victory over Antony. Cicero's motion of the 1 January promised increased allotments to the veterans of the VIIth and VIIIth legions, whom Octavian had recalled to the standards, and liberal assignations to the legionaries, raised in or since 49, who had deserted Antony; money and other privileges were also voted (*Phil.* v. 53). Pansa's agrarian law doubtless embodied the terms of this motion.[117] But even now senatorial generosity was restricted and insincere. Nothing was promised to the new recruits, or to the provincial armies; and once it appeared that Antony had been decisively beaten, the senate tried to fob off the veterans of VII and VIII with half the donative promised; it was Octavian's march on Rome that brought about a tardy repentance; only then did it vote to pay the full sum to the veterans, and to his other soldiers too (n. 110). It would certainly have been wise for the senate to have followed the precedent set by Sulla, and to have adopted the practice which Smith supposes to have been normal. The evidence shows that it did not.

In the eyes of the optimates it cost too much money to buy land (cf. n. 146), while redistribution of the public domain violated the sacred rights of possessors and the just law of inequality, and shook the very foundations of the state.[118] In 59 neither objection could be raised to

---

alleged precedent from 180 BC is nothing of the kind; Livy xl. 43. 4 f. merely means that Q. Flaccus triumphed with the soldiers he had been permitted to bring back from Spain (cf. 35 f., esp. 36. 10), not his whole army; for a late parallel cf. Plut. *Luc.* 36. 4. Cf. Meier. *Athen.* 1962, n. 14.

[114] Cic. *de leg. agr.* ii. 54 is characteristically perverse.

[115] Plut. *Pomp.* 48. 1, *Luc.* 42. 6, *Caes.* 14. 3 6 and 8; Dio xxxviii. 5. 4. On 'exercitus Caesaris' (*Att.* ii. 16. 2) see now C. Meier, *Historia* 1961, 79 ff.

[116] App. ii. 125, 135, 141, iii. 87; Nic. Dam. F 130. 103. But see also n. 90.

[117] Cic. *Phil.* vii. 10, xi. 37, xii. 29, *Fam.* xi. 20, 21. 1.

[118] Cic. *de offic.* ii. 73, 78, *de rep.* i. 43. But Sulpicius, presumably the great jurist (*cos.* 51), wrote 'dividi tamen esse ius plebei rura largiter ad adoream' (Varro *LL* v. 40, amended by Lachmann).

Caesar's first agrarian bill; but it was feared that the popularity accruing to its authors would make them too powerful;[119] such a danger need never have arisen, if the senate itself had initiated similar measures. Force or the threat of force was necessary to overcome senatorial opposition. The soldiers had to look to their generals to apply this coercion, though few generals were both ready and able to exercise it.

But did the soldiers really desire or need land? Hugh Last expressed what I take to be a prevalent opinion that 'military service was the occupation of their choice, to be protracted as long as possible',[120] and that when the time for discharge at last came, what would have suited them was a pensions scheme (a device which incidentally did not occur to Augustus or his successors). Heitland, who recognized more clearly than most writers of his day that the legionaries were rustics, thought that they desired an easy life as proprietors and that the excitements of warfare unfitted them for the patient economy of farming.[121] Most recently, Gabba and Smith have suggested that on the whole they regarded land allotments as pieces of real estate, assets 'easily converted into money, rather than as a means of gaining a livelihood'.[122] How far are these views to be accepted?

In the first place, it seems to me that Last's view rests on an exaggerated estimate of the normal length of military service. The Table of Heraclea (v. 90) suggests that, as in the second century, six years with the legions was regarded as a normal term.[123] Most of the men Sulla recruited from the land and resettled there had served him for only two years, though many had doubtless fought in the Social war. Metellus Pius and Pompey disbanded legions in 71–70 after seven to ten campaigns. The soldiers Pompey demobilized in 61 had mostly been serving only since 68 or 67. The twenty legions which fought for the triumvirs at Philippi consisted mainly of men enlisted in 49–48; yet they could be said to have served their full time.[124] In 36 soldiers who had been recruited for the *bellum Mutinense* in 43 demanded and obtained their discharge on the same ground (n. 128). None of these veterans had been so long in the army that they need have forgotten how to work in the fields.

---

[119] Plut. *Cato Minor* 31; Dio xxxviii. 2. 3.   [120] *CAH* ix. 134.

[121] op. cit. (n. 63), 175 f.   [122] Smith, 1958, 52; cf. Gabba, 1973, 128 = 1976, 47 f.

[123] Steinwender, *Philol.* 1889, 285 ff., argued from (i) Livy xxvi. 28; (ii) xlii. 33 f.; cf. xxxiv. 49 (Ligustinus' regular service, 200–195 BC); (iii) xxxix. 39; (iv) xl. 36; cf. xxxix. 20, 30, 33; (v) App. *Iber.* 78, that 6 years was usual practice in the third and second centuries. Steinwender's other arguments, and those of E. Cavaignac, *Rév. de Phil.* 1951, 169 ff., are more fragile. The text in Polyb. vi. 19. 2 is uncertain, and even if '16' is read there, evidence remains that so long a term of service was unusual. Cf. *IM* 400 ff. *Contra* L. R. Taylor, *JRS* 1962, 24, App. *Iber.* 78 does not suggest any innovation in 140. Lucilius' 19 years (490 f. M.) must be quite exceptional.

[124] App. v. 3; Dio xlviii. 2. 3; cf. in general *IM* 488 f. on the triumvirs' legions. App. iii. 42.

6   There were indeed soldiers who preferred to remain in the army or were not content to settle down on farms. In 68 the so-called Valerians who had gone out to Asia in 86 were mutinous; their discharge was authorized; in 67 they disbanded, but in 66 they joined up again with Pompey (Dio xxxvi. 16. 3, 46. 1). (There is no record that they were offered land as an alternative.) According to Caesar (*BC* i. 86), Pompey's men in Spain looked on discharge as a reward in itself; yet some of them found their way to fight for Pompey once more in the east (iii. 88. 3). Appian tells us that in 44 veterans from Caesar's old viith and viiith legions rallied to Octavian when they remembered 'the toils of agriculture and the profits of military service' (App. iii. 42). They were survivors from two legions which Caesar had taken over on becoming governor of the Gauls in 59 BC (*BG* viii. 8. 2), and though we must in my judgment suppose that all Caesar's legions, depleted though they were in the 40s, had received new recruits during the Gallic wars, it is likely that many of these men had served for an exceptionally long time; they had also found their service exceptionally lucrative. This isolated statement on the attitude of certain veterans has little force when contrasted with the other evidence that shows how anxious they were to retain the allotments granted or promised by Caesar (n. 116). In 42 after Philippi the triumvirs decided to settle their time-expired soldiers in Italy, except for those who desired to remain in the army. The volunteers numbered 8,000. Their army consisted of twenty full legions (App. *BC* iv. 108; cf. 107), about 100,000 men; allowing for heavy losses and for new recruits of 43–42, not entitled to discharge, I would put the number of the time-expired at under 50,000 (n. 124). Even on this basis it was only about one man in six who wished to protract his service, though most of them had been in the army for no more than seven years.

7   On some occasions the soldiers actually demanded discharge. I have already referred to the mutiny of the Valerians (n. 71). From their later conduct it would seem that they did not truly desire to return to civil life, but were seeking to put pressure on Lucullus for a larger share in the spoils. In 51 the Senate tried to consider the right of Caesar's legions to discharge (Cic. *Fam.* viii. 8. 7), and in 50 it was widely believed that they were war-weary and would desert Caesar in the event of war.[125] The belief was quite false, yet it was entertained by Pompey himself; and he, if anyone, should have understood the normal and natural wishes of soldiers after prolonged and arduous campaigns. In 49 the ixth legion, one with the longest service, actually mutinied; the men claimed that they were exhausted. Dio held that their real

---

[125] Caes. *BC* i. 6. 2; Plut. *Caes.* 29. 4, *Pomp.* 57. 4; App. ii. 30. Cf. Rice Holmes, 1923 iii. 2 n. 2.

motive was dissatisfaction with Caesar's refusal to permit them to plunder at will; and they openly demanded payment of a promised donative.[126] But is it not possible that a wave of temporary war-weariness passed through the legion? Lucan, for what his evidence may be worth, suggests that they desired peace as well as *praemia* (v. 243, 270 ff.); these perhaps conflicting motives may have operated on different men, or on the same men at different moments. In 47 there was a more general mutiny of the veterans; again they demanded discharge, and again Dio and Appian say that they were really seeking donatives.[127] It is of interest that Caesar did on this occasion release some soldiers—'those who were fairly well versed in farming and could make a living' (Dio xlii. 55. 1)—perhaps later recruits with the keenest taste for agriculture, or more substantial farmers who had been conscribed in Cisalpina. It must be stressed once more that the Gallic veterans are probably untypical of the soldiers of the late Republic. In 43 legions raised in or after 49 were described as 'bello confectae', and it was proposed to reward them with discharge and exemption from future call-ups (Cic *Phil*. v. 53). In 36 Octavian had to face mutinies from his veterans in Sicily, and he was obliged to discharge 20,000 who had served at Mutina and Philippi and whose time had expired. Some of these men were no doubt former soldiers of Brutus and Cassius, recruited by Caesar in or after 49 and incorporated in the three legions Octavian brought home from Philippi; but service as recent as 43 sufficed for discharge. Again it would seem that not all of them genuinely wished to return to civil life; some volunteered anew and were formed into a special legion. Their number we may compute at about 5,000. Thus, of those disbanded in 36, three men out of four were tired of the military life.[128] If we look forward, we find that the length of service under Augustus was one of the chief complaints of the mutineers on the Rhine and Danube in AD 14.[129]

Republican soldiers did not show such a zest for civil wars as the professional armies in AD 68–9 and later. (Yet though they were risky and repugnant to sentiment, they brought the prospect of largesses and relaxation of discipline.) In 83 Sulla gained over the legions of Lucius Scipio, partly when it was made to appear that Scipio had frustrated the hopes of peace.[130] At the onset of the struggle in 49 Italians were reluctant to enlist under Pompey, as they thought that Caesar's terms were reasonable (Plut. *Pomp*. 59. 2); and Caesar played on the general

[126] App. ii. 47 (500 *den.*); Dio xli. 26 ff.; cf. Rice Holmes, 1923 iii. 109.
[127] Cic. *Att*. xi. 21. 2, 22. 2; Plut. *Caes*. 51; Suet. *Caes*. 70; App. ii. 92 ff.; Dio xlii. 30. 1, 52 ff. Cf. Plut. 37 for trouble in 48. Cf. Rice Holmes, 1923, iii. 232–40.
[128] App. v. 128 f., Dio xlix. 13 f., 34; Oros. vi. 18. 33.
[129] Tac. *Ann*. i. 17. 2 f., 31. 1, 36. 3. Note 16. 1, 'nullis novis causis'.
[130] App. i. 85; Florus ii. 9. 19. Plut. *Sulla* 28 (cf. Sall. *Hist*. i. 91) alleges corruption.

desire for peace even in addressing the soldiers (n. 83). This propaganda may have stimulated Pompeian desertions (Caes. *BC* i. 74; App. ii. 42). Caesar also paraded his care to avoid shedding the blood of Romans fighting for his enemies (i. 72, 81 f., iii. 86. 4, 90. 2), remembering no doubt that there were neighbours and kinsmen on both sides (i. 74), and though his own troops sometimes did not share this sentiment (i. 81 f.), it affected them on other occasions (i. 74), and Lepidus could pretend that his troops in going over to Antony in 43 had shown 'consuetudinem suam in civibus conservandis communique pace'; he must have thought that it provided an excuse for his conduct that was at least plausible. It is in fact clear that in 44–43 Caesar's Gallic veterans were generally averse to fighting each other, that in 41 it was the soldiers through their officers who tried to patch up the conflict between Octavian and Lucius Antonius, and that in 40 the veterans forced Octavian and Antony to come together.[131] Among other reasons the recrudescence of war endangered their possession of lands. In 36 Octavian had to promise the mutineers that he would fight no more civil wars. Tacitus' judgment is also to be noted: 'populum annona, militem donis, cunctos dulcedine otii pellexit' (*Ann.* i. 2). 'Cunctos' includes the soldiers; they too desired peace—if only as the guarantee of the rewards they had won.

But is it true that it was not so much land that veterans wanted as the cash value of land? The suggestion does not seem very plausible. Flavius and Caesar himself proposed that the new revenues derived from Pompey's conquests should be used to purchase lands for veterans.[132] If in fact what the veterans desired was cash, in addition to the gratuities they had already received from Pompey, how much simpler it would have been to enact that further bounties should be paid to them out of the state's new income. Why was it taken for granted by Caesar as Dictator, by the senate in 43, and by the triumvirs that the best way of satisfying veterans on discharge was not that of augmenting their monetary rewards but of allotting lands to them, though the purchase of land was no less costly than increased bounties, and confiscations perpetuated discord in the state? An answer is not hard to give. The veteran might squander ready money, and in that case he would remain a discontented and dangerous element in the community, or he might try to invest it, and he then had no sound alternative to buying land for himself; there were no gilt-

---

[131] Nic. Dam. F 130. 115 ff.; App. iii. 42 (44 BC); Cic. *Fam.* x. 35. 1; cf. App. iii. 84 (Lepidus' army), but cf. *Fam.* x. 33. 3 (Pollio's) (43 BC); App. v. 20–4; Dio xlviii. 11 f. (41 BC); App. v. 57–64 (40 BC); v. 124, 128 (twice in 36 BC). Cf. now W. Schmitthenner, *Hist. Zeitschr.* 1960, 12 ff., esp. on the role of the officers. The importance Dionys. Hal. (xi. 42–4) assigns to centurions in a military revolt probably reflects experience in our period.

[132] Cic. *Att.* i. 19. 4; Dio xxxviii. 1. 5.

edged securities, no life insurance, while business and trade were precarious and outside the experience of all but a few soldiers; most of them were farmers or farm-labourers by origin. The allocation of land was thus not in Last's phrase 'a haphazard expedient',[133] but the most natural course to adopt.[134]

Naturally not all the military colonists made good. The more feckless among them might decide to realize their assets before even giving a fair trial to farming. Sulla made his allotments inalienable, probably for a term of years, but the rule seems to have broken down.[135] Caesar followed his example, and Brutus and Cassius vainly sought popularity with the veterans by proposing to annul this safeguard.[136] We know that some Caesarian veterans soon tired of agriculture (App. iii. 42). We know too that many of the Sullan settlers had failed by 63 (n. 47). That is not astonishing. The decay of the yeomanry before 133, the failure of the Gracchan scheme, must be remembered. Why should it be supposed that in the adverse economic conditions of the years between 80 and 63 (p. 252) small farmers should have been more successful than their predecessors but for defects derived from their having served in the army? The Sullan colonists were inevitably unpopular, and it is a familiar fact that a class which is unpopular as a whole is easily branded with the worst qualities of its worst members. We can well believe that some of Sulla's soldiers were spendthrifts who looked back with regret to the violence and plundering of civil war (Sall. *Cat.* 16. 4); but they need have been no more than a small minority. There must be some truth too in Lepidus' reported allegation that some of them had been fobbed off with poor land—'paludes et silvas'.[137]

The size of allotments is seldom recorded reliably, but probably varied between 25 and $66\frac{2}{3}$ *iugera*, according to the fertility of the soil. Farms of this size could be worked by the settler himself with the aid of his family or of a few slaves, whom he would have been able to purchase from his share in booty or from the cash donative he had also received, but would hardly have yielded an adequate return, if he had leased them to tenants or committed management to a *vilicus*. The meagre evidence of veterans' tombstones, especially in the territories of triumviral or Augustan colonies at Beneventum and Ateste, suggests that they often lived on their farms in the countryside and were not *rentiers* domiciled in the cities; of course residents in a town could also work fields in its close vicinity.[138] Officers would receive larger

---

[133] *CAH* ix. 137. Keppie, 1983, 126 n. 127, collects the little evidence for veterans in urban occupations.

[134] Cf. Lucan i. 343–5, vii. 257 f.　　　[135] Cic. *de leg. agr.* ii. 78.

[136] App. iii. 2, 7.　　　[137] Sall. *Or. Lepidi* 21–4; cf. Cic. *de leg agr.* ii. 68–70, iii. 2.

[138] Keppie, 1983, 91 ff., largely supersedes *IM* 295 ff., but not the remarks on Sullan allotments, ibid. 309 f. Plut. *Cr.* 2. 8 alleges allotments by Marius of 14 *iugera*.

allotments, and they could indeed become *rentiers* if they chose: the choice would be not unnatural and would not prove that the settler was incapable of farming himself. We have a glimpse of what might happen in one of Horace's Satires (ii. 2. 112 ff.). Ofellus, a substantial working farmer, has lost his lands to the soldier, Umbrenus; he remains as a tenant on part of his former land. I get the impression that Ofellus still rented a fairly large farm; surely then Umbrenus was an officer, who would have been given more acres than a common soldier. Ofellus surveys the future and says of Umbrenus:

> Illum aut nequities aut vafri inscitia iuris,
> postremum expellet certe vivacior heres.

The land may pass to Umbrenus' heir, but he may lose it through incapacity or through 'ignorance of the subtle law'. The last phrase may remind us that when military settlers did not make good, it was not always from ignorance of agricultural techniques.[139] Like all small farmers, they would in any event have had no option but to borrow in a bad season, and if that were followed by others, they would have been unable to repay the loans and ultimately have forfeited the ownership or enjoyment of their farms; this process cannot have been effectively hindered by the provision imposed by the Gracchi, Sulla, Caesar, and perhaps in all cases, that debarred them from alienating the allotments by sale, at least for a period of years. Still, the triumviral and Augustan colonies may have been on the whole successful. At any rate Augustus boasts that twenty-eight colonies he had founded in Italy were flourishing in his reign (*RG* 28. 2).

It may be said that Augustus' decision in 13 BC to substitute cash bounties on discharge for the land allotments 'the soldiers were always demanding' (Dio liv. 25. 5) reflects the government's experience that the soldier did not make a good farmer. More probably it was due to the impossibility of continuing to provide farms in Italy without disturbance of property rights.[140] Moreover, in AD 14 the mutineers complained that on discharge they were dragged away to widely scattered lands 'ubi per nomen agrorum uligines paludum vel inculta montium accipiant' (Tac. *Ann.* i. 17). Augustus had then not given up the practice of settling veterans on the land outside Italy. At all times in the Principate veterans received lands. The mutineers did not object in principle to this: it was the remoteness and poor quality of the lands actually assigned against which they protested. Probably they were

---

[139] Cf. perhaps the corrupt text in App. i. 27. 124; see Cic. *Caec.* 6 (law's delays), II *Verr.* iii. 27 (hardships litigation imposed on working farmers). Cf. n. 53.

[140] See e.g. Suet. *Aug.* 56. 2; cf. *Tib.* 29 ('singulis'); *ILS* 244. 17 ('privatarum') for imperial respect for private interests.

mostly Italians and would have been well content with farms in Italy. By the time of Nero, when the legionaries had come to be provincial by origin or adoption, it was settlement in Italy far from their homes that they disliked (Tac. *Ann.* xiv. 27.). Military colonies in the provinces were anything but failures. In Africa, for instance, colonists who had served twenty-five years, much longer than most Republican legionaries, helped to push forward the area of cultivation and peaceful order.[141] This hardly fits the notion that the peasant soldier was incapable in favourable economic conditions of earning his livelihood after his army service by a return to the land.

I do not indeed follow J. Kromayer[142] in arguing that the successive settlements of veterans in Italy between Sulla and Augustus restored the class of proprietors and reduced the preponderance of *latifundia*. It will suffice to say, firstly, that in each successive redistribution of lands, while some large estates were broken up, others were formed for the benefit of influential partisans of the victor and that perhaps most of the military colonists only replaced other middling and small farmers; and, secondly, that the economic factors may have remained adverse to small farming; if so, the effects of land distribution may have been ephemeral. There is some reason to think that under the Principate the number of small, independent farmers continued to fall. We cannot expect to hear much of this decline. No seditious tribunes could any longer voice their grievances; and as Roman armies were to an ever-increasing extent recruited in the provinces, the government had less reason to be concerned with the military consequences of a diminution in Italian manpower.

V

The Roman revolution, then, effected no permanent changes in the agrarian society of Italy. At best a number of those rural workers who had served in the legions bettered themselves individually. They had never fought in the interests of their class. There was no doctrine or programme to give the peasantry a sense of solidarity, and the leaders sought not to direct the rural masses in efforts to secure clearly conceived social changes, but simply to reward their own soldiers for their own ends. None the less, it was the wretchedness of the population from whom the army was recruited that enabled leaders whose primary concern was their own enrichment or aggrandizement to threaten and finally to subvert the Republic. Modern historians

---

[141] F. A. Lepper reminded me also of the evidence that imperial legions had their territories or *prata*; cf. e.g. Rostovtzeff, 1957, ch. VI, nn. 65, 74, 78, 81.

[142] *Neue Jahrb. f. kl. Altertums* 1914, 145 ff. See *contra IM*, ch. XIX.

properly devote their skill to elucidating the aims and ambitions of these leaders, their intrigues and combinations. Yet their designs could not have been accomplished if they had failed to find followers, and we need also to consider why the soldiers showed so little attachment to the old order.[143]

Moreover, since Augustus and his successors did no more than the senatorial government to ameliorate the condition of the rural poor, they too were confronted with the same problem that the senate had failed to solve; they too, in Tiberius' words, had to hold a wolf by the ears (Suet. *Tib.* 25). Augustus sought to restore stability (Suet. *Aug.* 28. 2), and for this purpose it was no less important to secure the loyalty of the troops than that of the old governing class. Here too his success was long-lasting, though not complete, as the mutinies of AD 14 and the revolts of 68–9 were to show. He was able to use more than one expedient. All the soldiers were bound to the emperor by the religious ties of the military oath and a personal oath of fealty.[144] There was also an aura of divinity about him. All commands and commissions, down to the centurionate, were in his gift; and he could hope to ensure that the soldiers would find no one to lead them in rebellion (ch. 1 n. 137). The conditions of service were improved. Caesar had doubled the pay of the common soldier, and Augustus seems to have greatly increased that of the centurions,[145] who in revolutionary times were the natural spokesmen and leaders of the troops (cf. n. 131). Donatives were given on suitable occasions. At the end of his long service the soldier could now expect a bounty in cash or an allotment of land; he was no longer discharged into destitution. All this cost money. In the Republic the optimates had been apt to meet any claims on behalf of the 'improbi et egentes' with the cry that the treasury could not afford them.[146] How could it when the 'boni et beati' needed so much from public funds?[147] In a single year as governor of Cilicia Cicero saved about enough from his allowances 'salvis legibus' to pay a legion.[148] Augustus found it necessary to reinstitute direct taxation of well-to-do Italians (in the form of the *vicesima hereditatium*) in order to pay discharged soldiers their *praemia*. It was much resented.[149] Even in the

[143] Schmitthenner, op. cit. (n. 131), 3.
[144] Cf. p. 439. See especially P. Herrmann, 1968.   [145] Brunt, *PBSR*, 1950, 67.
[146] See especially *de offic.* ii. 72–9; cf. *de leg. agr.* ii. 10 (obviously insincere), 15, *Att.* i. 19. 4 (specious), ii. 3. 3, 16. 1, 17. 1, *Sest.* 103, *de dom.* 23, *Tusc. Disp.* iii. 48, *ad Her.* i. 12. 21.
[147] Sall. *BJ* 41. 7; *Or. Macri* 6; Plut. *Cato Minor* 18. 1.
[148] *Fam.* v. 20. 9 (2,200,000 HSS). Piso apparently with legality invested his allowance of 18,000,000 at Rome (*Pis.* 86; cf. 61). Pompey was voted 24,000,000 for his six legions in 52 (Plut. *Caes.* 28. 5, *Pomp.* 55. 7): more than enough (cf. *IM* 714). Governors made legal profits from sums voted 'cellae nomine', II *Verr.* iii. 195, 217. For sheer peculation cf. *de imp. Cn. Pomp.* 37. Cf ch. 1 n. 110.
[149] Dio lv. 24. 9–25. 6, lvi. 28. 4–6. Cf. on the *centesima* Tac. *Ann.* i. 78, ii. 42. 4.

last struggle of the Republic the rich, as Cicero complained, were reluctant to pay *tributum*.[150] They were to find that the price they had been unwilling to pay for retaining their liberties had to be paid, after those liberties had been lost, to preserve order and stability. In refusing to satisfy the needs even of those 'miseri' whom they were obliged to arm, the Republican ruling class had displayed not only a lack of social sympathy which is conspicuous in their policy as a whole, but also a lack of prudence that was fatal to their power and privileges.

[150] Cic. *Fam.* xii. 30. 4; *Brut.* i. 18. 5. Cf. *de offic.* ii. 74.

APPENDIXES

I. Areas of Recruitment for the Republican Army

All Italy	87 BC	Plut. *Mar.* 41 (Cinna)—not at Rome
	84–82	App. i. 76 f., 81, 86 (Marians)
	83–82	App. i. 86 (Sulla)—not at Rome
	52	Cic. *Mil.* 67 f., Caes. *BG* vii. 1; Ascon. 34. 5 C.; Dio xl. 50. 1
	49	Caes. *BC* i. 7; App. ii. 34
	43	Cic. *Phil.* v. 31 (Cisalpina excepted, as D. Brutus had already levied troops there), vii. 13, 21; xii. 16; xiii. 5, 23, xiv. 5, *Fam.* xii. 5, 2; App. iii. 65, 91
	41	App. v. 27, 74
Urbs Roma	90	Dio, fr. 100; for freedmen cf. *Per.* Livy lxxiv; App. i. 49; Macr. i. 11. 32.
	83 (?)	App. i. 82. 373; but cf. p. 254
	63 (?)	Dio xxxvii. 35. 4 (tumultuary levy by Cicero, cf. n. 60)
	49 (?)	Caes. *BC* i. 14. 4 ('circa urbem')
	43	Cic. *Phil.* x. 21, *Fam.* xi. 8. 2.
Cisalpina (cf. Harmand 257)	90	Plut. *Sert.* 4
	87	App. i. 67. 308
	83	App. i. 86. 393
	63	Cic. *Cat.* ii. 5
	58–57	Caes. *BG* i. 7, ii. 2
	54–52	Caes. *BG* v. 24, vi. 1, vii. 1 (cf. 7. 5, 57. 1)
	50	Dio xl. 60. 1
	49	Caes. *BC.* i. 18, cf. iii. 87. 4 ('plerique ex coloniis Transpadanis'); cf. for Opitergium, Lucan iv. 462; Florus ii. 13. 33; *Per.* Livy cx
	44–43	Cic. *Phil.* v. 36, xii. 9 (D. Brutus); vii. 21 (Antony)
	41	Dio xlviii. 12. 5
Etruria	87	App. i. 67; Plut. *Mar.* 41. 2
	44	App. iii. 42; Dio xlv. 12. 6
	43	Cic. *Fam.* x. 33. 4, *Phil.* xii. 33; App. iii. 42, 66
		Cf. levies by Lepidus in 78 and Catiline in 63

Picenum (cf. E. Gabba, 1973, 90)	83	Vell. ii. 29; Plut. *Pomp.* 6
	63	Cic. *Cat.* ii. 5; Sall. *Cat.* 30
	49	Cic. *Att.* viii. 12B. 2; Caes. *BC* i. 13–5
	43	App. iii. 66, 72, 93
Umbria	64	Cic. *Mur.* 42
	49	Cic. *Att.* viii. 12B. 2; Caes. *BC* i. 12
		Cf. also *ILS* 2231
Ager Sabinus	49	Suet. *Vesp.* 1. 2
Latium/Campania	87	App. i. 65. 294 with 66. 302
	63	Sall. *Cat.* 30
	49	Cic. *Att.* viii. 11B. 2 (Camp.), ix. 19. 1 (near Arpinum); Caes. *BC* i. 14 etc.
	44	Cic. *Att.* xvi. 8. 1, 9; Nic. Dam. (Jacoby no. 90) F 130. 136–8; Vell. ii. 61. 2; App. iii. 40; Dio xlv. 12. 2
	44–43	Cic. *Phil.* vii. 22 (by Antony) Cf. also Cic. *de leg. agr.* ii. 84; *ILS* 2225
Marsi, Paeligni, Marrucini	83	Plut. *Crass.* 6. 3
	49	Caes. *BC* i. 15, 20, ii. 24, 27, 28. 1, 29. 3, 34. 3, 35. 1
	43	Cic. *Phil.* vii. 23 Cf. Hor. *Odes* iii. 5. 5
Samnium	44	Cic. *Att.* xvi. 11. 6 with 8. 1 Cf. *ILS* 2234
Lucania and Bruttium	55	Pliny *NH* ii. 147
	49	Caes. *BC* i. 30.
Apulia	49	Cic. *Att.* vii. 12. 2; Caes. *BC* i. 24 Cf. EJ[3] 368, *ILS* 2224; Hor. l.c.

(The alleged disqualification for military service of Picentes, Lucanians, and Bruttians after the Hannibalic war (*IM*, p. 280) naturally has no bearing on the situation after the enfranchisement of Italy. The Lucanians at least could provide numerous soldiers in the Social war (Diod. xxviii–xxxix. 13), and had continued to furnish troops for Rome's armies (ibid. xxxvi. 8. 1).)

Note also legions named Sorana, Sabina, Mutinensis. For soldiers' homes in the Italian towns cf. Plut. *Pomp.* 43. 2; Sall. (?) *ad Caes.* i. 8. 6; *RG* 3, where Augustus says of some veterans 'remisi in municipia sua'; for this practice, cf. *IM* 297, 300, 304 f., 318–27, 329, 337 f., 342, 349–52, 356, 366, 609. In *IM* I argued that not only the allied communities before 90 but the various communes of Roman citizens both before and after that date, as well as the Cisalpine communes which received the *ius Latii* in 89, were responsible for raising troops under the *dilectus*, see pp. 37, 408, and App. 19, especially 631–4; thus, when a *dilectus* was ordered in any region or in all, the instructions went to the local magistrates. Note, in addition to the texts there cited, Dio. xxxviii–xxxix. 12; Caes. *BC* i. 23. 2: 'magnus numerus equitum

Romanorum et decurionum quos ex municipiis Domitius evocaverat'; ii. 29. 3: 'municipia [sc. in Italy] diversis partibus coniuncta'; i. 15. 2: 'milites imperat; mittunt' [sc. the people, or rather the magistrates, of Cingulum]; cf. more generally Cic. *Cat.* ii. 24: 'florem totius Italiae ac robur educite. Iam vero urbes coloniarum ac municipiorum respondebunt Catilinae tumulis silvestribus'; for the 80s, App. i. 66, 76; for 43 BC Cic. *Phil.* vii. 23, viii. 4 (indicating that fines might be imposed on towns for disobedience), xii. 7, 10. In 44 Octavian had indeed made a direct appeal to Caesar's veterans settled in Campania, but also sought the co-operation of the council at Calatia, Nic. Dam. F 130. 136 f. So too in Cisalpina Caesar 'provinciae toti quam maximum potest militum numerum imperat', where the 'whole province' equals the *municipia* and *coloniae*, cf. Cic. *Phil.* v. 36 with xii. 9. Some of these texts also refer to the collection of money from the towns (cf. also Dio xli. 9. 7; App. ii. 34; Caes. *BC* i. 6. 8), and supplies were evidently obtained in the same way (Caes. *BC* i. 18. 4; Vitruv. ii. 9. 15).

The triumviral *legio Urbana* was probably not a legion raised at Rome in 43 but one that was left for the defence of the city (App. iii. 19; Obsequens 69), see Ritterling, *RE* xii. 1587.

II. The Settlement of Marian Veterans

The book *de viris illustribus* 73 records that Saturninus as tribune, presumably in 103, proposed that veterans should each receive 100 *iugera* in Africa, and overrode the veto of his colleague Baebius by violence. A colony at Cerceina (*Inscr. Ital.* xiii. 3, no. 7) may have been founded in implementation of this law. J. -L. Ferrary, *Mél. Wuilleumier*, 110, notes that Cic. *de leg. agr.* ii. 38 ff. does not refer to the existence of any *ager publicus* in Africa, and infers that it had probably all been distributed among Marian veterans. I am not persuaded by this argument, but no refutation is possible. The question whether Marian veterans were also settled in Africa outside that province is entirely separate. I contended in *IM*, App. 12, that this could not be deduced from the fact that some African communities under the Principate commemorated Marius as *conditor*: it was native Africans that he had settled in them. To the parallels I gave (p. 579) one could add Pompey's foundations at Pompaelo (Strabo iii. 4. 10), Lugdunum Convenarum (Jerome, *adv. Vigilantium* 4; Strabo iv. 2. 1), Gadara (E. Schürer, *Hist. of Jewish People in the Age of Jesus Christ* ii. 134, revised Eng. tr.), and of course his foundations in Pontus (A. H. M. Jones, *Cities of the Eastern Roman Provinces*[2], 159). In Spain, Bracara Augusta, which only attained Latin status under Vespasian, celebrated Augustus as *conditor* (*CIL* ii. 2421). The prevalence of the name Marius in parts of Africa (P. Garnsey in Garnsey and Whittaker, *Imperialism in the Ancient World*, 250) suggests that Marius actually enfranchised native Africans on some scale. I therefore adhere to the view propounded in *IM* for the reasons given there.

De viris illustribus, now evidently referring to the year 100, also reports that Saturninus proposed to found colonies in Sicily, Achaea, and Macedon, and to appropriate the *aurum Tolosanum* to the purchase of lands; that seems to me the kind of detail that is unlikely to have been fabricated. We need not assume that no colonization was to be in Italy, or that the list of provinces given is complete. None in fact was founded in Sicily, Achaea, and Macedon, but Eporedia in Cisalpine Gaul is dated by Velleius (i. 15) to 100, and another colony was established by Marius in Corsica (Pliny, *NH* iii. 80; Sen. *Cons. ad Helv.* 7. 9). The settlement at Cerceina may also have been authorized under this law rather than under that of 103. Appian also alleges that it was proposed to distribute land which had (it was pretended) been conquered from the Gauls (who therefore had no surviving title to it) by the Cimbri 'in what is now called Gaul by the Romans' (i. 29). Gabba ad loc. holds that Appian means Cisalpine Gaul, but this seems to me improbable. It was not remotely plausible that the Cimbri had annexed any land there, and the word 'now' rather suggests that Appian was thinking of what was still in his own day indubitably 'Gaul', as distinct from Cisalpina, which had long since constituted the *regiones* of Liguria, Transpadana, Venetia, and Aemilia within Italia, even though the term Cisalpina was still in non-technical use. It is of course immaterial that in Transalpina too no colonies were actually founded, and that there is no mention of Italian smallholders on the soil. All this is not to say that there were not also to be colonies in Cisalpina as in Sicily etc.; Appian too has given a very imperfect account of the law.

Cicero happens to tell us that Saturninus' law empowered Marius to grant Roman citizenship to Latins and perhaps other Italians (the number does not concern us here) enrolled in the colonies to be founded, and to report a case in which the validity of the grant to T. Matrinius was impugned in the courts on the basis that it was contingent on the foundation of the colonies and that they had not been founded (*Balb.* 48). The last statement is not true, *if* Eporedia or the Corsican colony or Cerceina were founded under the law in question. It would perhaps have been enough for the prosecutors of Matrinius if the colony for which he was registered had never been founded, and Cicero might have supposed that none had, if almost all which had been designed had been abortive, and particularly those to be sited in Italy.

It would be imprudent to assume that the plan of which we have such fragmentary information was confined to colonization in the provinces (including Cisalpina) and that it did not provide for viritane allotments as well as for colonies. The *Perioche* of Livy lxix in fact writes of a 'lex agraria', though this does not prove, especially given the character of the source, that there was also to be viritane settlement as under other agrarian laws. From Appian's account of the disturbances the proposal caused we can only discern that it was to benefit rural citizens (i. 29, 32, where they are also called *Italiotai*, which in the context should not designate Italian allies; 30. 134, 136; cf. 32, 143), as distinct from the urban plebs. An anecdote in Plutarch (*Crassus* 2) envisages Marius as himself concerned in the distribution of 14 *iugera* apiece to his veterans. This was surely in Italy. M. H. Crawford, *RRC* 629 f., thinks that the 'enormous' issues of coinage in 99–97 suggest that the *lex agraria* of

100 was put into effect and that 'Rome struck money specially for the purpose, to finance the viritane settlement of Marius' veterans'. This seems plausible.

We may conclude that as a result of Saturninus' two laws, though very few colonies were founded and none is recorded in Italy, some Marian veterans were settled *viritim* in the province of Africa, and others in Italy. There had been distant precedents for the viritane settlement of veterans (n. 4), but it was of course novel that the settlement should be forced through by popular agitation, and that to some extent it was to be effected outside Italy. Marius (or Saturninus) showed Sulla the necessity of rewarding veterans in this way, without (any more than Sulla) devising any system of such *praemia* for the future; and it was left to Caesar and his successors to resume making grants of provincial land.

6

LIBERTAS IN THE REPUBLIC

I. Some rival modern views: the supposed contrast of *libertas* and *eleutheria*; in fact to both Greeks and Romans freedom conceptually and in practice meant different things to different people. **II.** *Libertas* basically opposed to legal servitude, but also to lesser forms of private subjection; hence it admitted of degrees. The acceptance of slavery generated conceptions of the superior morality and social dignity of the free man, and inhibited development of the notion of freedom as an inalienable natural right. **III.** Ambiguity in the ascription of *libertas* to communities; either independence of external control or the freedom of citizens from internal despotism; in either case both for Greeks and Romans it admits of degrees. **IV.** Personal *libertas* rests on positive laws; though not identical with citizenship; not an abstract idea, but (as in England) a set of rights gradually acquired. **V.** The contrast drawn by Constant between ancient and modern concepts of freedom not wholly satisfying. (i) Greeks and Romans did not oppose the state, as an impersonal entity, to the individual: the state was the citizens. (ii) Many of the individual liberties comprised in Constant's ideal belonged to the Romans, more or less unchallenged and unrestricted, and therefore not consciously valued as liberties. Freedom of thought, of worship; attempted regulation of private morals (which could be regarded as detracting from freedom); individualism inherent in private law; freedom of association; economic *laissez-faire*. **VI.** Negative and positive sides to both Roman and Greek freedom (positive freedom equivalent to power). 'Doing what you please' not the only aspect of *eleutheria*, but a view of freedom even more abundantly illustrated in Latin usage. Freedom of speech at Rome. **VII.** Both Romans and Greeks could treat laws as at once restrictions and guarantees of freedom; nothing peculiarly Roman in the conception that freedom rests on the laws, which in any case derive at Rome from the people's will. **VIII.** Moderation or self-restraint can qualify *libertas* and is therefore not inherent in it; partisan distinctions between *libertas* and *licentia*. **IX.** Falsity of view that *libertas* comprises respect for *auctoritas* in popular conceptions; Cicero himself, who speaks for the aristocracy and does not express 'the Roman' conception (as if there were one), regards the liberty of the people and the authority of the senate as countervailing forces and wishes the former to be a mere sham. **X.** He values the liberty, i.e. the power, of senators, but senatorial liberty also excludes the preponderant *auctoritas* of individuals. **XI.** The *libertas*, i.e. particular rights—even 'sovereignty'—valued by the people generally. Protection of the citizens from magistrates. **XII.** Equal liberty before the laws (with comparison of Athens). **XIII.** The *ius suffragii*; elections. The people's jurisdiction. **XIV.** Legislation. The connection of legislative power with the people's *commoda*. **XV.** Possibility that *libertas* could connote economic independence. **XVI.** Obstacles to democratic freedom. Extinction of political freedom in the Principate.

I

IN the political struggles of the late Republic frequent appeals were made on all sides to *libertas*. For Syme they were essentially fraudulent. 'Liberty and the laws are high-sounding words. They will often be rendered, on a cool estimate, as privilege and vested interests.' The name of liberty was usually invoked in defence of the existing order by the minority of rich and powerful oligarchs. 'The ruinous privilege of freedom' was extinguished in the Principate for the higher good of 'security of life and property'.

Other scholars, sometimes perhaps writing under Hegelian influence, and taking more account of the individual rights guaranteed to citizens by the laws, have idealized 'the Roman' concept of freedom, limited by law and morality, and inseparable from Roman respect for authority and discipline, which they admire in the Roman way of life; they can represent it as wholly reconcilable with obedience to the will of a small ruling class or even of the emperor held by their inferiors in due esteem; they sometimes contrast it with the wild licence supposedly inherent in the Greek concept of *eleutheria*, the right of men to live as they please.[1]

Both types of analysis take too little account of the predominantly aristocratic character of our literary sources and pay insufficient attention to evidence that shows liberty as a term that could express the interests and views of the common people, as well as of feuding oligarchs. Moreover, though Syme was right in holding that on the lips of the nobility it often veiled their selfish attachment to power and its perquisites, he was wrong in my judgement in suggesting at least by insinuation that it was no more than a catchword, proclaimed in conscious cynicism, and that some, perhaps most, of them did not sincerely believe that the liberty or power they possessed under the Republican constitution was essential to the public good. In the same way the common people were surely attached to the different personal and political rights which their spokesmen subsumed under the name of liberty by sentiment and tradition, as well as by consciousness of the

---

[1] See *RR* 2, 59, 154–6 ff., 513. Contrast accounts of Kloesel, Schulz and Bleicken, discussed later. Wirszubski's treatment is more balanced, and I seldom disagree with it. De Ste Croix 366–8 has some admirable remarks.

concrete advantages which these rights secured to them. But the liberty or liberties of the aristocracy and of the plebs were not always congruent with each other. The very notion of liberty (whatever word be used to denote it in any language) is full of self-contradictions. Both conceptually and in practical application *libertas* meant different things to different people. So did *eleutheria*. There was, and could be, no single Roman and no single Greek idea of freedom, though to a very large extent the same range of meanings or applications is to be found in the thought and practice of both Romans and Greeks. In particular there is nothing peculiarly Roman in the beliefs that freedom within society is at once based on, and restricted by, law, while the contention that deference to the authority of a superior is inherent in the very definition of Roman *libertas* is perverse.

II

In Rome, as in Greece, freedom is primarily the legal status opposed to slavery. Already in the Twelve Tables the free man and the slave are sharply distinguished, and in all legal writings *libertas* generally means the status of one who is not a slave, but sometimes the actual grant to a slave of free status.[2]

Most philologists agree that *liber* and its Greek equivalent *eleutheria* have the same Indo-European root, *leudheros. Yet the terms for slave in Indo-European languages have no common root. Both *doulos* and *servus* seem to be borrowings. Normally men did not enslave their own co-nationals; for example, in the earliest Roman law, long obsolete in historic times, though a citizen could be sold into slavery for debt, he had to be sold outside Roman territory (Gell. xx. 1. 46 f.). Perhaps early Greek and Latin speakers borrowed the terms for slaves from the alien peoples among whom they made slaves. In Sanskrit the term used is actually taken from that of a foreign people in north-west India (Dasa); the Germans once called their slaves *wealh* (cognate with Welsh); our 'slave' and its equivalents in other modern European languages recall the importation of 'Slav' bondsmen from the Black Sea into medieval Italy. It seems to be beyond doubt that the term *liberi*, the free persons of the household (*familia*) subject to its head (the *paterfamilias*), is the plural of *liber*; but if the facts are as stated, it cannot

---

[2] *FIRA* i². 23 ff. (II, 1a, v, 8, VII, 12, VIII, 3, 14, XII, 2a). F. de Martino, *St. econ. di Roma antica*, 1979, 69 ff., denies that slavery existed in primitive Rome, since there are no reliable records of its existence, as if there are any reliable records for any social institutions earlier than the XII Tables. As in Homeric Greece, one would expect to find slaves as domestic servants from the earliest times. Slavery was already of vital economic importance in the Hannibalic war (*IM* 66 f.), and no doubt furnished more and more of the labour force as Roman dominion in Italy expanded.

have denoted in origin the free members of the household as distinct from the slaves. On a frequently but not universally accepted view the common root of *liber* and *eleutheros* is to be connected with a group of words in Indo-European languages, to which the German *Leute* (people) belongs: the *liberi* are the natural increase of the family, and the god Liber was once a numinous power of natural growth. Of course these etymological speculations were unknown to the ancients. Whatever had been the most primitive sense of *liber* or *eleutheros* was long forgotten. The man so designated was simply not a slave.[3]

The slave was in almost all respects a piece of property, to be bought and sold, given away, or bequeathed, like any other animal. The owner could force him to work, chain him, flog him, put him to death at his own discretion, allow him to breed or not as he chose. The children of the slave mother belonged to the mother's owner. Slave parents had no assured marital or family life. Under the Principate the law was to give slaves a little protection against brutality from their masters, but that is no more than the laws of other states have done in forbidding cruelty to animals. Slaves had of course always been protected from ill-treatment by third parties: the owner could sue for reparation, just as when he sustained wrongful damage to any other property.[4]

Not all the disabilities of the slave were peculiar to him. The *paterfamilias* was in law arbiter of life and death over his *liberi*. Like slaves, they could own no property. They could at one time be sold like slaves, and it was still possible in the second century AD if they committed a civil wrong, for which the *pater* was necessarily liable, for him to avoid paying damages by handing them over to the aggrieved party (*noxae datio*): they were then said to be 'in eius mancipio' (in his ownership) and to be 'in the position of slaves' (*servorum loco*). The poor man, who had no means to pay compensation, might have no choice

---

[3] *TLL* s.v. *liber*; so P. Chantraine, *Dict. de la langue gr.* and H. Frisk, *Gr. etym. Wörterbuch*, s.v. ἐλεύθερος, and Walde–Hoffmann, *Lat. etym. Wörterbuch* s.v. *liber*; J. Pokorny, *Indogerm. Wörterbuch*, 1959, 684 f.; the kinship of *liber* and *eleutheros* is doubted by Ernout–Meillet, *Ét. dict. de la langue lat.*, s.v. *liber*, and denied by Pohlenz, 1966, 181 n. 4. I derive other suggestions in the text from E. Benveniste, *RÉL* x 429 ff., xiv 51 ff., and *Le Vocabulaire des inst. indo-eur.* i, 1969, 321 ff.; for the origin of *schiavo* etc. see Ch. Verlinden, *L'Esclavage dans l'Europe mediévale*, ii, 1977, 999 ff.; the thesis concerning *servus* is doubted by Chantraine, and Ernout–Meillet favour the implausible connection made in antiquity with *servare* (Just. *Inst.* i. 3. 3).

[4] Finley, 1980, ch. 2, esp. 70 f. Note Sen. *de clem.* i. 18. 2: 'cum in servum omnia liceant, est aliquid quod in hominem licere commune ius animantium [!] vetet' (cf. 17. 1), and Pius' rescript (*Coll.* iii. 3. 2): 'dominorum quidem potestatem in suos servos inlibatam esse oportet nec cuiquam hominum ius suum detrahi: sed dominorum interest, ne auxilium contra saevitiam vel famem vel intolerabilem iniuriam denegetur his, qui iuste deprecantur', circumscribing the rights of individual masters for the common interests of all and of public order (cf. Posid. *FGH* no. 87 fr. 108 c, f on the causes of the first Sicilian slave revolt). For imperial protection of slaves in general see Buckland 36–8.

but to surrender a son in this way. These quasi-slaves could be emancipated, as slaves could be. Indeed the *pater* himself could emancipate sons in his power; it is significant that they are then said, in the Twelve Tables, to be 'free'. Complete subjection, even to one's own father, hardly seemed compatible with freedom.[5]

In the early Republic the poor would enter into a contract (*nexum*) which somehow made them the debt-bondsmen of their creditors. Livy supposed that these *nexi* could be kept like slaves in a private prison, chained, and flogged. According to the annalists, their condition occasioned the first secession of the plebs and the establishment of the tribunate. For long, however, nothing was done to end the servitude of the *nexi*. The annalists held that M. Manlius in 385 used his own resources to deliver debtors from their bonds, claiming to be a champion of liberty, but was actually accused by the tribunes of aiming at tyranny and put to death as an enemy of freedom. Two more generations passed before the contract of *nexum* was abolished by the *lex Poetelia*, and those then in bondage were released. Livy describes this reform as a new beginning of freedom; the first had been the overthrow of absolute monarchy.[6]

In reality this was not the end of bondage for debt. Under Roman law it always remained possible for the creditor to obtain a judgement of the court whereby he could take into custody the debtor who had not made repayment.[7] This *addictio* was a useful mode of coercion

[5] The XII Tables declared: 'si pater filium ter venum duit, filius a patre liber esto' (Gaius i. 132); cf. *Dig.* xxxii. 50. 1; *CJ* v. 4. 18, viii. 49, ix. 51, 13. 4; Sen. *Controv.* vii. 4. 4. In general see Gaius i. 123–41, esp. 138–41, iii. 104, 114, iv. 75–80; Papinian in *Coll.* ii. 3. 1. By Justinian's time *noxae datio* of free persons was no longer allowed (*Inst.* iv. 8. 7).

[6] Livy viii. 28. 1; Varro, *LL* vii. 105; Cic. *de rep.* ii. 59. Varro shows that the nature of *nexum* was already a matter of doubt and dispute for the jurists M'. Manilius (*cos.* 149) and Mucius (presumably Q. Scaevola, *cos.* 95); it is unlikely that the highly coloured accounts of the plight of *nexi* in Livy (ii. 28. 7, vi. 14. 3, and 10, 17. 2, 27. 8, 37. 7, viii. 27) and Dionysius rest on more than the vaguest recollections transmitted orally; they probably reflect later experience of the condition of some *addicti* (n. 7), and cannot be used to define the archaic legal institution. Analogies from other social systems suggest that the *nexi* were not, like *addicti*, defaulters under court judgements, but men who had bound themselves to service in return for a loan which it was not expected that they would repay. Cf. Finley, 1981, ch. 9. The modern literature is immense.

[7] Livy xxiii. 14. 3; Cic. II *Verr.* ii. 63, *Flacc.* 45, 48; *FIRA* i². no. 19. xxi f., 21. lxi; F. von Woess, *SZ* 1922, 485 ff., 523 ff.; Schulz, 1951, 26, remarks that some rules of classical law are unintelligible if *addictio* is forgotten (see his sections 78, 372, 529 f., 700, 792, 880). Quint. *Inst.* vii. 3. 26 refers to the 'addictus, quem lex servire donec solverit iubet'; cf. v. 10. 60; Ps.-Quint. *Declam.* 311; *HA. Hadr.* 18; and Sallust and Columella cited in the text. The jurists never mention this, perhaps because a pact between creditor and *addictus* was (despite Quintilian's 'lex') informal, or because it would never give rise to a suit in court; the *addictus* would have no means to sue for non-fulfilment, and the creditor had the sharper remedy of returning him to bonds. Varro's testimony (*RR* i. 17) may be explained as in the text, or by the hypothesis that he meant by *obaerarii* a class of persons in contractual bondage for labour service, like the *nexi* of old (n. 6). It is probable that the rich always preferred slave labour when cheap and plentiful; the increased supply of slaves (other Italians) resulting from Rome's conquests in the late fourth century may help to explain why they then were ready to concede the abolition of *nexum*. See also ch. 1 n. 107 with text.

against the debtor who was solvent but refused to discharge his obligation. However, since the creditor had to maintain such an *addictus* (*Dig.* xlii. 1. 34), it would have involved futile expenditure in the case of the man with no resources, unless he could be made to work. Quintilian and another rhetorician (Ps.-Quint. *Declam.* 311) indicate that *addicti* were 'in servitude' until they had worked off their debts, and Columella says that they were kept in prisons (*ergastula*) while labouring on the great estates (i. 3. 12). He actually designates them by the old name of *nexi*. Livy indeed often treats the *nexi* of old times as *addicti* (e.g. vi. 14. 3 and 10); his pictures of their plight are probably drawn from what was known in historic times of that of *addicti*. In 63 indebted peasants complained that through the savagery of the money-lenders and the praetor they had lost their personal freedom as well as their property (Sall. *Cat.* 33). The stock of slaves in Italy must have been temporarily diminished in the 60s by the losses owners had sustained in Spartacus' revolt, and they may have been the more tempted to fill the gaps in their labour force by reducing debtors to a kind of servitude. Varro (*RR* i. 17. 2) in the 30s writes as if there were then no debt-bondsmen (*obaerarii*) in Italy, as there were in some lands overseas. The explanation cannot lie in any change in the law, since *addictio* was always permitted; moreover, Columella again attests forced labour for debt in the Italy of the Principate. It may be that the huge demand for legionaries in the years from 49 made it impracticable for creditors to detain debtors, who could easily escape by enlistment; whereas by the time of Columella and Quintilian there was little recruiting in Italy, and indeed the emperor Tiberius had been reluctant to allow the penniless and vagrants to join up (Tac. *Ann.* iv. 4).[8]

Some citizens would also bind themselves by contract as *auctorati* to serve as gladiators and submit themselves to servile discipline by their employers.[9]

We cannot tell how commonly poor men fell into servitude in one of these forms. But numerically such bondsmen were far less important than chattel slaves. As early as the Hannibalic War there must have been adequate slave labour to keep up the production of necessary supplies, with perhaps 11 per cent of the citizen population serving in the legions. In the late Republic slaves *may* have comprised three sevenths of the inhabitants of Italy.[10]

Chattel slavery was not only the most common, it was also the most perfect form of servitude in Roman society. There was some justifica-

---

[8] *IM* 413–5; more fully, Brunt, *Scripta Class. Israelica*, 1974, 90 ff.
[9] Sen. *Ep.* 37. 1; Petron. 117; other evidence in Mommsen, *Ges. Schr.* iii. 9 n. 4.
[10] *IM* 67 and ch. x (highly conjectural estimates).

tion for saying that men who were not chattel slaves, though subject to the power of another, were in some sense free. The *liberi* in the power of their *paterfamilias* had most of the rights and obligations of citizens *sui iuris*. They could vote and hold office; they could serve in the army, as slaves and even freedmen normally could not; they could marry, and their children were of free birth. Marriage was permitted also to those *in mancipio* (Gaius i. 135), and presumably to *addicti* and *auctorati*; and perhaps these classes had, like the *liberi in potestate*, protection as citizens against arbitrary punishment by magistrates. The *liberi* automatically acquired full independence (if males), becoming *sui iuris* once death removed the *paterfamilias*; the *filius in mancipio* would be freed by the praetor, when he had worked off his debt, and the *addictus* may have had some chance of securing freedom by his labour;[11] the *auctoratus* was free, if he survived to the end of the period for which he had bound himself to fight. The slave who was manumitted enjoyed as a freedman only limited citizen rights: the liberation of other bondsmen restored to them the title of free birth.

Thus there could be degrees of freedom or servitude. This was true of communities as well as individuals. Aphrodisias was granted freedom by Rome 'on the same basis as a community with the best right and legal status which has freedom and immunity bestowed by the Roman people' (n. 31). By analogy with the *paterfamilias* a state can be entirely free if it is 'sui iuris ac mancipi' (n. 25). The *paterfamilias* had total control over his *familia*: Rome is the freest of states because of its imperial dominion (n. 30). Liberty is independence and, indeed, power (nn. 70–2).

The existence of slavery and other forms of servitude coloured the thinking of both Romans and Greeks about freedom in various ways. (1) The degradation of many slaves made it natural to connect freedom with morality: a free man was, or should be, a better kind of man than a slave. (2) Freedom as a legal status raised the dignity of its possessor, however poor, over that of the slave; it gave him some compensation for the superiority of material conditions that some slaves might enjoy, and inhibited the growth of any sense of common interest in the labouring class, which included both slaves and free men. (3) It was manifest that freedom of status depended on the positive law of a man's own state; the notion that freedom was a natural right due to human beings as such, though sometimes suggested, could gain little credence and had no practical effect.

(1) We read in Homer that when a man is enslaved he loses half that excellence (*aretē*) which makes him truly a man (*Od.* xvii. 322 f.). For

---

[11] Papinian in n. 5; cf. n. 7.

Aristotle the natural slave, one who deserves to be a slave, is a man whose intellectual and moral quality assimilates him to an animal, and who needs in his own interest to be under the perpetual tutelage of a master.[12] This doctrine was no doubt partly founded in experience. Most slaves known to Aristotle were barbarians who seemed immeasurably inferior to Greeks. In any case enslavement doubtless tended to debase a man. Hence slaves were depicted as typically lowspirited, cowardly, idle, shy, dishonest and mendacious. A free man of low moral quality was called in Greek '*aneleutheros*', unfree, a term not used of actual slaves. *Eleutheria* and *eleutheros* occasionally denote the excellence in character expected of a free man;[13] Terence uses 'liberum ingenium atque animum' (*Ad.* 828) in the same way, probably translating from the Greek, for Romans more naturally say 'worthy of freedom'. The Greek *eleutherios* and Latin *liberalis* have the same sense, along with their derivatives, though both come also to mean 'liberal' or 'munificent', virtues which the slave, having no property, had no means to practise. By contrast *servilis* is a term of moral opprobrium. The slave might, indeed, display qualities above his station, and for Aristotle himself he was then entitled to freedom; Terence makes someone say 'I have converted you from my slave into my freedman, because you served me with the character of a free man [*liberaliter*]' (*Andr.* 38). In sum, for both Greeks and Romans freedom could acquire moral overtones. The subjection of a whole people could be defended on the ground that it was unfit for independence, and merely lost the licence to do wrong,[14] while imperialists could justify their dominion on the ground that they were worthy to rule (e.g. Thuc. i. 76). However, though the manumission of slaves could be justified by their worth, it was not suggested that a free man should be deprived of his legal status because he was morally unfit for it.

(2) Kunkel somewhere remarked that the contrast between master and slave was omnipresent and vivid in Roman daily life: this was no less true in that of a Greek city. This must have made a man more intensely conscious of the value of whatever freedom he possessed. His own rights were more precious by contrast with the rightlessness of the slaves around him. No doubt this gave a special emotive force to 'freedom' and 'slavery', when they were employed as political slogans. In Rome society was always hierarchical. Senators or Equites had their own privileges, for instance their own form of dress and reserved seats at the games. But even the humblest citizen had his own social esteem

---

[12] *Politics* i. 2, 5, etc.
[13] Pohlenz, 1966, 47 ff. Dem. viii. 51, xviii. 242 show this view to have been familiar to the general public.
[14] Cic. *de rep. ap.* Aug. *Civ. Dei* xix. 21.

and rank (*dignitas*), which set him at least above the slaves. This doubtless explains why it was that the free poor gave but little aid to slaves when they rose in revolt, and why their champions were reluctant to seek servile support, though both classes may appear to us victims of a common exploitation.[15]

(3) The Founding Fathers of the United States declared: 'We hold these truths to be self-evident, that all are created equal, that they are endowed by their Creator with certain unalienable rights, that among these are life, liberty and the pursuit of happiness.' Sophistry reconciled these affirmations with the ownership of slaves.[16] ('How is it', asked Dr Johnson, 'that we hear the loudest yelps for liberty among the drivers of negroes?'). Greeks and Romans hardly ever embarrassed themselves with the notion that freedom was a natural or divine right, which their acceptance of the institution of slavery denied.

Slaves could indeed not be treated entirely as if they were things, not human beings. The law recognized their humanity in making them liable to punishment for crimes, in accepting their evidence (given under torture) in the courts, and in permitting their masters to manumit them; by a peculiarity of Roman law, unparalleled in the Greek world, manumission by due legal process gave them the status of citizens, subject to certain disabilities which did not extend to their descendants born in freedom. All this made it evident that there was a certain artificiality in slave status. So did the mere fact that men of free birth, Romans included, could be enslaved through war, piracy, and kidnapping. Roman law prescribed that the captive would, on return to the territory of Rome or of a friendly state, normally recover freedom and citizenship.[17] Enslavement might be just bad luck (Plaut. *Capt.* 302 ff.), and it was a commonplace, which the orator could take over from philosophers, that fortune, not nature, made men free or slaves;[18] not that this is likely to have made free men in general entertain any real doubts about the justice of their own superiority to slaves.

Some Greek thinkers had asserted that all men were born free, and that slavery was unjust as an institution, though without demanding its actual abolition: slavery was so deeply rooted in the economic organization and traditions of the Graeco-Roman world that this was

[15] During the Sicilian slave revolts the free poor gloated at the misfortunes of the rich and plundered on their own account but did not join the rebels (Posid. *ap.* Diod. xxxiv. 2. 48, xxxvi. 6, 11). A few free men joined Spartacus (App. i. 116. 540, 117. 547; other texts cited ad loc. by Gabba prove nothing); this was hardly significant. Catiline would not enlist slaves (Sall. *Cat.* 56. 5), though governments did so in crises, e.g. Rome in the Hannibalic war.

[16] For an explanation see J. P. Grene, *All Men are Created Equal* (inaugural lecture, Oxford, 1976).

[17] *Postliminium*; see e.g. Buckland 302 ff.; anyone who redeemed the captive had a lien on his person till the cost was repaid, and presumably would exact labour from him.

[18] Sen. *Controv.* vii. 6. 18; Quint. *Inst.* iii. 8. 31.

never thought of. Roman jurists of the imperial period were also to say or imply that all men were free by the law of nature.[19] This is apparently the law that nature has taught to all animals, which leads them to procreate and rear their young, and also to desire freedom instinctively.[20] Freedom can be defined by one jurist as 'a natural faculty of doing that which everyone wished to do, unless there is some hindrance in force or law.'[21] We shall see that this concept of freedom as *per se* unrestricted is no more alien to Romans than to Greeks. Law itself imposes limitations on it. It does not of course follow that any of the limitations were unjustified. Slavery is for the jurists an institution of the *ius gentium*, the law of nations, and that law can be viewed not only as the body of rules that all peoples use, but as established by natural reason. Now instinct is common to all animals, but reason is peculiar to man.[22] In affirming that slavery was contrary to the instincts of nature, the jurists were not then suggesting any moral condemnation of it, nor were they implying that the law of nature in this sense was what the Stoics held it to be, the rational and divine regulation of the world, a conception that does indeed appear in other juristic texts. And even Stoics accepted slavery; ubiquitous as it was, how could it not be part of the providential order determined by reason?[23] It is another matter if the teaching of the Stoics, who recognized that the divine reason was immanent in every man, and that the slave was as capable of virtue as the free man, perhaps conduced to some amelioration of the legal status of slaves. This development in any case belongs to the Principate, and it was then (if at all) that Stoic influence could have affected it. And at no time was the abolition of slavery proposed, even by those Greek thinkers who had challenged its justice and to whose theoretical objections Aristotle had offered a theoretical reply. They alone had suggested that freedom was a natural human right, without drawing any practical conse-

---

[19] Greek theoretical criticisms of slavery are chiefly known from Aristotle's reply in *Pol.* i. For natural freedom in Roman jurisprudence see *Dig.* i. 1. 4 *pr.* (Ulpian), xii. 6. 64 (Tryphoninus); xl. 11. 2 (Marcian); l. 17. 32 (Ulpian); nn. 21 f.

[20] *Dig.* i. 1. 3 (Ulpian) xli. 1. 1–5 (chiefly Gaius); Cic. *de leg. agr.* ii. 9, *de rep.* i. 55; Tac. *Hist.* iv. 17. 5: 'libertatem natura etiam mutis animalibus datam, virtutem proprium hominum bonum [as of rational beings]'.

[21] *Dig.* i. 5. 4 *pr*: 'libertas est naturalis facultas eius < faciendi > quod cuique facere libet, nisi si quid vi aut iure prohibetur. (1) Servitus est constitutio iuris gentium, qua quis dominio alieno contra naturam subicitur.' Florentinus goes on to accept the etymological connection of *servus* with *servare* (n. 3), and he may have thought that the 'natural faculty' to kill one's captives at one's pleasure was rationally limited, 'iure gentium', by the practice of preserving their lives and exploiting their labour.

[22] *Dig.* i. 1. 9 (Gaius); i. 1. 4 (Ulpian).

[23] Stoic natural law: *Dig.* i. 3. 2 (Marcian quoting Chrysippus); cf. 1. 1 *pr*: 'ius est ars boni et aequi' (Celsus), 1. 1. 1, 10 (Ulpian), 1. 11 (Paul). Stoic acceptance of slavery: *SVF* ii. 1118, iii. 351–3; Cic. *de offic.* i. 41.

quences, and this was not a notion that had any significant part in Greek or Roman thinking.

Of course in any state that recognized slavery the free man who was illegally enslaved had to be given means of redress. At Rome a person *de facto* in slavery normally had no access to the courts, but a free man could appear on behalf of one who claimed entitlement to liberty, and under the Twelve Tables he was subject to less pecuniary risk than in other litigation; Gaius (iv. 14) explained this on the ground that the law favoured the restoration of his rights to the free man wrongfully held as a slave. Many later rules of Roman law exhibit the same *favor libertatis* to slaves who had a legal claim to manumission under a will or contract,[24] but were in danger of being defrauded of their rights by an inequitable interpretation of the law. In principle all these rules were designed to uphold a man's legal title to freedom, which he had been unjustly denied, and do not illustrate any lurking belief that freedom was due to every man under the law of nature. Manumission too was regarded as a *beneficium*, and it was a mark of virtue to bestow *beneficia* on those, including slaves, who deserved them by their individual merits. But an admission that some slaves should be freed implied no condemnation of slavery.

III

Communities, like individuals, could be described as free or 'sui iuris ac mancipi'.[25] The application of the term was ambiguous. It might refer either to their external relationships or their internal organization. A state could be regarded as free if it were not subject to the rule of another state, or if the citizens had rights against their own rulers and were not enslaved to their despotic will. In both applications freedom might be more or less complete. No distinction between Greek and Roman ideas on these matters can be drawn.

Peoples who were subject to the arbitrary will of a single man or a small group of men were held to be deprived of freedom, as their condition was analogous to that of slaves. Thus for the Greeks the subjects of the absolute Persian king were his slaves. Romans contrasted *libertas* with both *regnum* and the *dominatio* of a faction. No matter if the despot was benevolent: 'freedom consists not in having a just master, but in having none' (Cic. *de rep.* ii. 43). On this view the fall of the monarchy at Rome was the beginning of freedom.[26] The

---

[24] e.g. sale 'ut manumittatur', Buckland 628 ff.
[25] Cic. *ad Brut.* 24. 4; cf. Sen. *de benef.* iii. 20. 1.
[26] Sall. *Cat.* 6 f.; Livy ii. 1; Tac. *Ann.* i. 1 all connect the institution of the annual and collegiate consulship with liberty.

very name of king was detestable;[27] and Sulla and Caesar could be seen as 'kings' and destroyers of liberty. Some nations indeed loved their chains: 'few desire freedom, the greater number prefer just masters'. For Greeks that was a mark of barbarism; Cicero too could contemptuously say that Jews and Syrians were 'born to servitude'.[28] But the Romans could pretend that they were conferring a boon on Macedonians (as Greeks) in abolishing their popular and national kingship and dividing them into four artificial republics. 'All nations were to know that the arms of the Roman people were not employed to enslave free peoples but to liberate others from slavery.'[29]

Internal freedom admitted of degrees. It could be predicated of a community whose citizens had only a limited share in their own government, provided that they had some rights guaranteed by their laws. Thus the Spartans boasted of their freedom (Hdt. vii. 104). Roman internal freedom, traditionally associated with the foundation of the Republic, admittedly increased as ordinary citizens acquired further rights. Cicero could claim that oratory flourished in 'every free people', as it did at Rome (*de orat*. i. 30); it was the mark of a truly free state that decisions were taken after public discussion, which was influenced by the arts of persuasion (p. 45).

National freedom may also consist in independence of foreign rule. From this standpoint Sallust could say that in their struggles for independence under royal government the Romans were already fighting for liberty (*Cat*. 6. 5 f.); in the next breath he makes them win liberty by overturning the monarchy (7. 3). Similarly Herodotus could speak of the Persians as not being slaves to others, since they had a national king (ix. 122). Freedom from arbitrary rule at home and freedom from foreign domination did not necessarily go together, as Livy observed (ii. 23. 2). The enemies of imperial Athens in the fifth century claimed that she had enslaved her allies, Athenian apologists that she not only protected their freedom against the barbarians but enlarged it by conferring on them the democratic freedom in their internal affairs which she enjoyed herself (n. 32).

The independence of a state had to be fought for (e.g. Sall. *Or. Lepidi* 4). It rested on power. According to Cicero, 'Rome far excels other

[27] e.g. Cic. *de rep*. ii. 53: 'pulso Tarquinio nomen regis audire non poterat [populus Romanus]'; there is no contrary testimony. When Cicero refers (i. 54 f.) to men's affection for kings, he has in mind their patriarchal position in some other societies (cf. Plato, *Laws* 680e, 690a) or the conception of the ideal monarch of Greek political theory, whose rule was secure because his outstanding virtue won the love or consent of his subjects (see e.g. M. Griffin, *Seneca*, 1976, 144). 'Sullanum regnum': e.g. Cic. *de har. resp*. 54, *Att*. viii. 11. 2; Sall. *Or. Lepidi*. Whether or not Caesar aspired to the title, he had in effect made himself *rex* for Cicero (*de offic*. iii. 83 etc.).

[28] Sall. *Ep. Mithr*. 18; Livy xxxvii. 54. 24; Cic. *de prov. cons*. 10.

[29] Livy xlv. 18. 1. None the less Romans did not scruple to acknowledge and protect vassal kings.

states in the prerogative of freedom'; she 'alone is and has always been in the highest degree free'. What meaning can be found in this rhetoric? Only that Rome's power made her uniquely free of any external constraint. 'Other nations can bear servitude, but liberty is proper to the Roman people', since by divine will Rome rules over all other races.[30] This was the freedom that some Greeks are said to have pined for in 192: Greek 'honour [*dignitas*] consists in that freedom which rests on its own strength, not on the will of others' (Livy xxxv. 32. 11). Very different was the freedom that Rome had just bestowed on the Greeks: unable, as Rhodian envoys are made to acknowledge, to defend it with their own arms, they relied on those of Rome (xxxvii. 54. 25).

Freedom of a community from external control also admitted of degrees. It could be restricted by treaty obligations and power relationships. Hellenistic kings would recognize the 'freedom' of cities that accepted their 'friendship' or 'alliance', and often specify the rights comprised within this all-embracing term: free cities would have their own constitutions, laws, and courts, would be immune from taxes, and have no governors or garrisons imposed on them. The cities which had acquired hegemonies in fifth- or fourth-century Greece had often given similar undertakings. None of these promises held good when the suzerain had the power and need to disregard them. Rome bound herself in the same way to respect the freedom of cities within her dominions by contracting formal treaties with them or by unilaterally conceding privileges to them by law or decree of the senate. As freedom was vague and undefined in itself, it did not necessarily include all the specific rights that might be associated with it. Free cities, for example, might be subject to taxation; or their right to impose their own taxes might be curtailed by exemptions for Roman or Italian residents. Aphrodisias enjoyed freedom *optimo iure*: by implication other free cities had less. But all which had a treaty relationship with Rome or possessed a charter conferred by people or senate were, at least in theory, exempt from arbitrary interferences in their own internal affairs by the holders of Roman *imperium*. In practice even unprivileged cities must normally have enjoyed local self-government. The Roman governor had not time or staff for frequent interpositions of his authority. In Cilicia Cicero gratified the Greeks by promising them autonomy, the use of their own laws and courts. It is not to be supposed

---

[30] Cic. *de leg. agr.* ii. 29, *Rab. Post.* 22, *Phil.* vi. 19, cf. II *Verr.* v. 164, *Cat.* iv. 24; Brunt, *Laus Imperii* IV–VI. In 52 the Gauls allegedly hoped to obtain 'imperium libertatemque' (*BG* vii. 64). On coins Libertas wears a diadem (*RRC* no. 391. 3), or is crowned by Victory (391. 1), or appears on the obverse with Victory crowning Rome on the reverse (449. 4; Crawford's interpretation seems to me mistaken).

that his predecessors had taken all or most cases into their own jurisdiction, but only that they had intervened whenever it suited them; Cicero promised, as a matter of principle, that he would not do so. This was a matter for his own discretion, where unprivileged cities were concerned; treaties and charters guaranteed the favoured communities against the governor's intrusion. But even this freedom was precarious; if in the judgement of the Romans a free city misbehaved, a treaty could be denounced and a law or senatorial decree rescinded. The ambassador of the free Achaeans remarked in 184 that their treaty afforded them no security, since *imperium* belonged to Rome (Livy xxxix. 37. 13).[31]

Moreover, no less than Athens, 'the tyrant city', and Sparta, the professed champion of Greek liberty, Rome tended to insist that her subjects or 'allies' adopted the forms of internal government that she approved. In the fourth century many Greeks had come to identify freedom with democracy; instances still occur in Roman times, but Rome did not tolerate democracy except in outward forms.[32] It is thus not true, as Last said (*CAH* xi. 436), that the 'free' cities in her empire were merely 'deprived of untrammelled control of international relations, with the right to declare peace and war at will'. For Tacitus they were only nominally free (*Ann.* xv. 45. 1), and Pliny writes of the 'remaining shade and surviving name of freedom' still left to Athens and Sparta (*Ep.* viii. 24. 4). In their time the scale of Roman supervision over the cities' internal concerns was marginally increasing, but it had always been true that the Greeks had never had more freedom than their Roman rulers conceded; Romans would naturally have concurred in Plutarch's comment (824 c) that more might not have been good for them.

The imperial jurist Proculus, after saying that a free people is one

---

[31] See generally Jones, 1940, chs. VI, VII; freedom divorced from tax immunity, ch. VII nn. 33, 35. Rights associated with freedom: Tod, *Greek Hist. Inscriptions* 123, 15 ff.; Polyb. iv. 84, xv. 24. It was the mark of all free peoples to live under their own laws, adopting Roman only by their own choice: Cic. *Balb.* 20–2, but the *lex Antonia* allows free Termessus use of its own laws and presumably courts only 'quod advorsus hanc legem non fiat' (*FIRA* i². 11. 8), and probably few had, like Chios, jurisdiction over Romans (*SIG*³ 785). Aphrodisias: Sherk 28B. 7. Cilicia: Cic. *Att.* vi. 1. 5, 2. 4).

[32] Sparta: Thuc. i. 19, 144. 2, v. 82. 1; cf. Spartan actions after the King's Peace. Athenian apologists often represented their support of democracy in 'allied' cities as championship of freedom: Lysias ii. 55–7; Isocr. iv. 104–6, xii. 68; Plato, *Menex.* 242a, 243a, 244c; I do not believe that Athenian politicians ever admitted what was in Thucydides' view the truth, that their rule was tyrannical. Alexander fulfilled his promise to liberate the Greeks of Asia by installing democracies (Arrian, *Anab.* i. 18; cf. Diod. xvi. 91, xvii. 24); in fact they were his subjects. For freedom as democracy see Jones, 1940, ch. x esp. pp. 170 ff.; in *ILS* 31 (Lycia) *libertas* translates democracy, and Pergamum, a free city, honoured a Roman governor in 46 for restoring 'its ancestral laws and unenslaved democracy' (ibid. 8879; cf. Magie 156, 417). On the decay of democracy under the influence of the kings and of Rome see de Ste Croix, 1982, App. IV.

not subject to the power of another people, adds that it may none the less be bound by treaty 'alterius populi maiestatem comiter conservare' —'to respect loyally the greatness of another people'. This clause appeared, for example, in the treaty made by Gades with Rome, and Cicero construed it as marking the subordination of Gades to Rome (*Balb*. 35–7). Proculus comments that though it does indeed imply the superiority of one party, the other is none the less free, just as clients are free, though unequal to their patrons in influence, rank, and sheer strength.[33] Some scholars suppose that the limited and precarious freedom that Rome granted was rooted in typically Roman social structure and ideas, and was so unfamiliar to the Greeks that they misunderstood what the Romans meant when they professed to be upholding the freedom of Greek cities. There is no warrant for this view. Centuries earlier the Spartans had professed to maintain the freedom of their allies without scrupling to impose on them oligarchic control when they had the opportunity, just as much as Rome did (n. 32). 'Perhaps all kings', wrote Polybius (xv. 24. 4), 'begin their reigns by making nominal offers of freedom to everyone'. Such professions had once been made for deception, but long experience had exposed the harsh truth that no power would readily leave full independence to states that it could dominate. Local self-government was probably all that most Greek beneficiaries of royal or Roman grants of freedom had come to expect, and all that Rome would accord.

For their part Romans were perfectly conscious that such freedom was not freedom in the fullest extent, and they could also use that ambiguous word, *libertas*, to designate the sovereignty that they sought to abridge. Cato, for instance, said that the Rhodians were to be excused for not wishing to see Rome utterly subdue Macedon, in the fear 'that under our single rule they might be in servitude to us: I consider that it was for their own *libertas* that they adopted this view' (Gell. vi. 3. 15). Caesar does not hesitate to admit that the Gauls who resisted him were fighting for freedom, even the Aedui (*BG* vii. 37), who were allies of Rome by treaty (i. 33): 'all men have a natural urge for liberty and hate a condition of servitude' (iii. 10). The very reason why Proculus had to insist that the inferiority of a dependent ally or client did not involve loss of freedom was that the restraints that flowed from such inferiority were naturally conceived to be inconsistent with freedom. There is no ground for holding that the grants of liberty made to dependent cities by Rome embody a peculiarly Roman concept that liberty as such is a status properly limited by some higher authority.

---

[33] xlix. 15. 7. 1: 'etiamsi neque auctoritate neque dignitate neque viribus pares sunt' (codd. 'neque viri boni nobis praesunt').

They show only that for Romans, as for Greeks, 'liberty' could be convenient shorthand for privileges that fell short of that full independence which both the Greek and Latin terms also connote.

IV

Freedom, as we have seen, could never be for Greeks and Romans, who accepted slavery, an inalienable right inhering in the human personality: it necessarily denoted privileges that reposed on positive law, including custom. Misleading statements made by Cicero have induced the thesis that for the Romans it was actually coterminous with citizenship,[34] not necessarily that of Rome, since the Romans of course acknowledged that foreigners could be free, but also of any other state recognized by Rome. This thesis has been refuted: in Levy's formulation 'liberty was the precondition of citizenship, and citizenship its guarantee'.[35] Suffice it to note here that the Campanians, who were deprived of Roman citizenship for some time after 211, and the Junian Latins under imperial law, were both free, though stateless.[36] However, for Romans and for Greeks, liberty came to mean more than the legal status of a man who was not in some kind of bondage. If a community was said to be free when its citizens had some share in determining their own civic obligations, this freedom can be resolved into the rights of the citizens. *Political* freedom of the individual citizen can indeed be equated with his citizenship; Romans often associated their right or rights (*ius* or *iura*) with their *libertas*, or used the terms interchangeably. Thus Cicero apostrophizes the personal security guaranteed to Romans by the Porcian and Sempronian laws with the words: 'O nomen dulce libertatis! O ius eximium nostrae civitatis'. The latter phrase in itself illustrates how this or any other right which Romans identified as liberty did not belong to a man as such but was the special right ('ius *eximium*') of a Roman citizen.[37] The rights of

---

[34] See endnote 1.   [35] *SZ* 1961, 142 ff.

[36] See e.g. Sherwin-White, 1973, 211, 329 ff.

[37] Cic. II *Verr.* v. 163 ('dulce': *Cat.* iv. 24, *Att.* xv. 13. 27; Pollio in *Fam.* x. 31. 3; Livy i. 17. 3, xxiv. 21. 3); for 'ius eximium' cf. n. 30. *Ius* (or *iura*) *libertatis* and the collocation of *ius* or *iura* with *libertas* refer to protection of the citizen's person (e.g. II *Verr.* i. 7, ii. 16, v. 143, *Rab. perd.* 11 f., *Sest.* 30; Livy iii. 56. 8–10), electoral rights (*de leg. agr.* ii. 29), participation in comitial trials of political offenders (Livy xxxvii. 52. 5), free speech (*Planc.* 55; cf. 33), and eligibility for office (Sall. *Cat.* 37. 9). Sallust contrasts 'ius a maioribus relictum' with 'hoc a Sulla paratum servitium', and refers to the tribunes, who are always connected with freedom (n. 109), as 'vindices omnis iuris' of the citizens (*Or. Macri.* 1, 22); in *BJ* 31. 16 f. *libertas* and *ius (populi)* are mere variants; freedom to vote on legislative proposals of tribunes is here to the fore; cf. section xiv. Cf. Cic. *ap.* Ascon. 76–8 C.; where he first describes the origin of the tribunate and other *iura* (cf. Sall. *Hist.* i.11), and cites 'Porciam [legem] principium iustissimae libertatis [protection for the person; cf. endnote 8], Cassiam qua lege suffragiorum ius potestasque convaluit [cf. n. 103], alteram Cassiam quae populi iudicia firmavit [pp. 340 f.] *Iura populi* is a term equivalent to *libertas* in Sall. *Cat.* 38. 3, *Or. Lepidi* 11, 16, 23.

Roman citizens were of course not entrenched in a written constitution any more than those of British citizens,[38] since at Rome, as in this country, there was no such constitution: they rested on particular customs and statutes, which could be modified or repealed by new legislation, in accordance with the rule of the Twelve Tables that whatever the people last enacted was binding in law.[39]

The legal rights that Romans most explicitly and commonly subsumed under the title of freedom are of two types: immunity from arbitrary coercion and punishment by magistrates, and some degree of participation in political power. Neither derived from any abstract conception of freedom and its value, such as that which underlies, for instance, the American Bill of Rights: indeed they both originated in early times innocent of political theorizing. Specific liberties were sought and obtained to protect their holders against oppression and to secure their material interests. It does not follow that an appeal to liberty was never anything but a cloak for such advantages. The 'name of liberty was sweet', if only because men instinctively wish to live as they please. The right of citizenship was the more prized because it was 'eximium', setting the Roman above the slave and the foreigner. His freedom made him less subject to the will of others or better able to enforce his will on them. Independence, power, superiority to the less privileged were enjoyed most of all by the aristocracy, but the humblest citizen had some share in them. Without ever formulating any more or less coherent notion of freedom as an ideal, and least of all the doctrine that the individual has a right to develop his own personality as he thinks best, within the limits of social order and justice, Romans could value liberties they possessed for these reasons, as well as for the concrete material interests they might assume; and they could seek new rights, like the secret vote, in the name of freedom, by analogy with or extension of those which they already enjoyed. Bleicken (1972, 38) suggests that the significance of appeals to liberty at Rome was the less because they were made in particular situations by men acting from personal motives, and embodied no abstract idea of liberty. The motive of those who invoked the name of liberty is not very material to judging the effect of the appeal on those to whom it was made, and the absence of an abstract idea of liberty will not seem of much importance to Englishmen.

A limited similarity may be seen between the Roman experience and our own. It could be boasted in 1816 that 'liberty is the chief distinction of England from other European countries'. However, then (as now) it consisted only of a bundle of legal or customary rights with

[38] See endnote 2.
[39] Livy vii. 17. 12, ix. 34. 6; Cic. *Balb.* 33, *Att.* iii. 23; cf. n. 34.

no constitutional guarantee (n. 38). Even the Bill of Rights passed in 1689, 'our greatest constitutional document since Magna Charta',[40] enumerates only those rights which had recently been infringed by royal prerogative, to the disadvantage of interests which preponderated in Parliament. Freedom of worship, and of religious belief and expression, are certainly regarded as important elements in our liberty, but they were secured in full over a long period, and not so much from recognition of the principle that men ought to be free to hold, propagate, and practise whatever religious faith answers to their own convictions, as because it became politically expedient to make concessions to those who would not conform to the established religion. This is characteristic of the way in which English freedom 'slowly broadened down from precedent to precedent'.

V

It is of course true that our concept of freedom has ultimately come to embrace many activities to which it was not consciously related by the Romans, or indeed by the Greeks. This was partly at least because in medieval and early modern times the individual had been subjected to restraints which were not imposed effectively or at all in antiquity, or not felt as limitations of freedom, because consciously or unconsciously they were taken to be inevitable; the effect of social tradition may be in this respect as strong as that of physical laws which constrict the power of a man to do as he pleases, but are not normally seen as limiting his freedom. It was when changes in conditions made these restraints irksome that their removal in modern Europe was demanded in the name of liberty. New restraints, imposed by law, are always naturally opposed as infringements of liberty by those who suffer from them. So it was at Rome. Although in general Roman freedom is political in character, novel attempts to control private behaviour could be denounced as inimical to freedom.

Benjamin Constant observed that the mere size of the modern state made it impossible for men to enjoy that continuous and direct part in government which Greeks and Romans were prone to identify with liberty, and that his own contemporaries were more concerned than the ancients to limit the intrusion of the state into private life; political liberty itself, in the sense of the power that citizens could now exercise only in periodic elections, was for him chiefly valuable because it could

---

[40] D. Ogg, *England in the Reigns of James II and William III*, 141 ff. Note the use of 'liberties' in English to denote 'privileges, immunities or rights enjoyed by prescription or grant' (*Oxford Dict.* s.v., whence the quotation of 1816).

be used to obtain institutional guarantees for private freedom.[41] At first sight Constant's view of ancient liberty may seem hardly applicable to Rome, since most Romans in the middle and late Republic could take no direct and continuous part in public affairs. But they had had more opportunity to do so in earlier times, when Rome's territory and population were relatively small, and that was surely the formative period when Roman ideas of freedom evolved. However, Constant's comparison between ancient and modern ideas of liberty, though not devoid of truth, is not satisfying.

(*i*) Neither Greeks nor Romans conceived the state as an impersonal entity which could be sharply contrasted with the individual citizen. Aristotle represented what they all thought in describing it as a kind of partnership between the citizens or free men (*Pol.* 1252[a]1, 1279[a]21). Officially Athens *was* 'the Athenians', and Rome 'the Roman people of the Quirites'. The Latin words 'civitas' or 'res publica' may be translated as 'state', but fundamentally the former means 'the quality of being a citizen' or 'the body of citizens', and the latter 'that which belongs to or concerns the people'; it may best be rendered 'commonwealth'. 'To be free' and 'to possess a commonwealth' are for Cicero (*Sest.* 81) equivalent expressions.[42] The citizen was, as it were, a shareholder in the state, and at Rome, as at Athens, men thought it quite proper to take dividends from its property: the state lands and revenues, Cicero tells the people, belong to them.[43]

Of course the state laid heavy burdens on the persons and sometimes on the property of the citizens. Romans could treat conscription and taxation as marks of servitude. But it was more manifest than it has often been in the modern era that the defence of the community in war, for which these burdens were imposed, conduced to the safety of the citizen, when the consequences of defeat might be massacre or enslavement; in his own interest and in that of all who were dear to him the individual might feel a more unconditional commitment to his community. This devotion was indeed diminished or obliterated if he considered that the organization of his community was injurious to him. This was the origin of the internal conflicts (*stasis*) so prevalent in Greek cities, and therefore of the development of Greek political theory, which was not primarily concerned with the nature and validity of the citizen's obligation to his state, the question which has

[41] *De la liberté des anciens comparée à celles des modernes*, 1819.

[42] Hellegouarc'h 545 n. 2 assembles texts connecting *libertas* and *res publica*; note esp. Cic. *Phil.* x. 7 f., where 'ius rei p.' is *libertas*. Officially the Romans state remained a *res publica* even in Justinian's usage (Brunt. *JRS* 1977, 116); Tacitus occasionally uses both terms to mean the Republic (*Hist.* i. 16, 50, *Ann.* i. 3, 4, 33, ii. 82); cf. Suet. *Aug.* 28. 1 (contrast 2).

[43] Cic. *de leg. agr.* ii. 48, 55, 80–2, 85; C. Gracchus *ap.* Gell. xi. 10. 3. Badian, 1967, brings out how the empire was exploited to meet the cost of 'popular' measures.

tended to dominate modern political theory, but rather with the form of state which would best guarantee his welfare. It is indeed obvious that once Rome had acquired imperial power the individual Roman would not have had cause to identify his own good with the survival of his state, which was no longer in peril; but in the formative period of Roman history he must have been subject to the same apprehensions as Greek citizens, and the outlook thus engendered could have persisted after the conditions that created it had passed away.[44] The annalists of early Rome did in fact suppose that civic burdens, which were always resented as marks of servitude when imposed by an autocrat or a foreign power, had been grievous to the poor in the fifth and fourth centuries; perhaps they were importing into that period feelings aroused in the time of overseas wars (see endnote 3). At any rate Romans as well as Greeks apparently felt no tension between the freedom of the individual and the authority of the state, provided at least that the individual had some share in that authority, and was not oppressed by it.

(*ii*) In actual fact the Roman state interfered much less in the private activity and beliefs of individuals than did the authorities of both state and Church in the subsequent periods to which Constant looked back, or than states do in our time. Romans could practise some activities in ways later regarded as essential to individual freedom, without themselves prizing such freedom as a right, perhaps just because it had never been contested. Moreover, the effective power of the state, even under the Principate, to curtail men's private liberty was very limited.

In the late Republic freedom of philosophical, religious, and even political speculation was unchecked.[45] Any supposed attempt to substitute monarchy for the Republic could be treated as a crime worthy of death, but there was nothing to hinder Cicero from making a case in his *de republica* for the thesis that ideally it was the best form of government. By contrast in the Principate, if the relative merits of different constitutions were discussed at all, it became necessary to decide in favour of rule by a single man of supreme wisdom, such as the emperor could be deemed to be; and though the old teaching that monarchy could easily degenerate into tyranny, the worst kind of government, could not be forgotten, it was unsafe, at times when the emperor could fit any delineation of the tyrant to his own head, to expose its evils or even to represent as tyrannical the conduct of a

[44] Eur. fr. 360 Nauck, esp. 39 f.; Democ. 252 D. (in Diels–Kranz, *Fr. der Vorsokratiker*, ii); Thuc. ii. 60. 2–4; cf. Sall. *Cat.* 6 on early Rome: 'libertatem patriam parentesque armis tegere'.

[45] For I. Berlin, *Four Essays on Liberty*, 1969, 118, remarks that the studies of social and political theory 'spring from, and thrive on, discord'. In suppressing discord the Roman Principate dried up their sources.

former ruler, which too closely resembled that of the reigning prince. Books were to be burned for containing such seditious views and their authors put to death, and philosophers who gave them currency were expelled from Rome. Such restrictions on freedom were almost unknown in the Republic.[46]

It is true that in 92 the censors banned the teaching of Latin rhetoric within Rome, but it was soon flourishing without further impediment (Suet. *de rhet.*, esp. 1). In 155 old Cato persuaded the senate to dismiss as rapidly as possible an Athenian embassy composed of philosophers, whose lectures (he thought) were turning the aristocratic youth of Rome away from their old respect for laws and magistrates; the chief offender was presumably the Academic sceptic, Carneades. Both philosophers and rhetoricians were expelled from the city in 161 and 154 (or 173).[47] But in Cicero's time there was no restriction on philosophic speculations. He himself adopted Carneades' views. Epicureanism he abhorred, refuting its doctrines and denouncing its tendency to corrupt morals, but it never entered his head that it should be legally proscribed. It may be relevant that theoretical beliefs did not necessarily affect the practice of men who embraced them. Epicurus inculcated political quietism, but his teaching was ignored by such followers as L. Piso (*cos.* 58) and Caesar's assassin, C. Cassius.[48] The traditional cults presupposed the beliefs that gods existed, and in human form, that they would afford men aid and protection, that their favour could be procured by prayers and sacrifices, and that they gave signs, which men might acquire the skill to interpret, of their approval or disapproval of proposed actions, and so made it possible to avert disasters; in various ways all the philosophic schools impugned these conceptions. The Epicureans denied that the gods intervened in human affairs. Stoics tended to assert the ineluctability of fate. Most philosophers decried anthropomorphism. The sceptics of the Academy doubted everything; Cicero, an augur himself, would expose divination in particular to devastating criticisms. But such subversive discussions were confined to small circles; though they were published in books, we can assume that the circulation was restricted by their price, the lack of

---

[46] Tac. *Ann.* i. 72, iv. 34 f., *Agr.* 2 f., etc.; book-burning was first authorized under Augustus ('res nova et inusitata de studiis', Sen. *Controv.* x. *pr.* 3–5); cf. F. H. Cramer, *Journ. Hist. Ideas* 1945, 157 ff.). Men were not free to write candidly of reigning emperors (*Ann.* i. 1, *Hist.* i. 1), and indictments of past tyrants could be treated as aspersions on the current ruler, if his conduct were similar; even ideal comparisons of the true and virtuous monarch with the tyrant could be dangerous. The expulsions of philosophers from Rome under the Flavians belong to this context.

[47] A. E. Astin, *Cato the Censor*, 1978, 174 ff., for full discussion.

[48] Cf. Lucret. ii. 1–61. A. Momigliano, *JRS* 1941, 149 ff., collects evidence for Epicureans in politics; his suggestions that they were active *as* Epicureans and that the ex-Pompeian Cassius was simultaneously converted to Epicureanism (Cic. *Fam.* xv. 16) and to the cause of Republican freedom are quite implausible. See also O. Murray, *JRS* 1965, esp. 173 and 178 ff.

literacy, and the complexity of the subject matter. Philosophy, as Cicero remarked (*Tusc. Disp.* ii. 4), 'was content with a few judges and shunned the multitude', and Lactantius was surely right in glossing this (*Div. Inst.* iii. 25) with the observation that it required so much preliminary study that it was beyond the reach of women, slaves, artisans, and workers on the land. Even under the Principate it was only the speculations of political theory that were curbed. It could indeed be felt that the very diversity of theological systems, to say nothing of the impiety of some, might undermine faith in the cults among the vulgar,[49] but there was all the less risk of this, since the enlightened were one and all ready to conform externally and set their inferiors an improving example; as the efficacy of traditional forms of worship was thought to depend on the exactitude of their performance and not on the mental attitude of the worshippers, it was unnecessary 'to make windows into men's souls'.

In public even Epicureans and sceptics would practise the cults, and sceptics would actually affirm the truth of the beliefs implied, for which they could find no rational justification; they were of course equally unable to refute them. For such conformity there might be various explanations. Those who adopted a spiritual conception of divinity might regard acts of conventional worship as symbolizing their genuine reverence for it. The Epicureans too claimed a true piety, though their enemies alleged that at heart they were atheists, and that fear of popular opprobrium made them hypocrites. In some minds there was doubtless a lurking suspicion that the generally received beliefs were true; it was then a kind of insurance to act as if they were. But it was probably a common view among the élite that, however erroneous the superstition of the masses might be, it served a necessary social purpose. Cicero sometimes stressed, and exaggerated, the utility of the state religion for purely political ends (ch. 1 n. 51). In public he asserted the age-old and long-enduring claim that it was by Rome's special devotion to her gods that she had acquired by divine favour her imperial dominion (ch. 1 n. 98). We can hardly estimate the effect of this conviction on the morale of Roman soldiers. It could also be held that religion was the indispensable basis for social morality (ch. 1 n. 101). It is hard for us to see the connection, since in most of the cults there was no moral implication, and no explicit ethical instruction was attached to any; for instance, no dogmas warning the wicked of eternal punishment. Perhaps it was felt that if the force of tradition were weakened in the religious sphere it would also be undermined in every other. At any rate Varro, who adhered to a philosophic theology

[49] Varro *ap.* Aug. *Civ. Dei* vi. 5; hence philosophic theology is not for the *forum*; cf. Cic. *de nat. deor.* i. 61, *de div.* ii. 28.

remote from that which he himself could regard as prevalent superstition, was none the less anxious that all the traditional rituals should be kept up and revived. In the same way Cicero, after expounding a sort of Stoic pantheism in the first book of his *de legibus*, inconsequentially proceeds in the second to prescribing a code of sacred laws modelled with only minor amendments on Roman tradition. In his later works he reverted to Academic scepticism, but Cotta, his mouthpiece in *de natura deorum*, still insists on the necessity of maintaining the established religion, and even (as later sceptics would do) his acknowledgement of its truth; while in *de divinatione*, after traversing all the arguments in favour of the official Roman modes of divination or of any claims that the gods revealed their will or the course of future events to men, he declares at the end that there must be no change in the ancestral institutions.[50]

Cicero made no provision for censorship of speculative beliefs in his ideal code of laws, unlike Plato (whom he had in mind), perhaps because they had so little effect on practice. But he did not allow freedom of worship. Foreign cults were to be admitted only if the state sanctioned them.[51] There was in fact a long tradition of naturalizing them, and then in such ways that they were harmonized with Roman modes of worship (Dion. Hal. ii. 19). In 186 secret and presumably orgiastic Bacchanalian rites had been repressed on avowedly moral grounds. Occasional efforts were made in the late Republic and Principate to ban the introduction of certain oriental religions, though in course of time they all obtained the sanction of the state. With the exception of Judaism and Christianity they were all compatible with the continued recognition of the ancestral gods. Not indeed that the state enforced any worship on private individuals; conformity only became necessary if men accepted offices which entailed sacral functions; it was not until Decius made the first systematic attempt to root out Christianity that all men were required to sacrifice to the gods as proof that they had not defected to the new faith. In any case, in comparison with medieval and modern rulers even the emperors lacked the machinery to impose religious uniformity. They were best able to undertake this task when abetted by the zeal and organization of the Church. One may recall Tacitus' remark on astrologers, 'a class of men which our state will never tolerate or forego' (*Hist.* i. 22). Toleration was not a principle of government, except in so far as each subject people could normally retain its own ancestral religion; in practice there was a large measure of freedom for men to worship, as well as to believe, as they chose.

[50] See endnote 4.
[51] Latte, 1960, 270–84, 342 ff. (for earlier reception of foreign religious practices, ch. VII). Cf. also J. A. North, *Proc. Camb. Phil. Soc.* 1979, 85 ff., on the Bacchanalia.

Cicero's code also gives the censors power to prohibit celibacy and to regulate the morals of the people (*de leg.* iii. 71); he actually exhorted Caesar, who had assumed the unfitting role of *praefectus morum*, to encourage procreation and repress sexual misbehaviour (*Marc.* 23), and Augustus was to attempt to carry out this programme. However, in the period of the Republic for which we have evidence, men were not compelled to marry and have children, and the supervision over morals that traditionally belonged to the censors was not exercised continuously, nor did it compare in strictness with the control imposed in later times by ecclesiastical jurisdiction; in any case it chiefly affected (as did Augustus' marriage laws) the upper classes. It was their luxury that a series of sumptuary laws, attested from 217 to Augustus' reign, sought to curtail. None seems to have proved enforceable.[52]

Of course these enactments, like the intermittent severity of censors, represent attempts by the state to regulate private life. But it is an error to suppose that no one ever protested against them as infractions of liberty. In 195 when it was proposed to repeal the Oppian law that prohibited displays of female finery, according to Livy, Cato, in defending the law, had to meet the claim that its repeal was justified in the name of liberty; in his view it could more properly be styled licence. This is one of the texts sometimes adduced to prove that 'the Roman conception of liberty' comprised the principle of due restraint and moderation (p. 320). It is relevant that the people did not endorse Cato's judgement: they repealed the law.[53] In 97 the tribune Duronius, urging the repeal of another sumptuary law, is represented as saying: 'you have been bound and restrained by the bitter bonds of slavery, by the law that commands you to live soberly . . . What use is freedom, if we are debarred from ruining ourselves with luxury, if we wish?' He was expelled from the senate by the censors. Here again proof is found that the Romans rejected so anarchic a conception of freedom. But the voters had adopted Duronius' proposal (Val. Max. ii. 9. 5). Moreover, the inefficacy of sumptuary laws which remained on the statute book shows that they were not in sufficient accord with the real sentiments of the citizens. The emperor Tiberius pronounced their futility (Tac. *Ann.* iii. 53 f.). For Tacitus any kind of moral legislation, however well justified by degeneration in social behaviour, is coercion

---

[52] Laws of 217, 215, 182, 161, 143, 115; a Licinian law before 103, and Antian of 68 (?); Sulla, Caesar, and Augustus all legislated in this matter (evidence in Rotondi, *Leges publicae populi romani*). Cf. ch. 1. n. 74. Cic. *Att.* xiii. 7 shows, *contra* Dio xliii. 25. 2, that Caesar's measure was ineffective. Augustus' marriage laws: *IM*, App. 9.

[53] Livy xxxiv. 1–8, esp. 2. 13. According to Livy the advocates of repeal were in fact arguing for the liberty of fathers and husbands to keep women under their subjection without state intervention (7. 11–13)!

(*Ann.* iii. 26. 1); even Numa had 'bound the people down by religious cults and divine law', (26. 4), and the enactments by which Augustus visited childlessness with financial pains and penalties, to say nothing of his harshness towards adultery, constituted 'stricter bonds' (28. 3).

Hence, it is not true, as Schulz held, that 'freedom to the Romans *never* meant the capacity to do or leave undone what one pleased, to live at one's own sweet will' (my italics);[54] this was certainly a view of freedom that some Romans entertained; and we shall see that this meaning was often inherent in usages of *liber* and its derivatives. It may seem the stranger that Schulz should have fallen into this error, since he himself delineated 'the extreme individualism' that pervaded Roman private law, for example the law of marriage, of associations (when there was any community of rights and obligations, as between coheirs or business partners, each person concerned 'must be at liberty to escape from the union and its limitations at any time'), of ownership, and of succession: he depreciated those obligations which did restrict a man's absolute control over his property. In analysing the classical law concerning contracts of hire, he remarked that it corresponded to social and economic conditions in which the *beati possidentes* preponderated, with the result that the rules of law suited their interests: 'parties were perfectly free to form the contract as they liked, which in this case means as the capitalist liked.' A 'generous freedom of disposition' was accorded to the testator: it seems to have been more generous under the Twelve Tables than it became as a result of praetorian and legislative modifications, some doubtless introduced to prevent men from exercising their rights in ways which had never been envisaged when the fifth-century code was drawn up, and which remained offensive to general opinion.[55] Still, one may question whether Schulz should have subsumed under liberty legal rules in which, though the modern theorist can detect its operation, the Romans themselves failed to enunciate it explicitly; they were not clearly conscious of it as a 'principle' to be respected, perhaps because it was so little infringed. To some modern thinkers the right to private property has appeared to be an essential part of freedom, perhaps its guarantee. Cicero, who thought that it was one of the chief purposes of social and political organization to ensure that each man 'retained his own', and who

---

[54] Schulz, 1936, 140 f.

[55] Schulz, 1936, 146 ff., 1951, 102 ff. (eulogizing the 'purely humanistic law of marriage . . . as a free and freely dissoluble union of two equal partners for life'). Law of hire: ibid. 542–6. Praetorian restrictions on testator's freedom: 266 ff.; cf. also provisions of *leges Voconia* (169) and *Falcidia* (40) and of Augustan marriage laws. The praetor also limited the testamentary rights of freedmen in the interest of patrons. The spendthrift could be deprived of disposal of his property (ibid. 200–2). In old days the censors could penalize a man who farmed his land badly (Gell. iv. 12). See n. 3 for restraints on slave-owners.

deplored some measures of land distribution or relief of debtors as assaults on property (though their advocates certainly never attacked it in principle), only hints at a connection between property and freedom; it may be that *populares* argued that the poor were not truly independent if they owned nothing.[56]

The Twelve Tables allowed citizens to form associations (*collegia*) with what rules they pleased, provided that they did nothing deleterious under public law. In the late Republic they were active at riots in Rome, and the senate dissolved them in 64. This was an usurpation of legislative authority. Clodius' law of 58 reasserted and perhaps extended the right of association. He could have appealed, as Cicero so often did, to ancestral custom, but also, as for his other measures, to liberty, a word ever on the lips of *populares* like himself. Men could have become aware that the right was part of their freedom, once they had been deprived of it. Caesar and the emperors were to impose new restrictions. *Collegia* now required a governmental licence granted only on certain conditions. It may be doubted if the rules were invariably operative, but the change illustrates the abridgement of freedom under the Principate.[57]

The *collegia*, though some consisted of men following the same trade, seem to have served primarily social and religious purposes; unlike medieval guilds they had no legal power to monopolize production, determine standards, or fix wages and prices. In general the state too made no attempt to regulate economic activity.[58] *Laissez-faire* prevailed, though it was not an axiom of economic theory, of which there was virtually none,[59] nor grounded on doctrines of personal freedom.

For example, though the state imposed port dues and taxes on sales, it was only to raise revenue. Protection of trade and industry was almost unknown. When the state did intervene, it was with little success. Prohibitions or limitations of lending money at interest were of small or transient effect.[60] The apparatus for economic controls did

---

[56] *de offic*. i. 20 f., 51, ii. 73, 78, iii. 21–4, *de rep.* i. 49 on property rights; see endnote 3 and *Phil*. xiii. 1 for faint association with *libertas*; cf. pp. 347 ff.

[57] XII Tables: Gaius, *Dig*. xlvii. 22. 4. Numa was supposed to have instituted *collegia* of artisans (Plut. *Numa* 17; Pliny, *NH* xxxiv. 1, xxxv. 159), and the tyrant Tarquinius Superbus to have dissolved numerous associations as seditious (Dionys. iv. 43). *SC* of 64 and Clodius' law: Cic. *Pis*. 9; Ascon. 7 f. C.; Dio xxxviii. 13; for Clodius and *libertas* see nn. 142, 158; Caesar and Augustus: Suet. *Caes*. 42, *Aug*. 32. For exhaustive treatment see F. M. de Robertis, *Il diritto associativo rom.*, 1938.

[58] See also ch. 3 pp. 176 ff.   [59] Finley, 1985, ch. 1.

[60] Cato, *de agric. pr.*: 'maiores nostri sic habuerunt et ita in legibus posiverunt, furem dupli condemnari, feneratorem quadrupli.' Allegedly interest rates were limited and finally prohibited by the XII Tables (Tac. *Ann.* vi. 16) and plebiscites of 357, 347, 342 (Livy vii. 16, 27. 3, 42. 1); a *lex Marcia* of unknown date was passed 'adversus faeneratores, ut si usuras [perhaps at an excessive rate] exegissent, de his reddendis per manus iniectionem cum eis ageretur' (Gaius iv. 23). For contentions on the question in the second century Astin (n. 47), pp. 319–23 App. i. 54.

not exist. The state was strong enough to perform the vital functions of mustering troops and raising money to pay for them, but for very little else. It did not even assist the plaintiff in bringing a defendant to court or in executing the court's judgement.[61] The penal laws were dormant, unless private citizens would come forward to prosecute offenders. No doubt it was on this account that sumptuary laws were inoperative. Rome itself was unpoliced before the Principate. But the administrative feebleness of the state persisted even then. For instance Domitian could not carry out his restrictions on viticulture (Suet. *Dom.* 7. 2). With a larger bureaucracy fourth-century emperors did seek to regiment economic life. Diocletian set maximum prices for virtually all goods and services; infraction was to be visited with death; the empire (it is said) was deluged with blood; but in the end his edict had to be withdrawn. Many sorts of men were to be bound to their hereditary vocations, but the laws were often evaded, and we cannot be sure how effective they were.[62] The autocrats of this time had an army of officials to do their will, which the Republican government had lacked, but they could not keep these very officials under control.[63] As for Republican times, there was no need at Rome for any agitation to sweep away in the name of freedom the innumerable regulations of economic activity which characterized the medieval and early modern periods: they did not exist.

No doubt social pressures restricted the individual far more than the state did. To J. S. Mill they represented the most insidious danger to liberty. Of this most Romans in all probability would hardly have been conscious. Following Panaetius, but as always exercising his own judgement, Cicero actually laid down that the 'decorum' required of a good man was to be found in conduct that met with the approbation of his fellows (*de offic.* i. 99); in illustrating this doctrine, he takes examples from Roman proprieties, which could differ from the Greek examples Panaetius would have given, for instance the ban on nudity (ibid. 127, 129); and it is he, no less than Panaetius, who holds that the established customs and conventions of a society are binding rules, and that we may not treat as exemplary the deviations of a Socrates or an

232 says that a ban on usury stood in the statutes in 89; it had clearly become obsolete on the principle that laws could be repealed 'tacito consensu omnium per desuetudinem' (Julian, *Dig.* i. 4. 32. 1); Caesar's law 'de modo credendi possidendique intra Italiam' similarly fell into abeyance (Tac. l.c.), as had the law *de modo agrorum* partially revived by Tiberius Gracchus. Cf. ch. 3 nn. 106–11 with text.

[61] Kelly, 1966, ch. 1.

[62] Lact. *de mort. persec.* vii. 6. 7; A. H. M. Jones, *Later Roman Empire*, 1974, ch. XXI.

[63] See e.g. *Cod. Theod.* viii. 5 *passim*; the more scattered evidence from the Principate (S. Mitchell, *JRS* 1976, 106 ff.) indicates the earlier prevalence of similar abuses. Nero and later emperors could also not make effective rules to prevent extortions by publicans (Tac. *Ann.* xiii. 51; Ulpian, *Dig.* xxxix. 4. 12 *pr.*).

Aristippus (ibid. 148). His tone is not polemical, and he doubtless counted on general assent. Of course eccentricity was far from uncommon among the high aristocracy, of whom we happen to know more than of the rural and municipal gentry, to say nothing of the mass of the population, and the most open contravention of traditional rules of behaviour does not seem to have injured nobles in their political careers. How often, if at all, they asserted their right as free men to set these rules aside we cannot tell.

VI

I now turn to modern claims that the Romans had their own distinctive conception of freedom, as not merely subject to necessary restraint but comprising restraint as an element inherent in its very nature, and far different from the Greek conception of *eleutheria*.

Wirszubski remarks that 'freedom, comprising as it does two different concepts, namely "freedom from" and "freedom to", neither of which admits of any but general definitions, is a somewhat vague term'.[64] A man would be absolutely free if he were (a) free *from* all human restraints and (b) free *to* realize all his desires, subject only to physical limitations. Since such absolute freedom is obviously unattainable, he will think it enough if he is (a) free *from* all human restraints except those which he consciously or unconsciously accepts, and (b) free *to* realize his desires so far as they are compatible with those restraints. It is clear that these 'negative' and 'positive' conceptions of freedom to a great extent overlap. The slave owner is free *to* make his slave work for him as he pleases in proportion as he is free *from* any constraints of law or public opinion. But the 'positive' conception may go further. Ancient thinkers, however far they exalted the authority of the state, had not indeed evolved the notion of some moderns that the liberty of the real self can be promoted when the state compels the individual to do for his own true good what he does not consciously wish to do. But it is also a positive conception of freedom which identifies it with a share in political power. Both Greeks and Romans held that in one sense it did consist in the exercise of political rights; of course this sort of liberty might also be the guarantee of negative liberty, e.g. freedom from arbitrary punishment. It is no less clear that the freedom, negative or positive, of one man or set of men may be the slavery of another man or set of men. The freedom of the master is correlative with the servitude of his chattel. Political rights may signify power for some, subjection for others. The underprivileged may

---

[64] Wirszubski 1; cf. Berlin (n. 45), ch. III.

complain in the name of liberty if they suffer restraints from which others are exempt or if they lack power which others enjoy. Thus a connection arises between freedom and equality. Romans spoke of *aequa libertas*. Equally the privileged may claim that their own liberty is abridged by new restrictions, which may actually enlarge the liberty of the rest. In practice liberty means different things to different people, and becomes the battle-cry of opposed sections of the community. It would be extremely surprising if all Greeks or all Romans had agreed even among themselves on the specific rights through which freedom negative or positive was to be realized. Living in a multitude of cities with varying social structures and political systems, each of which was liable to bitter civil conflicts, the Greeks could hardly be expected to have any single and concordant view. But Romans too, who lived through the struggles of the early and late Republic, are no more likely to have been in agreement. Those who contrast Greek and Roman ideas seem to be really contrasting Athenian democratic ideas, which they sometimes misunderstand, with those held, not by all Romans, but by Roman aristocrats. Of course, since the Roman political system was very different from Athenian democracy, it is easy enough to show that there were differences in the rights that Romans and Athenians saw as constituents of freedom. I may give one paradoxical instance. It was Romans, not Athenians, who treated personal protection against magisterial power as an important element of freedom. This was because the *imperium* of Roman magistrates made them potentially oppressive, as magistrates could not be in the Athenian democracy. Athenians did not need the *ius provocationis* or the tribunician *auxilium*. Particular forms of liberty are valued most when they become necessary in practice to protect men from some kind of coercion inimical to their desires and interests.

As we have seen, Schulz denied that *libertas* ever meant doing as you please. He held that limitations were inherent in the Roman conception; this is a very different matter from acknowledging that different Romans saw the necessity of limiting their own freedom in different ways, and still more that of others. He also claims that '*libertas* is a truly Roman conception, clear, limited, practical, somewhat matter-of-fact' (n. 54). Yet neither he nor anyone has been able to delineate this clear, unitary conception with any precision. He and others delight in contrasting it with the licence supposed to characterize Greek *eleutheria*. For instance, Hellegouarc'h set off the egalitarian and democratic view of freedom supposedly prevalent in Greece, which he took to be essentially negative (as if belief in the sovereign power of the people could be so construed), against the positive view of the Romans, positive apparently because it included the notion that free men owe deference to their superiors! It will be seen later that Romans of all ranks could treat deference to the authority of others as antithetic to their own *libertas*, and it may be suspected that scholars who cannot discern this are foisting on the admired Romans their own ideal.

Schulz specified one particular limitation inherent in *libertas*, which would illustrate how Romans moralized the concept: they recognized that 'one symptom of the liberty of a human being is that he grants liberty to others'. Kloesel (pp. 134 f.) and Wirszubski (p. 8) more or less agreed. Of course such recognition of human rights by slave-owners is quite unthinkable. Schulz adduced only one text in support of this absurdity, and he misunderstood it.[65]

Certainly the conception that in Hobbes' words 'a free man is he that . . . is not hindered to do what he hath the will to do' was current in Greece. Thus at Delphi manumitted slaves were entitled 'to do what they wish and run off wherever they want' (e.g. Collitz, *GDI* 1685–7). In his *Republic* Plato portrayed a democratic city full of liberty and of freedom of speech, in which everyone was allowed to do whatever he wished; he would then satisfy every desire without regard to law and morals in a society unrestrained by any authority (557 f., 562–4). In the *Laws* again he censured the 'total' freedom at Athens in much the same way (698–701), while conceding that some degree of freedom, or some compromise between freedom and complete subjection, is beneficial (701e; cf. 694a, 697c). On the same footing Aristotle once suggested that Sparta alone had grasped the necessity of forming the character of her citizens; elsewhere men lived as they pleased (*EN* 1180^{a}24 ff.). He says that this was one, (not the only), democratic conception of freedom (*Pol.* 1310^{a}27 ff., 1317^{b}11). It is obvious that Plato disapproved of freedom as he describes it, while Aristotle indicates that true freedom is not to be found in mere absence of restriction; there are hints that he regards the free man as one obedient to the law or reason in his breast (*EN* 1128^{a}32, *Met.* 1075^{a}19). But we need not doubt that 'doing as you like' was one conception of freedom common among the Greeks. We shall see that this was just as true of the Romans.

---

[65] Schulz, 1936, ch. VIII. Livy xxxvii. 54. 6, from a *Rhodian* speech to the senate: 'rerum natura disiungit [the Rhodians from king Eumenes], ut nos liberi etiam aliorum libertatis causam agamus, reges serva omnia et subiecta imperio suo esse velint'; Schulz says that only the second half of the sentence comes from Polyb. xxi. 22, but the first half is simply a rhetorical antithesis to the second, and the ideas are Greek. The Rhodians are not granting freedom to others, but arguing that the Romans in conformity with their general policy of liberating Greeks should not subject any Greek cities to Eumenes; they are pleading the cause of other *Greeks*, as distinct from barbarians (ch. 54. 11), who can properly be handed over to a king. The argument is also reminiscent of the *topos* on the common interest of democratic and therefore free cities in Dem. xv. 18–21. Respect for others' freedom is approved in Livy vii. 33. 3, xxiii. 12. 9, but these and other texts cited by Wirszubski 8 n. 5 do not show that it was conceived as part of one's own. Cf. also Kloesel 128 ff.; Wirszubski 35, 112; Hellegouarc'h 542 ff.

The Stoics took the negative sense of freedom and gave it a different twist. Cicero writes, in formulating their views: 'What is freedom but the power to live as you wish? Who then lives as he wishes, except the man who lives aright?' He whose life is not directed by moral principles is a slave to material things outside his own control and to his own passions. Only the wise man is free, because in accordance with the divine reason within him he conforms himself to the dispensations of a beneficent providence and does not see them as constraints, like the Christian submitting to God, 'in whose service is perfect freedom'[66] The Cynics inculcated the doctrine that in order to be free a man must rid himself of all desire for material goods or anything that fortune could deny.

Throughout lands of Greek culture, perhaps including Italy, popular preachers disseminated such ideas.[67] Now Ennius wrote (fr. 300–3 V.):

> sed virum virtute vera animatum addecet
> fortiterque innoxium stare adversus adversarios;
> ea libertas est, qui pectus purum et firmum gestitat;
> aliae res obnoxiosae nocte in obscura latent.

> It is proper for a man to live inspired by true manliness and to stand against his adversaries strong and blameless; it is freedom when he bears a pure and steadfast heart; all else is servile, hidden in the darkness of night.

Kloesel held that this cannot be a mere translation from Ennius' Greek model, Euripides' *Phoenix*, for then the Greek lines would have been preserved by an excerptor, like so many other Greek aphorisms on freedom! Kloesel inferred that Ennius was setting out a truly Roman conception of freedom in which the limits imposed by moral rectitude are inherent. But there is no other clear instance of this loaded sense of *libertas* in Latin, except in writers who were subject to Stoic or Christian influence;[68] it is in fact a more natural usage for Greek *eleutheria*. There is not the slightest objection to supposing that Ennius reflects the moralizing of Greek teachers of his day. Similarly the apophthegm recommended to orators that he must be deemed free who is no slave to vice (*ad Her.* iv. 23), is clearly one of several borrowed from the Greek schools.

---

[66] *Parad. St.* 34; *de offic.* i. 70. Freedom often has this sense in Seneca and Marcus Aurelius; see esp. Epict. iv. 1.

[67] See e.g. Diog. Laert. vi. 71; Dio Chrys. xiv, lxxx. However, Cynicism hardly penetrated Rome in the Republic (D. R. Dudley, *History of Cynicism*, 1937, ch. vi). Epicurus too said that 'the greatest fruit of self-sufficiency was freedom' (Bailey, fr. 77), and Epicureans claimed to free men from (superstitious) fear (Cic. *de nat. deor.* i. 56), but freedom is not prominent in Epicurean teaching.

[68] Kloesel 126 ff. But see *TLL* s.v. *libertas* 1315. 70–1316. 43.

Greeks also took a positive view of freedom. Admitting that it was fundamental to democracy, Aristotle identified it in effect with the sovereignty of the majority.[69] Jacqueline de Romilly observed that Greeks could regard dominion over others as an extension of freedom.[70] Romans could share this way of thinking. As we have seen, the unqualified freedom that Rome possessed as a state derived from her imperial strength. Within the state too power and liberty are assimilated. Scipio Aemilianus could say that *dignitas* (worth and rank) sprang from integrity, *honor* (office and distinction) from *dignitas*, *imperium* from *honor*, and *libertas* from *imperium*. In other words a man was most free when he had the fullest right to enforce his own will. Similarly the emperor Tiberius spoke in the senate of the great and unrestricted ('tam libera') power with which he had been vested. He could be charged with destroying the liberty of the magnates, when he curtailed their influence in the courts.[71] Cicero refers to the people's 'ius potestas libertasque' in one breath. You will not satisfy the people's desire for *freedom*, he argues, by giving them only a little *power*. Catiline is made by Sallust to adjure his associates to reclaim their freedom: he means a share in the influence, power, offices, and riches of which they had been deprived.[72] Livy represents the favourites of Tarquin as complaining that their loss of power amounts to servitude (ii. 3. 3). The 'excessive liberty' of the people, of which aristocrats complain in his story, is identical with their 'excessive power' (iii. 57. 6, 59. 1 f.). So too in private life the 'freedom' of the husband consists in his control over his wife (xxxiv. 2. 2).

It is indeed power that enables men, within the bounds that they possess it, to do as they like. But this anarchic conception of freedom cannot be seen as typical of Greek democratic thinking. Plato merely produced a model of the conditions that would result if men acted on this principle, and in sheer prejudice made it the principle of democracy. His 'never-never' world is not even a caricature of the Athenian system, which imposed heavy and unchallenged obligations on the citizens to serve the city with their persons and property. It is ludicrous to find 'the Greek conception' of freedom, as if there were any unitary Greek conception of it, in his account, and then to contrast it with the

---

[69] *Pol.* 1317ᵃ 40 ff. Here and elsewhere (e.g. 1261ᵃ32, 1275ᵃ22, 1275ᵇ2, 18, 1279ᵃ8) Aristotle stresses that free citizens take turns in ruling and being ruled; in fact at Athens neither this principle nor the concomitant use of sortition and payment of officials applied to those with the highest responsibilities, which they might exercise for years on end, while real power often belonged rather to 'orators', who also might guide the assembly for long periods; all were men of property.

[70] *Thucydides and Athenian Imperialism*, 1963, 81.

[71] *ORF²*, fr. 32 (p. 132); Suet. *Tib.* 29; Tac. *Ann.* i. 75 (on which see Kelly, 1966, ch. 1; de Ste Croix, 1982, 366 f.).

[72] Cic. *de leg. agr.* ii. 29, *de rep.* ii. 50; Sall. *Cat.* 20. 5 ff.

ordered liberty approved at Rome. It was a share for all citizens in political rights that Greek democrats prized above all as constituting their freedom, and Romans too subsumed such rights, naturally not the same as in Athens, under liberty.

In fact, however, to judge from linguistic usage, the purely negative sense of freedom was more congenial to the Roman mind than to the Greek. Unlike their Greek equivalents, *liber* and its derivatives denote mere absence of restraint in a great variety of contexts. A few illustrations will suffice. In Republican Latin arms and shoulders may be free to carry weapons (Caes. *BG* vii. 56. 4), houses are free of occupiers (Plaut. *Cas.* 533), and a bed free of a wife (Cic. *Att.* xiv. 13. 5); access is free, if unimpeded (*Bell. Alex.* 30. 5); a man is free, when unoccupied (Cic. *Fam.* vii. 1. 4), and then his time too is free (*de orat.* iii. 57); Seneca complains that a throng of clients leaves the patron no freedom (*Brev. Vitae* 2). Men can be liberated from hope, fear, and bias.[73] On some philosophical views death frees the mind from the body, and the mind then comes 'in liberum caelum'; for then its vision is unclouded. Or again, the philosophical sceptic is free from the laws of dogmatic systems. Similarly the writer or orator can be free from rules of diction or rhythm.[74] In law land can be free of servitudes or easements (and other obligations); *libertas* is a technical term in this sense. If condemned to death, a man may receive 'liberum mortis arbitrium', the right to choose how he will die (Suet. *Dom.* 8. 4). For a lawyer a man's *arbitrium* or *voluntas* is free when he may act without instructions from another.[75] The *filiusfamilias* or slave may receive free, i.e. unrestricted, power to manage his *peculium*.[76] According to Severus Alexander 'libera matrimonia esse antiquitus placuit': that meant that no limitations could be placed on the right of the spouses to divorce.[77] There were precise rules for the making of a valid will, but Trajan confirmed the privilege of soldiers to make wills 'in any manner they wish'; this was called 'libera testamenti factio', a term also used when freedmen were exempted from their normal testamentary obligations to their patrons.[78] For Caesar the Suebi enjoyed 'freedom in life: from boyhood they are altogether unaccustomed to duty and discipline and act entirely as they please' (*BG* iv. 1. 9).

This negative sense of freedom is perfectly apparent in Roman political usage. The protection for the person which the laws secured to Roman citizens was regarded as liberty, because it freed them *from* certain forms of coercion. The ballot enabled voters to exercise 'that

---

[73] Sall. *Cat.* 4. 2: 'mihi a spe, metu, partibus rei publicae animus liber erat'.
[74] Cic. *de senect.* 80, *Tusc. Disp.* i. 51, v. 33; cf. *TLL.* s.v. *liber*, 1284. 20 ff.
[75] e.g. *Dig.* i. 7. 28, iii. 5. 18 (19). 2.   [76] e.g. *Dig.* vi. 1. 41. 1.
[77] *CJ* viii. 38. 2.   [78] *Dig.* xxix. 1. 1, xxxviii. 2. 47. 2.

freedom which consists in doing whatever they wish'. These words of Cicero (*Planc.* 16) show that 'doing as you like' was at least one sense of *libertas* perfectly acceptable to Romans in a political context. A *libera legatio* entitled a senator to travel abroad on his private business 'sine procuratione . . . sine mandatis, sine ullo rei publicae munere' (without charge, restrictions, or public duty): i.e. he could do as he pleased.[79] Freedom of speech for a senator meant that he could speak what he felt without being subject to fear or pressure; Cicero would certainly have concurred with Tacitus that it existed 'when you are allowed to think what you please and to say what you think'.[80] Liberty of speech merges into a more general independence, proper to senators at least, which means that a man must be free to choose his own course of action. Valerius Maximus groups 'libere dicta aut facta' in a single chapter (vi. 2).

A 'free tongue' is an expression used by Naevius (*com.* 112 R^2) and by others after him. Plautus writes of 'libertas orationis' (*Bacch.* 168). There is no necessity to multiply testimonies to this kind of usage in Latin; they are extremely common.[81] Some have thought that as the Romans did not feel the need of a single word, like the Greek '*parrhesia*', to denote freedom of speech, they valued it little.[82] It seems to me more striking evidence of the importance they attached to it that the word *liber* can be used *tout court* to mean 'speaking one's mind', unlike equivalent words in Greek, English and other languages; thus Horace has 'liber amicus' for 'candid friend',[83] and Quintilian can refer to the Athenian comic poets as 'liberrimum genus hominum'.[84] Such freedom of speech can go too far, and may then be stigmatized as licence; it is, however, significant that even in excess it can still be described as liberty.[85] Admittedly in most cases where *libertas* corresponds to '*parrhesia*', the specific reference is made clear in the context.[86]

Freedom of speech is most often claimed as a due to senators, and vital to them, but that is perhaps an accident of our evidence: Cicero and other upper-class authors were most concerned with senatorial rights. However, in his defence of Plancius, Cicero answers the prosecutor's complaint that Plancius' father had made too 'rough' a

---

[79] *de leg.* iii. 18, disapproving of the privilege.

[80] Tac. *Hist.* i. 1; cf. *Agr.* 2 f.; cf. Cic. *Phil.* i. 27, iii. 5, xi. 3, etc.

[81] *TLL*, s.v. *libertas* 1314. 70 ff.

[82] Nepos, *Timoleon* 5. 3 renders *parrhesia* as 'talem libertatem . . . in qua cuivis liceret de quo vellet impune dicere'. On the Greek ideal see A. Momigliano, *Dict. of Hist. of Ideas* ii. 1973, 256 ff.

[83] *Sat.* i. 4. 132; cf. 3. 51: 'at est truculentior et plus aequo liber: simplex fortisque habeatur'; 4. 90.

[84] *Inst.* xii. 2. 22; cf. x. 1. 65; Hor. *Sat.* i. 4. 1–5.

[85] Hor. *Ep.* ii. 1. 145 ff., on Fescennine farces; *Ars Poet.* 281 f. on Old Comedy. Cf. Quint. *Inst.* xi. 1. 67, xii. 9. 11 ff., on forensic abuse.

[86] e.g. Cic. *Rosc. Amer.* 9, *Sest.* 123, *Planc.* 33, *de orat.* iii. 4.

remark by saying that though he had perhaps spoken with too much freedom, if the prosecutor, Juventius, were to contend that that was intolerable, he would rejoin that it was intolerable for men not to respect the freedom of a Roman Eques. 'Where is our famous tradition, where that equity in rights, where the ancient freedom which, though oppressed by the evils of civil strife, ought by now to have raised its head and to have at last revived and set itself erect?' Freedom of speech is an ancient right, which he can illustrate by the gibes made by the auctioneer Granius (whose occupation was not very respectable) against men of the highest eminence in the generation before the Social war; the elder Plancius was at most too keen on sticking to equestrian rights and freedom.[87] Cicero does not indeed assert that the humblest plebeian properly had the same liberty as a Plancius or even a Granius: that was not necessary to his argument (and would not have accorded with his own prejudices). But in law the Eques can have had no peculiar title to say what he thought, which the poorer citizen lacked, and we simply do not know that humble people would themselves never have claimed the right. Of course persons of higher rank would have objected, just as Juventius objected to Plancius' behaviour. Valerius Maximus thought it improper that the son of a freedman should have freely inveighed against Pompey as 'carnifex adulescentulus' (a teenage hangman). Pompey had indeed to endure insults ('licentia') from all sorts of people; Valerius views this as a conflict between his massive 'auctoritas' and their 'libertas'. Quintilian held that what would be freedom of speech in persons of high degree would be licence in others. The remark is evidence only of upper-class prejudice.[88] Moreover, Valerius and Quintilian both wrote under the Principate, when popular rights had vanished.

Admittedly the citizen had no right to address the people on public affairs. Meetings (*contiones*) at which they were debated could be summoned only by a magistrate, and no private person could speak at them except on his invitation. This did not mean that all sorts of views on controversial issues were not freely ventilated, even though it is likely that magistrates seldom chose to call on humble citizens to give their opinions, which most of them would doubtless have been unable to do. However, the people at large could declare their sentiments in collective acclamations, and Cicero lamented that they, as well as the

---

[87] *Planc.* 33, 55. For 'too freely' Hor. *Sat.* i. 4. 103, ii. 8. 37 (cf. n. 83). Cato's 'lingua acerba et immodice libera' (Livy xxxix. 40. 10) did not injure his career.

[88] Val. Max. ix. 6. 8, vi. 2. 4; Quint. *Inst.* iii. 8. 48. Cf. Cic. *Font.* 40 on Gallic 'ad male dicendum licentiam'. The 'maledicus' was too readily taken to be 'liber', Quint. ii. 12. 4 f. *Licentia* is also a technical term of rhetoric for reproaches 'cum apud eos quos aut vereri aut metuere debemus, tamen aliquid *pro iure nostro* dicimus' (*ad Her.* iv. 48 f.; cf. Quint. ix. 2. 27); cf. Thuc. iii. 38; Dem. ix. 3 f.

leading men, had lost their freedom, when it had allegedly become unsafe for them to express themselves in this way.[89]

Thus it is untrue that in the Republic freedom of speech was not associated with the Roman conception, or rather with some Roman conceptions, of *libertas*, nor is it legitimate to argue *e silentio* that it was properly confined to men of rank.[90] We simply cannot tell that it was not valued by ordinary commoners. Of course it would often have been imprudent for them to exercise it in a manner adverse to those with the power to hurt or help them. But that is no less true in every society, including those which in principle prize freedom of speech most highly.

Nor is it significant that freedom of speech was subject to certain legal limitations, as it usually is. In our own country, for instance, it is limited in various ways, notably by the law on defamation, but we do not conclude that the right does not exist at all. A clause in the Twelve Tables was understood in antiquity to have made it a capital offence to defame a man with opprobrious songs (*carmina*); it would be characteristic of early Roman law if this was interpreted in a literal and restrictive sense, and therefore did not cover defamation of any other kind.[91] But the capital penalty must have fallen into desuetude, when the poet Naevius (*c.*200) was merely imprisoned for his abusive lampoons on leading men, and only released by the tribunes after he had apologized (Gell. iii. 3. 15). Horace supposed that the ribaldry of Fescennine verses attracted a flogging (n. 85). No cases are recorded. Persons defamed from the stage could sue for damages. Lucilius was notorious for the bitterness with which in his satirical verses he assailed men of note: Horace thought that he escaped with impunity because he was a man of substance himself and protected by Scipio Aemilianus and his friends.[92] There is no proof that the Sullan law *de iniuriis* covered libel or slander before imperial times. The praetor gave a civil action against anyone who uttered or instigated *convicium*, but *convicium* was not any kind of abuse: it seems to have meant originally the concerted shouting of insults, and always denoted chanting or bawling in public.[93] One may doubt if such suits were ever at all common;

[89] *Contiones*: StR i³. 197 ff. Acclamations: Cic. *Sest.* 123, *Phil.* ii. 64 (the people only free to groan); Val. Max. vi. 2. 6; A. Cameron, *Circus Factions*, 1976, 157 ff., for popular demonstrations at the Games, even in the Empire.

[90] Cic. *Fam.* ix. 16. 3 treats it as integral to *libertas*, and we cannot be sure that many of low rank would not have thought the same.

[91] *FIRA* i². p. 52. esp, Cic. *de rep.* iv. 12, *Tusc. Disp.* iv. 4.

[92] *Sat.* ii. 1. 65 f. (note 79 ff. for libel actions of his own time); Trebonius *ap.* Cic. *Fam.* xii. 16. 3; A. Watson, *Law of Obligations in the Later Roman Republic*, 1965, ch. 16.

[93] *Convicium*: Dig. xlvii. 10. 15. 2–12. Cf. H. Usener, *Kl. Schr.* iv. 356 ff.; Lintott, 1968, 8–10; Kelly, 1966, 21–3. E. Weber, *Peasants into Frenchmen*, 1977, ch. 22, discusses similar practices surviving in 19th cent. France, which served to enforce obedience to traditional *mores*. General

there would be safety in numbers when a crowd shouted maledictions, and the responsibility of the organizer might be hard to prove. Moreover, the praetor could refuse a suit unless he judged the insults to be 'adversus bonos mores', against accepted standards. The procedure gave no remedy for written libels, nor probably for the mellifluous slanders of orators like Cicero. The praetor's general edict allowing suits for injury to a man's personality did no doubt cover defamation,[94] yet Cicero's invectives, and some of Catullus' poems, suggest that there was virtually no fear among men of standing in the Republic that they might have to compensate the victims of their most mendacious abuse; at worst their language might be censured as 'too free' (n. 87). It would be servitude, said Cicero (*Sulla*, 48), if you could not speak against anyone you wished. As for the poor, to sue them would have been futile: they had no means of paying damages. Under the Principate indeed things changed; defamation was more strictly repressed, and if directed against the emperor or leading men, assimilated to treason.

VII

It is often held that for the Romans, unlike the Greeks, the limits imposed by law were of the essence of freedom. This is yet another false contrast between Roman and Greek ideas. Certainly Greeks could write as if there was an antithesis between freedom and law; thus Herodotus said of the Spartans that 'though free, they are not free in all respects: above them is set a master in the law'.[95] If the jurist Florentinus also opposes law to freedom (n. 21), that is written off as a borrowing from Greek theory. But other Romans expressed themselves in similar fashion. Sallust describes a primitive people as 'without laws or government, free and unconfined' (*Cat.* 6. 1). A character in Plautus' *Trinummus* (1032 f.) complains that nowadays no one cares what the laws sanction: corruption is approved by custom and 'free from the laws'. A dictator is 'free and released from the bonds of the law' (Livy iv. 11. 3). For Cicero the people at large or the Equites are 'free from' a law, when it is binding on senators alone (*Cluent.* 151, *Rab. Post.* 12).

To be sure the Romans did not see laws as necessarily constricting freedom. On the contrary the liberties they prized were themselves

edict *de iniuriis*: Gaius iii. 220; *Dig.* xlvii. 10. 25 ff., which also concerns the special edict (Augustan?) 'ne quid infamandi causa fiat'.

[94] Tac. *Ann.* i. 72. Cf. the Augustan extension of the Sullan *lex de iniuriis* to cover libels against anyone, *Dig.* xlvii. 10. 5. 9–11, 6; Suet. *Aug.* 55.

[95] Hdt. vii. 104; cf. Eur. *Hec.* 864 ff.; Plato, *Laws* 698b, 699b. Berlin (n. 45) 148 quotes Bentham's view that every law is an infraction of liberty.

based on the laws. They could therefore speak of liberty and laws in the same breath (n. 96). It was obvious enough that the alternative to the rule of law was that of sheer force. For Cicero the violence of Clodius' gangs subverted both freedom and laws (*Mil.* 77). So did the tyrannic power (*regnum*) that Caesar usurped. But laws might either guarantee or deny men the right to act as they wished, and it cannot be concluded that all Romans accepted that legal restraint was inherent in the very idea of freedom. Scholars who believe this lay too much weight on Cicero's argument: 'in a state held together by laws' it is essential that the laws be scrupulously observed by the courts; that is the bond that secures the *dignitas* of senators and Equites (whom he was addressing), and the basis of liberty and the source of justice: 'we are all slaves of the laws in order that we may be free'. It is in the laws that the privileges of the orders and the competence of the courts have their origin; 'it is by the laws that we obtain all our blessings, rights, liberty, and our very survival'. His aim was to persuade the jury that the terms of the statute under which his client was accused must be strictly respected, however inequitable this might seem, and for this purpose he introduced the generalities in which he no doubt expected their ready concurrence and from which he drew his more controversial conclusion. But it cannot be inferred that his audience regarded true liberty as in its very nature limited by law. The point was that the positive laws provided the guarantee of the specific rights in which Romans discerned their liberty, and he particularly emphasized not so much liberty *tout court* as the privileges of the higher orders.[96]

In this there was, moreover, nothing peculiarly Roman. Cicero was embroidering the same theme as a Greek orator, who, after proclaiming the necessity of law for human society in terms to be quoted with approval by a Roman jurist (*Dig.* i. 3. 2), illustrates this by showing how various Athenian institutions rest on the laws ([Dem.] xxv. 15–27). Though that orator does not indeed explicitly make freedom depend on the laws, he remarks that if everyone were permitted to do as he liked, Athenian life would resemble that of wild beasts (20; cf. 25). And Aeschines did remind a court of what they had *often* heard, that it is the laws that preserved the persons and polity of citizens in a democracy, as distinct from a tyranny or oligarchy (i. 4 f.), while Demosthenes opined that no one would gainsay the proposition that Athens owed to the laws all her blessings, her democratic system, and her freedom (xxiv. 5). One may also recall the claim that Thucydides imputes to Pericles, that in the Athenian democracy private differences

---

[96] *Cluent.* 146–55. For association of law(s) and liberty see also n. 37 and e.g. *Mil.* 77, *Phil.* xi. 36, *de offic.* ii. 24, iii. 83; Sall. *Or. Lepidi* 4, *Or. Philippi* 10; Livy ii. 1, iv. 15. 3, xxxiv. 26. 7, xxxix. 27. 9, xlv. 31. 4, 32. 5. See n. 151 (Cato).

are settled in accordance with the laws under which all are equal (this is the *aequum ius* of the Romans), and that for all their freedom the citizens are law-abiding in public affairs, obedient to magistrates and laws, principally from fear and 'not least to the laws prescribed for the assistance of victims of wrong-doing, and to those which are unwritten, whose violation brings social disapproval'.[97] The innumerable indictments for illegal proposals (*graphai paranomon*) at Athens confirm the importance of respect for the laws in Athenian democracy. Cicero was echoing a commonplace of the Athenian courts, a commonplace because it was manifestly true at Athens and Rome alike, as in every civilized state which possesses any measure of freedom.

We must also bear in mind that to a Roman lawyer a *lex* (or *plebiscitum*) is 'what the people [or plebs] commands and establishes' (Gaius i. 3); according to Julian (*Dig.* i. 3. 32), 'the laws are binding on us only because they have been accepted by the judgement of the people'. These dicta come from the second century AD, when much of the substantive law in force had actually been made by emperor or senate, without formal concurrence by the people: they preserve Republican theory, when it had ceased to have practical significance. Indeed imperial jurists grounded the legislative competence of the emperor himself on the basis that he had received his *imperium* from the people.[98] In the same way the decemvirs, according to tradition, had power to legislate delegated to them by the people; likewise Sulla, though he preferred to obtain comitial ratification for his enactments. For the most part the powers of the magistrates and some other institutions of public law had never been established by statute; they rested on immemorial convention; but in this case, as Julian held, their validity could be supposed to depend on tacit and universal consent (loc. cit.). As for the important modifications in statute law due to Republican praetors, had they not corresponded to the general will, they would hardly have outlasted the innovator's own year of office, if they had escaped a veto when made. No Roman actually said, as Swift did, that 'freedom consists in a people's being governed by laws made with their own consent', but this principle is implicit in the Roman system, under which the people could not in perpetuity be bound by the laws that it had enacted or the conventions it had accepted, but had in general the power to set them aside by new legislation (n. 39); the conception that law is a divine ordinance, which men may not

---

[97] Thuc. ii. 37, iii. 37. 3 with Gomme's notes. The sentiments expressed by orators in court are more probative of what ordinary Athenians actually thought; cf. K. J. Dover, *Greek Popular Morality*, 1974, 8–10; on their attitude to law see further 184–7, 306–9. Similarly what Cicero says in speeches reflects the views of his audience (or reading public).

[98] Brunt, *JRS* 1977, 107 ff.

tamper with, appears in philosophical and even in juristic theory (*Dig.* i. 3. 2), but it has no place in the Republican constitution.

VIII

Again, according to Kloesel (128 ff.) and others, moderation is part of the very idea of *libertas* and distinguishes it from licence. Now Roman writers certainly commend the moderate use of freedom and reprobate its excess, but the very texts concerned often employ *libertas* as a neutral term (like Plato's *eleutheria*), describing a condition that is to be approved or condemned according to the use men make of it; to qualify freedom as moderate or excessive implies that moderation is no part of the meaning of the term.[99] It could be argued that men who were unaccustomed to freedom or at a primitive stage of their development were unfit for it; they needed to be kept under tutelage, or to be given freedom only in a modest measure.[100] However, since *libertas* was a 'dulce nomen' (n. 37), and most men craved for it, and yet recognized that a total relaxation of all restraints was incompatible with the social order, the term could undoubtedly be used, like its equivalents in other languages, to refer to that degree or kind of freedom which was acceptable; anything beyond those limits could be denigrated as 'licence', a term which itself originally meant only what is permitted, and which is sometimes used in this neutral sense; in that case it too denotes a right which can be abused (*Dig.* iii. 5. 37) or carried to excess (Gaius ii. 228). Thus Livy certainly identifies *libertas* as freedom subject to just restraints when he writes (xxiv. 25. 8) that 'it is the nature of the masses to serve abjectly or to lord it with arrogance; freedom lies between, but they do not know how to establish it with moderation or to maintain it.' Elsewhere he notes that it is not only the masses that may miss the golden mean: 'to show moderation in guarding freedom is a hard task; professing to desire equality, each man lifts himself up to press his fellows down; to avoid living in fear themselves, men deliberately make themselves the objects of fear, and in repelling wrongs, we inflict them on others, as if we must either do or sustain injury' (iii. 65. 11).

However, what was true liberty and what was licence depended on a man's point of view; Republicans or popular spokesmen could predi-

---

[99] e.g. Cic. *Qu. fr.* i. 1. 22 ('tam immoderata libertas'), *Cael.* 43, *Planc.* 43; Livy iii. 57. 6, 67. 6, xxiii. 2. 1 ('licentia plebis sine modo libertatem exercentis' at Capua), xxiv. 4. 1, xxxiv. 49. 8, xlii. 14. 8; *Bell. Afr.* 54; nn. 83–8.

[100] Cic. *de rep.* ii. 55 ('modica libertas'); Livy xlv. 18. 6 ('libertatem salubri moderatione datam'). Peoples unready for freedom: Livy ii. 1. 3–6 (Romans under the monarchy), xxiv. 24. 2, 27. 5, xxxix. 23. 13. Cicero suggests that on the fall of Tarquin the Romans abused liberty, being unaccustomed to it, *de rep.* i. 62 (cf. Sall. *Hist.* i. 29: 'insueti libertatis').

cate licence of the abuse of power by kings and their agents or favourites, by the holders of *imperium*, or by the nobility;[101] aristocrats, the excesses of democratic assemblies or of seditious tribunes, or simply of popular sovereignty.[102] For men of high degree it is licence if they are insulted by their inferior (n. 88), if the voters demand a secret ballot,[103] if the plebs insist on bringing their oppressors to trial (n. 114). For some males it is found if women wish to be released from restrictions (n. 53).

What some classed as licence, others claimed as indispensable liberty, e.g. the ballot (n. 103). Clodius persecuted Cicero on the ground that he had violated the personal security in which citizens saw their liberty; he dedicated a shrine to Libertas on the site of Cicero's town house. For Cicero his own condemnation, and the violence by which Clodius dominated the streets, were breaches of liberty, and the shrine was an honour to Licence (n. 142). An apologist for the tranquillity of the Principate, when there was no need for debate, since the all-wise autocrat determined everything (Tac. *Dial.* 41. 4), could explain the decline of oratorical eloquence on the basis that it had always been 'the nursling of licence, which fools call liberty' (40. 2), another statement that has been seriously adduced to show the Roman conception of freedom; one might wonder if Tacitus really disagreed with Cicero's dictum that 'eloquence has always flourished and reigned most of all in every free state, and especially in those which enjoy peace and order' (*de orat.* i. 30).

IX

Again serious misconceptions arise from the doctrine advanced by Schulz that 'the Roman state never omitted to uphold the principle of

---

[101] Kings etc.: Livy ii. 3. 3, xxvii. 31. 5 ff., xxxiv. 48. 2, xlv. 32. 5; Sall. *Cat.* 6. 7. Magistrates etc.: Livy ii. 37. 8; Sall. *BJ* 31. 22 (cf. 'lubido' in 31. 7, 40. 3, 41. 5, 42. 4); *Or. Macri.* 16.

[102] Cic. *Flacc.* 16, *de rep.* i. 44, iii. 23 (democracy 'dicitur libertas, est vero licentia'); Livy ii. 27. 12, 29. 9, iii. 53. 6, v. 29. 9, vi. 40. 7, xxiii. 2. 1, 4. 5, xlv. 18. 6; Phaedrus i. 2. 1 ff.

[103] Cic. *Sest.* 103. For ballot laws constituting freedom see *de leg. agr.* ii. 4, *Planc.* 16, *de leg.* iii. 34 ff., *de amic.* 41; *RRC* nos 266. 1, 292, 1, 403, 413, 426. 2, 437; Ascon. 78 C. (n. 37). Bleicken, 1972, 38, urges that we cannot deduce from these laws that they were motivated by an 'abstract idea of equal political liberty'; secret voting was not treated as a 'new norm', but gradually introduced for different kinds of comitial business; this indicates that each law was designed to suit particular circumstances. So too in this country it was on the principle of the right of the middle class to representation that the Reform Act of 1832 was advocated; the principle was applied in 1835 to the government of boroughs, but not until 1888 were the counties administered by representative bodies. Cf. Endnote 2; it is an unwarranted assumption that a principle is not operative if it is brought into operation slowly and piecemeal. Neither in Rome nor in England indeed was the principle that resulted in the creation of new liberties an 'abstract idea', even though such an idea as equality of rights could be invoked *ad hoc* to support what was desired for more practical reasons.

authority; and, truly, individual freedom is impossible in the long run without authority', or in the words of Biondi, which he quotes with approval: 'Liberty and authority are not mutually exclusive; each presupposes the other; liberty is more effective in proportion to the strength of authority; without authority it is anarchy, in the same way as authority without liberty is tyranny.' For Kloesel, whom Wirszubski more or less followed, 'in every conception of freedom, so far as true freedom, not *licentia*, is involved, the concept of authority has its place, and this is true with altogether special strength of the Roman concept', since 'an aristocratic valuation of personality dominated the whole of public and social life at Rome', excluding equality and requiring social gradations. Hellegouarc'h held authority at Rome to be the guarantor of freedom.[104] All these writers seem to be suggesting not simply that in any ordered political society, and specifically in the Roman, we must expect respect for law and government, whereby some liberties are preserved, but that there is no incongruity between liberty, at least as the Romans perceived it, and submission to higher power, and that this submission is inherent in the very concept of *libertas*, or in any just notion of freedom. It will, however, become apparent that Romans, like everyone else, could discern an incongruity between the 'principles' of liberty and authority, and seek to establish a balance between them.

Heinze's famous essay on *auctoritas* is of course always cited. He described it as the influence that belonged to those whose opinions and advice were sought and usually prevailed, especially to the *principes* distinguished for the offices they had held, and for their age, experience, ability, and services to the state. But he was content to remark that *auctoritas*, which he sharply differentiated from *potestas* or *imperium*, did not infringe freedom, since anyone could still decide for himself whether to seek and adopt the advice of those who possessed it; this of course does not imply that you take the advice simply because you think it reasonable; you defer to the views of a man with *auctoritas* because he is the man he is.[105] But Schulz mixed this up with submission to superiors, some of whom had the legal power to enforce their will; Romans would conform to the directions of the *paterfamilias* (he forgot that the son might be 'freed' from his power), the magistrates, the senate, the emperor, the jurists of eminence: the consequences of *auctoritas* 'are obedience, order, discipline; reasons for its dictates are not required, nor could many people check or understand

---

[104] Schulz, 1936, 165, 187 f.; Kloesel 8 ff.; Wirszubski 35; Hellegouarc'h 543.

[105] R. Heinze, *Vom Geist des Römertums*, 1960, 43 ff. However, the early *patrum auctoritas* and that of the *tutor* were legal powers; and *senatus auctoritas* meant more than mere advice. See also p. 43 and ch. 1 endnote 4.

them, if given.' Through such conformity the Romans 'combined *liberty* with bondage'!

Last too claimed that '*libertas* was not, like *eleutheria* according to some accounts, an unfettered freedom, but rather, like *principatus*, which was one of its constitutional counterparts, freedom from arbitrary rule' (*CAH*. xi. 436). Both he and Schulz referred to the denomination of cities as free when their freedom was really limited by the paramount authority of Rome. But, as we have seen (p. 293), this freedom was qualified, and inferior to that of a city like Rome herself, which was fully independent; such cities were free only in so far as Rome did leave them to act as they chose. Both also held that Roman *libertas* was compatible with the regime established by Augustus; this of course accords with the claims made by or on behalf of many of the emperors; Seneca, for instance, flattering Nero, could write of 'the happiest form of the commonwealth, in which there is nothing wanting for the most perfect freedom but licence to destroy ourselves' (*de Clem*. i. 1.). Tacitus himself allows that Nerva at last combined 'res olim dissociabiles, principatum ac libertatem' (*Agr*. 3); yet in fact the rights in which Cicero and his contemporaries had thought liberty to consist were attenuated, or disappeared, under the Principate, and *libertas* could be used to designate the Republican system with the implication that it had been lost in the new order (n. 42).

Let us, however, revert to the Republic. In the *Philippics* Cicero continually claims to be representing the cause of the authority of the senate, the liberty of the people, and the preservation of the commonwealth from Antony's designs of domination. We know from his political programme in the *pro Sestio* that he held that all good men should defend the ancestral constitution under which the senate was to rule with the magistrates as its executive servants; ideally the senate would protect and extend the liberty and interests of the common people.[106] Such statements do not, however, show that even Cicero supposed that respect for authority was inherent in the very notion of

---

[106] *Sest.* 137; our ancestors 'senatum rei p. custodem, *praesidem*, propugnatorem, conlocaverunt; huius ordinis auctoritate uti magistratus [cf. *Phil*. vii. 12; and Pompey *ap*. *Fam*. viii. 4. 4, 8. 9] et quasi ministros gravissimi consili esse voluerunt; senatum autem ipsum proximorum ordinum splendorem confirmare, plebis libertatem et commoda tueri atque augere voluerunt'; cf. *ad Her*. iv. 47 for the view that 'senatus est officium consilio civitatem iuvare, magistratus est officium opera et diligentia consequi senatus voluntatem; populi est officium res optumas [sc. in legislation] et homines idoneos maxime suis sententiis dilegere et probare'. Texts cited by Kloesel (e.g. *Phil*. iv. 5, x. 23, xiii. 33, 47, *de div*. i. 27) which link *auctoritas senatus* with *libertas populi* do not justify his claim that even on an optimate view the former guarantees the latter, but only that they are compatible. In *de Dom*. 130 Cicero contrasts the tranquil time when popular freedom was combined with senatorial direction ('gubernatio') of affairs with the Clodian terror, which (he alleges) had destroyed both. This is of course *ex parte*, and Clodius would have had a partially plausible reply.

liberty, still less that Romans in general shared the same view. Authority and liberty might be consonant, but Romans could detect conflicts between them.

Cicero himself adopted the theory that the ancestral constitution was of the 'mixed' kind, or rather balanced fairly between monarchical, aristocratic, and democratic elements. In his *Republic* he sketched the evolution of this system. Already under the monarchy, not only the senate but the people too had limited political rights.[107] This was only a mere taste of liberty in the sense of power, enough to titillate the appetite and not satisfy it (ii. 50). Once Tarquin had been overthrown, they demanded more. It was prudent on the part of Valerius Publicola to make some concessions to them; by granting the people freedom in moderation, he more easily maintained the authority of the leading men.[108] Most decisions were taken by the senate, whose control was fortified by the *patrum auctoritas*, the rule that every act of the *comitia* required the sanction of patrician senators (ii. 56). (In the ideal code Cicero later proposed (*de leg.* iii. 28) he would have gone further, giving decrees of the senate the force of law.) The people were still not content; the proper balance between the power of magistrates, the authority of the aristocratic council, and the freedom of the people, which would secure stability, had not yet been attained (*de rep.* ii. 57). Hence the further agitation for the creation of the tribunate designed 'to reduce the power and authority of the senate' (59). Not that this aim was achieved immediately; the senate continued to enjoy the highest authority, with the compliance and obedience of the people (61). In his later half-hearted defence of the tribunate as an essential element in the mixed constitution, Cicero remarks that it was originally devised as a compromise 'to make the humbler citizens *believe* that they were on a level with the leading men', and that although some real measure of freedom had to be granted, there were then many excellent institutions (he was probably thinking again primarily of the *patrum auctoritas*) which still made the commons yield to the authority of the leading citizens (*de leg.* iii. 24 f.). It is implicit of course that the tribunate was, as it is elsewhere described, a bastion of Roman freedom;[109] and it is therefore to be noted that Cicero should say that

---

[107] A system can be mixed without being balanced (*de rep.* i. 69, ii. 43). Rome, which was the model (i. 70), evolved towards a balance of the different elements present from the first (ii. 2, 37). For the senate under the monarchy, ii. 23; for the people's right to elect or confirm a new king, 24, 31, 33, 35, 37 f., and to hear appeals, 54. Cicero accepts the tradition that Ser. Tullius devised the centuriate assembly, 39 f. Servius' supposed dependence on popular support (Dionys. iv. 40) probably explains Accius' words (*ap. Sest.* 133): 'Tullius qui libertatem civibus stabiliverat'.

[108] *de rep.* ii. 53–5; contrast i. 62, perhaps drawn from an annalistic presentation of an extreme patrician view.

[109] Cic. *de leg. agr.* ii. 15 ('tribunum quem maiores praesidem libertatis custodemque esse voluerunt'), *Rab. perd.* 1–14, *Sest.* 30, *de orat.* ii. 199, Sall. *Or. Lepidi* 13, *Or. Macri* 26 (cf. p. 345);

it made men think that they were equal to the aristocrats; liberty implied some degree of equality. Deference to one's superiors is no part of the freedom they wanted, even by his account. The increase in popular liberty which the tribunate was thought to secure was tolerable for him, only in so far as it was inoperative, either because the senate could still baulk the tribunes, or because the tribunes themselves might calm rather than excite popular demands (ibid. 23). In the same spirit Cicero's ideal code defeats the purpose of the ballot, which the plebs prized as a constituent of freedom (n. 103), but 'which had deprived the best men of their *auctoritas*' (ibid. 34), by providing that men of rank may inspect the votes; he explains (39) that this 'grants the appearance (*species*) of freedom, and preserves the *auctoritas* of the aristocrats (*boni*). Livy expresses the same outlook in saying of the timocratic organization of the centuriate assembly (p. 343) that while no one *appeared* to be barred from voting, all power lay with the leading citizens (i 43. 10).

So far from thinking of *libertas* as inherently moderated by respect for superior authority (or moral principles), Cicero did not hesitate to use the term (*de rep.* i. 67) to translate *eleutheria* in paraphrasing Plato's denunciation of democratic licence (*Rep.* 565 ff.). No democrat, he rejects the democratic contention that all citizens should have equal rights; it contravenes the principle that equality is itself inequitable, because it excludes distinctions of degree, and in any case equality is never realized, as the people itself creates inequalities by grants of special powers and honours to particular persons. On this principle he approves of the timocratic organization of the centuriate assembly; it accorded with the rule, always to be observed, that the greatest number should not have the greatest power; the preponderance of voting strength lay with those who had the greatest interest in ensuring that the state was in 'the best condition'. One is reminded of the contempt he expressed in a speech for the 'uncontrolled freedom and licence' of Greek assemblies dominated by ignorant men, 'artisans, shopkeepers, and all that scum'; how different from the Roman *comitia* organized in classes, which voted only after they had heard *auctores*, the men with *auctoritas* who would advise on the business duly laid before them.[110] Greek critics of democracy had condemned the power vested in the lower class by the Athenian system just as strongly, and Cicero's insistence on proper gradations of rank echoes the preference of many

Diod. xii. 25. 2; Livy iii. 37. 5 ('tribuniciam potestatem, munimentum libertatis'), 45. 8 ('tribunicium auxilium arx tuendae libertatis'; cf. endnote 8 with text). Cf. pp. 21 ff. and esp. Polyb. vi. 16. 4 f. and ch. 1 n. 39.

[110] *de rep.* i. 43, 53 (*contra* 49), ii. 39 f., iv. 2, *de leg.* iii. 44; cf. Livy i. 43. 10: 'sed gradus facti, ut neque exclusus quisquam suffragio *videretur* et vis omnis penes primores civitatis esset', and n. 164 with text; Cic. *Flacc.* 15–18 (where he ignores the the tribal assembly!)

Greek thinkers for 'geometric' equality, in which men enjoyed rights proportionate to their excellence, whether excellence were to be defined in terms of birth, property, or moral attributes.[111]

Cicero's views are not then peculiarly Roman, but representative of attitudes common to both Greek and Roman aristocrats. It is obvious that they were not shared by all Romans; had that been so, the accretions to the power of the people which are examined later, and the line taken by the *populares* of the late Republic, would be incomprehensible. Cicero himself alludes to a very different Roman conception, when he makes the advocates of democratic liberty argue that unless the people are in effective control of the state, there can be no *res publica* that satisfies the meaning of that term as *res populi* (*de rep.* i. 39). This argument cannot come from a Greek source, because it derives from the literal sense of a Latin term for which there was no Greek equivalent.[112] To Cicero no doubt full democratic liberty was licence (*de rep.* iii. 23). The liberty conceded to the people at Rome was tolerable only in so far as it was specious. But even in his conception of the Roman system the liberty of the people and the authority of the senate are countervailing forces, which must be balanced in such a way as to content the people but permit the senate to preponderate. All this is totally incompatible with Kloesel's inference from his views (p. 125) that '*libertas* without *auctoritas* founded on *dignitas* as its correlative is unthinkable to the Roman'. Not only must we reject the assumption that Cicero speaks for 'the Roman': in his own way of thinking popular respect for *auctoritas* is indeed essential to a well-ordered state, but it is not inherent in *libertas*, by which it is actually threatened.

Except in harangues when he is deliberately appealing to popular sentiments, Cicero is no witness to Roman views on liberty which prevailed outside his own class. Just as one-sided are the opinions that Livy puts into the mouths of patrician spokesmen contending against the development of plebeian rights. Thus, we are told, they resisted a proposal that the plebs should usurp the senate's prerogative by granting a triumph, on the ground that the state would be free and the laws operate 'equally', only if each order kept its own 'majesty', and an agitation against prolonged military service aroused their ironical comment that Roman liberty was being construed as involving disrespect for senate, magistrates, laws, ancestral customs and institutions, and military discipline. This *ex parte* statement has actually been

---

[111] See e.g. Aristotle, *Pol.* iii. 5. 8–10, 7. 1–6, v. 1. 2 f.; F. D. Harvey, *Cl. et Med.*, 1965, 101 ff.; C. Nicolet *ap. La filosofia greca e il diritto romano*, i (Acc. Lincei, 1976), 111 ff.

[112] In *de rep.* i. 47 f., Cicero's mouthpiece Scipio allows that the people can hardly possess freedom under an aristocracy any more than under a monarchy, however beneficent (cf. ii. 43). Cf. Tac. *Ann.* vi. 42.

adduced to show that the true Roman conception of liberty comprised such respect.[113] With imaginative plausibility the annalists made out that the patricians would long resist any additional right which the people demanded, but once they had been forced to concede it, they would accept it as constituting liberty, but argue that anything more would be licence. Thus 'equal liberty' had been secured by the publication of the law code, but it would be licence if the people were enabled to bring magistrates to account for violating the laws. Admittedly freedom involved the right of the people to elect whom it wished, but it was deplorable that this freedom should not be subject to the constraint of open voting. What Livy says of the attitude of the patricians of old was not less true of optimates in the late Republic: 'they thought that any provision for the liberty of the plebs detracted from their own power' (iii. 55. 2). Naturally, however, they would appeal to popular notions of liberty when it suited their own ends. According to Livy, the sovereign electoral power of the people (which could be invoked to justify infringements of the legal conditions for eligibility in the interest of popular figures like Marius, or for the conferment of extraordinary commands in the late Republic) was held by the patricians to warrant the electors returning two patrician consuls in defiance of the law. Adopting a 'popular' standpoint, Cicero in 63 could criticize a 'popular' agrarian bill for its derogation from their electoral rights, and contend that his own banishment by the people in 58 was a violation of the liberty due to every Roman citizen.[114]

X

Of course Cicero too was passionately attached to liberty, the liberty of the senators. The authority of the senate was itself a nullity if it could not take decisions without fear or pressure.[115] Every member should be able to voice his genuine opinions with some chance of swaying the issue. Senatorial freedom was indissolubly linked with senatorial *dignitas*. Cicero could say in 63 that the enactment of Rullus' agrarian bill would place the senate at the mercy of his land commissioners and their followers and that the senate would therefore lose both *libertas* and *dignitas*.[116] This kind of apprehension was frequently realized from the time of the formation of the first 'triumvirate'. The military force at the disposal of the 'triumvirs' and the street gangs organized by

[113] Livy iii. 63. 10, v. 6. 17 (Kloesel 144); cf. perhaps viii. 34. 7–10.
[114] Impeachments: Livy iii. 53. 6–10 (cf. Dionys. vii. 22. 2, 50); Elections: vi. 40. 15–41. 3; cf. endnote 5.
[115] See endnote 6.
[116] *de leg. agr.* i. 22; cf. nn. 117, 118. The *dignitas* of the senate is often on his lips (e.g. i. 27). So too the *dignitas* of the *res publica* can be associated with its *libertas* (*Phil.* iii. 19); cf. n. 30 with text.

Clodius rendered the senate helpless. In such conditions Cicero could say that the commonwealth (*res publica*) no longer subsisted,[117] since in his judgement it was properly vested in the direction of the senate (n. 106). In 57 senators deterred from attendance by riots complained that the house had no freedom of judgement. In 55 Cicero could write to Lentulus Spinther that 'the objective on which we had been set, after holding the highest offices and performing the greatest exertions, of exhibiting *dignitas* in stating our opinions and *libertas* in administering public affairs, has been totally eliminated; I have suffered no more than everyone else; there is no choice but to fall in with the dynasts, whom we cannot influence, or to express dissent to no effect'.[118] Caesar and Hirtius could play on the same theme by alleging that in January 49 the senate was deprived of freedom by terror of Pompey's soldiers.[119]

Under Caesar's autocracy Cicero lamented that 'if *dignitas* consists in holding sound opinions on public affairs, with which good men agree, mine is intact, but if it lies in the ability to realize them or at worst to advocate them freely, not a vestige of it is left'. At the same time Servius Sulpicius averred that the regime deprived men of their 'freedom' in promoting the interests of their friends. Pollio's claim that he had learned in these circumstances 'how delightful liberty is and how wretched is life subject to a master' rings true.[120] As Cicero pointed out in 43 to Calenus, under a despot even his partisans could not count on continuing influence (*Phil.* viii. 12). Many prominent Caesarians were among the 'Liberators' who killed Caesar or joined them later (p. 500). But soon the menaces of Antony subverted the independence of the senate.[121] Cicero was to pretend then that he had always exercised the freedom required of a senator (*Phil.* i. 27). The facts belie him (p. 486). In 62 he had declared that it was his practice 'to speak his mind freely in the senate, to have regard rather to the interest than to the will of the people, to give way to none and to stand in the path of many'. From 63 to 59 he exhibited such independence, not least in his relationship with Pompey, and after his return from exile he hoped to resume it, but he was soon reduced to silence or subservience. Admittedly he was speaking in 62 as a consular and one of the *principes*.[122] His *dignitas* was superior to that of most senators. It was legitimate to seek 'to be equal in freedom to the rest, but first in

---

[117] e.g. *Att.* ii. 21. 1, *Qu. fr.* i. 2. 15 (59), iii. 4. 1, 5. 4 (54). Cf. n. 42 for connection of *resp.* and *libertas*.

[118] *de dom.* 10, *Fam.* i. 8. 3 f. (cf. *Att.* iv. 6. 1 f.), ii. 5. 2.   [119] *BG* viii. 52. 4, *BC* i. 3. 5, 9. 5.

[120] *Fam.* iv. 14. 1, 5. 3, x. 31. 3 (Pollio's avowal of his love for Caesar shows that he was not simply ingratiating himself with Cicero).

[121] *Att.* xiv. 14. 3 f., *Fam.* xi. 7. 2, *Phil.* iii. 6, etc.

[122] *Sulla* 25; for Cicero's independence in 62–59 and later loss of it (despite his protestations in *Planc.* 91–4) see pp. 478 f., 486 f. *Principes*: Gelzer, 1969, 44 ff.; more fully, L. Wickert, *RE* xxii. 2014 ff.

honour'. But here the first proposition is as significant as the second.[123]
And the freedom of a senator to take the political line he chose could be
compromised by binding commitments to others. Cicero could allege
that the consuls of 58 had lost their liberty of action by their infamous
bargain with Clodius, while Clodius could suppose that by accepting
an extraordinary command Cato had barred himself from denouncing
any others of the same kind.[124]

The liberty prized by senators was of course incompatible with the
domination of a faction like the first 'triumvirate' or the despotism of a
single man. It meant an effective share in political power. In this sense
it was indeed associated with *auctoritas*, that of the senate as a whole,
and for many of its members their own personal influence. But there is
no sign that senators themselves felt that their individual liberty
involved respect for the *auctoritas* of *others*.

A true senator, said Cicero, was one whose mind was not determined
by an *auctor* but was respected for himself. Tiberius surely understood
this kind of feeling when he gave out that he wished to be called *suasor*,
not *auctor*; senators liked to think that they were prepared to make
decisions on the basis of advice.[125] This did not of course imply that
they would not on occasion rely on the judgement of leading men they
esteemed as distinct from mere argumentation. They were called on to
speak by rank, and doubtless the junior members commonly followed
the guidance of one or more of the *principes*. But this was not invariably
so. On 5 December 63 the senate was successively swayed by the
oratory of Caesar and Cato, who were respectively only praetor and
tribune designate. In 61 it was none of the consulars but the praetorian
Q. Cornificius, a man of little note, who first stimulated the senate to
take cognizance of Clodius' alleged incest. In 50 the great majority
rejected the lead given by the chief optimates and voted for a
compromise between Pompey and Caesar.[126] *Auctoritas* was sinister if it
required mere submission. Brutus and Cassius told Antony that 'to free
men no authority belongs to one who utters threats'; they would not
object to his being a great man in a free commonwealth, but set their
own liberty at a higher rate than his friendship. Brutus would later
write that he and his associates could have obtained benefits and
honours from Antony as 'a kind master', but that this would not have
been consonant with freedom; no one should have more power than
the laws and senate. Few senators of his generation would readily have
tolerated the pre-eminent *auctoritas* of which Augustus was to boast.[127]

[123] *Phil.* i. 34; cf. Cato (quoted in n. 149.)   [124] *Sest.* 69; cf. 60, *de dom.* 22.
[125] Cic. *de leg.* iii. 40; Suet. *Tib.* 27.   [126] Sall. *Cat.* 50 ff.; Cic. *Att.* i. 13. 3; ch. 9 n. 94.
[127] *Fam.* xi. 3. 3, *ad Brut.* 24. 4 f.; in his commentary Shackleton Bailey impugns the
authenticity of the latter letter, but with no compelling reasons as against 25. Brutus had

In the Republic superiority of talents and achievements tended to evoke jealousy. It was only on an aristocratic conception that liberty could be said to have originated in the fall of the monarchy, which in the Roman tradition resulted in but a small accretion to the political rights of the people; but the royal power was now shared equally between the annual consuls,[128] and in consequence the direction of affairs passed to the senate. The subsequent multiplication of offices, the restrictions on re-election, the aversion to prolonged prorogations and to extraordinary commands, all illustrate the proclivity of the senate to deny any of its own members to acquire too manifest a pre-eminence. If the *cursus honorum* in itself created distinctions of degree, it was a derogation from liberty, as Servius Sulpicius implied,[129] that under the Caesarian regime men would no longer be able to seek office in due sequence. Within the limits that these distinctions imposed, the senators showed some regard for that connection between liberty and equality which, as we shall see, coloured the popular conception, though it was only a measure of equality in their own number that they valued. The new servitude of the Principate was manifest in AD 14, 'when all, casting off equality, awaited the orders of the prince' (Tac. *Ann.* i. 4).

XI

But attachment to liberty, including liberty in the sense of political rights, was not the exclusive concern of senators in the Republic. It was also the watchword of 'popular' politicians, and must therefore have had some appeal to the masses. Cicero himself played on it, when for his own ends he wooed their support. Very probably it was slogans and arguments of *populares* from the Gracchi onwards that annalists retrojected into their accounts of the early struggles between patricians and plebeians. *Populares* sought to show that it was their ideas of liberty that had triumphed in the times of 'our wise ancestors', and that it was optimates who deviated from the traditions by which Rome had grown great.[130] It would be a gross error derived from our excessive dependence on the partisan opinions of Cicero to suppose that *populares* did not make as much play with *mos maiorum* as their opponents. The

proclaimed his devotion to liberty as moneyer in 54 (*RRC* 433) against Pompey's dominance; cf. Quint. *Inst.* ix. 3. 95. On *RG* 34 see Syme, *RR* 320–2.

[128] Note Livy iv. 5. 5: 'quod aequandae libertatis est, in vicem annuis magistratibus parere atque imperitare licet'; cf. Dionys. iv. 74; Cic. *de leg.* iii. 5; n. 69.

[129] *Fam.* iv. 5. 3. Access to office, at least for those with the census qualification (Nicolet, *JRS* 1976, 20 ff.), is represented in the annals of the early Republic as an element in equal liberty (p. 337).

[130] See endnote 7.

ius provocationis, the tribunician prerogatives, the legislative supremacy
of the assemblies independent of senatorial authority, all belonged to
ancestral usage, and were contravened by, for example, repression
under cover of the *senatus consultum ultimum* or by the legislative
innovations of Sulla effected by force. It is characteristic that in 58
Clodius restored the right of free association, which was supposed to go
back to Numa and which the senate had abrogated in 64 by sheer
usurpation of legislative power (n. 57). Tiberius Gracchus could claim
that his agrarian law implemented an old enactment forced through in
response to popular demands and then set at naught (App. i. 8), and
that it embodied a traditional policy of keeping up the stock of soldiers
by settlements of the poor on the land. The rights and material
interests of the common people could all be subsumed under, or closely
associated with, *libertas*. Thus while optimates could raise the cry of
liberty in danger when they saw or affected to see the prospect of
despotism, *populares* could do so more regularly, because popular
liberty was continuously threatened by oligarchic dominance. It was
probably because of the more distinctly popular nuance of the term in
most of the great conflicts of the late Republic that Cicero omits it from
his catalogue of the principles on which all 'good' men could agree,
especially as the freedom he prized himself was inherent in the *senatus
auctoritas*, whose maintenance is for him the most vital of all these
principles (pp. 55 f.).

In the popular conception liberty consisted partly in protection
under the laws for the ordinary citizen against arbitrary punishment
by magistrates. Their unfettered *imperium* is represented as 'excessive
and unendurable in a free state', as was the very *cognomen* 'Imperiosus',
assumed by T. Manlius Torquatus.[131] The palladium of freedom in
this sense was thought to reside in the right of appeal to the people (*ius
provocationis*) from sentences of execution, flogging, and heavy fines, and
in the right of the tribunes to intervene between the magistrate and a
citizen whom he sought to coerce (*ius auxilii*). The origins and
development of these rights are swathed in obscurity. The former,
established by tradition as early as the foundation of the Republic, still
needed confirmation at least by a *lex Valeria* of 300, which was in Livy's
view necessary because hitherto the great resources (*opes*) of the few
had counted for more than the freedom of the commons, and even this
law merely declared an infringement to be wrongful, without prescribing any sanction; it was only in the early second century that three
Porcian laws were passed, of uncertain date and content, which not
only supplied this deficiency but seem first to have made the right

---

[131] Livy iii. 9. 2–5, vii. 4. 2. A contrast between *libertas* and *imperium* recurs in his history.

operative outside the city of Rome, and to have prohibited the use of rods (but not of canes) for flogging in the army; in my view generals were never debarred from inflicting the death penalty on soldiers under their command. Even then the right was sometimes violated and needed further strengthening by a law of Gaius Gracchus (ch. 4, section VI).[132]

At one time the real guarantee of personal security probably lay in the readiness of the plebs in the city to give physical aid to the citizen in danger,[133] later in respect for the legal prerogative of the tribune to intervene, or (since he could act only within the city) in the possibility that a tribune would impeach the offender before the people after he had demitted office; the people could doubtless condemn him at its discretion for wrongdoing, even if no specific sanction had been appointed by law. Even Sulla left the tribunes with their *ius auxilii*, but he may have deprived them of the right to bring charges before the assembly; this might explain Macer's complaint in 73, as given by Sallust, that citizens in the country had no protection from magistrates. If so, it was restored in 70 by the *lex Pompeia Licinia*, since it was exercised in 63 by the tribune Labienus against Rabirius.[134]

'O nomen dulce libertatis! O ius eximium nostrae civitatis! O lex Porcia legesque Semproniae! O graviter desiderata et aliquando reddita plebi Romanae tribunicia potestas': Cicero's famous apostrophe in arraigning Verres' execution of a citizen (II *Verr.* v. 163), while it indicates the value that was set on liberty in the sense of personal protection under the law, must not be taken as suggesting that such protection exhausted the popular conception of liberty. It is significant that Cicero appeals to laws that the people had enacted. The tradition made it perfectly clear that it was only the sovereignty of the people in legislation that had secured them liberty in this form.

The *ius provocationis* presents us with a puzzle. There is no certainly authentic instance of trial on appeal by the people, except for the archaic proceedings against Rabirius.[135] Otherwise we know only of

---

[132] See endnote 8. [133] See endnote 9.

[134] Sulla deprived tribunes of their power 'iniuriae faciendae' (Cic. *de leg.* iii. 22), removing their right to initiate legislation (*per.* Livy lxxxix), at any rate without the senate's sanction, and limiting (we do not know how) the *ius intercessionis* (Cic. II *Verr.* i. 155; Caes. *BC* i. 5, 7), perhaps too debarring them from bringing impeachments before the people; that would explain why citizens outside Rome, where the *ius auxilii* did not extend, were defenceless (Sall. *Or. Macri* 26); this may also explain Cicero's words quoted in the next paragraph; the need for tribunician impeachments was felt because in its absence there was no guarantee of observance of the Porcian and Sempronian laws.

[135] Gelzer, *Kl. Schr.* ii. 202 f., *Cicero* 76–8, right against R. A. Bauman, *The Duumviri in the Roman Criminal Law and the Horatius Legend*, 1969. The appellate proceedings that followed Rabirius' capital condemnation by *duoviri* had terminated; Cicero was defending Rabirius on a charge brought by Labienus, for which the penalty was a fine; Cicero's suggestions that Rabirius' *caput* was in danger when he spoke need be taken no more seriously than expressions in *Quinct.* 8, 49.

trials by the people in the first instance on impeachment. In the pre-Gracchan period non-political criminal charges were tried by magistrates with their *consilia*, and citizens they condemned were apparently unable to seize at a straw of escape through the people's clemency (ch. 4, section VI). It seems to follow that the supposed right of appeal was continually infringed. How then could it have been regarded as the palladium of Roman freedom? An analogy may be found in our own Habeas Corpus Act. Most persons who are arrested have no need to resort to it, because the very existence of the procedure it provides inhibits their indefinite detention without trial. In the same way the *ius provocationis* probably deterred *arbitrary* punishments of citizens; on the other hand, tribunes would not intervene at the time, or seek retribution later, if a citizen were punished after fair trial for a common crime, or if in their judgement he was manifestly refusing to obey lawful commands, e.g. by resisting conscription, given that the levy was being equitably administered.[136] On the other hand, when charges were political, magistrates and their assessors (a *consilium* composed of men of their choice) could not be trusted to decide impartially on the life or status of defendants who might be their political adversaries, and only the people were competent to decide, acting not on appeal but in the first instance. It was then only political charges that Polybius had in mind, when in his analysis of the balance of the Roman political system he twice asserts that the people alone could pass capital sentences; the repression of common crimes would not have come within his purview.[137] The *ius provocationis* and the *ius auxilii* safeguarded this system. The arbitrary repression of Tiberius Gracchus' partisans by the consuls of 132 was a deviation from accepted practice. As a result Gaius Gracchus entirely prohibited the capital condemnation of any citizen (whatever the charge, and whether or not he appealed) except by authority of the people, i.e. except after trial by the people or (as became more usual) by a court established by statute.[138] This Sempronian law was now in turn the chief guarantee of freedom. Because Verres held it in contempt, all Romans, Cicero could aver, thought that 'their rights, interests, protection, and indeed their entire liberty' depended on his condemnation. No matter that he was not on trial for this crime, for Roman courts did not necessarily decide either by the law or the facts relevant to the specific charge; moreover, Cicero promised that if Verres

---

[136] Bleicken, 1955, 78–83; Taylor, *JRS* 1962, 19 ff.

[137] Polyb. vi. 14. 6, 16. 2: it was only political offenders who would regularly escape death by voluntary exile.

[138] The banishment of Popilius (GC 32) shows that he was deemed to have broken the existing laws. Cf. Clodius' actions against Cicero.

escaped condemnation by the court, he would as aedile impeach him before the people for his violation of citizen rights.[139]

Cicero often paid lip-service to liberty in this sense, and indeed incorporated the *ius provocationis* and *ius auxilii* in his ideal code of laws.[140] But it was of prime importance to the humbler citizens: aristocrats were seldom at risk from the *imperium* of magistrates. The action of the consuls in 132 is only one case in which the ruling class demonstrated their lack of respect for the principle involved. Even after Gaius Gracchus' law, they were able to set it aside under cover of the *senatus consultum ultimum* (cf. p. 16). It was obviously reasonable that the magistrates should repress by force as public enemies men who had taken up arms against the state, but in 121 the consul Opimius then proceeded to execute those who had already surrendered; and his acquittal on impeachment before the *comitia centuriata*, dominated by the well-to-do, who prized order above freedom, gave his action the strength of a precedent, which was more than once followed.[141] The prosecutions of Rabirius in 63 (n. 135) were 'popular' attempts to deter such violations of liberty in the future. To no avail: in the same year Cicero executed the Catilinarian conspirators without trial. Hence Clodius could assail him as 'a tyrant and thief of liberty', secure his banishment by the plebs, and dedicate the site of his house to Libertas.[142] In my view Cicero remained thereafter unpopular with the plebs.[143] Of course he complained bitterly of his own banishment without trial (*de dom.* 80), but in 44 he was just as ready as before to approve of the summary execution of low-class rioters.[144]

XII

Cicero himself taught that it is the very essence of law (*lex*) that it binds all alike (*de leg.* iii. 44), though he did not concede the democratic contention that all citizens must have equal political rights (n. 10). However, 'the private man should live with his fellow citizens in accordance with a fair and equal system of law [*aequo et pari iure*], not in grovelling submission to others nor lifting himself above them', and the wise statesman will see to it that 'each man keeps his own with equal legal rights [*aequitate iuris*], and that the weaker citizens are not defrauded on account of their low status, while the rich are not

---

[139] II *Verr.* i. 13 f., v. 163, 172 f. Schulz, 1936, 174, is perverse.

[140] *de leg.* iii. 6; cf. n. 132.   [141] GC 44–7, 50 f., esp. Cic. *Part. Or.* 104.

[142] For Cicero they were not entitled as *hostes* to the protection of citizens under the law, *Cat.* iv. 9 f. Clodius' dedication: *Sest.* 109, *de dom.* 108–11, *de leg.* ii. 42 (really to Licentia).

[143] Ch. 9 n. 76.

[144] *Fam.* ix. 14. 7 f.; one may doubt if it was welcome 'infimo cuique'. For the circumstances see Weinstock, 1971, 364 f.

prevented by unpopularity from retaining or recovering what is theirs'.[145] In Roman tradition this ideal was largely realized by the decemvirs' codification of the laws in the Twelve Tables. Cicero's account implies that the greater part of the code was based on the principle of equality, when he refers to the two last tables as unfair, citing the prohibition on marriage between patricians and plebeians, a derogation from that principle removed almost at once (*de rep.* ii. 63). He does not bring out that the codification was supposed to have been the product of prolonged popular agitation and to have marked a further stage in liberty. This is clear in the annalists.

Livy, evidently following an 'optimate' source, held that after the overthrow of the monarchy the commands of the laws were already more potent than those of men, and that both freedom and equality of rights (*ius aequum*) had been attained. Dionysius even makes Servius Tullius uphold the latter ideal; however, in his account the kings had discretion in interpreting the laws, which were not published nor fully known to the citizens in general, and the consuls retained this discretion; hence popular spokesmen still had to agitate for equality under the laws, which he calls indifferently *isegoria* and *isonomia*, as a security for freedom.[146] Granted that men could no longer trample on the rights of others because they stood high in the favour of a king, a state of affairs that was allegedly observable later in regal Macedonia,[147] the annalists themselves supposed that the plebs could still be unfairly treated. Hence the work of the decemvirs could be described as that of equalizing 'freedom' or legal rights. Equality in freedom and in legal rights clearly has the same meaning.[148] The fragments of the Twelve Tables show that in general this principle was realized in form, as far as the private rights of citizens were concerned, though admittedly those without property were at a grave procedural disadvantage (Gell. xvi. 10. 5). It is noteworthy that under the code only the people was authorized to pass *privilegia* against named individuals.[149]

We are reminded of the famous statement of the Athenian democratic ideal in Euripides' *Supplices* (430 ff.): 'first of all, when the laws are not common to all, but one man rules and keeps the law to himself, there is no equality; but once the laws are written, the weak and the

---

[145] *de leg.* iii. 44; cf. *de offic.* i. 124: 'privatum autem oportet aequo et pari cum civibus iure vivere', ii. 85: statesmen should provide 'ut iuris et iudiciorum aequitate suum quisque teneat et neque tenuiores propter humilitatem circumveniantur neque locupletibus ad sua vel tenenda vel recuperanda obsit invidia', a principle reaffirmed by a third-century jurist (*Dig.* i. 18. 6. 2).

[146] Livy ii. 1. 1–6; cf. n. 147; Dionys. iv. 9. 9, 11. 2, 72. 3, x. 1, 29. 4 f.

[147] Livy ii. 3. 3; cf. xxxix. 27. 8 f., xlv. 32. 5.

[148] Livy iii. 31. 7, 34. 3, 56. 9, 61. 6, 67. 9; Tac. *Ann.* iii. 27. Cf n. 37.

[149] Cic. *de leg.* iii. 44, *de dom.* 43, *Sest.* 65. Dispensations from the law were at first granted by the people, later by the senate (Ascon. 58 C.; *StR* iii³. 337).

rich have the same right, the weaker when abused can reply in kind to the man of fortune, and with justice on his side the inferior triumphs over the great man. Freedom is found in this too: "Who wishes to bring before all some useful plan he has?"; then he who desires to do so wins fame, while he who has no such wish holds his peace. What is fairer for a city than these things?' The second of these constituents of Athenian 'equal freedom' never existed at Rome, but the first is enshrined in the Twelve Tables. Perhaps later writers placed the achievement of the code in a conceptual framework borrowed from the Greeks; perhaps the legislators themselves were influenced by models from the Greek cities in the west (rather than from Athens);[150] Nepos was certainly following a Greek source when he made Timoleon say that under the system he had created at Syracuse 'it was a form of liberty, if everyone were permitted to resort to the laws in accordance with his own desires' (*Tim.* 5. 2). But in any event it seems plausible to hold that the codification itself, and the equality between citizens which on the whole the code upheld, sprang from conditions similar to those which had produced similar effects in Greek cities, and that Romans, who found liberty inherent in the *ius provocationis* and the *ius auxilii*, institutions peculiar to themselves, were capable of independently discerning it in what the Greeks called *isonomia*. The insoluble question of derivation is of lesser importance, compared with the undoubted fact that Romans adopted the view that equality before the law was essential to their freedom. This view is probably implicit in Cato's dictum that 'we should have common enjoyment of right, law, freedom, and the commonwealth, but of glory and honour in accordance with the individual's own achievement'. The most liberal or egalitarian society might not object to the distinction that this dictum allows.[151]

Finley, commenting on 'the boldness and rarity' of the Athenian ideal expressed by Euripides, says that the Romans never attained it in the Republic and that the emperors rejected it.[152] He has traduced the Republic, though not the Principate. The *idea* was accepted, even by Cicero.

In *practice* men of wealth and standing had many advantages. Even when the laws had been published, the modes of procedure were not, until the aedile Cn. Flavius rectified this in 304. The forms of process most usual in early Roman law required litigants to wager a sum of

---

[150] So F. Wieacker, *Vom röm. Recht*[2] 1961, 46 ff.

[151] *ORF*[2], fr. 252: 'iure, lege, libertate, re publica communiter uti oportet, gloria atque honore, quomodo sibi quisque struxit' (cf. Cic. *Phil.* i. 34). Ter. *Ad.* 183 'libertatem aequam omnibus' might come from a Greek source.

[152] Finley, 1981, 84.

money which the poor can hardly have afforded; they were only
gradually superseded in the late Republic by the formulary system in
which there were no wagers. At all times in the Republic, the plaintiff
had to bring the defendant to court, and the successful litigant to
execute the court's judgement, without assistance from the state. This
must have made it hard to obtain justice from a more powerful
adversary, unless he were sensitive to the censure of public opinion.
Freedmen were severely limited in the claims they could make against
their former owners, though not against other citizens. (In Athens they
were not even citizens.) Courts might be open to the influence and
power of magnates and to bribes from the rich. Men of rank and
wealth were best able to retain the services of the most learned jurists
and most eloquent advocates. However, Finley himself allows that at
Athens too the principle of equality before the law was for similar
reasons not always realized in practice. As in modern democratic
societies, wealthy litigants enjoyed substantial advantages. At Rome
they were no doubt still better able to exploit their superiority.[153]

Bleicken remarks that the idea of legal equality could not become
'the engine of historical development' because of the inequalities that
prevailed in Roman society.[154] These inequalities surely increased as
Roman dominion and wealth expanded. No doubt ideas contribute
most to promote political and social changes when they harmonize
with material changes; at Rome those changes accentuated disparities
in property and power. But that does not mean that the ideal of 'equal
liberty', once it had been, however imperfectly, embodied in equality
before the law, was more or less submerged in Roman consciousness by
that respect for rank, authority, and patronage which Bleicken is apt to
think to have been commonly preponderant among inferiors in Roman
society; his evidence is valid only for what their superiors expected. He
himself has to allow that some measure of 'equal liberty' in a political
sense was obtained by plebeians in the struggle of the orders.

We do not of course know how they actually argued their case;
annalistic representations necessarily mirror the ideas of their own age.
By their account spokesmen for the plebeians contended for their
eligibility to the highest offices on the basis that they should be open to
all men of ability for the purpose 'aequandae libertatis' (Livy iv. 5. 5);
it was contrary to 'aequum ius' if plebeians were denied the chance of
imperium (vi. 37. 4), and it was a remarkable evidence of plebeian

---

[153] Kelly, 1966, chs. 1–3, illustrates the various advantages of the rich in litigation. He
conjectures that *convicium* (n. 93) may have restrained the powerful from disobeying the law;
hardly, if they lived in Rome and wreaked injustice through agents and slaves in distant parts (cf.
IM App. 8). Freedmen: p. 418.
[154] Bleicken, 1972, 24 ff. As always he overestimates the significance of clientship.

liberty, when one of their number for the first time dedicated a temple, defying the arrogance of the nobility (ix. 46. 5–8). No doubt it was also in recollection of Italian claims in 90 that a Latin representative in 340 was made to claim that one consul each year should be a Latin, in the name of liberty and 'aequatio iuris', since 'ubi pars virium, ibi et imperii pars est' (viii. 4. 3). All this may also remind us of complaints in the late Republic of 'paucorum dominatio', and of Cicero's assertion, appropriate to a parvenu, that office was open to the 'virtue and industry' of all citizens (*Sest.* 137). Naturally Cicero knew very well that it was accessible only to men of substantial property (n. 129) though he might well have said that that could be acquired by virtue and industry, and that the nobility had a preponderant share; but we must beware of supposing that an ideal which had very limited effect is of no importance at all; and we may recall that even in democratic Athens the poor were not eligible for all offices, and certainly lacked the leisure and education required for the political leadership that the 'orators' supplied. The ideal reappears in the justification probably advanced for C. Gracchus' extension of judicial rights to the Equites: it conduced 'ad ius libertatis aequandae' (Florus ii. 1). The reservation of the best seats at games to senators in 194 was also resented as a diminution of equal liberty, and so probably was the similar privilege restored to Equites by the *lex Roscia*.[155] It was in the Principate that the *ideal* was discarded; the hierarchical order was then strengthened, and eventually equality before the law was lost.

XIII

In the early Republic Rome also took halting steps towards democratic freedom in virtue of the electoral, judicial, and legislative rights of the assemblies, which were also to be swept away in the Principate; these rights, as Sallust would make Macer say (see below), constituted the *ius* and *maiestas* of the people. *Maiestas* is a vague term and may be rendered in this context by such equally vague terms as sovereignty or supremacy. In its electoral capacity the people was the fount of honour,[156] and could even assert its right to choose magistrates not qualified by law for office (n. 114). It could pardon offenders who appealed to it (n. 133), and itself determine capital charges including those of *perduellio* or *maiestas*, a crime so ill-defined that the assembly

---

[155] Livy xxxiv. 54. 5; Plut. *Cic.* 13; Pliny, *NH* vii. 117. The Roscian law 'restored' the privilege (Cic. *Mur.* 40; Vell. ii. 32), or 'confirmed' it (Ascon. 78 C. where Cicero's claim that the people demanded both this and the Aurelian law of 70 is implausible).

[156] 'Omnis potestates, imperia, curationes ab universo populo Romano proficisci convenit': Cic. *de leg. agr.* ii. 17; cf. 27 f. See endnote 10.

could construe it by its own pleasure. Its legislative competence was unbounded (n. 39); Polybius remarked that it could pass laws depriving the senate of traditional prerogatives and dignity and damaging to senators' property (vi. 16); the Gracchi and later *populares*, without claiming for it the normal direction of affairs on the pattern of a Greek democracy, would in fact propose enactments affecting every public concern. It is true that it could act only on the initiative of a magistrate and that there were various ways of obstructing its will. However, on a traditional view accepted by Polybius (vi. 16), the tribunes were expected to elicit or express that will, and *populares* would be ruthless in overriding obstructions on the ground that it should be decisive (pp. 21 ff.). When a tribune was accused of violating the people's *maiestas* by employing violence to pass a law, it was argued in his defence, on the footing that the law had the people's approbation, that '*maiestas*, which consists in a kind of grandeur of the Roman people in the retention of its power and right, was rather increased [by his action] than diminished'.[157] Not surprisingly Clodius carried a measure in 58 designed to ensure the people's freedom to reach its decisions unimpeded by vetoes or religious obstruction.[158]

This popular liberty entailed the *ius suffragii*. This constitutes another reason for rejecting the view that it was coterminous with citizenship (p. 296), seeing that from the fourth to the second centuries there were citizens (whom Mommsen called half-citizens) *sine suffragio*, possessed of only the private rights of citizens. We may reasonably guess that it was at the demand of the communities concerned that they were gradually raised to equality (pp. 104 f., 136 ff.). Intermittent proposals to abolish the rule whereby freedmen, or most of them, were registered only in one or all of the four urban tribes and to transfer those resident outside Rome to the appropriate rural tribes, in which their votes could have more weight, were also probably advocated (for whatever motive) in the name of 'equal liberty', while a plan to remove them from the tribal rolls altogether and thus to deprive them of the vote was abandoned on the objection that it was tantamount to taking away *both* their citizenship *and* their liberty.[159] The liberty sought by the Italians in 90 was also a share in the political rights of Romans, and

---

[157] Cic. *Part. Or.* 105; cf. J.-L. Ferrary, *CRAI* 1983, 556 ff.

[158] Cic. *Sest.* 56: 'eam legem quae omnia iura religionum, auspiciorum, potestatum, omnis leges quae sunt de iure et de tempore legum rogandarum, una rogatione delevit'; cf. *de har. resp.* 58 (note 'intercessionem removit') etc.; the vague rhetoric in all Cicero's allusions does not reveal (any more than Ascon. 8 C.; Dio xxxviii. 37) the precise purport of the law, which evidently did more than restrict the use of religious obstructions.

[159] Livy xlv. 15. 4; Treggiari, 1969, 37 ff. The first to attempt this, Ap. Claudius the censor, is portrayed as a demagogue (Livy ix. 46. 10 ff.), and the later proposers, P. Sulpicius Rufus, Cinna, Manilius, and Clodius, ranked as *populares*. Cf. n. 169.

it must have been on the plea of equal liberty that the newly enfranchised allies took up arms in 88–87 to resist the attempt to confine them to tribes whose votes would count for little. Obviously neither the centuriate nor the tribal organization fulfilled the ideal of equal voting power for all citizens, but an ideal can be entertained, though realized very imperfectly.

The second board of decemvirs infringed liberty, according to Dionysius (xi. 1–3), not only by its oppressive administration but by retaining office without elections. Cicero argues that the provision in his model code of laws that the senate should consist of ex-magistrates and not be chosen by censors is 'popular', since it ensures that the senate is recruited indirectly by election (*de leg.* iii. 27). It corresponded to practice in the post-Sullan period, but even earlier those who had held certain offices were entitled to attend the senate before they had been formally enrolled by censors, and censors were expected not to pass them over at the next enrolment without good reason. After Sulla censors could still eliminate men from the roll; it was characteristic of the popular standpoint that Clodius legislated in 58 to institute safeguards against their making arbitrary judgements.[160]

Political liberty meant the right of the citizens to vote *as they chose*. When adopting an insincerely popular stance, Cicero could declare that it was for the whole people alone to confer every kind of magisterial power, and that any derogation from this right was a diminution of liberty: citizens must be free to vote for whom they pleased (n. 114). It is clear that in elections candidates had to woo the suffrages of people of all sorts (ch. 8, section V). The introduction of the ballot by a series of laws was thought to free their votes from influence and pressure (n. 103).

Of these ballot laws that which, according to our information, was most strongly resisted by the nobility was the Cassian law of 137, which extended secret voting to popular trials, except those for treason; the exception was not removed until 106, when the tribune C. Coelius apparently thought that he was most likely to secure the conviction of C. Popillius Laenas for *maiestas* (*ad Her.* i. 15. 25), if the voting were secret (Cic. *de leg.* iii. 36). The trial of Popillius was the first of a series in the next few years of impeachments before the people of generals who were held to have disgraced Roman arms. Among them was Q. Servilius Caepio, whom the people first deprived of his command (Ascon. 78 C.), an act, it is said, without precedent since the deposition of Tarquin (*Per.* Livy lxvii); it was followed by another Cassian law excluding from the senate anyone so deprived or convicted by the

---

[160] *StR* ii³. 418 ff.; Ascon. 8 C. etc. for Clodius' law, which was repealed in the optimate reaction of 52 (Dio xl. 57).

people. Cicero, giving the 'popular' view, lists both Cassian laws as notable accessions to the power of the people; by the first 'suffragiorum ius potestasque convaluit', while the second 'populi iudicia firmavit'; and he collocates them with the Porcian law, 'principium iustissimae libertatis' (Ascon. loc. cit.). In Polybius' view the people's right to try political offenders was an important democratic element in the constitution (n. 137). According to Valerius Antias, the accuser of Scipio Africanus in 187 maintained that 'no citizen should be so eminent that he could not be questioned by the laws, and that nothing served so much to promote equal freedom as the liability of the greatest men to stand trial'; his story of the affair is suspect, but none the less it reflects first century ideas of popular freedom.[161] The accountability of ex-magistrates to the people on impeachment, normally by a tribune, was not only the guarantee of the private citizen's personal security from arbitrary coercion, but was essential to that ultimate control by the people which the *populares* championed, as the leaders of the plebs were supposed to have done in the time of the struggle of the orders. In those days, according to the annalists, it had been keenly contested; to the plebeians it was liberty, to the patricians licence (n. 114). The patricians had indeed succeeded in ensuring that capital charges could be heard only by the centuriate assembly, and not by the tribes, which could only impose fines. This was to prove a safeguard in later times for nobles like L. Opimius in 120 (ch. 1 n. 25), who was thought to have acted in the interest of the whole propertied class.

Despite the flurry of impeachments in the last decade of the second century, the procedure was by then falling into abeyance with the constitution of permanent courts, or of courts constituted *ad hoc* to deal with political offences such as that established by the Mamilian law for misconduct in the Jugurthine war. But these courts were themselves set up by the people, and sometimes as in this case, on the motion of 'popular' tribunes. Another 'popular' law, the Appuleian, created a permanent court to hear charges of *maiestas*, before which the younger Caepio could be indicted for obstructing by violence the will of the people, while Norbanus, prosecuted for his own resort to violence in the 'popular' interest, could be exonerated on the ground that he was fulfilling that will. The *iudices* under both the Mamilian and Appuleian laws were Equites; their attitude might not be very different from that prevalent in the centuriate assembly, and it may have been supposed that they would be less susceptible to the influence of the nobility, especially in the circumstances of the time. It was also an advantage that prosecution in such courts did not depend on the initiative of a

---

[161] Livy xxxviii. 50. 5–8 (see Scullard, 1973, App. IV); cf. xxvi. 2. 16.

tribune.[162] In the absence of a public prosecutor almost any male citizen, and not merely one aggrieved by the alleged delinquent, could prefer a charge on behalf of the state. Men who made a business of this activity, stimulated by financial and other rewards, could acquire an infamous reputation as delators (Cic. *de offic.* ii. 50), especially in the Principate, like the sycophants of democratic Athens, where the same system had been adopted. We may, however, recall that the author of the Aristotelian *Constitution of Athens* (9. 1), who ascribed the origin of the practice there to Solon, regarded it as one of his three most democratic innovations. It is of course unlikely that at Athens, any more than at Rome, accusers were often humble people. At Athens indeed the jurors were paid and might be poor men; in Rome there was always a property qualification. Still, it remains true that the judicial system of the late Republic ensured that members of the ruling class could be brought to account either before the people or before courts not composed of their own peers. It was only under the Principate that senators became free of such control by their inferiors. The ideal of *aequa libertas* had then been abandoned altogether.

XIV

Of all the rights of the people in their assemblies the most momentous, though at times little exercised, was that of legislation, since it was by passing laws that the commons could gain material benefits; to say nothing of popular enactments in the late Republic, it was by earlier legislation that *nexum* was abolished and the *ius provocationis* secured. Dionysius thought that from the first the people, then voting by *curiae*, had had the power to enact laws (ii. 14); by removing this power, Tarquin the Proud destroyed liberty (iv. 81. 2 f.); it was restored with the Republic (iv. 75. 4, v. 2. 2 f., vii. 56. 3); indeed the new system was approved by an assembly (iv. 84. 3). Although in his view it was aristocratic, he makes a patrician 'lover of freedom' declare that freedom consists in government by consent (xi. 11. 2; cf. 15. 3), and another acknowledge that the right to legislate was proper to free men (ix. 44. 6). I take it that these and other similar texts in Dionysius and Livy[163] relating to the early Republic, whether or not the facts they purport to give are authentic, derive from annalists writing after the Gracchi and reflect the sentiments current in the late Republic, especially among the *populares*, a term that Livy uses of spokesmen for plebeian rights during the struggle of the orders, and that Dionysius

---

[162] J.-L. Ferrary (n. 157) has an interesting discussion. Cf. ch. 4 for qualifications of *iudices*. The plebeians qualified under the *lex Plautia* of 89 probably had to be persons of some substance.
[163] Livy iv. 5. 2; cf. vi. 27. 6 ff.

renders by *demotikoi*; thus, he so characterizes the consuls of 449, Valerius and Horatius (xi. 43), whose tenure of office in Livy's view was 'popularis', because they passed laws for the freedom of the plebs (iii. 55).

Popular liberty in this sense was restricted under patrician ascendancy. No decisions could be taken by the *curiae* or centuries without ratification by the patrician senators (*patrum auctoritas*). Dionysius supposed that originally the tribunes of the plebs were themselves elected by the *curiae*; it was therefore of great advantage to the plebs when the elections were transferred to the tribes, which were also not liable to obstruction by patrician augurs (ix. 41, 49). Legislation, however, belonged in the Republic only to the centuriate assembly of the whole people; the tribes could do no more than pass *plebiscita* which had no binding force. This meant that legislation could be initiated only by the patrician magistrates who presided over the centuries, not by the tribunes who represented the plebs. Moreover, as Dionysius frequently observes, the common people had almost no power in the centuriate assembly, which was dominated by men of property, with whose support (he thought) the patricians were able so long to maintain control (xi. 45. 3). Originally 18 centuries of Equites and 80 of the first property class had an absolute majority of the 193 centuries; when they concurred, citizens of the middling sort would not even be called to vote, and the very poor, the *proletarii*, were brigaded in a single century, which would vote last, if at all, although on Dionysius' estimate they comprised perhaps half of the citizenry; probably this estimate was not far wrong for the time of the Hannibalic war, and the disproportion must have increased thereafter. In fact the centuriate assembly never lost this timocratic character; though there was a 'democratic' change, which can be dated between 241 and 218, of which Dionysius was aware, it did not amount to much; henceforth the centuries of the first class voted before the Equites, and they now numbered only 70, two for each of the thirty-five tribes, with the result that an absolute majority required at least some votes of the second class.[164] Nor would it have made any significant difference if proposals attributed to Gaius Gracchus and put forward later had been carried, whereby the centuries would

---

[164] iv. 20. 5, vii. 59. 7, viii. 82. 6, x. 17. 5; xi. 45. 3. *Proletarii*: iv. 18. 2, vii. 59. 6 (cf. Livy i. 43. 11); *IM* 24, 64–8. Democratic change: iv. 21. 3; cf. Brunt, *JRS* 1961, App. II. For the subsequent system cf. Cic. *de rep.* ii. 39. In elections a candidate needed an absolute majority to be returned; Cic. *Phil.* ii. 81 proves that this was attainable once the second class had voted. Cicero's boast that he was unanimously returned as praetor and consul (*de imp. Cn. Pomp.* 2, *de leg. agr.* ii. 4) means only that he had the votes of the Equites and the first two classes. Of his competitors in 64, C. Antonius beat Catiline only by a few votes; on this occasion all or nearly all the centuries must have been called to decide between them.

have been called in a random order and not in the rank of property classes.[165]

Hence it was vital, if the true will of the whole people was to prevail, that the right of legislation should be granted to the tribes, which at one time were more truly representative than the centuries, and which could vote on bills that the tribunes laid before them, and that the enactment of laws should not be subject to ratification by the patrician senators. Livy makes tribunes argue that 'equal liberty' means the right of the people to legislate as it chooses (n. 163); in the context this demand relates to the tribal assembly.[166]

The actual development is obscure. The *patrum auctoritas*, though never abolished, was reduced to a formality (Livy i. 17. 9) by a *lex Publilia* of 339, the work of a 'popularis' dictator, and a *lex Maenia*, probably later than 292; Sallust makes Macer say that this freed the people's votes.[167] *Plebiscita* were given binding force, we are told, by a *lex Valeria Horatia* of 449, by another *lex Publilia* of 339, and by the *lex Hortensia* of *c*.287. The last of these measures is unquestionably historical, though the circumstances in which it passed are largely veiled from us by the loss of the narratives of Livy and Dionysius. Whether the earlier laws are mere inventions or their purport has been inexactly transmitted, a matter of endless scholarly dispute, it is enough for our purpose to note that Livy conceived that the 'popular' consuls of 449, whom he credits with the reform, promoted the cause of liberty by putting the sharpest of weapons into the hands of the tribunes (iii. 55), a weapon, as Sallust's Macer was to say, to be used for liberty (see below). Dionysius took the view that they gave power to the 'plebeians and the poor'.[168]

The tribal assembly itself cannot have been fully representative of the people in 287, and must have become increasingly less representative;[169] in the last century of the Republic it seems to have been

---

[165] If we credit Sall.(?) *Ep. ad. Caes.* ii. 8, C. Gracchus considered this scheme, anticipating Manilius in 66 and Ser. Sulpicius in 64 (Cic. *Mur.* 47, testifying to the indignation of the municipal gentry).

[166] See n. 163. Livy iii. 55, viii. 12. 14 f. also treats any increase in the power of the tribal assembly as popular.

[167] *Or. Macri* 15; cf. Cic. *Planc.* 8 (*ius populi*). Publilian law: Livy viii. 12. 12 ff.; the Maenian is after 298 (Cic. *Brut.* 55) and was presumably noticed in Livy's third decade.

[168] Livy iii. 55 (cf. Dionys. xi. 45), viii. 12, *Per.* xi: 'plebs propter aes alienum post graves et longas seditiones ad ultimum secessit in Ianiculum, unde a Q. Hortensio dictatore deducta est'; cf. Dio, fr. 37 on the preceding agitation for a moratorium in repayment of debts; Gaius i. 3 etc. briefly record the law giving *plebiscita* the force of *leges*. For later jurists this was the operative law; moreover, the relevant events would still have been remembered in outline by the earliest annalists, writing some three generations or less afterwards.

[169] Taylor, 1960, Part I (with maps). The 14 rural tribes created between 387 and 241 had larger territories and ultimately at least more registered citizens than the first 17 rural tribes close to Rome, except for those among the latter which (especially Pollia) acquired substantial

dominated by the urban plebs (p. 25 f.), while the centuriate assembly continued to reflect the views of the more affluent. But not even opponents of the power or liberty of the people ever took the point that neither assembly could truly be regarded as the people. And they too, while always seeking to curb or nullify the exercise by the 'people' of its rights, were bound by respect for constitutional convention, on which the authority of the senate was itself based, to pay lip-service to its sovereignty; thus in 106 Lucius Crassus, cajoling a popular audience, could acknowledge that 'we [senators] can and ought to be subject [*servire*] to you all', i.e. to the people as a whole (Cic. *de orat.* i. 225). This conception of popular sovereignty was identified by *populares* with liberty. Thus the Gracchi, according to Sallust, sought to reassert the people's liberty (*BJ* 42. 1); it must have been as clear to him as it is to us that they had claimed its right to legislate without restriction on matters of every sort (p. 33). This is a leading theme in speeches which he attributes to 'popular' spokesman. They stand at least in name for the people's rights (*Cat.* 38) acquired in the early Republic and therefore sanctioned by *mos maiorum*, the Roman equivalent to constitutional law. Thus Memmius reminds the people of the *ius* and *maiestas* won in the secessions of old (*BJ* 31. 17); both had been violated by oligarchic tyranny (31. 1 and 9); the people must throw off 'slavery' and resume their liberty by asserting their rights in the interest of the commonwealth (*passim*), in the particular instance by overriding the senate in its conduct of relations with Jugurtha. The Gracchi, falsely accused of aiming at regal power, had been the people's true champions (31. 2, 7 f.). Lepidus declares that under Sulla's despotism the people has been stripped of *imperium*(!), glory, and right, with the result that the citizens are exposed to illegal entrenchments on their private rights; they are enslaved (*Or. Lep.*, esp. 11). Macer again, in agitating for the restoration of the rights that Sulla had taken from the tribunes (n. 134), laments the people's loss of liberty under the domination of his successors (1 and 6). Liberty is not simply the right to vote—for they can still at elections designate their masters (6), nor security against arbitrary ill-treatment, which had supposedly been secured by the first secession (1); though Macer suggests that even this had been lost by citizens outside Rome itself (n. 134), he treats with contempt the notion that personal security constitutes sufficient free-

exclaves. The distribution of the enfranchised Italians among the rural tribes after 90 only produced new inequalities. We must suspect gerrymandering, but do not know how it worked nor in whose interest. The number of citizens voting in an urban tribe was evidently greater than that of those voting in a rural tribe, and individual votes therefore less valuable; this must be the explanation of attempts to allow freedmen to be registered in rural tribes of their residence (which of course also presuppose that some freedmen lived in towns other than Rome or had farms); cf. n. 159.

dom (26). What is required is the restoration of the tribunician power as a weapon ('telum'; cf. Livy iii. 55) to be used for freedom (12), which must not be bartered for the meagre corndole with which the senate had tried to assuage discontent (19). In 63 Cicero himself, suiting his sentiments to those of a mass audience, would speak of the 'ius potestas *libertasque*' of the people, which was not to be abated by any surrender of its own prerogatives or of those of tribunes (*de leg. agr.* ii. 29 f.). Once again liberty cannot be dissociated in the eyes of its possessor from power.

XV

Liberty in the sense of popular power, whether that which formally belonged to the plebs at least after the Hortensian law, or that which the plebs was believed to have exerted by agitations before its legislative rights had even in the annalistic tradition been conceded, was certainly the means by which the unprivileged extracted material advantages (*commoda*) from the ruling class, and it is not surprising that *libertas* and its *commoda* are sometimes associated.[170] Some of these *commoda* were undoubtedly subsumed under the concept of liberty in other senses; the *ius auxilii* and *ius provocationis*, 'equal liberty' under the laws, whose codification and publication were thought to have been forced on the patricians by popular clamours, the abolition of *nexum*, and (we may add) the freedom of clients from oppressive demands by patrons, which was secured by legislation of the late third century (ch. 8 nn. 108 f.). It was also by the power of the people that 'equal liberty' was obtained for plebeians in office-holding, and that the introduction of balloting gave them greater freedom to vote as they pleased. Naturally the various measures of relief for the poor ascribed to plebeian leaders of the early Republic, or promoted by Flaminius' agrarian distributions, and by the Gracchi and their successors, were at least products of that *libertas* which could be identified with popular sovereignty. Moreover, it could be held that the property and revenues of the Roman state were the possessions and income of the citizens (cf. Cic. *de leg. agr.* ii. 55, 80–2); Tiberius Gracchus urged that it was just that the land of the community should be distributed in common, sc. that individual citizens should be given shares in what belonged to them, and Gaius probably deployed a similar argument for the application of public funds to grain distributions (Florus ii. 1); it may well be that they contended that the people was free to dispose of its own. Since the freedom of Rome as a state was connected with its imperial strength (n. 30), Tiberius might also have contended that his agrarian law, designed to ensure that more land should

---

[170] Hellegouarc'h 556.

be in the possession of free men available for service in the army, whose numbers guaranteed that strength, instead of being cultivated by slaves, was conducive to Roman freedom.

But is there yet another possibility, that distributions of land and grain or the relief of debtors were actually seen as enhancing or creating freedom? It could have been said that grain distributions at Rome made the recipients less dependent on bounties from the great houses, while limitations on the rate of interest, moratoriums on the repayment of loans, or reductions of the capital due to be repaid, freed debtors from creditors; the last claim was unquestionably made on behalf of those who had fallen into a condition of bondage analogous to that of the *nexi* of old (n. 7).

Kloesel thought that this conception did emerge in relation to the establishment of peasant proprietors on the land (n. 171). He cited a speech of Servius Tullius in Dionysius (iv. 9. 8), in which that king proposed to share out public land among the poor 'in order that, free men as you are, you may not labour as hirelings for others, but farm your own land and not that of others'. This is redolent of the notion of upper-class Greeks that it was servile to earn one's livelihood by taking wages, since the wage-earner had no true independence. Cicero repeats this idea, but in a passage in which he *may* be simply following the Greek Panaetius. I am not aware of any other explicit statement of it in Latin. It is quite another matter that upper-class Romans commonly shared the contempt expressed by their Greek peers for manual labour, including in my view the actual cultivation of the soil, as distinct from landowning; this contempt was felt for 'banausic' occupations of all kinds (retail trading too), irrespective of the legal or economic status of the persons engaged in them.[171]

Still, Kloesel may have been right.[172] As he remarks, Sallust says that the Gracchi began to champion freedom and expose the crimes of the oligarchs (*BJ* 42. 1); now, though it is true that Gaius Gracchus

[171] De Ste Croix, 1981, 179–208; for reasons given in *JRS* 1982, 160 f., I do not think that the upper-class opinion that wage-labour was servile in itself does anything to show that it was not of considerable economic importance, if only because the poor can have often had no alternative to accepting wages when offered, even though they too felt that it was a loss of independence. In *JRS* 1980, 99 f., I sought to refute the view that Roman law assimilated *mercennarii* to slaves; were this true, it would of course prove that men gained freedom by being taken out of the class of wage-earners. It is also clear that those engaged in 'banausic' work either did not share the upper-class prejudice against it (so F. M. de Robertis, *Lavoro e lavoratori nel mondo rom.*, 1963, 21–41), or at any rate had no choice but to live by means they despised. On Cic. *de offic.* i. 150 f., see Brunt, *Proc. Camb. Phil. Soc.* 1973, 26 ff.; on contempt for cultivation of the soil, ibid. 11–13.

[172] Kloesel 42 ff., discounted by Wirszubski 44 ff., and Bleicken, 1972, 35 n. 58, for lack of evidence. There is indeed no force in Kloesel's suggestion that opponents of agrarian distributions were answering the claim of reformers that they made for liberty by taxing them with the design of aiming themselves at despotic power; this imputation surely countered the assertion by reformers of *libertas* in the sense of the people's sovereignty.

fortified the *ius provocationis* and that his famous judiciary reform could be represented as an extension of 'aequa libertas' (Florus ii. 1), his brother was especially associated with agrarian reform, and he himself continued the work and also instituted the grain dole, while the context in which Sallust sums up their achievement is that of a description of the miseries of the poor: the freedom they stood for should be related to their efforts to alleviate social distress. Appian tells that the poor feared that in the event of Tiberius' death 'they would no longer enjoy equality in citizen rights but would be forced into being the slaves of the rich' (i. 15). Lepidus' speech links the loss of freedom under Sulla with the ejection of the poor from their homes (4, 12, 24) and with the abolition of the corn dole, which left the people destitute, deprived even of slave rations (11), as well as with disregard of the rule of law. Tiberius Gracchus also lamented that men who had fought for Rome had lost their own homes (Plut. *Ti. Gr.* 9), and Cicero himself was to mention in the same breath 'private hearths' and 'the rights of liberty' (*Phil.* xiii. 1). All this is little to show that *libertas* could connote economic independence, but we must recall how little the sources preserve of the sentiments to which *populares* appealed.

In any case, *libertas* as the sovereignty of the people was not just the instrument by which the people had secured various benefits: it had also been sought, according to annalistic tradition, for the sake of those benefits. This is written large in the accounts of the struggle of the orders in Livy and Dionysius. Cicero draws on this tradition when he suggests that there would have been no pressure to create the tribunate, had the senate provided relief for debtors who were being reduced to bondage (*de rep.* ii. 59), and Sallust when he explains the first secession of the plebs and the institution of the tribunate and other rights for the plebs by cruel and oppressive administration of the patricians (*Hist.* i. 11). No doubt the tradition was in large measure the product of annalistic imagination, but the very nature of the tribunate and of the organization of the plebs, as a kind of state within a state, virtually implies a bitter class conflict. At least the secession of *c.*287, and the circumstances that provoked it, must have been in the recollection of the earliest annalists, if not recorded in the pontifical annals at the time, and we can then safely say that the *lex Hortensia*, which finally established popular sovereignty, was the issue of a debt agitation (n. 168). In the late Republic too restoration of the full tribunician power was demanded in the 70s for the sake of freedom, but, according to Cicero (I *Verr.* 45 f.), it gained its force from discontent with provincial misgovernment (which is perhaps not easy to credit) and judicial corruption, for which no remedies could be expected unless tribunes recovered their former rights to initiate reforms; we may perhaps think that the masses were more concerned with the abolition or inadequacy of the corn dole and indeed the failure of the government to maintain supplies of grain for the market (Sall. *Hist.* ii. 45), and by the lack of protection for citizens outside Rome (*Or. Macri* 27).

We may then well believe that ordinary citizens valued their political rights in the consciousness that they had afforded, and might continue to afford, all sorts of other benefits, just as senators must have valued the liberty that inhered in the senate's authority for the power and perquisites that they individually derived from it. But in neither case need we assume that liberty had not also come to be regarded as a good *per se*, partly by its association with other advantages, penetrating men's minds at a deeper level than that of conscious calculation, and partly for the *dignitas* that it bestowed on its possessors. Senators enjoyed general respect and deference, but the common people could also rejoice that these grandees had to humble themselves in soliciting their votes. Each citizen had his share in the *maiestas* of the people.

XVI

If all this be true, we cannot say that there was no Roman conception of *libertas* that did not comprise democratic ideas. It is of course obvious that the seeds of democracy sown in the early Republic never came to fruition. The extension of Roman territory and the growth of citizen numbers, to say nothing of the peculiar defects of the Roman assemblies, were insurmountable hindrances, given that no one so much as thought of introducing the representative principle. The 'strength of the plebs', as Sallust observes, was 'disunited and dispersed' (*BJ* 41. 6). The people could act under the constitution only on initiatives from above, and though these were forthcoming they were for long infrequent, and always intermittent; there was no organized party with a continuous existence, ever intent on enabling the people to give effect to its will. Most aristocrats were always at one in desiring to keep real power in their own circles and the people, which was bound to commit the exercise of government to persons within a limited class qualified by property, education, training, and tradition, seldom had the chance to choose for office members, either nobles or new men, who would act against the common interests of that class, still less to fill the senate with them. We need not doubt that most citizens felt a respect passed on from generation to generation for the senatorial order under whose direction Rome had grown great, but such respect did not always outweigh all other interests and passions, nor was it thought to be inherently connected with *libertas*. *Auctoritas* was a restriction on *libertas*, and the abuse of aristocratic power inspired ebullitions of protest and hatred. It was aristocrats who then spoke of popular licence.

These ebullitions resulted in violence on both sides and ultimately in civil wars, in which the antagonists could all claim to be defending freedom, which they conceived in different ways. Seneca was to observe that it was futile for Brutus to hope that it could be restored in a state where so much was to be gained from both ruling and submitting to slavery, and which could no longer be brought back to its former condition, once the old morality had been lost; there could never again be equality of civic rights and a stable system of law, when so many thousands of men were ready to fight not for their liberty but for subjection to a particular individual (*de benef*. ii. 20). He implied that political liberty, taken to depend on sound morality and respect for law, was doomed before the institution of the Principate and was incompatible with it (cf. n. 42). Of course Tacitus and others could admit that liberty, in the attenuated sense of freedom for men of rank to think and speak as they chose, could be maintained by a benevolent prince; but even this measure of freedom was precarious: it reposed on the will of one despot and might be revoked by his successor.[173] For Tacitus too loss of equal rights was important: in AD 14 'all men [he is thinking of men of rank] abandoning equality awaited the orders of a ruler' (*Ann*. i. 4). Like Seneca, he saw that Romans in effect prized other things more than freedom; the plebs were won over to the new system by cheap food, the soldiers by rewards, all by the desire for *otium*; even the survivors of the old nobility were seduced by prospects of offices and wealth (i. 2). However, while the higher orders retained a share in the government, if only as servants of the monarch, and the new system respected their material class-interests, the people forfeited not only its electoral, judicial, and legislative rights, but eventually 'equal liberty' before the laws. It is symptomatic that Caesar himself abrogated that freedom of association which Clodius had confirmed, and that Augustus (or Tiberius) would invest the consular prefect of the city with arbitrary powers of coercion not only over slaves but over 'that disorderly element among the citizens whose audacity could be deterred only by force' (*Ann*. vi. 11). This was one step along the path that would lead to the imposition on the humble of penalties once thought appropriate only to slaves, and bind them to the soil in the interests of treasury and landowners. The optimate critics of the Gracchi were proved right; attempts to 'restore' the power of the people led on to monarchy, and monarchy destroyed popular freedom more completely than senatorial.

[173] Wirszubski 167–71.

7

AMICITIA IN THE LATE ROMAN REPUBLIC[1]

I. A modern conception that *amicitia* denotes political association contrasted with Cicero's ideal of *amicitia* as founded on virtue and the common value set on the pleasure derived from the relationship. *Amicitia* can certainly denote affection, and though it entails *officia* it is more than a relationship requiring the interchange of services (not necessarily political). Its range extends from genuine intimacy and community of principles (or at least pursuits) to forms of outward courtesy. **II.** These forms can coexist with political opposition and secret hostility. Nominal friendship does not indicate readiness to assist a 'friend'. Overt *inimicitiae*, as distinct from *occulta odia*, rare. Men can preserve the forms of friendship with avowed enemies of their other friends. *Amicitia* and *inimicitiae* in political trials. *Amicitiae* cannot be identified with political alliances, and private obligations to friends are far from furnishing the chief explanation for political alignments.

I

N describing a close political union Sallust observes 'haec inter bonos amicitia, inter malos factio est' (*BJ* 31. 15).[2] This remark may be taken as a text for a fashionable interpretation of *amicitia* in the late Roman Republic. Professor Lily Ross Taylor writes that 'the old Roman substitute for party is *amicitia*', and that 'friendship was the chief basis of support for candidates for office, and *amicitia* was the good old word for party relationships'.[3] Again, Sir Ronald Syme says that '*amicitia* was a weapon of politics, not a sentiment based on congeniality', and he maintains that 'Roman political factions were welded together, less by unity of principle than by mutual interest and by

---

[1] This paper, of which I read a version to the Cambridge Philological Society in 1964, was suggested by reading F. Lossmann, *Cicero u. Caesar im Jahre 54: Stud. z. Theorie u. Praxis der röm. Freundschaft* (1962); cf. my review in *Cl. Rev.* 1964, 90 f. I have also been helped by the valuable collection of material in J. Hellegouarc'h, *Le Vocabulaire latin des relations et des partis politiques sous la République* (1963). The present version is revised, and some material has been transferred to ch. 9.

[2] Cf. *BJ* 41. 6: 'nobilitas factione magis pollebat, plebis vis soluta atque dispersa in multitudine minus poterat'; Cic. *de rep.* i. 44, 69, iii. 44, and esp. 23: 'cum autem certi propter divitias aut genus aut aliquas opes rem p. tenent, est factio, sed vocantur optimates'. See also Hellegouarc'h 99 ff.; M. I. Henderson, *JRS* 1952, 115; ch. 9 *passim*, and pp. 446 f. below.

[3] Taylor, 1949, 7 f.

mutual services (*officia*), either between social equals as an alliance, or from superior to inferior, in a traditional and almost feudal form of clientship: on a favourable estimate the bond was called *amicitia*, otherwise *factio*'.[4] On this view, if a Roman called a man *amicus*, it meant that he was a political ally, or a member of what in eighteenth-century England could have been described as the same 'connection'.

This sort of relation is one described by Cicero as 'non amicitia sed mercatura quaedam utilitatum suarum' (*de nat. deor.* i. 122). The theoretical account of true friendship which he offers in the *Laelius* or *de amicitia* is strikingly different. It is 'voluntatum studiorum sententi-arum summa consensio' (15), arising not from our consciousness of our own deficiencies or from our need for reciprocal services: it springs rather from natural affection and benevolence, from which in turn reciprocal services result.[5] This affection is one of the bonds that unite any human society, but in an intenser form it subsists only between two or at most a few men. Between them it is certain to last only if they are good men, whose character and views do not 'alter when they alteration find'.[6] It is only on the foundation of virtue that genuine and durable affection can be based, a friendship inspired by mutual good faith (*de amic.* 65) and goodwill and by reciprocal recognition of merits (20), and cemented by similarity of character (*mores*) and pursuits (*studia*) (27, 74); the friends are frank, though courteous to each other, loyal and unsuspecting (65–6); they share, and ought to share, each other's joys and sorrows (22, 45–8); they serve each other without keeping an account of profit and loss (58); a man will do more for his friend than he would do for himself, and should even deviate from the strict path of justice, if his friend's life or reputation is imperilled,[7] though naturally he will do, and will be asked to do, nothing absolutely shameful (56–61; cf. 40); in short the true friend is an image of oneself (23), or indeed a kind of second self—'tamquam alter idem' (80; cf. 92).[8]

In this essay Cicero was presumably drawing on Greek philosophy, and W. Kroll, who held that *amicus* means in the everyday language of

---

[4] *RR* 157, ch. II.   [5] *de amic.* 19–32; cf. 51.

[6] Ibid. 18–20, 50, 65, 79–84; cf. Arist. *EN* 1156^{b}6 ff.

[7] F. Schulz, 1936, 237, aptly cites II *Verr.* 3, 122, 152.

[8] For *mores* cf. Nepos, *Att.* 5. 3; though Atticus' sister married Quintus Cicero, he was more intimate with Marcus, 'ut iudicari possit plus in amicitia valere similitudinem morum quam affinitatem'. Common *studia*, see below; cf. also *Cluent.* 46: 'iam hoc fere scitis omnes quantam vim habeat ad coniungendas amicitias studiorum ac naturae similitudo'; examples, *Lig.* 21 (Tubero), *Fam.* i. 7. 11, 9. 23 f (Lentuli), iii. 13. 2 (App. Claudius), v. 13. 5, 15. 2 (Lucceius), xiii. 29. 1 (Plancus), *de fato* 2 (Hirtius), *Ac. praef.* and i. 1 (Varro). Hellegouarc'h 174 ff. misses the common sense of intellectual pursuits. Frankness, *Fam.* xi. 28. 8. Courtesy in complaints, iii. 11. 5. Image, Lossmann (n. 1) 33 ff. compares Arist. *MM* 1213^{a}7 ff. Second self, *Fam.* vii. 5. 1 (Caesar), *Att.* iii. 15. 4 (Atticus), *ad Brut.* 23 (=i. 15). 2 (Brutus), *Att.* iv. 1, 7 (Pompey on Cicero).

the time no more than a political follower, was content to explain that
we find Roman practice in the strongest contradiction with Greek
theory.[9] Cicero's source or sources cannot be identified with certainty;
he does not here name any source, in the way that he names Panaetius
in the *de officiis*, and neither internal evidence nor Gellius' statement[10]
that he had apparently used Theophrastus on friendship proves who
the writer or writers were that he was following; it is obviously possible
that he was not slavishly following any source, even though he was
influenced by one or more Greek philosophical treatments of his
subject.[11] It is true that he was not an original thinker and that where
he is concerned with the more abstract philosophic themes, metaphys-
ics, physics, and the like, he perhaps does no more than expound the
doctrines of others, whether or not he indicates his own approval or
dissent. But it is another matter to suppose that he adopted the same
procedure when writing of practical morality or politics. Here he
expressly claims independence. 'It would be very easy', he says in *de
legibus* (ii. 17), 'to translate Plato, which I would do if I did not wish to
express myself.' Even in the *de officiis*, where he avows that he is mainly
following Panaetius, it is plain that he does so only because and in so
far as he can adopt the views of Panaetius as his own, and confirm and
illustrate them from Roman experience.[12] This was possible because
Panaetius himself had written not about the duties of the ideal *sapiens*,
but about those which should be performed by men who could
conventionally be regarded as good in the workaday world (i. 46, iii.
14–16). So too in the *Laelius* Cicero makes it clear that the good men
who alone can enjoy true friendships are not necessarily philosophic
sages but men, like Scipio and Laelius, who are good in the plain man's
sense;[13] he cites other models from Roman history.

The doctrine of the *Laelius* was certainly not the mere product of
Cicero's philosophic studies in old age. In a youthful work he defines
friendship as 'the will that good things should accrue to the man loved
for his own sake, combined with a like will on his part', and adds that
'as we are here speaking of lawsuits, we take into account not only
friendship but also its fruits, so that it would seem to be sought for their
sake as well'. 'There are some', he proceeds, 'who think that friendship

---

[9] *Kultur der ciceronischen Zeit*, i. 55 ff.

[10] i. 3. 11; *contra* Philippson (*RE* viiA. 1163 ff.) he clearly held that Cicero used Theophrastus,
but he need not be right. F. A. Steinmetz, *Die Freundschaftslehre des Panaitios* (*Palingenesia* iii), 1967,
an admirable analysis of *de amicitia*, has strengthened the case for Panaetius as at least Cicero's
chief source.

[11] Cf. V. Pöschl, *Röm. Staat u. gr. Staatsdenken bei Cicero*, 1962, 23 n. 27 on *de republica*.

[12] Panaetius, the main source of i–ii (cf. iii. 7: 'quem nos correctione quadam adhibita
potissimum secuti sumus'; *Att.* xvi. 11. 4), is criticized explicitly in i. 7, 9–11, 152, 161, ii. 16, 86,
iii. 33.

[13] *de amic.* 18–21, 38; cf. 39. 100–4.

should be sought only for its utility, others for its own sake alone, others again who value it on both counts.'[14] This distinction, which reappears in a letter to Appius Claudius (*Fam*. iii. 10. 7–9), between two types of friendship, not mutually exclusive, is somewhat different from Aristotle's, who had held that friendship was of three kinds: what attracted us in a man might be either the good, the useful, or the pleasant.[15] But the pleasures of friendship also constituted a theme well known at Rome; it was a rhetorical *topos* that 'maximum bonum est amicitia; plurimae delectationes sunt in amicitia' (*de inv*. i. 95); such terms as *iucundus* and *suavis* are often used to describe friendly relations, and Aristotle's classification underlies Cicero's explanation of the fact that Catiline had so many friends; in the *pro Caelio* (12–14) he says that Catiline was able to do them services, his company gave them pleasure, and to all appearances he was a man of many virtues; it accorded with Roman experience.

A sharp contrast between Greek theory and Roman practice is indeed out of place in Cicero's day. Roman thinking was already permeated by Greek ideas. Like many others of his class, Cicero had been versed in Greek philosophy long before he began to write on it more or less systematically,[16] and he could take such knowledge for granted in others; thus in writing to Appius Claudius long before he composed the *Laelius*, he can refer to the books of learned men on friendship as a matter of common knowledge (*Fam*. iii. 7. 5, 8. 5). Cicero himself took the moral and political principles he had adopted from Greek thought so seriously that in 49 BC, for instance, he examined over and over again how he should act in accordance with them; as Gelzer remarks, 'this way of thinking sprang from his deepest convictions'.[17] At the same time it is implausible to suppose that the Romans, whose word for friendship (as Cicero points out)[18] derives from *amo*, had no native acquaintance with genuine affection of a non-sexual kind. Cicero contended that in general the Romans were better practitioners in moral and political life than the Greeks,[19] and that the experience of a Roman statesman gave him special competence to write on political theory,[20] although the virtue Romans drew from

---

[14] *de inv*. ii. 167; cf. 157.

[15] *EN* 1156ᵇ16 ff. It is characteristic of one difference between Greek and Roman society that Cicero does not bring up Aristotle's point that friendship for utility is proper to the business man.

[16] *de rep*. i. 7, 13, *Fam*. iv. 4, *Brut*. 308 etc.; for later studies in leisure *Ac*. i. 11, *Att*. ii. 16, 3, etc. For other Romans see E. Zeller, *Phil. d. Griechen* iii/i⁴. 550–6 with numerous references, esp. *Ac*. ii. 4 f. (Lucullus), *Fam*. iv. 3. 3; cf. 2. 2 (Ser. Sulpicius), xv. 4. 16 (M. Cato, whom in *de fin*. iii. 7 Cicero depicts in Lucullus' library 'multis circumfusum Stoicorum libris').

[17] *RE* viiA. 995. cf. Brunt. *JRS* 1986, 12 ff.

[18] *de amic*. 26. Cf. Hellegouarc'h 146 f. for *amor* as equivalent to *amicitia*, e.g. *Att*. xiv. 13B. 1, *Fam*. i. 8. 2, 9. 6, *Qu. fr*. iii. 5. 3 f. Cicero supposed that Brutus was very fond of him ('me tam valde amat', *Att*. xii. 14. 3).

[19] *Tusc. Disp*. i. 1–3; cf. *de rep*. iii. 7, *de leg*. ii. 62.   [20] *de rep*. i. 13, *de leg*. iii. 14.

nature, tradition, and experience could be matured and deepened by the study of Greek doctrines.[21] Thus in his view Romans had a special aptitude for ethics and politics, the most important parts of philosophy.[22] It would be strange then if Cicero, holding as he did to the superiority of Romans in practical morality, would have been content in his old age merely to copy out Greek doctrines from a book, if they were totally irrelevant to the actualities of Roman life as he knew them in a long career. The *Laelius* is constantly illustrated from Roman life and it should be taken seriously as an expression of Roman experience.

It is beyond question that *amicitia*, for whatever reasons the relationship was formed, was not a relationship either of mere affection or of mere reciprocal interest; if it was more than an empty name, it bound the friends together in bonds of obligation and honour. It was supposed to be founded on *fides*, or, as Cicero says in the *Laelius* (92, 97) and quite casually in a forensic speech (*Quinct.* 26), on *veritas*. The author of the rhetorical work *ad Herennium* (iv. 19) ranks betrayal of friends with breach of an oath or violence to parents among acts of moral obliquity; a man can be condemned for destroying political harmony, good faith, friendship, and the public interest. In giving practical recommendations to the orator, Cicero remarks that he may appeal to considerations of both expediency and morality (*honestas*); friendships, 'which are determined by affection and love', come under the second head (*Part. Or.* 83–8). The duties (*officia*) that friends owe to each other are mentioned so often that I need cite no evidence here; many of the relevant texts will be quoted later. Following Panaetius, Cicero acknowledges special obligations first to the fatherland, and then in descending order to parents, children, kinsmen; but he then stresses the ties that bind us to friends, especially to those with whom we are united by 'similitudo morum' (*de offic.* i. 58). However, men could find themselves under apparently conflicting obligations, and had to decide which were the strongest in the complexity of actual circumstances. It was a breach of duty either to fail in doing for a friend what you might do for him rightly or to do for him what was not just; you should never prefer your own advantage to the claims of friendship, a practice which all too often led to the dissolution of the specious friendships of politicians (*de amic.* 33, 63), nor those claims to the interests of the fatherland or the requirements of law and justice.[23]

The passage I have already cited from the *pro Caelio* is only one of

---

[21] *de rep.* i. 13, iii. 4–6. Hence it is a public service to expound Greek doctrines, *de nat. deor.* i. 7, *de div.* ii. 1–4, *de fin.* i. 10, *de offic.* i. 155.

[22] *de rep.* i. 33, *de nat. deor.* i. 7, *de offic.* iii. 5.

[23] *de offic.* i. 58 f., iii. 43, *de amic.* 35–43, 61. Steinmetz (n. 10) 66 ff. is no doubt right that Cicero was polemizing against partisans of Caesar or Antony who justified their conduct in the name of friendship, but see pp. 380 f.

many in the speeches and letters in which *amicitia* is not restricted to a
connection founded solely on mutual services and common interests,
still less to membership of the same faction. It is easy but one-sided to
quote such statements as Cicero's 'idcirco amicitiae comparantur ut
commune commodum mutuis officiis gubernetur'.[24] Even when only
utility is mentioned, what is stressed is often not so much the services
actually rendered as the constant and known will or readiness to
render them,[25] and the sense of *amicitia* is not exhausted by *officia*; thus
Trebatius is not only 'plenus offici' but also 'utriusque nostrum
amantissimus' (*Fam.* xi. 27. 1). And *amicitia* often purports to describe
sincere affection based on a community of tastes, feelings, and
principles, and taking the form, where opportunity permits, of continuous and intimate association (*vetustas, familiaritas, consuetudo*).[26] It is
immaterial for my present purpose whether such affection always
existed where it was professed: I am concerned for the present only
with the meaning of the term.

Here Cicero's correspondence with Appius Claudius is of special
interest. It needs no proof that the *amicitia* was purely political, a
matter of expediency. It is therefore the more striking that Cicero
chooses to represent it as something more. He tells Appius that if it is
the mark of the greatest shrewdness 'omnia ad suam utilitatem referre',
nothing could be more useful to him than a union with a man of such
ability and influence as Appius, but he proceeds: 'illa vincula, quibus
quidem libentissime astringor, quanta sunt, studiorum similitudo,
suavitas consuetudinis, delectatio vitae atque victus, sermonis societas,
litterae interiores'. Even to Caelius, Appius is represented as 'suavis
amicus et studiosus studiorum etiam meorum'.[27] Thus their friendship
is depicted as more than a political connection: it is based on their
common intellectual pursuits and the delight they take in each other's
conversation and company. He later writes to Appius in the spirit of
the *Laelius*: 'propono fructum amicitiae nostrae ipsam amicitiam, qua
nihil est uberius (*Fam.* iii. 13. 2). Similarly he tells Lucceius that he
would greatly desire to live in his society; 'vestustas, amor, consuetudo,
studia paria; quod vinclum, quaeso, deest nostrae coniunctionis?' (v.
15. 2), and in 62 he writes to Pompey that if his services have not yet

---

[24] *Rosc. Amer.* 3.

[25] E.g. Sall. *Cat.* 20. 4: 'idem velle atque idem nolle, ea demum firma amicitia est'; *Fam.* v. 2. 3,
v. 7. 2, xi. 28. 1 (Matius refers to *perpetua benevolentia*), *Planc.* 5, etc. Cf. Hellegouarc'h 181 ff.; but
his view that '*Voluntas* est donc le terme propre à désigner la notion d' "opinion politique"' (183)
is at once too narrow and too weak; *voluntas* connotes the will to realize one's opinions and they
need not be political. For *benevolentia* in true friendship see e.g. *de amic.* 19 f.

[26] On these and other such terms see Hellegouarc'h's analyses, 68 ff. *Consuetudo* could naturally
be hampered by separation; cf. *Fam.* xv. 14. 2 and p. 357 on Matius.

[27] *Fam.* iii. 1. 1 (Appius dear to Cicero 'propter multas suavitates ingenii, officii, humanitatis
tuae'), 10. 9 f., ii. 13. 2.

brought them close together, politics will certainly cement their union; he hopes that on his return Pompey will allow him 'et in re publica et in amicitia adiunctum esse', 'to be united with him *both* in politics *and* in friendship'; a similar distinction is often made.[28] By his own account these hopes were fulfilled; in 61 he refers to their 'multa et iucunda consuetudo'; in 56 he publicly claims not only political co-operation but 'hanc iucundissimam vitae atque officiorum omnium societatem'; in 50 he speaks not only of Pompey's services to himself but of 'consuetudinis iucunditas'; their union is marked by 'amoris atque offici signa'; and in 49 he regards himself as bound to Pompey by 'merita summa erga salutem meam', by 'familiaritas', and by 'ipsa rei publicae causa'.[29] Similarly in the *Brutus* (1 f.) he recalls how much he lost by the death of his friend Hortensius in 50—'consuetudo iucunda, multorum officiorum coniunctio', and wise advice in the political crisis. The *officia*, when distinguished from political collaboration, must refer to personal or private services; the sense of loss on the death of a man from whose intimacy Cicero claims that he derived pleasure and private profit was enhanced ('augebat molestiam') by the fact that he was also a political associate. 'Semo, litterae, humanitas' (cf. *Fam.* iii. 9. 1) were recognized as qualities which might make even a disreputable man a welcome associate on whom the name of friend could be bestowed (II *Verr.* iii. 8). I need hardly do more than refer to Cicero's relations with Caelius, Cornificius, or Papirius Paetus, with whom he might indulge in rallies of wit.[30] From Trebatius he derived 'non mediocri . . . voluptate ex consuetudine nostra vel utilitate ex consilio atque opera tua' (*Fam.* vii. 17. 2).[31] Cicero represents his friendship with Matius, who as early as 53 is described as 'suavissimus doctissimusque' (*Fam.* vii. 15. 2), as beginning not with reciprocal services but with mutual affection (*amor*), which at first did not ripen into intimacy only because their different ways of life kept them apart;[32] then came the time when Matius rendered valuable help to Cicero in the civil war, and at last, after his return to Italy, they lived on terms of familiarity; they often spent many hours 'suavissimo sermone', and Matius encouraged Cicero to write philosophical works. 'Omnia me tua delectant', says Cicero, 'sed maxime maxima cum fides in amicitia,

---

[28] *Fam.* v. 7; cf. *de fin.* iii. 8 on Lucullus 'mecum et amicitia et omni voluntate sententiaque coniunctus'; *de orat.* i. 24: 'M. Antonius, homo et consiliorum in re p. socius et summa cum Crasso familiaritate coniunctus'; *Fam.* xii. 15. 2 (Lentulus writes): 'homo mihi cum familiaritate tum etiam sensibus in re p. coniunctissimus' (Hellegouarc'h 70 misinterprets both the last texts), *Planc.* 95, etc.

[29] *Att.* i. 16. 11 (cf. 17. 10), *de dom.* 28, *Fam.* iii. 10. 10, *Att.* viii. 3. 2.

[30] *Fam.* ii. 12. 1, viii. 3. 1, xii. 18. 2, ix. 15. 1 f.

[31] For Trebatius cf. also *Att.* ix. 9. 4, x. 11. 4, *Fam.* vii. 19 f., xi. 27. 1, *Top.* 1–5.

[32] Cf. *Fam.* xv. 14. 2.

consilium, gravitas, constantia, tum lepos, humanitas, litterae' (*Fam.*
xi. 17).

Above all of course there is Atticus, whom Cicero says that he loves
for his virtues next to his brother; Atticus is the partner of his studies;
they share the same joys and griefs; when Atticus is away, Cicero lacks
not only his advice but 'sermonis communicatio quae mihi suavissima
tecum solet esse', and yet even then he sees him as if he were present, so
clearly does he perceive the fellow-feeling of his love.[33] In the same
way he tells Lucceius that even when parted, they will seem to be
united 'animorum coniunctione iisdemque studiis' (*Fam.* v. 13. 5). One
is reminded of the dictum in the *de amicitia* (23): 'amici et absentes
adsunt'. Atticus, so Cicero believes, cares for his interests more than for
his own (*Att.* xii. 37. 3), just as Laelius is made to say that a friend
should. 'Quid dulcius quam habere quicum audeas sic loqui ut
tecum?', asks Laelius (*de amic.* 22). Cicero could speak with Atticus as
with himself (*Att.* viii. 14. 2); indeed Atticus is a sort of *alter ego*. The
phrase was borrowed from the Greeks, but it was in common use;
Cicero applies it also to Caesar and to Brutus, and Pompey used it in
public of Cicero.[34]

It is a similar relation between Laelius and Scipio that Cicero
portrays in the *de amicitia*. 'In Scipio's friendship', says Laelius, 'I found
agreement on politics, advice in private affairs, and repose full of
delight.' They shared the same house, the same life, the same
campaigns, the same travels; they were occupied in leisure in the same
philosophical inquiries. They enjoyed 'that in which lies the whole
strength of friendship, the most complete agreement of wills, pursuits,
and opinions'.[35] Kroll cites one of these texts to justify his statement
that 'Cicero makes Laelius say that for his friendship with Scipio
political agreement was essential'. This distorts Cicero's meaning; he is
rather suggesting that the political agreement which did subsist
between Scipio and Laelius itself flowed from their perfect accord in
character, which was the main basis of true friendship. Of course
Laelius emphasizes that such friendship is uncommon; the bonds of
affection can unite only two or at most a few persons (*de amic.* 20), and
there is no certainty that such affection will endure unless the friends
are good men, a doctrine that Cicero alludes to in writing to Appius
(*Fam.* iii. 10. 7, 13. 1–2). But the rarity of true friendship is not a
peculiarity of Roman society; it is probably true among all peoples,
and in all ages.

In professing his renewed friendship for Crassus, Cicero writes to
him: 'has litteras velim existimes foederis habituras esse vim, non

[33] *Att.* i. 17. 5 f., v. 18. 3, viii. 6. 4, *Fam.* vii. 30. 2.
[34] *Att.* iii. 15. 4; cf. n. 8.   [35] *de amic.* 15, 79, 103 f.

epistulae' (*Fam.* v. 8. 5). Professor Taylor cites this to support her statement that 'friendship for the man in politics was a sacred agreement'. Although in fact many political friendships were short-lived and insincere, there is no doubt that she has hit off the meaning of the term *foedus*. Treaties were ratified by solemn oaths and to break them was perjury. But it is wrong to confine the sacredness of friendship to political connections. Catullus uses the same metaphor of his relations with Lesbia, in a passage where *amicitia* stands for *amor*, just as *amor* may replace *amicitia* (n. 18); he prays

> ut liceat nobis tota perducere vita
> aeternum hoc sanctae foedus amicitiae.[36]

According to Sallust, indeed, it was one mark of the depravity of his age that 'ambitio multos mortalis falsos fieri subegit, aliud clausum in pectore, aliud in lingua promptum habere, amicitias inimicitiasque non ex re, sed ex commodo aestumare, magisque voltum quam ingenium bonum habere' (*Cat.* 10. 5). This indictment of the political morality of his times was hardly intended to be of universal application; we are not to suppose that Sallust thought that no Romans of his day recognized that *amicitia* involved sacred obligations.[37] The common practices of private life, not least the frequency with which men rewarded with legacies the services they had received in life, show how strongly the *fides* on which *amicitia* was based still worked on men's minds; the prevalence of *fides* in business life explains many of the institutions of Roman law. A friendship contracted *ex commodo* could easily involve the recipient of benefits in an obligation to repay them in circumstances when it was no longer in his interest to do so. A friend has a duty to give good advice (*Att.* iii. 15. 4), and when necessary to lend money (*Fam.* xiv. 1, 5, 2. 3) or to perform all manner of other services. The recognized moral element in political friendship made it possible for Cicero to appeal to Caesar as his friend in 49 to let him prove himself 'bonus vir, gratus, pius' in his relationship with Pompey (*Att.* ix. 2A. 3). But those who were guided in any measure by a sense of obligation could easily recognize that their obligations to their friends were transcended by their obligation to their *patria* (n. 23); and this in turn made it natural for seeming friends to excuse political differences with a plea that covered a divergence of their own interests.

In its highest form, true affection between good men, *amicitia* was durable even among politicians because they were *ex hypothesi* men who

---

[36] Catullus 109; cf. 76. 3, 87. 3. Many parallels for such *foedera* can be found, *TLL* vi. 1004–6. Cf. Hellegouarc'h, 38 ff. for *foedus* being cognate with *fides*, on which *amicitia* rested (*de amic.* 65).

[37] Cf. Schulz, 1936, ch. xi (of which Professor P. W. Duff reminded me); M. Gelzer, *Kl. Schr.* i. 70 ff.

shared the same correct moral and political principles. Others aspired or pretended to such a genuine and lasting intimacy, when in reality they were linked only by common tastes or interests; and the hollowness of their connection was not exposed unless their interests diverged. In the meantime this secondary form of friendship might assume a close familiarity, as between Cicero and Caelius, and involve obligations to render mutual services. But not all who called themselves friends were so closely bound together. Wherever courtesies and services were interchanged, the urbanity of social etiquette extended the use of the term *amici* to persons with whom no sort of intimacy subsisted, *Amicitia* had imperceptible gradations in quality and degree;[38] yet even the 'ambitiosae fucosaeque amicitiae'[39] which 'fructum domesticum non habent' took their name by external analogy from the true affection which is the primitive significance of the word.

Like ourselves,[40] the Romans might politely describe as a friend a person with whom they had no familiarity, but to whom they had, or professed to have, nothing but goodwill at the time. Cicero calls both the censors of 70 BC his friends, but in almost the same breath remarks that he was intimate with only one of them (*Cluent.* 117). In 43 he declared that there was no consular (not even his old enemy, L. Piso) 'quin mecum habeat aliquam coniunctionem gratiae, alii maximam, alii mediocrem, nemo nullam' (*Phil.* viii. 20). It was surely the merest commonplace, understood by all, that 'consuetudines victus non possunt esse cum multis' (*Mil.* 21). In letters he bestows the name of friend on far too many people to warrant the supposition that he even expected his correspondents to think that they were all his close associates.[41] The author of the *Commentariolum* observes that a candidate may be free with the title of friend and give it to anyone who manifests his support; but from such supporters is to be distinguished 'quisque domesticus ac maxime intimus', though others may be confirmed in allegiance; 'adducenda amicitia in spem familiaritatis et consuetudinis' (16–23); even if he be not Q. Cicero, the writer was well versed in the manners of the age. Many who belonged to the

---

[38] Cf. *de inv.* ii. 168: 'amicitiarum autem ratio, quoniam partim sunt religionibus iunctae, partim non sunt, et quia partim veteres sunt, partim novae, partim ab illorum, partim ab nostro beneficio profectae, partim utiliores, partim minus utiles, ex causarum dignitatibus, ex temporum opportunitatibus, ex officiis, ex religionibus, ex vetustatibus habebitur'.

[39] *Att.* i. 18. 1. The qualities of his friendship with Appius listed on p. 356 above were 'domestica' (*Fam.* iii. 10. 9).

[40] The *New Eng. Dict.* iv. (1901), 545 f. recognizes that 'friend' may be 'applied to a mere acquaintance, or to a stranger, as a mark of goodwill or kindly condescension on the part of the speaker', and that it may mean 'one who is on good terms with another, not hostile or at variance'.

[41] *Fam.* xiii. 71: 'etsi omnium causa quos commendo velle debeo, tamen cum omnibus non eadem mihi causa est'.

governor's *cohors*, or who paid morning visits of respect to the great houses, were *amici* only by courtesy.[42] More accurately, some were clients, but this was an appellation resented like death by all with any pretensions to rank or affluence.[43]

Such *amici*, drawn from the plebs, may well be regarded as political followers, yet it may often have happened that no ties of either interest or obligation bound them closely to any one political leader, and that they owed but a shifting allegiance. In the higher ranks of society, while the term *amicus* no more implied cordiality than that of 'honourable friend' in the House of Commons, it did not even denote political association, as the latter does. Courtesy or expediency often required that one senator should style another as his friend, despite serious disagreements in politics, merely because he had no wish for a personal quarrel, and at times because a genuine personal liking subsisted among those who were not in political accord. Moreover, in the network of relationships between leading senators, men incurred obligations to different *amici* or patrons whose policies and interests subsequently diverged, and were then confronted with a conflict of duties arising from the private relationships. With some the public interest might outweigh all private claims, as it was supposed to do (n. 23). Others might prefer to act *ex commodo* rather than *ex fide*, veiling private advantage with the cover of those obligations which best suited their own selfish aims. Thus, while *amicitia* always professed to be different from and superior to political alliance or allegiance, in the real world of public life it is commonly a good deal less. In the second part of this essay I propose to illustrate its complexity or ambiguity in political affairs.

II

Courtesy often outstepped the bounds of even temporary political co-operation. In May 44 Cicero privately described Antony's conduct as negligent, dishonourable, and pernicious, while assuring him of his constant love: no one, he said, was more dear to him in the existing political juncture (*Att.* xiv. 13. 6, 13A). Thus covert enmity and opposition were cloaked by polite professions of concord and amity. In his speech of 2 September Cicero still claimed to be Antony's friend while openly criticizing his conduct of affairs (*Phil.* i. 11 f.). This was indeed too much for Antony; he made an insulting reply (*Phil.* v. 19 f.). Cicero professed surprise: 'quid est dictum a me cum contumelia, quid

---

[42] M. Gelzer, *Kl. Schr.* i. 102 ff.

[43] *de offic.* ii. 69; cf. Sen. *de benef.* ii. 23. 3. Genuine friendship could of course subsist between men who were not completely equal in rank (*de amic.* 71 f.).

non moderate, quid non amice?' (ii. 6; cf. i. 27). He expected his
hearers or readers to accept that political opposition was compatible
with friendship, if there were no abuse. Before demonstrating how
much further he could go when provoked, he adds: 'I made serious
complaints on policy, but said nothing of the man, as if I had been
contending with Marcus Crassus, with whom I had many grave
disputes, and not with the most worthless of cut-throats' (ii. 7).

The allusion to Crassus is interesting. Crassus believed that it was
Cicero who prompted the charges made against him in 63 of complicity in Catiline's plot (Sall. *Cat.* 48. 9), and Cicero thought that Crassus
worked against his return from exile and intrigued against him before
Luca.[44] But this mutual hostility was hardly ever avowed. In 61
Crassus tickled Cicero's vanity with a deceitful encomium (*Att.* i. 14.
3 f.), and in 58 it was Clodius who said that Crassus was an enemy to
Cicero, not Crassus, who was content with declining to use his good
offices on Cicero's behalf; it was, he said, for the consuls to act (*Sest.*
39–41). Thus there was no overt quarrel, and in exile Cicero could
advise his brother, if accused of *repetundae*, to ask Crassus to defend him
(*Qu. fr.* i. 3. 7); on his return there was no need for formal reconciliation with Crassus, still less with Pompey, as Plutarch (*Cic.* 33. 5) and
Dio (xxxix. 9) wrongly assert; Cicero had only to repress his sense of
the wrongs Crassus had done him, until at last Crassus insulted him
personally in defending Gabinius; then his pent-up wrath broke forth,
and it was this sudden breach that had to be formally healed (*Fam.* i. 9.
20), a breach caused by mutual abuse. Thereafter, Cicero, who still
regarded Crassus as 'hominem nequam' (*Att.* iv. 13. 2), could write to
him, not implausibly, of their 'vetus necessitudo' (*Fam.* v. 8). It may be
added, as a curiosity to those who think that political ties were
hereditary, that Crassus' son Publius was an ardent admirer of
Cicero.[45]

Again in 43, when Cicero was trying to galvanize the senate into
resisting Antony effectively, the reprobate still had his friends and
spokesmen in the house, notably Q. Fufius Calenus (*Phil.* v. 6, xxi. 18,
etc.). Cicero had never had a good opinion of the man, once a
'levissimus tribunus plebis' (*Att.* i. 14. 1, 6) and an apologist for Clodius
(*Phil.* viii. 16), though he had admired his father (ibid. 13) and in the
very year of his tribunate had used influence with him on behalf of P.
Sestius (*Fam.* v. 6. 1); even in 49 he received him in his villa (*Att.* ix. 5.
1). Calenus was perhaps hostile to Cicero's pardon in 47 (if his name
may be read in *Att.* xi. 8. 2); at any rate there was an open quarrel,
which Calenus sought to make up in a letter which Cicero found

----

[44] *Fam.* xiv. 2. 2; i. 9. 9.
[45] Ibid. v. 8. 4, xiii. 16. 1, *Qu. fr.* ii. 8. 2; Plut. *Cr.* 13.

tasteless (xv. 4. 1), but to which he must have replied with polite assent.
For now Calenus is 'vir fortis ac strenuus, amicus meus' (*Phil.* viii. 11),
and if Cicero attacks his views, he professes to do so more in sorrow than
in anger; he is careful to avoid abuse (viii. 17, 19) and to express pleasure
when for once their opinions coincide (xi. 15). He only fears that 'ita
saepe dissentio ut . . . id quod fieri minime debet, minuere amicitiam
nostram videatur perpetua dissensio' (x. 2). It was only in extreme cases
that the wickedness of a man's public conduct could be, or alleged to be,
the basis for personal hostility (*de prov. cons.* 24). If the courtesies were
observed, a nominal friendship might survive political disagreements,
unless they were too continuous, or degenerated into personal assaults.
In the same spirit Cicero could reject the suspicion that he had differed
from Appius 'animorum contentione, non opinionum dissensione; nihil
autem feci umquam neque dixi quod contra illius existimationem esse
vellem' (*Fam.* ii. 13. 2).

With Caesar he could claim *familiaritas* and *consuetudo* going back to
the days of their youth.[46] In December 63, despite Cicero's commitment to oppose 'popular' measures and Caesar's avowed stance as a
'popularis', he spoke of him in complimentary terms. Late in 60 he
hoped to make Caesar 'meliorem', and complacently reports an
assurance that Caesar would value his counsel. Although his disapproval of the conduct of the triumvirs in 59 was avowed, and led them
to effect Clodius' *transitio ad plebem*, with the menace to Cicero's security
that this conveyed, Caesar continued even thereafter to offer posts to
Cicero, which implied that there was no personal breach between
them.[47] Formally his friendship with Pompey remained beyond
question intact. It was therefore not implausible for Cicero to claim in
56: 'ita dissensi ab illo [Caesar] ut in disiunctione sententiae coniuncti
tamen amicitia maneremus' (*de prov. cons.* 40 f.; cf. 25).[47] The fact or
appearance that Caesar had promoted or connived at his banishment
in 58 justified men in supposing that Cicero was now bound to regard
Caesar as an enemy; Cicero pretended to deny his responsibility, and
appealed to Pompey as witness that Caesar approved of his recall, and
had thereby repaired any wrong Cicero had suffered (ibid. 43); in any
event (he argued) Caesar's services to the state were such that any
private rancour must be laid aside, and the honours which the senate
had voted him with Cicero's support wiped out the memory of their
earlier political discord and would have necessitated a reconciliation, if
any reconciliation had been called for (ibid. 23 ff.).

The language he used to the senate in delineating his relationship
with Caesar, however false we may think it, must at any rate have

---

[46] *de prov. cons.* 40, *Qu. fr.* ii. 14. 1, *Fam.* i. 9. 12.
[47] *Cat.* iv. 9, *Att.* ii. 1. 6, 3. 3 f., 18. 3, 19. 4 f., *de prov. cons.* 41.

corresponded to normal conceptions of the ways in which amity could be preserved, or restored, between political adversaries. In fact by 56 Cicero was obliged to bow to the dictates of the triumvirs. But in private he now professes the warmest feelings for Caesar in particular, especially in letters to his brother Quintus and to Trebatius, both of whom were serving in Gaul; he even tells Quintus that he loves Caesar as much as Quintus or their children (iii. 1. 18). These letters, indeed, could easily have fallen into Caesar's hands (iii. 1. 21; cf. 6. 2, 7. 3), and perhaps the recipients were actually expected to relay his gushing sentiments to Caesar. Still, he could express satisfaction to Atticus with the regard that Caesar showed for him (*Att.* iv. 15. 10, 16. 7, 19. 2). No doubt Caesar, who wrote to him three times from Britain, treated him with exquisite courtesy, besides lending him 800,000 sesterces.[48]

Gelzer supposed that Cicero fell under his charm. That may be doubted. Late in 50, Cicero makes it clear that it was for his political security that he had had to join Pompey, and therefore to cultivate Caesar (*Att.* vii. 1. 2 f.). As Pompey's relations with Caesar cooled in 51, so Cicero ceased to refer to him with warmth; the loan was a particular embarrassment which he was anxious to repay, but never did. Though advocating peace in 50–49, Cicero then regarded Caesar as 'perditum latronem' (*Att.* vii. 18. 2; cf. vii. 11, 13. 1), and in his intimate correspondence with Atticus there is not a word of sorrow that his duty to the state or to Pompey may involve him in mortal conflict with a man he had once loved. Yet he still kept up friendly correspondence with Caesar himself for a time, as with several of his partisans,[49] who looked after his interests while he was with Pompey, and helped to secure his restoration;[50] and for years they lived on terms of close familiarity, seeming cordiality, and concealed mistrust.[51]

[48] On the relations between Cicero and Caesar from 56, Lossmann (n. 1), with full discussion, and Gelzer, 1969, 138 f., take a different view from mine. Cicero's apologia: *de prov. cons.* 23–43; cf. *Fam.* i. 9. 12–18. The loan: *Att.* v. 1. 2, 4. 3, 5. 2, 6. 2, vii. 8. 5.

[49] Correspondence with Caesar, *Att.* vii. 22. 3, viii. 2. 1, 3, 2, 11. 5, ix. 6A, 11A, 16. 2; their meeting, ix. 18. Relations with Balbus and Oppius, vii. 3. 11, viii. 15A, ix. 7A, B, 13A, x. 18. 2; with Trebatius ('a quo me unice diligi scio'), vii. 17. 3 f., *Fam.* iv. 1, *Att.* ix. 9. 4, 12, 15. 4–6, 17. 1, x. 1. 3, 11. 4 (still in early May 'vir plane et civis bonus'); with Matius, ix. 11. 2 (and often linked with Trebatius), *Fam.* xi. 27. 3; with Caelius, *Fam.* viii. 15 f., *Att.* x. 9A; with Antony, who professed the warmest affection, x. 8A, 10. 1, xi. 7. 2, and visited him, x. 11. 4, as did Curio, x. 4. 8; cf. 16. 3. In Pompey's camp he received a letter from his son-in-law Dolabella, written in Caesar's, *Fam.* ix. 9.

[50] *Fam.* xi. 27. 4 (Matius), 29. 2 (Oppius), xv. 21. 2 (Trebonius); for Antony, Balbus, Oppius, Hirtius, Pansa, Trebatius, Vatinius cf. *Att.* xi. 5. 4, 6. 3, 7. 2, 8. 1, 9. 2, 14. 1, 18.

[51] *Fam.* xi. 27 f. (Matius), 29; cf. *Att.* xvi. 12. 1 (Oppius), *Fam.* vii. 19. 1, xi. 27. 1, *Top.* 1 ff. (Trebatius). *Fam.* vi. 12. 2 (46 BC): 'omnis Caesaris familiaris satis opportune habeo implicatos consuetudine et benevolentia sic ut, cum ab illo discesserint, me habeant proximum. hoc Pansa, Hirtius, Balbus, Oppius, Postumius plane ita faciunt ut me unice diligant', cf. ix. 16. 2 (their *amor* is genuine), vi. 10. 2, 14. 3. References to his teaching rhetoric to Hirtius and Pansa are particularly common. In 44 he hoped to turn Hirtius into an optimate, *Att.* xiv. 20. 4, 21. 4; but for distrust of Hirtius, Balbus, and Matius at this time see xiv. 1. 1, 21. 2, 22. 1, xv. 2. 3.

No doubt both they and Cicero were at times angling for political advantage with each other; still, there were all the outward marks of affection in their intercourse, and a community of cultural interests helped to bridge or veil differences of political outlook. So too he could receive Caesar himself as a friendly guest and discuss *belles-lettres* with him (*Att.* xiii. 53). That did not prevent him exulting in the despot's assassination, the 'banquet' of the Ides of March, in which he only regretted that he had had no part (*Fam.* x. 28. 1).

It was not only Cicero who behaved in this way. Varro in Spain commanded a Pompeian legion in 49 but 'amicissime de Caesare loquebatur' (Caes. *BC* ii. 17); like Cicero and many others, he had old ties with each of the rivals; it was often hard for such men to opt for either side. Lentulus Spinther could actually plead for Caesar's clemency on the ground of their old friendship and the numerous benefits Caesar had conferred on him (ibid. i. 22). Caesar could negotiate through his own supporters and their friends in the Pompeian camp (i. 26. 3, iii. 57. 3); and the Pompeian L. Scribonius Libo, with whom he claims no personal amity (i. 26), was at least a more suitable intermediary than Bibulus, who was actually his personal enemy (iii. 16. 3), one of a small knot of such men, whom Caesar differentiates from his other adversaries (see below); Octavian made a similar distinction among those who held out against him at Perusia in 41 (App. v. 38, 40, 49). It was also a common friend of Antony and Octavian who reconciled them at Brundisium when they were on the point of hostilities (ibid. 60 ff.).

Caesar's personal relationships with political adversaries deserve remark.[52] By family connections he was a Marian, and it is said that Sulla was hardly persuaded not to proscribe him; that did not prevent his marriage in 68 to a granddaughter of Sulla and of Sulla's like-minded colleague in the consulship of 88. He first made his oratorical reputation by prosecuting the Sullan proconsul C. Cornelius Dolabella, whose counsel included his cousin, C. Aurelius Cotta, and attempting that of C. Antonius Hybrida, whose candidature for the consulship of 63 he was later to support. Suetonius remarks that the first act generated ill will (*Caes.* 4. 1); however, as we shall see, prosecutions, though they necessarily implied or produced hostility with the defendant and probably his closest kin, did not betoken any political commitment; hence there is no reason for special surprise that the college of pontifices composed of optimates co-opted Caesar in 73. In the 60s he seems often to have been associated with Crassus, and yet to have done much to ingratiate himself with Pompey, though their mutual animosity was an open secret; he was able to bring them

---

[52] Evidence not given here, or in ch. 9, IV will readily be found in Gelzer, 1968.

together in 60, and again at Luca in 56, when their ill will to each
other had again become patent (pp. 482 ff.).

As soon as he had begun to engage in political activity, he had
pursued 'the path that is accounted popular' (Cic. *Cat.* iv. 6). This did
not involve him in personal enmity with all or most of the optimates.
On 5 December 63 he could almost sway the senate to clemency in
dealing with Catiline's accomplices. It is true that Q. Catulus and C.
Piso tried to inculpate him in the plot, but each had private grudges
against him; Caesar had tried to encompass Piso's condemnation for
repetundae, and Catulus could not forgive him for his defeat in the
election to the chief pontificate (Sall. *Cat.* 49), perhaps not simply
because it was a slight to his *dignitas* but because he believed Caesar to
have won unfairly, by bribery (cf. Suet. *Caes.* 13). Bibulus too became
his personal foe during their joint aedileship (Caes. *BC* iii. 16. 3), when
Caesar had appropriated all the credit for their joint expenditure
(Suet. 10). Caesar also names Cato among his personal enemies in 49,
whose attitude he distinguishes from those of warmongers such as
Metellus Scipio and the consul L. Lentulus, men allegedly actuated by
private greed and ambition (*BC* i. 4, 7). Cato had actually proposed
that he should be surrendered to the Germans, whom he had in Cato's
view perfidiously attacked (Plut. *Caes.* 22); this was naturally proof of
the most bitter hostility, but whether it originated in Cato's exceptional rigidity of political principle or in his private connection with
Bibulus we cannot be sure. Caesar, like Balbus (*Att.* viii. 15A. 1),
complained that these enemies had alienated Pompey from him; he
referred to them as those who had once been their common enemies,
but it is far from clear that Bibulus and Cato had ever had a formal
rupture with Pompey (cf. n. 64); it must have been healed, if it ever
occurred, in 52, when both had advocated that Pompey should be sole
consul in the interests, as they saw it, of the commonwealth, since only
Pompey could restore order at Rome. Aware that Cicero would not
countenance the course he had taken, Caesar could still urge him not
actually to join Pompey and thus inflict a graver injury upon their
friendship; he would not treat Cicero's refusal to espouse his side as in
itself fatal to it.[53] Similarly, in August 44 Brutus and Cassius formally
protested to Antony in terms like those of a diplomatic note sent by one
state to another with which it preserves technically 'friendly relations';
they declared that, though preferring their own freedom to his amity,
they did not mean to provoke him to acts of hostility.[54] Avowed

[53] *Att.* x. 8B, written after the interview from which Cicero concluded 'hunc me non amare'
(ix. 18. 1).
[54] *Fam.* xi. 3, esp. at 4: 'nos in hac sententia sumus, ut te cupiamus in libera re p. magnum
atque honestum esse, vocemus te ad nullas inimicitias, sed tamen pluris nostram libertatem quam
tuam amicitiam aestimemus'.

political adversaries, they were not yet *inimici*. Courtesies were kept up on the brink of civil war—or even beyond.

If *amicitia* may connote no more than outward courtesy, it can also indicate readiness to render effectual aid. When Cicero describes two consular candidates of 65 as 'destitute of friends and reputation' (*Att.* i. 1. 2), he surely means only that they lacked actual support. None of the consulars, he told Lentulus Spinther in 56, was Lentulus' friend besides Hortensius, M. Lucullus, and himself; some were covertly unfavourable, others did not conceal their anger against him. But it can hardly be supposed that the 'obscurius iniqui' or even the 'non dissimulanter irati' were abusive of Lentulus; the latter actually included the consul Marcellinus, who declared that except on the Egyptian question he would vigorously defend Lentulus' interests. The man whom Cicero calls 'the perpetual enemy of his own friends' was one who evidently undermined them while professing amity.[55] The term *amicitia* is indeed ambiguous within a wide range. To determine its exact nuance in any particular context requires tact and discrimination, and it is often found where we have not sufficient knowledge of the circumstances to discriminate.

Certainly complex personal relationships could cut across political discords, and *amicitia* does not necessarily connote, though it may involve, collaboration in public affairs, still less consistent membership of a faction. It may seem inconsistent with this that in the *Laelius* Cicero remarks that ordinary friendships, those which are not based on mutual recognition of genuine virtue, are liable to break down, when the political interests and views of the friends are no longer harmonious. But this is not the only possible cause of rupture; it may also follow from a change in men's characters and tastes.[56] It is clear from what has been said that there might also be not so much a dissolution as a weakening of the ties of friendship; familiar intercourse or political co-operation might degenerate into external politeness. Much would depend on the particular circumstances of a breach and on the temperament of the friends. Naturally it was always a possibility that strong political opposition would be taken as a personal affront. Thus the optimate adversaries of the 'triumvirs' supposed that Cicero's move against them early in 56 would offend Pompey and make Caesar his bitter foe (*Fam.* i. 9. 10; cf. *Att.* iv. 5. 2), and that he would forfeit the friendship of both (which is not quite the same as incurring their hostility) by his sudden quarrel with their associate, Crassus (ibid. 20);

[55] *Fam.* i. 9. 2 (probably L. Domitius Ahenobarbus; cf. Shackleton Bailey ad loc.): for Spinther's 'obtrectatores' (*Qu. fr.* ii. 2. 3) see also i. 5B. 2, 7. 3; Marcellinus i. 1. 2. The Egyptian question and Lentulus' complex connections are more fully discussed on pp. 484 ff.
[56] *de amic.* 33 ff., 63 f., 77 f.

we shall see, however, that men tolerated attacks by a friend on their associates and expressions of amity and esteem to their antagonists. In the *Verrines* (II. iii. 6) Cicero appears to imply that sharp political differences entailed personal feuds, when he asks Hortensius, 'an tu maiores ullas inimicitias putas esse quam contrarias hominum sententias ac dissimilitudines studiorum ac voluntatum?' But the large inference we may be tempted to draw from these words must be rejected in the light of the other evidence. The context should be considered. By prosecuting Verres Cicero was undoubtedly engaging in hostilities with him, and Hortensius had apparently censured this on the ground that he had no private quarrel to plead in justification. Cicero answers that one who had violated *fides*, religion, and the rights and liberty of Roman citizens, besides oppressing Rome's subjects, was the enemy of all good men and had earned the detestation of the Roman people.

Hostility was always due to such a putative 'inimicus patriae', for example P. Clodius. It would then be reciprocated. Cicero could boast of the hatred in which he was held by the 'perditi'. Sallust makes C. Aurelius Cotta allege that he had incurred 'maximas inimicitias pro re publica'.[57] The fatherland indeed took precedence of all private ties. On this footing Pompey could answer Caesar's appeal to their long friendship with the plea that what he had done 'rei publicae causa' should not be a matter for reproach: 'semper se rei publicae commoda privatis necessitudinibus habuisse potiora'; Caesar too should refrain from injuring the commonwealth in his desire to injure his private enemies.[58] Cicero, in arguing that it was right for him to have laid aside any personal quarrel with Caesar because of Caesar's great services to the state, certified by the honours the senate had paid him, could adduce famous examples of patriots who had agreed to terminate their feuds for the public good.[59] Equally men were bound to subordinate to this consideration the obligations of friendship. Q. Aelius Tubero and other friends of Tiberius Gracchus had acted admirably in abandoning him when they saw him 'rem publicam vexantem'. The young Lentulus Spinther took pride in deserting his crony Dolabella and his kinsman Antony 'from greater love for the fatherland'.[60] It was in this way that former friends of Caesar could

---

[57] *de prov. cons.* 24, *Fam.* i. 9. 10 (Clodius), *Cat.* ii. 11; Sall. *Or. Cottae* 6.

[58] Caes. *BC* i. 8. 3. Cf. n. 23.

[59] *de prov. cons.* 18 ff.; cf. *Flacc.* 2, *post red. Quir.* 23; and see *Fam.* v. 4. 2 and *post red. sen.* 25 for Metellus Nepos' quarrel and reconciliation with Cicero. The reconciliation of M. Aemilius Lepidus and M. Fulvius Nobilior followed their election as censors in 179 (cf. Livy xl. 45 f.), and can be explained on the basis that the censors could do nothing except in agreement (Mommsen, *St R* ii³. 339); Scullard, 1973, 179 ff., adopts an interpretation of the facts which defies all the evidence. See also n. 95.

[60] *Fam.* xii. 14. 7.

justify their part in his assassination or their subsequent plaudits of the deed (see below). Naturally it was a matter of subjective judgement whether the vital interests of the commonwealth were involved in any particular issue; not every political difference of opinion necessitated a breach in friendship. In 49 Caesar, pretending that the war had been occasioned by the machinations of his personal foes, took the view that those who refused to support him might yet honour the claims of friendship by neutrality and still enjoy his amity, whereas the Pompeians maintained that they were fighting for the commonwealth, and that all who were not with them could be treated as its enemies.[61]

It is true that in many instances friendships had been dissolved by less grave dissensions, such as competition for office. This was to be regretted. However, despite the frequency of electoral contests, we do not find the leading men at Rome in Cicero's time (of which we know most) persistently involved in mutual hostilities. Cicero pronounced it disgraceful if on such occasions former friends became open enemies and resorted to *iurgia, maledicta, contumeliae* (n. 56). Here Scipio Aemilianus was the model; he gave up his amity with Q. Pompeius when the latter cheated C. Laelius of the consulship, and that with Q. Metellus Macedonicus because of some political difference, but 'utrumque egit graviter ac moderate et offensione animi non acerba' (*de amic.* 77). Elsewhere Cicero speaks of the 'sine acerbitate dissensio' between Scipio and Metellus, though he classes Metellus among Scipio's 'obtrectatores et invidi'.[62] Now *invidi* are often distinguished from *inimici* (cf. n. 55); thus Cicero often describes the *boni*, with whom he sought to co-operate, as his *invidi*.[63] Such people who harbour 'occulta odia' (*Fam.* i. 9. 5) may be 'insidiosi amici', but they are not 'aperte inimici'.[64] Despite the contrary statements of some late writers, I do not doubt that Scipio and Metellus continued to speak of each other with outward courtesy, even when their intimacy had been broken; otherwise it is hardly conceivable that Scipio's kin and friends should have let Metellus' sons act as his pall bearers. And, however this may be, their differences did not extend to every political issue; Metellus,

---

[61] Raaflaub, 1974, esp. 293 ff.   [62] *de offic.* i. 87, *de rep.* i. 31.

[63] E.g. *Att.* i. 19. 6, 20. 3, ii. 1. 7, 16. 2, iii. 7, 2. iv. 1. 8. In iv. 5. 1 f. (cf. *Fam.* i. 9. 5. 10, 20) he writes with resentment of the nobles who shared his political aims but who were envious of or secretly unfriendly to him, and who even 'fondled' Clodius, when he too was working against Pompey; Bibulus and Hortensius were presumably among these nobles, and it is clear that there was no open breach between Cicero and them. *De prov. cons.* 19 distinguishes *alieni* from *inimici*, *Fam.* i. 9. 17 from *amici*.

[64] *de dom.* 29, II *Verr.* 5. 182, *Mur.* 45, *Fam.* iii. 10. 6. In 56 Pompey spoke to Cicero of Curio, Bibulus, and 'ceteris suis obtrectatoribus' and of 'nobilitate inimica' (*Qu. fr.* ii. 3. 4); but their hostility was covert; cf. *Qu. fr.* ii. 1. 1, 5. 3. Note Caelius in *Fam.* viii. 14. 2: 'sic illi amores et invidiosa coniunctio [of Caesar and Pompey] non ad occultam recidit obtrectationem [as might have been expected] sed ad bellum se erupit'.

like Pompeius, to whom he was at one time hostile, was united with the friends of Scipio in opposing Tiberius Gracchus.[65]

Inimicitiae, open and avowed, were imprudent and surely rare—most common, if we may believe Cicero, with *novi homines*.[66] In 54 Cicero could actually assert that Pompey, who had given as much offence as most men of his day, had not an enemy in the state except P. Clodius (*Fam.* i. 9. 11)! This was false, but cannot have been flagrantly implausible (cf. n. 64). *Inimicitiae* might be formally denounced and formally composed.[67] Save in the exceptional cases in which they were warranted by patriotic duty,[68] they arose from personal injuries, which might include those sustained by one's father or close kin and friends. Political contentions did not in themselves suffice, unless they were accompanied by personal abuse or damage to a man's status and dignity, such as that suffered by Metellus Nepos at the time of his breach with Cicero (*Fam.* v. 2. 6 ff.). To prosecute or testify against a man on charges that threatened his *caput* or *existimatio* was necessarily a hostile act, which might initiate a feud if one did not exist already. This was perhaps the most common cause of enmity, or its most flagrant manifestation. A man might also become the enemy of one who in his view had given an unjust legal decision against him,[69] or against a competing candidate who unfairly got the better of him, for instance by bribes. L. Torquatus and his son became enemies of P. Sulla when corruption gave him the victory over the former at the polls; they then sought and obtained his conviction (*Sulla* 90). Cicero's own bitter invective against Catiline and C. Antonius Hybrida in 64 was inspired by the malpractices whereby they hoped to beat him in the consular election. The hatred that both Catulus and Bibulus felt for Caesar can be explained by their belief that he had treated them unfairly. As we have seen, the breach between Scipio Aemilianus and Q. Pompeius had a similar origin.

There is no evidence that competition in itself betokened any pre-existing hostility or turned rivals into personal enemies. Cicero was so

---

[65] Val. Max. iv. 1. 12; Pliny, *NH* vii. 144; Plut. *Mor.* 202 A. Astin, 1967, 311 ff., believes them. See also pp. 466 ff.

[66] II *Verr.* 5. 180 f. (with instances). Asinius Pollio said that Cicero 'maiore simultates adpetebat animo quam gerebat' (Sen. *Suas.* vi. 24). Suetonius held (with examples) that Caesar was always ready to compose his enmities (*Caes.* 73). Syme, 1964, *Sallust* 22, cites no evidence for his assertion that nobles took pride in often inherited feuds.

[67] On *inimicitiae* (hostile acts or declarations) cf. Hellegouarc'h 186 ff.; the singular is used only by modern scholars. R. S. Rogers, *TAPA* 1959, 224 ff., discusses the formalities, mostly from imperial evidence; *Fam.* v. 2. 5 shows that there might be doubt in Cicero's time whether hostilities existed, requiring formal reconciliation. Hereditary: e.g. Ascon. 62 f. C.; *de offic.* ii. 50, *Ac.* ii. 1. M. Brutus' hatred of Pompey, who had put his father to death, is a striking instance (Plut. *Pomp.* 64. 3).

[68] *de offic.* ii. 50, *Sull.* 6 f., *de prov. cons.* 24, *Fam.* i. 9, 10.

[69] *Div. Caec.* 55–8 (but cf. II *Verr.* 1. 15), II *Verr.* 3. 7.

far from having been an enemy of Catiline before 64 that in the previous year he had thought of defending him in the courts with a view to mutual assistance in their candidature (*Att.* ii. 1). Once Antonius had been elected as his colleague, he obviously made up his quarrel with him, and was to appear for his defence in 59, of course without any love of the man. It is indeed very seldom that we have any list of candidates. But in 184 the names of five patrician and four plebeian competitors for the censorship are given by Livy (xxxix. 40): they included two Scipios, and on Scullard's theory (which I do not accept) two of the plebeian candidates also belonged to their faction; on any view it is impossible to suppose that whatever combinations there may have been between any two of them, such as that which obtained between those who were elected, M. Cato and L. Valerius Flaccus, personal enmities inspired the 'contentio dignitatis' among them all. In the notorious election for the consulship of 53 (p. 427) two of the candidates combined, but there is nothing to show that they were already on bad terms with the rest, any more than Cato was at feud with his fellow-optimates, M. Marcellus and Ser. Sulpicius, who defeated him for the consulship of 51.

We must not suppose that hostility to any particular person involved hostility to all his associates, or that friendship with him excluded enmity with them. Antony's hatred for Cicero is said to have extended to all his friends (Nepos, *Att.* 10. 4). Cicero could refer to those who were enemies not only of P. Sittius but of his friends as well (*Fam.* v. 17. 2). But such an attitude was surely exceptional and called for remark. Cicero says that it was his own resolve not to assail the friends of his enemies, especially those of humbler station (*Att.* xiv. 13B. 3). When he quarrelled with Metellus Nepos, he could depute common friends to negotiate a reconciliation (*Fam.* v. 2. 8); his efforts failed, but his letter to Nepos' brother Celer indicates that their relationship, though chilly in the extreme, was not formally hostile. In 57 Nepos agreed to give up the feud (*Sest.* 130, *Fam.* v. 3), but still backed Cicero's bitter foe P. Clodius (*Sest.* 89), who was his brother-in-law. Cicero himself could support the same candidate as Clodius in 59 (*Att.* ii. 1. 9) and plead for the same defendant in 54 (n. 78). In 59 Pompey was friend of both Cicero and Clodius (ibid. 22. 2), and Atticus had 'marvellous conversations' with Clodius, which he reported to Cicero (9. 1, 22. 1 and 4). Atticus' lifelong generosity in befriending mutual enemies was remarkable, but he only carried further what was accepted, that there was no obligation to hostility with a friend's enemies, nor to amity with his friends. After Luca Cicero was bound by ties of friendship to both Caesar and Pompey; that did not impede a temporary rupture with Crassus (see above), and Lentulus Spinther, who was also their friend, thought that his reconciliation both with Crassus and with Caesar's protégé Vatinius demanded explanation (*Fam.* i. 9. 19 f.); moreover, Cicero continued to assail Caesar's father-in-law L. Piso and Pompey's associate Gabinius. Admittedly his relationship with Caesar inhibited him from actually prosecuting Piso (*Pis.* 81 ff.), and Pompey ultimately obliged him to undertake Gabinius' defence; his denial that he acted under pressure (*Rab. Post.* 32 f.) was utterly insincere (*Qu. fr.* iii. 1. 15, 2. 2, 4. 2 f.), and can have convinced nobody. But Cicero's special insecurity fettered his independence to an unusual degree; Appius Claudius, whose daughter had married Pompey's son, was perfectly free to assail Gabinius (*Qu. fr.* iii. 2. 3). Cicero too remained a bitter enemy of P. Clodius, though reconciled to Appius (*Fam.* i. 9. 19).

Cicero excused his reconciliation with Gabinius with the apophthegm that he was not ashamed if his enmities were mortal while his friendships were everlasting (*Rab. Post.* 32). This was a proverbial expression (Livy xl. 46. 12). Not only the supposed interest of the state (n. 59) but personal advantage might bring former foes together. Hostility was as fragile as amity, or more so; it was embarrassing for men who might often meet in the same circles, one reason why no one would readily involve himself in the feuds of his own associates.

It has already been noted that criminal accusations furnish the most striking evidence for personal rancour. But no less notable is the reluctance and infrequency with which leading members of the ruling class undertook such prosecutions. It was legitimate to avenge one's kin in the courts, or to prosecute in the interests of the Republic or of injured subjects.[70] But in Cicero's day it was no longer in vogue for men of rank and influence to appear as accusers,[71] and there had been cases, it was held, in which defendants had been acquitted out of prejudice against powerful enemies who assailed them in the courts.[72] Young men indeed might seek to establish an oratorical reputation by prosecuting, as L. Crassus had done in securing the conviction of C. Carbo (Cic. *Brut.* 159); Cicero's triumph over Verres is the most famous instance.

There was said to be more honour, and there was certainly more *gratia*, to be won from acting for the defence. To prosecute once might be enough, or too much; in old age Crassus repented of ruining Carbo (II *Verr.* iii. 3). At the outset of his career at the bar Cicero abjured any

---

[70] For what follows cf. generally *de offic.* ii. 47, 49 ff. Pliny, *Ep.* ix. 13. 2 ('materiam insectandi nocentes, miseros vindicandi, se proferendi') corresponds to Republican practice. Cf. Gelzer, 1969, 83 f.

[71] 'Principes' once appeared 'pro sociis', now only 'imperiti adulescentes', *Div. Caec.* 63 ff.; cf. II *Verr.* 3. 6, *Cael.* 73 ff., *de offic.* loc. cit. (last note); Quint. *Inst.* xii. 6. 1, 7. 1 ff.

[72] *Font.* 23 ff., Sall. *Cat.* 49. 2, *Ascon.* 60 C.

desire to rise by the misfortunes of others, and though he secured primacy by accusing Verres, he represented his prosecution as a defence of the Sicilians, to whom he had a duty as their patron; he hoped that it would be his last appearance as accuser, as it was his first; and in fact he only acted as prosecutor once more, against T. Plancus in 52. In his opinion it was inhumane to accuse a personal enemy on a charge of which he was innocent, but you might properly defend a man you believed guilty, 'modo ne nefarium impiumque', a qualification that meant little; he had himself been prepared to defend Catiline for *repetundae*, though his guilt was crystal clear (*Att.* i. 2. 1). At most it was permissible to indulge in frequent indictments of 'inimici rei publicae'.[73] No doubt others took a sterner view and were more intent on seeing the laws observed; for that purpose, in the absence of a public prosecutor, delation was indispensable. The accusers of Murena in 63 included the upright Cato, who had no private or public quarrel with him (*Mur.* 64), and C. Postumus, his father's friend, who had previously been connected with him by neighbourly goodwill (ibid. 56), as well as Ser. Sulpicius, who was naturally incensed that Murena had beaten him at the polls, as he supposed, by sheer bribery. Cicero speaks of numerous persons who were 'the common enemies of all defendants', ever ready to bear witness on charges of *ambitus*: their testimony counted little with the courts and alienated the people; it was not the way to rise in public life (*Planc.* 55). M. Iunius Brutus, a second-century prototype of imperial delators, who set out to be a Roman Lycurgus, was regarded as a disgrace to his family (*Brut.* 130). It was clearly unusual that Gaius and Lucius Memmius were 'accusatores acres atque acerbi' and seldom appeared for the defence (ibid. 136); the former, it is true, all but reached the consulship (App. i. 32). But it was more typical that, so far as we know, Hortensius appeared as prosecutor only twice, whereas he is recorded as counsel for the defence on seventeen occasions,[74] and that Marcus Crassus, an assiduous pleader (*Brut.* 233), is not known to have prosecuted at all. A man of low birth and mediocre talent, Q. Arrius, could reach the praetorship, because he served so many defendants in time of need, including some whose political prospects were at risk (ibid. 243).

Cicero says that if the friends of Servius Sulpicius had been debarred from representing Murena, when Sulpicius charged him with *ambitus*, neither he nor Hortensius nor Crassus nor any other counsel could

---

[73] See *de offic.* ii. 49 f.; e.g. *Rosc. Amer.* 83, *Div. Caec.* 1–4, II *Verr.* i. 98, ii. 10, 179, v. 189, *Rab. perd.* 1, *Sull.* 3–10, 49, *Vat.* 5 ('cum in hac civitate oppugnatio soleat . . . defensio numquam vituperari'), *Reg. Deiot.* 30, *Sull.* 81. Plancus, *Fam.* vii. 2. 2; Dio xl. 55. 4. Restored by Caesar, he was a partisan of Antony and reviled by Cicero (*Phil.* vi. 10 etc.)—who was on ostensibly cordial terms with his brother Lucius (*Fam.* x. 1–24).

[74] *RE* viii. 2470 ff. (v. der Mühll).

have been found for the defence, so widely did Sulpicius' *gratia* extend. He claims that he himself had done all in his power to bring about Sulpicius' election. Sulpicius construed it as a breach of friendly obligation that he should then defend Murena. Without reason, according to Cicero: Sulpicius himself was ready to advise men who were nothing to him in their suits with his own friends, and on the same footing Cicero would have been entitled to represent Murena, even if he had not been (so he says) an old intimate of Murena as well. (In later years Cicero and Sulpicius were certainly still, or again, on amicable terms.) Between clients and patron in the courts there need have been no antecedent ties. According to Cicero, Marcus Antonius (*cos.* 99), like himself, had frequently defended men with whom he had not the least connection ('alienissimos'); he also makes him say that once advocates had undertaken such cases, if they wished to be esteemed good men they must no longer regard their clients as *alieni*, but use all their eloquence to gain for them the sympathy of the court.[75] As in the trial of Murena, they might have friends on the other side. In 54 Cicero was doubtless prepared, if need be, to defend any of the four candidates for the consulship, who might be accused of bribery (of which each was equally guilty), for he counted all as his friends.[76]

L. R. Taylor wrote of 'the unending prosecutions brought from political motives by [a man's] personal enemies'. In fact most of the *principes* in Cicero's time had not been arraigned in the courts, nor arraigned others.[77] Cicero says that a good man would not wish to ruin a citizen even by making him bankrupt (*Quinct.* 51); of course he was not thinking of circumstances in which personal enmity already subsisted. 'All of us', he says, 'rush in unison to rescue from dangers' men of eminence like Murena, 'and all who are not their declared enemies earnestly discharge the duties of the closest friends, even to those with whom we have the least connection, if their *caput* is in danger' (*Mur.* 45). The trial of M. Scaurus in 54 affords a signal illustration. In order to bar his election as consul, which he hoped at that time to secure for his brother Gaius, Appius Claudius instigated a charge of *repetundae* against him. Scaurus' counsel included not only Cicero but his bitter enemy and Appius' brother P. Clodius, as well as Hortensius, M. Messalla (*cos.* 61), M. Marcellus (*cos.* 51), and M. Calidius. Nine consulars, among them Cicero's enemy L. Piso, deliv-

---

[75] *Mur.* 7–10. *De orat.* i. 184 depicts the jurisconsult 'praesidium clientibus atque opem amicis et prope cunctis civibus lucem ingeni et consili porrigentem'. Antonius: *de orat.* ii. 200; cf. 191 f. Cicero's practice: 'tantum enitor, ut neque amicis neque etiam alienioribus opera, consilio, labore desim' (*Fam.* i. 9. 17).

[76] *Qu. fr.* iii. 1. 16; he preferred Messalla, iii. 6 (8). 3. All indicted, iii. 2. 3.

[77] Taylor, 1949, 7. Pompey was charged with *peculatus*, Crassus with *incestum*, both before they had risen to eminence. Caesar prosecuted only in his youth.

ered or sent in laudations of the accused. Other notables of lower rank supplicated the jury on his behalf: they included Milo and the son of C. Memmius, one of Scaurus' rivals for the consulship. Plainly this heterogeneous assortment did not constitute a political faction; the scene shows the general unwillingness of the aristocracy to encompass or see the ruin of one of their own class.[78] It is also characteristic that the prosecution was conducted by young men of inferior lineage.

Of course it was by defending men who were not already his friends, and indeed by making it clear that his services were available to all who might require them (*Comm. Pet.* 22), that an orator could extend his connections and influence: 'alieni' who owed their acquittal to him were 'alieni' no longer.[79] It was no less expedient that he should handle his opponents as gently as his client's interests permitted. In seeking to oblige some, you must be careful not to offend others: the point seemed self-evident to Cicero (*de offic.* ii. 68). He says that in defending Murena he will always keep his friendship with Sulpicius in mind (*Mur.* 10). In the same speech he ridicules Cato's philosophic views, but implies the highest opinion of his integrity and *auctoritas* (58 ff.). At the trial of Scaurus he spoke with great respect of Appius, with whom he was newly reconciled. I have noted eleven instances in which he professes friendship with the prosecutors of his clients,[80] not to speak of adverse witnesses,[81] and even when he does not go so far, he prefers to apply to them kind or laudatory terms, to avoid the hostility that might arise from contumely.[82] His personal attacks on the integrity of Verres' principal counsel Hortensius, with whom he had often appeared on the same side (*Div. in Caec.* 44), are quite exceptional, and were no doubt occasioned by the use that Hortensius made of his political authority as well as of his eloquence on Verres' behalf; it was therefore necessary to discredit him as far as possible.[83] One might suppose that a feud resulted, but in 66 Cicero, while countering Hortensius' objections to the Manilian law, was already speaking of him in honorific terms (*de imp.* 51); after 63 they often co-operated both

---

[78] *Mur.* 45; Ascon. 18–20 C. Cf. perhaps the trial of Catiline in 65, ibid. 87 with *Sull.* 49, 81. For Gruen (1968 *passim*, 1972, chs. vii–viii) most prosecutions by senators were politically motivated; he explains away the readiness of 'so many individuals of such varied political attitudes' to defend Scaurus by the hypothesis that they thought it in their common interest not to allow a man to be debarred from standing for office by a charge of *repetundae*; this is sheer fantasy (1972, 334 ff.).

[79] Gelzer, 1969, 70 ff.

[80] See (i) *Font.* 36; (ii) Ascon. 60 f.C.; *Brut.* 271 (*pro Cornelio*); (iii) *Cluent.* 10, 118, *Brut.* 271; (iv) *Mur.* 3, 7, 10; (v) *Sull.* 2, 47; (vi) *Flacc.* 2; (vii) *Cael.* 7, 25; (viii) *Planc.* 2 ff., 58; (ix) *Scaur.* 31; (x) *Rab. Post.* 32; (xi) *Lig.* 21. The bitter attacks on Hortensius in the *Verrines* are exceptional and did not preclude a hollow friendship later. L. Torquatus' taunts did indeed make him threaten to renounce friendship, *Sull.* 21 f., 47, but his moderation on this occasion was not unique, ibid. 49.

[81] *Planc.* 56; Ascon. 60 C. f.   [82] *Tull.* 3, *Rab. perd.* 25.

[83] e.g. *Div. in Caec.* 23, I *Verr.* 15, 35–40, II *Verr.* iii. 7–9, iv. 6, 126, v. 173–7.

in politics and in forensic practice, and in the *Brutus* (1 ff.) Cicero
pronounces a posthumous eulogy on his old rival. Here he also lauded
the memory of L. Manlius Torquatus (ibid. 265), who had in 62
assailed his 'regnum' in the courts with perhaps almost as much
opprobrium as Cicero had vented on Hortensius.[84] Cicero says
nothing in his *pro Sulla* of the allegation that he had undertaken Sulla's
defence only because of the interest-free loan Sulla was ready to let him
have (Gell. xii. 12), but it may well have been suggested without proof
by Torquatus, and passed over by Cicero when he published his speech
in order not to give further currency to a report he could not refute.
But Torquatus' attack on Cicero was probably as untypical of the
behaviour of advocates as Cicero's onslaught on Hortensius. When
Favonius prosecuted Nasica, he was content with slight censure of
Cicero for defending him (*Att.* ii. 1. 9). And a more or less professional
advocate, like Cicero, whose influence rested to some extent on his
forensic practice even after he had reached the consulship, had reason
not to speak in ways that might debar him from taking another brief.
In 56 he could successively defend L. Calpurnius Bestia on a charge of
ambitus brought by M. Caelius,[85] and M. Caelius in the speech still
extant on charges laid against him as a reprisal by Bestia's son.

Thus the appearance of an orator as counsel for the defence is no
clear proof of his political affiliations, and an accuser might act out of
private hostility,[86] the desire to make a name, or even care for the
public weal; we can never assume that his aim was to strike at a
member of a rival faction. I cannot, for instance, agree with Badian's
thesis that M. Antonius is to be seen as an ally of Marius because he
defended Manius Aquillius, Gaius Norbanus, and Marius Gratidianus;[87]
his strenuous resistance to the popular tribune of 99, Titius, when he
was consul, is a better indication of his political stance in the 90s (*de
orat.* ii. 48). To explain his defence of Norbanus in particular, we need
not go behind the reason Cicero gives (*ibid.* 200), that he had
obligations to his former quaestor;[88] no doubt he spoke with passion,
but we may recall that Cicero makes him hold that the orator must be
like the actor (*ibid.* 193), 'his whole function suiting with forms to his
conceit, and all for nothing'; this was of course Cicero's view,
corresponding to his own practice (*Orat.* 132).

---

[84] *Sull.* 21 f., 40, 48.
[85] *Qu. fr.* ii. 3. 6; Cicero had previously appeared for C. Antonius Hybrida, when accused by
Caelius, once his youthful protégé, and again his friend after Cicero secured his own acquittal; see
R. G. Austin's introduction to his edition of *pro Caelio*, 1959.
[86] Hortensius could even profess to assume that this was the one legitimate reason, II *Verr.* iii. 6.
[87] Badian, 1964, 46 f. So far as his reconstructions of political alignments depend on similar
evidence, E. Gruen (n. 77) builds on sand. See also pp. 459 ff.
[88] Cf. *Div. Caec.* 61, *Planc.* 28.

The task of the advocate was to put his client's case in the way most likely to sway the jury. In 66 Cicero denied that his own utterances in court could be taken as proof of his personal sentiments (*Cluent.* 138–42). Antonius, he recalls, had been careful not to publish his forensic speeches, lest they be quoted against him. Cicero was less prudent, but no doubt reckoned on his readers' comprehension. His statement is relevant to the extreme 'popular' principles which he too voiced when defending C. Cornelius in 65; he certainly would not have endorsed them at any time after he appeared as a champion of senatorial authority as consul in 63; and already in political speeches he had concurred with the optimates in resisting the annexation of Egypt and an attempt to extract public moneys from Faustus Sulla, allegedly embezzled.[89] It is true that he also advocated the Manilian law and in doing so pronounced a great encomium on Pompey, but even then he referred in honorific terms to eminent optimates on the other side. Cornelius had been Pompey's quaestor; and some hold that his prosecution was an indirect attack on Pompey, whose interests Cicero was protecting. This is highly speculative. It is true that the indictment was backed by five optimate consulars, and that in 56 Vatinius alleged that by his defence Cicero incurred the ill will of the optimates; Cicero replied that Cornelius was his old friend and that his action had not prevented his election to the consulship with the enthusiastic support of all the best people (*Vat.* 5 f.). They presumably included the common enemy of Cornelius and Pompey, C. Piso (*cos.* 67), who by making Cicero his legate gave him facilities for canvassing in Cisalpine Gaul (*Att.* i. 1. 2). It appears to me that the nobles who assailed Cornelius had their reasons for doing so, independent of any political connection he may have had with Pompey, whose attitude to his reforms is not on record, and that they will have understood well enough that Cicero was bound to do all in his power as an orator to save his client.[90] It was another matter indeed when the orator employed not only the sophistries of his art but his *auctoritas* to win his case, as Cicero was later to do on some occasions.[91] And of course there might be instances in which he expressed his true opinions in a forensic speech, as when he appeared for Sestius. But we need other evidence, such as Cicero supplies in intimate letters or theoretical treatises, to discern when this is so.

I have tried to show in Chapter 9 that in Cicero's time, though there was a fundamental division among politicians between those ready to impugn the authority of the senate as the true governing body of the

[89] *Cic. Orationum Schol.*, ed. Stangl, 91–3; Asc. 73 C.
[90] For a different interpretation see M. Griffin, *JRS* 1973, 196 ff., cf. p. 471 below.
[91] *Mur.* 2, 59, 86, *Sull.* 2–4, 10, etc.

state and those who would uphold it, so far as they had the means, the politicians of whom we know most almost all took the most variable courses, at least when this issue was not at stake, and that there were no large, durable, and cohesive political factions; nor is there any proof that they had existed in earlier generations. It is apparent that the usual character of friendship in the political class did not favour the formation of such factions. Even when political friendship amounted to more than the exchange of formal courtesies, and created actual obligations for reciprocal support, it was unstable (*de amic.* 64) in so far as men found themselves subject to conflicting claims from different friends or subordinated all such claims to their own selfish aims or to their conceptions of the public good; nor did it attach them to the interests of those associates of their friends with whom they themselves had no direct tie, or implicate them in hostility to their friends' own enemies. It never required them, even in moral terms, to direct their political conduct in sole conformity with private obligations. That is not to say that *ceteris paribus* they did not often seek to gratify their friends, sometimes no doubt because this appeared to suit their own advantage. Moreover, men who could not clearly discern where their patriotic duty lay, or who did not scruple to ignore it, might be guided to some extent by consideration of their private relationships. This happened in some cases on the outbreak of civil war in 49.

The unscrupulous Caelius said that in peaceful controversies one should take the more honourable part, and in civil wars the stronger and safer, but he also explained his choice of Caesar's side by his friendship for Curio and hatred of Appius.[92] Pollio acted in a rather similar way, by his own account, avoiding the camp where his personal enemies were too strong. It was only later that he came to love Caesar '*summa cum pietate et fide*'.[93] Cicero once said that the only men who joined Pompey in flight were those who had cause to fear Caesar's hostility, a transparent exaggeration at best (*Att.* ix. 19. 2), and Plutarch alleges that Pompey had more followers from personal allegiance than from public principle (*Pomp.* 61. 4). For Syme Labienus himself would serve as an instance; this may be doubted (ch. 9 n. 114). Caesar, of course, would have his readers believe that the war was provoked by the factious hatred of his personal enemies (*BC* i. 4 etc.), a partial view we must be wary of accepting.

The difficulty of accounting for men's behaviour at this time mainly by their feuds and friendships is that many had friends and enemies on both sides. Labienus, Lentulus Spinther, Varro, Cicero himself, and

---

[92] *Fam.* viii. 14. 3; cf. 16, 17. 1.

[93] *Fam.* x. 31. 2: 'cum vero non liceret mihi nullius partis esse, quia utrubique magnos inimicos habebam, ea castra fugi in quibus plane tutum me ab insidiis sciebam non futurum'.

doubtless a host of others were friends of both Caesar and Pompey, and many more must have had close connections in the opposing camp; even Balbus, Caesar's confidant, was permitted not to appear in arms against his old benefactors, Pompey and the consul Lentulus Crus, and actually to manage the affairs of the latter at Rome.[94] Both the leaders made play in their propaganda with appeals to public interest and constitutional principle, and affected in their private negotiations to be ready to subordinate their own advantage to the common good (pp. 490 f.). M. Brutus, whose father Pompey had put to death, had not been on speaking terms with him, naturally enough; now he joined his camp, obviously 'rei publicae causa'.[95] It is not likely that he stood alone. Though professions of patriotism may be 'the last refuge of a scoundrel', it would be unwise to assume that they were always insincere. Men do not appeal to standards that no one observes, and hypocrisy serves no purpose where virtue is not to be found.

Cicero's own hesitations are significant. He speaks of the 'causa bonorum' and the 'turpitudo coniungendi cum tyranno', yet he often questioned whether resistance to Caesar could succeed, or whether Pompey's victory would not be marred by cruelty and lead no less than Caesar's to a 'Sullanum regnum'; he would have preferred a compromise peace. His mind endlessly revolved not only the public good, but his own self-interest and his duty to Pompey as a friend, continually emphasizing and consciously overstating the benefits he owed him. In the end he seems to have concluded that only Pompey's victory would ultimately assure the restoration of the Republic.[96] Later he could say: 'erat obscuritas quaedam, erat certamen inter clarissimos duces; multi dubitabant quid optimum esset, multi quid sibi expediret, multi quid deceret, nonnulli etiam quid liceret';[97] he himself doubted all these things at once. A man without scruple would surely in these circumstances have chosen his own advantage against all ties, public or private; but a man of honour might resolve his problem by the claims of friendship, because he could fairly plead that he could not see clearly what his public duty was.

Such a man perhaps was Matius, 'temperatus et prudens . . . semper auctor oti', as Cicero wrote at the time (*Att.* ix. 11. 2). If we accept his own claims, he disapproved of the war and of Caesar's case, and he gained nothing from Caesar's victory, rather suffered financial loss; he followed Caesar as a friend, not as his political leader. He mourned his death, and his critics said that he was putting friendship before the

---

[94] *Att.* viii. 15A, 2, ix. 7B, 2.
[95] Plut. *Brut.* 4. The influence of Cato (not himself an old 'adherent' of Pompey) may well have been decisive, but can hardly be ascribed merely to Cato being his mother's stepbrother.
[96] Brunt, *JRS* 1986, 12 ff.   [97] *Marc.* 30; cf. *Lig.* 19.

Republic by grieving for a tyrant; his reply was in effect that Caesar had been no tyrant and that there was no proof that his killing had been of public benefit; he still claimed to be as good a patriot as anyone.[98] One might indeed think that the man who wished everyone to feel the bitterness of Caesar's death let private affection weigh too much with him, and that Cicero was right in suspecting him of rejoicing at the general confusion which ensued (*Att.* xiv. 1. 1).

An Eques who had not sought a political career, Matius cannot be regarded as typical of those who did. More significant is the behaviour of men who took part in Caesar's assassination or gave it their approval. Some, like Marcus Brutus and Cassius, were former Pompeians, but others had been adherents of Caesar. Among the conspirators themselves they included Ser. Sulpicius Galba, who was perhaps disappointed in his expectation of a consulship, but also C. Trebonius, whom Caesar had honoured with that office, and D. Brutus, who was one of his special favourites, and who could have counted on being one of the leading men under a Caesarian monarchy. They were reproached for disregarding the obligations of friendship and betraying their leader; Cicero would justify them, as no doubt they justified themselves, for their fidelity to the commonwealth, of which they claimed to be the 'Liberators'. It must be borne in mind that their enterprise was dangerous; in the end it cost them their lives, and this might well have been the immediate issue of the attempt. It is not plausible that they risked so much simply 'in envy of great Caesar', to gratify personal grudges and ambitions, as malignant enemies sometimes alleged. At worst it might be said of them that, like Caesar himself, they set their own *dignitas*, which his 'tyranny' subverted, above the public good, but in fact they did not distinguish it from the liberty of the Republic. The senate itself, full of Caesar's nominees, indemnified them. Others who had served Caesar against the Pompeians, like the young Q. Hortensius or the new man Staius Murcus, who must have owed his rise entirely to Caesar's favour, were to join their standards, or countenanced their cause until Octavian and Antony became masters of Rome (pp. 500 f.). In writings after Caesar's death, especially the *Laelius*, Cicero lays much weight on the priority of duty to the commonwealth over private ties; but we should not conclude that this is special pleading in their cause; rather, their actions illustrate the truth of his contention. He was representing the Roman tradition: the good man was true to his friends, but not to the extent that he was bound to assist them in doing wrong, and above all

---

[98] *Fam.* xi. 27 f., on which see A. Heuss, *Historia* 1956, 53 ff., and B. Kytzler, ibid. 1960, 96 ff.; I do not wholly agree with either, but any interpretation of Matius' views must probably remain subjective. See also Steinmetz (n. 10) 70 ff.

not in dereliction of the supreme duty to the fatherland, than which there could be no graver example than the imposition of despotic rule.

Matius' own loyalty to Caesar and his memory betokens a friendship which cannot be simply analysed into 'mutual interest and mutual services' and takes us back from the world of political faction towards that realm of ideal friendship with which I started. The range of *amicitia* is vast. From the constant intimacy and goodwill of virtuous or at least of like-minded men to the courtesy that etiquette normally enjoined on gentlemen, it covers every degree of genuinely or overtly amicable relation. Within this spectrum purely political connections have their place, but one whose all-importance must not be assumed. They were often fragile, and ties of private friendship could transcend their bounds. The clash of social and economic interests between sections, the constitutional principles in which such interests might be embedded but which men had often come to value for their own sake, the fears, ambitions, greed, and even principles of individuals deserve no less consideration than the struggles of factions, whose stability is exaggerated, when their existence is not simply imagined (Chapter 9). To the historian of ancient Rome, however, if he is not concerned only with the power-struggle but with every aspect of the people's life and thought, the moral ideal which informed the concept of *amicitia* and the polite civilities which social conventions required from all but the few who were declared enemies merit attention for their own sake.

8

CLIENTELA[1]

I. Prefatory remarks on varieties of relations of dependence; the nature of *clientela*; the excessive importance modern scholars attach to it. **II.** The silence of Polybius and Cicero *de officiis*; the general character of *gratia*; the rarity of allusions to Roman *clientelae* in Republican evidence; Caesar on clientship in Gaul; the foreign *clientelae* of Romans (to be considered only as evidence for the nature of Roman clientship); the distinction of clientship from *amicitia* and *hospitium*; patronage not restricted to the nobility of patrons; conflicting obligations of clients. **III.** Clientage in early times; the evidence of Dionysius; the meaning of *patronus* and of *fides*; modern exaggerations of the subjection both of freedmen and of clients (who must be distinguished); the supposed patriarchal relations of patrons to clients in early times; clientship in the struggle of the orders. **IV.** Evidence from the middle Republic for mutual obligations of patrons and clients; a relaxation of ties inferred from legal institutions; other signs of the disintegration of a putative social harmony produced by clientage; independence of the plebs before and in the Gracchan period. **V.** The supposed electoral importance of clientage greatly overrated. **VI.** The minor role of clients in civil broils of the late Republic. **VII.** Irrelevance of clientage to the behaviour of the soldiery. **VIII.** The erroneous conception of the *princeps* as universal patron. The increased importance of private patronage after the fall of the Republic. Conclusions.

---

[1] This essay challenges current views of the importance of patronage, reflected for instance in Syme, *RR*, Badian, 1958, and Gruen, 1974, which derive above all from von Premerstein, 1900 (*RE* iv. 123 ff.) and 1937, and Gelzer, 1969 (the slightly revised version of a monograph of 1912); it is notable that in his later and detailed narratives of events in the late Republic Gelzer himself put little emphasis on it. I am indebted for comments on earlier drafts especially to the late M. W. Frederiksen and to Andrew Drummond. The earliest of them antedated Rouland's work of 1979, perusal of which has not led me to make any substantial changes. In my view his discussion of early clientship is vitiated by credulity in the 'testimony' of annalists; he even takes speeches in Dionysius and Livy to be authentic. I am also not convinced by his thesis that clients were later found mainly or chiefly in the urban plebs, not in the rural population, given the evidence (of which he is aware) of patronage over Italian towns, and therefore over the local gentry. Evidence for urban clients is unbalanced by Martial and Juvenal; and in any event texts relating to the Principate can be used only with caution for the Republic.

I

Relations of dependence are found in all societies. They may be defined and upheld by the law. The slave-owner possesses legal power over his slaves (not necessarily as absolute as at Rome), and he may retain a legal right to their services after manumission, as at Rome. Serfs have legal obligations to lords, whose lands they may cultivate and to whose jurisdiction they may be partially subject. Dependence may also rest on sheer force, like that which *mafiosi* employ to bring people under their 'protection', or on the economic pressure which in certain circumstances the landlord can exert on his tenants, the creditor on debtors, or the employer on wage-earners. The authority of the superior may be subtly reinforced by respect imbued by habit and tradition for his birth, education, achievements, and supposed wisdom. Within the same social sphere one man may defer to another of greater age, station, or real or reputed talent, with influence by which he can assist the advancement of those he favours. This last kind of gradation inevitably exists in the most democratic and egalitarian societies; for instance, in our own the preferment of men in political parties, in the professions, and in business companies is likely to turn on the approval of those who have already risen higher. At Rome it was proper for young aristocrats to model themselves on respected figures of an older generation (nn. 14–16), whose political support they could then hope to obtain. However, subordination of this kind will naturally diminish or disappear, as the inferior himself advances, though he may continue to harbour sentiments of regard, affection, or gratitude. On the other hand, where dependence results from a lasting disparity of power, it may endure throughout a man's life and be transmitted to his children. In a stable society which is also highly stratified we may expect to find in some degree a tradition of subservience to all members of a higher class, even to those who do not enjoy any legal or economic control over all who manifest it. In our own country, for example, the gentry and persons in the higher professions could for long count on deference from the lower classes, not confined to those on whom they could bring pressure individually. This subordination tends to break down when and if the lower classes perceive more or less clearly that their interests diverge from those of the higher, and acquire the means to organize and protect themselves, by violence or the exercise of political and other legal rights, or by a combination of both methods.

During the early struggles of patricians and plebeians at Rome, and again in later periods of the Republic, the common citizens were patently able to use their political rights, and sometimes force, in this way. It may be noted that Cicero thought that all men, Romans included, sought equality before the law (*de offic.* ii. 42; cf. ch. 6, section XII). None the less Roman society was on the whole both stable and stratified. There were great inequalities in wealth. Many were economically dependent on the rich as tenants or wage-labourers or artisans producing for their needs. The higher orders monopolized political and military offices and rights of judication at Rome itself, while local oligarchies ruled the municipalities. Men of rank could enjoy that *auctoritas* which enabled them to make their wishes prevail in default of legal powers of enforcement. Knowledge of the law was restricted to a few experts. The successful litigant was left to execute the civil judgements of the courts, and this may often have been hard, if he could not deploy sufficient force. Social gradations were marked by distinctions in apparel and ornamentation and in reserved seats at the games, distinctions which the masses could occasionally resent (ch. 6 n. 155). Ideally to a conventional upper-class Roman like Velleius, 'the humble would look up without fear to the powerful, who take precedence over them without feeling contempt'. In his view the ideal was realized under the beneficent rule of Tiberius.[2] By then the ordinary citizens had in effect lost their political rights; so long as they had possessed them, they had less cause for subservience. But probably respect for superiors had always been normal.

Velleius expected men of station to be respected by all those beneath them. He was not specifically concerned with the relationship between patrons and freeborn clients, which was peculiar to Roman, or Italian, society. Described at some length by a Greek observer, Dionysius of Halicarnassus, this had imposed more or less defined obligations on both parties. They rested not on law but on *fides*, trust or good faith, required by custom. They were hereditary on both sides. Accepted in the first place (we may suppose) to suit the reciprocal interest of the parties, they might be strengthened or loosened in proportion to the extent to which they continued to answer to those interests, but they might also be perpetuated by social opinion and unreflecting habit. The patricians of old, and later the patricio-plebeian nobility, which enjoyed for generations the greatest power, political and economic, to afford aid and protection, or to inflict injuries, must have been in the best position not only to retain that general deference due to their rank but to accumulate the largest number of clients in the strict sense. Their hereditary patronage could extend to whole communities. *Hospitium* (n. 28) and *amicitia*, connections, which in themselves did not entail subordination, but which also reposed on *fides*, might approxi-

[2] ii. 126. 3; cf. Tac. *Dial.* 40. 4 (cited by Woodman ad loc.).

mate to clientship, where one party was permanently superior to the other in influence and resources.

Gelzer propounded the view in 1912 that 'the entire Roman people, both the ruling circle and the mass of voters whom they ruled, was, as a society, permeated by multifarious relationships based on *fides* and on personal connections, the principal forms of which were *patrocinium* in the courts and over communities, together with political friendship and financial obligation . . . The most powerful man was he who by virtue of his clients and friends could mobilize the greatest number of voters'.[3] He was consciously resurrecting the theory of Fustel de Coulanges, who had traced to Rome's earliest days the form of patronage (*patrocinium*), which was certainly an important feature of society in the late empire, and who held that it furnished part of the explanation of the origin of feudal institutions in France.[4] Since Gelzer wrote, this way of thinking has become increasingly dominant. Roman nobles have actually been assimilated to feudal barons, and the armies of the civil wars conceived as formed from their retainers. In a recent treatment of the Roman constitution Bleicken prefaces his account of political institutions with an analysis of clientship; he seems to suppose that most citizens were clients, and 'clientship absorbed the political will of the citizens, which was conditioned by the social mechanisms consequential upon it.'[5] The Roman system can then be viewed as oligarchical without qualification; it becomes possible with Syme more or less to disregard the powers of the assemblies and the sentiments and interests of the masses.[6] I have tried to show in Chapters 1 and 6 that this conception blinds us to the realities of the great crises of the late Republic. The theory rejected in Chapter 9 that Roman politics were dominated by long-lasting factions of great families allied by kinship and friendship, or eventually by the adherents of dynasts like Pompey, rests in part on the premiss that they could simply manipulate the votes of masses of dependants. Even Meier, though critical like Gelzer of this theory, expatiates on the importance of personal connections of kinship, patronage, and friendship.[7] It is a relief to turn to Nicolet's balanced survey of Roman institutions, in which clientship is allotted only a limited place.[8]

[3] Gelzer, 1969, 139.
[4] *Hist. des institutions de l'ancienne France, les origines du système féodal*, 1890, 205 ff.; cf. 255 ff. on the late empire.
[5] *Die Verfassung der röm. Rep.*, 1974, 20; on 138 ff. he depreciates the role of the people. Similar exaggerations pervade Bleicken, 1972, 64 ff., and 1975, 268 ff.
[6] Syme, 1962, 71.
[7] Meier, 1966, ch. ii. Gelzer's factions (1969, 123 ff.) are only shifting combinations.
[8] He devotes only 10 out of 450 pages in *Rome et la conquête du monde méd.*, 1977, i. 227 ff., to patronage; the book provides the best modern brief analysis of political, social, and economic institutions.

In my view, as argued in other chapters, it is evident that the great conflicts of the late Republic resulted from divergencies of interest and sentiment between the senatorial nobility at large on the one hand, and (at various times) the Italian allies, the Equites, the urban plebs, and the peasantry on the other; it was also because the senate had failed to win the hearts of the mass of the rural population that the soldiery, mainly recruited from that population, displayed so little loyalty to the government, and were ready to obey the treasonable orders of generals, to whom they were attached not as clients to patrons, but rather as mercenaries to *condottieri*, and to whom they looked for rehabilitation as peasant farmers, cherishing the aspirations habitual to the class from which they were drawn (Chapter 5). The leaders who for whatever motives placed themselves at the head of dissident movements were indeed themselves chiefly aristocrats, but they relied for support not so much on personal connections and influence as on the kind of following that political reformers may secure in any age by the attractiveness of the measures they seek to carry. This is the only interpretation of Roman politics which is commended by the ancient sources.

In considering the strength of personal connections, we must be careful not to assimilate *amicitia* or *hospitium* too closely to clientage. Admittedly both terms might veil the real dependence of one party on the other; there is, however, nothing to show that they imposed the specific obligations said to be incumbent on clients, and men of some social standing resented the appellation of client, which implied a subordination incompatible with their sense of their own dignity (n. 31). In Chapter 7 I have tried to show that the political ties of friendship were often loose and transient. As for *hospitium*, it is a reasonable assumption that it was the term most readily applicable to what was really patronage exercised by Roman magnates over the aristocratic families which commonly controlled the peoples allied or subject to Rome. The surviving evidence documents this kind of relationship most fully for provincial communities, but we can readily suppose that it often subsisted between the great houses at Rome and the *domi nobiles* among the Italian allies before the Social war (see e.g. Cic. *Phil*. xi. 27), as later we find it attested with the Italian municipalities. In that case, however, it is highly relevant to any assessment of the strength of the ties so established that they did not prevent the widespread revolt of 91–90; it was then primarily the Latin cities that remained loyal, and their loyalty can surely be explained not in terms of the personal connections of their *principes* with Roman aristocrats, which the rebel *principes* must also have had, but by the solidarity of kinship with the Roman people, which distinguished the Latins from the other allies and was the basis of special privileges they already possessed.

If we turn to clientship in the strict sense, the star witness on its importance, Dionysius, who lived at Rome under Augustus, held that it had been the chief factor in preserving social harmony in the good old days, forgetting that this harmony had not been very manifest in the time of the struggle of the orders, but that it had been dissolved in the age of Gaius Gracchus (ii. 11). But of course the Gracchi only revealed more clearly cleavages which had long been present, if largely latent. I shall argue that the authority of patrons had never in any period of which we are informed extended in Gelzer's words to 'the entire Rome people', and that it was being progressively eroded before the Gracchi set to work. It is indeed remarkable how rare are the references to clientship within the citizen body in the last century of the Republic. But the first notable silence is that of Polybius,[9] who observed the Roman scene at the very time when, if we trust Dionysius, the institution of clientship was in its heyday.

II

In regarding the Roman constitution as the finest example of the mixed constitution beloved of Greek theorists, Polybius recognized the importance of the democratic element within it (pp. 18 ff.). According to Walbank, this doctrine 'blinded him to an extraordinary degree to the elaborate texture of political life which throughout [his lifetime] ensured the domination of the nobility';[10] Walbank does not add that Cicero, who was after all a practising politician, took a similar, supposedly doctrinaire, view. He does not explain his criticism, but presumably he had in mind the prevalent notions that the domination of the nobility rested on the ability of the great houses in their putative alliances to combine in mobilizing their dependants, especially at elections, so as to control the assemblies. It is fair to say that Polybius focuses attention too much on the formal powers of the different organs of government. He does not even make explicit the fact that senators and magistrates were of a class distinguished by birth and wealth, though he may have made this clear in his lost 'archaeology'. In any case his Greek readers would have taken for granted that the leading

---

[9] Perhaps Polybius mentioned clientship in his account of the regal period, which was fairly detailed to judge from fragments in vi. 11a, as did Cicero (*de rep.* ii. 16); like Cicero (ii. 2, 30, 37), he insisted on the gradual and experimental development of the Roman system (vi. 10. 13 f.), and may have furnished details on particular institutions at the putative moment of their inception (cf. iii. 87. 8), if they were not given as a sequel to the general analysis in vi. 12–18; somewhere he evidently explained who patricians were (x. 4. 1), just as he gave information on Roman priesthoods (xvi. 13. 11); and he surely noticed the Roman practice of group voting, strange to Greeks. Not that Cicero's narrative in *de rep.* ii is wholly dependent on Polybius. Cf. Walbank's *Commentary* i. 635, 663 ff.

[10] Walbank, *Polybius*, 1972, 155.

men at Rome were of this type, as in their own cities, including those which still retained democratic forms.[11] Naturally Polybius was aware of the truth, and brings it out incidentally both in his famous account of Roman aristocratic funerals, which implies that many at least of the great men at Rome belonged to families that had held office for generations, and in allusions to their contemporary riches and luxury.[12] From their own military and diplomatic contacts with Rome Greeks were familiar with the powers of senate and magistrates, which are continually exemplified in Polybius' narrative, but they were less likely to know of the prerogatives of the people, which were more conspicuous in internal affairs, and which were better understood by Polybius as a result of his long residence at Rome. In my judgement he was right in recognizing their importance, though he himself remarks that the aristocratic element in the 'mixture' was the largest at Rome, by contrast with Carthage (vi. 53).

As he was long associated with Roman aristocrats, it is not at all likely that he was blinded to the true extent of their power; his eyes were not closed to social and economic realities. Thus among the devices by which the senate was able to control the people, he notes its right to superintend the public contracts, in which 'everyone' invested, and the senators' monopoly of judication in the most important civil suits (vi. 17); by the 'people' he means of course the most affluent citizens outside the senate (pp. 148 ff.), whose votes, as he may well have observed in a lost part of his work, preponderated in the centuriate assembly (cf. n. 9). Implicitly, he was drawing attention to social and economic modes of senatorial control. He also has various allusions to social *mores*.[13] It is therefore the more striking that in the extant part of his work he never refers to patronage, not for instance in accounting for the influence of Scipio Africanus and Scipio Aemilianus. He traces the rise of the former to his reputation for valour, beneficence, liberality, and courtesy, and of the latter to the popularity he earned by generosity, courage, and other virtues.[14]

It is true that he contrasts Aemilianus' conduct in youth with that of his peers, who commonly sought favour by advocacy in the courts and by formal visits to the houses of leading men, and Gelzer brought this into connection with patronage by suggesting that they were paying court to their 'protectors'.[15] But the deference envisaged is not the

---

[11] Jones, 1940, 166–8.   [12] vi. 53 f., xxxi. 25–9.

[13] vi. 3. 3; e.g. 11a. 4, 52–6; cf. Cic. *de rep.* iv. 3 and n. 14.

[14] x. 3 f., xxxi. 25–9.

[15] Gelzer, 1969, 104. In imperial times Fronto (Haines ii. 152 = *Ver.* ii. 7) shows his consciousness of the difference in making out that a younger senator showed him the same respect as a client *or freedman* would. We may compare the relationship to that of senior members of a modern Cabinet with younger aspirants to office.

subordination of hereditary clients to patrons; it is simply that of relatively young men to their elders and betters in the same social stratum, which is common to all societies and would have been well understood by Greek readers who knew nothing of clientage. In his *de officiis* Cicero prescribes conduct appropriate to members of the landed élite (i. 150 f.), adapting the views of the Greek Panaetius; he enjoins the young to revere and take the advice of their most respected elders, men conspicuous for moral rectitude and public services, and especially of those vested with legal powers; equally it is the duty of these men to supply counsel and guidance to the younger generation. He is certainly not thinking of the special relationship of clients to patrons, which he does not mention; his precepts, which surely correspond to traditional Roman social morality, as observed by Polybius, would apply to scions of the highest aristocracy, for example to the young Brutus, who associated with Cato and took him as a model. Cicero remarks that by winning the approval of those who already enjoy public respect a man can inspire in the people the expectation that he will himself act on the same principles.[16] Polybius' young nobles were behaving as he was to recommend. They hoped to rise by the *merita* and *gratia* on which the emperor Tiberius could suggest that candidates for the consulship might rely (Tac. *Ann.* i. 81).

Gratia signifies not only a favour done to others, and especially a favour done in return for those received, and the gratitude evinced in such a requital, but also the influence that accrues to men with a claim on the gratitude of others. Its ambivalence reflects the reciprocity of services and obligations which was characteristic of Roman society. This reciprocity is of course illustrated in the relationships between patrons and clients, and between friends, but it has a wider range. For Cicero beneficence or liberality (such as the Scipios displayed), though a virtue to be practised on its own account, is no less expedient than honourable, since it also reaps rewards from the gratitude that it evokes. It is due, he holds, in particular to kinsmen, friends, and fellow-citizens; he makes no reference to clients, nor of course to patrons, since it is the duties of men of high station that he is concerned with; at most he notes that grateful recollections of favours received may be transmitted to future generations, but without any hint that he has in mind the transmission of hereditary dependence. He dwells rather on liberality and aid given to the people at large. In his moral vein he depreciates the prodigality so common in Roman public life on the provision of feasts, shows, building, and the like, and recommends

---

[16] *de offic.* i. 122 f., 147–9, from that part of his work which most closely follows Panaetius on τὸ πρέπον (*decorum*), ii. 46 f. (with Roman *exempla*). Cf. Schulz, 1946, 56–8, on the relations between eminent jurists and novitiates, all of the higher classes.

readiness to give services rather than freedom with the purse; however, services should be available not merely to those with whom special connections already exist but to as many as possible. Most men, he observes, are prone to bestow benefits on persons, evidently of substance, from whom they can expect a prompt and speedy return, yet the gratitude they procure hardly extends beyond the beneficiaries themselves and perhaps their children. The poor, or at least the deserving poor, are more likely to be grateful, but they need help from many quarters, and hope for similar favours in the future; by assisting a single honest man among them, you can gain a reputation that will earn the goodwill of the rest. Clearly he is not contemplating the creation of permanent and exclusive hereditary ties, like those of traditional clientship; men of substance resented the very name of client, while the poor needed more than one protector. Moreover, influence derives as much from the hope of future benefits as from the obligations incident to those previously received.[17] Similarly, in idealizing senators in early times, he says that they would give their services, advice, and material aid to individual citizens, without specifying that this assistance went to existing clients or brought others within their patronage (*de rep.* ii. 59).

Hence Sallust's reference to the 'few powerful men under whose influence most people had passed' ('pauci potentes quorum in gratiam plerique concesserant') need not relate solely or primarily to the patrons of clients. Rather the contrary: in the very same context he writes of struggles for power between men pretending to act on behalf of senate or plebs ('sub honesto patrum aut plebis nomine'); as elsewhere, he is concerned with the political followers of the optimate or popular leaders; and here, so far from mentioning the personal loyalty that magnates might inspire in their dependants, he sneers at the greater facilities for doing injuries to humble folk that wealth affords. From an optimate standpoint Cicero divides politicians into the true champions of property rights and the public good and demagogues who in offering specious benefits to the masses fail to win the *gratia* they seek because they forfeit the goodwill of property owners.[18]

Patronage certainly figures in some lists of the concomitants of aristocratic power (n. 139). Thus Sallust makes Marius enumerate among the advantages of the nobility the resources of their kin by blood and marriage and their numerous clients, but also their ancient

---

[17] *de offic.* i. 42 ff., ii. 52 ff., esp. 63–70.
[18] Sall. *Hist.* i. 12, *Cat.* 38, *BJ* 41 f.; in *Hist.* i. 11 he also explained the early movement of the plebeians against the patricians by the oppressive government of the latter; Cic. *Sest.* 96 ff., *de offic.* ii. 79.

lineage and the brave deeds of their ancestors; by implication these in themselves strengthen their hold on the people; later it is only their pride of birth and their riches that Marius depreciates (*BJ* 85. 4 and 38), and the allusion to the importance of patronage is isolated in Sallust's unquestionably authentic works.[19] In his idealization of the good old days he tells how the foremost men pursued true glory in the service of the state and acquired true friendships by their readiness to confer benefits, without adding that they would protect humble dependants (*Cat.* 6. 5, 9. 1); once corrupted by the greed for money which they squandered in luxury and by unscrupulous ambition (e.g. *Cat.* 3–12), they would not only enrich themselves by monopoly of the profits of empire (*Cat.* 20. 7, *BJ* 31. 9, 19) but oppress the impoverished plebs, which was impotent to resist them, not because they could mobilize dependants to do their will, but because they were organized and the plebs leaderless until the Gracchi came forward (*BJ* 41 f.) Their patronage is not adduced to explain their exclusive hold on the highest offices (*Cat.* 24. 6, *BJ* 63. 7); indeed Sallust proffers no explanation, but he conveys the impression, except in the single allusion cited above to the nexus of family connections and to *clientelae*, that it lay in their wealth and in the general respect felt for their ancestral fame.[20]

In fact clientship appears infinitely more often in modern than in ancient writings. Exclude references to patronage over (*a*) freedmen; (*b*) provincials and foreign communities; (*c*) persons represented in the courts (who admittedly incurred obligations to their advocates, but might be their equals or superiors in rank and were in that case certainly not their clients), and the lexica then register only some fifty allusions to clientship in Italy in all the works of Cicero and Sallust; about a third concern individual clients of one or more persons (chiefly Cicero's).[21] Clients are also found rather seldom in inscriptions both Republican and imperial; the inscriptions do indeed confirm that the institution was not confined to Rome but was known in other Italian communities.[22] Mass all this evidence together, and throw in references to other forms of connection, as Gelzer did, and it seems impressive; scattered over a thousand pages of Latin, it does not naturally suggest that political power was based on these connections, especially as the ancient writers often afford explicit indications that it was founded on sectional interests.

[19] His (?) second letter to Caesar also notes that the nobility had inherited 'gloriam dignitatem clientelas' (11. 3); here high lineage extends the respect they enjoy beyond their own clients.

[20] See generally Earl, 1961, chs. I–IV.

[21] I count only allusions to *cliens, patronus*, and cognates; the phrase 'in fide[m]' is ambiguous but also not common. No doubt some *amici* or *hospites* were clients in all but name, but we often do not know enough of the circumstances to be certain of this.

[22] See endnote 1.

The Caesarian *corpus* never expressly mentions Italian clients, though the tenants mustered by L. Domitius Ahenobarbus in 49 along with his slaves and freedmen *may* have been his clients (*BC* i. 34). Caesar has, it is true, much to say of clientship in Gaul, and his use of the term shows that he detected some analogy with the Roman institution; however, he is clearly bent on making the differences clear. In Gaul by his account the common people were virtually slaves; debt, taxation, and oppression by magnates forced them to place themselves in servitude to nobles, who had all the same rights over them as (Roman) masters over their slaves (*BG* vi. 13). Festus says that the Gallic *ambactus*, a word used by Ennius, was equivalent to slave (4 L.), and according to Caesar, the greater the lineage and wealth of a Gallic notable, the larger was his retinue of *ambacti* and clients (vi. 15). Elsewhere he collocates clients and debt-bondsmen; the latter could be mobilized for war by their lords; we hear the same of clients alone (i. 4, vii. 4, 32, 40). Before Caesar's time it had been the custom for a man's favourite slaves and clients to be immolated on his funeral pyre (vi. 19). Clients thought it sinful to desert their patrons in the extremity of ill fortune (vii. 40). In return for such devotion they received protection: it was an ancient usage that none of the commons should lack aid (*auxilium*) against the more powerful; no magnate would let 'his own people' be oppressed and defrauded; that would be an end of his influence (vi. 11). A similar class in Aquitania called *soldurii* surrendered themselves to the 'friendship' of lords, with whom they shared the good things of life and whom they held it shameful to survive (iii. 22). It may be that Caesar has confused various types of servitude in Gaul, but what he calls clientship is evidently one of them. The entire subordination of the Gallic client to his lord arises because humble Gauls have no such protection in the law and the tribunician *ius auxilii* as Roman citizens. They must look to one magnate to defend them from the rest. What Caesar tells of Gallic clientship suggests by implication what Roman clientship was not.

Roman magnates too were often hereditary patrons, or in name *hospites* or *amici*, of the subjects or allies of the Roman people, of kings, peoples, cities, and individuals, both in Italy before the enfranchisement of the Italians and beyond the seas,[23] and we may assume that when the terms patronage or clientship are applied to these relationships, they are used in the Roman sense; what we learn of these 'foreign *clientelae*' can therefore be used as evidence for the Roman institution. In fact we hear more of them than of clientship within the citizen body. This may in some degree be an accident of the surviving evidence,[24]

---

[23] Gelzer, 1969, 86 ff. Harmand, 1957, assembles data. App. ii. 4 says that all subject peoples had patrons (προστάται) at Rome.

[24] References proliferate in the *Verrines* and no doubt distort the balance of the evidence.

but it may also be due to the fact that foreigners lacked the political rights whereby citizens could independently influence political decisions at Rome, and were thus in greater need of the aid that Roman patrons could give. I shall not discuss how far such patronage affected Rome's administration of the subjects or foreign relations. My concern is with the effects of patronage in Roman internal affairs.

No doubt the *dignitas* of a Roman grandee was enhanced by the mere number of his foreign clients. This was probably always an important incentive to the extension of patronage (cf. Plaut. *Men.* 574); in the Principate it is hard to think of any other reason why the great houses continued not only to maintain patronage in the provinces (Tac. *Ann.* iii. 55) but also to support so many hangers-on in the city of Rome (n. 155); by that time clients could hardly afford them any useful political support. In the Republic too foreign clients, though they might perhaps assist Roman patrons financially (cf. n. 107), could have little impact on political decisions, or on military issues. In 48 Dolabella tartly observed that Pompey's boasted patronage of kings and nations had not prevented the loss of Italy and Spain (Cic. *Fam.* ix. 9. 2). Admittedly in Spain his extensive connections were to revive and drag out resistance till Munda and beyond, but they could not secure Caesar's defeat.[25] The votes, and ultimately the arms, of Italians were decisive; relatively few provincials fought in the civil wars.[26] Provincial clientship was perhaps of most material value to the clients, though their hopes of favour and protection were not always fulfilled, as the Sicilians discovered in Verres' time. Brutus exacted usurious interest from his Cypriot clients, and Cicero did not welcome the grant of the Latin right or of citizenship to his dear Sicilians,[27] any more than Pompey sought to elevate his Transpadane clients from Latin to Roman status.

Given the paucity of explicit evidence on clientship in the late Republic, modern scholars discourse more vaguely on other *necessitudines* based on *fides* (*Näh-und-Treuverhältnisse*), *amicitia* (Chapter 7), and *hospitium*.[28] There can be no doubt that these terms may disguise a

---

[25] Gelzer, 1969, 96; add Caes. *BC* i. 61. 3 for Pompey's name inspiring fear as well as affection; note too 74. 5, *B. Alex.* 58 f. against the view that loyalty to Pompey had much to do with the movement against Q. Cassius. Dio xliii. 30. 1, xlv. 10. 1; App. v. 143 best illustrate the strength of his Spanish connections. But Caesar too had Spanish clients and complained that his favours to them did not produce proper devotion (*B. Hisp.* 42). No doubt many Spaniards had conflicting obligations, and made (as it happened) an imprudent choice between them.

[26] *IM*, App. 29.

[27] Brunt, *Chiron* 1980, 273 ff.; (esp. ii *Verr.* iv. 89) Cic. *Att.* vi. 1. 5, xiv. 12. 2. Gelzer, 1969, 88 ff., illustrates services that some patrons did render to provincial communities.

[28] *Hospites*: Wiseman, 1971, 33 ff.; *TLL* s.v. *hospitium*; cf. n. 82 with text; Harmand, 1957, ch. ii. Lyso of Patrae could entertain Cicero and tend his sick freedman Tiro, services not comparable with Cicero's protection of his business interests (*Fam.* xiii. 19. 1); cf. Shackleton Bailey on *Fam.* xiii. 78, and for Cicero's often specious references to friendship, on xiii. 27.

degree of social dependence, but this can only be determined by scrutiny of the particular circumstances, which are not always clear. Let us look at some instances. Cicero warmly commended to his brother M. Orfius, an Eques who was a notable of Atella and influential beyond his home town, and who was at the time serving under Caesar. Atella was a town in Cicero's patronage, and its leading men, like Orfius, may well have been individually his clients: the ties between a Roman magnate and a municipality were doubtless strong in proportion to the strength of his ties with the chief local figures. Cicero describes Orfius simply as a person connected with him in his own right ('necessarium per se'). The connection evidently did not extend automatically to Cicero's brother. As a military tribune in Caesar's army, Orfius probably had incurred heavier obligations to his general. Another such connection of Cicero was the young C. Trebatius from Velia (*Fam.* vii. 20. 1), who was to attain great eminence as a jurist. Cicero had received him 'in amicitiam et fidem', and commended him to Caesar, in the hope that the latter would enrich him from the spoils of Gaul. He writes: 'totum denique hominem tibi ita trado de manu, ut aiunt, in manum'. This language is hyperbolical. Subsequent correspondence shows that Trebatius remained Cicero's friend as well as Caesar's, and it would be injudicious to suppose that he was simply transferred in such a way as to be at Caesar's entire disposal: he was not 'Caesar's man' any more than he had been Cicero's. *Commendatio* in itself did not have that effect; Cicero could also 'wholly commend and transfer' himself to the young Curio: 'nunc tibi omnem rem atque causam meque totum commendo atque trado'.[29] But Cicero's numerous letters of commendation (*Fam.* xiii *passim*) illustrate the help that such friends as Trebatius might obtain from their superiors; it could actually extend to more or less delicate pressure on magistrates who were to determine their rights in litigation.[30] Advocacy in the courts or legal advice were other services that might be rendered, but they might not only fulfil the pre-existing obligations of a patron or friend, but (as Gelzer showed at length) enlarge the circle of his connections. The practice of procuring *privilegia* from the senate in a thin house, circumscribed by the *lex Cornelia* of 67 (Ascon. 58 C.), is probably another example of the operation of patronage in a broad sense.

Orfius was Cicero's *necessarius*, Trebatius his *amicus*; like *hospes*, these could be courteous appellations for connections which presuppose

---

[29] Orfius: Cic. *Qu. fr.* ii. 13 (12). 3. Trebatius: *Fam.* vii. 5. 3; cf. 17. 2; parallel case in Caes. *BC* ii. 57. 1. For Trebatius as intermediary between Caesar and Cicero in 49 see *RE* viA. 225 ff. (Sonnet). Cicero and Curio: *Fam.* ii. 6. 5.

[30] G. E. M. de Ste Croix, *Br. Journ. Sociol.* 1954, 33 ff.

dependence, when there was great disparity between the parties in status and influence. But it is significant that they might be preferred to language that unveiled that dependence. Men of wealth and standing, Cicero says, thought it 'like death' to be called clients; they might even be reluctant to accept favours that bound them too closely to the benefactor and looked for a return.[31] Only two of his correspondents who belonged to this class style themselves clients, in conscious self-abasement, when imploring his help, and these very men he urbanely and perhaps sincerely addresses as his friends.[32] In his youth, when himself an Eques, he had assimilated clients to freedmen and slaves (n. 87). It was then natural that the description should be abhorrent to all Romans whose *dignitas* made them cherish their independence. In an epigram of Pubilius (B. 5) to 'accept a favour' is itself to 'barter freedom', and Brutus would not sell his liberty for the benefits Antony might grant (*ad Brut.* 24. 4). Romans whose social status was sufficiently assured evidently resented the claim to subservience that clientship might seem to convey.[33] We have no access to the mentality of the lower classes in this regard, unless Publilius speaks for them, but they might well have wished to model their attitude on that of their betters. Was not a client 'in obsequium plus aequo pronus' (Hor. *Ep.* i. 18. 10) destitute of that *libertas* which many or almost all Romans valued? It may be said that terminology is of little importance in assessing the realities of the relationship between a Trebatius and his more powerful friends, but this may not be true. Though friendship might persist over generations in Roman as in any other society, we are not told that it involved any hereditary *obligations*, as clientship did, and it was certainly in the discretion of friends to decide when and how far they would reciprocate services rendered. The nuances of the mutual connections of Romans are obscured when friends of lesser degree are treated as no more than clients.

It may also be imprudent to assume that even clients faithfully observed the theoretically hereditary force of their obligations, which is attested by Dionysius and confirmed by some inscriptions.[34] In fact very few literary texts of the Republic relate to inherited *clientelae* in Italy. It is patent that though the great noble dynasties presumably had the largest number of clients, this did not invariably suffice to

[31] Cic. *de offic.* ii. 69; cf. Sen. *de benef.* ii. 23. 3.

[32] *Fam.* vi. 7. 4, vii. 29. 2; contrast vi. 5. 4, 6. 2, 9. 1 (Caecina); xiii. 17. 1 (Curius); his correspondence with them suggests some real familiarity. *Fam.* v. 9. 1 is merely jocular.

[33] Note Mart. ii. 55: 'Vis te, Sexte, coli: volebam amare./ parendum est tibi; quod iubes, colere:/sed si te colo, Sexte, non amabo.'

[34] Dionys. Hal. ii. 10. 4; *ILS* 6094–6100 (*hospitium* too was hereditary); Gelzer, 1969, 22 f. Collaterals might have patronal claims; cf. Brunt, *Chiron* 1980, n. 8 on II *Verr.* iv. 79–81; but Orfius was *necessarius* of Cicero and not of his brother.

sustain their power and influence. Some of them failed to supply consuls for long periods, perhaps as a result of early deaths in successive generations, but perhaps also because of the exceptional incapacity of their representatives, or of extravagance that diminished the resources available for munificence to the people at large.[35] For instance, M. Aemilius Scaurus, consul in 115, who became the first man at Rome by his own efforts, belonged to one of the most splendid patrician clans, but for three generations none of his forebears had attained office, and he had to repair his economic fortune before embarking on a political career.[36] Probably the loyalty of hereditary clients was impaired when the patron lacked the wealth and power to render them much assistance. In 50 the young Tiberius Claudius Nero, the scion of a patrician house that produced no consul between 202 and the future emperor Tiberius in 13 needed the help of the governor of Bithynia to confirm his ancestral patronage there and to bind his clients with new favours (*Fam.* xiii. 64). Under Sulla's dictatorship the Roscii of Ameria deserted their numerous old patrons, who included some of the chief aristocrats at Rome, for the more effective aid of Sulla's freedman and favourite, Chrysogonus.[37] Inherited sentiments of loyalty counted for less than the possession of resources and influence, combined with the disposition to use them, for the aid and protection of dependants.

> Perseverance, dear my lord,
> Keeps honour bright; to have done is to hang
> Quite out of fashion, like a rusty mail
> In monumental mockery.

Men who came to the fore by their personal talents were thus well placed to acquire an extensive patronage; their clients must either have been previously independent, or have had ties with other patrons (which, as we shall see, were not necessarily dissolved by the new connection). There is perhaps some exaggeration in Valerius Maximus' report (ix. 15) that the oculist Herophilus, by posing as Marius' grandson, gained the allegiance of numerous veteran colonies and other townships and of 'almost all the *collegia*', but it suggests that Marius, though a new man, had a widespread patronage, which is not astonishing, since he had been seven times consul and was acclaimed as saviour of his country. Sulla himself came from a branch of the Cornelii, which had not attained the consulship for two centuries; if his son Faustus, who himself does not seem to have enjoyed political

---

[35] Brunt, *JRS* 1982, xxxi–xxxiii.

[36] Ascon. 23 C.; *de vir. ill.* 82; Val. Max. ii. 10. 4; Cic. *Mur.* 16.

[37] 'Cum *multos* veteres a maioribus Roscii patronos hospitesque haberent, omnes eos colere atque observare destiterunt ac se in Chrysogoni fidem et clientelam contulerunt' (*Rosc. Amer.* 106).

influence incommensurate with his youth, could be described as a man 'with the greatest resources and numerous kin by blood and marriage, connections, and clients', the explanation must lie in his father's personal dominance.[38] Pompey's large *clientela* (n. 144) must likewise have been in part the result of his own unique military and political career; it is true that his father Cn. Pompeius Strabo already had many dependants in Picenum, but Strabo himself, though perhaps a collateral of the parvenu consul of 141, was at best of praetorian descent. Not surprisingly, we know most of the patronage of Cicero; his preeminence at the bar and his consular rank enabled him to furnish valuable aid and protection; individuals apart, he was patron of the Sicilians, of Arpinum, Capua, Reate, Atella, Cales, Volaterrae, Arretium, and all the towns from Vibo to Brundisium, not to speak of his close connection with the great publican companies, whose leading members would obviously have been styled friends.[39]

Nor was patronage confined to nobles and new men, like Marius and Cicero, who rose to exceptional authority. It might belong to senators of much lower status, like P. Sestius, or to such persons as the *latifondista* C. Quinctius Valgus, patron of Aeclanum, or M. Satrius, patron in 44 of all Picenum and the Sabine country ('o turpem notam temporum'), neither of whom is known to have entered the senate. To say no more of Chrysogonus, a mere freedwoman of the Manlii boasts of the great number of her clients (n. 22). Naturally Atticus too had his clients. So within their home towns did many *domi nobiles* like the Roscii of Ameria; the *graffiti* at Pompeii afford many examples (n. 127).[40] It will appear in section V that the electoral support of municipal gentry was important to candidates for office at Rome, but perhaps not so much because of their humble dependants as because they might persuade friends and neighbours of the same status as themselves, who had the means to travel to the city and whose votes would count more in the centuriate assembly, to support the same candidates as they did. Such men, like the Roscii, might themselves be clients of great Roman houses. But we cannot assume that there was always or usually any unbroken line of dependence. Atticus, for example, obviously owed no allegiance to anybody.

---

[38] *Cluent.* 94. Cf. p. 474 on Faustus.

[39] *Div. Caec.* 2, *de offic.* ii. 50, *Att.* xiv. 12 (Sicily), *Sest.* 9, *Pis.* 25 (Capua), *Cat.* iii. 5 (cf. Sall. *Cat.* 26. 4), *Scaur.* 27 (Reate), *Qu. fr.* ii. 13. 3, *Fam.* xiii. 7. 1 (Atella), *Planc.* 97 (Vibo etc.), implied for Cales (*Fam.* ix. 13. 3), Volaterrae (xiii. 4. 1, *Att.* i. 19. 4, as for Arretium; cf. *Caec.* 97); we can hardly tell how far his patronage of communities derived from defence of local magnates like Caecina or C. Curtius (*Fam.* xiii. 5). Patronage of his native Arpinum can be assumed (cf. *Fam.* xiii. 11 f.). Publicans: e.g. *Qu. fr.* i. 1. 6, 32–5, *Fam.* xiii. 9, 65. 2. Provincial clients and *hospites*: *Cat.* iv. 23, e.g. Dyrrachium (*Planc.* 41). Syme says that Cicero lacked clients (*RR* 16)!

[40] *ILLRP* 523 (Quinctius); Cic. *de offic.* iii. 74 (Satrius), *post red. sen.* 20 (Sestius), *Rosc. Amer.* 19 (a Roscius), *Att.* i. 12. 2, 20. 7, x. 8. 3 (Atticus). Cf. Harmand 1957, 79–82.

Indeed it is highly questionable how far clients in general stood in an exclusive relationship to particular patrons. The Roscii had many noble patrons (n. 37). A. Caecina was a client both of the Pompeian Cicero and by a hereditary attachment of the Caesarian consul of 48 P. Servilius Isauricus.[41] At one time Marius was apparently a hereditary client of both the Metelii and the Herennii, not a consular family (Plut. *Mar.* 4 f.). Even a freedman could have a patron other than his ex-master.[42] Generals became patrons of the peoples they subdued, but thereafter these clients could choose additional patrons; Syracuse and other Sicilian cities had many besides the Marcelli. Colonies were in the patronage of their founders (*deductores*), but as the foundation was normally entrusted to triumvirs, they had more than one from the start, and the Caesarian charter of Urso, in part at least tralatician, permits the council, subject to certain restrictions, to co-opt patrons in addition to the founder and his descendants. The Sullan colony of Pompeii had several patrons in 62. Co-optation is probably attested in an inscription of Fundi (not a colony) not later than 152. Cicero boasted that after his consulship Capua made him sole patron (n. 39); this was clearly unusual, and it cannot have remained true after Capua received colonial status by favour of Caesar in 59 and of the land commissioners appointed under his law.[43] It is simply inconceivable that Cicero was sole patron of all the other towns mentioned earlier. Pompey had clients in Transpadane Gaul; perhaps all the cities there that owed their Latin right to his father were bound to him,[44] but he never advocated their enfranchisement as Caesar did, and we may guess that as proconsul Caesar conferred many benefits on them and continued to hold out the prospect of their promotion to citizenship; in 50 he could count on Romans there, including the ex-magistrates of the Latin communities, to vote for his *protégés* (*BG* viii. 50. 3, 52. 1): he did enfranchise the Latins, once master of Rome (Dio xli. 36. 3), and the region was an important source of recruits for his legions (*BC* iii. 87. 4). By 49 he had stronger claims than Pompey on their support, and if they were already voting at his behest, we cannot infer that this was what clients normally did for patrons; they had singular expectations from his favour.

[41] Cic. *Fam.* vi. 7. 4 ('me veterem tuum, nunc omnium clientem'), xiii. 66. 1.

[42] Treggiari 223.

[43] Gelzer, 1969, 87; further items for Sicily in Brunt, *Chiron* 1980; Cicero's suggestion that Verres could substitute himself for certain patrons in Sicily (II *Verr.* 4. 89) is delusive. Pompeii: Cic. *Sull.* 60. Fundi: *ILLRP* 1068. Urso: *ILS* 6087, xcvii, cxxx: the restrictions were perhaps Augustan, (cf. Dio lvi. 25. 6), and interpolated in the text of Caesar's charter. In AD 223 Canusium had 40 patrons, *ILS* 6121.

[44] *Fam.* viii. 4. 4, *Qu. fr.* ii. 3. 4, a result perhaps of his campaign in 877, more probably of the *lex Pompeia* of 89 (Ascon. 3 C.; Seager, 1979, 2, says that 'it was designed to extend [Pompeius Strabo's] influence'; by parity of reasoning the *lex Iulia* of 90 was designed to make all new citizens clients of L. Caesar!

The plurality of patronage has of course been noted before, but its significance has not been brought out. It necessarily meant that if the patrons were discordant the loyalties of the clients were divided. Thus in civil wars many communities and individuals might have ties with both warring parties; the dilemma of Massilia (Caes. *BC* i. 35) cannot have been unique. In Italy itself all the towns, it is said, offered prayers for Pompey when he was seriously ill in 50, and thanksgivings when he recovered. Perhaps this demonstrated primarily the universal popularity of a national hero, but Pompey must have been patron of at least as many towns as Cicero. Yet even in Picenum there was little resistance to Caesar in 49, and the adulation for the victor was no less fervent when he had driven Pompey out of Italy.[45] A similar dilemma in a less acute form could confront clients when their patrons competed for office. It may be noted that Pompey himself had to resort to bribery or force to secure the election of a candidate he preferred (Cic. *Att.* i. 16. 12), and even for his own in 55. There is indeed no sign that in this period the mobilization of clients had anything more than a marginal effect at elections (section V), whether because patrons could not ensure their loyalty or because loyal clients could never constitute a decisive proportion of the electorate. It may be observed that the great noble families were still as successful as they had ever been in filling the consulship, and we cannot therefore explain their previous preponderance by the hypothesis that the votes of their dependants had once mattered more.

Clients, like friends, if faced with a conflict in their personal obligations, had to make a choice, and that choice might be determined by consideration either of the relative strength of those obligations taken by themselves, or of their own advantage, or of the public interest, or, of course, by mixed motives. We must not assume that their views of the public interest counted for nothing. It might actually affect their choice of patrons. The adoption of Brutus and Cassius as patrons of Teanum and Puteoli after Caesar's death looks like a declaration of adherence to the Republican cause (ch. 1 endnote 1). If we can believe Cicero, it evoked widespread enthusiasm in Italy, including Cisalpina. There Brutus could have acquired clients as governor in 46, but there is no like explanation of Cassius' patronage among the Transpadani.[46] Only those towns in the region which Antony actually held by force failed to back the senate.[47] Years later

[45] Vell. ii. 42; Plut. *Pomp.* 57; Dio xli. 6. 3; cf. Cic. *Att.* viii. 16. 1, ix. 5. 4.

[46] Cic. *Phil.* ii. 107, *Fam.* xii. 5. 2; cf. ch. 1 n. 9.

[47] They included Bononia, 'in Antoniorum clientela antiquitus' (Suet. *Aug.* 17. 2); the *deductores* (Livy xxxvii. 57) had, so far as known, no living descendants in the male line. But Antony founded a colony there (Dio l. 6); that can hardly have suited the existing citizens, and I wonder if he was not simply patron of the new colony.

Brutus was still honoured at Mediolanum as the champion of freedom (Suet. *Rhet.* 6). Clientship might then be the effect rather than the cause of political affiliations, just as personal friendships and enmities could be terminated in changed political conjunctures on the basis or pretext of political principles.

To summarize the argument thus far, it appears that our authorities do not justify the modern hypothesis that the influence exercised by the great aristocratic families at Rome over hordes of dependants was of great significance for the understanding of Roman politics. Patronage was not confined to those families, and its acquisition was as much a consequence as a cause of ascendancy in the state. It was sometimes or often shared, and then established no exclusive claim to allegiance. It is mentioned rather seldom in our sources, and they offer quite different explanations (examined in other chapters) of the great conflicts of the late Republic and the course they took. In later sections I shall discuss more fully the part that clients supposedly played in these conflicts. But first I shall consider what is known or believed of clientship in pre-Gracchan ages. It is in part because scholars suppose it to have been the foundation of aristocratic power in early Rome that they are ready to assume that it survived in some degree so long as that power continued. Their conception of the structure of society and politics in the second and first centuries is coloured by the picture they have drawn of archaic conditions; and no one should deny that ancestral custom had a strong effect on the mentality of Romans. However, in fact very little is known of early clientage; and there are sufficient indications that even in the fifth and fourth centuries the majority of citizens could show their independence of patrons, and that thereafter the ties that bound patrons and clients together became still looser.

III

The antiquity of clientage is beyond dispute. The ancients themselves made Romulus its creator. Cicero said that he had the plebs distributed into clientships of the leading men ('habuit plebem in clientelas discriptam'); Cicero promised to show the advantages of this later, but if he did so it was in a lost part of his *de republica* (ii. 16). In the light of the less ambiguous statements on Romulus' work in Festus (262 L.), Dionysius (ii. 9. 2), and Plutarch (*Rom.* 13), that Romulus divided the plebeians as clients among the patricians, the suggestion that Cicero *meant* that the plebeians were already clients before the city was founded can be dismissed. According to Dionysius, each plebeian was allowed to choose his own patron. Both he and Plutarch purport to describe the first organization of the Roman community and the very origin of clientship. Naturally no one will now believe that it was deliberately instituted in this way, but the construction of the Roman annalists has commonly been taken as proof of an authentic tradition that at the first all plebeians were clients of the patricians.[48] Modern scholars also tend to think that they were clients of patrician *gentes* as such, whereas the ancient writers explicitly state that they were assigned to individual patrons, admittedly on a hereditary basis; in historic times there is certainly no evidence for patronage exercised by *gentes*.[49] More important, the moderns often deny that the clients, and therefore the plebeians, originally had citizen rights, however limited. This contention has no foundation in the 'tradition', which knows nothing of the enfranchisement either of plebeians in general (as distinct from their acquisition of particular rights withheld from them in early times) or of clients in particular; for instance, the annalists told that in the early Republic plebeian clients supported the patricians with their votes. Moreover, although Dionysius claims that the social harmony maintained by patronage lasted till Gaius Gracchus, and therefore by implication that till then the support given by clients to patrons remained of political importance, the annalists also conceived that in the struggles between patricians and plebeians many of the latter could be sharply differentiated from the clients of the patricians, and therefore that it was no longer true that all plebeians were their dependants. This must be correct; otherwise it would be impossible to understand how some of the plebeians won full parity as nobles with the patricians, or how the citizens in general acquired the personal protection under the laws and the political rights which they undoubtedly enjoyed from the early third century. The 'tradition' casts no light on the putative process whereby many at least of the plebeians had escaped the ties of dependence by which all were supposedly once bound; we may of course conjecture that they had been liberated by the disappearance of patronal families. This is speculation; and we may

[48] So recently F. de Martino, *Misc. Manni*, 1979, 681 ff., but see above all Premerstein, 1900, whose dogmas and conjectures largely derive from Mommsen, *Röm. Forsch.* i. 355 ff., and *StR*³ iii. 54 ff., one of those constructions in which Mommsen displayed his imaginative power to create almost *ex nihilo*; they have been more or less repeated by other scholars, e.g. with some variations by M. Lemosse (*RIDA*, 1949, 46 ff.), C. W. Westrup (ibid. 1954, 451 ff.), and Badian, 1958, 1–13 (with occasional and rather tender criticisms); for this and other theories cf. Richard, ch. 1 and 157 ff.

[49] Dionys. ii. 10. 2 says clients were to τῶν ἀναλωμάτων [of patrons] ὡς τοὺς προσήκοντας μετέχειν, 'as if related by birth', not as 'belonging to the *gens*'; cf. Botsford, *Roman Assemblies*, 1909, 27 ff., against Kübler, *RE* vii. 1178 ff., whose own discussion shows that there is no evidence that freeborn clients belonged in any sense to the *gens*. The simile in Cic. *Tim.* 41 (cf. *de leg.* i. 23) does not prove that *quasi gentiles* was a term applicable to any class of persons at Rome, and no Latin expression exists for persons belonging to a *gens* but *gentiles* (on whom cf. Cic. *Top.* 29 with Brunt, *JRS* 1982, p. 3).

wonder if there was any genuine recollection of conditions in which all plebeians were clients, anterior to the conflicts beginning in the early fifth century, when this can no longer have been true.

All modern accounts of Roman clientship rely heavily on Dionysius (ii. 9–11). He professes to be recording the laws of Romulus, the historicity of which must be in doubt. Was he none the less drawing ultimately on laws of the regal period? A record of these 'laws', some of which on Dionysius' own admission (ii. 24. 1, 27. 3) were originally unwritten, was evidently kept in the pontifical archives, but few will take this to be proof of their authenticity.[50] The rule mentioned by Dionysius that a patron or client convicted of impious and unlawful actions against each other was liable to be killed for 'treason' by anyone who pleased as a victim to Zeus Katachthonios might be seen as a retrojection of a supposed provision in the Twelve Tables that the patron who wronged his client was to be *sacer* and his life therefore forfeit,[51] but the authenticity of this provision is itself suspect (p. 409). The 'impious and unlawful actions' include acting in the lawcourts and voting against each other, or being ranked among each other's enemies; it is hardly credible that all such conduct was ever prohibited by law, and Dionysius' assertions that clients were to assist patrons in the cost of magistracies and not to vote against each other, perhaps in courts but more probably in the *comitia*,[52] are patent anachronisms for the regal period. It seems most likely that Dionysius or his source found a validation in fictitious laws for customs which they took to be characteristic of the 'good old days'. We cannot in fact be sure that all the customs he describes were authentic. In historic times it seems that the founders (*deductores*) of colonies and the generals who reduced foreign peoples to submission were necessarily the patrons of the communities concerned,[53] which could subsequently choose additional patrons; Dionysius makes out that communities, like individuals, could always choose their patrons. But he is right that the relation of patrons and clients was hereditary, and there is confirmation of his statement that patrons were authorized by the senate to compose communal

---

[50] *Leges regiae*: FIRA i². pp. 3 ff.; for authenticity, A. Watson, *JRS* 1972, 100 ff; A. Drummond remarked to me that his medieval parallels suggest, contrary to his own view, that social bonds would be given legal definition gradually, if at all. J. P. V. D. Balsdon, *JRS* 1971, 18 ff., discredited the theory that Dionysius drew on a political pamphlet, but even if he is wrong, the source of that pamphlet could have been 'laws' in the archives.

[51] It would be another anachronism if he meant *Dis Pater* (Wissowa 309 ff.; Latte 246 ff.). See also A. Watson, *CQ* 1979, 439 (unconvincing). Cf. n. 75.

[52] The context of the sentence suggests that he has trials in mind, but in what early courts would there be voting? He certainly thought that there were magistrates under the kings, and later (n. 82) often refers to clients voting at elections.

[53] Gelzer, 1969, 63; Cic. *de offic.* i. 35 (the Syracusans would hardly have taken Marcellus as patron out of love for him!). Cf. n. 43.

controversies.[54] He was realistic in writing of the zeal with which the magnates would maintain and extend their patronage, but surely idealizing, when he speaks of the marvellous goodwill that once subsisted between them and their clients.

Dionysius makes various statements about the early relationship between patrons and clients in legal processes. Patrons were (1) to explain to their clients the laws of which they were ignorant; (2) to sue on their behalf if they were wronged, e.g. on contracts; (3) to defend them in both civil and criminal cases. Furthermore, patrons and clients might not (4) bring accusations nor (5) bring witness against each other. Mommsen held that (4) could relate only to civil suits, since in his view there were no private prosecutions for crimes in early Roman law, a thesis since impugned by Kunkel.[55] Some infer from (1) and (3) that clients could not appear in the courts themselves and must then have lacked the full rights of citizens,[56] but the prohibition in (4) implies that they could take independent action, except against patrons, and of course Dionysius himself credited them with the voting rights of citizens. In the historic period clients were still debarred from appearing as counsel or witnesses against patrons, though this restriction apparently vanished in time (pp. 417 f.), and the right of freedmen to sue their patrons was limited, but not that of freeborn clients. In classical law citizens could be legally represented by a *cognitor* or *procurator*, or in certain circumstances by a *tutor* or *curator*; such legal representatives were not necessarily patrons.[57] No doubt patrons were always under a moral obligation to assist clients in the courts;[58] the legal rules reported by Dionysius, if they ever existed, became obsolete in course of time.

Dionysius says more generally that the patron was to care for his clients as for his own sons. We must not infer that like *filiifamiliarum* they had no property. That conclusion would certainly be incompatible with his own assertions that they were expected to contribute to the costs sustained by patrons in dowries, fines, ransoms, and public services. Of such contributions there are recorded instances, real or fictitious.[59] Plutarch, however, says ultimately it was thought demeaning for men of high degree to take money from clients.[60] In fact, as we shall see, demands for gifts were resented, and restricted by law (p. 422).

[54] *ILS* 5946; Cic. II *Verr.* ii. 122, *Sulla* 60–2. Horace credibly pictures a Regulus settling disputes between individual clients (*Odes* ii. 5. 53).
[55] Kunkel, 1962, chs. III, VIII, XIV f.
[56] A. Magdelain, *RÉL* 1971, 103 ff. (with other implausible conjectures), followed by Richard 161 etc.
[57] M. Kaser, *Röm Zivilprozessrecht* 152 ff.   [58] e.g. Plaut. *Men.* 574 ff.
[59] Fines: Livy v. 32. 8, xxxvii. 60. 9. Cf. n. 107.
[60] *Rom.* 13. 6. Evidently Dionysius is not his sole source.

Cicero tells of a foreigner residing in Rome as an exile who had applied to a Roman 'quasi patronum'; he died intestate, and the patron claimed the estate; in the proceedings he illuminated the *ius applicationis*, which was quite obscure and unknown (*de orat.* i. 177). Now under the Twelve Tables the patron did not enjoy the right of intestate succession even to a freedman who had a *suus heres*, i.e. a member of his family who had been subject to his *patria potestas*, and he never in historic times had such a right in the case of a freeborn Roman client. Nor are the terms *se applicare* (as distinct from *se commendare* or *se dare*)[61] and *ius applicationis* ever used elsewhere of a Roman coming under the patronage of another Roman. The *ius* in question would not have been obscure if the client had been a Roman freedman or *ingenuus*. But he was a foreigner, who doubtless died without natural heirs, and the patron evidently argued, presumably with success, that he had the same right to his estate as if he had been his freedman intestate in similar circumstances. The text has no relevance to patronage over freeborn Romans.

Dionysius compared clients (*pelatali*) with the *thetes* of archaic Athens and the *penestai* of Thessaly (ii. 9. 2); the latter were serfs, and he also uses the term *penestai* to denote the Etruscan serfs (ix. 5. 4). This terminology has helped to generate a modern theory that clientship was originally a kind of serfdom (*Hörigkeit*). It is supposed that the first clients were peoples conquered by Rome and distributed as dependants among the patrician *gentes*, together with freedmen and their descendants, that the latter long remained under the absolute authority of their former masters, and that their status reveals what that of other clients had been; the conquered were subject to the unfettered control of the Roman state, and *therefore* to that of their particular patrons! It is admitted that patrons never had the same authority over freeborn citizens who voluntarily sought their protection (by a procedure unwarrantably styled *applicatio*), and that they eventually lost it over other clients of free birth and later over freedmen. In fact, as we shall see, there is no good evidence that they had ever possessed it over citizens, whether of free or servile birth, nor is there any record of the change assumed. The only kind of bondage attested at Rome apart from slavery is debt-bondage, abolished in 326 or 313, though forced labour could be exacted in various relationships arising from contract or delict (pp. 285 f.). The theory is certainly alien to Dionysius' own conceptions, for what they are worth; he observed that the Romans improved on the Greek patterns he cites; clients were not treated as virtual slaves, like Thessalian *penestai*, nor despised as mere hirelings,

---

[61] Ter. *Eun.* 885, 1039; Gell. v. 13. 2; cf. n. 37.

like Athenian *thetes*; there was a relationship of mutual goodwill (ii. 9). The theory rests neither on his account of clientship nor on any direct testimony, but on assumptions and deductions which do not bear critical examination.

We may begin by noting that it is not sustained by the terminology of the Romans themselves. No certain inferences, for instance, can be drawn from the original meaning of *cliens*, which is as obscure as its etymology.[62] *Patronus* obviously comes from *pater*; and therefore, it is argued, the patron once had the same authority over clients as the *paterfamilias* (head of the household) always possessed over his slaves and children. An adventurous supplementation of lacunae in Festus simply derives from this hypothesis and cannot properly be adduced in proof of it.[63] By contrast, Dionysius had learnt that the significance of the word derived from the fatherly care of the patron for his dependants (ii. 9. 3). This may be true. It is already used figuratively to mean 'protector', like *pater* itself, by Plautus,[64] as it was by Metellus Pius when he called the tribune Q. Calidius, a new man, patron of his proud family because he had secured the recall of Numidicus from exile.[65] The special application of the word to a pleader in the courts may always have had the same sense, though it may go back to days when patrons normally assisted their clients in legal proceedings; naturally in the historic period, when *patronus* in a special sense means pleader, it is not correlated with *cliens*. For instance Cicero's appearance in 63 as counsel for Piso, the consul of 67, in a *repetundae* trial did not make Piso his *cliens*. Gelzer indeed suggests that the term *patronus* was reserved for advocates of high rank, but there are too many exceptions to this supposed rule.[66]

---

[62] It is generally held to be cognate with Greek κλύω (listen) or κλίνομαι (lean on); cf. Richard 159 f. Rouland 19 ff. derives it from *colere*.

[63] Festus 253 M. reads 'patr[onus a patre cur ab antiquis dictus sit, manifestum: quia ut liberi, sic enim clientes] numerari inter do[mesticos quodammodo possunt]': 'why the term patron [derived from *pater* was used by the ancients is clear; it was because like the sons, the clients too could be] counted among ho[usehold people in a way]'. Lindsay 300 rightly spurns this conjectural reading.

[64] Neuhauser, *Patronus u. Orator*, 64 ff., is useful here. Note the collocation in this sense in Plaut. *Capt.* 444; Ter. *Ad.* 456. Even slaves or freedmen can be 'patrons', i.e. protectors, of their own masters or ex-masters, Plaut. *Asin.* 652, *Cas.* 739, *Rudens* 1266, and a man may be 'patron' of others' slaves (*Rudens* 705).

[65] Cic. *Planc.* 69. Drusus (*tr. pl.* 91) was 'senatus . . . paene patronus' (*Mil.* 16). The usage is common (cf. last note). Livy writes of a patron or patrons of the army (iii. 29. 2, xxii. 29. 11, 30. 2, with assimilation to *pater*; cf. 34. 6) and of the plebs (ii. 9, vi. 18. 14).

[66] *Contra* Gelzer, 1969, 71, Cicero so designates not only P. Antistius (*Brut.* 226) but L. Fufidius, C. Licinius Macer, and Q. Arrius (ibid. 113, 238, 243), himself while still an Eques (*Rosc. Amer.* 5), and the Caepasii (*Cluent.* 57). I doubt if *cliens* is normally used, as client in English, for the person represented by an advocate in court; *de orat.* i. 51, 174, *Brut.* 97 may rather illustrate the practice of patrons appearing for clients in the normal sense of the latter term, and *Fam.* v. 9A. 1 is ironic.

An individual who voluntarily became a client was said, as we have seen, 'se commendare [dare] in fidem alicuius' (n. 61); but in Cicero's time this certainly did not mean that he surrendered himself to the patron's absolute control (n. 29 with text). There is no proof that it had ever had this meaning, nor indeed is this alleged by advocates of the theory under consideration. But have they any reason to hold that such control appertained to the patron of a conquered people? Such a people, on submitting 'in fidem populi Romani', was indeed subject to the absolute *dicio* of Rome.[67] Moreover, *fides* was associated with power when Romans spoke of the *fides* of the magistrate (e.g. Suet. *Rhet.* 1) or that of *iudices*. Since such a community was also in the *fides* of its patron, does this not suggest that at one time it was as much in his power as in that of the Roman state? This must be answered in the negative. Plainly it is not true that patrons had such power in the historic period, and it cannot be inferred from the terms used that their position must originally have been stronger. The Roman state, being subject to no higher authority, had absolute discretion how to treat a community that had surrendered to its *fides*, and so had the general as its representative at the time when he accepted the surrender, but it does not follow that once Rome had defined the status of that community, he and his descendants as patrons still had like power. *Fides* cannot be equated with *potestas* (which could itself be limited, as in the case of minor magistrates); we must bear in mind the phrase *do fidem*, used when a solemn promise was given, the mutual *fides* expected of friends, and the development of the word to denote a moral quality of trustworthiness. In the light of these usages the *fides* ascribed to magistrates and *iudices* surely indicates that they had a trust in the exercise of power. We may then suppose that the client was 'in fide patroni' because it was a matter of good faith that the patron should protect his client. Though the patron is never said to be 'in fide clientis', Dionysius thought that the client owed a certain faith to his patron, and Plautus speaks of 'clientium fides' (*Men.* 576). But such terms as 'fealty' and 'allegiance', which conjure up the legal obligations of medieval vassals to their lords, including that of military service, are hardly apposite to the relationship.[68] In historic times the

[67] Badian, 1958, 4–7, 156; cf. Walbank on Polyb. xx. 9. 10; E. Gruen, *Athen.* 1982, 510 ff.

[68] Watson, 1975, 47–51, 101, 105; Cicero's references to the *fides* and *potestas* of *iudices* are irrelevant to the position of patrons (*Font.* 40; cf. *Quinct.* 101, *de dom.* 1). *Fides*; bibliography and survey of views, F. Wieacker, *SZ* 1963, 20 ff. Elsewhere (*Vom röm. Recht*[2] 1961, 14) he suggested that *fides* was a constraint on another person with supernatural sanctions, at first magical and then divine. Whatever be thought of hypotheses on *fides* in its most primitive character, its actual usage in historic times in relation to clients or friends must be connected with its more general application in Roman society (see the text), and with e.g. Cicero's definition, which is free of all supernatural colouring or affinity with *potestas*: 'dictorum conventorumque constantia et veritas' (*de offic.* i. 23); we cannot assume that it retained nuances from a remote past.

patron had no legal claims on his clients, and there is no proof that he had ever had any.

It is sheer fantasy to infer from the hereditary character of patronage and from the legend of Romulus' distribution of plebeians as clients that the plebs, including conquered peoples, were at one time all clients of patrician *gentes* as such; still more to suppose that they were ruled by the head of the *gens* (himself a figure constructed by modern scholars) in much the same way as the *familia* was ruled by the *paterfamilias*. But did the latter have any legal authority over his clients? It has been contended (*a*) that he long retained absolute power over freedmen as well as slaves, and (*b*) that this points to his having once enjoyed as much power over other clients. Neither proposition can be justified.

(*a*) Three anecdotes used to be commonly cited to show that as late as the first century BC the patron still possessed the right of life and death over his freedmen, but it has now been proved that they have no evidential value. Cicero had no effective means of coercing a refractory freedman. It was apparently the Augustan *lex Aelia Sentia* that first made freedmen liable to legal penalties for 'ingratitude', and then only by action in the courts.[69] Re-enslavement is occasionally attested, but not before Claudius.[70] As early as the Twelve Tables the freedman could acquire and devise property; the patron inherited from him only if he died intestate without a *suus heres*; it was later that the praetor gave the patron limited rights of inheritance against the terms of the will, if the freedman had no heir of the body. The patron's restricted right of intestate succession is similar to that of agnates or *gentiles*; and just as under the Twelve Tables the nearest agnate becomes *tutor legitimus* of the freeborn minor, for whom his father had appointed no *tutor* by will, so in like circumstances did the patron of the freedman's son; it was the right of the *tutor* in both cases to administer and preserve the property which would pass to him if his ward died (*Dig.* xxvi. 4. 1 *pr.*, 4. 3 *pr.*); there is no implication that the freedman remained a member of the patron's *familia*, any more than the freeborn minor belonged to the *familia* of the nearest agnate. As patrons evidently had no title to hinder freedmen from making wills adverse to their interests,[71] they can hardly have had coercive power over them at the time of the Twelve Tables; and it is an unfounded conjecture that they had possessed it earlier.

It is true that, according to Servius Sulpicius, masters could impose

---

[69] Treggiari 71 ff. against e.g. Kaser, *SZ* 1951, 88 ff.

[70] Buckland 422 ff. On supposed domestic jurisdiction over freedmen (and clients) in *Dig.* xlvii. 2. 90 see Brunt, *JRS* 1980, App. 7; Watson 1975, 107 f.

[71] *FIRA* i². p. 41 (texts assembled under A and B).

excessively onerous obligations on freedmen at the time of manumission, until their rights were limited by the edict of Rutilius Rufus, praetor *c*.118. But his statement can and probably does mean that such obligations had earlier been made binding by oath or *stipulatio*; this would hardly have been necessary if freedmen were as such subject to the absolute jurisdiction of patrons.[72] Under the Principate a governor might have to intervene to enforce *obsequium* to the patron (*Dig*. i. 16. 9. 3). Naturally we do not know what was the position of the freedman in times for which no testimony exists, and we may adopt any hypothesis we like, provided that we do not claim that in the time of the Twelve Tables or later freedmen were hardly differentiated from slaves. The *lex Cincia* of 204 BC (n. 109) is indeed reported to have excepted from a general ban on the acceptance of gifts those gifts which came 'a servis quique pro servis servitutem servierunt', and an ancient commentator remarked that here the term *servi* comprises freedmen, but the meaning was surely that gifts were allowed from 'slaves and those [free men] who were thought to be slaves, who *have been* in servitude', i.e. those who were no longer in either category.[73] In any case the freedman's long-existing right to devise property is conclusive that in legislation of this date he cannot have been assimilated to a slave.

(b) Even if the freedman had once remained in subjection to his patron, that would furnish no proof that this was also true of the freeborn client. In later Latin the freedman is seldom called a client, and we find two separate correlations, *patronus/cliens* and *patronus/libertus*.[74] The term *patronus* had different connotations for each pair, at any rate in the later law, when the freedman was limited in his rights against the patron in ways that the freeborn client was not. The fragments of the Twelve Tables preserve no traces of any status 'between freedom and slavery'. They contrast free men (citizens of course) and slaves (VIII. 14), without admitting an intermediate class

---

[72] Treggiari 68 ff. Cicero's claim that of old patrons could command freedmen not less than slaves (*Qu. fr.* i. 1. 13) would relate to practice, not law, and need not be true.

[73] *Vat. fr.* 307. P. Stein, *Athen.* 1985, 143 ff., who collects evidence of the *lex Cincia* (n. 109) and discusses various interpretations of this text, thinks that the gifts allowed are from those still *servi* or *liberi bona fide servientes*, but this seems to me implausible in itself (there would have been no need to legitimate such gifts), and an unnatural construction of the perfect tense.

[74] See e.g. Cic. *de inv.* i. 109: 'servis libertis clientibus'; *Caec.* 57: 'aut cliens aut libertus'; *Dig.* xlvii. 2. 90: 'libertus vel cliens'. 'Libertinus cliens' (Livy xliii. 16. 4; Suet. *Caes.* 2) is an unusual collocation. Writing on 'in ius vocatio' (cf. n. 94) Ulpian says: 'patroni hic accipiendi sunt, qui ex servitute manumiserunt' (*Dig.* ii. 4. 8. 1). This is patently the normal meaning in legal texts, and we can assume it even where it is not explicit, e.g. probably in the rule that the patron of either party may not sit on juries under the Sullan law *de iniuriis* (xlvii. 10. 5 *pr.*) or in xlviii. 19. 28. 8 (heavier penalties for crimes committed against those with whom special relationships subsisted). Patrons and freeborn clients are designated in the Gracchan *repetundae* law by a periphrasis (n. 89). Cf. Rouland 79 ff.

(even that of freedmen), and among free men, they distinguish only between those with and without landed property, (*adsidui* and *proletarii*, I. 4, 10)) and between patricians (*patres*) and plebeians (XI. 1); the household (*familia*) consists only of sons and *slaves* (XII 2a), and the power of life and death, which presumably needed no legal sanction in relation to slaves, is expressly conceded to the *pater* over the sons alone (IV. 2).

However, the legal dependence of the client on the patron in the time of the code has been inferred from the only 'fragment' of the Twelve Tables in which the relationship is allegedly attested. Virgil mentions among other sins, not all of them subject at any time to legal penalties, but punishable in the after-life, 'fraus innexa clienti' (*Aen*, vi. 609). In his commentary Servius claims that there was a provision in the Twelve Tables: 'patronus si clienti fraudem fecerit, sacer esto.' Mommsen took this to imply that the client had no right to sue his patron for civil wrongs, but that instead the magistrate could proceed against the patron on a capital charge. If convicted, he would then be *sacer*: i.e. anyone could kill him with impunity (cf. Festus 424 L.). Mommsen connected this with Dionysius' statement that under the laws of Romulus either patron or client who violated the reciprocal obligations which he had listed and which included a bar in either party appearing against the other in court (p. 403), was to be treated as guilty of treason and to be sacrificed to Zeus Katachthonios. However, he thought that Servius was in error in imputing the rule to the Twelve Tables, apparently supposing that it belonged only to the so-called laws of Romulus. For this contention he gave no explicit reason, but remarked that there is no trace of the application of the rule in practice and that in the historic epoch it was obsolete. That is of course no less true of some other rules in the Tables, notably those concerning the sale of insolvent debtors into slavery beyond the Tiber (iii. 5). Still, the Tables themselves strongly suggest that there was at their date no bar on clients proceeding against their patrons in the courts, any more than under the classical law (p. 418). They plainly allow all free citizens the right to sue for reparation of wrongs under various heads (i. *passim*, vii. 8, viii *passim*). This is compatible with the putative bar, only if we assume either that no citizens were clients, and that it was after the codification that any clients obtained citizen rights, or that clients were specifically prohibited from proceeding against their patrons, though not against other citizens. But no such specific prohibition is on record (except in Dionysius' account of the laws of Romulus), and it is manifestly incredible that no citizens needed or secured patronal protection, or that there was a mass enfranchisement of clients after *c*. 450, of which we hear nothing. Moreover, 'fraudem facere' can mean only 'do harm', and it would be bizarre if the all-powerful patronal class had on the one hand safeguarded its members from all pecuniary claims for delict on the part of clients, and on the other exposed themselves to a capital penalty for offences so undefined that (as Mommsen held) it must have been at the court's discretion to determine in what conditions it was due. There must then be grave doubt whether Servius' ascription of the rule in question to the Twelve Tables is correct (at least if it carries with it the implication that Mommsen discerned); but, if it really came from the 'laws of Romulus', it may be quite apocryphal.[75]

All this is not to deny that in early times humble citizens needed protection from patrons, not least in matters of legal process, and that in practice they were unable to proceed in the courts against their own protectors, who equally could doubtless coerce them effectively enough, without invoking the machinery of law. Admirers of 'the good old days' would give a moral colouring to the hard realities of dependence and would say, for instance, like Gellius (xx. 1. 40), that no misdeed had once been accounted worse than the proved plundering of a client; the next step was to embody a prescription of social morality in a fictitious royal code of law. Be this as it may, it is certain that in all periods for which reliable evidence exists the dictum of the imperial jurist Proculus holds good: 'we recognize our clients as free men, although they are not our peers in authority, rank, or resources'.[76] The rest is surmise.

Economic dependence must usually have lain beneath the subordination of clients to patrons. On one theory it took a special form in the earliest time. Festus explained the use of *patres* to mean senators as well as fathers partly by the fact that 'agrorum partes ad [tribuerant tenuioribus] perinde ac liberis'; the supplements are guaranteed by Paul's epitome: 'they had assigned parts of their lands to humbler persons as to their children. (288 f. L.)' The etymological explanation is fanciful, and it may be doubted if Festus' antiquarian source had access to any reliable tradition about the earliest Roman society. We might perhaps place more confidence in the ancient belief that the *heredium* owned by an individual and transmissible to his heir was originally only two *iugera*, and infer that most land belonged to the state or the *gentes*. It is a further inference drawn by modern scholars from Festus that at first only patrician *gentes* owned lands and that plebeians as their clients could at best receive from them revocable holdings. This was clearly no longer true, if it ever had been, in the early Republic,

---

[75] In *Röm. Forsch.* i. 384 Mommsen took Servius' fragment of the XII Tables to be genuine, but see *Strafr.* 566, *StR.*³ iii. 82; also Kunkel, 1962, 41 n. 153. Servius had no cause to tell us what Dionys. ii. 10. 3 asserts, that the faithless client was also liable to penalty (under Romulus' laws).

[76] *Dig.* xlix. 15. 7.

since the success of the plebeians in winning equal rights is incomprehensible except on the assumption that some of them were men of substance, and in the conditions of those days, landowners.

The theory derived from Festus' text has been supported by consideration of 'precarious possession' in the lawbooks. An owner could grant such possession of any property, including a farm: the possessor was protected against eviction by a third party, but not against the owner, who could resume the grant whenever he pleased. No connection is made by the jurists between such possession and clientage. They represent precarious grants as acts of liberality or kindness; no payment was due. Very possibly some clients were the beneficiaries. None the less, it is of course inconceivable that grants of this kind had their origin in the systematic assignment of lands to clients on this footing, in days when patrons could clearly not have afforded to dispense with rent in money or kind from the estates in which their economic and political power rested. We may, if we choose, *conjecture* that the practice of requiring a recompense for precarious possession had disappeared in later times. (It may be noted that the occupiers of public land also had only precarious possession and that they were liable to pay rent to the state (App. i. 7), but different rules could well have applied to public land than to private.) It is also true that precarious grants of property were not necessarily, or perhaps commonly, proof of sheer generosity. A debtor would often transfer title of his property to a creditor by *fiducia*, on the footing that if the debt was repaid when due it must be restored to him; as the small farmer had no means of paying, if in the interim he lost the enjoyment of his farm, it might be arranged that he should retain it by precarious possession until payment was due. The benefit to the creditor was recovery of the principal lent, with interest. But there is nothing to show that this sort of arrangement was one made chiefly by patrons with their clients.[77]

The most reliable tradition on the typical conduct of landowners in early Rome tells us nothing of patriarchal benevolence, but shows them working their estates with the labour of citizens whom they had

---

[77] *Precarium*; Steinwenter, *RE* xxii. 1814 ff., and Michel 128 ff., who both take the view I contest. Michel conjectures that custom might require the precarious *possessor* to make periodic gifts (130); cf. his Part III for reciprocal gifts in societies at a pre-contractual stage, a practice that has left traces in Roman laws and customs. Presumably, too, *stipulatio* could be used to obligate such a *possessor* to rent or services, as to obligate a debtor to pay interest on a loan contracted by *mutuum*; the contract of *locatio–conductio* was of relatively late date. But there are no texts; hypothesis is heaped on hypothesis. In classical times a creditor would acquire his debtor's property by *fiducia* and then allow him precarious possession of it as the means of getting his capital back with interest; this was the economic incentive, rent not being due (Gaius ii. 60; cf. Steinwenter 1816).

reduced to debt-bondage (*nexi*).[78] As for later times, it may be that tenants or free wage-labourers were sometimes or often clients of their landlords or employers, but I do not recall that this is ever documented. Roman writers on agriculture presuppose that landowners will adopt purely economic criteria for the best exploitation of their holdings and will commonly rely on slave labour; they never hint that their decisions might be affected by obligations to clients. In the first century AD Columella offers some discussion of the relative advantages of leasing farms and of keeping them in hand with slave gangs; if they are leased, he recommends that the tenants should be, not clients as such bound by special ties of loyalty or affection to the owner, but country-bred, long associated with the lands they cultivate, and diligent in their work (i. 7. 3 f.). The relationship of tenant to owner appears in all the evidence to be contractual and not 'precarious'.

The 'tradition', as we have seen, bids us believe that all plebeians were once clients of the patricians, but not that they were destitute of all citizen rights. I shall not enter into controversies on the origin of the plebs, a 'Serbonian bog, where armies whole have sunk'.[79] Whether or not the 'tradition' was right on both points or either, and whether or not it reposed on genuine recollections, it is also clear that if we give it credit, we must also believe that from the early fifth century there was a mass of plebeian citizens who could be distinguished from the clients of the patricians. As for the latter, it is presupposed, particularly in what Dionysius tells us, that they included men of substance. It was only to such men that noble patrons could turn for useful material assistance, and it was only their votes that counted for much in the centuriate assembly; moreover, the indigent do not litigate, and all that we hear of the aid that patrons might furnish to their clients in legal processes surely relates to property owners. Yet it is precisely persons in this class whom we might expect to have chafed at a condition of dependence. It will in fact appear that the ties between patrons and clients were gradually relaxed, a process that we can occasionally illustrate from the middle period of the Republic, as well as by contrasting what is known of the relationship that still subsisted in that time with that which is revealed later in juristic texts (pp. 416–20) If the hold that patrons originally had over their clients was in reality greater in the beginning than in my view the scanty evidence justifies us in supposing, its later relaxation naturally suggests that patronal authority provoked discontent, which whittled it away. This would be a process not easy

[78] Ch. 6 n. 6. [79] Richard is exhaustive.

to terminate, in conditions in which the lower orders of society still had the means to carry it further.

To revert to the early Republic, we are told that some great houses, the Claudii and Fabii at least, had hosts of clients; according to Dionysius, the latter could raise an army from their own clients to fight for Rome, just as in the tale of the Sabine Appius Herdonius nearly capturing Rome in 460 his force was composed of clients and slaves. Camillus' clients are said to have formed 'a great part of the plebs'.[80] It is worth noting that Livy has nothing of the same kind after his first decade, save that in the suspect story of the trial of the Scipios he mentions their 'magnum agmen amicorum clientiumque'. A strange tale of Suetonius, that some early Claudius (whose identity cannot be determined) had a diadem set on his statue at Forum Appii and tried 'Italiam per clientelas occupare', is evidence that this kind of design could at any rate be the subject of legend or of invention developed from a picture of society that may be legendary.[81] Both Livy and Dionysius make out that clients sometimes gave important backing to the patricians in the struggle of the orders. What historic truth these reports have may be doubted. Ogilvie thinks 'Livy preserved nothing of value about the primitive *clientela*. Instead he gives a picture of it at work as it must have been in the first century BC.'[82] This judgement seems to me to rest on the common exaggeration of the strength of *clientela* in the later time, and in particular on the false belief that powerful men could often raise armies from their own retainers (cf. section VII). It is far more likely that intermittently aware, as they were, that conditions in the early Republic were very different from those which prevailed later, the annalists guessed that the dependence of clients on patrons was then far greater (as Dionysius clearly implies), and produced an imaginative reconstruction of political life in the fifth century which did not in this respect accord at all with their own experience. It may not have been wholly wrong. How did some fifty patrician clans[83] retain control of the state for 150 years after the fall of the monarchy? No doubt they commanded general respect, so long as they monopolized experience in military leadership and (so it may have been believed)

---

[80] Livy ii. 16. 4 (cf. iii. 56. 1), 49 (with parallels cited by Ogilvie, esp. Dionys. ix. 15), v. 32. 8; Dionys. x. 14. 1. Numbers are wildly inflated; cf. de Martino (n. 44) 702 f.

[81] Livy xxxviii. 51. 6. Note also xxiii. 3. 2, 7. 10 (Capua). On Suet. *Tib.* 2 see Premerstein, 1937, 18; Taylor, 1960, 137.

[82] Livy ii. 35. 4, 56. 3, 64. 2, iii. 14. 4, 16. 5, 58. 1, vi. 18. 5; cf. Dionys. ii. 62, v. 7. 5, vi. 51. 1, 59. 3, 63. 3, vii. 18. 2, 21. 3, 54. 3, 64. 3, ix. 41. 5, x. 15. 5, 27. 3, 40. 3, 41. 5, xi. 22, 30. 1, 33. 1, 36. 2, 38. 4, xiii. 5. See Ogilvie's *Commentary* on Livy (pp. 479 f.) and his Addendum. Dionysius thought that whole armies could be composed of patricians and their clients (vi. 47. 1, vii. 19. 2, x. 4. 3); the Fabii sustained Rome's war with Veii thus (ix. 15); Livy has nothing of this.

[83] Mommsen. *Röm. Forsch.* i. 71–127.

in the skills required to propitiate the gods; a people struggling for survival would not lightly cast off their leadership. But it would be helpful to suppose that they also had substantial voting support given by their dependants.

Still, the plebeian leaders must have been economically and politically free of their control, and in the end they won the backing of a majority of the citizens for their own ambitions, largely (if the tradition is sound) by linking them with the satisfaction of the grievances of the masses. The majority might have consisted partly of clients of the patricians who would not always vote as their patrons directed, partly of clients of the plebeian leaders themselves,[84] partly of entirely independent citizens. So too the *nexi* were either clients whom their patrons failed to protect or men with no patrons to protect them. On any view the patricians had lost their putative patronal relationship to all plebeians, or else this relationship did not suffice to assure their loyalty. Both the dependence of the masses on aristocratic patrons and the social solidarity acclaimed by Dionysius as its result had already broken down. So much at least the tradition shows. The last secession of the plebs *c.*287 must be historic (ch. 6 n. 168), and it is alone enough to prove the existence of a grave social cleavage. But the evolution of the plebs as a kind of state within a state and of the tribunate tell the same story, as does the abolition of *nexum*. If the prolonged success of the patricians in preserving their supremacy suggests that they could rely on numerous clients, their ultimate failure is conclusive that the majority of citizens felt no obligation to obey their behests. The struggle of the orders resulted in the acquisition by the common people not only of personal protection under the law, which tended to make them somewhat less dependent on the aid of patrons, but of significant political rights, by which they were able on occasion to impose their common will first on the patricians, then on the nobility which was to be formed by an amalgamation of the patricians with the greater plebeian houses. Patronage inevitably came to be of less political importance through the exercise of these rights.

IV

No doubt Dionysius preserves some features of patronage in early times which survived later (ii. 10 f.). His statements can be accepted in so far as they are confirmed by more reliable evidence (see below). On this basis we can say that patrons were expected to give their clients legal

---

[84] Livy supposed that Sp. Maelius had his clients (iv. 13. 2).

advice to assist them in the courts, a matter of considerable importance when success in litigation depended both on knowledge of the
law and on social and economic strength; that they might arbitrate
between them (n. 54); that they would in all sorts of ways represent
the interests of communities in their *fides*. Patrons and clients were
expected not to take hostile action against each other in the courts. In
certain circumstances clients were morally bound to render their
patrons material aid. We may credit Dionysius' unsupported statement that they were also to vote for them when they stood for office.
He does not claim that they were equally bound to vote for any other
persons, or on legislative and judicial questions brought before the
assemblies, as their patrons might direct, but respect for the trusted
authority of men of rank, ingrained affection, economic dependence
and mere habit might make them ready to take the advice that
patrons offered, at least when their own interests or consideration of
the public good did not furnish compelling reasons to reject it; and
men and communities might have several patrons, who were not
necessarily in agreement. There was of course no question of their
being bound to fight for their patrons; the legend of the Fabii at the
Cremera (n. 82) is isolated; until the civil wars armies were raised
normally by the levy enforcing the duty of citizens to serve their
country, and we shall see that clients do not figure largely in the
gangs or legions of the first century. In that period indeed clients
appear seldom or inconspicuously in the ancient texts, as distinct
from modern accounts, even in circumstances where we should most
expect to find them prominent if those accounts are true, for example
in elections (section V). Moreover, there are indications in the
Republican sources and in the silences of later juristic texts that the
ties binding patrons and clients were progressively loosening from the
late third century. The development of popular movements and the
increased opportunities for material gains available to the higher
orders both contributed to disintegrate such solidarity between patrons and clients as had existed in early times, which even then had
not prevented the tensions apparent in the struggle of the orders.

Dionysius himself allows that this disintegration occurred in C.
Gracchus' time (ii. 11. 3). In imperial times Gellius records an old view
that clients had a higher claim on *fides* than *hospites*, and both than
cognati (sc. all blood-relatives);[85] the jurist Masurius, whom he
quotes,[86] reverses the order between clients and *hospites*; these texts
warn us not to assimilate *hospitium* (or *amicitia*, which is not mentioned)

[85] Gell. v. 13; cf. xx. 1. 40.
[86] In the last of his three books on *ius civile*, thought to be dependent on a work of Q. Mucius
Scaevola, *cos*. 95 (Schulz, 1946, 156). Did Mucius too write of *past* obligations of patrons?

to patronage. Gellius also quotes Cato as saying of his own day that a man testifies against *cognati* on behalf of a client, but not against clients. According to Cicero (*de senect.* 32), Cato still fulfilled his duties to fatherland, friends, clients and *hospites* in old age. But Cato also said that men placed ('habuere') a patron next to a father. The change of tense is significant; he is now referring to the past; the loyalty of clients was not what it had been. In the next century the writer of the treatise *ad Herennium*, after referring to 'societates atque amicitiae', recognizes special duties 'in parentis deos patriam hospitia clientelas cognationes adfinitates'; the order is perhaps arbitrary.[87] Gellius also quotes Caesar on his principle of setting clients above *propinqui*. Perhaps that had become eccentric. Sallust has not a word of care for clients in his eulogies of the old Roman morality. Catalogues given by Cicero, Horace, and Seneca of those to whom we have special obligations include friends but ignore patrons and clients altogether;[88] nor are clients expressly mentioned as proper recipients of liberality in Cicero's long discussion of that topic (*de offic.* ii. 52–71), though it is plain that in his view benefactors expected gratitude. Naturally we have nothing in our upper-class sources from clients to show how they viewed the relationship.

Dionysius' statement that patrons and clients would not bear witness against each other is confirmed by Cato for the patron; both doubtless refer to evidence given voluntarily. Under laws that set up *iudicia publica* witnesses summoned by the prosecution could be bound to testify. But the Gracchan *repetundae* law barred the summons of anyone who, or whose ancestors, had been *in fide* of the defendant or his ancestors, or of anyone who, or whose ancestors, had held *in fide* the defendant or his ancestors; such persons could also not act as prosecuting counsel. The law thus enforces the old moral code, though it implies that hereditary ties might have been severed; a man's ancestors might have been clients, when he himself was not. Curiously, there is no like disqualification for jury service, as there is for kinsmen of the accused and fellow-members of a club or guild (*sodalitas* or *collegium*). Perhaps this was an oversight; Roman laws are

[87] *Ad Her.* iii. 4. Ter. *Ad.* 529 has the order: 'cliens amicus hospes'. Cicero promised Crassus in 54 to look after his friends, *hospites*, clients (*Fam.* v. 8. 5). Friends first intrude, then take a higher place than clients; finally clients drop out of such lists (nn. 88, 139). Cic. *de inv.* i. 109 distinguishes between (*a*) kinsmen and friends and (*b*) slaves, freedmen, clients, and suppliants, 'quibus indignum [est] nos male tractari'; clients are associated with freedmen and even slaves in *post red. sen.* 20, *Parad.* 46; Tac, *Hist.* i. 4, *Ann.* iv. 59, xiv. 61; Mart. vii. 62; Fronto ii p. 152 Haines.

[88] *de offic.* i. 53–8 from Panaetius, but Cicero adapts his doctrines to Roman conditions where necessary. No clients in lists of persons to whom special obligations are due in *Part. Or.* 80 (parents, friends, *hospites*); Hor. *Ars Poet.* 312 ff. (*patria*, friends, parents, brothers, *hospites*); Sen. *Ep.* 95. 37 (parents, children, friends, *hospites*, *patria*). For Sallust Romans in the good old days showed their virtue to parents (*Cat.* 6. 5), friends (9. 2), and above all to the *res publica* (6–9).

not invariably well-drafted. There were probably similar provisions in the law on *ambitus*, under which Marius was tried in 116, and which may be earlier.[89]

This incident justifies a digression. Herennius refused to bear witness against Marius on the plea of being his hereditary patron. At this time then a senator could still be counted a client. This is also implicit in the *repetundae* law, since most defendants would be senators or ex-magistrates with a claim to be enrolled in the senate, together with their sons, though former *tribuni militum*, who would not necessarily be of senatorial family, were also liable.[90] Herennius, it may be noted, had no exclusive claim to Marius' allegiance, for he also seems to have been a client of L. Metellus. However, Marius had already shown so little respect for the ties of clientship that he had as tribune ordered the arrest of Metellus, then consul. He also resented Herennius' plea as derogatory to his own dignity, averring that he had ceased to be a client on election to office, evidently at least from his election to the tribunate.[91] It was his view that was to prevail: in Cicero's time no senator is ever called a client by Roman writers. It is regrettable that modern scholars do not always follow their usage, and thus preserve the gradations of social distinction which it reflects. Practice does indeed seem to have changed again in the Principate; Tacitus could describe men of high rank as clients, and though they themselves might have spurned the appellation, a Gallic magnate of the third century evidently had no objection to being styled 'amicus et cliens' of a Roman governor.[92]

The provisions that mention clientage in the second-century laws on *repetundae* and *ambitus* also seem to reflect a dying social order. No restriction in later legislation is recorded on patrons and clients (as distinct from freedmen)[93] suing or prosecuting each other or giving hostile evidence. Caesar's or Augustus' law *de vi* prohibited a freedman, but not a client, from bearing witness against patron or his son. The *senatus consultum Calvisianum de repetundis* of 4 BC excludes nomination of a *iudex* who is so related to the accused by blood or marriage that he could not give evidence against him under the *lex Iulia iudiciaria*, or whom the accused swore to be his enemy; as the *iudices* are necessarily senators, there was no cause to refer here to clients (much less freedmen). However, the *lex* in question (apart from provisions regarding kinship) merely ruled that *freedmen* and patrons might not be

---

[89] *FIRA* i². no. 7 vv. 10, 22, 33; Plut. *Mar.* 4 f.
[90] Sherwin-White, *JRS* 1982, 19; cf. p. 198.   [91] Plut. *Mar.* 4 f.
[92] Tac. *Hist.* iii. 66, *Ann.* iv. 2, 68; *CIL* xiii. 3162 (Thorigny).
[93] *FIRA* i². no. 68, v. For exclusion of kin see ch. 9 n. 8. Law relating to witnesses: Kaser, *RE* va, 1049 ff. Cf. n. 74 on Sullan law *de iniuriis*. Vis: *Dig.* xxii. 5. 3. 5, 5. 4; in 5. 3 *pr.* the patron is significantly absent; cf. *Coll.* ix. 2; *ILS* 6087, xcv (Urso), where *patronus* is correlative to *libertus*.

compelled to give evidence against each other (this also applied to the freedmen of patrons' children, parents, or spouse), but apparently did not exclude such evidence given voluntarily, and in any case did not concern the freedmen's freeborn descendants, still less clients with no taint of servile blood. A similar provision occurs in the Caesarian charter of Urso, which is in part tralatician. So too it is only the freedman, and not his freeborn descendants, who under the praetor's edict (which is generally held to have been little altered after the Republic) is debarred from suing patron, or his children or parents, except with the praetor's sanction (which would be forthcoming unless the action was *famosa*). The freedman could also sue his patron for *iniuria atrox*, for instance if he had received a severe beating. (Some scholars hold that this concession is 'post-classical'; that would have the implication, which I find bizarre, that freedmen were better protected by the law in the increasingly hierarchical society of the late Empire.) He was also permitted to defend his property rights against the patron.[94] But he might not charge him with a crime, except for murder of his kin, adultery with his wife, or treason.[95]

In all this there is not a word of freeborn clients. Their right to proceed against patrons seems to be quite unrestricted. They are actually mentioned no more than five times in the *Digest*.[96] It may be said that all this evidence is imperial, and that the fewness of allusions to clientage in the legal texts fails to show that it was not more important in the Republic. But literary testimony proves that great men continued to have just as extensive patronage as in the past in the time of Tacitus, Martial, and Juvenal (n. 155). The juristic texts are mostly of still later date, but there is no reason to think that the social and economic importance of patronage was diminishing: it was to reach its apogee in the late empire (nn. 4, 156).

Perhaps it might be thought that the jurists would not be concerned with a relationship that created obligations of *fides* not enforceable in the courts. However, the case-law in which the *Digest* abounds is full of allusions to the social context of litigation. Moreover, other relationships of *fides* generated or influenced numerous institutions of Roman law, such as *fiducia, fideipromissio, fideicommissa*, some of which go back to

---

[94] *Dig.* ii. 4. 4. 1, 4. 8. 1–10, 12, xxxvii. 15, 2, xlvii. 10. 11. 7, xlviii. 2. 11. 1 (cf. xliii. 16. 1. 43), 5. 39. 9. In iv. 3. 11 the *humilis* too is barred from the *actio de dolo* against a man of high degree, e.g. a consular (but not a patron as such); Garnsey, 1970, 181 ff., thinks this may be Augustan; the second century seems to me more likely.

[95] xlviii. 2. 8, 2. 11 *pr.*, 4. 7. 2, 5. 39. 9. Cf. n. 129.

[96] vii. 8. 3, ix. 3. 5. 1, xxviii. 9. 3. 6 (texts which show that clients might get free lodging and maintenance; the reference to Rutilius in vii. 8. 10. 3 indicates that this was a Republican practice; it was not only freedmen and clients who could benefit; cf. Michel 42–55), xlvii. 2. 90 (n. 70), xlix. 15. 1 (n. 76 with text); xlvii. 10. 15. 23, without naming clients refers to their *adsectatio*.

the second century BC or beyond; it was probably in the third that the praetor began to give binding effect in law to some at least of the consensual *bonae fidei* contracts. Ties of *amicitia* are mentioned quite often; they sometimes affect legal rights and obligations, and indeed originated some legal institutions like *mandatum*.[97] But no such influence of clientship can be detected.

The draftsmen of second-century laws did think it appropriate, as we have seen, to give legal force to the mutual obligations of patrons and clients, but their successors did not. We may contrast their attitude to the relationship between patrons and their *freedmen*. The honour morally due from the freedman to his former master is never forgotten: 'the freedman and the son should always treat the person of the patron and father with honour and veneration'.[98] No such consideration operates with regard to patrons and freeborn clients. The law of guardianship affords one illustration. Servius Sulpicius declared that its purpose was no longer to preserve the property during a minority for the next heir, but to protect the minor himself (*Dig.* xxvi. 1, 1 *pr.*). If a minor has no *tutor testamentarius* or *legitimus*, his kinsmen or father's friends and freedmen, but not his patron or client, have a right, and in some cases an obligation, to apply to the praetor for the appointment of a *tutor*. Nor is there any suggestion that a patron would be the appropriate choice, whereas the patron of a *freedman's* son, if also his intestate heir, would be his *tutor legitimus* (*Dig.* xxvi. 6. 2, *pr.* 1). Now appointment of a *tutor* by the praetor went back to the *lex Atilia*, earlier than 186 BC (Livy xxxix. 9. 7); significantly he had to obtain the concurrence of a majority of the tribunes (Gaius i. 185), the traditional guardians of the common people. Diodorus, presumably drawing on Posidonius, tells of a praetor, probably L. Sempronius Asellio (*c.*96), who was outstanding for his justice, and who would commonly name himself; he also took great care in succouring victims of oppression; the context suggests that he would hinder *tutores* from pillaging the estates of their wards (xxxvii. 8. 4). In that case the safeguards devised by the *lex Atilia* had not always been effective. Perhaps the legislator had had it in mind that patrons were not to be trusted with the property of their clients under age; at any rate it is clear that the law never treated them as the natural candidates for guardianship.

Similarly, if a free man in slavery does not exercise his right to proclaim his title to freedom, a parent or kinsman may act on his behalf, and so may a patron on behalf of his freedman, but not a patron on behalf of a freeborn client (*Dig.* xl. 12, 1–6). Or again

[97] Michel 555–77 (though not all his texts expressly mention *amici*); see esp. 568 on *tutela*. Note *Dig.* iii. 1. 1. 2, xxxix. 5. 5.

[98] *Dig.* xxxvii. 15 *passim*, esp. 9.

servitudes can be exercised or retained through slaves, tenants, friends, and *hospites*, but not through patrons or clients (xliii. 19. 3. 4; cf. 1. 7 f.).

All this surely betokens that the ties between patrons and clients had weakened in the Republic, and were not given legal force even in the Principate, when there is reason to believe that patronage was acquiring or regaining greater importance.

In the old days, according to Horace (*Odes* iii. 5. 52) patrons would arbitrate between their clients, and according to Dionysius, would interpret the law for them and represent them in court. In Plautus' *Menoechmi* (571 ff.) we read 'that a summons to appear in court is directed not only to the defendants but to his patron too'. 'Our ancestors', declared Cicero, 'did not wish even the humblest citizen to be in want of a *patronus* to plead his cause.' The patrons of Sextus Roscius at least engaged the young Cicero to defend him on their behalf. Cicero recalls that the houses of jurisconsults like Sex. Aelius (*cos.* 198), Manius Manilius (*cos.* 149), and Quintus Mucius (*cos.* 117), and still earlier worthies, were thronged with men who would consult them not only on the law but on the marriage of daughters, purchase of farms, cultivation of the land, and any obligation or business. However, their doors were open not only to clients but 'to all citizens'.[99] Cicero himself would refuse no one an audience.[100]

By their practice jurists, still more orators, could increase their *opes* and *gratia*;[101] their aim was not simply to fulfil hereditary obligations but also to extend their influence, and perhaps to render a public service. The magnates needed ample room in their mansions to accommodate visitors,[102] but though many of these would be clients who, according to Pliny (*NH* xxxiv. 17), would set up statues of their patrons in the *atria*, many would also be 'friends', often men of rank, going on the round of salutations which is best attested for the Principate,[103] but which had already become the vogue in Polybius' day (n. 14). Gaius Gracchus and Drusus, tribune in 91, had to divide such 'friends' into three categories, those they received singly, in groups, and *en masse*.[104] Although both belonged to great families, hereditary patronage cannot explain why they were courted by

---

[99] Cic. *Mur.* 10, *Rosc. Amer.* 5, 28, 30, 77, 149, *de orat.* iii. 133 (cf. i. 199 f.), *de leg.* i. 10–12; Hor. *Ep.* ii. 1. 103. Thrasea Paetus would devote himself to 'clientium negotia' on retiring from public life (Tac. *Ann.* xvi. 22).

[100] *Planc.* 66; cf. *Att.* ii. 22. 2.   [101] *de offic.* ii. 65 f.; cf. *Mur.* 23 ff.

[102] E. Wistrand, *Eranos* 1970, 191 ff., *Opera Selecta*, 1972, 469 f. Cf. *de offic.* i. 139; Stat. *Theb.* i. 146.

[103] Friedländer, *Sitteng. Roms*⁹, 1919, i. 223 ff. (Eng. tr. from 7th edn., *Roman Life and Manners*, i. 195 ff.). Rouland 557 ff. seems willing to treat *salutatores* of rank as clients! The same *salutatores* would visit rival candidates for office (*Comm. Pet.* 35).

[104] Sen. *de benef.* vi. 34.

exceptional numbers of visitors: most of these men were not family dependants but political followers or time-servers attracted to them by the great power they had temporarily acquired by their legislative programmes.

In Cicero's day moral obligations might sit lightly on patrons. He speaks of it as an admirable practice of the past that Rome's great men would prosecute governors for despoiling their provincial clients. In fact the numerous patrons of the Sicilians did little to protect their dependants against Verres: some actually aided the culprit. If provincial patronage had afforded effective aid to the subject, oppressive government would have been less common.[105] No doubt the magnates were readier to advise and sustain citizens and citizen communities: they had votes.[106] (This was perhaps one reason why the Italians were so bent on obtaining voting rights in and after 90.) The claims of *fides* counted for less than selfish interests; perhaps that had also been true in the 'good old days'!

Dionysius thought that patrons and clients had once given each other mutual aid of a material kind (ii. 10. 2). No doubt the free meals and *sportulae* that clients at Rome could obtain from the great houses in the Principate (n. 109) were not unknown in the Republic. Legal texts show that lodging and maintenance might be given (n. 96). But Cicero says that most men of his own class preferred to confer benefits on the rich, who were best able to reciprocate (*de offic.* ii. 69). Plautus had made the same suggestion (*Men.* 578 f.). In the Principate it seems to have been common for men to make provision for maintaining their poor freedmen (*Dig.* xxxiv. 1); otherwise their patronage was ultimately lost (xxxvii. 14. 5). But we hear of no such arrangements for their freeborn clients.

What of the material aid that clients, according to Dionysius, had once rendered patrons? Livy has a tale that in 187 L. Scipio's kin, friends, and clients offered to pay his fine (n. 59). I know of no later instance of *Roman* clients acting in this way. We never hear in the historic period of their contributing to a candidate's electoral expenses. *Provincial* clients undoubtedly gave their patrons pecuniary assistance; for example, the Sicilians helped Cicero to bear the costs of the aedileship in 69.[107] Plutarch thought that patrons came to be ashamed to demand such subventions (n. 60). Probably he had read that the practice had ceased, but his explanation need not necessarily be credited. It may be that Roman clients resented claims

---

[105] *Div. Caec.* 66–9; cf. Brunt, *Chiron* 1980, 273 ff.

[106] e.g. Cic. *Att.* iv. 15. 5 with Varro, *RR* iii. 2. 3. This practice continued in the Principate (nn. 156 f.).

[107] Plut. *Cic.* 8. Shatzman 86, and Badian, 1958, 161, give further evidence.

on their pockets. And they had the voting rights to curtail them by law.

Macrobius tells us that 'inasmuch as many took the Saturnalia as an occasion to make greedy and presumptuous demands for *munera* from their clients, and this burden fell heavily on the poor, Publicius, tribune of the plebs, enacted that only wax tapers should be sent to men of greater wealth'.[108] This law seems to belong to the same period as the Cincian law of 204, which forbade advocates to take fees, a prohibition that was not in the end very effective. The law had a wider scope: Cato, according to Livy, said that it was designed to prevent the commons from becoming tributary to the senate, and it restricted 'dona et munera' in general, except between persons within specified degrees of kinship and between patrons and *freedmen*; in the later law the latter could be required to maintain indigent patrons and their children (*Dig.* xxv. 5. 18 ff., xxix. 2. 73). Once again no such rules apply as between patrons and clients. The Publician law, which I take to be earlier, concerned only gifts at the Saturnalia, the Cincian gifts at all times. Neither stopped patrons bestowing *sportulae* on clients, and in the Principate we still find clients making small regular presents to patrons; we cannot be sure whether the Cincian law actually allowed gifts of limited value, or was inadequately enforced. In any event it is clear that the people wished to relieve clients of burdens; the legislation can hardly have been welcome to patrons in general, even though Q. Fabius Cunctator backed the Cincian law.[109]

Horace portrays a grasping landowner who entrenches on the land of his neighbours and drives them by violence from their farms, though they are his own clients (*Odes* ii. 18. 23. ff.). Whether or not such behaviour was common, it is beyond question that in one way or another the rich were enlarging their private holdings of land in the pre-Gracchan era and annexing more and more of the public domain. If the peasants who were thus deprived of their livelihood were not clients, it follows that clientage was far from extending to the whole body of the commons; if they were, patrons failed to give them protection. The large landowners, moreover, preferred to employ slaves in cultivation rather than humble dependants. It was in these conditions that Tiberius Gracchus could carry his agrarian bill. Like his brother, he and their few associates among the nobility naturally had their own clients, but they must have been outmatched by those of

---

[108] Macrob. i. 7. 33; cf. Mart. x. 87. 5; 'cereus aridi clientis'.

[109] Cic. *de orat.* ii. 286,, *de senect.* 10; Livy xxxiv. 4. 9; *Vat. fr.* 260–316; see M. Kaser, *Röm. Privatrecht*², 602 ff.; cf. n. 73 above. Advocates' fees: Tac. *Ann.* xi. 5 f. and commentaries thereon. The small gifts that peasants brought to a grandee's villa in Mart. iii. 58. 33 ff. may illustrate a custom that could have been onerous. Martial also refers to gifts from clients in iv. 88. 4; viii. 33. 11, xiii. 27. But it is imprudent to use imperial texts for the Republic, cf. p. 440.

their adversaries, who preponderated in the aristocracy. In fact we hear almost nothing of clients on either side. The massed supporters of Tiberius were clearly rustics who hoped for allotments, just as those who thronged round his brother were prospective beneficiaries of his programme.[110] Gaius of course appealed also to the urban plebs, the Equites, and the Italians. If their opponents too could eventually mobilize equestrian or Italian support (Sall. *BJ* 42. 1), it was surely when Equites or Italians (cf. App. i. 19), or some sections among them, felt that their own interests were prejudiced by the reformers. Neither then nor in the case of later popular proposals do we hear of appeals to clients either by *populares* or by optimates. The antagonists play on sectional interests, or invoke political principles: they can seldom rely on the allegiance of personal followers (cf. section VI).

The Gracchi were not of course the first to force through laws against the opposition of the greater part of the nobility, who, it must be assumed, had the most clients. We may think of Flaminius' agrarian law, and of the Claudian law of 218 (p. 173), or of the Porcian laws on *provocatio* (ch. 6 endnote 8), and not least of the introduction of the ballot for elections in 137, for popular trials except in cases of *perduellio* in 137, for legislation in 131, and for trials of *perduellio* in 107 (see p. 340). Obviously the ballot diminished the ability of patrons to bring pressure on client voters; however, we must bear in mind that all the laws mentioned except the last, and also Tiberius Gracchus' agrarian law, were passed by open voting.

We must not indeed regard the ballot as crucial to the independence of the assemblies in the post-Gracchan period. It is significant that Sulla did not repeal them; he thought it enough to deprive tribunes of their rights to initiate legislation and perhaps to bring criminal prosecutions before the assembly (ch. 6 n. 134). The ballot did not remove any sense of moral obligation or sentimental attachment to patrons that clients may have felt: it only restricted intimidation. Still, the laws indicate that patrons were thought to be resorting to such pressure, and not merely trusting the loyalty of their dependants, and that this was resented, if not by the clients themselves, then by independent voters, who were sufficiently numerous to carry them. Bleicken's comment that the ballot destroyed the relation of the assemblies to the real social structure based on clientage is perverse.[111] It exaggerates the effects of secret voting, and blurs the truth that an effective majority of voters were already not invariably, if ever, the mere tools of noble patrons. The ties of clientship, so far as they existed,

---

[110] Vell. ii. 7. 3 (mentioning C. Gracchus' clients); Plut. *Ti. Gr.* 13. 2; cf. 12. 4 for their friends and freedmen. Gracchan supporters: Asellio *ap.* Gell. ii. 13; App. i. 10, 21; Plut. *C. Gr.* 6. 3, etc.

[111] Bleicken, 1975, 278 ff.

were too weak to keep the masses obedient, when patrons were responsible for, or oblivious to, grave social and economic grievances. The oligarchs could actually become the objects of popular hatred, as shown in the last two decades of the second century.[112] This was at least as much a part of the social reality as personal allegiance, and clearly had much more effect on the course of events. Equally the patronage that the great houses presumably had over Equites and the gentry of the Italian towns (disguised or attenuated as it might be under the names of friendship or *hospitium*) did not inhibit the conflicts of the senatorial and equestrian orders or the revolt of the allies. It is only in elections to the higher offices that it seems plausible to see the strength of aristocratic patronage. But here too closer investigation suggests that its importance is usually exaggerated.

V

It was in elections, especially to the consulship, that the nobility generally continued to dominate the assembly. Five out of six consuls throughout the period from 199 to 49 were of consular descent. Most of the rest belonged to well-established praetorian houses. When mere parvenus were returned, they were usually leagued with influential aristocrats. It was exceptional when Marius was elected for 107 against the united opposition of the nobility. In the same decade three other new men were returned, and what with Marius' repeated re-elections, only twelve members of consular lineage were successful.[113] The hatred that the nobility had inspired among the masses by their cruel suppression of the Gracchi and their partisans cannot fully account for this, since in the centuriate assembly it was citizens of substance whose votes were normally decisive. Imputations of corruption and the military disasters brought on by incompetent aristocratic commanders had for the time weakened the prestige of the nobility, and the influence of patrons could not avail against the supposed interests of the commonwealth (n. 112).

It seems to me erroneous to believe that patronage was more than one factor in accounting for the normal preponderance of noble names in the list of consuls. Very few even of the greatest families could secure the office in each successive generation. Some of them fell into

---

[112] Sall. *BJ* 5. 1, 16. 2, 30 f., 32. 5, 40. 3, 65. 5, 73; Plut. *C. Gr.* 18. The elections of Marius and of other *novi* (in 105 and 104; Billienus too was nearly successful, Cic. *Brut.* 75) as consuls, the trials under the Mamilian law, and the impeachments of aristocratic generals in the last decade of the century variously illustrate the resentments of the common people, and to some extent of men of substance outside the senatorial order.

[113] Brunt, *JRS* 1982, 1 ff. Hopkins, 1983, ch. 2, presents more schematically but with great force the limits within which consular families monopolized high office.

prolonged oblivion. Their own dependants could not save them from this fate; of course they could never have been sufficiently numerous to assure them of a majority of the polls, and it is a matter of speculation how far their close friends could bring out their clients to vote as they directed. The reputed merits of individual candidates must have had some effect on the electorate. In my judgement there was a general proclivity to prefer men whose ancestors had served the state well. And the inherited wealth of the nobility enabled them to acquire *gratia* among the people at large.[114] Impoverishment probably often explains the eclipse of some lines, like that of the Aemilii Scauri (n. 36).

Legitimate munificence could be supplemented by sheer corruption. Numerous attempts were made to repress this by law. To say nothing of earlier legislation, a law of unknown date and authorship constituted a permanent court for charges of *ambitus*, by which Marius was tried in 116 (Plut. *Mar.* 5). The provisions of a presumably Sullan law were sharpened by the *lex Calpurnia* of 67, under which the consuls elect for 65 were to be unseated and disqualified for office. This too proved insufficiently effective; the senate in 64 recommended a further measure, which a tribune vetoed, but Cicero in 63 succeeded in passing a new enactment. Again this did not suffice: in 61 the senate vainly tried to promote more rigorous legislation. It appears that a systematic organization had developed through the agency of *sodalitates* or *collegia sodalicia* with tribal *divisores* to distribute and *sequestres* to hold the cash, whose members were 'enrolled' ('conscripti') and brigaded in decuries; they could also be used for violence and intimidation. In 56 the senate decreed that they should be dissolved, and that in case of disobedience the penalties of *vis* should apply. This decree, once more, had no force, but it seems to have been the basis of a law enacted by Crassus as consul in 55 against such *collegia*, under which men were certainly charged with corrupt practices.[115] However, both bribery and violence reached a crescendo in 54 and 53. As sole consul Pompey passed yet another law in 52, which Velleius thought effective (ii. 47); and

---

[114] Shatzman 84–90, 159–65; on the Domitii Ahenobarbi and Metelli see Brunt, *Latomus* 1975, 84 ff. Gelzer, 1969, 110 ff, recognized the magnates' need for wealth without bringing out the implication that the support of friends and clients could not assure success. Note the collocations in Ter. *Ad.* 502: 'potentes dites fortunati nobiles' and *Heaut. Tim.* 227: 'potens procax magnifica sumptuosa nobilitas'; Sall. *BJ* 85. 4 ('cognatorum et adfinium opes') no doubt implies that kinsmen by blood and marriage would help from their own resources. Munificence: Cic. *de offic.* ii. 52–64. Individual distinction: ibid. ii. 45–51, 65 f. (military, oratorical, juristic in descending order; cf. *Mur.* 20–42).

[115] Mommsen, *Strafr.* 865 ff. Sullan law: Schol. Bobb. on Cic. *Sulla* 7, 78 St. *Lex Calpurnia*: *MRR* ii. 142. *SC* of 64 and *lex Tullia*: Ascon. 83, 88 C.; Cic. *Mur.* 3, 47, 67, 71 (the *lex Fabia* cannot be precisely dated); *MRR* 166. *SC* and *rogatio* of 61: Cic. *Att.* i. 16. 12 f., 18. 3. *SC* of 56 and *lex Licinia*: Qu. *fr.* ii. 3. 5, *Planc.* 36–48 with Schol. Bobb. 152 St.; cf. Gruen, 1974, ch. VI. On the legislation in general and esp. on the last law: Taylor, 1949, 62 ff. is helpful. *Divisores*:

certainly we hear nothing of corruption in the last three years of the free Republic.

Gruen suggests that its prevalence in the post-Sullan era is often exaggerated on the ground that it is only actually attested in nine years and that 'formal charges grew out of the campaigns' in only four. More generally candidates for the consulship were returned 'as patrons, benefactors, and heirs of illustrious *gentes*', occasionally as adherents of others who had a similar following. In fact, however, we can seldom judge why the electors preferred particular candidates, if only because we often do not know whom they rejected; we have no information, or virtually none, about the circumstances of most elections.[116] The multiplication of senatorial decrees and laws on corruption is alone proof that the evil was rampant. The difficulty of obtaining convictions must have deterred prosecutions; Murena, for example, was pretty clearly guilty, yet he was acquitted. There were obvious disadvantages of incurring dangerous enmities by bringing accusations unlikely to succeed. Gruen remarks that imputations of bribery might be unfair, but they must have had at least the plausibility that derived from the frequency of the practice.

Some of the cases in which such allegations were made have particular significance because they imply that it was true, or plausible, that candidates of the highest lineage or attainments, or their most influential supporters, could not dispense with corruption. Thus Cicero suggested that in the elections of 70 Q. Hortensius and Q. Metellus Celer relied on largess from Verres' coffers; yet the former was leader of the bar, and the latter the scion of a family which had enjoyed unexampled electoral success for two generations; however, he had been a candidate for the praetorship of 74, and if all had gone smoothly for him, should have been praetor that year and consul in 71. One of the disqualified candidates in 66, whom the voters had preferred to an Aurelius and a Manlius, was P. Autronius, who was not of consular descent. For all his personal popularity and resplendent birth Caesar in 60 thought it prudent to enter into a coalition with L. Lucceius (who was at best of praetorian lineage): Lucceius' role was to furnish cash in their joint behalf. (It did him no good; Caesar was returned along with

---

StR iii³. 196 (esp. Cic. I *Verr.* 22 f., *de har. resp.* 42, *ap.* Ascon. 74 C. *Att.* i. 16. 12, *Planc.* 45–8 and 55). *Sequestres*: Cic. *ap.* Ascon. 83 C., *Planc.* 38. *Decuriae* and *conscriptio*: *Planc.* 45, 47. *Sodalitates*, once respectable associations for sacral and convivial purposes (Cic. *de amic.* 45, *de orat.* ii. 200, II *Verr.* i. 93, *Mur.* 56) had come to denote organizations for political ends (perhaps *Comm. Pet.* 19) and, in fact, for corruption (*Planc.* 46). Cf. ch. 9 n. 8.

[116] Gruen, 1974, ch. IV, esp. pp. 127 ('Ties of patronage, which bound the voting populace to the dominant clans of the aristocracy, remained unbroken.') and 159–61; the chapter is a tissue of speculative explanations for the return of particular candidates, which also rests on his belief in aristocratic factions. But it contains the evidence for what follows on consular elections; it is his interpretations that need to be treated with caution.

his political and personal foe, Bibulus.) Pompey had in the previous year resorted to bribes to secure the return of his protégé Afranius. He himself and Crassus, it may be noted, had to employ outright violence for their own election as consuls of 55. Most remarkable of all is the electoral campaign of 54.[117] Three of the candidates were of consular houses, M. Aemilius Scaurus, Cn. Domitius Calvinus, and M. Valerius Messalla; the fourth, C. Memmius, had the backing of Caesar and Pompey, who also gave initial and (it was thought) insincere support to Scaurus. The latter could appeal to the greatness of his father's name, which still counted with 'country people' (*Att.* iv. 16. 6), but he had also lavished his wealth on aedilician games. Domitius and Messalla too had displayed munificence, and Domitius' claims were urged by many friends. Yet he and Memmius thought it advisable to make an infamous pact with the consuls, who were somehow to help engineer their return; and all four resorted to bribery to an extent that doubled the rate of interest. All were accused of the offence, and ultimately Messalla (who was returned with Domitius), Scaurus, and Memmius were convicted.

These men, it is patent, could not depend simply on birth, connections, and patronage for success. Among the consular candidates in 65, the patrician P. Sulpicius Galba was being plainly refused support; neither he nor L. Cassius Longinus was a serious rival to Cicero in the following year despite their lineage. (Admittedly no Galba had been consul since 145; another member of the house, backed by Caesar, failed in 50.) In 65 two other candidates of consular family, Q. Minucius Thermus and D. Iunius Silanus, are described by Cicero as poor in reputation and friends; however, he notes that the former had gained by having been *curator* of the Via Flaminia, presumably because the post had given him the opportunity to confer benefits and win *new* personal adherents, rather as Murena was to ingratiate himself with voters in Umbria by his conduct of the levy there (Cic. *Mur.* 42). It is no part of my contention that *gratia* acquired in such ways (as by munificence), did not count: it is very different from hereditary patronage. (It may be that Thermus was actually elected for 64; certainly Silanus was returned in 63.)[118] In all these accounts of electoral campaigns we hear nothing of clients, unless in the reference to the *éclat* of Scaurus' name with the country people. Our best evidence, however, comes perhaps from the *Commentariolum Petitionis*,

---

[117] See esp. Cic. *Att.* iv. 15. 7, 16. 6, 17. 2, 5, *Qu. fr.* iii. 1. 16, 2. 3, 3. 2, 6. 3, 7. 3; Ascon. 18–20 C. Cf. p. 475. Scaurus and Memmius were convicted in 52 (App. ii. 24), Messalla, acquitted *de ambitu* in 51, was condemned *de sodaliciis* (Cic. *Fam.* viii. 2. 1, 4. 1).

[118] *Att.* i. 1 f. (cf. Shackleton Bailey on Thermus' possible identity with C. Marcius Figulus, *cos.* 64); Ascon. 82 C.; *Comm. Pet.* 7.

and certainly from the speeches in which Cicero defended Murena and Plancius on charges of corruption. Here too there is little to suggest that patronage did much to decide elections.

The former work is at least well-informed about conditions in the late Republic, whether or not its attribution to Quintus Cicero be accepted. It purports to advise Cicero on canvassing. As a new man Cicero naturally had no hereditary clients unless in his native Arpinum. How far he had yet personally secured the extensive patronage which he eventually possessed (n. 39) we cannot say with precision, but he already had a claim of gratitude for services rendered to the publicans, most Equites, many *municipia*, *collegia*, and *sodalitates*, and various individuals (3, 8, 16–20, 33, 50, 55). They must, however, all be constantly reminded of their obligations (38), and it is not only benefits previously received that are likely to affect votes but the prospect of favours to come (22, 26, 40, 49). Cicero must personally canvass all and sundry (41 ff.); we know that he adopted this precept in 65 as far afield as Cisalpine Gaul (*Att.* i. 1. 2). He was then plainly hoping for indications of support from the nobility and from Pompey; the pamphlet bids him cultivate consulars, nobles, and other senators (4–6, 29), while contriving to suggest that his return will be agreeable to Pompey (cf. ch. 9 n. 50).But he must also woo persons of influence in their own towns and regions, and freedmen in the city itself.[119] It is evident that some of these could deliver more votes than their own, but also that they would not themselves necessarily act at the command of noble patrons. Even freedmen are taken to be potentially independent; as for municipal gentry, they were likely to have had connections with several of the great families at Rome, and could doubtless steer a delicate course between them if those families were themselves not united. Cicero's success will rest partly on his own reputation and his energy in the canvass, partly on the zeal of his friends, partly on popular sentiment (16; cf. 41 ff.). It is in the last context that we find the only allusion to his own clients. He must show that he is loved by his friends, fellow-tribesmen, neighbours, clients, freedmen, and *slaves* (17)! Their enthusiasm will prove to others that he deserves their votes; his *gratia* among men who know him will be proof of his *merita*. Similarly in his defence of Murena there is only one allusion to clients (in that of Plancius there is none):

[119] *Comm. Pet.* 24, 29 (freedmen; some leading men in urban *collegia* (cf. 30) would be in this class), 30–2; Cicero can count on some, apparently *municipales*, 'propter suam ambitionem, qui apud tribules suos plurimum possunt', presumably men, like Plancius, themselves aspiring to a senatorial career; others have influence 'apud aliquem partem tribulium' (ibid. 32); since many or most rural tribes were since the Social war geographically fragmented, it is in fact rather unlikely that anyone (even a Roman aristocrat) had influence extending to the whole tribe; cf. n. 125. See also pp. 126 f., 128.

Murena canvassed with a cortège, partly consisting of clients, neighbours, fellow-tribesmen, and Lucullus' soldiers, with other humble citizens, who, the prosecution doubtless alleged, were mere hirelings. The votes of the poor, among whom we must reckon soldiers, counted for almost nothing in the centuriate assembly: Murena's purpose was to parade the good opinions he inspired. Cicero claims that the soldiers' commendations of his military prowess carried *auctoritas* with the electorate at large.[120]

In the end Cicero carried every century of the first two property classes and the Equites, which gave him the absolute majority required (ch. 6 n. 164). Sallust implies that the ill-repute of his two principal rivals, Antonius and Catiline, both nobles, who relied on corruption if we believe Cicero (*ap.* Ascon. 83 C.), induced the nobility to support him (*Cat.* 23), and Plutarch was surely right that fear of disorder brought all respectable people to his side (*Cic.* 10); that best explains their unanimity.

Murena and Plancius were each prosecuted for corrupt practices by defeated competitors, who argued *inter alia* that only bribery could explain why they had not been preferred for their more splendid lineage. Cicero, who was able to reply in the case of Murena that his descent was not truly inferior to that of the prosecutor, Servius Sulpicius, rejects this contention: the people had to be wooed; they were capricious, volatile, unpredictable; they had often preferred to nobles men inferior both in rank and in other respects for reasons that in retrospect still remained obscure; moreover, the prosecutors of Murena and Plancius had been insufficiently assiduous and deferential in courting their favour.[121] The prosecutors also claimed that they were superior in ability and previous services to the state; Cicero compares the past careers of the rivals to subvert this assertion.[122] Both sides assumed that *merita* in public life mattered as well as *gratia*. But as to *gratia* Cicero stresses Murena's munificence (which may have contravened the law) to the whole plebs, and the benefits he had personally conferred on Umbrian towns and on Romans with affairs in Transalpine Gaul; he does not speak of inherited patronage (and neither Murena nor his adversary Sulpicius may have had much of that). By contrast Sulpicius had offended 'men of rank and influence in their own neighbourhoods and towns'. Here again there is a suggestion that local magnates could influence votes in their home districts, but

---

[120] *Mur.* 37 f., 69–72. The soldiers were not even numerous (*contra* Gruen, 1974, 129), some 1600 men (*IM* 457). Parallels: *Att.* iv. 16, 6, Livy xlv. 35. 8 f.

[121] *Mur.* 15–17, 35 f., 43–8, 53, *Planc.* 6–18, 31–5, 50–3. Cf. *Comm. Pet.* 11. The end of elections by the people released senators 'largitionibus ac precibus sordidis' (Tac. *Ann.* i. 15).

[122] *Mur.* 18–34, 41 f., *Planc.* 13, 27 f., 61–3, 67, 77.

also that they were independent themselves.[123] Plancius too enjoyed powerful backing not only from his father's publican friends but from his compatriots at Atina and populous places in the vicinity. Cicero recalls that he had had similar regional support in his own electioneering. Plancius' influence among his neighbours was partly inherited, partly due to the favours he had himself bestowed. It was, according to Cicero, traditional for men to be liberal to their own tribesmen, to win them over ('conficere') for their friends, and to expect friends to do the same for them. Bribery in such circumstances was an absurd imputation.[124]

Cicero claims that he could name the person by whose efforts ('studio') any tribe had been carried in the aedilician election at which Plancius was returned. This boast should not be taken too seriously. If the electoral behaviour of the people as a whole was incalculable, that must also have been true of most of the voting units. Few tribes can have been at the disposal of a single magnate. L. R. Taylor pointed out that both Caesar and his irreconcilable adversary, L. Domitius Ahenobarbus, were registered in the Fabian tribe and that both surely had much influence within it; in most tribes there must have been many such persons.[125] There is a similar exaggeration in a letter Cicero wrote to D. Brutus in 43, urging him to win over for a particular candidate the equestrian centuries 'in which you are sovereign' (*Fam.* xi. 16); in this case it seems likely to me that Cicero assumed that these centuries strongly approved of the 'tyrannicide' of Caesar, and would follow advice tendered by Brutus, the most eminent of the 'Liberators' still in Italy at the time. The extensive canvassing to which he himself, Murena, and Plancius all had resort, the importance of munificence and bribery, the weight attached to the past careers of candidates, all go to show that election did not turn on the support of a handful of powerful patrons. The magnates could not even rely on the obedience of their own freedmen.[126] The votes of humble clients, who might often be mere dependants of a single family, could seldom affect the issue, at least in the centuriate assembly, but a display of their loyalty

---

[123] *Mur.* 37, 42, 47, 72–7, *Planc.* 67; cf. *Comm. Pet.* 30–2.

[124] *Planc.* 19–22, 45, 48, cf. Mur. 69. *Vicinus* and cognate words are as common in Cicero, in reference to Italians, as *cliens*. On *tribules*, StR iii³. 197 (surely overstating the familiarity among them in this period; cf. n. 119).

[125] *Planc.* 48; cf. Taylor 1949, 62 ff.; she quotes *Phil.* ii. 4, where Cicero alleges that in 50 Antony could not have carried a single tribe without Curio's help, but that probably refers to Curio's influence as a popular tribune. Cf. n. 119.

[126] Dionys. iv. 23, 6 supposed that freedmen and their posterity would vote for their patrons (cf. Rouland 86). Most freedmen were confined to the four urban tribes, and rich freedmen may actually have preponderated in the centuries of those tribes in the higher *classes*; in Succusana and Esquilina at least there might have been no senators or equestrian *iudices* enrolled in AD 5 (EJ 94a. v. 33). If the nobility could generally count on freedmen backing their patrons, that might provide a paradoxical explanation of their consistent opposition to the redistribution of freedmen in the rural tribes (Treggiari 37 ff.). But some freedmen seem to be independent.

might impress uncommitted voters.[127] Men of higher status undoubtedly had connections with Roman aristocrats, and could bring out their own associates to vote with them, but they had to be courted directly, probably because those connections, often better described as relationships of *amicitia* or *hospitium* rather than of clientage, were so varied and so likely to result in conflicting obligations that they were free to make their own choice. Patronage was only one of many factors that affected voting behaviour, and the evidence does not warrant the conclusion that it counted more than any other; rather it suggests that it was of subordinate importance.[128]

VI

In the late Republic violence became endemic. How far could the magnates rely on the allegiance of clients?

Many stories of the adventures of men proscribed in the 80s and 40s illustrate the loyalty or treachery of wives, kinsmen, freedmen, and slaves. I can find only a solitary case in which a man was harboured by his client;[129] one might add that a former client of P. Clodius revenged his patron by revealing Cicero's whereabouts to Antony's cutthroats (App. iv. 19). A faithless client is said to have cut off Gaius Gracchus' head.[130] 'Friends' occasionally appear in the stories, and some may in reality have been dependants.[131]

In the second century the praetor found it necessary to protect men forcibly ejected from their possessions by the interdict *de vi*. In Cicero's time still sharper remedies were devised against the illegal use of armed force. They expressly relate to ejection by a man's *familia* or *procurator* as well as by himself. The *familia* consisted of the slaves, and in the 70s misdeeds effected by armed gangs of slaves on distant estates had become common (Cic. *Tull.* 8–11). The term *procurator* could include a tenant, neighbour, client, or freedman, but any such person exposed his principal to legal action only as his agent and not as a direct

---

[127] Electioneering at Pompeii in the first century AD may present some analogies to that of Republican Rome. J. L. Franklin, *Pompeii, the Electoral Propaganda*, AD 71–9 (Mem. of Amer. Acad. Rome) 1980, concludes that clients could be expected to vote for their patrons, unless their loyalty was divided between more than one (106 f.), but that they did not consistently follow patrons' lead in voting for others, and sometimes had to be incited to do their duty (111 ff.). Support from neighbours is also attested (92 f.). Clients often recommend the good qualities of their patrons to uncommitted voters. Cf. P. Castren, *Ordo Populusque Pompeianus*, 1975, 127 ff.

[128] See endnote 2.   [129] App. iv. 18; cf. Val. Max. ix. 11. 6.

[130] App. i. 26 with Gabba ad loc.

[131] App. i. 60–2, 72–4, 95 f., iv. 12–29, 36–51; Dio xlvii. 3–11; cf. Vell. ii. 67. 2: 'fuisse in proscriptos uxorum fidem summam, libertorum mediam, servorum aliquam, filiorum nullam' (nothing on clients). Anecdotes in Val. Max. iv. 7. 1–6 relate to similar conditions. Tac. *Hist.* i. 81, iii. 73 f., 86 does tell of patrons hiding with clients in AD 69.

consequence of the other relationships named (Cic. *Caec.* 57). By
Cicero's account Caecina was dispossessed by a band of armed men,
some of whom were free (ibid. 20); they may have been clients of his
adversary, but in any case we may suppose them to have been hired
labourers (cf. Varro, *RR* i. 17. 3), who as such would have been so
economically dependent on their employer as to perform his illegal
orders.[132] In any event clientage had long existed, and had once been
a more vital element in Roman society than it was by this time; the
spread of rural violence was clearly a new phenomenon requiring new
remedies in the second and first centuries, to be associated with the
increased use of slaves. In scenes of political violence slaves also
frequently appear.

Gruen indeed makes out that in the broils in Rome itself patrons
often called on the strong arms of their clients. This is characteristic of
the modern fashion of superimposing clientship on the evidence. Turn
to the pages in which his admirable index registers clients, and you will
seldom find them in the texts cited. In particular, Lintott's careful
analysis of the composition of the gangs that operated in Cicero's
Rome shows how rarely they are mentioned.[133]

In 121 the consul Opimius used troops to suppress C. Gracchus and
his followers, whom I take to have been his political partisans (n. 110).
He also ordered senators and Equites to arm themselves, and the latter
to turn out each with two armed slaves. By analogy, it was probably
slaves rather than clients who bore clubs when attending on the
senators who lynched Tiberius Gracchus.[134] On the popular side
Saturninus, who can hardly have had extensive patronage, is recorded
to have formed gangs from rustics, many or most no doubt Marius'
veterans, who hoped to benefit from land allotments under Saturninus'
legislation. His enemy Caepio opposed force to force, aided by 'boni
viri'. Once the *senatus consultum ultimum* had been passed in 100, senators
and Equites appeared in arms, as in 121, presumably with many
followers, equipped from the public arsenals, and drawn, so Cicero
says, from all orders; some perhaps came from distant Picenum.
Probably clients were among them, but they were mobilized by order
of the consuls.[135] It is interesting that, as again in 88–87, the urban

---

[132] *IM* 551 ff.; on legal remedies see now B. W. Frier, *Rise of the Roman Jurists*, 1985, esp. 51–7.
Changes in the praetor's edict concerning the interdicts *unde vi* and *de vi armata* (Lenel, *Edictum
Perpetuum*[2] 461 ff.) did not affect the principle that the transgressor was liable for acts done under
his mandate, e.g. by *filiusfamilias* or *mercennarius* (*Dig.* xliii. 16. 1. 20). Freedmen, but not clients,
are debarred from use of the former edict against patrons, though given the protection of an *utile
interdictum*, but not of the latter, presumably because armed violence breached public order as
well as their private rights (xliii. 16. 1. 43).

[133] Gruen 439 ff., 501; Lintott, ch. vi.   [134] Plut. *C. Gr.* 16. 3; cf. 14. 4, *Ti. Gr.* 19. 5.

[135] App. i. 29–32; cf. Cic. *Rab. perd.* 20, 23. Caepio: *ad Her.* i. 12. 21. Note also lynching of
Furius (App. 33). In both 88 and 87 the old citizens, sc. those living in Rome, sided with the

plebs seems to have sided chiefly with the optimates. Perhaps we may identify them with that section of the city population which Tacitus describes as 'the sound section of the people attached to the great houses', contrasting them with 'the low rabble' (*Hist.* i. 4. 3). The grain doles were as yet not free, and in any case they never supplied all the needs of the poor at Rome; many must have relied on largesses from the great houses. We may then allow that on these occasions nobles could invoke the support of clients, though of men whose loyalty could have been inspired not so much by sentiment as by economic dependence. In the post-Sullan era we find nothing of similar support for the optimates; conceivably the urban plebs were alienated by Sulla's abolition of corn distributions, short-lived as it was, and by the senate's failure to ensure the cheap supply of grain for the market (pp. 75, 172, 179).

In 90 the younger Drusus, who could employ a client to arrest the consul (Val. Max. ix. 5. 2), may well in virtue of his birth and exceptional wealth have enjoyed extensive patronage, though Diodorus (xxxvii. 10) thought that his own and his father's reputation had won him universal favour. In fact he needed to gain popular backing by proposals for distribution of land and grain. It was not on hereditary clients that he relied when violence ensued on his proposals. Seneca says that he was 'surrounded by a huge concourse from all Italy' (*de brev. vitae* 6. 1). Of course Italians backed him because he proposed their enfranchisement. The oath that they allegedly took to him, if authentic, bound them to pursue both his interests and *their own*, and to esteem him their greatest benefactor if they obtained the citizenship (Diod. xxxvii. 11). Granted that 'benefactor' (*euergetes*) represents the Latin *patronus*, this obligation went beyond that of traditional clientship, which had also not been ratified by oaths, and it held only on condition that Drusus could fulfil his promises.

Sulpicius Rufus in 88 had a guard of 600 Equites (p. 156), who were doubtless accompanied by slaves. As he belonged to a somewhat *déclassé* patrician house, we cannot suppose that they were his hereditary clients, a title that Equites were anyhow prone to resent (n. 31); they were clearly his political sympathizers. He could also depend on the new citizens (n. 135).

In 63 Cicero did have a bodyguard of clients from Reate.[136] But on

optimates against Sulpicius and Cinna (App. 55, 64); perhaps Appian is right that they simply wished to preserve their voting superiority. It may also be inferred from App. 58 that Sulpicius did have some support from town dwellers. App. 55 alleges that his aim in redistributing the new citizens was only to obtain their support as 'servants' for his other purposes. 'Servants' in my judgement means that they would be his political followers, not his clients; in any case this is probably a hostile misinterpretation of his intentions.

[136] Cic. *Cat.* iii. 5; cf. Sall. *Cat.* 26. 4, 49. 4.

5 December armed Equites protected the senate, and the government
relied mainly on the levy to put down Catiline's rising (Sall. *Cat.* 30,
36. 3). The plebs is said to have favoured Catiline (37) till it was
alienated by fear that the conspirators would set the city on fire (48). It
was therefore only a few of Lentulus' freedmen and clients who
planned his rescue, though in the end they did not attempt it (50. 1).
In the final battle Catiline was surrounded by his freedmen and
tenants (59. 3). Similarly in 49 L. Domitius Ahenobarbus enlisted his
slaves, freedmen, and tenants (Caes. *BC* i. 34). Tenants might well
have been clients of their landlords, but the choice of the term brings
out their economic dependence based on a contractual relationship,
not the tie of *fides*.

Clodius made himself master of the streets in and after 58 with gangs
composed, according to Cicero, of slaves, hirelings, and criminals.
Cicero was capable of calling freedmen slaves, and we may question
whether Clodius had the resources to hire men on a large scale. In fact
there is reason to believe that by making the corn distributions free,
enlarging the number of recipients, and restoring the right of association to the common people Clodius acquired genuine popular support.
At times he could bring out shopkeepers and artisans, some of whom
constituted a sort of urban middle class, in demonstrations, especially
when the market price of grain rose high. Most of them may well have
been freedmen, but in that case we have further proof that noble
patrons lacked control even over their former slaves. Naturally Clodius
must have had his own clients, but there is no actual allusion to them,
and they would surely have been outmatched by those of the
optimates, if the optimates had been able to rely on such dependants.
They had to turn to gladiators to fight it out with Clodius' gangs.
When Cicero was recalled from exile by a *lex* in 57, it was passed by the
centuriate assembly (which hardly ever legislated), presumably because the approval of the masses in the tribal assembly would have
been hard to obtain; and respectable people swarmed in from all parts
of Italy to vote for it and to overawe Clodius and his followers; they
must have had numerous attendants, but once more these may have
been slaves rather than clients.[137] Sestius had previously, it is true,
mobilized his freedmen, clients, and slaves on Cicero's behalf, to little
effect (Cic. *post red. sen.* 20), and later Pompey brought up retainers

---

[137] Brunt *ap.* Finley, 1974, sections VI f.; cf. Lintott ch. VI. The activity of similar gangs in the
60s (e.g. Ascon. 45, 59 C. f.) had led to the senate's dissolution of the *collegia* of humble people,
which Clodius legitimated and organized more efficiently in 58 (ch. 6 n. 57). I doubt if hired
operae were numerically significant in the gangs; where would the money have come from? On
Cicero's recall see Gelzer, *Cicero* 148 f.; I do not believe Cicero's own assertions that *all* sections of
the people welcomed it with enthusiasm.

from Picenum and Cisalpina for his own protection (*Qu. fr.* ii. 3. 4). C. Cato too is said to have employed clients against Asinius Pollio, a minor brawl (Sen. *Controv.* vii. 4. 7). That is all; in general the evidence suggests that it was political partisans or slaves who took the chief part in the gang-warfare of the 50s. It is significant that in the final encounter between Clodius and Milo each was escorted by armed slaves, a usual occurrence in those days, according to Asconius (31. f. C.); they had two or three freeborn companions, who were conceivably clients, perhaps styled 'friends'.

Much weight is often placed on Cicero's statement that in 59 everyone was promising to protect him against Clodius with their friends, clients, freedmen, slaves, and purses. This is a formula, which recurs in jest when Cicero implores Atticus to do everything possible to make sure that Cicero does not lose the legacy of a valuable library![138] It looks as if clients were traditionally included among the resources at a man's disposal. An anonymous writer of the time recommends orators to traduce adversaries in the courts by dwelling on their 'vim, potentiam, factionem, divitias, incontinentiam, nobili-tatem, clientelas, hospitium, sodalitatem, adfinitates'. In other such catalogues of resources and connections clients sometimes appear, but not invariably.[139] Such texts certainly show, what I do not doubt, that clients might in various circumstances aid their patrons. They do not tell us how common and effective such assistance was when it came to blows. The promises made to Cicero in 59 were not fulfilled; perhaps they could not have been. The dialogue in *Henry IV Part I* comes to mind:

GLENDOWER.   I can call spirits from the vasty deep.
HOTSPUR.   But will they come when you do call for them?

VII

Modern scholars are, however, fond of saying that in the late Republic patrons were actually able to raise troops from their clients or converted their soldiers into clients by the benefits they bestowed on them.[140]

---

[138] *Qu. fr.* i. 2. 16, *Att.* i. 20. 7.

[139] *ad Her.* i. 8; cf. nn. 87 f., 138; Cic. *Cluent.* 94, *post red. sen.* 20, *Parad.* 46, *Part. Or.* 87; Sall. *BJ* 85. 4. Note also collocations with *vicini* or *tribules* in Cic. *Caec.* 57, *Mur.* 69, *post. red. Quir.* 3, *Sest.* 10 (though they might be *amici* rather than *clientes*). Clients are omitted in somewhat similar catalogues in *Cluent.* 202, *Vat.* 31, *Fam.* ii. 13. 2, iii. 10. 9.

[140] Premerstein, 1937, 22 ff.; cf. Syme, *RR* 15; Harmand, 1967, 445 (who demonstrated the peculiar devotion to Caesar of his Gallic soldiers, e.g. 272–98, 442–94). *Contra* Gruen, 1974, 365 ff.

In fact, allusions to the enlistment of clients in the armies are extremely sparse.[141] The normal mode of recruitment was conscription, and even when men volunteered for foreign wars, as for service under Marius in 107, it was probably the prospects of booty that attracted them. If they joined up in response to an appeal from their patron, they might remain under the standards after he had returned home; and most generals took over the command of armies already in being. As for civil wars, coercion was certainly one method used to procure soldiers in 83, and it is the only attested method by which both the Pompeians and Caesar raised troops in 49. It may be remarked that Caesar could hardly have overrun Italy with two or three legions in the first three months of that year, if the nobility opposed to him had indeed been 'barons' able to summon retainers from their fiefs; this feudal terminology is wholly inapposite to conditions in Republican Italy.[142] The generals never failed to tell their soldiers that they were acting 'rei publicae causa', and it was on the basis that they had been legally invested with command that the soldiers were sworn to obey them; just because their title to such obedience could fairly be challenged when they did not appear to be truly acting 'rei publicae causa', they would sometimes try to bind the soldiers with a new oath, but the military or any other oath has nothing to do with traditional clientage. What effect either political propaganda or oaths had on the minds of their men is dubious. Certainly mutinies and desertions occurred.[143] On the whole the legionaries, though in a few instances influenced by the personal charisma of a leader (Caesar above all), behaved like the mercenaries of *condottieri*; it was gratitude for material rewards, and still more the expectation of benefits to come, that sustained their loyalty; and as there was no prospect of largess after defeat, they would abandon commanders who seemed to have little chance of victory.

Since much is generally made of Pompey's enlistment of clients in Picenum in 83, it is worth examining, whether his later military and political career can be explained by his continued ability to call up clients in Italy. It is a conjecture that can neither be proved nor refuted that he again recruited them in Picenum and Cisalpine Gaul for repressing Lepidus' revolt.[144] All that is clear is that the senate needed his talents for the purpose, as for the Sertorian war, and vested him with extraordinary commands, which of course entitled him to levy

---

[141] Ch. 5 n. 87; sections III–IV document much that follows in this section. Conscription: *IM*, ch. XXII (esp. 408 f.) and App. 20. Marius' volunteers: Sall. *BJ* 84.

[142] Syme, *RR* 12, and Gruen, 1974, 102, use such terms.

[143] Cf. Harmand (n. 140) and Botermann, 1968.

[144] So Badian, 1958, 277. Gelzer, 1969, 93 ff., is exhaustive on Pompey's *clientelae*.

troops in the usual way. It was popular clamour that secured him the commands against the pirates and Mithridates; once again he was authorized to conscribe legions, and in the east he took over those which had been raised by others in previous years. He enriched his troops in service, and after his return was bent on obtaining land allotments for them. But he could not effect this purpose, till he found in Caesar an agent ruthless in overcoming opposition. The strong arms of his veterans forced through Caesar's agrarian legislation.[145] It is obvious enough that the veterans were not simply or primarily fulfilling the obligations of *fides*: they were promoting their own interests. Gelzer once wrote that in 59 'the triumvirs controlled the largest *clientelae* and circles of friends'. This seems to be a misconception (which Gelzer himself ceased to entertain); their dominance rested on force, not only that supplied by the veterans but very soon by the proximity of Caesar's own army in Gaul.[146] Within Rome itself when Clodius turned against him, Pompey's control and personal security were temporarily jeopardized by Clodius' gangs, but then his veterans, preoccupied no doubt with farming, were not normally available to protect him; only once do we hear of his summoning 'a large band', presumably of clients (not necessarily his old soldiers), from Picenum and Gaul for the purpose (Cic. *Qu. fr.* ii. 3. 4). In 56 he and Crassus employed violence for their election as consuls, but then Caesar sent home soldiers on leave to assist (Dio xxxix. 31. 2). When civil war approached, Pompey is said to have boasted that he had only to stamp his foot to raise an army; very probably he was encouraged by the universal demonstrations of affection for him throughout Italy on the occasion of his grave illness in 50.[147] Within a year it transpired how easily the Italian towns would turn to fêting Caesar. We need not of course think of Pompey as being patron, still less exclusive patron, of all the communities concerned, though probably enough his patronage far exceeded that of Cicero (n. 39). In any case, if he relied on the allegiance of clients, events proved that he was sadly mistaken. He had to resort to conscription, and it was unpopular, for instance in Campania (Cic. *Att.* vii. 13. 2), where some of his veterans had presumably been settled. He had high hopes of Picenum,[148] but the

---

[145] Plut. *Pomp.* 48. 1; Cic. *Vat.* 5.

[146] Gelzer, 1969, 124; in *Caesar* 67 ff. he gives a correct account, with a bare mention of the *hetairiai* of the triumvirs (Dio xxxvii. 54. 3, 57. 2; Plut. *Crassus* 14. 2), which did not justify his earlier view; cf. pp. 473 ff. Cic., *Att.* ii. 16. 2 imagines Pompey saying later in 59: 'I shall hold you down with Caesar's army'; no doubt Caesar was already holding a *supplementum* for his provincial legions, of which three were in Cisalpina; C. Meier, *Historia* 1961, 79 ff., rightly rejects Gelzer's interpretation of 'army' as figurative.

[147] Plut. *Pomp.* 57; cf. 60. 4, Cic. *Tusc. Disp.* i. 86, *Att.* viii. 16.

[148] Cic. *Att.* viii. 11A, 12A–C; Caes. *BC* i. 12–18, 23 f.; cf. *IM* 474 f.

towns in this putative fief of his family opened their gates to Caesar's small army without a blow; Auximum, which had recently honoured him as patron (*ILS* 877), would not exclude 'C. Caesarem imperatorem, bene de republica meritum, tantis rebus gestis', the other towns followed suit, including Cingulum, which his partisan Labienus had organized and endowed, and many of the soldiers whom his agents had enlisted were to serve Caesar. Caesar's testimony (n. 148) is partial, but the facts speak for him. There was no enthusiasm for Pompey. And not a hint either in narratives of the war or in Cicero's correspondence of the importance of his patronage.

As for Pompey's soldiers at this time (which included two legions that had seen some service under Caesar), some from the five legions who surrendered in Spain made their way east to fight for him again; Pompey regarded them as the most reliable of his troops at Pharsalus, but they constituted only a few cohorts, evidently not a full legion.[149] Earlier, by Caesar's account, there had been almost daily desertions from Pompey's army, none from his own. Perhaps it was not unfitting that in the end Pompey was assassinated by one of his former officers.[150].

Neither Dionysius nor any other ancient writer intimates that it was a traditional duty of clients to render military aid to patrons. In foreign wars it was the citizen's duty to bear arms for the state, and civil wars had not been conceived in the old days. It would have been a novel development in the late Republic if patrons had claimed a moral right to the services of clients either in street warfare or in campaigns. Occasionally they did call on them with success, but no ancient source suggests that this was normal, or that the armies of the civil wars were composed of men who had been from the first, or became, the clients of their commanders; the bonds of loyalty are clearly delineated, and are quite different.

VIII

Octavian (or Augustus) must have inherited and acquired, in virtue of his adoption, power, and wealth, a *clientela* that exceeded all others. But there is nothing to show that this was one of the chief factors in his gaining and keeping control of the state.[151] That control rested, most

---

[149] Caes. *BC* i. 87, iii. 4, 88.   [150] Ibid. iii. 61, 104.

[151] *Contra* Premerstein, 1937, ch. II, who bases this view partly on a thoroughly exaggerated assessment of the importance of clientship in the Republic, partly on his interpretation of the so-called *Gefolgschaftseid* taken to Octavian in 32 and to later emperors; cf. Harmand, 1957, 157 ff. Syme, *RR*, acknowledges a special debt to Premerstein in his preface, and follows him on the oath; he sees Augustus as leader of a Caesarian party based on patronage, but elsewhere (esp. chs. XXIX and XXXIII) rightly shows how he sought universal consent by his policies.

obviously, on military force, and, like other dynasts since Sulla, he needed to win and retain the fidelity of the soldiers by material rewards. But force (or fraud) was not the sole, nor ultimately the most solid, basis of his supremacy; rather, this was the universal consent of which he boasted with perhaps not much exaggeration, and which he earned by restoring order and stability and devising a system that perpetuated it, and above all, satisfied the general ideology of the upper class.

In 32 men throughout Italy and the western provinces swore an oath of fealty to him. Similar oaths were to be taken to his successors. In some formulations they bound the swearers to pursue the emperor's enemies by land and sea to the death. Premerstein derived this oath (which sometimes expressly sets up a hereditary obligation) from clientage. But clients were not traditionally bound by oaths at all. The oath of 32 and the later oaths 'in verba principis' are *sui generis*, with some analogy both to the soldiers' oath of obedience (though civilians too took the former) and to the oath to protect Caesar taken by senators (who clearly did not thereby become his clients); there are Hellenistic parallels too. We certainly cannot infer from these oaths that all were clients of Augustus and his successors.[152]

That would be a bizarre conception. Cicero thought it monstrous that L. Antonius should be designated patron of the thirty-five tribes, i.e. of all the citizens (*Phil.* vi. 12, vii. 16). The designation was really meaningless. What clients expected from a patron was special favour and protection in their relations with others. The patron of all would be useful to none. In fact the emperor, who was in theory the leading citizen, had in a private capacity clients of his own, either inherited or acquired before he had attained the imperial station; they could be distinguished from the subjects at large.[153] As ruler he could also be regarded as having the whole state and all the citizens in his care and protection. He could from this standpoint be officially entitled *pater patriae*.[154] We have seen that the term *patronus* can be used in the same sense without any correlation with clients (nn. 64–6). This explains why Velleius (ii. 120. 1) can call Tiberius, even in Augustus' lifetime, 'perpetuum patronum Romani imperii'. The appellation is very rare and unofficial. Only in this metaphorical sense was the emperor the universal patron.

The patronage of others, however, increased rather than diminished in the Principate. Grandees continued to have individuals and commu-

---

[152] Herrmann, 1968, giving all the evidence which has accumulated since Premerstein wrote.

[153] Suet. *Aug.* 56. 4; Pliny, *Paneg.* 23. 1; for communities Harmand, 1957, 159 ff. Rouland 500 ff. rejects Premerstein's view on similar grounds with further evidence.

[154] Cf. J. Béranger, *Recherches sur l'aspect idéologique du principat*, 1953, 252 ff. The term *prostates* need not translate *patronus* in a technical sense. See also A. Alföldi, *Der Vater des Vaterlandes in röm.*

nities as clients. It is to some extent no doubt an accident of our evidence that the subject matter of Martial's and Juvenal's verse yields more information than any Republican writings about the 'turba clientium' (Sen. *Ep.* 76. 15) in the city of Rome itself, and that there is a far greater abundance of inscriptions documenting the patronage exercised over cities and tribes in the empire.[155] But not entirely: destitute of political rights, men were now in greater need of protection from those who had power and influence. The more that decisions were taken in the emperor's closet, or by officials whom he appointed and who enjoyed his favour, the stronger was the impulse to seek the aid of those who had the best access to authority. Public careers no longer depended on citizen votes but on the imperial will, yet the emperor himself could often know little or nothing of candidates for preferment, and they naturally solicited the favour of those whose commendations he might respect. At every stage the hierarchical structure produced a chain of dependency.[156] This process culminated in the late empire, when the humble would entrust themselves to the patronage of those who had the power to defend them against official oppression. If Fustel de Coulanges was right to detect the roots of feudalism in Roman patronage, it was patronage of a kind that thrived in these conditions (n. 4). It may conceivably have resembled that which had existed in early Rome, but there was no continuity between the one and the other. Dionysius, the star witness for the importance of clientship in the Republic, himself supposed that the solidarity it created in society had been dissolved in the Gracchan era; and we have seen indications that the bonds of clientship had been loosened earlier and had not been sufficiently strong even in the fifth and fourth centuries, to uphold the monopoly of power once enjoyed by the patricians, who in his account originally held all the plebeians in their patronage.

Denken, 1971, 40 ff. I also do not think it appropriate to say with Z. Yavetz, 1969, *Plebs and Princeps*, 152, that *largitiones* made the emperors 'in a sense *patroni* of the entire urban plebs'; the corn dole was a state institution administered by senatorial prefects, and of course clients of noble houses were not excluded. Largess to both plebs and soldiers helped to make them loyal subjects; the term clients is never used.

[155] See esp. Tac. *Ann.* iii. 55; cf. ii. 55, iii. 9, iv. 2, 34, 59, 68, xiii. 47, xiv. 61, xv. 22, 32, *Hist.* i. 4, 12, 81, ii. 72, iii. 66, 73 f., 86. For communities see Harmand, 1957, 159 ff. (patrons include emperors and members of their families). Such documents as EJ 354–6, 358a, make the hereditary nature of the connection explicit. Martial and Juvenal show how at Rome clients attend the levees of patrons, escort them in the streets, and get meals and trifling gifts (*sportulae*) in return. Tacitus refers to advocates obtaining the patronage of towns and whole provinces (*Dial.* 3. 4, 5. 4, 41. 2) as well as individuals; their houses were thronged with men courting their favour (6. 2); they acquired as a result wealth (8), *dignitas*, and far-flung fame (5. 4, 7, 13. 1).

[156] R. P. Saller, *Personal Patronage under the Early Empire*, 1982.

Many factors would have tended to weaken the authority of patrons in the Republic. The obligations that clients owed them were moral, but morally the claims of the state came first, and obligations to patrons could conflict, when men had more than one patron, a common occurrence. They were correlative with the duty of patrons to aid and defend their clients, and the loyalty of clients would be undermined, when patrons failed to afford such support or themselves inflicted injuries. The need for protection by the great families was reduced in so far as citizens obtained equal protection under the laws (which was indeed never complete) and political rights to further their own aims. We do not even know what proportion of the citizen body at any time, for instance during the struggle of the orders or in the contentions of the late Republic, ever stood in a relationship of hereditary dependence to noble or other patrons. It is unjustifiable to assimilate to this relationship that which obtained between a political leader and the following he secured by a programme of reforms, or that which resulted from the extensive *gratia* procured by munificence to the people at large, or to sections of it, or from the achievements of a sort of national hero such as Pompey. Modern accounts of patronage indeed conceal how elusive is the evidence for its strength. The references to it are somewhat rare; and it is not conspicuous where we should most expect to find it, above all in relation to elections. Respect for and deference to the aristocracy as such, who had (it could be supposed) made Rome great, is not the same as submission to particular noble patrons; and at times it could give way to popular hatred of the nobility. In any event the dominance of patronage in Italian society, binding both individuals and communities by hereditary ties to the Roman nobility, is a hypothesis utterly incompatible with the most clearly attested facts of the history of the late Republic: the discord between senate and Equites, the great Italian revolt, the popular legislation promoted by a few nobles but opposed by most of their order, the introduction of the ballot, land distributions, corn doles, etc., and the behaviour of the soldiery in the civil wars. In the last century of the Republic, says Sallust (*BJ* 41. 5), 'the nobility made a passion of their rank, the people of their liberty; everyone sought gain, pillage, rapine for himself'. Sallust saw no social solidarity founded on subservience to superior station. His picture is perhaps overdrawn. But the revolution was surely brought about not by the clash between magnates relying on their personal adherents, but by the success of rival politicians who were, or were thought to be, champions of the rights and interests, which could be construed as liberty or independence, of entire sections of the Italian population, the allied communities, the Equites, the urban plebs, and the peasantry from whom the legions were recruited, who could all suppose that they were contending in their own cause and not in that of individuals or families to whom their allegiance was due.

9

FACTIONS

I. The supposed existence in pre-Gracchan or pre-Sullan times of large, cohesive factions composed of allied families; thereafter of adherents of personal leaders. The lack of explicit testimony to vouch for this theory. The ties of kinship and friendship in 'routine politics'. The solidarity of families and effect of marriage-ties considered. Neither the *Fasti* nor political trials afford inductive proof for the theory. **II**. The attested character of the small coteries round L. Crassus, Scipio Aemilianus, the Gracchi, and Scaurus. **III**. The post-Sullan age. The optimates. Pompey's supposed faction. Crassus, Caesar, Cicero, and their connections. Alignments after 59. **IV**. Alignments 49–42: no parties existed of men bound with a personal allegiance to Pompey or Caesar; the variety of motives which influenced the behaviour of sections and individuals. Developments after Caesar's death. **V**. General conclusions.

I

Accordingto the Romans themselves, there were from time to time bitter conflicts which divided the whole state, in the early Republic between patricians and plebeians, and from the Gracchi onwards between optimates and *populares*, the champions of the authority of the senate and the rights of the people; knowledge of these later dissensions coloured the reconstructions of the early struggles which the annalists concocted. Mommsen is often belaboured for treating the antagonists as if they formed parliamentary parties familiar in his own day. Many of his critics adopt (with various modifications) the conception that originated with Münzer that throughout the Republic political life was dominated by contests for office and influence between coalitions of aristocratic families: kinship and friendship rather than differences on public policy or purely egoistic aims tended to determine the conduct of politicians; thus were formed factions so extensive that three or four might divide the entire senatorial order, lasting perhaps for generations. Münzer had not scrupled to describe them as parties, and his disciple Scullard, who briefly and correctly premised that there were at Rome no party organizations or 'tickets' of the modern type, and preferred to write of 'groups', none the less gave them much of the cohesiveness and permanence of parties. Syme acknowledged a special debt in his *Roman Revolution* to Münzer, whose ideas suffuse the whole work; it is perhaps the brilliance of his interpretation of Roman politics in the period after Sulla and especially after Caesar's death that has done most to make them prevalent in English scholarly writing. In fact their correctness has commonly been presupposed without argument; Scullard, however, attempted an explicit justification in the first edition of his *Roman Politics*, and in the Foreword to the second edition stated objections with characteristic fairness, and tried to meet them, as Gruen had already done. Dissent had been voiced in a few English works, for instance by implication in the original version of Chapter 7 in 1965, but it was left to Christian Meier, following in the footsteps of Gelzer (whose views are too often confounded with Münzer's), to develop the fullest critique.[1]

In what follows I shall argue that factions of the kind postulated were at best small and evanescent in the time of Cicero and that there is no sound reason for believing that they were more extensive and permanent in earlier times, for which there is much less evidence. In my opinion each individual Roman politician normally took his own course, influenced no doubt by the ties of kinship and friendship to which the school of Münzer attaches overwhelming importance, but as much by merely personal ambition or his own judgement of the public good, which men were prone to identify with the sectional interests that divided optimates from *populares*. I have naturally borrowed some points from Meier, with whose views on this question I am in general agreement.[2]

According to Scullard, the solidarity of the *gens* or, when and if this was dissolved, that of the family was the basis of political divisions at Rome. Each *gens* or family would act together to further its own dignity and power, and for this purpose would enter into alliances with other *gentes* or families, often cemented by intermarriage, and held together in any case, sometimes for generations, by reciprocal acts of friendship, imposing obligations of continuing mutual support. Moreover, the great houses enjoyed the allegiance of large numbers of their

---

[1] See Münzer, 1920; Syme, *RR*; Scullard, 1973 (quotations come from his Foreword and pp. 1–30); Gruen, 1968 (esp. the introduction) and 1974 (esp. ch. II). For reservations and criticisms see Gelzer's reviews of Münzer and Scullard's first edition (1951) reprinted in his *Kl. Schr.* i. 196–210; Meier, 1966 (with my review in *JRS* 1968, 229 ff.), esp. 7–63, 162–200, and his admirable analyses of events 91–80 and *c*.60 in chs. VI f.; Scullard's Foreword cites many other discussions.

[2] Evidence not given here may be readily found in standard works on Roman history, in *MRR*, and in the articles in *RE* on individuals (those by Münzer are replete with accurate information) and in Gruen's well-indexed books.

inferiors, whether or not formally designated as clients, who were attached to them by manifold forms of assistance, economic, legal, and political. 'This far-reaching nexus of personal and family relationships and obligations . . . underlies the basis of Roman public life.' Here no significant place is allowed either to the egoistic aims of individuals or to genuine differences on the interest of the state. In his later defence of the theory Scullard defined the sort of 'group' he had in mind as consisting of '(a) a noble and those of his fellow nobles whom ties of family or friendship bound to him and (b) the actual men who on a given occasion recorded their votes for him'. This definition is of course consistent with the view that there were no more than shifting combinations of politicians backed by equally shifting combinations of voters. Scullard himself seems to think that the primary function of his groups was that of managing elections; however, he maintains not only that 'various blocs of the electorate tended to vote over considerable periods for candidates of certain families', but that the groups tended to survive between elections, acting together for all sorts of purposes, and that they 'provided the basis of a noble's political power'; he allowed in the second edition that their composition might have been more fluid than he had previously made out, but still contended that the rivalries between them were the essence of political conflict, in pre-Gracchan times at least.

He and others supposed that in those times groups formed around leading patrician clans such as the Fabii, Aemilii, and Claudii, or a great plebeian house, the Fulvii; other scholars, impressed by the success of the Metelli in obtaining fifteen consulships between 143 and 52, freely write of a Metellan faction in that period, supposedly prominent even in years when no consular of the family was active.[3] No factions are designated by ancient writers as Fabian, Metellan and the like, and it should seem wildly implausible that clans or families no less proud of their lineage ever accepted the leadership of Fabii, Metelli, etc.; however, it is no essential part of the theory that they did; the 'Fabian' or 'Metellan' factions may be taken as convenient modern labels for coalitions of the kind postulated. Scullard himself saw that this conception of family coalitions did not suit the copious evidence for Cicero's time, and suggested that factions then consisted rather of 'devoted followers' of ambitious individual *principes* like Pompey: it still remains possible in his view to stress the importance of kinship by blood and marriage and of the obligations of friendship in determining the composition of groups of this putative new type. In fact the

---

[3] See e.g. Badian, 1958, 212, and 1964, 34–70 (from *Historia* 1957). Nothing is heard of any Metellus from 98 to the Social war, when Metellus Pius appears; *pr.* 89, he was not yet among the *principes*. The other consular Metelli of Cicero's time do not seem to have been men of great force.

evidence suggests to me that in all periods groups tended to form around prominent individuals like Scipio Aemilianus, M. Scaurus, or L. Crassus, though on my assessment they were both smaller and less cohesive and durable than those posited by the school of Münzer, and could rest on a community of sentiments as well as on the ties which they represent as stringent; as for Cicero's time, not even a Pompey could command the loyal allegiance of many 'devoted followers'.

It is true that Scullard's conception of groups attached to individuals seems to find some confirmation in the allusions of our sources to Marians, Cinnans, Sullans, Pompeians, and Caesarians. But these terms almost invariably denote men who were following or had followed one of the leaders named in civil wars,[4] when there was necessarily a polarization of the political *élite*, derived in my view from the conflicts between optimates and *populares*; for the purpose of victory each side had to accept the leadership of a single man. Rullus, tribune in 63, does indeed seem to have designated all who approved of Sulla's settlement as Sullans; Cicero speaks as if Rullus included persons like himself who had at the time remained neutral, and he characterizes Rullus as a Marian, though he was presumably too young to have taken part in the war (*de leg. agr.* iii. 7). This is wholly exceptional. The 'Pompeian' senate maligned by Antony in 43 (*Phil.* xiii. 28; cf. 33, 38) designated the senators who had fought with Pompey in 49. But among them were men like Cato, who had spent their lives in opposition to Pompey, and who sided with him in 49 only because in their eyes this was the way to prevent Caesar from seizing power.

Scullard recognized that there was no Latin term for the kind of group that he had in mind. He replied that this was the less surprising as 'even in Cicero's day political groups were referred to with considerable lack of clarity'. The truth is that there is no hint in the sources of groups of the sort he postulates for that time too. The divisions in the state which Cicero and Sallust recognize are between optimates and *populares*, or senate and plebs (p. 32 f.). The term *factio* certainly denotes a political combination, but one of which the writer disapproves, not a more or less respectable coalition for electoral and similar purposes. For Sallust the nobility as a whole is a faction operating for the advantage of the whole class, and oppressing the other citizens, whom they can dominate by reason of their cohesiveness (*BJ* 41. 6). Sallust and others can also write of factions formed by an individual or by a number of individuals in league with each other, but always in a pejorative sense. One of them was the band of conspirators organized by Catiline, in 64 on his false chronology, which included L.

---

[4] See *TLL* and the indexes to Cicero and Caesar s.nn.

Cassius Longinus, who was a candidate for the consulship of 63 in competition with Catiline himself.[5] The use of the term never seems to imply a long-enduring alliance of families or individuals. Münzer's school naturally thinks of Cato as the leader of a coterie of friends and kinsmen in the late Republic, but Sallust, whose admiration for Cato's high morality hardly makes him an apologist for his politics, avers that he did not contend 'factione cum factioso' (*Cat.* 54. 6). It remains an objection to their view that the feature of Roman politics they think of paramount importance could not be clearly described in the language of the Romans themselves.

Although our sources do not attest any such combinations as they construct, Scullard claims that their existence is proved directly for the period for which Livy's narrative is extant 'by the bitter personal and factional struggles' which it records. In fact Scullard has superimposed his own interpretation of political controversies on Livy's description of them. For example, when Livy mentions 'the faction adverse to the Scipios' (xxxviii. 55. 3), he means that there was a combination, perhaps quite temporary, of their opponents, which he implicitly condemns by his use of the term 'faction', without the slightest hint that it consisted of allied families; 'the Scipios' naturally refers simply to Africanus and his brother, Lucius, not to a family group formed around them. The objection that the postulated coalitions and electoral blocs of the second century are not mentioned in the sources is answered by Scullard in the suggestion that the annalists on whom Livy directly or indirectly drew need not have included in their narratives descriptions of 'internal politics in the sense of factions within the nobility'. But Livy does certainly describe 'personal' struggles, such as those in which the Scipios were involved, as well as apparently impersonal controversies, like that on the repeal of the Oppian law (xxxvii. 1–8), without mentioning family alliances. Are we to believe that all the annalists were either ignorant of the real working of Roman politics or that they suppressed their knowledge of it? Gruen, apparently with Scullard's approval, adopted the first alternative, suggesting that they might not be aware of 'back-stage manœuvres'. This is inconceivable, as several of them belonged to the political élite.

---

[5] R. Seager, *JRS* 1972, 53 ff., showed that the word often has a verbal sense, the act of combining, whence it comes to mean the group engaged in this activity. I doubt if it ever denotes simply 'influence' (for which *auctoritas* and *gratia* were the natural terms), or 'dissension' (Caesar only links 'factiones dissensionesque', *BG* vi. 22. 3), or 'intrigue', which was of course one of the reprehensible procedures of a faction. Seager might have stressed more strongly the almost invariably pejorative nuance of the term. On Sallust's use of *factio* see esp. K. Hanell, *Eranos* 1945, 263 ff.; in *JRS* 1968, 231, I did not recognize that he sometimes applies it to small coteries (*Cat.* 32. 3, 34. 2, 51. 40, 54, 6; cf. n. 33 on Scaurus) without any implication that they had prolonged life. *Partes* seems to be used when the state is deemed to be cleft into 'two parts', as in civil war (e.g. Cic. *Phil.* v. 32) on its imminence (n. 6), or when men are divided on the gravest policy issues.

No one need doubt that underhand machinations sometimes occurred; Polybius, who chooses to tell little of internal politics, refers to the intrigues of the friends of Flamininus in 198–197 (xviii. 10 f.), of course without the least intimation that they constituted a group of the Scullard type or that they persistently acted together on all occasions. However, on Scullard's theory the groups existed above all for electoral purposes; their members would mobilize friends and clients, and no doubt (as he admitted) woo the support of independent voters, to get their own candidates in. Thus year by year the existence and cohesion of the factions would have been perfectly patent; the annalists could not have been ignorant of practices which must have been open and respectable, and had no motive to conceal them. It is then very odd that not a vestige of all this has survived in Livy's account.

In Cicero's time we find only shifting combinations composed not so much of whole families permanently leagued together as of individuals often working each for his own personal ends and not bound in allegiance either to a group or a single leader. No doubt the political scene was then very different from what it had been in the pre-Gracchan era, when recorded domestic controversies were relatively rare, and apparently less bitter. Differences were perhaps most apt to arise over questions of foreign policy. What Christian Meier usefully categorizes as 'routine politics'[6] preponderated, that is to say contests over the filling of magistracies and other official posts, and over a multitude of minor questions that concerned Rome's relations with other communities within and beyond her own dominion. It was only in and after 133 that deep divisions were created in the body politic, when *populares* emerged to threaten the authority of the senate and on occasion the economic and social interests of the senatorial order.[7] At times too Marius and later 'dynasts' acquired influence or domination that evoked the fear and jealousy of other *principes* to a far greater extent than a Scipio had done in earlier generations. These new conditions undoubtedly affected even routine politics. Senators, when they did not oppose popular or over-powerful politicians in what they saw as the interest of their own order or that of the commonwealth, perhaps sinking private feuds or rivalries for the purpose, might seek to

---

[6] See Meier's index (p. 330) s.v. 'Regelmässige Politik', esp. pp. 7–23; e.g. note the honour paid by Pompey's friend M. Pupius Piso, *cos.* 61, to Pompey's bitter enemy C. Piso, cos. 67 (Cic. *Att.* i. 13. 2). Probably men of differing political complexions often supported each other in contests for offices and the like, in fulfilment of private obligations. Caelius thought it noteworthy that in the election of 50 at which Antony was returned as augur 'plane studia ex partium sensu apparuerunt; perpauci necessitudinem secuti officium praestiterunt' (*Fam.* viii. 14. 1). Optimate kinsmen of the young Marian Caesar begged him off in the Sullan proscriptions (Suet. *Caes.* 1. 2); and optimate *pontifices* co-opted him as a colleague in 72 (cf. *MRR* ii. 113 ff.).

[7] See ch. 1 Section iv.

avail themselves of their power to further their own advancement; and even issues of foreign policy might be settled in ways that tended to suit or obstruct the designs of demagogues or dynasts. Still there were many years in which routine politics proceeded as of old and were not overshadowed by popular agitations or by the ambitions of dynasts. Hence it remains significant that large and durable groups, formed either round a great family or round a single leader, do not impinge on us in the sources, which are now relatively copious.

Why should we suppose that there had been such a transformation in the political scene that in an earlier period there were long continuing coalitions within and between *gentes* and families, of which there is also no explicit documentation, and that their rivalries underlie all political decisions? The school of Münzer found this doctrine on the assumed solidarity of kindred and friends. Now in the time of Cicero even close kin were sometimes divided, while friendships were often fleeting or so nominal that they involved neither sincere identity of views nor overt co-operation. The tie that linked friends, and also patrons with clients, was the moral tie of *fides*, but men do not always put the claims of moral obligation above their own personal advantage; moreover, individuals could find themselves under conflicting obligations to different friends (and indeed kinsmen), just as both individuals and communities could have several patrons and might be torn in duty between them. It seems unlikely that these limitations on the effectiveness of men's bonds to friends or patrons were not operative at all times in some degree, though perhaps the use of the words *necessarii* and *necessitudo* in reference to the relationships with both kin and friends suggests that the bonds had originally been tighter. Enough has been said on friendship and clientship in Chapters 7 and 8; here I shall primarily discuss the ties of kinship.

It is no part of the doctrine under consideration that the solidarity of families was based on mutual affection, which must often have subsisted at least among close kin, though it was perhaps a commonplace to speak of 'solita fratrum odia' (Tac. *Ann.* iv. 60. 3); rather, it was the result of social convention or moral sense. Solidarity is likely to have been strongest between those most nearly related. In the Gracchan *repetundae* law it is plainly implied that no person could be expected to act impartially in the process if he were connected with either party to the suit by kinship relations extending as far as second cousins, fathers or sons-in-law, stepsons and stepfathers, or by common membership of a *sodalitas*, or by hereditary patronal ties. (It is curious that we hear little elsewhere of *sodalitates*, which probably originated as aristocratic social clubs, but which by 55 had degenerated into associations for the distribution of bribes at elections (ch. 8 n. 115);

they had evidently ceased by that time to be significant features of upper-class society.) Whereas later legal rules analogous to those in the Gracchan law do not recognize the relevance of either patronal ties (except where freedmen are concerned) or those of *sodales* to the duties of citizens to take part in legal processes as *iudices*, advocates, or witnesses, in the developed classical law among those entitled to sue on another's behalf, a right which was much restricted, there appear kinsmen within the same degrees as those prescribed in the Gracchan statute, and they could also not be *required* to give evidence against each other, though they were not debarred from bringing civil suits or criminal charges against each other. Thus the law marks out persons of specific affinities, which extend beyond but also do not go so far as membership of the same patrilineal family or *gens*. These legal definitions surely correspond to prevalent conceptions of the extent of duty towards kinsmen. Cicero too in determining the hierarchy of special obligations places in order of precedence those to parents, spouses, children, siblings, first and then second cousins, by blood and marriage, and all who share the same familial rites and tombs; there is perhaps a reservation when he speaks of 'kinsmen with whom we are on good terms and with whom our lot is generally shared'. He also dilates on the mutual obligations of friends without making it clear how these stand in comparison with those towards kinsmen (other than parents) if a conflict should arise.[8] However, in Roman morality the fatherland had the highest claim of all on citizens (pp. 40 f.).

That did not mean that kinsmen and friends did not commonly assist each other in competition for offices or in other matters in which merely private interests seemed to be at stake, subject to any conflicting obligations they might have to other kinsmen or friends. But even if this attitude prevailed in routine politics, wherever the public good was in men's judgement at variance with private claims, it was the former that should have taken precedence. And in so far as men neglected moral considerations, they could have been guided purely by those of personal advantage. Moreover, where public issues became a matter of debate in assembly or senate, which was often the case, politicians could hardly have won much general support by obtruding their own private obligations or interest, but must have at least argued in the name of the public good. It is an unwarranted assumption that such arguments really counted for less than the combinations of families.

For Scullard 'the *gens* with its subdivision into *familiae* formed the basis on which political life was organized'. Now in Roman private law

---

[8] See endnote 1.

the family is the nuclear family in which the *paterfamilias* exercises authority over his descendants and over its property; on his death each surviving son acquires absolute and independent authority of the same kind. The family as an entity consisting of all descendants of a common ancestor in the direct male line has no functions, though all these persons have certain rights as agnates to intestate succession and to guardianship of women of the same line. As for the *gentes*, whatever role be assigned to them in the process by which states like Rome had come into existence, their functions in historic times are shadowy. Patrician and some plebeian *gentiles* who shared the same *nomen* supposed themselves to have a common ancestor, but as they invented fictitious eponyms, it is evident that their true descent was lost in the mists of antiquity; moreover, many plebeian bearers of the same gentile *nomen* did not even affect to be of the same blood. In circumstances that were probably extremely rare they had the right of succession to any member of the *gens* who died intestate; the jurist Q. Mucius Scaevola (*cos.* 95) found it necessary to define the *gentiles* who could exercise this right in such a way that they did not need to prove common descent, which many or all would presumably have been unable to do.

Gentiles had certain common rites, and there are a few allusions collected by Scullard to meetings of *gentes* or families which took place for sacral or legal functions.[9] He conjectures that political action might be concerted at these meetings. That would be plausible, if it were clear that they did act in concert. There is, so far as I know, only one instance on record: in 193 all the Cornelii supported the candidature of P. Scipio Nasica for the consulship (Livy xxxv. 10. 9). But they cannot have been in such accord the next year when he was actually elected, with his own cousin L. Scipio as a competitor (ibid. 24. 5). The relationship to each other of the numerous families of this *gens* must have been very remote; even the connections between members of the single family of the Lentuli (which ultimately held more consulships than any other noble family) elude our enquiries, and it is certain that

---

[9] Scullard 8 f. On *gentes* see, however, endnote 2 and Brunt, *JRS* 1982, iv–ix. Some had their own *sacra*; nevertheless *sacra privata* had to be kept up by the principal beneficiaries under wills, and some sought by chicanery to evade the burden (Cic. *de leg.* ii. 48 ff.). For the *familia* as a subdivision of the *gens* see *StR* iii³. 16 n. 2, but in this sense it seems to have no place in Roman law, in which the *familia* consists of all those subject to *patria potestas* (and thus not brothers who are *sui iuris*), and more specifically the slaves of the household. At one time on the death of the *pater* the *sui heredes* would inherit in common and administer the property jointly (Gaius iii. 154a), but as early as the Twelve Tables coheirs could go to the courts for a division of the inheritance (iv. 17a; *Dig.* x. 2. 1. *pr*); the case of the Aelii Tuberones, who lived from a single farm held in common in the second century (Plut. *Paul.* 5; Val. Max. iv. 4. 8), was probably commemorated not only for the poverty of a noble family, but for the rarity of so primitive a practice. C. Gracchus (p. 452) uses the word *familia* in yet another sense, comprising kin bound together closely by natural affection (the use of *familiaris* as a synonym for friend probably derives from this, though in Cicero's time it could be used in mere courtesy), see p. 452.

in the first century they did not all act together. The Claudii Pulchri
and Nerones could both trace their descent to the famous censor of 312,
but whereas the former held at least one consulship in each generation,
the Nerones gained none between 202 and the election of the future
emperor Tiberius in 13; the Pulchri lacked the will or influence to
advance the cadet branch, whose kinship, unless refreshed by intermarriage, became more distant with each generation. No doubt there
was more co-operation, the closer the relationship (and some *gentes*
were reduced to a single line); even so, it would not always amount to
entire agreement. Thus in 102 two cousins, Q. Metellus Caprarius and
Q. Metellus Numidicus, could not as censors agree to exclude
Saturninus from the senate (App. i. 28). Members of the same family
could compete for office, like the Scipios in 192; two Sempronii (of
different families) both stood for the censorship in 184 (Livy xxxix. 40).
We cannot say how commonly this happened, since we seldom have
lists of candidates even for Cicero's time; this means incidentally that
we can hardly ever assess the significance of the return of any
particular candidate, since we do not know whom he defeated. Many
other examples of division within *gentes* or families will appear in the
sequel.

It is well known that Romans without male heirs of the body often
adopted sons to prolong the family line, whose nomenclature preserved
the memory of their original descent, if they came from a different *gens*,
as in the case of P. Cornelius Scipio Aemilianus; of course nomenclature does not reveal where adoptions occurred from within the *gens*,
and they may have been frequent. However, in many recorded cases of
adoption from outside the *gens*, the choice does not seem to have been
made because no *gentilis* was available, for example in the second and
first centuries there was a host of Cornelii Lentuli, not to speak of
Cornelii of other families, yet Lentuli adopted a Clodius (*cos.* 72) and a
Claudius Marcellus, ancestor of the consul of 56. Neither adoptive
father nor adoptive son can have felt overwhelming attachment to the
gentile link. No doubt the man adopted was often compensated by an
ample inheritance for his loss of the ancestral name; this might explain
why a Calpurnius (*cos.* 61) had transferred himself into the undistinguished family of the Pupii. It may also be remarked that Gaius Gracchus
declared in 122 that if he and his son did not survive, the *familia* of his
father and of Scipio Africanus would be rooted out (*ORF*[2], fr. 47). But
there must have been Gracchi of a collateral line, whose descendants
are attested under Augustus. Gracchus' sentiments are those of a man
for whom family solidarity no longer includes all the offspring of a
common ancestor in the male line, but can embrace those of a
maternal grandfather, Scipio Africanus. However, the descendants of

Scipio's brother and cousin are not members of the same *familia* in his sense.

Believers in family factions attach great importance to intermarriage. So far as family affection is concerned, it may well be that Romans often felt as much of it for kinsmen on the mother's side as on the father's. Girls were usually given away at the age of puberty;[10] clearly such marriages were arranged, and not the result of sexual attraction or romantic fondness, which conceivably may have had some effect when mature women contracted later marriages. It goes without saying that at the time when a marriage was arranged the families concerned were on amicable terms. But it cannot be assumed that their main or only purpose was to cement a political association. The bride might be an heiress, or bring a large dowry under her husband's control. Presumably it was for economic reasons that aristocrats would sometimes wed women of families of no political consequence, and of course such reasons may often have counted or preponderated in other marriages too. Thus the immense wealth of the Metelli as well as their electoral success doubtless enhanced the attractions of their womenfolk. We cannot say how often *mésalliances* occurred, since so few marriages are on record at all; thus in the best-known epoch we do not know the name of even one wife for over half the sixty consuls between 78 and 49 inclusive, and many Romans married more than once. But we may note a few cases. M. Crassus (*cos.* 70, 55), himself the son of a Venuleia, married a Tertulla; the wife of L. Manlius Torquatus (*cos.* 65) came from Asculum, and L. Calpurnius Piso (*cos.* 58), descended on the mother's side from a citizen of Placentia, espoused the daughter of one P. Rutilius Nudus; the wives of M. Aemilius Lepidus (*cos.* 78), C. Scribonius Curio (*cos.* 76), and less surprisingly of A. Gabinius (*cos.* 58) were at least of non-consular lineage, and so were those of L. Marcius Philippus (*cos.* 57) and C. Claudius Marcellus (*cos.* 50), though admittedly they were cognates of Caesar. Atia, who was presumably not Philippus' first wife, was the daughter of a new man from Aricia, M. Atius Balbus, who had secured the hand of Caesar's sister; we may well suppose that just as some nobles married for money, others were ready to give their daughters or sisters to suitors who were content with little in dowry in order to raise their social standing.[11]

Like marriages between royal houses in modern times, those between noble families at Rome afford no proof of previous alliance or

[10] M. K. Hopkins, *Population St.* 1965, 309 ff.

[11] Metelli: Brunt, *Latomus* 1975, 624 ff. *Mésalliances*: Cic. *Att.* xii. 24. 2, *Sulla* 25, *Pis.* 62; Ascon. 4 f. C.; Suet. *Caes.* 50, 1, *Aug.* 3 f. There is no collection and analysis of all known senatorial marriages; if there were, it might or might not furnish a sufficient statistical basis for assessing their *probable* causes and effects; as it is, the practice of drawing quite speculative conclusions from particular marriages is methodically unsound.

future accord. Cicero remarked that 'old enmities are often discarded as a result of new marriage-connections' (*Cluent.* 190); *a fortiori* they might unite men whose relations had been simply distant in the past. They might equally fail to preserve harmony, and even cause discord.

Tiberius Gracchus was doubly connected with the Scipios through his mother Cornelia, the daughter of Africanus, and his sister Sempronia, the wife of Aemilianus; yet the latter and his friends proved to be hostile to the tribune's policy. This hostility is often linked with Tiberius' own marriage to the daughter of Appius Claudius, Scipio's chief opponent, who was also to be Tiberius' chief supporter. The date of this union is uncertain, and it might even have been part of an abortive plan to heal the discord between Scipio and Appius. It perhaps gained Tiberius influential backing, but his previous marriage-connections did nothing to maintain a putative political alliance of the past. If it be true that there was no love between Aemilianus and his wife (App. i. 20), that personal factor may have helped to promote political dissension. The younger Drusus (*tr.* 91) and Q. Servilius Caepio each married the other's sister; the breakdown of both marriages led to divorces, and to public as well as private enmity. By divorcing his wife Mucia in 62 for misconduct, Pompey alienated her half-brothers, Metellus Celer and Nepos, who had hitherto collaborated with him; he then sought a marriage-connection with his adversary Cato, but unsuccessfully.[12] Cicero also noted that divorce was often the consequence of new enmities arising between kinsmen (*Cluent.* 190). In his time divorce had become rather common; no doubt in the second century it was less frequent, but matrimonial discord may have been just as common before social convention tolerated the easy dissolution of the marriage-tie, and just as apt to generate quarrels between kinsmen.

All this should make us hesitate in inferring, when we happen to know that two men were related by marriage, that they and their families had been or were to be long allied in public life.

In order to ascertain who belonged to any given group, Scullard and others suppose that members of the same families who are frequently found as colleagues or frequently succeed each other in office were allied to each other. They explain this partly by supposing that the presiding magistrate had great influence over the electorate and could thus procure the return of his political associates. Now it may be that in the early Republic the electors could do no more than accept or reject the names of candidates he submitted to them. But this had certainly

---

[12] Badian, 1964, 40 ff.; R. Seager, 1979, 73.

long ceased to be true.[13] At most he could exclude candidates whom he had some reason for regarding as disqualified.[14] This was a rare occurrence, and there is no clear instance of his barring a political opponent as such. In the Hannibalic war by Livy's account Q. Fabius Cunctator did indeed *persuade* the centuries not to return as consuls men unequal, as he claimed, to the military crisis.[15] Livy also records that in 185 a presiding consul did his utmost by canvassing to promote the election of his brother. He was successful, but his procedure could be held incompatible with the impartiality expected of the presiding magistrate.[16] There were various means by which the magistrate could try to affect the voting.[17] Cicero avowed that in 63 he had given all the aid to Ser. Sulpicius proper to a friend and a consul (*Mur.* 7). What this was is not stated: it was not efficacious. In Cicero's lifetime there is no evidence that support given by consuls to would-be successors was common or that it was ever decisive. One case in the previous generation stands out. As consul in 88, Sulla, having made himself master of the city by military force, could not prevent the return of Cinna, who was known to be an ill-wisher (Plut. *Sulla* 10). This can well be taken as an illustration of the rule, not an exception to it. Indeed Scullard himself, holding that his 'groups' alternated in dominance, is obliged to admit that from time to time a member of one had to declare his adversaries elected. Equally he concedes that colleagues did not invariably belong to the same group; since his assignment of families to groups is nothing but conjectural reconstruction, this may have been far more usual in the second century than he allows. As for the later period, the consuls of 70, 63, 61, 60, 59, 57, 51, and 50 were all either opponents or at least not in complete accord; and disagreements between the censors of 65 made it impossible for them to complete the performance of their duties.

[13] E. S. Staveley, *Historia* 1954, 193 ff., revived a theory that the *interrex* retained this power to the last. Would the plebs in the time of the struggle of the orders have left it to a magistrate who was not elected and always a patrician? Strong evidence is needed to make this credible. It is not forthcoming; naturally construed, Livy xxii. 34. 1 with 35. 11 f. (216) and Dio xxxix. 31 (55) refute the theory. It would also have been pointless for Milo to continue bribing the electorate in the interregnum of 52 if the *interrex* could nominate the consuls. Pompey was indeed then returned 'ex s.c.'; I take it that the *interrex* prevailed on the centuries to vote only for him. This was an altogether extraordinary occasion. See Ascon. 33, 36 C.

[14] Volcacius in 66 (Ascon. 89 C.; Sall. *Cat.* 18. 3), Sentius Saturninus in 19 (Vell. ii. 92), and therefore conjecturally C. Piso in 67 (Val. Max. iii. 8. 3) had such reasons.

[15] Livy xxiv. 7–9 (214); he also reports strange doings at the elections of 216 (xxiii. 3–5), 210 (xxvi. 22), and 209 (xxvii. 5 f.), illustrative *prima facie* of public concern for the efficiency of the high command; Scullard (ch. III) interprets the data to fit his theory of groups: mere speculation.

[16] Livy xxxix. 32; cf. xl. 17. 8 for a parallel, but in 193 the presidency of a Cornelius did not avail a candidate from his *gens* (xxxv. 10. 9).

[17] For exhaustive discussion see W. Rillinger, *Der Einfluss des Wahlleiters bei der röm. Konsulswahlen von 336 bis 50 vor Chr.*, 1976 (rather too credulous of data in Livy's first decade, which none the less conform with the conclusions that the presiding magistrate had no decisive influence).

If we had as little evidence for Cicero's time as for the second century, and made deductions from the *Fasti* and from family relationships in Scullard's manner, there would be curious results. In 72 and 71, 57 and 56 one Lentulus succeeded another as consul; mutual support would be postulated. In fact Cn. Lentulus Clodianus (*cos.* 72) was as censor in 70 to expel his successor P. Lentulus Sura from the senate, nor did any other Lentulus supplicate for that man's life in 63, while the consul of 56, Cn. Lentulus Marcellinus, was to thwart the ambitions of the consul of 57, P. Lentulus Spinther (pp. 484 f.). As Pompey and Crassus were colleagues in the consulship both in 70 and 55, we should infer that they were continuously allied. Caesar's connection with them would follow from the marriage of his daughter to Pompey, and that of L. Calpurnius Piso, elected consul under Caesar's presidency for 58, from Caesar's union with Calpurnia. As a member of the same *gens* M. Calpurnius Bibulus would belong to the same group; it would be confirmation that he was Caesar's colleague in every office. Bibulus would carry with him his own father-in-law M. Cato and L. Domitius Ahenobarbus, Cato's sister's husband; it would be no accident that Domitius reached the praetorship under Caesar's presidency and the consulship under Pompey's, when Cato too was elected praetor. If it were recorded that Bibulus and Cato recommended Pompey's sole consulship in 52 and fought with him in 49, the chain of proof would be complete. But the existence of this group could be traced back to the previous generation: in 89 Pompey's father had been consul with L. Cato at elections directed by L. Iulius Caesar, who in 89 shared the censorship with Crassus' father. This farrago of half-truths and falsehoods is precisely analogous to fashionable reconstructions of earlier factions.

Gruen, who conceded the fallibility of such procedures, but still held to the existence of family factions, sought to determine their composition (in so far as it could not be inferred from attested kinship) by an investigation of political trials. He premised that it was for factional reasons that men appeared for the prosecution or the defence. This is highly questionable (cf. pp. 370–7). Men would rally to the defence of all but their open enemies, and declared enmity, which must not be equated with political dissension or covert dislike and jealousy, was rare. As for prosecutors, we must remember that the Roman criminal law could only be enforced through private persons bringing charges; some accusers surely thought that they were performing a public duty by bringing wrongdoers to book. Others (we know) simply came forward to make a name for themselves. No doubt in either case they would abstain from imperilling personal friends or political associates. And we may readily grant that they would be most prompt to assail a private enemy or political opponent. Private grudges were perhaps most often operative. It was considered morally justifiable to attempt the ruin of a man who had himself injured the prosecutor or his father. Syme writes of 'inexpiable vendettas' between families.[18] But this is a patent exaggeration. In Rome there were no Capulets or Montagues. In the revolutions of medieval Italian cities entire families were banished or deprived of civic rights. Not so in Rome. There law and practice knew nothing of 'the passive solidarity' of the family. It was only in the dim past (so it was said) that all the Tarquinii had been expelled after the overthrow of the last king, Tarquinius Superbus. Only individuals were named in the proscription lists of the 80s and 40s. That was natural enough, when families were divided in civil wars. The triumvirs actually condemned their own kinsmen who had shared in the resistance to them. Sulla indeed thought it prudent to exclude sons of the proscribed from political life,[19] a measure upheld by Cicero in 63 as necessary for stability;[20] it was sons who had a recognized duty to avenge their fathers, and their vindictiveness might threaten public tranquillity.

The existence of family alliances cannot be inferred from the prosopographic data of which Münzer possessed magisterial knowledge, unless the presuppositions of his theory, and variants of it, are granted. We must first assent to the propositions that kinsmen normally acted together, and that attested friendship or collaboration between individual members of a family implies a family alliance. On this basis we identify the nucleus of a group. We may then discern a conflict between two such groups on the premise that if particular members of one are known to compete for office, to disagree on some question of policy, or to be personal enemies of members of another, the groups constitute factions regularly opposed to each other. If a person in another family is recorded as a friend of a member of one group, or serves under his command, or is perhaps remotely connected with him by marriage, or shares high office with him, or secures election under his presidency, or appears for his defence, or prosecutes one of his putative antagonists, his family may then be assigned to the same group, naturally with confidence proportionate to the number of instances in which these sorts of association are known. If dissension between kinsmen, or dissolution of friendships, happens to be on record, it may be treated as exceptional, though it would be hard to demonstrate the rule by any process of induction from other recorded

---

[18] *RR* 157; cf. 'feuds' in his index. Attested examples are only of enmities inherited from a father. Syme also writes (13): '*amicitia* presupposes *inimicitia*, inherited or acquired'; *contra* pp. 370–2.

[19] Sall. *Hist.* i. 55; Vell. ii. 88; Plut. *Sulla* 31.   [20] Cic. *Att.* ii. 1. 3; Quint. xi. 1. 85.

cases. It is hardly surprising that different scholars of this way of thinking differ on the composition of the factions, while concurring on their existence and importance, since individuals or families may be found in these kinds of association with more than one putative group. If the existence and importance of family factions were already certified, these differences might be ascribed to the deficiency of evidence. None the less they show that prosopographic data in themselves cannot be the basis of an induction that there were any large cohesive groups of the kind presupposed, still less that the entire political élite, was divided into a few warring factions. Yet clearly, if a group had but a small membership, its political significance is correspondingly reduced. In the complexity of the various constructions proposed the reader can easily lose sight of the fact that their foundations are all equally insecure. Family alliances are not reported in the sources; there is no name for them in Latin; the solidarity of kinsmen is probably exaggerated, and so is the durability of political friendships, at any rate if we look to the Ciceronian period; community of views between colleagues in office and between them and their successors is admitted to allow numerous exceptions; and in my judgement the nature of political trials is misconceived. The inferences from prosopographic data which are taken as reliable for the second century are of a kind that would lead to absurdly false conclusions for Cicero's time, when at last they can be checked by actual testimony to men's behaviour.

In the next section it will be contended that where we have a little more information than usual for pre-Sullan politics, it suggests that political divisions were of much the same kind then as later. Kinship and friendship were admittedly among the factors that influenced men's conduct, notably in 'routine politics', but individual advantage might preponderate, as might concern for sectional interests, which men could sincerely or hypocritically identify with that of the commonwealth; the public good always furnished the reasons employed to persuade those with no private commitments, probably the majority, and politicians were never obliged to follow a party line instead of making a personal decision on each question as it presented itself.

II

Our sources afford occasional glimpses from pre-Sullan times of the political affiliations and divisions of aristocrats, which tend to show that then as later they changed course and that though small coteries were formed they might be transitory.

The orator L. Licinius Crassus (*cos.* 95) made an early name for himself by prosecuting the Gracchan renegade C. Papirius Carbo, and advocating the foundation of Narbo, a continuation of C. Gracchus' policy of establishing colonies overseas; his speech in its favour detracted from the authority of the senate (Cic. *Cluent.* 140). It must have been about this time that he married the daughter of Q. Mucius Scaevola (*cos.* 117), who in his youth had been a friend of Scipio Aemilianus and probably an opponent of Tiberius Gracchus (see below), but who for all we know may have later backed C. Gracchus; the marriage, however, need have had no political significance. It has been supposed that Crassus was also closely associated with that man's cousin and namesake, who was his colleague in every office down to the consulship of 95; but it may be noted that this Scaevola as *pontifex maximus* obstructed Crassus' claim to a triumph. Crassus himself had at latest in 106, when he delivered a famous speech for the *lex Servilia Caepionis*, renounced any popular leanings and become a champion of senatorial interests (Cic. *Cluent.* 140, *de orat.* i. 225). In 91 he was the chief supporter of Drusus, who assumed the tribunate 'pro senatus auctoritate' (Cic. *de orat.* i. 24); this means in my judgement that he favoured not only the judiciary bill, to which Drusus was provoked by the condemnation of P. Rutilius Rufus (*cos.* 105), who had married his aunt, but his proposal to enfranchise the Italians (ch. 2, App. I).

It was Crassus' death in September that perhaps did most to frustrate Drusus' policy. Cicero presents him as the leading figure in a discussion of oratory supposed to have taken place ten days earlier. The dialogue *de oratore* is of course fictitious, but it seems unlikely that Cicero would have brought together as interlocutors men, all personally known to himself, who were not then at least on terms of amity, and though this alone did not invariably entail politicial collaboration, amity might hardly have survived sharp dissension on the issues Drusus raised, given the bitterness and violence which his programme evoked. The circle portrayed by Cicero is one with common cultural pursuits, and the absence of Drusus himself, and of his most prestigious backer M. Aemilius Scaurus, *princeps senatus*,[21] is enough to confirm that it was not his intention to include all Drusus' principal supporters; but we may still believe that the interlocutors were all among them, and in some instances this is certified.

Besides Crassus himself those supposedly present were his father-in-law Scaevola, Q. Lutatius Catulus (*cos.* 102), M. Antonius (*cos.* 99), whom Cicero categorically describes as a political ally and close

---

[21] Ascon. 21 C. f. Scaurus encouraged Drusus to propose his judiciary bill, but his indictment by Q. Varius indicates that he also backed Italian enfranchisement. But he was very old, and L. Crassus was doubtless the most energetic of Drusus' supporters.

personal friend of Crassus (i. 24), C. Iulius Caesar Strabo (a half-brother of Catulus), P. Sulpicius Rufus, and C. Aurelius Cotta, a nephew of Rutilius, eventually consul in 75. The last two are stated to have been associates of Drusus (i. 25), and Cotta fell a victim to Drusus' opponents under the Varian law, under which Antonius too was prosecuted. Catulus had indeed married the sister of Q. Servilius Caepio (*cos.* 106), whose son had become a personal enemy of Drusus as also of Scaurus (Ascon. 22 C.), and one of his chief political antagonists, but this only illustrates the fact that such family connections did not necessarily entail lasting political collaboration.

There are no grounds for supposing that the circle of L. Crassus were opposed by Marius and his friends.[22] Marius' attitude to Drusus' proposals is not recorded. Both Crassus and Scaurus had once been Marius' enemies, but they were among those who accepted that the public interest required his appointment to command against the Cimbri and Teutones (Cic. *de prov. cons.* 19). A reconciliation must have ensued: Crassus had given his daughter in marriage to Marius' son. Arguments (which I do not think probative) have been advanced to show that both Catulus and Antonius had been politically allied with Marius. Cicero represents Sulpicius as on friendly terms with him (*de orat.* i. 66). In 88 he was to form an *entente* with Marius for reasons which the dearth of evidence obscures, and both were to be proscribed after Sulla's *coup*. But the events of 88 and later years cannot be adduced to clarify political alignments in 91. The members of Crassus' circle themselves went different ways after his death. As tribune in 88 Sulpicius resisted the illegal candidature of his old friend Caesar Strabo for the consulship. After forcing his return in 87, Marius was to proscribe his chief opponents (Diod. xxxviii–xxxix. 5). They included Catulus and Antonius, and Caesar Strabo, together with P. Crassus (*cos.* 97), a kinsman of Lucius, and Caesar Strabo's brother L. Caesar (*cos.* 90), although Marius had himself married Julia, the sister of the future dictator's father, a second cousin of the Caesars he killed. (Cotta too was connected with this branch of the Caesars.) These men must have at least accepted the outlawry of Marius and of Sulpicius, once the friend of so many of them; Scaevola was the only senator to protest (Val. Max. iii. 8. 5); and the rest had no doubt taken a prominent part in the resistance to Cinna.

Marius himself had few adherents in 88. Besides his son and Sulpicius, a mere seven men were outlawed along with him in 88; of these only one is known to have been of praetorian rank, and one other

---

[22] What follows on events from 91 to 82 involves much disagreement with Badian, 1964, 1–33, 206–34. On M. Antonius cf. p. 376 f. I agree generally with Meier, 1966, ch. vi.

of noble lineage.[23] Under the dominance of Marius, Cinna, and Carbo in 86–82 only seven men held the consulship; besides Marius, C. Norbanus Flaccus was also a parvenu; the illegal iterations of Cinna and Carbo in the consulship may suggest that they had few devoted partisans of high position to reward. Cicero implies that the Marians and Cinnans were mostly new men (II *Verr.* i. 35), and in addressing a senatorial court (*Rosc. Amer.* 16. 136–8, etc.) he presents Sulla's cause as that of the nobility. In 82 the younger Marius ordered the massacre of senators he could not trust; the victims included a Carbo and the consul of 94 L. Domitius Ahenobarbus (App. i. 88), though another Ahenobarbus was to perish as a Marian at the hands of Pompey (*Per. Livy* lxxxix). (He is usually taken to be a brother of the optimate consul of 54, but is much more likely, given the apparent disparity of age, to have been a collateral.[24]) Thus in the 80s as in the 40s (see below) families were divided (cf. n. 23), though it is improbable that so many of the nobility were found on the Marian side as later on Caesar's; Sulla's first proscription list is said to have contained the names of only forty senators, including the four surviving Marian consulars (App. i. 93); most of his victims are for us anonymous, and therefore were probably not men of birth and rank.

All this is not to say that most senators were Sullans, except in the sense that they ultimately fought on his side or approved his victory. In 88 they must have condemned Sulpicius' resort to violence and the unprecedented transfer by popular vote of the eastern command to Marius from a magistrate. But few were probably ready to countenance the military coup, which was Sulla's answer to the pernicious laws carried by force. It is significant that all but one of his own senior officers would not follow him. The senate itself, perhaps, as Plutarch says (*Sulla* 9), terrorized by Marius and Sulpicius, perhaps to avert bloodshed and an evil precedent, more than once sent embassies beseeching him to stay his advance (App. i. 57). Plutarch (*Sulla* 10) had read that the senate disliked his proceedings after his capture of Rome; if true, this evidently applies not to measures by which he reinforced its authority but to the savagery with which he took vengeance on his enemies. It was the people who rejected his candidates for the consulship of 87 and returned Cinna, who was already known to be on bad terms with him, but Cinna may have enjoyed support not only among the 'many' senators who were to flee from Rome and join him in 87 (App. i. 66), but also from those who would later deplore his own resort to arms.

[23] M. Iunius Brutus and P. Cornelius Cethegus (who joined Sulla in 83–82; App. i. 60, 80 with Gabba's notes); the relation of the former to two other Marians, M. Brutus (*tr. pl.* 83) and L. Brutus Damasippus, and to the Sullan consul of 77 D. Brutus is unknown.

[24] For collateral Ahenobarbi see *RRC* i. 286.

The majority surely detested the 'domination of Cinna'. Out of twelve other consulars known to be alive at Rome in 87, Marius and Cinna put seven to death, together with some other notables.[25] We may easily imagine the bitterness felt by their numerous kin and friends, but it can only have been less in degree among the body of senators, who had lost so many of their most respected leaders. The iteration of consulships by Cinna and Carbo showed a grave contempt for law and custom. Cicero could say that the state was 'sine iure et dignitate' (*Brut.* 227) and that Sulla championed the 'honesta causa' (*de offic.* ii. 27), a view in which Sallust would probably have concurred (*Cat.* 11. 4).

Not that from 86 to 83 men were 'waiting for Sulla'.[26] There could have been no rational expectation that with a mere five legions he could overcome the forces which could be mobilized against him throughout Italy. Probably few fled to his camp in the east. Cicero recalled the despair his seniors had felt at the time (*Fam.* ii. 16. 6). The senate had indeed not entirely lost its freedom of action. It was still able to attempt mediation between Sulla and his enemies, though impotent to restrain the military preparations which the latter made.[27] The forms of the Republic were mostly observed. Some might hope for a gradual mitigation of the evils, or even to bring it about, if they could rise to be *principes* (Cic. *Cat.* iii. 25). L. Marcius Philippus (*cos.* 91) held that it was best 'to serve the time'; with M. Perperna (*cos.* 92) he took office as censor, perhaps with the very object of frustrating the effective enfranchisement of the new citizens, to which Cinna was pledged. To Scaevola (*cos.* 95) participation in civil war was the worst course of all.[28] The attitude of neutrals in 49, and of those who, like Cicero, thought it hopeless to protract the struggle with Caesar after Pharsalus, or who, would even, like Brutus, accept preferment from him, was no different from that of men who chose to remain at Rome from 86 to 83.

But when the intransigence alike of Sulla and his adversaries made war inevitable, and still more when it came to appear that Sulla had a good chance of victory, senators progressively rallied to his cause, among them Philippus and perhaps Perperna, and the 'Marians' felt that they could not rely on neutrals still at Rome, whom they slaughtered. Sulla's new adherents need not be despised as mere time-servers; earlier resistance to the Marians would have been not only dangerous but futile and pernicious to the state; war is an intrinsic evil,

---

[25] App. i. 72–4; it is not certain if A. Atilius Serranus was the consul of 106.

[26] See also J. P. V. D. Balsdon's cogent critique of Badian, 1964, 206 ff., in *JRS* 1965, 230 ff.

[27] App. i. 77; *Per.* Livy lxxiii. Note Meier's conjecture (1966, 233 ff.) on the sending of L. Flaccus to Asia.

[28] Cic. *Att.* viii. 3. 6; *IM* 93.

and hardly to be justified when there is no probability that the ends for which it is fought can be achieved. Even Philippus may have eventually opted for Sulla, not just because he judged that he would be on the winning side, but also because it was the side to which his natural sympathies inclined. Similarly the assassination of Caesar allowed Cicero and others to reveal their true sentiments. Sulla's legislation in 88 had already shown that he was likely to uphold the authority of the senate; and expectations that he would again follow the same course were ultimately to be fulfilled. His dictatorship was probably accepted as a temporary necessity. Many who had fought for him surely condemned his cruelty and contempt for process of law.[29] but in the end he must have contented them by restoring the old system with new safeguards for control by the senate.

In all these transactions we can sometimes discern small political groups, in which kinsmen by no means always stand together and which dissolve and form again, but we can also see that the majority of the nobility and senate would work, so far as they could, for the preservation of senatorial authority, which Sulpicius, Marius, and Cinna tended to subvert; and which Sulla, however personal were his aims, was ready to revive. All this seems to be equally true of the preceding and subsequent generations.

For the former Cicero names numerous friends of Scipio Aemilianus.[30] Those of his youth are said to have included Cato (*cos.* 195), Ti. Gracchus (*cos.* 177, 163), father of the tribunes, C. Sulpicius Galus (*cos.* 166), P. Scipio Nasica Corculum (*cos.* 162, 155). Among his own contemporaries Q. Metellus (*cos.* 143) and Q. Pompeius (*cos.* 141) broke away from him and became his jealous detractors; in inferior sources, which I do not believe (p. 369), they are represented as his personal enemies. C. Laelius (*cos.* 140) always appears as his closest intimate. P. Rupilius was his protégé. With his colleague as consul in 132 he persecuted the humble followers of Ti. Gracchus: Laelius was a member of the commission they set up for the purpose. Scipio himself had approved of the lynching of Tiberius, the son of his old friend and

---

[29] Cic. *Rosc. Amer.* 150–4, *de dom.* 43, perhaps reflecting the sentiments of senatorial *iudices* or *pontifices*, though the language in the former speech may well have been strengthened in the published version. Cf. Plut. *Sulla* 31; Oros. v. 21. If we believe the anecdotes in Plut. *Cato* 3 and *Brut.* 3, we may think that the boys Cato and Cassius vented opinions which their elders discreetly reserved for talk in private. See also Syme, *Sallust* 1964, 124, 177. Only the scholarly sophistry of modern times has made a statesman out of this historical Busiris.

[30] Evidence for political affiliations (as well as speculations) for the time of Scipio Aemilianus and Ti. Gracchus is fully given by Astin, esp. ch. VIII. See also Strasburger, *St. zur alten Gesch.* 946 ff. (= *Hermes* 1966, 60 ff.); D. C. Earl. *Tiberius Gracchus* 1963 (elaborating an interpretation adumbrated by Syme, *RR* 60) with my critique in *Gnomon* 1965, 189 ff., and the riposte to it by Badian, *ANRW* i. 1, 668 ff; cf. also J. Briscoe, *JRS* 1974, 125 ff. Münzer himself gave a balanced account of the Gracchi in *RE*, much to be preferred to the later extravagances of his school.

husband of his sister (Plut. *Ti. Gr.* 21), and his attitude must have
produced a personal enmity with Gaius Gracchus, with Tiberius'
father-in-law Appius Claudius (if it had not already arisen from their
previous opposition in politics), and with Gaius' father-in-law P.
Crassus Mucianus. In 129 Scipio was engaged in thwarting the activity
of the Gracchan land commission.

It is in that year, just before his untimely death, that Cicero places
the discussion of political theory between Scipio and a number of his
friends which forms the subject of the *de republica*. Besides Scipio and
Laelius he names as present M'. Manilius (*cos.* 149), L. Furius Philus
(*cos.* 136), Sp. Mummius, and some younger men, Scipio's nephew Q.
Aelius Tubero, the two sons-in-law of Laelius, C. Fannius (*cos.* 122)
and Q. Mucius Scaevola (*cos.* 117), and P. Rutilius Rufus (*cos.* 105).
The dialogue is certainly fictitious, and no credence can therefore be
given to Cicero's profession that he had learned its purport from
Rutilius in his old age (i. 13). It is quite another matter to deny that he
would not have eagerly listened to reminiscences about Scipio and his
contemporaries from Rutilius and also from Scaevola and his wife
Laelia (*Brut.* 211); if he chose to represent Rutilius as his informant, it
was doubtless because it was more dramatically appropriate to attribute to him the recollection of a theoretical discussion on matters in
which as a Stoic he might have had a peculiar interest.

Strasburger was surely right in holding that Cicero has inflated the
measure of the cultural standards and philosophic understanding
attained in Scipio's circle. But we need not follow him in supposing
that Cicero simply reconstructed a list of Scipio's friends through the
knowledge of his political associates and kinsmen which he had
acquired from histories or speeches of the time or from Lucilius' satires,
and perhaps threw in the names of some who were influenced by
Stoicism, on the basis that Scipio was a patron of the Stoic Panaetius.
The political affiliations in 129 of the younger interlocutors of Cicero's
dialogue, who were not then of much consequence, could hardly have
been ascertained from the sources suggested, and it may be noted that
Sp. Mummius, an older man but of no more than praetorian status
and surely not himself an important political figure, was brother of L.
Mummius, with whom Scipio had had differences in their censorship
of 142, and of whom he had spoken with open contempt (Val. Max. vi.
4. 2). Nor is it a convincing contention that Rutilius himself could not
have stood close to Scipio, on the ground that the former adopted
humane and the latter authoritarian views; both could be reconciled
with Stoic ideas, and we are not bound to assume that two friends
shared exactly the same principles (any more than Cicero and Atticus
did), or that Rutilius' outlook never changed after his youth. It is also

fallacious to argue that such and such a person can never have been a friend of Scipio because at some point he dissented from Scipio's policies. Rejection of Cicero's testimony by this kind of criterion is quite unjustified, all the more because we can see that already in this period men altered their political courses and entered into various and transitory political combinations.

Scipio's attested friends certainly include some who were related to him or to Laelius by birth or marriage. Cato's son was the husband of his sister Aemilia; Scipio Nasica Corculum was his distant cousin; both he and the elder Gracchus had married the daughters of Scipio's grandfather by adoption; Tubero was his nephew; and Laelius' two sons-in-law were among the other interlocutors in the *de republica*. It is, however, apparent that such private relationships did not guarantee unvarying political accord, and do not imply membership of a group enduring for decades. Cato had been an opponent of Scipio Africanus; so had Gracchus (we are told), but in such a way as not to interfere with personal admiration or prevent him much later from taking Africanus' daughter to wife. Cato and Nasica were locked in prolonged dispute on policy towards Carthage; it seems probable that Scipio agreed with Cato, but a difference on this impersonal issue need not have prejudiced the private amity of the cousins. From genuine or professed religious scruples Gracchus too had forced Nasica's abdication from his first consulship; and he was on good terms with C. Claudius Pulcher, his colleague as consul and censor, who for the school of Scullard belonged to a group adverse to that to which Scipio was hereditarily attached. Sulpicius Galus had had many associations with Scipio's natural father L. Aemilius Paullus; there had been a rift in 167, but this need not have been permanent; it is also irrelevant that Scipio was later on bad terms with Ser. Sulpicius Galba (*cos.* 144), who may not have been at all closely related to Galus.

The breach between Scipio and the tribune Tiberius Gracchus despite their double family connection has already been noted; it may be added that in marrying the daughter of Scipio's antagonist Appius Claudius, Tiberius was renewing or cementing the friendship that had subsisted between Appius' father Gaius and his own. In the conflicts generated by his tribunate other members of the kinship went different ways. Tubero, though a cousin of Tiberius, was one of the coevals who renounced their friendship with him (Cic. *de amic.* 37); not so another cousin, C. Cato (ibid. 39); however, he cannot have remained pro-Gracchan throughout his career, since he was to be one of the victims of the 'Gracchani iudices' under the Mamilian law of 109 (Cic. *Brut.* 128). Though P. Mucius Scaevola (*cos.* 133) at first gave his assistance to Tiberius, on one account only covertly (Cic. *Acad. Prior.* ii. 15), whereas his brother P. Crassus Mucianus (*cos.* 131) was openly a Gracchan, and though in 129 he was a leader of that 'part' of the state adverse to Scipio's (see below), Cicero could suppose that his young cousin Quintus remained a member of the Scipionic circle; it was in fact impossible for him to side both with P. Mucius and his father-in-law Laelius. It is true that later Quintus gave one daughter in marriage to L. Crassus, who first appeared as a *popularis*, and another to M'. Acilius Glabrio, who *may* have been tribune in 123 and an associate of C. Gracchus; we might then suppose that some years after Scipio's death he deviated from the line that Scipio's friends might have expected to follow. But we do not know that Crassus, still less Glabrio, were committed to popular policies when the marriages were contracted, and Cicero represents Scaevola in his old age as condemning both the Gracchi (*de orat.* i. 38). Laelius' other son-in-law did indeed turn his coat not once but twice; he earned his consulship in 122 by Gaius Gracchus' favour, and then took the lead in impeding Gaius' bill to enfranchise the Latins.

Let us turn to Scipio's attested adversaries. In 133 he was absent from Rome, but we know that he was to disapprove of Tiberius Gracchus' actions as tribune. Tiberius' chief and only known backers of high position were Ap. Claudius and Mucianus, the fathers-in-law of himself and of Gaius, and more discreetly the consul in office P. Scaevola. Modern scholars sometimes make out that he had the support of a powerful senatorial faction, bent simply on aggrandizing their own power, and even go so far as to depict him as a mere mouthpiece, though the sources unanimously see him as the true author of his own measures. It is no objection that he was not by age and rank one of the *principes*; we may recall that Drusus as tribune in 91 could be called 'almost patron of the senate' (Cic. *Mil.* 16), or think of the authority possessed by Cato from the time he was elected tribune for 62. My impression is that the majority of the senate were from the first unsympathetic to his agrarian scheme, and no doubt their hostility was aggravated by his subsequent procedures.[31] There is some confirmation in the composition of the triumvirate to which the distribution of land under the scheme was entrusted. If the scheme was to be implemented, it was vital that the work should be in the hands of those who sincerely wished it success. Tiberius therefore secured the election in the first place of himself, his young brother, and Appius. His

---

[31] It was probably because of attitudes prevalent in the senate that Laelius had earlier withdrawn some proposal which Plutarch (*Ti. Gr.* 8) thought analogous to Gracchus' agrarian bill, obtaining thereby a reputation for prudence. Scipio and his friends perhaps disapproved not of Gracchus' objectives but of the methods by which alone he could attain them and of the political discord which his plan provoked and which they had anticipated.

own place was to be filled by Mucianus; and when the deaths of Appius and Mucianus created other vacancies, no trusty consular was available to succeed them; it was some years before the new commissioners, M. Fulvius Flaccus and C. Papirius Carbo, attained the consulship (in 125 and 120); and the latter had by then deserted the Gracchan cause. P. Scaevola himself was either unwilling to take up the task or was thought unreliable; in fact, though he declined to suppress Tiberius by force, he had subsequently condoned the lynching, and was later to express by implication condemnation of the conduct of Gaius Gracchus.

It is true that Cicero asserts (*de rep.* i. 31) not only that Tiberius' tribunate and death had cleft the 'people' into two parts, but that the senate too was divided between the followers of Scipio on the one hand and of Appius and Mucianus, and thereafter of Scaevola and Q. Metellus on the other. The latter cannot, however, be regarded as leading a Gracchan faction; that does not fit the totality of what we know of Scaevola, and as for Metellus, we are told that he actually opposed both Tiberius, perhaps only late in his tribunate, and Gaius Gracchus (Plut. *Ti. Gr.* 14; Cic. *Phil.* viii. 14). The nature and origin of the cleavage within the senate in 129 are obscure. In the passage cited Cicero makes Laelius explain it by detraction and envy of Scipio, which he imputes to both Metellus and Scaevola. This explanation was dramatically appropriate to Laelius, and may also have been Cicero's. Anyone who outshone his peers, as Aemilianus or Scipio Africanus did, was bound to incur grave jealousy as well as to win high respect. No doubt there were senators who would tend to decry any policies that he championed, just because he was their champion; that would not of course entail that they were united on all other matters. But we must also note that the senate had made no effort to repeal Tiberius' agrarian law. That course may have seemed to the majority too unpopular to be safe or practicable; others may have thought that Tiberius had sought to remedy admitted evils, and that injudicious as his remedy had appeared when proposed, it was now best, given that it had passed into law, to test by experience whether after all it might prove efficacious. Scipio on the other hand was trying to frustrate the activity of the land commissioners. Thus there may have been a genuine disagreement on public policy between Scipio and others who were far from having been adherents of a powerful faction represented by Tiberius.

The personal and political relationships of men in that time were patently variable and complex. Another illustration may be given. Both Metellus and Q. Pompeius were former friends and later detractors of Scipio. But they also became mutual enemies, not later than 139, when Metellus was a hostile witness at a trial of Pompeius (Cic. *Font*. 23), in which conviction would have brought ruin. Yet both were taken as legates to Spain by Scipio's friend Furius Philus, who is also said to have been an enemy of both (Val. Max. iii. 7. 5; Dio. fr. 82). This can hardly be accepted as it stands; Furius could not have supposed that military operations could be conducted efficiently by three men divided by bitter reciprocal hostility. There must have been some sort of reconciliation. Pompeius as well as Metellus was a critic of Tiberius Gracchus in 133 (Plut. *Ti. Gr.* 14), and in 131 they were colleagues as censors and completed their magisterial tasks, for which agreement between the two censors was required.[32]

It will hardly be denied that Gaius Gracchus attained for a time a greater dominance than his brother ever did. Among his associates we can name M. Fulvius Flaccus (*cos.* 125), some of his tribunician colleagues, and for a short time C. Fannius, who turned against him after entering on his consulship in 122. But in the surviving extract of his speech on the mysterious *lex Aufeia* (Gell. xi. 10) he imputed corrupt motives to all the politicians who spoke in the rival interests of the kings of Pontus and Bithynia and to all who maintained a discreet silence. This was an invective on the honesty of the entire senatorial order, and strongly suggests that he felt himself to be a more or less isolated figure. In that case we must suppose that he owed the strength of his position to his own eloquence and capacity and to the support that he acquired outside the political élite. It was in his view 'the worst' citizens who had done his brother to death (*OFR*[2], fr. 17), but the senate as a whole had virtually condoned the killing; and it was by its will that Tiberius' followers, not his murderers, had been subjected to legal, or rather illegal, punishment.

We cannot tell how far the conflicts between leading men in Scipio's day arose from personal hostility or emulation, or from genuine disagreements of judgement on public affairs. Indeed this can never have been clear except to those who could read their minds; whatever their true motives, politicians always had to appeal in public to considerations of state in endeavouring to persuade senators or citizens who were not committed to follow them in any direction they chose to go. The evidence does not suggest that there were many so committed; on the contrary it appears that already in this age politicians could not count on the united support of their own kin on every issue nor on the constancy of their friends; not that dissent inevitably involved the

---

[32] *StR* ii[3]. 339. In my view this explains the famous reconciliation of M. Lepidus and M. Fulvius Nobilior after these old enemies had been elected censors for 179; the honour, the greatest in their careers, would have been empty if they had persisted in mutual obstruction. *Contra* Scullard 179 ff.

dissolution of friendship. Collaboration on one or two occasions need not imply a permanent alliance, and express testimony is almost always needed to certify that a man's kin or friends rallied round him, especially when large public issues were at stake. Nothing suggests the existence of large coalitions durably linked by kinship and friendship. As in the time of L. Crassus, it is individuals rather than families who appear to count, men who possessed what the Romans called *auctoritas*, inspiring a respect that reached far beyond those bound to them by personal ties, but which at the same time provoked envy and antagonism among those who sought equal or greater eminence.

Outstanding *auctoritas* hardly ever belonged to men who had not risen to the highest offices of state, and in consequence still more rarely to those who were not of high lineage. But noble descent and connections were the apanage of most consulars, who did not all attain the same degree of influence; more was required, distinguished services to the state, especially in war, or eloquence, which of course when exercised in the courts might place numerous individuals under obligations; to a lesser extent juristic expertise had similar utility.

We cannot perceive its sources in every individual instance. Cicero could say that M. Aemilius Scaurus, consul in 115 and for long *princeps senatus*, was able to direct almost the entire world by his nod. Though of patrician stock, he had raised himself from comparatively humble circumstances by his own ability. He married a daughter of L. Metellus Delmaticus (*cos.* 119), and may therefore have enjoyed the support of the Metelli, then at their apogee of electoral success, if indeed they were united, but it is clear that he himself and not any member of that family was the most influential figure of his time. However, the nature of his talents is not clear from the evidence. He had no great military exploits to his name, he was not a jurist, and though assiduous in the practice of oratory, he apparently had no special gifts or training to excel as a speaker; at best, like M. Crassus in Cicero's day, he may have extended the circle of those under obligation to him by constant activity and diligence in forensic work; ultimately, of course, his mere appearance as a *princeps* would assist the cause of any litigant he aided. Cicero creates the impression that men trusted his judgement, whereas Sallust regards him as *factiosus*, an intriguer, adept at forming combinations.

The appellation fits M. Crassus in Cicero's time; and he too by his liberality in making interest-free loans from his immense wealth, his zeal in canvassing for candidates, his forensic activity, and his ingratiating flattery had many senators beholden to him. We may also recall that mysterious figure P. Cornelius Cethegus, who in the 70s attained the authority of a consular without holding the office; of a low moral repute, and no more than an adroit pleader, he had (we are told) a thorough knowledge of affairs; nothing could pass in the senate without his approval, and men would secretly visit his house at night to implore his good offices.

Sallust too testifies to Scaurus' great influence and speaks of his faction, yet by his own account Scaurus (for motives which he slights) initially advocated military action against Jugurtha, when the allegedly venal majority of the senate, apparently including members of his faction, voted for merely diplomatic intervention; it was only at a later stage that he too in Sallust's view was corrupted by a huge bribe; and in the end he could so far distance himself from those who were arraigned for corruption before the courts set up by the Mamilian law that he could himself be appointed as one of their three presidents. It may then be doubted if even Scaurus, though the chief figure in the political scene of his day, was at the centre of any large, cohesive group. Certainly his faction, like the circles of Scipio and L. Crassus, did not survive him; the memory of his greatness and the connections he had built up were of some service to his late-born son in 54 as candidate (p. 475) and when on trial (p. 374), but this man was not a figure of the first consequence. The same can be said of Faustus Sulla; even the dictator could not pass influence on to a new generation.[33]

III

Let us now turn to the better documented post-Sullan age. It will not be my sole purpose in this section to show that political affiliations were often transient and that no formidable factions were organized round either families or powerful individuals, but also to illustrate from time to time how personal self-interest and political principle as well as ties of obligation to kinsmen and friends influenced men's conduct.

Sulla had ultimately restored and strengthened the senate's control over the state. At first the chief men in the senate were those who had fought on his side. Whether or not they had previously been his close political allies, or had disapproved of his methods and resented his temporary autocracy, they must have wished to uphold a system under which they possessed the greatest influence. The majority of *principes* in the next generation were surely no less attached to senatorial supremacy, which accorded with their interests but which they might see as a matter of principle. The natural inclination of all would also have been to uphold law and order at home, and the imperial power of Rome

[33] Scaurus: Cic. *Font.* 24, *Brut.* 110–12; Sal. *BJ* 15. 4 f., 28. 4, 29, 30. 2, 40. 4. M. Crassus: *Brut.* 233 (cf. 242 f.); Plut. *Cr.* 3, 7 (cf. n. 59). Cethegus: Cic. *Cluent.* 84 f., *Parad.* 40, *Brut.* 178; Plut. *Luc.* 5 f. Faustus: ch. 8 n. 38; p. 474.

overseas. They may be termed optimates. Their basic community of views did not of course exclude differences on 'routine politics', resulting from conflicting private ties and personal interests. On particular questions of policy they might also hold divergent opinions of the public good, without abandoning their commitment to senatorial control of the state.

Some thought it prudent at times to make concessions to popular discontents. Thus C. Aurelius Cotta as consul in 75 carried a law relieving ex-tribunes of the disqualification for higher offices which Sulla had imposed on them; he thereby incurred the hostility of extremists, who would have preferred to keep the Sullan system intact.[34] In 70 his brother, then praetor, met the agitation against the corruption of senatorial *iudices* by putting an end to the senatorial monopoly of the criminal courts; whether he acted as an instrument for Pompey's wishes is quite unclear.[35] In 73 the consuls thought it necessary to reinstitute on a small scale the corn doles which Sulla had abolished, and they were greatly enlarged by Cato as tribune in 62. Optimates had never approved of these distributions *per se*; the circumstances in which the law of 73 was passed are not known, except that in 74 there had been riots provoked by scarcity; Cato was surely prompted by the need to prevent a renewed upsurge of feeling at Rome in favour of Catiline, who was still in arms (cf. Plut. *Cato* 26).

It may also be noted that the chief men in the senate could not invariably command the determined support of the whole order. In 67 the tribune Cornelius carried laws which detracted from their influence and encountered strong resistance in the senate; five of the leading consulars thereafter tried to ruin him by criminal prosecution, but it was only their familiars among the senatorial jurors who voted for his conviction. Here indeed we have evidence that there were some lesser senators who would vote at the bidding of *principes*, but equally that their number was limited.[36] The shifts of opinion in the great debate of 5 December 63 on the fate of Catiline's accomplices illustrate how little the senate was governed by one or two powerful factions: it was susceptible to the force of argument. Nor was intransigent resolution ever a mark of its behaviour. Cicero had had much difficulty in

---

[34] Acc. to Cicero *ap.* Ascon. 78 C. they became 'inimicissimi' to Cotta. Sallust makes him say of his earlier career: 'maxumas inimicitias pro re publica suscepi' (*Or. Cottae* 4). *Inimicitiae* seldom resulted from merely political dissension (ch. 7 II); Cotta doubtless contracted them earlier in the exceptionally bitter conflicts of 91–90.

[35] Brunt, *Chiron* 1980, 285 ff.

[36] Ascon. 58–62 C. The consulars were Q. Metellus Pius (80), Q. Catulus (78), M. Lucullus (73), Q. Hortensius (69), and probably Mamercus Lepidus (77), not Manius Lepidus (66); cf. G. V. Sumner, *JRS* 1964, 41 ff. Full discussion in M. T. Griffin, *JRS* 1973, 196 ff.: I do not think it proved that Cornelius' prosecution was a disguised attack on Pompey, his 'putative' patron.

overcoming reluctance to take early and strong action against Catiline. In the 50s the senate succumbed to the argument of force.[37] On the eve and outbreak of the civil war in 49, most senators had small sympathy for Caesar, but would have preferred to keep the peace. In this instance it seems that the senate allowed itself to be overawed or manipulated by a very small number of determined men, enemies of Caesar or intimates of Pompey, but many more would finally take arms against Caesar in a war they had not wanted (see below).

Oligarchic control was menaced by the discontents of sections alienated by Sulla, the Equites, the urban populace, the dispossessed peasants. As early as 78 M. Lepidus made himself the spokesman of the plebs and attempted a military coup. He and his associate M. Iunius Brutus were defeated in the consulship of the optimates Mamercus Lepidus and D. Iunius Brutus. In Spain the Marian Sertorius had held out and stirred up a formidable provincial revolt. The bloodshed of the 80s had left the senate short of military talent (Cic. *Font.* 42 f.). It was necessary to employ the young Pompey to suppress both Lepidus and Sertorius. But it soon turned out that despite his Sullan past he was bent on securing a primacy in the state which was incompatible with the parity of dignity and influence which the other *principes* desired to maintain among themselves. He could not be denied the consulship of 70, though strictly ineligible, and in temporary conjunction with his colleague Crassus he carried a law restoring to the tribunes the plenary rights of which Sulla had deprived them.[38] This destroyed the barrier to popular legislation Sulla had devised; the Sullan system was now in ruins, all the more because clamour or violence in the streets, which the senate lacked military force to put down, could be used to overcome legal obstacles to further measures which the masses desired.

The initial beneficiary was Pompey. It was by popular demand that he received under the Gabinian law the great command against the pirates in 67, a demand that sprang from the scarcity of food which their depredations caused, not to speak of the damage they did to the interests of merchants and tax-farmers (p. 172). Caesar is said to have been the only senator who spoke for the law (Plut. *Pomp.* 25. 4). A veto was overridden by the mob. Pompey's swift success made him a popular hero. For this reason alone, Manilius' proposal that he should take over the war against Mithridates was probably irresistible. The most intransigent optimate leaders, Q. Catulus and Q. Hortensius,

---

[37] However, the tenor of Cic. *de prov. cons.* implies that some senators could be moved by arguments that the extension of Caesar's command was in the state's interest. On the publication of this speech see p. 47.

[38] *Per.* Livy xcvii; Ps.-Ascon. 189 St. As Pompey was chiefly responsible, the joint authorship of Crassus is ignored in Cic. *de leg.* iii. 22 (cf. I *Verr.* 44); Vell. ii. 30; Plut. *Pomp.* 22; cf. n. 61.

could not muster united opposition in the senate: four eminent consulars advocated the Manilian law,[39] so it was safe for Cicero, anxious though he was not to offend anyone of influence by taking a strong political stand (see below), to follow suit. But it would be imprudent to suppose that its advocates were not themselves moved by such arguments as he adduced: the public interest demanded that Rome should finish with Mithridates, and there was no one else obviously equal to the task (p. 172).

Once the victorious Pompey had returned to Rome, the optimates, led by L. Lucullus, could again try to reduce his authority to the level of that to which other *principes* might aspire. They baulked his efforts to secure lands for his veterans and the ratification of his eastern settlement. It was on this account that he formed the combination with Caesar and Crassus which we nickname the first triumvirate. As consul in 59 Caesar did not scruple to carry through the measures that Pompey required, by the strong arms of Pompey's veterans.[40] The legislation of Vatinius too was enacted in defiance of all legal obstructions.

Prima facie then Pompey rose to the consulship by the remarkable services he rendered first to Sulla and then in the 70s to the Sullan regime; but in 70 he adopted a popular role and subverted it; thereafter it was with popular support that he obtained his great commands in 67 and 66; and it was by turning to Caesar, a consistent and avowed *popularis*, and Crassus (n. 64), and by resort to violence that he procured his ends in 59. Cicero implies that all three, Pompey included, accepted the appellation *popularis*.[41] The grant to Caesar of a five-year command with a great army and control of north Italy meant that so long as the triumvirs remained in accord the optimates had no means of meeting force with superior force.[42] They even lacked the power to suppress the gangs with which from 58 Clodius was usually able to dominate the streets of Rome; Pompey himself then lost control in the city and was in more danger from these gangs, when Clodius had broken with him, than from the rancour of the optimates.

None the less some modern scholars suggest that Pompey owed his success to being head of a powerful aristocratic faction. Of this there is no hint in the sources. It is said that in 70 he had had less influence in the senate but more with the people than Crassus (n. 59), and that in 67 the senate was almost united against the Gabinian law (Plut. *Pomp.*

---

[39] Cic. *de imp. Cn. Pomp.* 51–68; the four consulars were P. Servilius Vatia (79), C. Scribonius Curio (76), C. Cassius Longinus (72), and Cn. Lentulus Clodianus (72).

[40] Plut. *Pomp.* 47 f., *Caes.* 14, *Cato* 32; App. ii. 10 f.; Dio xxxviii. 5 f.

[41] Cicero could regard Pompey as *popularis* in 60 (*Att.* i. 19. 4, 20. 2; cf. Badian. *Athen.* 1977, 233 ff.); for 59 cf. ii. 19. 2, 20. 4.

[42] Cf. Cic. *Att.* ii. 16. 2 (with Meier, *Historia* 1961, 79–84) See also p. 437.

25). We shall see that in and after 59 there appears to have been no large body of senators committed to support of the 'triumvirs' or of Pompey in particular, though both then and earlier individuals would accommodate themselves to political realities, so far as to accept posts in their gift or to avail themselves of their electoral backing. The basis of the modern theory is a set of prosopographic inferences. It is supposed that Pompey was significantly strengthened by families related to him by the bonds of marriage or friendship. Let us first consider connections of the former kind.[43]

Pompey had taken as his third wife Mucia, the half-sister of Q. Metellus Celer and Q. Metellus Nepos; both served him as legates in the 60s, and Nepos as tribune in 62 was ardent on his behalf. But it is unwarranted to speak of an alliance with the Metelli (Syme, *RR* 32). Whatever his relationship may have been with his senior colleague in Spain from 77 to 71, Q. Metellus Pius, whom he overshadowed, in 67 he affronted Q. Metellus Creticus (*cos.* 69), another distant cousin of Celer and Nepos. Moreover, when Pompey put Mucia away, Celer too turned against him, and was one of his strongest adversaries as consul in 60. Later, after the death of his next wife Iulia, Caesar's daughter, Pompey was to marry the daughter of Q. Metellus Pius Scipio, and Syme writes of 'the compact with Metelli and Scipiones' (ibid. 43b) but there were no other representatives of either family then of mature years and political consequence.

Gruen notes Pompey's connections by birth and marriage with 'the house of Sulla', with M. Scaurus, son of the consul of 115, and with the Memmii. He had once married Aemilia (his second wife), the sister of Scaurus and the stepsister of Sulla's only son Faustus, but she had died in 81. Faustus' own sister was married to L. Memmius, the father of C. Memmius, praetor in 58; L. Memmius' brother Gaius, who was killed when Pompey's quaestor in 75, was married to Pompey's sister, who bore him C. Memmius, tribune in 54, and who took as her second husband P. Sulla, the man elected to the consulship of 65 and disqualified for *ambitus*, who was to be a legate of Caesar in the civil war. The 'house of Sulla' is a misleading expression, since P. Sulla and two other members of the family implicated in the Catilinarian conspiracy (as he too was alleged to have been) were probably only distant cousins of Faustus, and are not known to have co-operated with him. Their connections with Catiline hardly suggest that they were partisans of Pompey, and after 65 P. Sulla, though still rich, had in any event no political standing. That is no less true of Faustus, who was too young to reach any office higher than the quaestorship (in 54), and not

---

[43] See e.g. Gruen 1974, 62 f.; Syme, *RR*, ch. III.

much less of Scaurus, at least until he was praetor in 56; neither seems to have possessed any marked ability to offset their youth. Pompey's nephew C. Memmius, as tribune, was along with Sulla, his stepfather, associated in prosecuting Gabinius (Cic. *Qu. fr.* iii. 3. 2), whom Pompey despite every effort ultimately failed to save. That Memmius' cousin as praetor in 58 had been vocal against Pompey's ally, Caesar; and if any marriage relationship is to explain this, it must be the union of his own sister with C. Curio (*cos.* 76), who along with his son took a leading part in opposition to the 'triumvirs'.[44] The praetor of 58 must later have changed front, as both Pompey and Caesar backed his unsuccessful candidature for the consulship of 53 (*Att.* iv. 16. 6), though Pompey was unwilling or unable to prevent his condemnation and exile for bribery. Scaurus, one of Memmius' rivals in the competition, suffered the same fate. Pompey had left him to govern Syria in 62, but there is no testimony to a subsequent political connection, until Pompey supported him too for the consulship of 53, perhaps insincerely; he was thought to resent Scaurus' marriage to his divorced wife Mucia (Ascon. 19 C.; *Att.* iv. 15. 7), and threw him over before the election (*Qu. fr.* iii. 8. 4). Memmius, Scaurus and P. Plautius Hypsaeus, whose condemnation for bribery in 52 Pompey also refused to avert (n. 49), are the only candidates whom Pompey is recorded to have commended after Pupius Piso (*cos.* 61), though he also stood behind Afranius and doubtless Gabinius; it is in fact curious how rarely we hear of the intervention of *principes* in any elections.

Thus Pompey's kinsmen were not all his consistent collaborators, and (except the Metelli) did not reach the highest office; their support could not much have augmented the strength of his 'faction'.

It is also suggested that the four consulars who supported the Manilian law and likewise Cicero, as well as the senators whom Pompey chose as legates in his various commands, were his political allies.

Of the former C. Lentulus Clodianus and L. Gellius had been censors in his first consulship; but it is a mere conjecture that they were chosen and acted at his will. Both were also among his legates in the 60s.[45] So too was Cn. Lentulus Marcellinus (*cos.* 56), and P. Lentulus Spinther (*cos.* 57) is well attested as his 'friend'. Hence an alliance with the Lentuli in general has been tentatively postulated by Syme (*RR* 44). But in 59 L. Lentulus Niger was an opponent of the triumvirs,[46]

---

[44] Cic. *Att.* ii. 24, *Vat.* 24, *Brut.* 218 f. Hence, after his clash with the Curios as friends of Clodius in 61 (*Att.* i. 16. 1; Schol. Bobb. 85 ff. St.), Cicero was again on good terms with them (*Att.* ii. 7. 3).

[45] *MRR* lists legates in this period.

[46] Cic. *Vat.* 25, *Att.* ii. 24. 2, iv. 6. 1. L. Lentulus Crus (*cos.* 49) should also not be classed as a previous adherent of Pompey because he had served under him in the 70s; Caes. *BC* i. 1–4 makes him appear quite independent.

and so was Marcellinus himself as consul in 56 (n. 71). In fact the
family had no political cohesion (p. 456). Gellius too was adverse to
Pompey in 59.[47] In fact none of the four consulars who spoke for the
Manilian law is known to have given Pompey any political backing
later. In 59 Curio was prominent in opposition (n. 44).

As for legates, it is far from clear that a governor normally chose
them for their political affiliations rather than for their talents or
character, or that they were subsequently bound to his allegiance.[48]
We may recall the choice made by L. Furius Philus (p. 468). In the 60s,
however grievous to the optimates was the popular legislation by
which Pompey obtained his commands, it was manifestly in Rome's
interests that her enemies should be subdued; men who took a
prominent share in the task could hope to win for themselves honour
and riches, as well as Pompey's favour, in the service of the state; and if
any apprehensions were entertained of Pompey attempting a military
coup, aristocrats on his staff were best placed to thwart it. Pompey's
choice was not then circumscribed by narrow political considerations.
We know the names of twenty of his legates in this time; they include
Gellius, Marcellinus, the two Metelli brothers, all of whom were later
to oppose him, and L. Valerius Flaccus, with whom his relations had
become so sour in 59 that he was suspected of engineering Flaccus'
prosecution for *repetundae* (Cic. *Flacc.* 14); Flaccus none the less became
legate of L. Piso (*cos.* 58), who as Caesar's father-in-law is naturally
taken to be an ally of Pompey. Of the other legates, L. Manlius
Torquatus (*cos.* 65) was at least not among those who favoured his
Egyptian ambitions in 56 (see below), and M. Pupius Piso, whom he
commended for the consulship of 61, did nothing effectual on his behalf
when in office, and actually operated against him (*Att.* i. 14. 6), and
thereafter disappears from view. By birth he was one of the Calpurnii
Pisones, another family not united politically; L. Piso (*cos.* 58) stood
with the triumvirs, but the young Cn. Piso had been Pompey's enemy
(Sall. *Cat.* 19); so was the consul of 67, who was treated with high
honour by Pupius (Cic. *Att.* i. 13. 2). Only two of Pompey's known
legates may be classed safely as his loyal adherents, L. Afranius (*cos.*

---

[47] Plut. *Cic.* 26. 1. The 'Pompeian' military man M. Petreius (*RR* 31 n. 6) was also against him
in 59 (Dio xxxviii. 3. 2).
[48] Three of Cicero's four legates in Cilicia had military experience, his brother Quintus, and C.
Pomptinus and M. Anneius (*Fam.* xiii. 57. 2), neither of whom are known as his special friends.
Acc. to *Pis.* 53 f., all L. Piso's legates in Macedon were ultimately estranged from him. Of 23 who
certainly or probably served as Caesar's legates in Gaul, 7 were dead or have disappeared from
our records by 49; admittedly 12 were thereafter his partisans (L. Caesar (*cos.* 64) and Ser. Galba
(*pr.* 54) were perhaps neutral, and Q. Cicero and Labienus followed Pompey), but only two
Caesarians, Antony and the insignificant P. Sulpicius Rufus, belonged to consular houses; the rest
had doubtless obtained unexpected riches and status by service with Caesar, and their
relationship to him cannot be taken as typical of that between legates and their commander.

60) and A. Gabinius (*cos.* 58), men of undistinguished birth, who owed everything to their connection with him and could hardly contribute independent influence to enhance his strength. Those mentioned later as his intimate advisers were also not men who counted for much in their own right.[49]

Cicero was never among these intimates, and complains from time to time how little he could understand the mind of his 'friend' Pompey.[50] Until he himself became consul, he hardly wielded much authority, whether or not Pompey's partisan. But there is no testimony or other good reason to justify placing him in that category. His advocacy of the Manilian law warrants this for him no more than for the four consulars. He may well have believed that the law was justified by needs of state for the reasons he gives (p. 172). No doubt he chose to make his first appearance in a *contio* on this occasion, just because it was a popular cause, to ingratiate himself with the electorate (*de imp. Cn. Pomp.* 1–3). The *Commentariolum Petitionis* says that it had been his aim to win Pompey's friendship or at least prevent Pompey's opposition to his advance (5), and that he ought to make it universally known that his election to the consulship would accord with Pompey's desire and interests (51); but it contains no evidence that Pompey himself signified his approval to anyone, and Cicero's own jocular allusion to Pompey's favour in the summer of 65 can hardly be taken seriously; at the time he was using the good offices of Pompey's enemy C. Piso for his canvassing in Cisalpine Gaul (*Att.* i. 1. 2). The *Commentariolum* admits that there were others he had alienated by his laudations of Pompey (14), but Cicero had been careful to minimize this risk, and in fact he had not lost Piso's goodwill. In advocating the Manilian law, as in

---

[49] Pupius: Dio xxxvii. 44. 3 presumably means that at Pompey's request the senate postponed the consular elections of 62 to allow Pupius to stand in person; if Pompey asked for postponement till his own return (Plut. *Cato* 30, *Pomp.* 44), which was probably as late as December, the demand was rejected. Cicero names as Pompey's special intimates in 56 P. Plautius Hypsaeus and L. Scribonius Libo. Plautius, of consular lineage, he would support for the consulship of 52 and then abandon to judicial condemnation (Ascon. 35 C.; Plut. *Pomp.* 55; Val. Max. ix. 5. 3). Libo, of old praetorian family, appears among his confidants in 49, along with L. Lucceius, Caesar's unsuccessful partner in the consular elections of 60, also of praetorian family (at best), and the Greekling Theophanes (n. 107). Note also Pompey's cousin C. Lucilius Hirrus, who with his fellow-tribune M. Coelius Vinicianus would have made Pompey dictator in 53; neither was of high lineage; Lucilius fought for Pompey, was pardoned by Caesar and perished in the proscriptions of 43; Coelius commanded under Caesar. The famous M. Terentius Varro, presumably of consular descent, served Pompey as legate in Spain in the 70s, in the pirate war, and again in Spain in 50–49, besides being a land commissioner under Caesar's laws of 59; but he seems to have been of no political consequence and never rose beyond the praetorship held in the 70s.

[50] e.g. *Att.* i. 13. 4, iv. 1. 7, 9. 1, 15. 7, *Qu.fr.* i. 3. 9, iii. 6 (8). 4, *Fam.* i. 1. 3, 2. 3. E. S. Gruen, *AJP* 1971, 1 ff. (cf. Brunt. *Chiron* 1980, 252 f.) against Cicero's supposed connection with Pompey in 70. *Comm. Pet.* 5, 14, 51 and *Att.* i. 1. 2 (see Shackleton Bailey ad loc.) do not show that Pompey promoted his election as consul. For the years 62–60 R. J. Rowland. *Riv. St. Ant.* 1976–7, 329 ff., is essentially right.

defending Cornelius, he had been careful to speak in honorific terms of the leading optimates, including Pompey's rivals or adversaries.[51] On the two other occasions before his consulship when he addressed the people, it was on the optimate side.[52] He could claim in 62 that at this time he was not yet deeply involved in politics, since he was preoccupied not only by forensic practice but by his aspirations for the highest office (*Sulla* 11). This statement, whether or not true, must have been credible; in other words it was plausible that a prospective candidate, at least if a parvenu, would seek to avoid political entanglements which might alienate electoral support. This was one way for a rising man to preserve his independence.

From 63 onwards Cicero could of course assume the role of one of the *principes*. This meant for him that he should speak his own mind on public affairs with the chance of being able to affect decisions.[53] Except when the interests of his client Cornelius had required him to justify the sovereignty of the people (Ascon. 71 f., 76–8 C.), he had never even in the past detracted from the authority of the senate, though he had on occasion bitterly assailed the arrogance of a few aristocrats;[54] now he frankly declared his optimate principles, and years later he could truly assert that as consul he had acted throughout by the will and advice of the senate;[55] if he also advocated 'concordia ordinum' or 'consensus Italiae', it was on the basis that the Equites and the propertied class in Italy would accept the direction of affairs by the senate, which on its part should respect the sentiments and interests of these elements in the state (*Sest.* 96–137). 'It had always been his desire', he was to say, 'that no one man should have more power than the whole commonwealth' (*Fam.* vii. 3. 5), and for him the senate was the proper representative of the commonwealth. Cato would have concurred.

It is true that as consul he made out that in opposing Rullus' agrarian bill he was protecting Pompey's interests (*de leg. agr.* ii. 24 f., 47–54, 60–2); but the contention was perhaps no less specious than the other sophistries by which he discredited the bill; agrarian legislation of any kind he abhorred (*Att.* ii. 3. 3). His resistance to the tribune Metellus Nepos in 62 was not that of a Pompeian partisan. When

---

[51] Ascon. 61 C.; Cic. *de imp. Cn. Pomp.* 20 f., 26, 51–63.

[52] Against Crassus' proposal (Plut. *Cr.* 13; cf. n. 63) to annex Egypt (Schol. Bobb. 91–3.; Cic. *de leg. agr.* ii. 41–4), and against the attempt to make Faustus Sulla disgorge public moneys allegedly in his possession (Ascon. 73 C.).

[53] It was now proper for him 'in senatu sentire libere, populi utilitati magis consulere quam voluntati, nemini cedere, multis obsistere' (*Sulla* 24). Cf. his complaints of the loss of such *dignitas* and *libertas* in *Fam.* i. 8. 3 (55) and iv. 14. 1 (46).

[54] e.g. *Quinct.* 31, I *Verr.* 36, II 1. 155, iii. 145, v. 126 f., 180 f., *Cluent.* 152. But see R. Heinze, *Vom Geiste des Römertums*, 1960 (first published in 1909), 87 ff.

[55] *Phil.* ii. 11. Hence his banishment was an assult on *senatus auctoritas* (*post red. sen.* 8, 20, etc.).

Pompey's return was imminent, he offered to be Laelius to Pompey's Scipio (*Fam.* v. 7). The terms of the letter suggest to me that they had previously had no close association. After Pompey's arrival their relations were at first distinctly cool (*Att.* i. 13, 14. 3), and Cicero was contemptuous in private and soon openly critical of Pupius, Pompey's protégé in the consulship (i. 13. 2, 16. 8). In fact Pupius proved disloyal (14. 6). Cicero clearly numbered himself among the optimates (13. 2 f., 16. 6–8, 18. 3); he deplored Pompey's popular stance (n. 41), despised Afranius, whose election to the consulship of 60 Pompey procured by bribery (16. 12), and expressed the highest commendation of 'his friend' Metellus Celer, the other consul of 60 (18. 3, 19. 4, ii. 1. 3); and yet Metellus took a leading part in obstructing Flavius' agrarian bill (Dio xxxvii. 50), which Pompey was bent on passing, to provide lands for his veterans (*Att.* i. 19. 4). Cicero himself proposed amendments which would have made the measure less effective, and his claim that he was satisfying Pompey was probably self-deceptive (ibid.). As for Pompey's other main objective, the ratification of his eastern settlement, of which Metellus was also an opponent (Dio xxxviii. 49), Cicero says not a word of it to Atticus, and surely gave Pompey no help. From July 61 Cicero could suppose himself to be on the friendliest terms with Pompey, whom the raffish dubbed Cn. Cicero (*Att.* i. 16. 10, 17. 10), apparently because Pompey was now at last willing to laud Cicero's achievements as consul and to lay aside something of his own 'popularis levitas' (i. 19. 7, 20. 2, ii. 1. 6); by the summer of 60 Cicero hoped to bring Caesar too over to the good cause (ii. 1. 6). All this shows that in his own estimation he was no partisan of Pompey, but his equal; moreover, their alliance was to be based on Pompey's adherence to Cicero's constitutional principles, not on the satisfaction of Pompey's personal demands. But this alliance existed only in Cicero's delusions. He was awakened to reality by the pact between the so-called triumvirs. Though not active in opposing their measures, Cicero made his disapproval patent, rejecting all their overtures. He did indeed, probably like many others, preserve the outward forms of personal amity with them, but his unconcealed hostility to their political conduct induced them at least to connive in his expulsion by Clodius.

Clodius, it need hardly be said, was no mere instrument of the 'triumvirs'.[56] By legitimating and organizing the *collegia* he secured a mastery of the streets at Rome which outlasted his tribunate, and before his year of office had expired in 58 he had come into conflict with Pompey and his protégé as consul A. Gabinius, though not with Gabinius' colleague L. Piso, Caesar's father-in-law, nor with Crassus;

[56] E. S. Gruen, 1974, 98 ff.; cf. *Phoenix* 1960, 120 ff.

at the same time he entered into some sort of *rapprochement* with the extreme optimates, who were ready to 'fondle' him in the hope of undermining Pompey's position.[57] None the less, Pompey and Caesar had assisted him in his adoption by a plebeian, and thereby enabled him to qualify for the tribunate; and it suited their aims that he removed both Cato and Cicero from the political arena at Rome.

Of course Clodius acted against Cicero from a personal grudge, but as Cicero justly reiterated, his action in putting the Catilinarians to death had been approved in advance by the senate, and the senate's authority was impugned when he was exiled for this alleged breach of the right of citizens to due trial on a capital charge (n. 55). It is clear that the senate was almost unanimous in protesting against his martyrdom in its cause; it was impotent to save him in 58 because the consuls, both supporters of the 'triumvirs', were leagued with Clodius, and there was thus no possibility of the senate passing the 'last decree' and calling on them to crush the force that Clodius commanded with superior force; moreover, Caesar, still outside Rome, indirectly pronounced his condemnation of Cicero's action in 63 (Dio xxxviii. 17), and neither Pompey nor Crassus would express any opposition to Clodius' measures. However, the senate virtually suspended all business until he should be restored,[58] hardly because he was personally much loved, but because its own authority was at stake. Its wishes could not be answered until Pompey had broken with Clodius and was prepared to organize respectable people throughout Italy to back Cicero's recall; and this he would do only when Cicero had given some kind of pledge not to assail his ally Caesar, and thereby procured Caesar's assent (*Fam.* i. 9. 9). It can hardly be doubted that his banishment had been effected in the first place with the sanction, however reluctant, of the 'triumvirs', who viewed him as a potentially formidable antagonist, but were ready to restore him once they were assured of his future good behaviour.

These transactions are not merely of interest in so far as they concern Cicero's biography. If the 'triumvirs' themselves concurred in his banishment, which almost the entire senate treated as derogatory to its authority, we have additional proof that they had little support in the senate, whose will was overborne because the consuls of 58, their partisans, refused to carry it out, and because Clodius' gangs and Caesar's army in any event, outmatched any force which the senate could muster (*Sest.* 35, 42). At the same time the subsequent breach of Clodius with both Pompey and Gabinius, but not with their associates, shows how uncohesive was the small faction supporting the triumvirs.

[57] *Fam.* i. 9. 10, *Qu. fr.* ii. 3. 4. The manœuvres are obscure.
[58] Brunt, *LCM* 1981, 227 ff. Gelzer, *Cicero* ch. IX, gives the evidence fully on his exile.

The senate as a body had indeed been reduced to a nullity by force. Naturally some of its members would adjust themselves to the circumstances. A board of twenty, of whom five were armed with judicial powers, was appointed to administer Caesar's agrarian laws (*MRR*, ii. 191 f.). Pompey and Crassus served on it; besides them only five names are recorded. They include a single consular, M. Messalla, who had when in office (61) earned Cicero's approval as a man of sound views, but he seems to have been a cipher. P. Vatinius, tribune in 59, and one of his colleagues, C. Alfius Flavus, a man of no significance, the consuls of 58, and one or two of Clodius' fellow-tribunes can be treated as partisans of the 'triumvirs'; perhaps too Caesar's legates in 58, among then Clodius' brother Gaius, and perhaps Ser. Sulpicius Galba; the rest (Labienus included) were of undistinguished families. Thus there is nothing to show that the 'triumviral' faction was at all numerous. Pompey himself brought few adherents to his cause. It is a *petitio principii* to speak of his aristocratic allies deserting him; there is no proof that in extolling his past achievements, approving the conferment of great commands upon him, or accepting from him commissions in which they could serve the state and themselves, aristocrats had ever pledged an alliance with him for the future. As for Caesar, he was a declared *popularis* (Cic. *Cat.* iv. 9); his espousal of popular causes, his eloquence, and his munificence had won him popular acclaim but could only foster suspicion in his own order (n. 63). Crassus no doubt had a greater pull over senators (n. 33); in 63 so many were under financial obligations to him that charges of his complicity with Catiline were not so much as given a hearing. But one who was neither a firm friend nor an implacable enemy but who readily changed his attitude at the bidding of self-interest was unlikely to have inspired devotion in others.[59] His wealth and proclivity for intrigue, which may well have made Pompey and Caesar sedulous to conciliate him, must also have generated mistrust; and I find no evidence that there was a group in the senate which consistently, if ever, followed his lead.

His relationship with Pompey is in itself a striking example of the permutations in the behaviour of almost all politicians of the age of whom much is recorded.[60] According to Plutarch (*Cr.* 6. 4, 7. 1), he was envious of Pompey from the first. Yet he combined with him in canvassing for the consulship of 70 and as his colleague in restoring the tribunician power. But then he failed to show the deference Pompey expected; a quarrel ensued, ostensibly ended by a public reconciliation

---

[59] Sall, *Cat.* 48; Plut. *Cr.* 7; perhaps it was precisely because of his quarrel with Pompey (n. 61) that he had more senatorial support.

[60] Ward, 1977, gives the evidence fully, though often too speculative on political alignments.

that proved hollow.[61] He did not support either the Gabinian or Manilian bills. He was thought to have promoted the extraordinary appointment of Cn. Piso to govern Nearer Spain in 65, because Piso was, like himself, Pompey's enemy.[62] Throughout Pompey's absence from Rome he was engaged in manœuvres, of which this was one specimen, to build up his own influence to counterbalance that of the man he sought to rival.

In some of these schemes he had the support of the young Caesar.[63] Both favoured the enfranchisement of the Transpadanes and the annexation of Egypt, and both appear to have been behind Rullus' agrarian bill in 63; in all cases the optimates were obstructive. Both also seem to have backed the election of Catiline to the consulship of 63; that gave some plausibility to charges, which there is no ground for accepting, that both were involved in his plot of 63, not to speak of a coup allegedly projected in 65, which in my judgement was hostile invention. While Caesar courageously argued against the execution of Catiline's accomplices, Crassus absented himself from the senatorial debate, not wishing either to deviate from 'popular' principles or to take a stand against his peers.[64] Despite his Sullan past he was now, like Caesar, taking a popular line. The optimates were naturally averse to popular measures, and had no more love for Crassus than for Pompey. The success of their opposition to Crassus' schemes shows how little real influence he had in the senate. There is no reason to think that he had it in mind to furnish himself with the means to confront Pompey in an armed struggle for power. No forces at his disposal

[61] Sall. *Hist.* iv. 58, 61; Plut. *Cr.* 12, *Pomp.* 22 ff. App. i. 121 (see Gabba ad loc.) is, as often (e.g. ii. 9–14), chronologically confused.

[62] Sall. *Cat.* 17. 7, 19; he is no doubt right that the optimates concurred in the appointment out of ill will to Pompey.

[63] Gelzer, *Caesar*, ch. 2, gives the evidence for what follows. R. Seager, *Historia* 1964, 338 f., decisively discredited the 'first Catilinarian conspiracy'; his scepticism on the second (ibid. 1973, 240 ff.) is unwarranted, but the complicity of Crassus and Caesar alleged by their enemies lacked proof or plausibility. A coup by Catiline would have given Pompey good reason for emulating Sulla, and have been their ruin had they been involved; Crassus would not have been so imprudent, and Caesar had no cause to embroil himself with Pompey. The sources for many transactions are meagre and biased, esp. on Caesar's early career (cf. H. Strasburger, *Caesars Eintritt in die Gesch.* 1938 = *St. zur alten Gesch.* 181 ff.). On Suetonius's life cf. ch. 1 n. 82; the story in 8 is incredible, though Caesar's later enfranchisement of the Transpadani (Dio xli. 36. 3; cf. Cic. *Att.* v. 2. 3) reflected earlier sympathy with their aspirations; and 11 on Egypt is a farrago of nonsense, which at best has a basis in truth if he backed Crassus' move for annexation (n. 52). He as well as Crassus may be the unnamed persons of Cic. *de leg. agr.* ii. 44 who had urged it in 65, and who were the real but covert authors of Rullus' bill, men feared by the senate (i. 16, 22, ii. 10, 20, 23, 65); the bill too in many respects corresponded to Caesar's agrarian legislation in 59 (*IM* 312 f.). Probably Crassus assisted Caesar with his creditors in 62 (Plut. *Caes.* 11, *Cr.* 7. 6; Suet. *Caes.* 18; App. ii. 8). If both also supported Catiline's candidature in 64 (Ascon. 83 C.), that gave some colour to hostile calumnies a year later.

[64] His absence from the list of consulars present in Cic. *Att.* xii. 21. 1 identifies him as the notable professed *popularis* who would not vote on the *caput* of a citizen (*Cat.* iv. 10).

could have equalled the strength of Pompey's veteran army. Rather it was a peaceful contest for influence after Pompey's return that he was preparing for. Pompey was a patron of the Transpadanes (ch. 8 n. 44): Crassus would have had superior claims to their gratitude if he had obtained the citizenship for them. The acquisition of Egypt and its wealth would have matched the conquests Pompey was making in the east. Rullus' bill would doubtless have provided lands for Pompey's veterans among others, but Crassus as commissioner for allotments would have gained much of the credit.

The association of Caesar with Crassus in manœuvres by which Crassus at least was trying to set himself up against Pompey is at first sight puzzling, since Caesar had supported the Gabinian and Manilian bills and was to join Metellus Nepos in 62 in demanding that Pompey be recalled to meet the threat from Catiline; he also urged that Pompey, not Catulus, should be commissioned to dedicate the temple of Capitoline Jupiter. He was collaborating with Crassus, yet in other ways ingratiating himself with Pompey. This was the easier, as Crassus was characteristically careful to work against Pompey only by indirect means, abstaining from any acts of overt enmity. The patron of the Transpadanes had no legitimate grievance if new benefits were conferred on his clients. The annexation of Egypt would not have entrenched on his functions in the east. He could not have complained (despite Cicero's pretences) if land had been available for his soldiers under Rullus' law; Caesar could have contended that it would actually suit his interests. The conduct of the young Caesar in these years is to my mind only an extreme case of the independence to which senators aspired, untrammelled by allegiance to any leader or faction.

Some ancient and some modern writers have believed that there was general fear that on his return from the east Pompey would seize power by arms; it seems unlikely to me that it was entertained by those who knew the man. Crassus himself left Italy in 62 in pretended apprehension, but went to Asia, where Pompey was already in absolute military control.[65] Presumably he hoped to do a deal with him, as in 70 and in 59. But he was disappointed; at that moment Pompey was meditating a *rapprochement* with the optimates, as his abortive overtures for a

---

[65] Plut. *Pomp.* 43; Cic. *Flacc.* 32; Crassus was back in Rome about the same time as Pompey or earlier (*Att.* i. 14. 1–4), and must have started on his return before he could learn that Pompey had disbanded his army. For alleged fears of Pompey see also Vell. ii. 40. 2; App. *Mithr.* 116; Dio xxxvii. 20, 44. Cic. *Fam.* v. 7. 1 (on which see Gruen, *Phoenix* 1970, 237 ff.) also indicates that some thought he might use his military power illegally; yet the firm action taken against the tribune Metellus Nepos in 62 might have furnished Pompey with an excuse for armed intervention, as did that against tribunes in 49 for Caesar, and seems to show that the senatorial leaders had no real apprehensions of a coup.

marriage connection with Cato show.[66] In the event they obstructed his desires, abetted by Crassus. It was Caesar as the mutual friend of Pompey and Crassus who brought them together in 60–59.[67] The insincerity of the latter was patent to Cicero, who remarked that the spectacle of Pompey addressing the people in July 59 without evoking any signs of their customary affection for him could please none but Crassus (*Att.* ii. 21. 3 f.). By 57 he was notoriously encouraging Clodius in activity hostile to Pompey, who could even suggest that Crassus was plotting against his life (*Qu. fr.* ii. 3. 4). At Luca Caesar had to reconcile them again. Crassus had now realized that wealth and intrigue could never make him the equal of his partners; his price was a military command in which he hoped to rival their fame.

The ill will of the optimates, of Clodius, and of Crassus between 58 and 56 gravely weakened Pompey's position. Though he received with senatorial assent a new commission, to organize the procurement of grain for Rome in 57, this was to allay popular agitation. How few and insignificant were his personal adherents is revealed by the senatorial debates early in 56 on the restoration of Ptolemy Auletes to the throne of Egypt; they also illustrate the disunity of the optimates and the entanglement of individuals in conflicting obligations to friends.[68]

In 57 the senate had allotted the task of restoring Ptolemy to P. Lentulus Spinther the consul, who was to be governor of Cilicia and Cyprus. Cicero's letters to him presuppose that Spinther counted himself one of the *boni* and could be expected to endorse Cicero's optimate ideal of *otium cum dignitate*, which Cicero proclaimed in 56 when defending P. Sestius; at the same time he continued to enjoy some sort of personal friendship with both Pompey and Caesar. The king wished the task to be entrusted to Pompey. The optimates were naturally opposed to his being given a new extraordinary command; Crassus shared this antipathy. A Sibylline oracle was 'discovered', and interpreted to mean that no army might be sent to Egypt. The tribune Gaius Cato gave it publicity; a distant cousin of Marcus, he had assailed the triumvirs in 59 (*Qu. fr.* i. 2. 15), but was now leagued with Clodius and covertly incited by Crassus.[69] If the oracle were to be observed, the restoration of Ptolemy would hardly be practicable. It

---

[66] Plut. *Pomp.* 44, *Cato* 30.
[67] Cic. *Att.* ii. 3. 3 confirms App. ii. 9; Dio xxxvii. 54 f.; Plut. *Pomp.* 47.
[68] Cic. *Fam.* i. 1–7, *Qu. fr.* ii. 2. 3, 3. 2, 5. 3 (4. 5); Dio xxxix. 12–6.
[69] Spinther and Pompey: *Fam.* i. 1. 2 f., 2. 3, 5B. 2, 7. 3, 8. 5, *Qu. fr.* ii. 2. 3. In *Fam.* i. 9. 11–18 Cicero can assume Spinther's approval not only of his accord with Pompey and with Caesar (another of Spinther's friends, Caes. *BC* i. 22), but also of his eulogy of Bibulus and his anti-triumviral motion on the *ager Campanus* (n. 75), and in general of his endorsement of optimate principles and of *otium cum dignitate* (ibid. 10, 21); nor could Spinther understand his reconciliation with Crassus or Vatinius (ibid 19 f.). C. Cato: Dio xxxix. 15. 3; *Qu. fr.* ii. 1. 2, 3. 3 f., 5. 3 (4. 5).

was thus adverse to the ambitions of Spinther as well as of Pompey. Since Spinther had assisted hardly less than Pompey in effecting Cicero's recall, this suited Clodius well; and C. Cato in fact tried to have Spinther deprived of his province. The optimates too mostly had no inclination to gratify Spinther. Conceivably they resented his personal amity with Pompey and Crassus. Probably they secretly agreed with the old Sullan consul P. Servilius Isauricus that no attempt at all should be made to restore Ptolemy; however, it was embarrassing for them to resile from a commitment already accepted (not without bribes from the king), and in January 56 Servilius apparently had no seconder, when the senate considered four other proposals, all for Ptolemy's restoration (*Fam*. i. 1. 3, 2. 1 f.): (1) by Spinther (advocated by M. Lucullus, Hortensius, and Cicero); (2) by Pompey (supported by the tribune Rutilius Lupus and by Pompey's close friends, including Volcacius Tullus (*cos*. 66) and Afranius (*cos*. 60); (3) by three legates, not excluding those already possessed of *imperium*, as Pompey was (proposed by Crassus); (4) by three legates, excluding holders of *imperium*. The last course was favoured by the consuls Cn. Lentulus Marcellinus and L. Marcius Philippus, by Bibulus, and by all other consulars present (*Fam*. i. 1). Those known to have been still politically active and not abroad at the time were C. Scribonius Curio (76), L. Gellius Publicola (72), Q. Metellus Creticus (69), Manius Lepidus (66), L. Cotta and L. Torquatus (65), L. Caesar (62), and Marcus Messalla (61): Curio was certainly involved, and so perhaps were all the rest.

Of these motions that of Crassus evidently had no support; and there was also no prospect of a vote in favour of Pompey (*Fam*. v. 6B. 2). Only two consulars spoke for it, neither a man of any weight; Volcacius, moreover, far from being Pompey's faithful adherent, was to remain neutral in 49. Among Pompey's intimates who urged it on his behalf Cicero names only two men of lesser rank, P. Plautius Hypsaeus and L. Scribonius Libo (n. 49). It was their activity that made men assume that Pompey coveted the command; with his usual reticence he would neither disavow them nor refuse to serve, while advocating Spinther's claims in public and professing constancy to his friendship. This attitude no doubt made it easier for Cicero, who was under obligations to both, to go on pressing Spinther's cause. But only two other optimate consulars concurred with him. Most together with the consuls agreed with Bibulus. Even Spinther's professed friends behaved as his ill-wishers and detractors (*Fam*. i. 7. 2 f., 2. 7 f.), notably Curio (4. 1) and that 'perpetual foe of his own friends' who may be identified with L. Domitius Ahenobarbus.[70] The consul Marcellinus

---

[70] See Shackleton Bailey on *Fam*. i. 9. 2.

proclaimed his readiness to protect Spinther's interests in any other matter (1. 2); he did in fact obstruct Cato's bill to deprive Spinther of *imperium* (*Qu. fr.* ii. 5(4). 2 f.; cf. 3. 1). As remarked above (p. 456), the Lentuli cannot be shown to have formed a political unit, still less to have been allies of Pompey, of whom Marcellinus was a prominent adversary to the end of his consulship.[71] The majority of the senate rejected Bibulus' motion. Spinther was entitled to act on the previous decree of the senate, but not to use force. Naturally he did nothing; it was left to Gabinius to bring Ptolemy back, employing his army in Syria in defiance of the oracle.

The complexity of alignments revealed in this affair could never have been inferred from prosopographic data, but need not have been unique. It is clear that Pompey did not have the backing of a powerful personal faction. The pact of Luca in 56 renewed 'triumviral' accord and dominance. But it still did not give their 'party' sway in the senate. It is quite incredible that two hundred senators attended the conference at Luca[72] or that the triumvirs could thereafter rely on any considerable body of support in the house. Violence was needed to secure the election of Pompey and Crassus as consuls for 55 and the passage of the Trebonian law which gave them great commands in Syria and Spain. Cicero complained that Pompey was the sole master and that senators had lost, if not their freedom of speech, their ability to influence the conduct of affairs, with the result that there was no longer a true commonwealth.[73] But if they were impotent, Pompey was often almost in the same predicament. Violence and corruption reigned.[74]

For the first time Cicero himself, who had tried on his restoration from exile to resume his independent role,[75] was now reduced by the vague threats of the dynasts to acting on their behest; he who had once been a leader had become a mere 'attendant' (*Att.* iv. 6. 2).[76] It was he who moved some of the unprecedented honours that the senate voted to Caesar.[77] We should not, however, conclude that a 'triumviral' party now had a majority in the senate; Caesar's astonishing successes in Gaul had enhanced the *laus imperii* listed by Cicero among the foundations of that ideal of *otium cum dignitate* which in his view all good men desired; and the eulogy of Caesar which he delivered in his speech

[71] *Qu. fr.* ii. 5. 3; Dio xxxix. 27–30.   [72] Ward, 1977, 265 n. 13.

[73] *Fam.* i. 8. 2–4, *Att.* iv. 18. 2, *Qu. fr.* iii. 5. 4.

[74] e.g. *Att.* iv. 15. 7. The consulship for 53 was not filled for 6 months, for 52 for nearly 3.

[75] e.g. *Fam.* i. 9. 7–10 (on section 9 see D. L. Stockton, *TAPA* 1962, 471 ff.); cf. his proclamation of optimate principles in defending Sestius.

[76] For his loss of liberty cf. *Att.* iv. 5 f., 18. 2, *Qu. fr.* ii. 8 (7). 3, 14 (13). 4, iii. 4. 1 f., 5. 4, *Fam.* i. 7. 7 and 10, 8. 2–4, 9. 17, ii. 5. Cf. his complaint in 59: *Att.* ii. 21. 1.

[77] Caes. *BG* iii. 35, iv. 38 (cf. Cic. *Balb.* 64, *de prov. cons.* 38), vii. 90.

de provinciis consularibus very probably corresponded to widely felt patriotic rather than to partisan sentiments, even though the most bitter optimates remained hostile.[78] Nor in adhering to the 'triumvirs' was Cicero joining a cohesive party. Lentulus Spinther, himself a friend of Pompey and Caesar, approved of Cicero's amity with them, but could not see that this entailed reconciliation with Crassus and Vatinius too (*Fam.* i. 9. 19 f.). Cicero continued to inveigh against Pompey's protégé Gabinius and Caesar's father-in-law L. Piso, so far as he dared; in the end Pompey pressed him into Gabinius' defence (to no effect) and Cicero lamented that he was not even free to hate.[79]

Cicero was certainly not the only man of note who decided after Luca not to kick against the pricks, as the coterie of M. Cato still did; others were ready to obtain their commendations for office, which were still insufficient without massive electoral corruption. That did not make them loyal partisans of Pompey or Caesar. We can perhaps guess their real feelings from Cicero's. He professed the warmest affection for Caesar. Yet on the imminence or after the outbreak of civil war he was to blame Pompey for raising up Caesar to be a danger to the commonwealth, and when indicting Caesar as 'an insane and wicked man who had never glimpsed the very shadow of honour' (*Att.* vii. 11. 1), he betrays no sorrow that it was one he had loved who so disgraced himself (pp. 363 f.); Pompey too had only turned into 'an admirable citizen' after his 'divine third consulship' in 52, when he had restored order in league with the optimates (vii. 1. 2–4). Vulnerable to the hatred with which the masses requited his contempt for them[80] and to the enmity of Clodius, Cicero had sheltered for prudence under the protection of the dynasts, to his own humiliation; he had forfeited the independence to which all senators aspired. Appius Claudius with his aristocratic lineage was one who could still retain it. He was at Luca, and in or before 51 married one daughter to Pompey's son, but another to Pompey's enemy and Cato's associate M. Brutus (n. 109); he could first try to protect Gabinius and then assail him; he could co-operate as consul in 54 both with L. Domitius Ahenobarbus, one of the most consistent adversaries of the triumvirs, and as censor in 50 with L. Piso; as a final curiosity it may be remarked that when in the interests of one brother he engineered the prosecution of Scaurus, his other brother P. Clodius, with whom he had at times acted in harmony, appeared (with Cicero among others) for the defence (p. 374). The manœuvres of such individuals cannot be explained in terms of factional combinations, however short-lived, or obligations to friends and kin, or in this

---

[78] Cic. *Sest.* 98, *Fam.* i. 9. 21 (with 14–8); cf. Brunt, *Laus Imperii* 159 ff.
[79] *Fam.* i. 9. 19 f., *Qu. fr.* iii. 5. 4; Ascon. 1 f. C.
[80] *Att.* i. 16. 11, ii. 3. 4, viii. 11D. 7, *Phil.* vii. 4; Ascon. 37 C.

instance by any principles at all; the personal advantage of the moment was everything.

IV

For the 40s our information on political alignments is exceptionally rich, thanks to the abundance of Cicero's correspondence and the detailed and generally reliable narrative of Appian for the events that followed Caesar's death. All the leading men pretended to be acting in the public interest; for example Lepidus claimed that his desertion of the senate's cause in 43, though forced on him by his soldiers, was justifiable in the name of peace and concord (Cic. *Fam.* x. 35); generals continued to make similar professions as late as 41 (App. v. 17). Contemporaries assumed that men would generally be governed by considerations of common advantage; senators, Equites, the urban plebs, debtors could be expected to adopt the same attitudes (nn. 93, 95). Though their predictions were sometimes falsified, we can see the strength of the desire for *otium* at almost any cost among the propertied class. Naturally it was easy for them to equate this with the public good. Others, however, would prefer to risk everything for Republican liberty. All kinds of personal hopes and fears were said to dictate the conduct of particular individuals. Families were divided and friendships sundered; or rather, friends in different camps could in a fashion preserve their old relations of private amity or renew them easily in the intermission of peace. It is seldom suggested that the obligations of kinship or friendship determined the choices that each man had to make for himself, and there is still less reason to hold that many considered themselves bound in a merely personal allegiance to Pompey, Caesar, or Caesar's would-be successors. To show all this it will be appropriate to examine the evidence, especially for alignments in 49, in somewhat greater detail.

Anarchy in the city had reached a crescendo in the riots of 52 ensuing on Clodius' murder. Pompey was the one man who could restore *otium*. The senate voted that he be made sole consul in 52 on the motion of Bibulus supported by his father-in-law Cato (Ascon. 36 C.; Plut. *Cato* 47). Together with L. Domitius, Cato's brother-in-law, and a few others they had been hitherto Pompey's most resolute opponents. They were also Caesar's personal enemies. According to Caesar himself, in 49 it was they, along with Pompey, his father-in-law Q. Metellus Pius Scipio, and the consul L. Lentulus Crus, who manœuvred or terrorized the senate into passing the decrees that left him no choice but to resort to arms. In 52 Pompey had married Scipio's daughter Cornelia, and then taken him as colleague in the consulship. But Cornelia had previously been the wife of Crassus' son; Scipio is not known to have been a member of Cato's coterie, and Caesar, though ascribing to both him and Lentulus disreputable motives for warmongering in 49, distinguishes them from his own personal enemies. The faction which on his view precipitated hostilities consisted of disparate elements and had come together only recently.[81]

The measures which they forced through the senate in January 49 were designed to ensure that Caesar must give up his provinces and army before the consular elections of that year, and to force him to stand in person for a second consulship; though he would no doubt be returned, there would be time before he assumed office to prosecute him in the courts, which would only be possible once he was no longer vested with *imperium*; condemnation would eliminate him from public life.[82] The extreme optimates could remember his consistent profession of 'popular' principles and the ruthlessness with which he had exercised his consular powers in 59. With his vastly increased wealth and prestige, the conqueror of Gaul could as consul for the second time subvert senatorial ascendancy completely. To prevent this by intimidating Caesar or in the last resort defeating him in arms, they needed the military strength which they supposed to be at Pompey's disposal. No doubt they reckoned that Pompey would be content with a mere primacy in the state, as his past conduct suggested, or that once he had lost the backing of Caesar, he would become dependent on them. It was perhaps the risk of this dependence that made Pompey himself slow to commit himself to a breach with his old ally. But it was surely true, as all the later accounts say, that he had come to fear that his own fame and influence were now overshadowed by Caesar's. By the end of 50 he was ready to fight rather than allow Caesar a second consulship. That, he said in December, adopting the optimate standpoint, would be 'the destruction of the constitution' (*Att.* vii. 8. 4).

The majority of the senate had no taste for war (see pp. 492 f.). No doubt many shared the view which Cicero voiced at times that the contest would be merely one for personal dominance between the two dynasts,[83] and like him would have purchased peace by conceding Caesar's demands, however unjustifiable they seemed. Once the die had been cast, some would opt for neutrality, others reluctantly take a side in a struggle they deplored.

---

[81] Caes. *BC* iii. 1–4; he later thought to use Scipio as an intermediary for peace (iii. 57; contrast 16. 3 on Bibulus). For the bellicosity and personal motives of some leading Pompeians cf. *Att.* ix. 1. 4, 11. 4, *Fam.* iv. 1. 1, vi. 6. 6, vii. 3. 2, xvi. 11. 2, 12. 2.

[82] Raaflaub, 1974 (with his article in *Chiron* 1975) gives an exhaustive and fully-indexed account of the preliminaries to war (in part obscure), the subsequent diplomacy and propaganda, and the aims and attitudes of many participants; on alignments see also Bruhns, 1978, and, esp. on Cicero, Brunt, *JRS* 1986, 12 ff. Documentation here is selective.

[83] e.g. *Att.* vii. 3. 4, viii. 11. 2; Caelius, *Fam.* viii. 14. 2.

Both leaders appealed to the public good and claimed to be champions of the free commonwealth.[84] These appeals can be termed propaganda, but propaganda served no purpose, unless it was conceived as affecting public opinion, and conciliating wider support.

Liberty was the ideal that both professed to serve. For the 'Pompeians' it was tantamount to the authority of the senate, which Caesar had set at naught first by inducing tribunes to prevent the expression of its will, and then by open defiance.[85] Cicero certainly believed, as did many others, that Caesar sought despotism.[86] In intimate letters he could also assert that there was little to choose between him and Pompey: 'each wished to reign'; Pompey aimed at a 'Sullanum regnum' (n. 83). Pompey and his principal allies made no secret of their intention to follow the example of Sulla; fearful proscriptions and confiscations would ensue on their victory, and freedom would be extinguished at least for a time.[87] Yet Sulla himself had in the end restored control to the senate. In the last analysis Cicero too presumed that this would be the result of a Pompeian victory.[88] We must surely endorse this judgement. Nothing in Pompey's previous career justified the apprehension that he would seek absolute rule for himself; in the war he was not fully master of his leading associates, and in victory he would have had to defer to them; and they were men either genuinely attached, like Cato, to the authority of the senate, or at least bent on maintaining and enhancing their own personal dignity and influence in the state.

As for Caesar, he admitted that he was fighting to preserve his own 'dignity', which might otherwise have been lost by contrivances of his enemies to have him condemned in the courts and driven from public life; he avowed that it was dearer to him than life; he says nothing of the thousands of other lives he sacrificed to it.[89] Yet his *dignitas*

---

[84] Thus Pompey urged Caesar to set the *res publica*, as he always did (!), before personal considerations: Caesar replied that he was acting in its interest (*BC* i. 8 f.). In general the Pompeians seem to refer more often to the public good; for their propaganda see Plut. *Cato* 53; App. ii. 37; for Caesarian n. 91. At Pharsalus both sides appealed to liberty (Dio xli. 56; cf. Caes. *BC* iii. 91), which meant different things to different people (ch. 6, x ff.).

[85] Pompey said in 51 'nihil interesse utrum C. Caesar senatui dicto audiens futurus non esset an pararet qui senatum decernere non pateretur' (*Fam.* viii. 8. 9). In 49 the Pompeians acted under the cover of senatorial decrees (e.g. *Att.* x. 8. 8).

[86] e.g. *Att.* vii. 7. 7, 11–13; cf. n. 97.

[87] e.g. *Att.* viii. 16, ix. 10. 2, 6, 11. 3 f., xi. 6. 2; cf. n. 98.

[88] For Cicero the Pompeian cause is 'bona' (*Att.* ix. 7. 3 f.), approved by the senate (n. 85), or the 'causa bonorum' (vii. 3. 3), even though the 'boni' might not deserve the name (*Fam.* vii. 3. 2); the war could be styled 'just and necessary' (*Att.* x. 4. 3); Caesar's victory would destroy the 'nomen Romanum', and Pompey would at least be the better 'rex' if he intended to follow Sulla's practices, of which Cicero always disapproved (x. 7. 1); still, even Sulla had restored 'ius' and 'dignitas' to the state (*Brut.* 227), and Caesar's rule proved far worse than Sulla's (*Att.* xi. 21. 3). See Brunt, cited n. 82.

[89] *BC* i. 9. 2 with Cicero's indignant comment (*Att.* vii. 11. 1): 'haec omnia facere se dignitatis causa. Ubi est autem dignitas nisi ubi honestas?'.

involved no pretension to dominance; the compromise peace that he continually offered would have made him the first man in the state but not its master.[90] And he too initially claimed to be champion of a cause, that of the sacred rights of the tribunes, traditionally associated with plebeian freedom, with the sovereignty of the people, and that of the liberty of the senate; in his construction of events it had been intimidated by Pompey's soldiers into taking actions which justified his march on Rome.[91] His conduct as dictator, and indeed the contempt he showed for the veto of a hostile tribune as early as April 49, proved that he really cared nothing for all this;[92] none the less, we cannot be sure that his propaganda had no impact; at Pharsalus a centurion in his army led the attack with the cry that 'we shall restore Caesar's *dignitas* and our own freedom' (*BC* iii. 91). This propaganda could hardly affect senators, who had no solicitude for tribunician or popular powers, and who could have thought that in January 49 Pompey's soldiers were only making it possible for the senate to declare its true will. But it must have made a greater impression that Caesar persisted even in 48 in offering a compromise peace, which would assure 'quietem Italiae, pacem provinciarum, salutem imperi' (iii. 57), all the more as his overtures were made from a position of apparent strength. Moreover, the contrast between his unexpected respect for life and property and the angry menaces of the Pompeians produced a movement of opinion in his favour.

In September 50 Caelius had predicted that if war broke out Pompey would have the backing of senate and *iudices*, i.e. the grander Equites, whereas Caesar could count on 'those who lived in fear or who had nothing to hope for', and on his incomparable army. Respectable people fled *en masse* from Rome when they heard that Caesar had occupied Ariminum. They feared that as despot Caesar would carry through a programme of cancellation of debts, redistribution of property, restoration of exiles, and forced levies of money. Cicero marked down as his supporters the urban plebs (which certainly favoured the old *popularis*), and all 'lost souls': those who had suffered or expected to suffer judicial or censorial condemnation, those oppressed by debt, and the *jeunesse dorée*, many of whom were doubtless subject to financial embarrassments.[93] But this kind of analysis was in part falsified. Even among the upper orders there had never been any

---

[90] So Cicero later recognized (*Fam.* vi. 1. 6).   [91] *BC* i. 1–7, 9, 22. 5, 32, 85.

[92] Dio xli. 15–17; Caesar shows the uncooperative attitude of the senate in *BC* i. 32 f.; Curio perhaps exaggerated his wrath (*Att.* x. 4. 8 f.); other texts in *MRR* ii. 259. In 44 Caesar was to display flagrant contempt for the tribunician rights of Flavus and Marullus.

[93] *Fam.* viii. 14. 3, *Att.* vii. 3. 5, ix. 7. 5. The attitude of the urban plebs explains why the consuls of 49 could not without troops return to Rome and seize the contents of the treasury (*Att.* vii. 21. 2).

enthusiasm for war. In December 50 the senate itself had voted by 370 to 22 for Curio's motion that both Pompey and Caesar should give up their provinces and armies, which, if operative, would have peacefully resolved the impending conflict.[94] Later in the month Cicero found a general disposition for peace at any price among the gentry immediately south of Rome, including both senators and Equites. To this end he himself would have conceded Caesar's demands, though he thought them outrageous. Both sides found it hard to raise recruits. This betokens not only that the peasantry were indifferent to the issues, but that the municipal oligarchies, whose assistance in the task of conscription was essential (ch. 5, App. I) did little to help. Early in 49 Cicero found them concerned only for their farms, money-bags, and little country houses.[95]

Caesar's ostentatious clemency allayed apprehensions that he would proscribe his opponents; for debtors he did nothing until the end of 49, and then relieved only property owners temporarily short of cash.[96] Curio and Caelius indeed warned Cicero not to count on his persisting in this moderation; his conduct at Rome cast some doubt on his sincerity (*Att.* x. 9A; cf. n. 91); and Cicero was still convinced that he would show himself a tyrant, or rather that he was already behaving as one, and fearful that in the end he would resort to massacres and confiscations.[97] Still, the danger of a Pompeian victory was much more evident to all who had not taken the Pompeian side. From the moment of his departure from Rome, Pompey had threatened to treat as traitors all who did not rally to what he saw as the cause of the commonwealth.[98] These menaces were continually reiterated in the Pompeian camp (n. 87). Thus neutrals as well as Caesarians were threatened in their lives and property. Moreover, the Pompeian evacuation of Italy meant that they could win only by blockading the peninsula with their command of the sea and provincial sources of food, or by fighting their way back. Though for Cicero the victory of either party would entail universal ruin, it was pretty clear that Italy

[94] App. ii. 27–31; Plut. *Pomp.* 58. It is clear that the senate would have preferred that Caesar alone should disarm.

[95] Conscription unpopular: e.g. *Att.* vii. 13. 2, ix. 19. 1. Note ix. 2A. 2; Cicero claims foresight 'de municipiorum imbecillitate, de dilectibus'; cf. ch. 5, App. I on the role of *municipia* in the levy. Desire for peace: vii. 5. 4, 7. 5, viii. 13. 2, 16 (note that the *iudices* turned against Pompey).

[96] *Clementia*: Weinstock, 1971, 233, gives all the evidence. Cicero doubted in 49 if Caesar's clemency was sincere or would last (n. 97); it persisted, but the implication that he had the moral and legal right as well as the actual power to punish or pardon adversaries was unacceptable to those who regarded his actions as treasonable. Debts: M. W. Frederiksen, *JRS* 1966, 128 ff.; for agitations after 49, *MRR* ii. 273, 286 f.

[97] e.g. *Att.* viii. 16. 2, x. 1. 3, 4. 2 and 8, 8. 2. Contrast Atticus' hopes in ix. 10. 9.

[98] Caes. *BC* i. 33. 1; Dio xli. 6. Caesar's letter in *Att.* ix. 7c was no doubt typical of his very different professions, first confirmed at Corfinium; he remained ready to treat all who were not against him as for him (Cic. *Lig.* 33); for the effect on opinion see e.g. *Att.* viii. 16, ix. 15. 3.

would suffer less if Caesar won.[99] The effect of this consideration on public opinion must have been very marked. The refugees of January 49 were soon flocking back to Rome, and Caesar was fêted in the towns which had recently demonstrated their affection for Pompey.[100] In 48 Caelius, whose personal hopes in adopting Caesar's cause had proved delusive, complained that he had no backing except from the few money-lenders (*Fam.* viii. 17. 2). Agitation continued for relief of debt in 48 and 47 (n. 96). Caesar ultimately had to assuage the distress by new remedies, later denounced by Cicero as breaches of property rights (*de offic.* ii. 83 f.). In particular he remitted house rents in Rome and Italy; the demand for this relief must have come not from the indigent but from middle-class people, principally perhaps from fairly prosperous shopkeepers and artisans.[101]

No doubt Caelius exaggerated, but just as there had been no upsurge of sentiment in favour of the Pompeians, so there was none on Caesar's behalf (n. 95); at most men were unwilling to resist a general 'who had deserved well of the commonwealth by his magnificent achievements' in Gaul (Caes. *BC* i. 13). His own military genius and 'incomparable army' were to decide the war.

In the end according to Dio (xli. 43), two hundred senators were found in Pompey's base at Thessalonica. This was only a third of the whole body, and to judge from the voting on Curio's motion and Cicero's testimony to the strength of pacific sentiment, most of them probably joined Pompey with as much hesitation and reluctance as Cicero himself. The conduct of the Marcelli is significant. Marcus, the consul of 51, had sought when in office to force the issue with Caesar when others, Pompey among them, were still opposed to a breach; yet in 49 he, unlike his brother Gaius, the consul of 49, favoured temporizing.[102] His cousin Gaius, the consul of 50, remained neutral. He had married Caesar's grandniece, but this connection can hardly explain his attitude, for it was he in December 50 who had on his own responsibility given Pompey a mandate to mobilize for war; Cicero ascribes it to sheer cowardice. (A younger member of the same family served Caesar in Spain, perhaps with dubious loyalty.)[103] We may suspect that most of the Pompeians felt that once armed conflict had begun they had no choice but to join Pompey, if senatorial supremacy were to be preserved. They included twelve consulars, whereas Caesar had the active aid of only three or four, and two of these, Gabinius and

---

[99] e.g. *Att.* viii. 11. 2 and 4, 16, ix. 4. 2, 7. 4, 9. 2, 10. 2 f., x. 8. 4.

[100] e.g. *Att.* viii. 16, ix. 1. 2, 5. 3, 13. 4.

[101] Frier, 1980, esp. ch. 11.

[102] Caes. *BC* i. 2. 2, Cic. *Fam.* iv. 7. 2.

[103] C. Marcellus: App. ii. 31 etc. (cf. Hirt. *BG* viii. 55 for an earlier move against Caesar), *Att.* x. 15. 2. On M. Marcellus (*qu.* 49, perhaps *cos.* 22), see *MRR* ii. 274.

M. Messalla (*cos.* 53), were among the ruined men whom he recalled from exile. Cicero later conveys the impression that in the lower ranks of the senate too there was more distinction among the Pompeians.[104]

Shackleton Bailey has listed all the individuals known to have been Pompeian, Caesarian, or neutral.[105] It must be observed that the senators who appeared at Rome in April 49 in response to Caesar's wishes were not disposed to co-operate with him and provoked his anger (so we are told); many of the neutrals were willing to wound but afraid to strike (n. 92). Among them were consulars, but these were men mostly inconspicuous in politics, or elderly; they included probably three connected by marriage with Caesar,[106] and L. Paullus (*cos.* 50), whose goodwill he was reputed to have purchased, and whose brother M. Lepidus, the future triumvir, was one of his partisans; both were sons of that Lepidus whom Pompey had helped to suppress in 77. Shackleton Bailey makes out that there were actually more nobles, by which he means men of consular lineage, in Caesar's camp than in Pompey's, but by his own criterion he has wrongly classified some of the Caesarians as nobles; his list also includes some restored exiles, and some who are named only because they held posts in Caesar's gift after Thapsus, when he was already employing ex-Pompeians; in general they tend to be younger men, and thus illustrate Cicero's remarks on the *jeunesse dorée* (n. 93). Of Caesar's 13 nominees to the consulship (from 48 to 42 inclusive) only six were of consular families, and this disproportion by Republican standards persisted throughout the triumviral period. It is therefore reasonable to hold that the greatest families on the whole were opposed to Caesar and his political heirs.

Real or reputed sectional sentiments and interests were recognized by contemporaries as factors in the great division that the civil war revealed or effected, but not factions bound together by ties of kinship or friendship or allegiance to the two chiefs. Most Pompeians were Pompeian perforce; on Caesar's adherents something will be said later. We need not doubt, however, that the war was brought on by the resolution of a small minority in the senate, no doubt mostly the same twenty-two who had voted against Curio's motion. Caesar himself

---

[104] *Phil.* ii. 37 f., 52–4, xiii. 28–30. The other Caesarian consuls were Cn. Domitius Calvinus and, perhaps, L. Caesar, who had been legate of his (remote) cousin in Gaul since 52 (*BG* vii. 65. 1, *BC* i. 8) and was to be *praefectus urbi* in 47 (Dio xlii. 30), but may have remained neutral in the interim. His son was a Pompeian to the last (*MRR* ii. 297). He himself had voted in 63 for the execution of his brother-in-law P. Lentulus Sura, and took some part in resisting Antony, the son of his sister (n. 120), who with difficulty begged him off in the proscriptions (*RE* x. 468 ff.).

[105] *CQ* 1960, 253 ff., which documents much that follows. Bruhns, 1978, ch. II, differs here and there, notably in regarding Ser. Sulpicius (*cos.* 51) as neutral, not Pompeian.

[106] L. Aurelius Cotta (*cos.* 65), a kinsmen of his mother, L. Calpurnius Piso (58), his father-in-law, and L. Marcius Philippus (56), his niece's husband and Octavian's stepfather, who had given his daughter in marriage to Cato.

ascribes the fatal decrees to the combination of Pompey with his personal foes and others who hoped to enrich and aggrandize themselves by victory. Cicero provides some confirmation that all but a few of the leaders (he excepts Pompey himself) were governed by personal ambition and rapacity or by their previous enmity with Caesar (n. 81). But this combination is itself typical of the only kind of faction which the sources ever attest, a temporary coalition called into being by a particular conjuncture. It would clearly be absurd to describe Cato and his circle as Pompeians in any sense save that of associates of Pompey in the civil war. The leading 'Pompeians' were a parcel of aristocrats, each with his own purposes. Caesar depicts them on the very eve of Pharsalus disputing over the honours and rewards to follow the victory on which they counted (*BC* iii. 83). None counted among Pompey's confidants: they were the praetorians L. Lucceius and L. Scribonius Libo, and the Greekling Theophanes of Mitylene.[107]

Cato's circle merits further examination. Syme has constructed a genealogical stemma to illustrate his aristocratic connections, and insinuates that they may afford an explanation of his political influence.[108] The stemma certainly shows that he was related by birth or marriage to many of the other leading optimates of his and the preceding and succeeding generations. It may, however, be surmised that a similar stemma of almost any leading aristocrat of the time would exhibit similar relationships.

The special authority that Cato enjoyed, without ever rising to the highest office, was surely the product of his unique combination of noble lineage, talent, industry, and high-minded resolution. Moreover, if the stemma were somewhat enlarged, it would contain the names of his distant cousin C. Cato, the seditious tribune of 56 (n. 69), and L. Marcius Philippus (*cos.* 56), the father of his second wife, who was a neutral in 49 and was stepfather of Caesar's grandnephew and heir, the future emperor Augustus. As it is, it includes the three daughters of Cato's half-sister Servilia, who married respectively the Caesarians, Lepidus and P. Servilius Isauricus (*cos.* 48), and the Pompeian, C. Cassius. Servilius, son of the Sullan consul of 79, had long been a political associate of his uncle, yet in 49 he joined Caesar for reasons of which we know nothing. After Caesar's death he was to take some part in the resistance to Antony, but made his peace in 43, and enjoyed a second consulship in 41. The son of the orator Hortensius also appears in the stemma; he fought for Caesar, though he was to perish with the Liberators at Philippi. Servilia's son M. Brutus who had come under Cato's influence, took the side of Pompey, although he had previously

---

[107] *Att.* ix. 1. 3, 11. 3; Caes. *BC* iii. 18.   [108] *RR* 23 f.

not been on speaking terms with the man who in 77 had put his own father to death.[109] In the light of all that we know of Brutus his attitude must surely be explained on the basis that he shared Cato's principles, not that he was simply moved by consideration of kinship. Neither family ties nor past political affiliations necessarily decided men's choice in 49.

Cicero was to say that Q. Aelius Tubero had felt bound to obey the senate and take arms against Caesar, as befitted a man of 'stock, name, family, and upbringing' (*Lig.* 21, 28). With this in mind we may allow that family connections or traditions could affect individual decisions. But Shackleton Bailey's lists show that some families, not to speak of *gentes* and cognates, were divided. The Marcelli afford one instance (p. 493). The kindred of Caesar himself were not united. His rather distant cousin L. Iulius Caesar (*cos.* 64) may have sided with him rather than taken a neutral stance; but that man's son Lucius fought against him *à outrance*.[110] Cicero thought that his brother Quintus, who as Caesar's former legate might incur Caesar's special resentment if he joined Pompey, was not under any obligation to make the same choice as himself (*Att.* ix. 6. 4). As for friendship, that between Caesar and Pompey had been among the most lasting known in the period; and there must have been many, like Cicero and Lentulus Spinther (n. 69), who had been friends of both the rivals, and who had other friends in the opposing camp (e.g. Caes. *BC* iii. 57. 1). It should be no surprise that men's decisions were not always predictable from the part they had previously taken in public affairs. Servilius is one case; another is Cn. Domitius Calvinus, active against the triumvirs as tribune in 59, consul in 53, although Caesar had backed his competitors, but now the commander of one of Caesar's armies, and later to earn a second consulship from the favour of Octavian and Antony. Equally men could deviate from the attitudes of their fathers. D. Brutus was consul in 77 and adverse to the popular movement led by Lepidus and the father of Caesar's assassin M. Brutus (with whom his relationship by birth may have been remote), but his son, Decimus, though prominent later in the conspiracy against Caesar, was at this time one of his legates.

In general it is almost impossible to be sure why any individual opted for one side or the other or for neither. Both at the time and later Cicero accounted for his own behaviour in different ways, even when

---

[109] Plut. *Brut.* 4; cf. also ibid. 2 on his close association with Cato, whose daughter he was to marry in 45.

[110] *B. Afr.* 88 f.; Suet *Caes.* 75. 3; cf. Cic. *Fam.* ix. 7. 1. Cf. n. 105. Families divided: Aurelii Cottae, Cassii Longini, Cornelii Sullae, Iunii Bruti, Pompeii Bithynici, Sulpicii Rufi, Terentii Varrones. Many 'families' (i.e. bearers of the same *nomina* and *cognomina*) appear united because they have only one or two known representatives.

he was not trying to deceive anyone but himself. In my judgement he finally chose to follow Pompey in the belief that this was his duty to the commonwealth. But he made many statements which contradict this, some deliberately one-sided if not false, others occasioned by the tumult of his emotions at the time. We cannot rely on any single expression of his opinions, still less then on what others said in exculpation of their own conduct, or on what was propounded in their defence or in criticism of them.[111] But all these apologias or imputations had to allege motives of a kind which everyone knew *might* have been determinant. On both sides there were some who hoped to aggrandize themselves or obtain riches or at least shake off the burden of debt for their share in victory; they had to try to pick the winner. Caelius, an optimate tribune in 52, intimated to Cicero in advance that he thought it prudent in the event of war to disregard principle and attach himself to Caesar as the likely victor (*Fam.* viii. 14. 3); later, when disenchanted with Caesar, he would claim that he had yielded to the solicitations of his friend Curio (ibid. 17. 1). It was, according to the ancient sources, for a bribe that Curio himself had gone over from the optimates to Caesar in 51.[112] Q. Ligarius, whose brothers and connections were in Italy and at least did not oppose Caesar, professed that he had taken the other side only because he was in Africa, where the Pompeians were in control (*Lig.* 4 f., 20); he was to be one of Caesar's assassins. T. Antistius, quaestor in Macedon, found himself, according to Cicero, under a similar necessity, though he would otherwise have been guided by the Caesarian C. Ateius Capito, whom he loved as his father (*Fam.* xiii. 29. 3 f.). Matius, an Eques, was later to declare that he had disapproved of Caesar's cause, yet had followed him as a friend (ibid. xi. 28. 2): Pollio, that he had joined Caesar only because he feared that in the camp of Pompey his safety would be in jeopardy from the intrigues of his enemies there (ibid. x. 31. 2 f.). Cicero accused C. Marcellus and Ser. Sulpicius of timidity: they might have retorted the same charge on him; and Sulpicius perhaps eventually adhered to Pompey, though his son was a Caesarian.[113] When Cicero heard of Labienus' desertion of Caesar (which Dio perhaps had some ground for ascribing to a personal quarrel), he assumed that Labienus judged that Caesar's march on Rome was a crime and that he was actuated by the public good; Syme's notion that Labienus was bound to Pompey

---

[111] Brunt, cited n. 82.

[112] The evidence is biased but cannot be refuted, despite W. K. Lacey, *Historia* 1961, 318 ff.

[113] Servius joined Pompey, according to Shackleton Bailey, remained neutral according to Bruhns (n. 105). I favour the former view. In 46–45 he served Caesar as a proconsul, but so did the ex-Pompeian M. Brutus. His relationship to the Caesarian P. Sulpicius Rufus is unknown and probably remote.

by an old allegiance, to which he was returning, simply did not occur to him, and has little plausibility.[114]

Obviously, even if we accept any or all of the explanations for the behaviour of a few individuals in the crisis, given by themselves or by others, we cannot generalize from them. They reveal only a medley of often incongruous motives: consideration of the public good and of the senate's authority, private friendship or hostility not only to the leaders but to members of their entourage, greed, venality, ambition, and pusillanimity. From such evidence we can draw no valid conclusions about the attitude of senators in general, let alone those of lower station. But contemporaries always presupposed that each man made his own decision: they do not hint that anyone was morally bound to a group.

In so far as they were guided by public principles, it is natural to assume that senators in general were attached to the supremacy of their own order and held it to be essential to the good government of the state. Before 49 few would have sincerely espoused popular ideas, and still fewer, one might guess, have credited Caesar's professed fidelity to them. On the other hand those who took his side need not have accepted the charges of his adversaries that he was already bent on seizing absolute power; this was a design that he did not admit, and considering his readiness for a compromise peace, did not yet harbour. There is no reason to think that there were any Caesarians who actually desired the establishment of a monarchy. Of those who believed that the victor would in any event make himself at least temporarily dominant, some might for personal reasons prefer Caesar's dominance to Pompey's; others might regard his victory as certain or probable, and for that reason choose to back the winner. Ambition, greed, or fear no doubt induced many to join either side. Many more, disapproving of both alike, preferred neutrality as the most prudent course. They probably composed the majority of the senate which met on Caesar's summons in April 49, though some still in Italy kept aloof. Even those who attended showed that they had no sympathy with Caesar, and simply desired peace.

The intransigence of Caesar's enemies compelled him to defeat them in the field before he could attempt any settlement of the state. It was then virtually inevitable for him at first to reserve to himself, as Sulla had done, the direction of affairs. But he progressively showed that, unlike Sulla, he was now unwilling to lay down the absolute power

---

[114] *Att.* vii. 12. 5, 13. 1, *Fam.* xiv. 2, xvi. 12. 4. Dio xli. 4 had read that he had a personal grudge against Caesar. Unless there had been such a personal quarrel, he could have expected Caesar to back him for the consulship. Caesar had already enriched him (*Att.* vii. 7. 6). *Contra* Syme, *Roman Papers*, ch. 7, his ties with Caesar must have become closer than any which may once have bound him to Pompey. Syme is so convinced that men must have been decided by such ties that he does not even consider Cicero's instinctive explanation of his deserting Caesar.

which the course of events had given him. He fulfilled to this extent the predictions that his enemies had made at the outset. The senate loaded him with honours, but he must have realized that this was lip-service. He could not count on the genuine goodwill of the Pompeians he had pardoned, nor of the former neutrals; and he would alienate some of his own partisans by his autocratic position and conduct. He did not even exert himself to affect a readiness to seak the co-operation of the senate, which, having lost most of its natural leaders, was perhaps less competent than usually to make a useful contribution to the tasks of government.

All power was concentrated in his hands. He appointed the army commanders and provincial governors. He nominated men to adminis- ter Rome itself. He controlled the public funds. His much advertised clemency did not conceal the truth that it lay with him alone to pardon his former adversaries or to leave them to rot in banishment. The assemblies were still summoned to elect magistrates, but in 44 he was empowered to name half of them, and in fact no one could be chosen without his approval. The senate was packed with men he selected. He still legislated through the people and consulted the senate (Dio xliii. 27), but Cicero found that he was registered as a draftsman of decrees passed at sessions at which he had not been present (*Fam.* ix. 15. 4). Constitutional forms were sometimes neglected altogether.[115]

For a time indeed hopes could linger that this 'reipublicae nox' (*Brut.* 330) would clear. In 46 Cicero could still conceive that Caesar himself perhaps wished for the restoration of the Republic but was circumscribed by temporary difficulties (*Fam.* ix. 17. 2). In his speech for Marcellus he exhorted him to undertake the task (26 ff.). Writing to Servius Sulpicius, who shared his own view (cf. *Fam.* iv. 5. 3), he says that Caesar's readiness to respond to the senate's intercession for Marcellus gives a faint 'speciem quasi reviviscentis rei p.' (iv. 4. 3). More significantly, he could expess the hope that Caesar desired 'ut habeamus aliquam rem p.' to Servilius Isauricus (xiii. 68. 2); even one of Caesar's partisans could be expected to feel no content in the existing state of affairs. But disappointment followed. Caesar's appetite for power grew with its exercise; and it became evident that he would never surrender autocratic control, at latest in 44 when he accepted the dictatorship for life.[116] It then proved that he had no party loyally prepared to sustain him.

---

[115] e.g. *Fam.* vii. 30. The *lex annalis* was also disregarded.

[116] As he was already dictator for ten years, i.e. till 36, and could have had the term renewed on expiration, in the rather unlikely event of his living so long, the dictatorship for life did not enhance his power but merely symbolized his intention of never surrendering it; hence it was plausible to impute to him the sayings 'nihil esse rem publicam; appellationem modo sine corpore ac specie; Sullam nescisse litteras, qui dictaturam deposuerit' (Suet. *Caes.* 77). To Republicans it

The assassins or Liberators included Pompeians whom he had pardoned and promoted, such as M. Brutus and C. Cassius, but also former adherents, notably C. Trebonius, whom he had made consul in 45, and D. Brutus, who was designated for 42 and was a special favourite.[117] Thus men who had followed him in the civil war and who were high in his favour could not endure the loss of independence. They were to find support later among other Caesarians, who had been advanced to posts of government in the provinces; throughout the east his nominees either joined Brutus and Cassius or failed to resist them.[118] On the morrow of his assassination the senate, filled as it was with men he had enrolled, promptly indemnified the authors of the deed and prohibited the creation of any future dictatorship. Whatever their private feelings, the other chief Caesarians found it expedient to accept these measures.

Antony, Dolabella, and Lepidus, unlike Octavian and Caesar's Gallic veterans, appear to have had no rancorous desire to avenge Caesar's death. Each no doubt hoped to avail himself of the confusion to establish a strong personal position in the state, Antony perhaps to succeed to his dominance. However half-heartedly, the senate with the Caesarian consuls Pansa and Hirtius at its head sought to prevent this in unison with the 'Liberators' as well as with Octavian. The complex circumstances in which this uneasy coalition broke down and in which Octavian came together with Antony and Lepidus to impose their

was relatively unimportant whether he also aspired (as I believe) to the title of *rex* and, like Hellenistic kings, actually assumed divine honours (cf. esp. J. A. North, *JRS* 1975, 171 ff.). As his monarchic power would not pass automatically to anyone else on his demise, his assassins could reasonably have supposed that the Republic would revive with his removal; and they might have been proved right if they had removed Antony too. The immediate abolition of the dictatorship after his death (App. iii. 23 etc.), and Augustus' prudent rejection of it in 22 (*RG* 5 etc.), show that its tenure was his chief offence.

[117] The conspirators are said to have numbered 60 (Suet. 80) or over 80 (Nic. Dam. *FGH* no. 90 F. 130. 59); for recorded names see Groebe, *RE* x. 255; App. ii. 115 identifies 5 ex-Caesarians, of whom Tillius Cimber had a brother in exile, presumably as a Pompeian, and 8 friends of Brutus and Cassius; but of these Ser. Sulpicius Galba had certainly been a Caesarian, and only Q. Ligarius is known to have fought on Pompey's side. Galba had been disappointed of the consulship (Suet. *Galba* 3. 2); he was one of only 4 men of consular lineage in the band.

[118] Of 9 known praetors in 43, all designated under Caesar, 4 were proscribed by the triumvirs (including a brother of L. Plancus). In the provinces C. Antistius Vetus (*cos. suff.* 30), Q. Cornificius, Q. Hortensius, Q. Marcius Crispus, L. Staius Murcus (of central Italian stock, cf. Syme, *RR*, 91), Caesar's appointees, joined the Liberators. So did L. Aemilius Paullus, whom Caesar had helped to the consulship in 50, the brother of Lepidus but neutral in 49, and a younger P. Lepidus. Of all these men only Hortensius and the Lepidi were of consular families. The jurist Pacuvius Labeo, probably of Samnite origin (W. Kunkel, *Herkunft u. soz. Stellung*, 1951, 32; cf. E. Badian, *Polis and Imperium, St. in honour of E. T. Salmon*, 1974, 152), adhered to Brutus and killed himself after Philippi (App. iv. 135); his son M. Antistius Labeo, the greatest of Augustan jurists, was notable for his free-spoken independence; cf. the hostility to the triumvirs shown by another eminent jurist A. Cascellius (Val. Max. vi. 2. 13), a senator probably from Etruria (Kunkel, 24–6).

joint despotism cannot be examined here. To stabilize their control of
Italy, they found it necessary to proscribe hundreds of their antagonists; many took refuge with Sextus Pompey, or with Brutus and
Cassius. The victims included Equites as well as senators; many were
doubtless municipal gentry who had compromised themselves by word
or deed in the previous struggle with Antony.[119] The senate itself had
been packed with new men from the Italian towns by Caesar. But even
men of this stamp could not be counted on as Caesarians who would be
loyal to the memory of the dictator and the cause of those who now
professed themselves to be his avengers: they might be numbered
among the proscribed.[120] No doubt the slaughter at and after Philippi
took a disproportionate toll from the ranks of old consular families,[121]
but among the accomplices or subsequent partisans of Brutus and
Cassius and the victims of the proscriptions known to us, the great
majority were of less distinguished descent (nn. 117–9).

After Philippi, as Tacitus remarked (*Ann.* i. 2), no Republican forces
were left. Some men of rank kept aloof from public affairs altogether.
Those who still sought honours, wealth, and influence had now to
attach themselves to a leader. It is at this stage that we can most
plausibly speak of parties, groups or factions with some sort of personal
'allegiance'. But the numerous desertions from Sextus and Antony to
Octavian may suggest that men were still apt to 'serve the time' rather
than to exhibit a consistent loyalty. Were they self-seekers who simply
took the side that they thought most likely to win? Not necessarily. The
Roman state survived; men might think it incumbent on them to
render it what service they could, however little they approved of the
inescapable conditions of public life. By the time of the final conflict
between Antony and Octavian they might judge the latter to be so
strong that for the sake of peace and stability it was best to work for his
speedy victory. Moreover, he now paraded as champion of old Roman
traditions which Antony flouted. Hopes could linger that he would in
the end relinquish absolute control and restore the old Republican
regime. This was what he found it expedient to do, at least in outward
show. In name he exalted the authority of the senate and professed to

---

[119] The number is uncertain: App. iv. 5, 7 gives 300 senators (130, *Per.* Livy cxx; 200 or 300,
Plut. *Cic.* 46, *Brut.* 27, *Ant.* 20), about a third of the total number which Caesar had inflated, and
2000 Equites; Drumann-Groebe, *Gesch. Roms* i[3]. list nearly 100 known names (senatorial or
equestrian), mostly preserved by App. iv. 12 ff., many with incomplete nomenclature; Syme, *RR*,
191 ff., selects examples. Only 5 were of consular lines. Some *domi nobiles* are mentioned; most
probably belonged to that class; cf. ch. 1 endnote 1.

[120] Cicero (*Fam.* x. 28. 3, xii. 5. 2) claimed in 43 that the senate was firm on the Republican
side, apart from the consulars; Ser. Sulpicius being then dead, the others were all former neutrals
or Caesarians; he praises only L. Caesar, but he was too mild against Antony, his sister's son.

[121] *RR* 205 f.

be its chief minister.[122] The façade he erected to veil his ultimate
supremacy was a tribute to the persistence of the Republican sentiments among those from whom he was obliged to enlist his agents and
assistants (senatorial and equestrian) in the task of government. He
could not and did not depend on the 'allegiance' of a mere party but
preferred to seek 'universal consent', promoting objectives which most
men in the highest orders could identify with the welfare of the
commonwealth (ch. I VII), and opening to individuals of varied
backgrounds the opportunity to advance their personal interests.

V

To conclude, in the post-Sullan era we do not find large groups of
politicians, bound together by ties of kinship or friendship, or by
fidelity to a leader, who act together consistently for any considerable
time. Individuals make personal decisions, guided no doubt at times by
their private obligations, but also by considerations of their own selfish
advantage or of the public good. For all these varied purposes they
may enter into short-lived combinations. What evidence there is for the
period between the Gracchi and Sulla suggests that politicians then
tended to behave in the same way. It is much harder, as the evidence is
so meagre, to determine how they had conducted themselves in still
earlier times. It is obviously true that the continual appearance of
'popular' reformers or agitators, whose proposals directly or indirectly
threatened the control of the senate and on occasion the economic
interests of its members, tended to rally the majority of senators,
especially the higher nobility, to defence of a common cause. The
exorbitant ambitions of a Marius or a Pompey would have the same
effect. These factors were not operative in any significant degree before
the tribunate of Tiberius Gracchus. 'Routine politics', which continued to be significant after 133, must have occupied most attention
until then. Private ties probably affected men's political courses more
strongly in, for instance, competitions for office when the welfare of the
state did not seem to be at stake. It is, however, implausible that on
more vital questions considerations of the public good never predominated. The greed and ambition of individuals must then too have
played their part. In default of testimony, it is imprudent to assume
that even in pre-Gracchan times loyalty to a group consisting of kin
and friends normally governed the behaviour of Roman aristocrats. Of
large, cohesive, and durable coalitions of families there is no evidence
at all for any period.

---

[122] Brunt, *Biblioteca di Labeo*, 1982, 236 ff., *CQ* 1984, 423 ff. Cf. pp. 67 ff.

CHAPTER 1: THE FALL OF THE ROMAN REPUBLIC

1. Acc. to Cicero, 'all Italy' was against Antony (e.g. *Phil*. iv. 9, vi. 18, vii. 1, 20, x. 19, xiii. 39, *Fam*. xi. 8. 2, xii. 4. 1, 5. 3), likewise Cisalpina (e.g. *Phil*. iii. 13, 38, v. 36, x. 21, xii. 9, *Fam*. xii. 5. 2), where only three cities adhered to him, Bononia, Regium Lepidi, and Parma (*Phil*. x. 10), the last after he had sacked it, killing the leading men for their Republicanism (xiv. 8 f., *Fam*. x. 33. 4, xi. 13B). Padua, the birthplace of Livy, who was to make his Republican sentiments plain (Tac. *Ann*. iv. 34), and Vicetia are singled out for their exceptional services (*Phil*. xii. 10; cf. D. Brutus in *Fam*. ix. 19. 2), but other cities furnished men and money (*Phil*. x. 21, xii. 9) and suffered devastations in the cause (x. 21, xii. 9). Cassius and D. and M. Brutus all had clients in Cisalpina (*Fam*. xi. 19. 2, xii. 5. 2); probably as at Teanum Sidicinum and Puteoli (*Phil*. ii. 107) approbation of the 'Liberators' had gained them patronage. Under Augustus M. Brutus was still honoured with a statue at Milan as 'legum ac libertatis auctor et vindex' (Suet. *Rhet*. 6); we may compare the memorial at Nursia to those who fell for liberty in the *bellum Mutinense* (Dio xlviii, 13). Cicero also alludes to the enthusiasm for liberty of the colonies, *municipia* and *praefecturae* in Italy (*Phil*. iv. 7, v. 25, vi. 18), and though action in Campania against Antony (ii. 99 f., xii. 7, *Att*. xvi. 11) may in part have been inspired by Octavian, and all Cicero's generalities are suspect of exaggeration, if not mendacity, since it was his cue to overstate the extent of zeal for his cause and thus make it appear safer to join it (cf. *Phil*. v. 31: 'bello autem dubio quod potest studium esse dilectus?'), specific references to local votes of men and money (vii. 23 f. for Firmum and the Marrucini) and the contributions of an individual Eques (viii. 4, xii. 7) have more weight. Probably the 18 cities designated by the triumvirs for veteran settlement and numerous victims of the proscriptions (ch. 9 n. 119) had been prominent in the struggle against Antony. The Republican consensus at Rome which Cicero alleges to have existed among the Equites (e.g. vii. 21, 27) hardly (as he claims) extended to all orders, even the plebs (vii. 2, xiv. 5, *ad Brut*. i. 3. 2); he himself excepts 'those unworthy of citizenship' (viii. 8) and privately admits the presence of internal enemies (*Fam*. xi. 25. 2, *ad Brut*. i. 9. 3, 10. 1). It was the *boni* he counted on, the men of property (*Phil*. xiii. 16), whose lives and fortunes were supposedly imperilled by Antony (iv. 9, v. 32, vii. 27, xiii. 47, xiv. 37).

2. The presiding magistrate consults the senate either on specific matters or 'de summa re p.' In the former case he cannot prevent senators speaking on other matters (e.g. Cic. *Att*. i. 13. 3, 16. 9, *Fam*. iv. 4. 3, viii. 4. 4, x. 28. 2) and even filibustering (*Att*. iv. 4. 3, Gell. iv. 10. 8), and he must ask their opinions in a fixed order of rank (consulars first etc.); after Sulla designate magistrates take precedence over ex-magistrates in each rank.

He does not normally put a motion of his own, but is free to select which motion made by another is to be voted on (e.g. Cic. *Qu. fr.* ii. 8. (7) 3; Caes. *BC* i. 2); if it is carried, he 'makes' a *SC* assisted by witnesses who 'scribendo adfuerunt' and who were doubtless in fact the draftsmen; if it is vetoed, it may still be recorded as a *senatus auctoritas* (*Fam.* viii. 8). Consuls have a prior right to all others in convening and consulting the senate; praetors take precedence over tribunes, but a tribune, when his turn comes, may raise the same business as a consul and make a different *SC* or *senatus auctoritas* (e.g. App. ii. 30). See *StR* iii³. 905 ff. In form decrees were merely advisory; and magistrates could on their own responsibility act on a *senatus auctoritas* if the veto could not be enforced (tribunes had no power outside Rome).

3. In Sallust's view (*BJ* 41 f., *Hist.* i. 12) the cleavage in the state, which evidently resembled that between patricians and plebeians in the early Republic (*Hist.* i. 11), followed a period of supposedly unique concord, began after the destruction of Carthage (or after Rome acquired world dominion, *Cat.* 36), and became patent when the plebs found leaders in the Gracchi, and again (*Cat.* 37 f.) after the restoration of tribunician power in 70. Though Sallust avoids the terms *populares* and optimates (very occasionally and sardonically he can write of *boni*), terms certainly in common use in his day and perhaps since that of C. Gracchus (cf. his words in *ORF*², fr. 17: 'pessimi Tiberium fratrem meum optimum interfecerunt', probably rejecting his opponents' claim to be 'the best people'), he has in effect the same dichotomy. Syme, *Sallust*, 17 f., rightly denies that he conceived of two organized parties; equally he attaches no importance to factions within the nobility (ch. 9 n. 5), whom he regards as generally united against popular demands. His works, together with some insincere rhetoric in Cicero's professedly 'popular' speeches (*de leg. agr.* ii and *Rab. perd.* with fragments of his defence of the popular tribune Cornelius), and retrojections of later polemics in annalistic accounts of early Rome in Livy and Dionysius, furnish our best evidence for the popular standpoint (see generally ch. 6, xi ff.). Earl, 1961, showed that Sallust did not himself adopt a partisan view; he could bring out the good qualities of both the Gracchi and the optimate Metellus Numidicus and the self-seeking of Marius, and contrast the integrity of Cato with the egoistic ambition of Caesar (*Cat.* 54). His approach is moralizing, which does not prevent him from discerning the social and economic causes of discord. His unhistoric idealization of old Rome and inaccuracies in recording the course of events do not invalidate his informed interpretation of Roman politics in the last century of the Republic. Syme (loc. cit.) calls it 'schematic and defective', epithets that best apply to an analysis of Roman politics that ignores or depreciates the grievances and aspirations of the common people.

4. *Auctoritas*: ch. 6, ix f., esp. n. 105. Tac. *Germ.* 11 delineates German chiefs in Roman colouring: 'prout aetas cuique, prout nobilitas, prout decus bellorum, prout facundia est, audiuntur, auctoritate suadendi magis quam iubendi potestate.' *Auctoritas* also derived from election to high

office: Cic. *de imp. Cn. Pomp.* 2. *Principes*: ch. 6 n. 122. L. Metellus (*cos.* 251, 247, and *pont. max.*) claimed that he alone of all Romans had achieved the ten greatest goals, 'primarium bellatorem esse, optimum oratorem, fortissimum imperatorem, auspicio suo maximas res geri, maximo honore uti, summa sapientia esse, summum senatorem haberi, pecuniam magnam bono modo invenire, multos liberos relinquere et clarissimum in civitate esse' (Pliny, *NH* vii. 139; not all his coevals would have agreed!). P. Crassus Mucianus (*cos.* 131) boasted of being 'ditissimus, nobilissimus, eloquentissimus', a jurisconsult, and *pontifex maximus* (Gell. i. 13. 9). Cato held that though citizens were equal in right they could attain eminence in *gloria* and *honor* by their own efforts (*ORF*², fr. 252); he endlessly sounded the praise of his own military achievements and integrity (ibid. 21–55, 128–35, 173–5, 203). The early monuments of the Scipios (*ILS* 1–7) commemorate their striving for 'honos fama virtusque gloria atque ingenium' (4), their offices and deeds. The great jurist Ser. Sulpicius (*cos.* 51) thinks of times before Caesar destroyed the commonwealth, when those of each rising generation 'rem a parente traditam per se tenere possent, honores ordinatim petituri essent in re publica, in amicorum negotiis libertate sua usuri' (Cic. *Fam.* iv. 5. 3). Such texts reveal aristocratic ambitions and their limits: no one dreamed of domination before Sulla, and few afterwards. A great noble who had held the consulship, like Ap. Claudius, distinguished by 'opibus, honoribus, ingenio, liberis, propinquis, adfinibus, amicis' (ibid. ii. 13. 2; cf. iii. 10. 9) would follow his own line in politics.

5. We hear more of debt agitation in the early Republic than later; notably it led to the abolition of *nexum* (ch. 6 n. 6) and the secession of the plebs in 287 (ibid. n. 168); cf. Brunt, *Social Conflicts*, ch. 3. (In that book I wrongly ascribed to the proto-*popularis* C. Flaminius a measure for relief of debts, but see *RRC* 610 ff., and another, like Mommsen, *Ges. Schr.* iii. 346, to C. Gracchus on the basis of a dark text in Nonius.) Personal execution for debt: ch. 6 n. 7. Land and other property could be transferred by *fiducia* as security for debt, to be recovered if the debt were repaid, and personal goods could be pledged to a creditor (Schulz, 1951, 400 ff.); it was probably by the former process above all that peasant owners lost their lands. For Caesar and the debt problem see M. W. Frederiksen, *JRS* 1966, 128 ff. Frier, 1980, esp. chs. 1 f., shows that the beneficiaries of rent remissions must have been persons of some means, who paid rent in arrears, not the very poor, who surely had to make down payments for a night's lodging; the former doubtless included shopkeepers and craftsmen.

6. Crawford, *RRC* 633 ff., collects the allegations of 'inopia aerarii'; the large reserve accumulated in the second century must have been dissipated in the 80s, and, given the number of legions in service in the 70s and 60s (*IM* 446 ff.), not replenished until Pompey brought in huge new revenues from the east (on which see Badian, 1967, ch. VI, though the truth underlying Plut., *Pomp.* 45.3 can hardly be ascertained); the data on the reserve in 49 in Pliny, *NH* xxxiii. 55 f., and Oros. vi. 15. 5 cannot be used, as Crawford shows. In my view complaints of 'inopia' in the mid-50s (e.g.

de har. resp. 60, *Balb.* 61) might have seemed plausible, if provincial surpluses were not regularly remitted to Rome and if the central accounts, which should have shown what was due, were confused. For criticisms of the extravagance of 'popular' measures see e.g. *Sest.* 103, *Tusc. Disp.* iii. 48 (on C. Gracchus), *de leg. agr.* i. 3 f., 12, ii. 10, 47 ff., *Att.* ii. 16. 4, 17. 1, 18. 1, ii. 3. 3, *Qu. fr.* ii. 6. 1, *Sest.* 55, *Vat.* 5–29, *Pis.* 4.

7.   Crawford, *RRC* 696 f., shows that the annual cost of a legion in the first century was officially estimated at 1,500,000 *denarii* before Caesar doubled legionary pay and 3,000,000 thereafter; however, he calculates pay for a legion of 4,400 men as only 524,880; at full strength the post-Marian legion of 6,200 would on the same basis have cost in pay alone no more than 700,000, but legions were often far below full strength (*IM*, App. 27). We must no doubt allow an indeterminate sum for the cost of supplies, other than those for food, clothing, and arms, which were deductible from the soldier's wage (Brunt, *PBSR* 1950, 50 f.), but Crawford must be right that the official estimate of a legion's cost included 'generous provision for an inflated corps of general's aides'; and probably no account was taken of the difference between real and nominal strength. This helps to explain how Caesar had funds to raise 4 new legions in 58–5 before the senate voted a further grant for their pay in 56 (*Balb.* 61; cf. *IM* 467). L. Piso (*cos.* 58) received 18 million for his government of Macedon, where he had 3 or 4 legions (*IM*, 469); he banked this sum at Rome, presumably at interest for his own account (Cic. *Pis.* 61, 86–8), and met all expenditure from local revenues. Such revenues were of course also at Caesar's disposal. It is far from clear that a governor was required to refund to the treasury the balance between what he had been voted and what he had actually spent. Cicero could legitimately save 2.2 million for his own pocket from the sum voted him for his Cilician command (*Fam.* v. 20. 9; cf. *Att.* xi. 1. 2, 2. 3). Was he entitled to appropriate the difference between the assumed and real cost of his two weak legions (*IM* 689)? Certainly governors could legally pocket the difference between the sum voted to them for purchase of food at fixed prices and that actually spent at the market price, if lower (II *Verr.* iii. 209 ff.), and the profit on such transactions would be potentially greater in proportion to the numbers of their troops and staff. Presumably there was no bar on governors investing for their own account public moneys they administered, provided that they ultimately accounted for and restored the capital. For vague charges of peculation or at least enrichment from public funds see n. 61 *Manubiae*: Shatzman 63 ff. (cf. *Historia*, 1972, 177 ff.); the enormous wealth of Pompey, and of Caesar after 59, illustrate the profits generals could make (ibid. 346 ff.; 389 ff.).

8.   In *de rep.* Cicero wrote by his own account 'de optimo statu civitatis et de optimo cive' (*Qu. fr.* iii. 5. 1). Though he agreed with most Greek political theorists in pronouncing monarchy, i.e. rule by the 'iustissimus et sapientissimus', to be the best of the simple forms of constitution (i. 43, 69, ii. 41, iii. 46 f.), he doubted if in practice a single man could be wise enough to govern by himself (i. 52)—the good kings at Rome had

actually taken the advice of the senate (ii. 15, cf. 35)—and suggested that subjection even to a just master was incompatible with freedom (ii. 43); moreover, like the other simple constitutions, monarchy was unstable; as at Rome under Tarquinius Superbus, it could easily degenerate into tyranny, the worst form of government (cf. ch. 6 n. 28). He therefore preferred the mixed or, rather, balanced system (i. 54, 69, ii. 64 f.), of which Rome by a gradual evolution beginning under the kings was the exemplar (ii. 1–65 cf. ch. 6 n. 105). In *de leg.* his aim is to set out the laws appropriate to the 'optimus rei p. status' expounded in the earlier treatise (i. 15, 20); the code of secular law prescribed in book iii makes no provision for vesting extraordinary power in any individual except (iii. 9) that in accordance with old Roman practice a dictator may be appointed for no more than six months in the event of serious war or civil strife.

A great part of *de rep.* was indeed devoted to an account of the *optimus civis*, but the very term *civis* excludes the notion that Cicero had in mind a man vested with monarchic power. He must be a statesman who can ride the fierce beast which the people is, and create the harmony needed for a state's preservation (ii. 68 f.); he is evidently to combine practical experience of affairs with philosophic insight, attributed to Scipio and his friends Laelius and Furius Philus (iii. 1–6); Cicero clearly intends it to be thought that he himself had these qualities (i. 3, 13). Philosophy shows that government must be founded in justice, it must then be exercised by men who are themselves ruled by reason and virtue (iii. 38–42) No doubt this means that the ideal statesman must have the same attributes as the good king such as Numa (v. 3), but it does not imply that he need possess regal prerogatives; in the renewed comparison between different constitutions which ensues (iii, 43–8), Cicero does not retract his approval of the balanced system. The claim that the ideal statesman must be master of law and *eloquence* (v. 5, 11) shows that in Cicero's view he must be capable not merely of giving just commands but of using the arts of persuasion in conditions of political freedom. The nouns by which he is designated, *rector, gubernator, moderator* with the corresponding verbs, can in Cicero's linguistic usage refer to the political administration, guidance, and leadership that may be exercised by *principes* who excel in *auctoritas* (cf. p. 43), and who possess *potestas* only by accident; they have no monarchic overtones (see esp. E. Lepore, *Il princeps ciceroniano*, 1954, ch. 2, for exhaustive proof). He influences men partly by moral example; this is the more important because the leading men in any society shape the general standards (i. 47, vi. 12, *de leg.* iii. 31).

'Laelius' makes out that in his day there was a good supply of men of this type (ii. 67); and Cicero, who had already written in *de orat.* iii. 63 of an 'auctorem publici consilii et regendae civitatis ducem et sententiae atque eloquentiae principem' who 'ad rem publicam moderandam usum et scientiam et studium suum contulisset', a description which patently foreshadows the 'moderator' of *de rep.*, had then named Scipio and three of his coevals as conforming to the ideal, and indicated (ibid. i. 211; cf. *de rep.* ii. 67) that there were many more. 'Laelius' does indeed suggest that in 129, the dramatic date of the dialogue, the crisis required Scipio's appointment as dictator; but the very use of that term implies that his authority would be temporary; his task would be 'rem publicam constitu-ere' (vi. 12). The new 'fragment' published by C. A. Behr, *AJP* 1974, 141 ff., gives no reliable grounds for questioning this interpretation. Nor is there any good reason to think that in 54, the year of composition, Cicero favoured resort to this expedient; certainly he showed no enthusiasm for the proposal then being ventilated that Pompey should be made dictator (*Att.* iv. 18. 2 f., *Qu. fr.* iii. 6. 4). Admittedly he was to approve of the way in which Pompey restored order in 52 as sole consul (*Att.* vii 1. 4), but Pompey's position then was well short of even temporary monarchic power, and in 49 Cicero evinces abhorrence of the design for *regnum* or *dominatio* which he sometimes imputes to Pompey. At that time he makes it clear that his 'moderator rei p.' is a model which *both* he *and* Pompey (and presumably all statesmen) ought to follow (*Att.* viii. 11, 1); since for all his conceit Cicero never saw himslf as sole ruler, this is alone proof that the term is not equivalent to monarch, and that he is not foreshadowing the kind of dominance Augustus was to exercise.

9. *Excursus on historical facts and evidence.* It seems to me beyond question that the aim of the historian is to discover 'how things really were', even if he recognizes that he can never achieve complete success. The assumptions and procedures that he adopts are essentially, however refined, identical with those we all make in our daily lives. Whatever theoretical objections Pyrrhonists may raise, we have to act on the basis that material things and other persons exist, that we know about them from the evidence of our senses, even though the evidence of one perception may need correcting from that of other perceptions and the judgements founded on perceptions are always fallible, and that actual events occur from their interaction, which we instinctively interpret in terms of cause and effect; by this we may mean that A can be regarded as the cause of B, because there is an observable correlation in sequence between events of type A and type B, but more often because we seem to grasp that A directly produces B by some kind of force or propulsion. It must be remembered that every event that has occurred even in the last second belongs to the past and is therefore a part of history: there is no distinction in principle between the propositions that Caesar was killed by Brutus and Cassius and that Smith has just been injured by a golf-ball. On such historical facts cf. G. Kitson Clark, *The Critical Historian*, 1967, ch. 6 (a work with which I am in general sympathy).

In ascertaining what we need to know (in the loose sense of that term applicable in daily life), we draw not only on our own perceptions but on those of others. We accept what they tell us, provided that experience has not seemed to show that they are generally mendacious, at any rate in the kind of report that is our immediate concern, or faulty in their recollec-tions, or incapable of giving accurate accounts of their own perceptions. Subject to similar provisos, we may also trust what they tell us of others' reports, while recognizing the probability that errors will enter into their transmission. Our chance of learning the truth always depends on access direct or indirect to the faithful report of an eyewitness. Documents are no more trustworthy than oral evidence without this guarantee; hence laws require that there should be witnesses to the sealing or signature of wills and other legal instruments, to prove their authenticity.

The historian ought to view his evidence in the same way. It is a curiosity that some who are familiar only with the normal practice of modern scholars in relying entirely on written sources find it disturbing when writers of 'contemporary' history resort to the interrogation of witnesses who have actually seen or heard what they report. Yet all history must ultimately be based on such first-hand reports. Historical documents must be known or reasonably assumed to have been authenticated by competent witnesses. Thus tabulated figures of industrial production rest on innumerable reports of clerks of the goods that left a factory. If the Roman historian treats the inscribed copy of a *lex* as evidence of what the Roman people enacted, it is because he supposes that it would not have been engraved and exhibited unless it had been authenticated from an archival copy, and that this copy in turn had been certified as correct (just how we do not know) on being deposited in the archives. (Decrees of the senate were certified by the senators named as present at their drafting.) But when history rests on earlier narratives, its reliability reposes on the availability, often at many removes, of first-hand information.

Very little of such information is directly accessible, especially to the historian of Greece or Rome. Even a Thucydides or a Caesar could have seen personally only some of the happenings they relate. They had to interrogate other witnesses. We do not know how skilful or thorough they were; Thucydides (i. 22) remarks that it was a hard task to discover the truth as the reports of eyewitnesses differed with their bias and recollections. Thus even contemporary sources are seldom 'primary'; and most of what we have is derivative. At best, like Polybius on the Hannibalic war, they may preserve a full record (with their own interpretations) of what they themselves found in contemporary sources; at worst, they provide meagre selections or summaries of fuller accounts, not necessarily contemporary, distorting them by sheer inaccuracy or through their ignorance of conditions in the times concerned. There are intermediate stages of unreliability, and at all of them bias, misunderstandings, and imagination may corrupt the tradition. If there is any element in the historian's craft that can justly be called scientific, it is perhaps to be found in the development of critical techniques to determine and apply criteria in the valuation of evidence.

In the last resort, however, the historian often trusts his intuition, guided by his general conception of what he takes to be relevant to his decision. Moreover, except where little is even reported (and this is not uncommon in classical history), he cannot repeat (or if he did, no one would be able to read through) all the facts or alleged facts of which he is aware; and there may also be so many that he himself could never have time to learn them all; he has therefore to select those which he considers significant from his own information, and to decide not to inform himself about others. All this is highly subjective, all the more as his judgement is likely to be affected by preconceptions derived from the ideas and experience of his own time, which may be alien to the times he studies. And this subjectivity cannot be excluded by adopting a model, if in the definition endorsed by Finley (*Ancient History*, 1985, 60) models themselves are 'highly subjective approximations in that they do not include all associated observations or measurements, but ... are valuable in obscuring incidental detail and in allowing fundamental aspects of reality to appear'. It is manifest that such models are abstractions and involve presuppositions, in themselves subjective, that there are certain fundamental aspects of reality. Moreover, they do not issue from empty minds: they are suggested by some prior subjective selection of 'facts', and are subject to testing by equally subjective examination of other 'facts'.

Still, the subjectivity of history remains only partial. No one thinks that the historian purports to record the past freely, as he imagines it, whatever claims may be made on behalf of the historical imagination. If that were so, he could spare himself the arduous task of investigating evidence, and proceed like the novelist, providing perhaps more entertainment and more universal insight into human nature. Tolstoy's description of the battle of Borodino is not deprived of value, if found to be discrepant with archival material; but the account given by a historian would be. The work of a historian, like that of a scientist, is subject to correction in the light of evidence that he has falsified, neglected, or simply not known about. Such corrections naturally imply that, however selective a historian's choice of facts or interpretation of them may be, there are objective facts to be discovered and appraised. It is such a fact that Brutus and Cassius killed Caesar; other facts can be brought into relation with this, and in principle new relevant facts might be revealed by further inquiry. It is thus that we think that we can at least come nearer to the truth about what actually happened. Models are not the only approximations to aspects of reality. In practice, however, the dearth of trustworthy evidence for the political history of Rome is hardly ever remediable by new discoveries; it is mainly on social, economic and cultural conditions that new epigraphic, papyrological, and archaeological finds cast light (they are also occasionally useful for administrative history); the material long known has been almost exhaustively examined, and new work, if it does not consist in exposing the errors of the past, often adds to their number.

CHAPTER 2: ITALIAN AIMS AT THE TIME OF THE SOCIAL WAR

1. The texts of Livy, cited on p. 95, seem to me to presuppose that a *ius migrandi* already existed, (perhaps extending to some non-Latins, Ilari 13), and to record that it was annulled in particular cases, and restricted

for the future (though not in the way Galsterer thinks), not abolished. For this and other privileges comprised in the Latin right see Jolowicz–Nicholas 58 ff., and with evidence and full discussion *REx.* 1260 ff. (Steinwenter); cf. *RC²* 108 ff.; see now on its early history esp. Humbert, ch. III, and for the Hernici, p. 92. *Commercium* entailed the right to inherit and own real property in the territory of the foreign state concerned; inheritances were likely to accrue as a result of *conubium* (which seems also to have extended to some non-Latins; cf. n. 70); Ulpian's dictum that Latins and *peregrini* have *conubium* with Roman citizens only 'si ita concessum est' (*Tit. Ulp.* 5. 4) probably refers only to later law, perhaps only to some Junian Latins. Originally, we are told, the members of the Latin and Hernican leagues all had *commercium* and *conubium* with each other as well as with Rome, which Rome terminated on dissolving the leagues (Livy viii. 14. 10, ix. 43. 23), a temporary measure (*RC²* 113). It was perhaps often when a foreigner with these rights had acquired land in Roman territory that he would migrate and take up the Roman citizenship: I can conceive of no ground on which his right of obtaining the Roman citizenship by migration should have been limited to cases in which he had come to reside in Rome itself, though it might be (*a*) that it was generally by personal application to the censors there that he could properly get himself enrolled on the list of citizens; (*b*) that the economic opportunities offered by residence at Rome were particularly attractive to immigrants. As to (*a*), however, in so far as municipalities were entrusted with the registration of citizens within their own territories, they may in practice have been able to enfranchise foreigners; cf. *IM* 170 f., 543 f. Enrolment of foreigners in a Roman colony would *eo ipso* give them citizenship; but the enrolment of colonists including Roman citizens was a matter for the discretion of the magistrates concerned.

2. G. Tibiletti, *Rend. Istit. Lomb.* 1953, 43 ff. Under the *lex Pompeia* of 89 the Transpadane peoples in general obtained the *ius* of 'ceterae Latinae coloniae, id est ut petendo magistratus civitatem Romanam adipiscerentur' (Ascon. 3 C.). But at that time the Latin colonies in Italy, including those of Transpadana, had already been raised to Roman citizenship by the *lex Iulia*. Galsterer 100 supposes that 'ceterae Latinae coloniae' refers to Latin colonies existing in 89 in Spain, Carteia (Livy xliii. 3. 104), and Corduba and Pollentia, whose Latin status is conjectural, which presumably did not benefit under the *lex Iulia*; for all these and future 'Latin colonies' a new privilege was now created. This seems a possible reading of the text, which might even mean that the *ius* belonged to all Latin colonies of Asconius' own time (cf. the charters of Latin *municipia* in Spain, see now *JRS* 1986, 147 ff.). It is more usual and natural to think that Asconius meant that the *ius* had previously belonged to Latin colonies. But confirmation of this cannot be extracted from what we know of the rewards offered to successful prosecutors under the Gracchan *repetundae* law, as under later *repetundae* laws; cf. Galsterer 94 ff. They are entitled to receive Roman citizenship with *militiae vacatio*, or else (evidently if they wish to retain their own) *provocatio, vacatio,* and certain

privileges as litigants (*FIRA* i². 7. vv. 76–86; cf. the fragment of a later law found at Tarentum, conveniently reprinted by H. B. Mattingly, *JRS* 1969, 140; Cic. *Balb.* 53 f.); the rewards for Roman citizens who prosecute successfully (vv. 87 f.) no doubt include *vacatio*. The second alternative is, however, not open to those who have been dictator, praetor, or aedile in their own communities. It is commonly supposed that they are excluded because the rewards offered are inapposite, since these ex-magistrates were already as such entitled to the Roman citizenship (which carried with it the *ius provocationis* but not, be it noted, *vacatio militiae*), or as Sherwin-White holds (*RC*² 216; cf. *JRS* 1972, 94 ff.), to choose between this and the other specific privileges. In Mommsen's supplements the ex-magistrates named are only those of Latin communities. It is a difficulty for these supplements that not all Latin cities had dictators, praetors, or aediles: in some the chief magistrates were *duoviri* (e.g. *ILLRP* 536, 545). No doubt the draftsman meant these titles to include all the chief magistrates in the communities concerned, but on that construction they are just as pertinent to non-Latin communities; the titles cannot show that the exclusion is limited to ex-magistrates among the Latins. The most natural interpretation of the exclusion is then that the alternative set of rewards was inapposite for those excluded, because they already possessed the particular privileges offered; in that case the *ius provocationis* etc. already belonged to ex-magistrates in all the allied communities. As there is no like exclusion in the previous clause offering citizenship, it would seem that they did not automatically possess citizenship as ex-magistrates; and of course no one thinks that any but Latins could acquire citizenship 'per magistratum'. If any were already citizens, their rewards would be the same as for other citizens (vv. 87 f.); there is no implication that the Latin *ius* mentioned by Asconius did not already exist, and none that it did. The only other possibility that occurs to me is that *if* the ex-magistrates specified are only those of Latin cities, i.e. if Mommsen's hazardous supplements are correct, and if they were already entitled to claim the Roman citizenship, the legislator actually wished to deny them the option that might otherwise have arisen for those who had procured a conviction for *repetundae* of taking other privileges instead; it was Roman policy that they should identify themselves with Rome. Cic. *Caec.* 100, *Balb.* 27 ff. show that it was contrary to the principles of Roman law that a man should be simultaneously citizen of Rome and of another state (as distinct from a mere *municipium* like Arpinum; cf. *de leg.* ii. 4 f.), including one *de facto* subject to Rome; the rule was breaking down in his time (cf. Nepos, *Att.* 3) and was abandoned in the next generation; and I cannot believe that it was applied to the Transpadane Latins in his day; no more then to Latin communities before 89.

3. Romans were enrolled in Latin colonies on foundation 'aut sua voluntate aut legis multa' (Cic. *Caec.* 98; cf. *de dom.* 78); the attraction of land allotments would probably produce enough volunteers normally. Since the colonies were intended to be *propugnacula imperii* in the midst of potentially or actually hostile peoples, it was essential that the colonists'

loyalty to Rome should be beyond question, and it is therefore improbable that many of the native population were enrolled (*IM*, App. 5); though eventually, as in the reinforcement of Cosa in 197, Italians other than Latins, provided that they had remained faithful in the Hannibalic war, could be enrolled (Livy xxxiii. 24. 8 f.); the colonists must generally, especially before 268, have been either Romans or Latins. But after the dissolution of the Latin league in 338, all but three of the original Latin cities had been incorporated in the Roman state, and the Latin colonies founded in the next generation or two must have been peopled chiefly by Romans; these Latin colonies would also in turn have had relatively few men to spare for subsequent foundations, if they were to fulfil their military functions. At each point of time Romans greatly outnumbered the Latins; in 225 the ratio was probably 2.5 : 1 (*IM*, ch. iv). Consequently the Romans should always have had a greater surplus for colonization; and in so far as land-hunger made both Romans and Latins desirous of enrolling, the Roman government had a stronger motive for satisfying those who had full political rights at Rome than those who lacked them. This consideration no doubt explains why in the viritane assignations of 173 Romans got 10 *iugera* apiece, Latins only 3 (Livy xlii. 4. 3 f.). Of course Romans forfeited their citizenship in going out to Latin colonies; but at a distance from Rome they had little opportunity of exercising the political rights of citizens, and they were free to manage their own communal affairs; *commercium* and *conubium* permitted retention of the most important private rights of Roman citizens. In *IM*, 29, 84, I conjectured that in the fourth and third centuries Romans furnished 75 per cent of the colonists, decreasing to 50 per cent in the second.

4. I gave my views on municipal autonomy in *IM*, App. 3 (cf. now ch. 2, App. III below), where there is an error on p. 534: in *FIRA* i². 7. 31 ('in terra Italia in oppedeis foreis conciliab[oleis, ubei ioure deicundo praesse solent, aut extra Italiam in oppedeis foreis con]ciliaboleis, ubei ioure deicundo praeesse solent') the subject of 'solent' is not 'praefecti iure dicundo' but 'whatever judicial authorities there may be' (Simshäuser 99). The subsequent investigations of Simshäuser and particularly of Humbert, chs. vii–ix, with whom I am in general agreement, tend to confirm my position, not least in regard to the use of municipal magistrates in census-taking. On Capua before its revolt see most recently M. W. Frederiksen, *Campania*, 1984. Sherwin-White showed against Rudolph that the *quattuorviri* and *duoviri iure dicundo* after the Social war possessed jurisdiction from the first (see now *RC*² 159 ff); as to the kind of limitations imposed in Gallia Cisalpina (*FIRA* i². 19 f., on which see now Simshäuser), which presumably conformed to those previously applied to the magistrates in the rest of Italy, it is relevant that in classical Roman law any recognized court, whatever the normal restrictions on its competence, could decide any civil suits if the parties agreed (*Dig*. v. 1. 1). On *coloniae c. R.* see *RC*² 82 ff. On magisterial titles in the older *municipia* see n. 82. I do not see why the presence of the octovirate in some Umbrian as well as Sabine communities shows that it must be of Roman invention,

not of local origin with Latinized name; some Umbrians could have borrowed institutions from Sabine neighbours, as Fulginiae and Assisium borrowed Etruscan *marones* (Vetter 233, 236 = *ILLRP* 550); cf. also E. Campanile and C. Letta, *Studi sulle magistrature indigene e municipali in area italica*, 1979 (though much of their work seems to me mistaken).

5. *Quattuorviri*, already found at Larinum in 83 (Cic. *Cluent.* 25), were so much the mark of a *municipium* that a rumour that the Transpadani had been ordered by Caesar to choose them meant that he was supposed to be granting them the franchise (Cic. *Att.* v. 2. 3); but *duoviri* (normal in colonies) also occur; A. Degrassi (*Scr. Var.* i. 99 ff.) and Sartori (cited n. 84) think that the anomalies may result from the previous institutions of the communes concerned. *FIRA* i². 18 (Tarentum) and 13 (Table of Heraclea, on which see *IM*, App. 2) 83 ff. illustrate the regulation of local institutions in Italy; those of colonies were prescribed by *leges* such as that of Urso (ibid. 21); though Caesarian and Spanish, it is in part tralatician (cf. LXII). So too the charters of Latin *municipia* in Spain (see now *JRS* 1986, 147 ff.) attest the uniformity imposed on their administration in Flavian times. The general tendency is to vest local government in the control of the local council, though the magistrates (from whom councils were recruited) are elected. We must assume much legislation of this kind, like that which prescribed juridical institutions after the enfranchisement of the Transpadani in 49 (*FIRA* i². 19 f.), to have been consequential from, if not comprised in, the *lex Iulia* (at least one minor matter was the subject of the *lex Plautia Papiria*; cf. n. 37) or from the subsequent grants of citizenship to the former rebels. Group voting: *FIRA* i². 24; it may be the key to distinction in some Sullan colonies (*IM* 306) between the new settlers and the old inhabitants; cf. the senate's attempt after 90 to segregate the new citizens in special voting units.

6. Gabba, 1973, ch. IV (= 1976, ch. III), sect. IX: his study first appeared in 1954 and is now superseded on this matter by Wiseman, 1971. On Sulla's new senators cf. ch. 3 n. 50 with text, and on the great number of *municipales* in the senate in 62, Cic. *Sulla* 24; it is obvious that in doubling the size of the senate Sulla was bound to recruit Equites, and in view of the hostility of those most active in politics *c*.90, especially those who controlled the communes that had taken his side. Caesar and the triumvirs, who raised the number to 900 and then to 1000, must have elevated many more of municipal eminence; Augustus continued the same policy (*ILS* 212. I 1 ff.). See Wiseman, ch. 1. He seeks to illustrate the process from prosopographical data. App. 1 purports to list newcomers to the senate by period, and App. II to identify the origins of many of them. There are many uncertainties and more than he admits. (*a*) The non-consular *Fasti* from 167 are very incomplete; many families must have been represented in the pre-Sullan senate unknown to us; hence a *nomen* recorded later is not necessarily that of a *novus*, unless that term be reserved for men of non-consular families. (*b*) A far greater proportion of senators certainly or probably living *c*.56 is known than of senators of a later generation (cf. ch. 1 n. 8); hence App. II cannot be used for a

statistical comparison of newcomers before and after 49. (*c*) Nomenclature is often an unsafe guide to origins. As a result of colonization both before and during the first century, Latin *nomina* were widely diffused throughout Italy, and may even have been adopted in non-Latin communes; for example, the name Tullius is borne by consuls of 500 and 81, yet Cicero came from Volscian Arpinum; in any event a Latin *nomen* is obviously compatible with Latin as well as with Roman status before 90. Moreover, from early days there had been Sabine and probably Etruscan elements in the Roman citizen body, reflected in *nomina* like Pomponius and Pompeius from Oscan *pumpe*, as Quinctius from *quinque*. Even the characteristic Central Italian suffix -*idius* in *nomina* is exemplified in the pre-90 senatorial *nomina* Aufidius and Didius, though there is a high statistical probability that bearers of such names were descended from persons enfranchised in the 80s. Non-Latin as well as Latin *nomina* are often widely diffused. This might be the result not only of the mix-up of landholdings consequent on colonization and the sale of confiscated estates in the first century, but also of inheritances; for example, a man such as A. Caecina of Volaterrae, who inherited land in Tarquinii, might move his domicile there. I do not mean to deny that there are numerous examples produced by Wiseman of the rise of families from particular *municipia*, and it may be that we can properly infer from his App. II, conjectural as many of the data are, that the magnates of communes which were Roman before 90 or which then remained loyal to Rome (especially Latin) had a better chance of reaching the senate than those of ex-rebel communes. This would not be surprising; the former would be more Romanized and less likely to have suffered economic ruin in the 80s.

CHAPTER 3: THE EQUITES IN THE LATE REPUBLIC

1. *Lex Roscia*: Porphyry on Hor. *Epodes* 4. 15 f.; A. Stein, *Der röm. Ritterstand*, 1927, 21 ff. *Lex Visellia*: Pliny, *NH* xxxiii. 32; *CJ* ix. 21. 1, 31. 1; freedmen were certainly excluded from the 18 centuries in the Republic (Dio xlviii. 45. 8); by the favour of dynasts or emperors, or illicitly, persons of servile taint could creep in (cf. Treggiari, ch. II, for the Republic). Pliny, xxxiii. 29–36, with its obviously false claim that only in 63 did the Equites become a 'tertium corpus in re p.', cannot in my view be a safe basis for any reconstruction of developments, *pace* J. L. Ferrary, *RÉL* 1980, 313 ff. (whose analysis of the *meaning* of section 34 I accept). See in general Nicolet, 1966, Part I, e.g. on the census required in the Hannibalic war (p. 66) and on the number enrolled in the 18 centuries (113 ff.), but cf. *IM* 700. I do not agree with him that the *collective* term Equites was restricted in the late Republic to holders of the public horse (cf. ch. 4 n. 40 with text on *tribuni aerarii*), see above all T. P. Wiseman, *Historia* 1970, 67, for lucid review of all the evidence and arguments: it may well be that the honorific term 'eques R.' was applied to *an individual* only in the restricted sense. Nicolet also denies that the law of 129 excluded senators from the 18 centuries (103 ff.), since the Gracchan *repetundae* law specifically bars

senators from jury service. This argument is not conclusive unless the law made *current* membership of the 18 centuries the positive qualification; and it fails if the law only required 'equestrian' property and birth, or embraced past as well as holders of the public horse, in which case senators, who would have held the public horse at least before admission to the senate, would have been eligible unless expressly excluded. Gelzer, 1969, 4 ff., has a useful sketch of the equestrian order.

2. See n. 106 for Lucullus' anti-equestrian measures in Asia. The allegations of his enemies (Dio xxxvi. 2. 2), that he was unduly prolonging the war, first made in 69, led then only to his replacement in Asia, which conformed to equestrian interests; in 68 he was also given a successor in Cilicia (*MRR* ii. 150 n. 7). It was hardly practicable for a general operating in Armenia to administer provinces to the west. In 67 the popular tribune Gabinius, later no friend of the publicans (n. 29), carried a law vesting Bithynia and Pontus in the consul M'. Glabrio, and discharging the 'Valerian' legions under his command, which had been in service since 86 (cf. App. *BM* 90); in fact Glabrio did not take over. Cicero says that the people thought 'imperi diuturnitati modum statuendum' (*de imp. Cn. Pomp.* 26). Since the Hannibalic war only Metellus Pius and Pompey in Spain had enjoyed so lengthy a tenure of command. This very probably aroused jealousy among other senators, and could not be justified by Lucullus' success; even before the disaster to Triarius in 67 it was manifest that his victories had been indecisive. Significantly Cicero fails to cite Lucullus in *Fam.* i. 9. 26 as a victim of the enmity of Equites; at most it contributed to his supersession. This note modifies App. III in the original version of this article and takes account of the objections to it raised by T. R. S. Broughton in his comments on it in the same volume.

3. Badian, 1972, ch. IV, is the best account of the Republican companies; for that given by Maria Rosa Cimma, *Ricerche sulle società di publicani*, 1981, see his criticisms in *Gnomon* 1984, 45 ff. But her book is valuable on public contracting under the Principate (ch. III) and for the discussion of the later juristic texts on publican companies (ch. IV), which have unfortunately been much abbreviated or altered by the Justinianic compilers of the *Digest*, but which at least tend to confirm what is stated in the text on their peculiarities. For other kinds of partnership recognized in Roman law, I may refer to any standard textbook, and especially to F. Wieacker, *SZ* 1952, 302 ff. and 488 ff. D'Arms, 1981, ch. II, ignores or minimizes the limits that legal rules imposed on 'commercial organization' in general; with the single exception of the public contracts they did not permit the construction of a 'rudimentary company law'. The juristic fragments in *Dig.* xvii. 2 do not even suggest that partnerships were formed more for commercial enterprises than for joint holdings of land.

Recently A. di Porto, *Impresa collettiva e schiavo 'manager' in Roma antica*, 1984, has argued that there was important scope for joint enterprises conducted through the agency of *servi communes*, whether as *institores* or trading with their *peculium*; in the latter case the liability of joint owners, like that of a single owner, was limited roughly to the value of the *peculium* or of the acquisitions made by the principal(s) through the agency of their slaves. It is plainly hard to conceive that any collective enterprises in which very large sums were invested were conducted in this way. Moreover, just as a *societas* could always be dissolved at the instance of any partner (subject to his meeting previously incurred liabilities), so the holders of any common property, including slaves, could at any time enforce its division. Finally, a slave entrusted with substantial investments was bound to expect early manumission; if this was not promised, or the promise was not fulfilled, he was unlikely to show the zeal and efficiency required for the success of a business. Unless therefore the owner or owners could find a succession of efficient slave managers, the enterprises concerned would hardly be long-lasting. Thus, whether or not di Porto's interpretation of the legal texts on which he relies (which do not in themselves indicate that the use of a *servus communis* was a frequent commercial phenomenon) wins acceptance, it cannot be concluded that the employment of slave managers did much to remedy the defects in the law of *societas* which tended to inhibit the establishment of large trading companies. (I myself believe that individual Romans of wealth very often invested relatively small sums in probably many different enterprises carried on by different slaves or freedmen.)

CHAPTER 4: JUDICIARY RIGHTS IN THE REPUBLIC

1. W. Simshäuser, 1973, 145–85. Beyond question municipal courts were authorized, e.g. under foundation charters, to impose heavy fines for infractions of the local constitutions. The Table of Heraclea disqualifies from municipal offices and membership of the *curia* any person condemned 'iudicio publico' in a local court, as well as anyone banished from Italy as a result of condemnation at Rome (*FIRA* i². no. 13. 135 ff.); it is patent that those in the first category have not been capitally condemned! Cf. *lex Ursonensis* (ibid. 21) CII, CV, CXXIII f., which doubtless show what we may understand in the Table by 'iudicium publicum', but which again do not refer to capital trials. The Oscan Table of Bantia is in my view still to be dated before 90 (ch. 2, App. IV). I am astounded that S. Bove should infer from the documents he published, *Labeo* 1967, 22 ff., that the magistrates of Puteoli in the Principate had the right to execute citizens, and by crucifixion (cf. Kunkel, *RE* xxiv. 781 f., *contra* F. de Martino, *Labeo* 1975, 211 ff.). (Suet. *Cl.* 34. 1 can refer to execution at Tibur of persons condemned by Claudius in that place.) The chief puzzle is that the first clause of the *lex Cornelia* concerned only offences of *sicarii* within the city of Rome (*Coll.* i. 1. 3). It may be that this was tralatician drafting, the process having originated long before Sulla in the need to preserve public order at Rome by penalizing the carriage of weapons there with malicious intent, and that subsequent provisions not only extended the scope of the *quaestio* to the use of poisons (clause 5, *Dig.* xlviii. 8. 3 *pr.*) but to murder by any means and in whatever place; for one tralatician clause, borrowed from a Gracchan law *totidem verbis*, see nn. 52 f.

2. The publication of the *editio princeps* of the *lex Irnitana* by J. Gonzales with an admirable commentary in *JRS* 1986, 147 ff., has enabled me to make a few last-minute adjustments in the text and notes of these essays. The overlap of its fragments with those of the *lex Malacitana* and *lex Salpensana* confirms what Mommsen had inferred from the latter documents that all belong to a standard form of charter for the Spanish towns on which Vespasian had conferred Latin status. We cannot of course be sure how far the regulations correspond to those made for Italian or provincial communes which had earlier received the Latin right. It is also not necessary to assume that in every detail the regulations were identical even for the new Spanish *municipia* with Latin status. For instance property qualifications for magistracies, curial rank and rights of judication, and perhaps the pecuniary limits fixed for the competence of municipal courts, may have been varied from one charter to another, to suit the varying affluence of different communes. In the *lex Irnitana* (LXXXIV) the local courts are restricted to civil cases in which 1000 sesterces or less are at stake; in Cisalpina with its large and prosperous cities the limit was 15,000 (*FIRA* i². 19. xxi f.). It is clear throughout that the local courts in Spain are to administer Roman private law in accordance with Roman procedure, subject to any specific provisions in the charters (esp. LXXXIII). Within the limits of his competence the local magistrate is empowered to proceed to the 'datio addictio' of a *iudex* or *arbiter* or the 'datio' of *recuperatores*; the distinction (cf. nn. 108 f.) is made in LXXXVI f. and LXXXI, though in LXXXIX 'dari' alone is used of the *iudex* or *arbiter*. It is his duty to make up decuries of persons to serve in these capacities, consisting either of decurions or of others qualified as prescribed by birth, property and age (LXXXVI). *Recuperatores* are always to be taken from the decuries, the litigants having defined rights of *reiectio* (LXXXVIII). As for the nomination of a *iudex* or *arbiter*, the litigants by agreement may choose their own man from the decuries, or (subject to restrictions) at large; if they do not so agree, a complicated process of *reiectio* from within the decuries is prescribed, but if either party will not co-operate, the other is free to nominate (LXXXVI f.). No doubt the much greater number of persons on the *album* at Rome made any such process of *reiectio* impracticable there; hence the resort to sortition (n. 107), where the parties could not agree on the choice of *iudex* or *arbiter*. The arrangements in the *lex Irnitana* suggest that the parties were encouraged to agree; probably their choice might usually fall on a man enrolled in the decuries, but it is plain enough that such agreement was not a precondition for trial *apud iudicem*.

CHAPTER 6: *LIBERTAS* IN THE REPUBLIC

1. Cicero maintains (*Balb.* 31) that the ancestral *iura* provide 'ne quis invitus civitate mutetur neve in civitate maneat invitus'; these *iura* furnish 'fundamenta firmissima nostrae libertatis'; in *de dom.* 77–80 he speaks of 'iure munitam civitatem et libertatem nostram'; what is valid in the

sophistries he deploys is that citizenship guaranteed through the laws the rights associated with Roman *libertas* (cf. II *Verr.* i. 7). In *Caec.* 95–104 he claims that the courts had refused to recognize a law of Sulla depriving the Arretines and (as the context shows) the Volaterrans of citizenship; it had apparently been argued that the standard form of *sanctio* in the statute, 'si quid ius non esset rogarier, eius ea lege nihilum rogatum', annulled the substantive provision in question. A *lex* (he claims) could not deprive any citizen of either freedom or citizenship; 'si semel civitas adimi potest, retineri libertas non potest'; this is simply false. Cicero's doctrine that the legislative authority of the people was fettered, despite the rule of the XXI Tables (n. 39) that 'quodcumque postremum populus iussisset id ius ratumque esset', might have seemed plausible on the footing that the code also forbade the magistrates to propose *privilegia*, sc. against individuals (Cic. *de leg.* iii. 11, 44; cf. *RE* xxiii. 19, Wesenburg), as distinct from bringing charges against them to be decided judicially by the *comitia centuriata*. We must also bear in mind that the verdicts of Roman courts were not subject to review, and that their conformity with law could not be assured. In the case discussed by Cicero, the *sanctio* in the Sullan law coupled with the *ius* relating to *privilegia* may explain the verdict. Lepidus (*cos.* 78), however, seems to have thought it well to confirm by a new law the citizenship of those affected by the Sullan law (Sall. *Or. Philippi* 14).

2. J. W. Gough writes in *Chambers Encyclopaedia*, s.v. liberty: 'The law of England does not recognize the liberty of the press as a special constitutional right, any more than personal freedom, or the right of public meeting, or other so-called 'liberties of the subject'; all rest on 'the general principle of the rule of law, which means that the government does not possess arbitrary power and no one can be punished unless convicted in the ordinary courts of a breach of the law', e.g. for infringing specific laws relating to libel, obscenity, copyright, Official Secrets, etc. Religious toleration has never been asserted as a principle but secured by a series of statutes passed at long intervals, progressively removing restraints on religious meetings and (later) the civic disabilities imposed on Nonconformists, Roman Catholics, and Jews.

3. In wartime, both Greek cities, and Rome (where there was virtually never peace) until 167, imposed direct property taxes; cf. *IM* 76, 641 f., for alleged complaints in the early period. Cicero thought that such taxation was a last resort, since it infringed property rights (*de offic.* ii. 74), and it was a basic principle of political organization 'ut sit libera et non sollicita suae rei cuiusque custodia' (78); cf. *Phil.* ii. 93: 'a tributis vindicare' (the verb suggests assertion of liberty). Of course Rome did not scruple to impose direct taxes on subjects, which Tertullian (*Apol.* 13. 6) treats as marks of servitude. Conscription at Rome was a constant grievance (*IM*, ch. xxii; App. 20, 21) and *vacatio militiae* was a prized privilege; but, unless in Livy v. 2. 8, the obligation to fight for one's own country is not treated as servitude, as conscription by a foreign state may be (e.g. Tac. *Agr.* 31, *Hist.* iv. 14). Rome and other western cities must always have demanded from citizens services, affecting both persons and

property, familiar in Athens as liturgies; for *corvées*, for instance, see the tralatician Charter of Urso (*FIRA* i². no. 21, xcviii); Dionys. iv. 81. 2 regards those ordered by Tarquin the Proud as proof of his tyranny. These liturgies or *munera* were essential to the administration of municipalities in the Roman empire; they were heavy burdens enforced by the imperial government; 'immunity' was coveted, but it is not normally, if ever, termed 'freedom' (see e.g. *Dig.* i. 5 f.), no doubt because traditionally such obligations had not been thought incompatible with civic liberty.

4. Piety of Epicureans: A. Festugière, *Epicurus and his Gods*, ch. iv; imputed atheism: Cic. *de nat. deor.* i. 123 (citing Posidonius); conformity of Stoics: Zeller, *Phil. d. Gr.* iii.⁴, 318 ff., esp. 322; of Pyrrhonists; Sext. Emp. *Adv. Math.* ix. 49 (cf. the curious affirmation of belief by Cotta speaking for the sceptical Academy in *de nat deor.* iii. 5); of philosophers in general: Origen, *Celsum* v. 35, 43, vi. 3–5, 17, vii. 6, 44, 66; Celsus urged the Christians that they could express their reverence for the true God through the traditional forms of worship, viii. 2, 66. For Varro's own theology, probably drawn from Antiochus of Ascalon, see Aug. *de Civ. Dei* vii. 5 f.; cf. iv. 31; yet he prescribed (in immense detail) adherence to the traditional cults, including private cults (vii. 3), see iv. 31, vi. 4 f., etc., as did Cicero in *de leg.* ii. 19 ff. (esp. 23); cf. *de nat deor.* iii. 5 f., *de div.* ii. 148. (In *de leg.* i–ii Cicero espoused a Stoicizing theology abandoned in his later works.)

5. Electoral freedom was of course limited by rules prescribing qualifications for office (cf. n. 129), including the *leges annales* and restrictions on re-election; the last were suspended in the Hannibalic war, when the people received the right 'quos et quotiens vellet reficiendi consules' (Livy xxvii. 6. 7), and were defied in the re-election of C. Marcellus for 152. There was a popular clamour for the irregular election of Scipio Aemilianus as consul in 147, on the basis that the people had sovereign power to disregard the law; to avoid accepting this, the senate had his candidature legitimated (App. *Lib.* 112; cf. Astin, 1967, ch. vi); a similar procedure was no doubt adopted to permit his second consulship in 134 (Astin 135 n. 5.). It is not known if such *privilegia* were obtained in advance for Marius' consulships 104–100, which were all irregular. Legal requirements were also ignored under the 'domination' of Cinna and often in and after Caesar's 'regnum'. In 184 the senate was resolute against an irregular election as justified 'nec iure ullo nec exemplo tolerabili liberae civitati' (Livy xxxix. 39. 6); here liberty is seen as necessarily comprising respect for the laws, not as popular sovereignty. For liberty as the right of the citizens to vote for and return whom they pleased cf. Cic. *de leg. agr.* ii. 16–25 (cf. n. 156), *Planc.* 16; Livy iii. 64. 5.

6. Livy iii. 59. 4; Dionys. vii. 25. 2. f., 30. 1–3, 48. 4, 58. 2 refer to popular pressure in the fifth century, including threats of prosecution for opinions voiced in the senate; perhaps this reflects later experience of such opinions being quoted outside to prejudice optimates, e.g. at trials. Livy iii. 55. 13 alleges that in 449 it was provided that decrees of the senate should be transmitted to the plebeian aediles for deposit in the temple of Ceres,

whose cult was peculiarly plebeian (Wissowa, 1971, 300); in historic times they were, however, placed in the *aerarium Saturni*. Caesar's rule of 59 that the proceedings of the senate (which recorded more than actual decrees) should be published (Suet. *Caes.* 20) was perhaps designed to expose senators to the force of opinion outside; Augustus rescinded it (Suet. *Aug.* 36); it was inappropriate to the new system, always adverse to popular rights. On the *acta senatus* see Kubitschek, *RE* i. 287 ff. Sherwin-White, *JRS* 1982, 21, remarks on various provisions in the Gracchan *repetundae* law concerning publicity, and enabling the people to 'exercise the passive force of public opinion'; F. Millar, *JRS* 1984, 19, adduces further instances, and has called my attention to the prescription of the Rubrian and Acilian laws (possibly 'popular') that treaties must be inscribed where they could be read and recited annually in a *contio* (Sherk no. 16, 11 ff.). All such regulations at least implied the responsibility of senate and magistrates to the people.

7. Popular *libertas* is the leitmotiv of speeches which Sallust puts into the mouths of Memmius (*BJ* 31), Lepidus, and Macer, and reappears inappropriately in that which he makes Catiline address to his aristocratic faction (*Cat.* 20); for Sallust it hardly mattered that the sentiments Catiline is made to utter cannot have been sincere, since he questions the sincerity of virtually all politicians (*Hist.* i. 12, *Cat.* 38). His cynicism was doubtless equally warranted in relation to Lepidus. The historical setting of Lepidus' speech is impossible, but it does not follow that Sallust has done more than retroject the propaganda that Lepidus did really use later, to stir up a formidable revolt. Whether or not the speeches of Memmius, Lepidus, and Macer have any basis in evidence known to Sallust of what they ever said (which cannot be determined), it must surely be assumed that Sallust knew enough to give us the kind of considerations they would have advanced to win popular support, and the sincerity of their own attitudes (which Sallust probably allows in the case of Memmius, *BJ* 27. 2, 30. 3) is irrelevant to the effectiveness of these considerations. As almost always, it is idle to write them off as rhetorical *topoi*; slogans or propositions become commonplaces, because they correspond with what many people feel and think. Hence Cicero too resorted to them in *de leg. agr.* ii and *Rab. perd.*, when affecting a popular stance. Bleicken's attempt to discredit Sallust's testimony (1972, 44 f.) is characteristically confused by his inability to perceive the reality of social conflicts, blinded as he is by acceptance of an aristocratic standpoint and by his infatuation with the importance of patronage, which even obtrudes into his treatment of *libertas* (64 ff.). Memmius and Macer both hark back to the struggle of the orders; Sall. *Hist.* i. 11 suggests that he discerned a recrudescence of old issues. Macer's *Annales* may underlie the anachronistic colouring of their accounts of that struggle in Livy and Dionysius, though the few fragments offer no confirmation. Appian's remarks on the old law 'de modo agrorum' in i. 8 were surely at least influenced by annalistic versions of the *lex Licinia Sextia*, whether or not there was also a second-century enactment.

8. According to the annalists, the *ius provocationis* on capital changes was established by a *lex Valeria* of 509 (Livy ii. 8 etc.) and confirmed by the *lex Valeria Horatia* of 449 (iii. 55 etc.) and the *lex Valeria* of 300 (x. 9); for appeals against fines over a permitted maximum see *StR* i³. 158–60. Most scholars discredit the first two of these laws as fictions. A sanction was first introduced by a *lex Porcia* (x. 9). According to Cicero (*de rep.* ii. 54), there were three Porcian laws with three different authors, which did no more than that; he also refers to Porcian laws in the plural in *Rab. perd.* 13; *Cat.* iv. 10, whereas in *Rab. perd.* 8, II *Verr.* v. 163 he speaks of only one, as do Livy and Sallust (*Cat.* 51. 39). We may infer that though there were three laws, one, presumably that which imposed a sanction, was regarded as most momentous, though it is reasonable to suppose that most magistrates would have complied even earlier with the prescriptions of the *lex Valeria* from a general respect for law, nor could tribunes ever have been debarred from impeaching offenders *ad hoc*. On the other hand, it is impossible to suppose that three laws were required simply to impose a sanction. They must have widened the extent of *provocatio*. The exact date of these laws is not known, but Porcii first appear in the *Fasti* from 211. One of the legislators was evidently a Porcius Laeca, whose descendants as moneyers in the late second century celebrated *libertas* and *provocatio* on their coins (*RRC* nos. 270, 301); in the second of these issues a citizen dressed in the *toga*, i.e. not a soldier, appeals against sentence by a magistrate in military attire. This strongly suggests that Laeca's law extended the right of appeal beyond the area within the *pomerium* and a mile beyond (*StR.* i³. 66 ff.) in which tribunes could operate, but only to citizens in civil life. It seems to me clear that the general retained the power to execute soldiers in Polybius' time (vi. 12; cf. 37 f.) and later (Cic. *Phil.* iii. 14; Plut. *Crassus* 10); on the other hand, he was forbidden to beat them with *rods* by 134 (*per.* Livy. lvii; cf. Plut. *C. Gr.* 9. 3); this may have been a novelty of a law perhaps advocated by Cato (Festus 166 L.). It is curious that Livy ignores all these statutes in his detailed narrative of events down to 167.

Cicero avers (*de rep.* ii. 54) that the right of appeal was (a) shown to go back to the monarchy by the archives of the pontiffs; cf. the legend of the trial of Horatius in Livy i. 26 (but the authenticity of such archives for early times need not be credited, and the trial of Horatius can be regarded as a mere paradigm of later practice), and (b) that it was attested by several laws in the XII Tables; but if that had been the case, it is unintelligible that so much later legislation was necessary. At best Cicero is guilty of rhetorical exaggeration; at no time was there any right of appeal against small fines or *poenae* entailed by condemnation in certain civil processes. Cf. next note. Probably he misunderstood the code. For instance, the provision he cites in *de leg.* iii. 11, 44 that only the 'maximus comitiatus', i.e. the *comitia centuriata*, could pass sentence 'de capite civis' was probably intended to inhibit the tribal assembly from attempting to exercise capital jurisdiction, and irrelevant to *provocatio*. In the historic period capital processes decided by the people were always a matter for the centuriate assembly; the tribes could only impose fines. Cicero may also have anticipated Mommsen in supposing that popular trials implied *provocatio*, whereas it has now been shown that in all historical cases, except that of Rabirius in 63, they were trials in the first instance, with a magistrate, normally a tribune, acting both as president and as prosecutor. If the views presented in ch. 4, VI are right, the *ius provocationis* was not in practice available to common criminals, but only to defendants whose alleged offence had a political colour, safeguarding them against the prejudices of a magistrate and his *consilium*; cf. n. 137. But even in this limited way it was along with the tribunician *ius auxilii*, considered a bulwark of freedom; cf. nn. 37, 109; and also Cic. *de orat.* ii. 199, *de rep.* ii. 55, iii. 44; Livy iii. 48 ('tribuniciam auxilium et provocationem . . . duas arces libertatis tuendae'), 56. 6, x. 9. 3–67, etc. and the coins cited above. For full discussion Bleicken, *RE* xxiii. 2444 ff.; Lintott (next note); it need hardly be said that this is a subject of endless controversy (cf. ch. 4, VI).

9. On Lintott's view (*ANRW* i. 2. 226 ff.) *provocatio* began as an appeal to the plebs for physical aid, and always remained an appeal to the tribes, which would not formally try the appellant by the comitial procedure for which only the centuriate assembly was competent (hearing cases in the first instance), but merely approved or disallowed the sentence. I cannot believe that the XII Tables formally sanctioned this, or that the theory can account for 'licere' in *de rep.* ii. 54. But texts he cites (e.g. Dionys. xx. 16; Livy xxvi. 33) actually attest decisions by the tribes; his account may then be right for the period after the *ius provocationis* had been prescribed by law, at latest from 300. Lintott suggests that presumably fictitious scenes of appeals to plebs or tribunes in annalistic narratives of early Rome (Livy ii. 55, iii. 58, viii. 33, ix. 26. 10) derive from later experience.

10. It was a partial concession to the principle that all 'potestates' emanated from the people that the great priestly colleges, at first filled by co-optation, came to be elective, by an assembly composed of 17 of the 35 tribes selected by lot. No doubt these tribes might commonly be a fair cross-section of the entire body, but it seems hard to explain the peculiarity of this practice, except on the hypothesis that the lot was supposed to indicate divine approval of the tribes it marked out, which was held to be requisite for the election of priests (Cic. *leg. agr.* ii 18) though this conception of the lot is little attested at Rome (Ehrenberg, *RE* xiii. 1465 f.). The *pontifex maximus* was thus elected in 212 and the *curio maximus* in 209 (Livy xxv. 5, xxvii. 8); a 'popular' bill to make all priesthoods depend on 'beneficium populi' in 145 failed to carry (Cic. *de amic.* 96), but one was passed in 104 by the tribune Cn. Domitius Ahenobarbus, actuated by personal reasons (Ascon. 21 C.; Cic. *de leg.* ii. 18) but probably *popularis* at the time (cf. Ascon. 80 C.); his law was naturally repealed by Sulla and revived by the 'popular' tribune of 63, Labienus (Dio xxxvii. 37). Cicero argues that the same procedure applied to any secular office would derogate from popular liberty (n. 113).

CHAPTER 8: *CLIENTELA*

1. Thus in Degrassi's collection of Republican inscriptions *cliens* occurs only
    in a freedwoman's boast of numerous clients (*ILLRP* 982). Some Delian
    dedications to patrons (359–63, 433) were no doubt set up by clients,
    though the dedicants do not so describe themselves; but in most cases a
    patron is clearly the former owner of freedmen, with whom he may have a
    common sepulture (e.g. 798, 927a, 946 f.); a freeborn client shares this in
    CIL vi. 14672, perhaps a unique record. The index to *CIL* vi registers 3 or
    4 clients in some 30,000 inscriptions from the city of Rome; one is a
    dedication by clients of Sulla (1390). Patrons occur very frequently: a
    sample shows that most were patrons of freedmen, the rest generally of
    communities or *collegia*; for Pompeii see n. 127. The standard form of
    index to *CIL* only notes patronage of communities (see e.g. *ILS* iii. 691 f.),
    which is common. *ILS* 6577 ('C. Manlio C. f. cens. perpet. clientes
    patrono') from Caere (early Principate) is exceptional; the monument
    shows clients sacrificing to the *lar* of the patron's *fundus*, according to R.
    Bianchi Bandinelli and M. Torelli (*L'arte dell'antichità classica*, ii. *Roma
    Imperiale*, no. 84), and they suggest that 'in the light of Roman legal
    conceptions there is clearly a representation of acceptance of a natural
    obligation, of entry *in clientelam* under the *manus* of a patron'; but only in
    imperial law did jurists recognize that persons 'in power' could have
    'natural' obligations (see e.g. Schulz, 1951, 460 ff.), and no jurist has ever
    supposed that in this period clients were 'in power' (*manus*)! Cf. W. W.
    Buckland and P. Stein, *Textbook of Roman Law*[3], 1966, 552 ff.
2. I have not mentioned in the text one matter perhaps pertinent, but
    obscure to me. In the centuriate assembly a tribal century of *iuniores*
    chosen by lot voted first, and its vote was announced before the election
    proceeded further. Cicero alleges that this *centuria praerogativa* had so much
    auctoritas that of the two candidates who obtained its vote for the
    consulship the one returned first was always successful, either at that
    election or (if the election were interrupted and resumed later *ab initio*) for
    the year in question (*Planc.* 49). Taylor, 1949, 204 n. 40, notes some
    exceptions from the Hannibalic war, but Cicero could hardly have made
    the allegation unless it had been at least generally true in his day. There is
    some confirmation in the promise made by two candidates in 54 to
    distribute corrupt rewards to voters in the prerogative century in the
    event of their return (*Qu. fr.* ii. 13. (14). 4). Cicero also suggests (*Mur.* 38,
    de div. i. 103, ii. 83) that the preference of this century was thought to
    manifest the divine will, as it was chosen by lot. Yet the remaining
    centuries were rarely unanimous, as in electing Cicero (ch. 6 n. 164); so
    not all of them would respect the omen. Why too was it only the
    candidate returned first by that century who was deemed to enjoy divine
    favour? Taylor 56 suggests that a 'bandwaggon psychology' was at work.
    That would seem to imply that whichever tribe was selected to vote first
    was thought to be representative of the feeling prevalent generally at least
    in the top classes of the centuriate assembly. Yet one would have supposed

that many of the tribes were too small and too susceptible to the influence of particular magnates to have been regarded as cross-sections of the electorate, unless indeed it was normally the case that one candidate was so preponderant in virtue of his *gratia* and *merita* that most voters would back him; it might then be that the remaining centuries were not so much following the example of the *centuria praerogativa* as casting their votes for the same reasons which had already influenced that century. In any event it is hard to see that its putative authority fits the view that patronage was decisive. The patrons who counted for most with the voters at large might have little influence in an unrepresentative tribe on which the lot happened to fall. See further Meier, *RE* Suppl. viii. 593 ff.

CHAPTER 9: FACTIONS

1. *Necessarii*: Hellegouarc'h, 1963, 77 ff. Gracchan law: *FIRA* i². 7. vv. 10 f., 19–26; cf. pp. 416 f. *Sodalitates*: Festus 382 L.; *ad Her.* i. 8; Cic. *de senect.* 13 (which shows that they might have sacral functions), *Qu. fr.* ii. 3. 5, *Planc.* 29, 36 f., 46. Cf. ch. 8 n. 115. *Kinship*: within the same degree of affinity as in the Gracchan law kinsmen could under the *lex Cincia* (204) and *lex Furia* (before 169) receive gifts and legacies which were otherwise barred (*Vat. fr.* 298, 301); their murder also constituted parricide under the *lex Pompeia* (*Dig.* xlviii. 9. 1); and they were excluded from acting as *iudices* under the Sullan *lex de iniuriis* (xlvii. 10. 5 *pr.*), and from being compelled to give evidence against each other in a criminal trial by a law of Augustus (xxii. 5. 4); cf. *lex Ursonensis* (*FIRA* i². no. 21, xcv). On the other hand in classical law it was only parents that men might not sue, or in general prosecute for crimes (ii. 4. 4. 1, xlviii. 1. 8–11); and the restricted right to take legal proceedings on another's behalf was conceded only to parents, children, siblings, husbands, parents and children -in-law, step-parents and stepchildren, and guardians. None of these rules differentiate between agnates and cognates. Originally in cases of intestacy where there were no *sui heredes* the nearest agnate had the right to succeed, and if he declined the members of the *gens* took the property. Evidently not all *gentiles* could prove descent from a common ancestor, for the jurist Scaevola (*cos.* 95) defined *gentiles* without specifying this condition (Cic. *Top.* 29). Gentile succession, attested in the late Republic (e.g. Cic. II *Verr.* i. 115), had become obsolete in Gaius' time (iii. 17). Already in the Republic the praetor would in certain circumstances give possession of intestate property to cognates (e.g. *Cluent.* 165). In imperial law at least kin to the sixth and even the seventh degree could benefit. No doubt this explains why gentile succession became obsolete; in this case too the circle of kindred recognized by the law is unusually large. At one time there was a taboo on intermarriage of kin extending to second cousins, which may be connected with the custom that within these limits kindred might kiss women on the lips (Polyb. vi. 11a. 4); but the rule was relaxed, probably in the third century, so that even first cousins could wed. Plutarch (265 D) thought that the change was to enable poor men to marry heiresses, but it

may reflect a loosening of kinship ties. In any event the legal rules, which obviously derive from current concepts of obligations to kinsmen, show that the sense of affinity extended beyond the nuclear family, but not to all who could claim the same patrilinear descent, and that it also encompassed connections on the mother's side and those most closely related by marriage. Cicero's hierarchy of special obligations (*de offic*. i. 53–9), even if taken from Panaetius (cf. the similar views of the Stoic Hierocles *ap*. Stob., ed. Hense and Wachsmuth, iii. 731, iv. 671–3), corresponds to the Roman ideas revealed by the legal institutions.

ADDENDUM
THE RIGHT OF CITIZENS TO OBTAIN REPARATION UNDER THE *REPETUNDAE* PROCESS

I have treated it as a possibility that citizens as well as *peregrini* could claim reparation for their own wrongs under the *lex Calpurnia de repetundis*. No proof can be given of this, but it seems to me certain that they possessed the right under the Gracchan law, identified with the *tabula Bembina*. This view, advocated by C. Venturini, *Studi sul* crimen repetundarum *nell' età repubblicana*, 1979, 82 ff., from whom I differ in certain particulars, goes against orthodox opinion derived from Mommsen (*Ges. Schr.* i. 1 ff.), though he himself later expressed some hesitancy (*Strafr*. 721 n. 4). By his supplementation of the opening clause of the inscription (v. 1), he excluded citizens from the categories of those whose wrongs could generate claims under the *repetundae* process. However, there appears to be no epigraphic objection to inserting the words '[quoi ceivi Romano]' before '[no]minisve Latini ...' It is beyond question that Roman citizens could take proceedings under the Gracchan law (vv. 22, 76 f.), but Mommsen held that they could do so, only when acting 'alieno nomine' on behalf of *peregrini*, and that it was a later development, first attested in the time when Sulla's law was operative, by which citizens too could seek reparation from the *repetundae* court.

Mommsen relied on a conjectural hypothesis that the *repetundae* procedure developed from a form of private action, *condictio pecuniae indebitae*, which *peregrini* could bring against ex-magistrates before the peregrine praetor, whose function, he supposed, was simply 'ius dicere inter cives et peregrinos', and who could therefore not entertain claims made by one citizen against another (*Strafr*. 721 f.). Of such private actions there is no evidence (though we should not expect any). More important, Mommsen's conception of the original jurisdiction of the peregrine praetor is ill-founded (D. Daube, *JRS*, 1951, 66 ff.). It is true that it was probably he who presided over the *repetundae* court under the Calpurnian law (cf. *tab. Bemb.* v. 12), but a statute could confer on any magistrate functions diverse from those which he normally performed. So too it could develop the law in a novel direction. Thus, even if Mommsen was right in his theory on the origin of the *repetundae* process, a theory no longer in fashion (Venturini, *loc. cit*.), any statute could have introduced innovations, and there could be no *a priori* ground for assuming that the right of citizens to take proceedings for their own wrongs in the *repetundae* court had not been introduced by legislation earlier than Sulla's.

Mommsen himself recognized that under Sulla's law citizens could seek redress against senators alleged to have taken money 'ob iudicandum' (Cic. *Cluent.* 104, cf. I *Verr.* 38 f.; Venturini 368 ff.). The inclusion of this offence in those actionable under *repetundae* law was atypical, since the claimant would hardly be a person from whom the defendant had taken money (in the form of a bribe), but one who had been wronged as a result of the corruption. It is then conceivable that special rules might have applied in these circumstances. However, as Venturini remarks (84), *Cluent.* 116 suggests that P. Septimius Scaevola who was condemned in 72 'frequentissimis Apuliae testibus' faced other charges brought by Italians, by then Roman citizens. I would add that in the trial of Verres, though Cicero commonly speaks as if he were acting only for the Sicilians, he also makes claims on behalf of citizens resident in Sicily (e.g. II *Verr.* ii. 16, 119, 176 f., 182, 185, iii. 36, 59–63, 93, 97, iv. 42 ff.). Similarly Flaccus was inculpated for depredations on citizens in Asia (*Flacc.* 70–93). Even Cicero's statement that the *repetundae* process had been devised primarily for the protection of *socii* (*Div. Caec.* 17 f., see below) implies that it was available to citizens as well. In the operation of the *lex Iulia* under the Principate, when increasing numbers of provincials had themselves secured the Roman franchise, citizenship was obviously no bar to claims of every kind for *pecunia capta*.

As for the Gracchan law allowing proceedings to be taken 'alieno nomine' (v. 6), the only fragment which casts any light on the circumstances envisaged seems to restrict the right to one proceeding on behalf of his own king, people, or fellow-citizen (v. 60), and therefore to exclude a citizen from acting on behalf of *peregrini*. Venturini, who sees this, supposes that there must none the less have been some other clause which entitled a citizen so to act (155 ff.), but I can discern no place among the lacunae appropriate for such a provision. Venturini adopts this view because he believes that there are three cases in which Romans did act on behalf of *peregrini* during the period in which the Gracchan law was operative. In this connection he allows that that law can have been modified by the Acilian, which some would identify with the Gracchan but which he dates (on grounds that I regard as speculative) to 111, whereas his three cases antedate that year. In two of them (*Font.* 38, *Fam.* ix. 21, 3) Cicero speaks of a Roman 'accuser'. However, even in the context of legal proceedings, Cicero can use the terms 'accusare' or 'accusator' loosely. Thus, he describes Hortensius as 'accusator' of P. Quinctius (*Quinct.* 8 f.), though he was no more than *patronus* of Quinctius' adversary in a civil action, and he speaks of the province of Sicily as 'accusing' Verres (*Div. Caec.* 54), though strictly he himself had brought the charges and was technically the accuser. In the third of Venturini's instances T. Albucius, who appeared against Q. Scaevola after his administration of Asia (*MRR* i. 523 f.) is not even named as accuser. Like the two so-called accusers, he may have been simply the patron of the claimants. Moreover, though in this and at least one other of the three the charges arose out of provincial administration, we do not know who the claimants were; if they were Roman citizens, then under the Gracchan law Albucius etc. were entitled to act 'alieno nomine' on their behalf. If they were acting on behalf of *peregrini*, it must surely have been under some statute amending the Gracchan law, whether the Acilian or one of which we have no record at all, a possibility that cannot be excluded (pp. 288 ff.). The right to proceed on behalf of *peregrini* had certainly been conceded to citizens by the law, Caepio's or Glaucia's, under which certain trials took place at the end of the first century; it is irrelevant to our present purpose whether this legislation had also withdrawn from *peregrini* other than Latins the right to sue for themselves as Venturini holds (419 ff.). As under the Cornelian law, it was then necessary to establish a procedure of *divinatio* to decide between rival prosecutors (*Div. Caec.* 62 f.). It is significant that no extant part of the *tabula Bembina* refers to *divinatio*, and that it is again hard to see where provision could have been made for it in the lacunae.

Very fragmentary clauses in the *tabula* (vv. 30–5) show that the praetor was required to assist claimants in collecting evidence and to enforce the attendance of not more than 48 witnesses whom they had called to support their case. But the writ of a praetor at Rome surely did not run outside the *ager Romanus* in Italy itself; he could hardly have trespassed on the administration of a provincial governor, nor unless expressly authorized, have entrenched on the autonomy of the Latins and Italian allies. The words extant or plausibly supplemented in v. 34 refer to the collection of evidence only 'in terra Italia in oppedeis foreis conciliab[oleis ubei ioure deicundo praeesse solent]', which should be interpreted in the sense indicated since the Latin and allied communities in Italy would hardly be designated by such terms, while the supplementation which requires the praetor to act 'extra Italiam' must surely be rejected. It is true that under the Cornelian law the prosecutor was enabled to impound incriminating documents in provinces (II *Verr.* i. 60, ii. 182, iv. 36, 149) and that under the Julian witnesses from beyond the seas could be compelled to attend (e.g. *FIRA* i.[2] no. 68 v. 95). We must presume that the later laws obliged provincial governors to co-operate in the process. The fact that under the *tabula Bembina* the praetor was to assist claimants gathering evidence within Roman territory in Italy, and surely only within that limit, in itself suggests that claims could arise from the activity of a delinquent there, prejudicial to citizens.

This official aid to claimants for *repetundae*, though limited as yet, illustrates the way in which they were favoured by comparison with a plaintiff in a civil action; the state did not intervene to enable him to seize documents or bring his witnesses to court. The praetor was also obliged to supply the claimant for *repetundae* on request with a *patronus* subject to his own approval of the person chosen (vv. 9–12). Most important of all, the state assumed responsibility for execution of judgement, if the defendant was condemned, whereas in private law the plaintiff had to execute judgement himself. The provision that the condemned defendant was to pay twice the sum he was adjudged to have wrongfully taken, though reminiscent of the *poena* prescribed in some civil actions for delict, also gave the procedure a deterrent effect. Moreover, a large equestrian court was probably less exposed to undue pressure by a powerful senatorial defendant and his friends than any *unus iudex* or *recuperatores*. It seems extremely unlikely that all these advantages were granted to *peregrini* and still denied to citizens under a law promoted by C. Gracchus, who was 'unus maxime popularis'.

It is true that in 70 Cicero could assert that the *repetundae* law was designed primarily for *socii*, 'nam civibus cum sunt ereptae pecuniae, civili fere actione et privato iure repetuntur' (*Div. Caec.* 17). This text in itself surely implies that the *repetundae* process was open to them under the Cornelian law, as we know from other evidence. In view of the various advantages of resorting to it, it must seem puzzling if they generally brought purely private actions. However, at the time when Cicero was speaking the *repetundae* court was manned by senators, who would commonly have been partial to their peers in the dock and who were in general estimation notoriously venal. Citizens might then well have preferred to have their claims settled by an *unus iudex*, in whose selection litigants had some share (pp. 228–30), and who was perhaps not necessarily a senator (p. 235); even if he were, the plaintiff might be able to procure the appointment of a senator of known integrity. Moreover, the quasi-statistical statement that Cicero makes is one of a kind whose correspondence to the facts his hearers or readers could hardly check. It would be quite another matter if, as Buckland maintained against received opinion (*JRS*, 1937, 37 ff.), it was virtually impossible for a citizen either in 70 or 123 to take private proceedings against an ex-magistrate in respect of his official actions. In conformity with the principle that an orator should never be patently mendacious (*de orat.* ii. 306), Cicero would certainly not have made an assertion (not even essential to his argument), which everyone would have at once seen to be absurdly false. None of the ingenious arguments of probability on which Buckland built his case can stand against this consideration. But unless the Gracchan law allowed citizens to claim for their own wrongs under the *repetundae* process, we should have to conclude, if he were right, that Gracchus left them without any redress at all for official depredations, while improving the chances of *peregrini* obtaining reparation.

One of Buckland's arguments merits notice. He reiterates that no case is on record of a citizen taking civil proceedings against an ex-magistrate. This is a good example of an argument from silence which has no force. The number of recorded civil cases from the Republican period in every category is so small that it is not in the least surprising that there is none in one particular category, in which the total number may well not have been large. A similar answer can be given to an objection, which some might raise against the view that reparation for citizens could be obtained under the Gracchan law (if not earlier). For the period between 123 and the Social war Gruen (1968, 305 ff.) lists ten certain and eight possible prosecutions for *repetundae*; we do not of course know what proportion of all prosecutions these constitute. In not one instance are we told what claims were made and by whom. Even when it is attested or probable that the prosecution arose from the administration of a province, it is only the orthodox presupposition that the claims of citizens were excluded that has made scholars take it for granted that the claimants were provincials rather than Roman publicans or *negotiatores* operating in the province. According to Cicero, the Sicilians had never until 70 sought redress from the *repetundae* court 'publico consilio' (II *Verr.* ii. 8); they were accustomed to endure oppression in silence (iii. 64). Yet many of Verres' predecessors had been accused and only two acquitted (ii. 155). Though we may harmonize these assertions by assuming that Verres was the first against whom Sicilian cities as such had acted, and that earlier charges had been brought by or on behalf of private individuals, the possibility exists that resident Romans had been among those individuals. Appian's allegation of collusion between prosecutors and equestrian *iudices* (i. 22) gains in plausibility if some at least of the prosecutors were Equites pressing their own claims. After his unjust condemnation Rutilius retired to the very province which was the scene of his alleged extortions; the charges against him might well have come not from provincial men of straw, but from Romans in Asia whose rapacity he had checked. The obscure Apicius, said to have been primarily responsible for his ruin (Posidonius F. 27 Jacoby), could have been the chief claimant against him. So too in a later time Gabinius, who had incurred the animosity of the publicans in Syria, may actually have been condemned on claims they preferred.

To conclude, under Gracchus' law citizens could obtain redress for extortions at their expense. This may have been possible under the Calpurnian law, but the transfer of judication for *repetundae* to Equites made it more likely that ex-magistrates would succumb to claims made against them by citizens, among whom Equites active in the provinces might well have been the most notable.

All this was written before the publication of J. S. Richardson's article in *JRS*, 1987, 1 ff., which produces arguments for holding that the procedure instituted by the *lex Calpurnia* gave redress to citizens and was still available to them as late as 70. This may well be so; his contentions do not undermine my thesis that Gracchus designed his new procedure for citizens as well as *peregrini*, and that it suited their interests, at least with equestrian *iudices*; indeed, it is rather less likely that it was not available to them, if their claims could already be heard by the *repetundae* court. (I do not share Richardson's doubts that the *lex Calpurnia* also offered protection to *peregrini*.)

INDEXES

References to pages also include the footnotes. Romans are designated by *cognomina*, when so designated in the text. Many incidental allusions to individuals are not indexed, and some individuals are registered only under their families. Dates of magistracies are given solely for identification.

I. PERSONS, PEOPLES AND PLACES

II. SUBJECTS